International Conference on Performance of
Data Communication Systems and their Applications
Paris, France, 14-16 September, 1981


Organized by
École Nationale Supérieure des Télécommunications (ENST)
and
Institut National de Recherche en Informatique et en Automatique (INRIA)


under the sponsorship of
AFCET, AICA, DGT, BELL-NORTHERN,
IEEE, IFIP WG7-3, IFIP TC6

Program Committee
M. Arato, D. Barber, P. Caseau, V. Cerf,
W. Chu, A. Danthine, P. Enslow, E. Gelenbe,
P. Green, P. Kuhn, J. Labetoulle, G. Le Molli,
O. Macchi, Y. Makino, E. Manning, R. J. T. Morris,
G. Pujolle *(Chairperson)*. M. Reiser, H. Rudin,
M. Schwartz, K. Sevcik, O. Spaniol,
A. Spizzichino, J. Vincent-Carrefour,
H. Zimmermann

NORTH-HOLLAND PUBLISHING COMPANY
AMSTERDAM • NEW YORK • OXFORD

# PERFORMANCE OF DATA COMMUNICATION SYSTEMS AND THEIR APPLICATIONS

Proceedings of the International Conference
on Performance of Data Communication Systems and
their Applications, Paris, France 14-16 September, 1981

edited by

## G. PUJOLLE
*École Nationale Supérieure des Télécommunications*
*Paris, France*

NORTH-HOLLAND PUBLISHING COMPANY
AMSTERDAM • NEW YORK • OXFORD

ISBN: 0 444 86283 8


*Published by:*
NORTH-HOLLAND PUBLISHING COMPANY — AMSTERDAM • NEW YORK • OXFORD



*Sole distributors for the U.S.A. and Canada*
ELSEVIER NORTH-HOLLAND, INC.
52 Vanderbilt Avenue
New York, N.Y. 10017

PRINTED IN THE NETHERLANDS

PREFACE

The International Conference on Performance of Data Communication Systems and their Applications, held on September 14-16, 1981, was sponsored by the Institut National de Recherche en Informatique et en Automatique (INRIA) and the Ecole Nationale Supérieure des Télécommunications (ENST). These proceedings contain the papers presented at the Conference. We are most grateful to the authors, to the session chairmen, to the panel participants and to the referees for their effort and for the role they assumed in bringing about the success of the Conference.

What is the state of the art in the areas of performance of data communication systems and their applications? Is the field of performance evaluation ready to accept the challenges coming from new, rapidly emerging systems as computer networks, local networks, satellite networks, distributed systems, etc.? This volume is organized to provide an answer to these questions.

These proceedings are organized into specialized areas including Access Control, Congestion Control, Communication Theory, Routing, Local Networks, New Telecommunication Services, Networks and Standardization, Modelling Theory and Queueing Systems, Realization, Protocol, Control in Networks, Network Evolution Measure and Performance. One important feature of the program is the international participation (18 countries).

The interaction between computer and data communication systems is very well-covered. The growing dependence on software and hardware is clearly illustrated. Finally, the continuing evolution of performance evaluation techniques is shown through the study of new transmission systems.

In summary, this book permits a broad in-depth coverage of the present and future state-of-the art in data communication systems on a world-wide basis.

G. PUJOLLE
Editor

# REFEREES

The assistance of the following referees is gratefully acknowledged

M.H. ACKROYD  (G.B.)

A.K. AGRAWALA (U.S.A.)

J.P. ANSART (FRANCE)

J.D. ATKINS (U.S.A.)

F.   BACCELLI (FRANCE)

J.P. BACH (FRANCE)

M.   BADEL (FRANCE)

J.S. BANINO (FRANCE)

T.A. BANK (BELGIUM)

Y.   BARD (U.S.A.)

A.   BELLONI (ITALY)

G.   BERNARD (FRANCE)

K.P. BHARATH - KUMAR (U.S.A.)

M.A. BONUCCELLI (U.S.A.)

P.   BOUCHET (FRANCE)

P.   BOYER (FRANCE)

A.   BRANDWAJN (U.S.A.)

W.R. BRAUN (U.S.A.)

W.   BUX (SWITZERLAND)

S.B. CALO (U.S.A.)

J.F. CHAMBON   (FRANCE)

M.   CHAMPEAUX (FRANCE)

A.   CHESNAIS (FRANCE)

C.   CHESNEAU (FRANCE)

C.M. CHIE (FRANCE)

W.   CHOU (U.S.A.)

G.   COHEN (FRANCE)

J.P. COUDREUSE (FRANCE)

T.   CZACHORKSI (POLAND)

J.   DAY (U.S.A.)

M.   DECIMA (ITALY)

B.   DELOSME (FRANCE)

M.   DEVAULT (FRANCE)

B.T. DOSHI (U.S.A.)

O.   DROBNICK (RFG)

D.   DROMARD (FRANCE

G.   DUROURE (FRANCE)

M.   EL DESSOUKI (EGYPT)

G.   FAYOLLE (FRANCE)

J.P. FERNOW (U.S.A.)

J.M. FEUVRE (FRANCE)

A.A. FREDERICKS (U.S.A.)

N.   GEORGANAS (CANADA)

M.   GERLA (ITALY)

A.   GIESSLER (RFG)

M.   GIEN (FRANCE)

R.   GONZALEZ (FRANCE)

M.   GOURGAND (FRANCE)

J.L. GRANGE (FRANCE)

D.   GRILLO (ITALY)

M.   GUILLEMONT (FRANCE)

T.   HASEGAWA (JAPAN)

J.   HAVERTY (U.S.A.)

G.   HEBUTERNE (FRANCE)

J.A. HERNANDEZ (FRANCE)

E.   HORLAIT (FRANCE)

V.A. IVERSEN (DENMARK)

J.B. JACOB (FRANCE)

R.   JOLY (FRANCE)

G.   JOMIER (FRANCE)

C.   KAISER (FRANCE)

F.   KAMOUN (TUNISIA)

M.   KATO (JAPAN)

H.B. KEKRE (INDIA)

P.   KERMAN (U.S.A.)

P.   KING (G.B.)

W.   KLEINODER (RFG)

H.   KOBAYASHI (U.S.A.)

A.   KONHEIM (U.S.A.)

M.   KUBIAK (FRANCE)

K.   KUMMERLE (SWITZERLAND)

A.   KURINCKX (FRANCE)

G.   LATOUCHE (BELGIUM)

M.   LEGROS (FRANCE)

G.   LE LANN (FRANCE)

C.   LEMIEUX (CANADA)

R.W. LUCKY (U.S.A.)

F.   MAGNEE (BELGIUM)

J.C. MAJITHIA (U.S.A.)

R.   MARIE (FRANCE)

J.W. MARK (CANADA)

I.   MITRANI (G.B.)

H.   MIYAHARA (JAPAN)

D.E. MORGAN (CANADA)

N.   NAFFAH (FRANCE)

A.   NILSSON (U.S.A.)

G.   NOGUEZ (FRANCE)

H.   NORA (FRANCE)

J.F. OMNES (FRANCE)

K.   ONO (JAPAN)

M.   PARISSE (BELGIUM)

G.   PAYET (FRANCE)

C.   PENN (FRANCE)

H.   PERROS (U.S.A.)

J.M. PITIE (FRANCE)

B.   PLATEAU (FRANCE)

J.   POSTEL (U.S.A.)

D.   POTIER (FRANCE)

J.R. RAY MC FARLAND (U.S.A.)

M.   RAYNAL (FRANCE)

J.W. ROBERTS (FRANCE)

E.C. ROSEN (U.S.A.)

D.H. ROUSE (U.S.A.)

I.   RUBIN (U.S.A.)

W.D. RUMMBER (U.S.A.)

A.   RYBCZYNSKI (CANADA)

M.   SCHOLL (FRANCE)

A.   SEGALL (ISRAEL)

D.   SERET (FRANCE)

J.M. SIMON (FRANCE)

R.C. SNARE (U.S.A.)

P.P. SPIES (RFG)

W.J. STEWART (U.S.A.)

B.W. STUCK (U.S.A.)

C.   SUNSHINE (U.S.A.)

I.   TODA (JAPAN)

F.W. TOMPA (CANADA)

S.   TUCCI (ITALY)

H.   TZSCHACH (RFG)

H.   VANTILBORGH (BELGIUM)

M.   VAUTRIN (FRANCE)

M.   VERAN (FRANCE)

A.   VIGHI (ITALY)

A.   WOLISZ (POLAND)

C.K. WONG (U.S.A.)

C.M. WOODSIDE (CANADA)

K.   YAKOV (USSR)

P.S. YU (U.S.A.)

J.   ZAMARLIK (FRANCE)

# LIST OF CONTENTS

Performance of Data Communication Systems
and their Applications, G. Pujolle (ed.)
© North-Holland Publishing Company, 1981

# A BUSY-TONE-MULTIPLE-ACCESS-TYPE SCHEME
# FOR PACKET-RADIO NETWORKS

Moshe Sidi and Adrian Segall[*]

Department of Electrical Engineering
Technion - Israel Institute of Technology
Haifa, Israel.

We consider a packet-radio network whose stations share a
communication channel and work with an algorithm similar
to the busy-tone-multiple-access protocol of ALOHA systems.
In this context, two problems are treated: distributed
routing and bandwidth allocation.

## THE MODEL

Consider a packet-radio network with given topology consisting of $N$ nodes, where
data may originate at any node and is forwarded via the network, according to some
routing strategy, towards its destination. Every node has a radio transmitter
with limited range and may act as a source of data as well as a repeater for data
arriving from and destined to other nodes. Originally we look at the situation
where all nodes in the network share a common wideband radio channel and we assume
for the purpose of this paper that all transmitters have the same transmission
range, say $R$. The nodes are equipped with omnidirectional antennas, in order to
facilitate rapid and convenient deployment as well as area coverage for mobile
terminals. Consequently, two nodes $i$ and $j$ can communicate directly if and
only if the distance between them is $R$ or less and then we say that they are
neighbors in the network. We denote by $N(i)$ the collection of all neighbors of
node $i$ and by $N^2(i)$ the collection of all neighbors of neighbors of node $i$,
excluding node $i$ itself and nodes that are in $N(i)$.

Packets that originate at traffic sources have to be routed through the network to
reach their destination and since packet transmissions are received by all neighbors, every transmitted packet should carry at each transmission the identity of
the neighbor to which it is intended. A node discards all received packets not
intended for itself.

The nature of a radio device used at each node, determines that a node may either
transmit or receive packets, but not both simultaneously. Therefore, whenever a
node $i$ transmits a packet to node $k$, node $k$ must not transmit at the same
time, and in addition, in order to avoid collisions of packets at the receiving
node, all neighbors of node $k$ must not transmit while node $i$ is transmitting.
For simplicity, we choose in this paper to inhibit the transmissions of all nodes
in $N(i)$ and $N^2(i)$ whenever node $i$ transmits a packet, this guaranteeing
successful transmission. This might be achieved by the following channel access
scheme: each nontransmitting node continuously senses the shared channel, and
whenever any activity is detected on this channel, it starts to transmit a signal
on a separate, narrow band channel, called the busy-tone channel. When the activity on the shared channel ceases, the transmission on the busy-tone channel is

* The work of A. Segall was conducted on a consulting agreement with the Laboratory for Information and Decision Systems, MIT, Cambridge, Mass., U.S.A., with
  partial support provided by the Office of Naval Research under Contract
  ONR/N00014-77-C-0532.

stopped as well.  It is assumed that the transmitters on both channels have the same range  R.

A node is allowed to start transmission of a packet only if it detects no signal on either the shared or the busy-tone channels.  Otherwise, the transmission is inhibited and the node reschedules the packet for transmission at some later time, incurring a random retransmitting delay.  At this new point in time the same procedure will be invoked.

Provided that the propagation delay of the carrier is negligible, the present scheme avoids conflicts in the network.  This is seen by noticing that according to this scheme, all neighbors of a transmitting node  i  are inhibited, since the shared channel is busy and also the neighbors of the neighbors cannot access the shared channel since all neighbors of node  i  transmit a signal on the busy-tone channel.

It is clear that a better scheme could be designed, in which not all neighbors and neighbors' neighbors of a transmitting node are inhibited, but only the node for which the packet is intended according to the routing procedure and its own neighbors.  However, in such a scheme, the neighbors of a transmitting node will have to decode the address contained in the transmitted message, before deciding whether to transmit a signal on the busy tone channel or not.  This decoding time may not be negligible, a fact that gives rise to conflicts.  In this paper we restrict our attention to the channel access scheme described before.

We may also note that this scheme is a natural extension of the Busy-Tone Multiple Access (BTMA) scheme [2], that was designed for an ALOHA network, to the case of general topology radio networks.

## COST FUNCTION  (Performance Evaluation)

In order to evaluate the performance of a given PR network we need to define a cost criterion.  In this paper the cost function is taken to be the average number of scheduled noncompleted transmissions, from the time a packet enters the network until it arrives at its destination.  Since every scheduled transmission that does not take effect results in a random delay (according to the channel access procedure described above), this average number of scheduled transmissions is also a good indication to the average delay in the network.

In order to express the average number of scheduled transmissions in terms of the network parameters, we need the following simplifying assumptions (some of which have already been mentioned):

(1)  The propagation time of the carrier and the time required to detect it are negligible, that is zero propagation and detection time are assumed.

(2)  At each node in the network, the random point process defined by the points of time when packets are scheduled for transmission (whether they were actually transmitted or not) is an independent Poisson process.

(3)  The average time required to transmit a packet by node  i  is  $1/\mu_i$  units of time (sec).

(4)  The shared and the busy tone channels are noise-free.

(5)  The buffers at each node are unlimited.

(6)  A node cannot simultaneously transmit and receive over the shared channel.

The critical assumptions are (1) and (2).  Assumption (1) ensures, as explained in the first chapter, that no conflicts are possible in the network because immediately after a node starts to transmit a packet (no two or more nodes may start transmission simultaneously because of the Poisson assumption), all its neighbors and the neighbors of its neighbors are inhibited. Therefore, whenever a packet is transmitted, it is successfully received (see also Assumption 4) by all the neighboring nodes, and in particular by the neighbor to which it is intended. Assumption (2) is based on extensive works [7] that checked its validity by simulation for an ALOHA network. It was shown there, that if the expectation of the rescheduling delay is large, then Assumption (2) is a good approximation. We still have to examine the validity of this assumption for more general topology configurations.

Now it is relatively simple to express the average number of scheduled transmissions of a given packet at node $i$, until it is actually transmitted (and then the transmission is certainly successful). Assumption (2) implicitly says that in steady state, the probability that a packet is actually transmitted when scheduled, is the same whether the packet is new or has been blocked before. For a node $i$, this probability is

$$P_{s_i} = 1 - \sum_{\ell \in A(i)} S_\ell^t / \mu_\ell \tag{1}$$

where $A(i) = i \cup N(i) \cup N^2(i)$, and $S_\ell^t$ is the average number of packets transmitted by node $\ell$ per unit of time (sec).

Equation (1) is derived from the following simple argument: Consider a very long interval of time $T$, and consider a packet that is scheduled for transmission by node $i$ in this interval. The probability that the packet is actually transmitted is the probability that this scheduled packet finds both the shared and the busy tone channels idle. The portion of time that at least one of these channels is busy during interval $T$ is:

$$\tau = T \cdot S_i^t / \mu_i + \sum_{\ell \in N(i)} T \cdot S_\ell^t / \mu_\ell + \sum_{\ell \in N^2(i)} T \cdot S_\ell^t / \mu_\ell . \tag{2}$$

The first term in (2) expresses the portion of time that node $i$ holds the channel, the second term is the portion of time that the shared channel is busy because neighbors of $i$ are transmitting, and the third term is the portion of time that the busy tone channel is busy because neighbors of neighbors of $i$ are transmitting.

It is clear that

$$P_{s_i} = \frac{T - \tau}{T} \tag{3}$$

and hence (1). Obviously, the condition for steady state is that $P_{s_i} > 0$ for all $i$.

Before proceeding, notice that in steady state, $S_\ell^t$ is also the average rate at which packets that are not destined to node $\ell$, enter it, and is the sum of the average rate of new packets entering node $\ell$ (from outside of the network) denoted by $S_\ell^n$, and the average rate of packets entering node $\ell$ from its neighbors (with destination other than $\ell$). The average throughput of the network is therefore:

$$S = \sum_\ell S_\ell^n \tag{4}$$

where the sum is taken over all nodes in the network. $S_\ell^t$ is calculated by using the law of flow conservation in the network, according to the particular routing scheme used in the network. The average number of scheduled noncompleted transmissions of a given packet at node $i$, is simply given by

$$D_i = 1/P_{s_i} - 1 \tag{5}$$

and averaged over the entire network becomes:

$$D = \frac{1}{S} \sum_i S_i^t D_i \qquad (6)$$

where the sum is taken over all nodes in the network.


## THE ROUTING PROBLEM

Generally, the routing problem in PR networks can be specified as follows: Given the network topology and the channel access procedure at each node, determine the routing at each node such that network performance is optimized. Determination of routing in PR networks, means that whenever a node $i$ decides to route a packet to its neighbor $k$, it attaches the identity of node $k$ to the packet. All neighbors of $i$ will receive this transmitted packet, but all, except for neighbor $k$, ignore it.

To specify the routing variables the following notations are used:

$\phi_{ik}(j)$ - routing variable, expresses the fraction of flow at node $i$ destined to node $j$ and relayed to neighbor $k$. By definition $\phi_{ik}(j) = 0$ for each node $k$ that is not a neighbor of node $i$, and also for $i = j$.

$S_i^n(j)$ - input flow, expresses the rate at which packets with destination $j$ enter node $i$.

$S_i^t(j)$ - total flow, expresses the total rate at which packets with destination $j$ transverse node $i$.

Clearly, the following relations hold for any node $i$ in the network:

$$S_i^t = \sum_{j \neq i} S_i^t(j) \qquad (7)$$

$$S_i^t(j) = S_i^n(j) + \sum_m S_m^t(j)\phi_{mi}(j) \quad . \qquad (8)$$

Given:            Topology, channel access scheme, $\{S_i^n(j)\}$ ;

Minimize:         Cost function, $D(S_1^t, S_2^t, \ldots, S_N^t)$ ;

Over:             $\{\phi_{ik}(j)\}$ ;

Constrained to: $\phi_{ik}(j) \geq 0$                        , $\forall i,k,j$ ;

$\sum_k \phi_{ik} = 1$                        , $\forall i,j$ ;

$S_i^t(j) = S_i^n(j) + \sum_\ell S_\ell^t(j)\phi_{\ell i}(j)$ , $\forall i,j$ ;

$S_i^t = \sum_{j \neq i} S_i^t(j)$                , $\forall i$ .

The constraint $P_{S_i} > 0$, $\forall i$, which is the condition for steady state, is ignored, since it is handled implicitly by the fact that $D \to \infty$ whenever $P_{S_i} \to 0$. We are interested in a quasi-static routing algorithm that is applied distributively [3] within the network. Actually we shall see that under some conditions, a distributed algorithm similar to those presented in [4,5,6] might be used to solve the routing problem presented above, so that the cost will be locally minimized. To show this, the following definition and two theorems are needed:

Definition: A set of routing variables $\phi$ is a set of non-negative numbers $\{\phi_{ik}(j)\}$, $1 \leq i,k,j \leq N$ such that

 (i)  $\phi_{ik}(j) = 0$, $\forall i \neq j$ and $\forall k \notin N(i)$ ;

 (ii)  $\sum_k \phi_{ik}(j) = 1$ ;

 (iii)  $\forall i,j$, $(i \neq j)$, there exists a route from $i$ to $j$. In other words, there exists a set of nodes $i,k, \ldots, m,j$ such that $\phi_{ik}(j) > 0$, $\phi_{k\ell}(j) > 0, \ldots, \phi_{mj}(j) > 0$.

Theorem 1: Let a set of input rates $\{S_i^n(j)\}$ and a set of routing variables $\phi$ be given. If the functions $\partial D/\partial S_i^t$, $\forall i$ are continuous, then the set of equations (9) has a unique solution for $\partial D/\partial S_i^n(j)$.

$$
\begin{cases}
\dfrac{\partial D}{\partial S_i^n(j)} = \dfrac{\partial D}{\partial S_i^t} + \sum_k \phi_{ik}(j) \dfrac{\partial D}{\partial S_k^n(j)} \;,\; \forall i \neq j \\[2em]
\dfrac{\partial D}{\partial S_j^n(j)} = 0 \;.
\end{cases}
\tag{9}
$$

Theorem 2: If the functions $\{\partial D/\partial S_i^t\}$ are continuous, then a sufficient condition that a set of routing variables $\phi$ will locally minimize $D$ is that for all $i \neq j$ and $k \in N(i)$, (10) will hold:

$$
\frac{\partial D}{\partial S_i^t} + \frac{\partial D}{\partial S_k^n(j)} \geq \frac{\partial D}{\partial S_i^n(j)} \;.
\tag{10}
$$

The proofs of the two theorems appear in the Appendix. Notice that condition (10) is equivalent to

$$
\frac{\partial D}{\partial S_k^n(j)} \geq \min_{\ell:\ell \in N(i)} \left\{ \frac{\partial D}{\partial S_\ell^n(j)} \right\} \;,\; \forall i \neq j \text{ and } k \in N(i) ,
\tag{11}
$$

with equality for $\phi_{ik}(j) > 0$. (To see this, multiply (10) by $\phi_{ik}(j)$, sum over $k$ and use (9)).

From (11) it is easy to see that it is possible to develop a loop-free distributed routing algorithm similar to the algorithms that are presented in [4,5]. In principle at each iteration of the algorithm, each node $i$ in the network increases (decreases) those routing variables $\phi_{ik}(j)$ for which $\partial D/\partial S_k^n(j)$ is small (large). Each iteration of the algorithm will be divided into two stages: (i) the update stage at which each node $i$ will receive $\partial D/\partial S_k^n(j)$ from its neighbors with $\phi_{ik}(j) > 0$, and will calculate $\partial D/\partial S_i^n(j)$ via (9); (ii) the rerouting stage at which the routing variables are modified according to the principle described above. If the cost function $D(S_1^t, S_2^t, \ldots, S_N^t)$ is convex, then such an algorithm leads to the global minimum cost. Unfortunately, the cost function obtained in Section 2 is not convex in general, so that such an algorithm will lead only to a local minimum.

Observe that each iteration of the algorithm requires transmission by each node of one control message per destination to each of its neighbors [5]. The scheme for sending these control messages over radio channels is a question for further research.

## BANDWIDTH ALLOCATION

In the previous sections we assumed that the shared channel is common to all nodes in the network, so that each node uses the entire bandwidth of the channel at each transmission. In this section, the following problem is addressed: For a PR network with a given total available bandwidth, can one improve performance by dividing this bandwidth? If the total bandwidth is divided into $L$ distinct channels ($L = 1$ corresponds to the situation considered in previous sections), each given node will transmit over one and only one of the $L$ distinct channels. However, in order to maintain the same neighborhood relations between nodes and the same connectivity degree in the network, it is required that each node will have $L$ distinct receivers. With this model, there will be $L$ sets of nodes in the network, each of them shares its common channel that is not interferring with any other channel. In order to avoid conflicts in this model, the channel access scheme described in Section 1 is applied in each of the $L$ distinct channels. In addition, a node that senses activity on the subchannel $\ell$ (where $1 \leq \ell \leq L$), transmits a signal over a corresponding busy tone channel, so that all its neighbors that use $\ell$ for transmission, except the transmitting node, will be silent for the period of transmission.

From the above description, it is clear that the probability of completed transmission at a node $i$ that uses the subchannel $\ell$ for transmission is given here by

$$P_{s_i} = 1 - \sum_{m \in B(i)} \frac{S_m^t}{\mu_m \cdot \delta_\ell} , \qquad (12)$$

where $B(i)$ is the collection of all nodes in $A(i)$ that use the subchannel $\ell$ for transmission and $\delta_\ell$ is the portion from the total bandwidth allocated to subchannel $\ell$. From (5), (6) and (12) we get that the average number of scheduled transmissions of a packet in the network is:

$$D = \frac{1}{S} \left[ \sum_{\ell=1}^{L} \sum_{i \in N_\ell} \frac{S_i^t}{1 - \sum_{m \in B(i)} \frac{S_m^t}{\mu_m \delta_\ell}} - \sum_{i=1}^{N} S_i^t \right] , \qquad (13)$$

where $N_\ell$ is the set of all nodes that use the subchannel $\ell$ for transmission. Since the term $\frac{1}{S} \sum_{i=1}^{N} S_i^t$ depends on the routing policy and not on the bandwidth management, and since $S$ is a constant, the cost function used in this section is reduced to:

$$D = \sum_{\ell=1}^{L} \sum_{i \in N_\ell} \frac{S_i^t}{1 - \sum_{m \in B(i)} \frac{S_m^t}{\mu_m \delta_\ell}} \qquad (14)$$

Determining $L$, $N_\ell$ and $\delta_\ell$, $1 \leq \ell \leq L$, so that the cost function $D$ will be minimized is a very complicated problem. In this section we present two simple results: (i) in a completely connected symmetric network (i.e. each node is in the transmission range of each of the other nodes) splitting of the main channel does not improve performance; (ii) an example in which splitting the main channel does improve the performance.

## FULLY CONNECTED SYMMETRIC NETWORK

Consider a network where all nodes are neighbors of each other. For simplicity assume that $\frac{1}{\mu_i} = 1$ and $S_i^t = S$ for each node $i$ in the network. Assume also that the main channel is split into $L$ separate channels. Then the cost becomes from (14):

$$D = \sum_{i=1}^{L} \frac{S|N_i|}{1 - \frac{|N_i|S}{\delta_i}} , \tag{15}$$

where $|N_i|$ is the number of nodes in the set $N_i$ of all nodes that share the i'th channel. Clearly $\sum_{i=1}^{L} |N_i| = N$ and $\sum_{i=1}^{L} \delta_i = 1$. When minimizing $D$ with the constraint $\sum \delta_i = 1$, one finds (by using the Lagrange multipliers technique) that for any $L$ and any partitioning of the nodes, the $\delta_i$ should be chosen as follows:

$$\delta_i = \frac{|N_i|}{N} , \tag{16}$$

and therefore the cost becomes

$$D_{min} = \frac{NS}{1 - NS} , \quad S < \frac{1}{N} , \tag{17}$$

which is the same cost as in the case when the main channel is not split at all. Therefore no improvement is noticed in the network performance by splitting the channel in this case.

## EXAMPLE OF PERFORMANCE IMPROVEMENT

Consider a cyclic network with $N$ nodes and $\frac{1}{\mu_i} = 1$ and $S_i^t = S$, $\forall i$. When the main channel is not split, the cost is (for $N \geq 5$):

$$D = \frac{NS}{1 - 5S} \quad \text{for } s < \frac{1}{5} , \tag{18}$$

because $|A(i)| = 5$, $\forall i$.

Assume now that the main channel is split in $L = 3$ equal portions, i.e. $\delta_1 = \delta_2 = \delta_3 = \frac{1}{3}$. Let the number of nodes in the network be a multiple of 3 (i.e. $N = 3k$ where $k$ is an integer). Assume that nodes $1,4,7,\ldots,3k-2$ use the first portion of the channel, nodes $2,5,8,\ldots,3k-1$ use the second part, and nodes $3,6,9,\ldots,3k$ use the third part. Then the cost becomes

$$D = \frac{NS}{1 - 3S} \quad \text{for } s < \frac{1}{3} , \tag{19}$$

since $|B(i)| = 3$, $i = 1,2,3$, showing an improvement in the network performance.

## REFERENCES

[1]  L. Kleinrock and F.A. Tobagi, Packet Switching in Radio Channels:  Part I - Carrier Sense Multiple-Access Modes and Their Throughput-Delay Characteristics, IEEE Trans. Commun., COM-23, 12, 1400-1416 (1975).

[2]  F.A. Tobagi and L. Kleinrock, Packet Switching in Radio Channels:  Part II - The Hidden Terminal Problem in Carrier Sense Multiple-Access and the Busy Tone Solution, IEEE Trans. Commun., COM-23, 12, 1417-1433 (1975).

[3]  A. Segall, The Modeling of Adaptive Routing in Data-Communication Network, IEEE Trans. Commun., COM-25, 1, 85-95 (1977).

[4]  R.G. Gallager, A Minimum Delay Routing Algorithm Using Distributed Computation, IEEE Trans. Commun., COM-25, 1, 73-85 (1977).

[5]  A. Segall, Optimal Distributed Routing for Virtual Line-Switched Data Networks, IEEE Trans. on Commun., COM-27, 1, 201-209 (1979).

[6]  A. Ephremides, Extension of an Adaptive Distributed Routing Algorithm to Mixed Media Networks, IEEE Trans. Commun., Com-26, 8, pp. 1262-1266 (1978).

[7]  L. Kleinrock and S.S. Lam, Packet Switching in a Multiaccess Broadcast Channel:  Performance Evaluation, IEEE Trans. Commun., COM-23, 4, 410-423 (1975).

## APPENDIX

### Proof of Theorem 1

Without loss of generality, let $j = N$ and delete the parameter $j$ in (9). Let $\underline{F} = (F_1, F_2, \ldots, F_{N-1})^T$ and $\underline{G} = (G_1, G_2, \ldots, G_{N-1})^T$ where $F_i = \dfrac{\partial D}{\partial S_i^t}$ and

$G_i = \dfrac{\partial D}{\partial S_i^n}$ for $1 \le i \le N-1$. With these notations we can write (9) as follows:

$$\underline{G} = \underline{F} + \Phi \underline{G} \ , \tag{A.1}$$

where $\Phi$ is a $(N-1) \times (N-1)$ matrix with terms $\phi_{i\ell}$, $1 \le i, \ell \le N-1$.

From (A.1) we have:

$$G_i = \sum_\ell (I-\Phi)_{i\ell}^{-1} \cdot F_\ell \ . \tag{A.2}$$

In [4, eq. A5], it is proven that the term $i,\ell$ of the matrix $(I-\Phi)^{-1}$ equals $\dfrac{\partial S_\ell^t}{\partial S_i^n}$ . Therefore the unique solution of (9) is

$$\frac{\partial D}{\partial S_i^n} = \sum_\ell \frac{\partial S_\ell^t}{\partial S_i^n} \cdot \frac{\partial D}{\partial S_\ell^t} \ . \tag{A.3}$$

Q.E.D.

## Proof of Theorem 2

Let $\phi$ and $\tilde{\phi}$ be two sets of routing variables with corresponding flows $S_i^t(j)$, $S_i^t$ and $\tilde{S}_i^t(j)$, $\tilde{S}_i^t$ respectively. Assume that $\phi$ satisfies (10) and that for all $i$, $|S_i^t - \tilde{S}_i^t| < \delta$ for $\delta > 0$. Then we have to show that $D(\tilde{\phi}) \geq D(\phi)$. Let $\delta$ be chosen so that the function $D$ is convex in the domain $|S_i^t - \tilde{S}_i^t| < \delta$ for all $i$, and define

$$S_i^t(\lambda) = (1-\lambda)S_i^t + \lambda\tilde{S}_i^t \ , \quad \forall \ i \ , \quad 0 \leq \lambda \leq 1 \ . \tag{A.4}$$

Therefore $D$ is a convex function of $\lambda$ in this domain so that

$$\left.\frac{dD(\lambda)}{d\lambda}\right|_{\lambda=0} \leq D(\tilde{\phi}) - D(\phi) \ , \tag{A.5}$$

and it suffices to show that

$$\left.\frac{dD(\lambda)}{d\lambda}\right|_{\lambda=0} \geq 0 \ . \tag{A.6}$$

From (A.4) we get that

$$\left.\frac{dD(\lambda)}{d\lambda}\right|_{\lambda=0} = \sum_i \frac{\partial D}{\partial S_i^t} (\tilde{S}_i^t - S_i^t) \ , \tag{A.7}$$

so that we have to show that

$$\sum_i \frac{\partial D}{\partial S_i^t} \tilde{S}_i^t \geq \sum_i \frac{\partial D}{\partial S_i^t} S_i^t \ . \tag{A.8}$$

To do this, multiply (10) by $\tilde{\phi}_{ik}(j)$ and sum over $k$ to get:

$$\frac{\partial D}{\partial S_i^t} + \sum_k \frac{\partial D}{\partial S_k^n(j)} \tilde{\phi}_{ik}(j) \geq \frac{\partial D}{\partial S_i^n(j)} \tag{A.9}$$

Multiplying (A.9) by $S_i^t(j)$, summing first over all $j \neq i$ and then over $i$, we obtain:

$$\sum_i \frac{\partial D}{\partial S_i^t} \tilde{S}_i^t + \sum_{j \neq i, k} \frac{\partial D}{\partial S_k^n(j)} \sum_i \tilde{\phi}_{ik}(j)\tilde{S}_i^t(j) \geq \sum_{i,j=i} \frac{\partial D}{\partial S_i^n(j)} \tilde{S}_i^t(j) \ . \tag{A.10}$$

From (8) we have that

$$\sum_i \tilde{\phi}_{ik}(j)\tilde{S}_i^t(j) = \tilde{S}_k^t(j) - S_k^n(j) \ . \tag{A.11}$$

Substituting (A.11) in (A.10) yields

$$\sum_i \frac{\partial D}{\partial S_i^t} \tilde{S}_i^t \geq \sum_{j,k} \frac{\partial D}{\partial S_k^n(j)} S_k^n(j) \ . \tag{A.12}$$

The only inequality used above was (A.9) and if we substitute $\phi$ instead of $\tilde{\phi}$ in (A.9) it becomes an equality (because of (9)), so that

$$\sum_i \frac{\partial D}{\partial s_i^t} s_i^t = \sum_{j,k} \frac{\partial D}{\partial s_k^n(j)} s_k^n(j) \quad . \tag{A.13}$$

Now (A.13) and (A.12) yield (A.8).

Q.E.D.

Performance of Data Communication Systems
and their Applications, G. Pujolle (ed.)
© North-Holland Publishing Company, 1981

ANALYSIS OF A LOCAL-AREA BUS SYSTEM WITH CONTROLLED ACCESS

Werner Bux

IBM Zurich Research Laboratory
8803 Rüschlikon
Switzerland

In this paper, we address the performance analysis of a
controlled-access scheme for local-area bus systems. The
operation is characterized by an alternating sequence of
time intervals required for scheduling the ready stations
and intervals where the actual data transmission takes
place. In the framework of the access scheme considered,
various scheduling disciplines are possible. Three major
examples are examined in the paper: fixed priorities, variable priorities, and "shortest-packet-first". Our analysis
yields explicit results for the mean packet-transfer delay
under the assumption that packets are generated according
to Poisson processes; packet lengths and scheduling times
can be generally distributed. Numerical results indicate
that the access method works very efficiently; comparison
of different scheduling disciplines gives insight into the
questions of fairness among the stations, and the potential
for performance improvement by sophisticated scheduling.

## 1. INTRODUCTION

Besides ring systems, busses or multipoint systems are attractive candidates to
provide the basic transport functions in local-area networks. In this paper, we
address the modeling and performance analysis of local-area bus subnetworks operating according to a controlled-access protocol. In contrast to random access, a
controlled-access scheme avoids any collisions of data on the transmission medium.
With the access protocol considered, this goal is achieved, as subsequently described.

Transmission of data packets occurs in the form of an alternating sequence of
scheduling and transmission intervals, as shown in Fig. 1. We refer to a pair of
scheduling and subsequent transmission intervals as constituting one "frame". During the scheduling interval, it is determined which of the attached stations have
data packets ready to transmit. These, and only these packets are transmitted in
the subsequent transmission interval.

Scheduling of the ready stations can be performed in a strictly centralized manner
by a controller polling each attached station in succession. A station responds to
the poll by notifying the controller of its possible intention to transmit a packet.
Actual packet transmission takes place within the subsequent transmission interval
and can be solicited by an extra poll. Obviously, this simplest realization of the
general principle leads to inefficient operation in case of comparatively long
propagation delays, and/or turnaround times, and a greater number of stations.

11

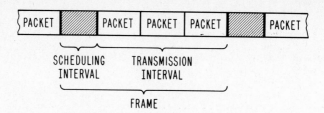

Figure 1
Operation Principle of the Access Scheme


This deficiency, and to a certain extent, also the need for centralization, is avoided in another realization of our general operation principle, the access scheme MLMA (Multi-Level, Multiple-Access) proposed by Rothauser and Wild [1]. In its simplest version, this method works as follows: Every station attached to the bus owns a "request field" within the first part of the frame. In its private request field, a station can indicate willingness to transmit a packet within the current frame. Thus, at the end of the request interval, full information is available about which stations want to make use of this frame. The actual transmission of the packets again takes place during the transmission interval and can be organized in (at least) two different ways: Either a controller solicits packet transmissions from the ready stations by a polling signal, or all stations are equipped to autonomously deduce from the request fields received when it is time to transmit.

The simple MLMA version described above is similar in concept to a bus-access method described and approximately analyzed by Mark [2], and to a contention-resolution method for computer-interrupt systems suggested by Taub [3]. Moreover, the general MLMA method [1] provides a solution to how stations can be very efficiently scheduled even if it has to be done based on long station addresses.

Concerning the order of transmission, a wide variety of different scheduling disciplines is possible. The simplest solution is, of course, for stations to transmit in a fixed order. To avoid the inherent unfairness of this fixed-priority scheme, variable priorities may be used. One may even conceive more sophisticated strategies: it would be possible, for example, that the stations during the scheduling interval not only signal their global desire to transmit, but also the lengths of their ready packets, thus enabling a controller to schedule the packets according to a delay-minimizing strategy.

In Section 2, we develop a queueing model to describe the type of operation discussed above, including the effect of the scheduling overhead. This model is analyzed in Section 3; first for a fixed-priority scheme, second, for variable priorities, and third, for the "shortest-packet-first" discipline. Section 4 presents and discusses numerical results.


2. THE QUEUEING MODEL

To determine the performance characteristics of the controlled-access scheme described in the Introduction, we subsequently develop a queueing model suitable to describe both the simple centralized method of scheduling and the MLMA technique.

As shown in Fig. 2, the bus is modeled as a single-server facility. Packets from

all stations which have been newly generated and not yet scheduled form the "distributed" queue $Q_0$. According to the operation described in Section 1, these new
packets cannot be transmitted within the current frame but have to wait until the
new frame starts. At this point, all packets in $Q_0$ simultaneously obtain a first
"service" phase of length S, the length of the scheduling interval. Following
this batch service, the packets are put into the station-specific queues $Q_1$ to $Q_K$
where they wait for their second, single-service phase of length B, the packet-
transmission time. With respect to the order of transmission, we distinguish between three different types of disciplines: *Fixed priorities*: The order of service
among the K queues is fixed, i.e., service is first given to all packets in queue
$Q_1$, then to $Q_2$, etc. *Variable priorities*: Priorities of the stations are systematically varied according to certain rules to avoid or, at least, reduce the inherent unfairness of the fixed-priority discipline. We consider two different types
of variable priorities called "cyclic priorities" and "complementary priorities",
see Section 3.2. *Shortest-packet-first*: A controller is assumed to have full
knowledge of the length of all packets the stations have ready to transmit. To
minimize mean queueing time, it then schedules the packets in the order of their
transmission time, i.e., length. This discipline is not considered as a really
practicable solution, but as an idealistic model to discover whether sophisticated
scheduling disciplines have a potential for significant performance improvement in
the framework of our bus-access scheme.

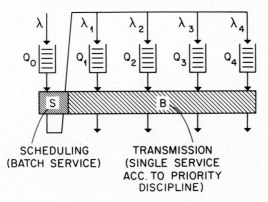

Figure 2

Queueing Model.   (K = 4 Stations; $\lambda_k$: Packet Arrival Rate at Station  k; $\lambda$: Total
Packet Arrival Rate; S: Scheduling Time; B: Packet-Transmission Time.)

Throughout the analysis, we assume that packets are generated according to Poisson
processes with rates $\lambda_1$ to $\lambda_K$; the aggregate arrival rate of all stations is denoted by $\lambda$. We impose no restrictions on the type of packet-length distribution;
in other words, the packet transmission time  B  is generally distributed with
probability density function b(t). (In case of non-negligible propagation delays,
we prolong the pure packet transmission time by the propagation delay between successively transmitting stations.) Furthermore, we assume that the scheduling interval is generally distributed with probability density function s(t). (For most
schemes, the scheduling interval is nearly or exactly constant; in case of the general MLMA scheme of [1], however, the request slot length varies from frame to
frame.)

## 3. ANALYSIS

In this section, we present exact analyses of the average packet transfer delay for the scheduling disciplines, described in the former section. The transfer delay of a packet is defined as the time interval from its generation until the end of its transmission.

### 3.1. Fixed Priorities

As described in Section 2, the order of service among the K station-specific queues is fixed here; following the scheduling phase, service is first given to all packets in queue $Q_1$, then to $Q_2$, etc. The order of transmission among packets of the same queue is assumed to be "first-come, first-served".

We derive the mean transfer time $t_f(k)$ of the packets from queue $Q_k$ by tracing a "tagged" packet of this queue on its way through the system. This technique has been successfully applied in the analysis of priority queueing systems, see, e.g., [4-6].

The transfer delay of the tagged packet consists of the following parts: The time until the start of the next frame, subsequently denoted as residual frame length $F_r$; the scheduling delay $S$; the delay $D_1(k)$ due to packets in the higher-priority queues $Q_1$, ..., $Q_{k-1}$; the delay $D_2(k)$ due to those packets in queue $Q_k$ transmitted before the tagged packet; its own transmission time $B$.

Taking expectations of these times we obtain

$$t_f(k) = E[F_r] + E[S] + E[D_1(k)] + E[D_2(k)] + E[B] \quad . \tag{1}$$

We subsequently show how the unknown terms $E[F_r]$, $E[D_1(k)]$, and $E[D_2(k)]$ can be determined.

### Residual Frame Length

The expectation of the residual frame length $E[F_r]$ can be derived as follows. If we denote by $F$ the total random frame length, then the following relation is known from renewal theory, see, e.g., [5]:

$$E[F_r] = \frac{E[F^2]}{2E[F]} \quad . \tag{2}$$

The first and second moments of the frame-length distribution, required in (2) to determine the residual frame length are subsequently determined.

We denote by $f_j(t)$ the probability density function of the length of the j-th frame. Furthermore, let $F_j^*(p)$, $S^*(p)$, and $B^*(p)$ be the Laplace-Stieltjes transforms of $f_j(t)$, $s(t)$, and $b(t)$, respectively.

The length of the j-th frame is given by the scheduling delay plus the sum of the transmission times of all packets which arrived during frame No. $(j - 1)$. Hence, the following recursive relation holds:

$$f_j(t) = \sum_{n=0}^{\infty} \{b^{(n)}(t)* \quad s(t)\} \int_0^{\infty} e^{-\lambda t} \frac{(\lambda t)^n}{n!} f_{j-1}(t)dt \quad , \tag{3}$$

where $b^{(n)}(t)$ denotes the n-th convolution of $b(t)$.

Transforming Eq. (3) yields

$$F_j^*(p) = \sum_{n=0}^{\infty} B^*(p)^n S^*(p) \int_0^{\infty} e^{-\lambda t} \frac{(\lambda t)^n}{n!} f_{j-1}(t)dt$$

$$= S^*(p) F_{j-1}^* \left( \lambda\{1 - B^*(p)\} \right) . \qquad (4)$$

We subsequently consider the frame-length distribution for the limiting case of j approaching infinity. Assuming that the limit of $F_j^*$ exists,

$$\lim_{j \to \infty} F_j^*(p) = F^*(p) \quad , \qquad (5)$$

we obtain the following functional equation for the Laplace-Stieltjes transform of the frame-length probability density function:

$$F^*(p) = S^*(p) F^* \left( \lambda\{1 - B^*(p)\} \right) . \qquad (6)$$

By differentiating Eq. (6) and taking values for p = 0, we finally obtain the following results for the first and second moments of the frame-length distribution:

$$E[F] = \frac{E[S]}{1 - \rho} \quad , \qquad (7)$$

$$E[F^2] = E[F]^2 + \frac{E[S^2] - E[S]^2 + \lambda E[F] E[B^2]}{1 - \rho^2} \qquad (8)$$

with $\rho = \lambda E[B] < 1$.

We remark that an alternative, though less direct way to derive Eqs. (7) and (8) is to make use of a result for the number of customers served during one cycle of a multi-queue system [7].

Delay Component $D_1(k)$
_____

The expectation of the delay $D_1(k)$ due to packets of higher priorities transmitted in the same frame as our tagged packet of priority k, is equal to the aggregate transmission times of such higher-priority packets generated *before* and *after* the tagged packet.

The mean number of packets from priority class $\nu$ which are generated, i.e., arrive in our queueing model after the start of the last frame but before the tagged packet, is given by

$$\psi_b(\nu) = \lambda_\nu E[F_e] \quad , \qquad (9)$$

where $F_e$ is defined as the elapsed frame length until the arrival of the tagged customer.

Again, it is known from renewal theory that the distribution of the elapsed frame length is equal to the distribution of the residual frame length. Therefore, we obtain

$$E[F_e] = E[F_r] = \frac{E[F^2]}{2E[F]} \quad . \qquad (10)$$

The mean number of packets from priority class $\nu$ which are generated after the tagged packet but before the start of the next frame, is given by

$$\psi_a(\nu) = \lambda_\nu \, E[F_r] \quad . \tag{11}$$

Therefore, the expectation of the delay component $D_1(k)$ due to packets of higher priority transmitted in the same frame as our tagged packet, is given by

$$E[D_1(k)] = \sum_{\nu=1}^{k-1} \{\psi_b(\nu) + \psi_a(\nu)\} \, E[B]$$

$$= \sum_{\nu=1}^{k-1} \rho_\nu \, \frac{E[F^2]}{E[F]} \quad . \tag{12}$$

As a side-glance, we want to stress that the mean number of packets of priority $\nu$ transmitted within the same frame as our tagged packet, is different from the overall average number of packets of priority $\nu$ transmitted per frame which is equal to $\lambda_\nu \, E[F]$.

Delay Component $D_2(k)$
_____

The delay $D_2(k)$ is due to packets of class $k$ which arrived after the beginning of the last frame but before the tagged packet. Its expectation is therefore given by

$$E[D_2(k)] = \lambda_k \, E[F_e] \, E[B]$$

$$= \rho_k \, \frac{E[F^2]}{2E[F]} \quad . \tag{13}$$

Mean Transfer Time $t_f(k)$
_____

We have now determined all components of the mean transfer time in Eq. (1). By substituting Eqs. (2), (7), (8), (12), and (13) into (1), we obtain

$$t_f(k) = \frac{1}{2}\left(1 + 2\sum_{\nu=1}^{k-1}\rho_\nu + \rho_k\right)\left\{\frac{E[S]}{1-\rho}\left(1 + c_s^2\,\frac{1-\rho}{1+\rho}\right) + \right.$$

$$\left. + \frac{\rho E[B^2]}{(1-\rho^2)E[B]}\right\} + E[B] + E[S] \tag{14}$$

with

$$c_s^2 = \frac{E[S^2] - E[S]^2}{E[S]^2} \quad . \tag{15}$$

The overall mean transfer time $t_f$ of the packets averaged over all stations, can be derived direct from Eq. (14):

$$t_f = \sum_{k=1}^{K}\frac{\rho_k}{\rho}\,t_f(k)$$

$$= \frac{1}{2}(1+\rho)\left\{\frac{E[S]}{1-\rho}\left(1 + c_s^2\,\frac{1-\rho}{1+\rho}\right) + \rho\frac{E[B^2]}{(1-\rho^2)E[B]}\right\} + E[B] + E[S] \tag{16}$$

$$= \frac{1}{2}\,E[S]\left(\frac{1+\rho}{1-\rho} + c_s^2\right) + \frac{\rho E[B^2]}{2(1-\rho)E[B]} + E[B] + E[S] \quad .$$

## 3.2. Variable Priorities

To avoid the inherent unfairness of the fixed-priority scheme (or at least to reduce it) it is conceivable to periodically alter priorities among the queues (stations). We subsequently consider two simple strategies of this kind: "cyclic
priorities" and "complementary prioritites".

### 3.2.1. Cyclic Priorities

Under this discipline, a queue which had priority p ($p\varepsilon\{1, 2, \ldots, K-1\}$) in
one frame assumes next-lower priority (p + 1) in the next; the station with lowest
priority K obtains highest priority 1 in the next frame. This scheme can be analyzed by a straightforward extension of the analysis of the fixed-priority discipline presented in Section 3.1., as subsequently shown.

Denote by $\hat{t}_p(x|i)$ the expected transfer time of a packet from queue $Q_x$ provided it
is transmitted while queue $Q_x$ has priority i. Furthermore, let $p_x(i)$ be the
probability that a packet from queue $Q_x$ is transmitted within a frame in which
queue $Q_x$ has priority i. Then, the mean transfer time of packets from queue $Q_x$
is simply given by

$$\hat{t}_f(x) = \sum_{i=1}^{K} \hat{t}_f(x|i) \, p_x(i) \quad . \tag{17}$$

The probability $p_x(i)$ is equal to the probability that a packet from station No. x
arrives during a frame in which queue $Q_x$ has priority i − 1 if i > 1, or priority
K if i = 1. Obviously, frame lengths are identically distributed, independent of
the current priority assignment. Hence, under our Poisson input assumptions, all
probabilities $p_x(i)$ are equal:

$$p_x(1) = p_x(2) = \ldots = p_x(K) = \frac{1}{K} \quad . \tag{18}$$

From Eq. (14), the expected transfer time $\hat{t}_f(x|i)$ of a packet transmitted when
queue $Q_x$ has priority i can be determined to

$$\hat{t}_f(x|i) = \frac{1}{2} \left( 1 + 2 \sum_{\xi=1}^{i-1} \rho_{1+(x-i+\xi-1)\bmod K} + \rho_x \right) \left\{ \frac{E[S]}{1-\rho} \left( 1 + c_s^2 \frac{1-\rho}{1+\rho} \right) + \right.$$

$$\left. + \frac{\rho E[B^2]}{(1-\rho^2)E[B]} \right\} + E[B] + E[S] \quad . \tag{19}$$

Introducing Eqs. (18) and (19) into (17), we obtain the mean transfer time of queue
(station) No. x under the cyclic-priority discipline

$$\hat{t}_f(x) = \frac{1}{2} \left( 1 + \frac{2}{K} \sum_{i=2}^{K} (K - i + 1)\rho_{1+(x-i)\bmod K} + \rho_x \right) \cdot$$

$$\cdot \left\{ \frac{E[S]}{1-\rho} \left( 1 + c_s^2 \frac{1-\rho}{1+\rho} \right) + \frac{\rho E[B^2]}{(1-\rho^2)E[B]} \right\} + E[B] + E[S] \quad . \tag{20}$$

### 3.2.2. Complementary Priorities

A second possibility to operate with systematically varying priorities is the so-
called "complementary priorities". Under this discipline, station No. x assumes

priority  x  for one frame, and priority (K + 1 − x) for the next.  Then it returns
to priority  x, etc.

Based on the same arguments as used for the analysis of the cyclic-priority discipline, it can be shown that for complementary priorities the mean transfer delay
for all stations is equal, independent of the traffic distribution among the stations.  The value of the mean transfer delay is equal to the mean delay averaged
over all stations in the case of fixed priorities, see Eq. (16).

### 3.3. "Shortest-Packet-First" Discipline

A conceivable kind of bus operation within the framework of our access method is
that stations not only make a global request for transmission, but also indicate
the packet lengths they intend to transmit.  In this case, a controller would be
able to schedule the packets according to a delay-reducing strategy, like the
"shortest-packet-first" discipline proposed in [8].  We subsequently study this
discipline to identify the range of possible performance improvement, rather than
to consider it as a practicable solution.

Under stationary assumptions, the frame-length distribution does not depend on the
order of service (whether service-time-dependent or not); therefore, we can use
similar arguments as in [9]: The mean transfer time of a tagged packet requiring
transmission time  t  is given by

$$t_f'(t) = E[F_r] + E[\sigma(t)] + E[S] + t \quad, \tag{21}$$

where $\sigma(t)$ is the aggregate transmission time of all packets shorter than  t  which
are transmitted within the same frame as our tagged packet.

The expectation of $\sigma(t)$ can be written as the product of the mean number $\chi$ of all
other packets transmitted within the same frame as the tagged packet, and the expectation of a random variable B' = f(B) defined as being equal to  B  (the random
packet-transmission time) if B < t, or equal to zero if B ≥ t:

$$E[\sigma(t)] = \chi \cdot E[B']$$
$$= \chi \cdot \int_0^t \tau\, b(\tau)d\tau \quad. \tag{22}$$

Using the same arguments that led to Eqs. (9) and (11), we obtain

$$\chi = 2\lambda\, E[F_r] \quad. \tag{23}$$

By substituting Eqs. (22) and (23) into (21) and averaging over the transmission
time  t, we obtain the mean transfer time for the "shortest-packet-first" discipline as

$$t_f' = \int_0^\infty t_f'(t)\, b(t)dt$$

$$= \frac{1}{2}\,(1 + q \cdot \rho)\left\{\frac{E[S]}{1-\rho}\left(1 + c_s^2\,\frac{1-\rho}{1+\rho}\right) + \rho\frac{E[B^2]}{(1-\rho^2)E[B]}\right\} + E[S] + E[B] \tag{24}$$

with $q = \dfrac{2}{E[B]}\displaystyle\int_0^\infty t\, b(t)\,\{1 - B(t)\}\, dt$ and $B(t) = \displaystyle\int_0^t b(s)ds \quad.$

Comparison of Eqs. (24) and (16) shows that the delay reduction is expressed in the term q in (24) which is a function of the packet-length distribution. The value of q is equal to 1 for constant packet-length, 2/3 for uniform packet-length distribution, 1/2 for exponentially, and $(C_b^2 + 3)/2(C_b^2 + 1)$ for hyperexponentially distributed packet lengths with squared coefficient of variation $C_b^2$. Numerical examples for the transfer delay are given in Section 4.

## 4. RESULTS

In this section, we present and discuss numerical results for the bus system analyzed under the various scheduling disciplines.

Figure 3 shows the normalized mean transfer delay as a function of the total offered traffic $\rho$ for a model with ten queues and fixed-priority scheduling. Further assumptions are that all stations generate the same amount of traffic and that packet lengths are exponentially distributed. For three different ratios of mean scheduling time E[S] to mean packet-transmission time E[B] the graph shows, respectively, the mean transfer delay of the highest-priority queue No. 1, the lowest-priority queue No. 10, and the mean delay averaged over all queues. Note, that for this and the subsequent examples, the scheduling time is assumed to be constant. We observe that the scheduling overhead can have a significant impact on delay which indicates that the inefficient, individual-polling method discussed in Section 1 should be used only in case of a small number of stations. Using the MLMA method, also described in Section 1, the ratio of scheduling overhead to packet-transmission time can usually be kept considerably lower than one, even for a great number of stations and relatively long bus propagation delays. Our analysis shows that under this condition, the access scheme considered represents a very efficient solution. As expected, the lowest-priority class No. 10 suffers a higher delay than the highest-priority class 1; however, the performance degradation is not dramatic.

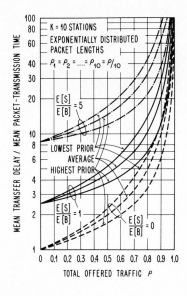

Figure 3
Normalized Mean Transfer Delay vs.
Total Offered Traffic for Fixed-
Priority Scheduling

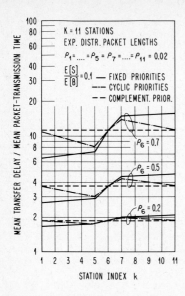

Figure 4
Normalized Mean Transfer Delay vs. Station Index. Comparison of Fixed-, Cyclic-, and Complementary-Priority Scheduling

If, nevertheless, an application requires avoidance of this different performance, variable priorities, as introduced in Section 2 and analyzed in Subsection 3.2 can be used. Figure 4 compares the various possibilities. It shows the mean transfer delay for all queues of a model with 11 stations. The underlying assumption is that all stations, except station No. 6 generate the same traffic value 0.02, whereas the offered traffic due to station No. 6 is equal to 0.2, 0.5, and 0.7. With *fixed* priorities, the delay grows monotonically with decreasing priority, e.g., with increasing values of the station index k. As we observe from the figure, the unfairness is reduced by the *cyclic*-priority scheme, however, it is not totally avoided: Station No. 7 - having the shortest "distance" from the highly loaded station No. 6 - suffers the longest delay. The mean transfer delay decreases from station No. 7 to station No. 5, i.e., with increasing "distance" from the highly loaded station No. 6. If the situation were such that all stations generated the same amount of traffic, then the cyclic-priority discipline would yield equal mean transfer delay for all stations. This can be immediately concluded from Eq. (20). As pointed out in Subsection 3.2.2, the *complementary*-priority discipline leads to equal mean transfer delays for all stations, independent of the traffic distribution among the stations.

Finally, Fig. 5 demonstrates what the performance gain could be by using a delay-reducing discipline. It shows the mean transfer delay as a function of the total offered traffic $\rho$ for three different packet-length distributions and two different scheduling disciplines: (i) packet-length-independent scheduling e.g., fixed, cyclic, or complementary priorities), and (ii) the "shortest-packet-first" discipline introduced in Section 2 and analyzed in Subsection 3.3 For non-constant packet lengths, "shortest-packet-first" leads to lower mean transfer delays; however, as can be seen from the figure, the performance gain is modest, even for a hyperexponential packet-length distribution with the high coefficient of variation $C_b = 2$. The reason why this gain is so small is because in the access scheme considered, "shortest-packet-first" scheduling is only performed among packets transmitted within the same frame and not among all waiting packets. This insight indicates that it is highly questionable whether the small potential of performance gain justifies any additional effort by using sophisticated scheduling.

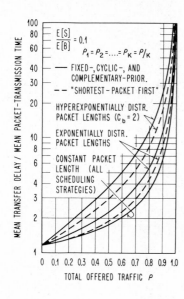

Figure 5
Normalized Mean Transfer Delay Averaged over all Stations vs. Total Offered Traffic. Comparison of Fixed-, Cyclic-, and Complementary-Priority Scheduling and "Shortest-Packet-First" Scheduling for Different Packet-Length Distributions

## 5. CONCLUSIONS

This paper presents the performance analysis of a controlled-access scheme particularly suitable for busses used in the local area. Major modeling goals were to take into account the overhead required for scheduling of the packets, and to study the performance characteristics of different scheduling strategies.

The major conclusions from a number of quantitative studies are: 1) Inherent to the simplest scheduling strategy, fixed priorities, is that low-priority stations suffer longer delays than high-priority ones. The analysis showed that these differences are usually not dramatic. For applications, where unequal service is undesirable, the unfairness can be reduced by cyclic priorities, or even totally avoided by complementary priorities. 2) Investigation of the "shortest-packet-first" scheduling policy revealed that only modest performance improvements can be expected from using sophisticated, delay-reducing strategies. 3) A comprehensive comparative study of different local-area subnetworks (token ring, slotted ring, random-access bus with CSMA-CD, controlled-access bus with MLMA) has shown that the access protocol analyzed in this paper represents an efficient scheme for a local-area bus system [10].

## ACKNOWLEDGMENT

The author would like to thank E.H. Rothauser for helpful discussions, and K. Kümmerle for reviewing the manuscript.

REFERENCES

[1] E.H. Rothauser and D. Wild, "MLMA: A collision-free multi-access method,"
    Proc. IFIP Congress 77, (North-Holland, Amsterdam, 1977), pp. 431-436.
[2] J.W. Mark, "Global scheduling approach to conflict-free multiaccess via a data
    bus," IEEE Trans. Commun. Vol. COM-26, 1342-1352, 1978.
[3] D.M. Taub, "Contention-resolving circuits for computer interrupt systems,"
    Proc. IEE, Vol. 123, 845-850, 1976.
[4] A. Cobham, "Priority assignment in waiting line problems," Operations
    Research, Vol. 2, 70-76, 1954.
[5] L. Kleinrock, "Queueing systems," Vols. I and II, (J. Wiley & Sons,New York,
    1975 and 1976).
[6] U. Herzog, "Optimal scheduling strategies for real-time computers," IBM J.
    Res. Develop., Vol. 19, 494-504, 1975.
[7] M.A. Leibowitz, "An approximate method for treating a class of multi-queue
    problems," IBM J. Res. Develop., Vol. 5, 204-209, 1961.
[8] S.S. Nair and M.F. Neuts, "A priority rule based on the ranking of the ser-
    vice times for the M/G/1 queue," Operations Research, Vol. 17, 466-477, 1969.
[9] T.M. O'Donovan, "The queue M/G/1 when jobs are scheduled within generations,"
    operations Research, Vol. 23, 821-824, 1975.
[10] W. Bux, "Local-area subnetworks: A performance comparison," Proc. of the IFIP
    WG 6.4 International Workshop on Local-Area Networks, Zurich, Aug. 27-29,
    1980. (To be published by North-Holland, Amsterdam, 1981.)

Performance of Data Communication Systems
and their Applications, G. Pujolle (ed.)
© North-Holland Publishing Company, 1981

A ROUTING ALGORITHM AND ITS SIMULATION ANALYSIS
FOR NETWORK INTERCONNECTION

Yuan-Chieh Chow                          Chuan-Lin Wu

Computer & Information Sciences        Electrical Engineering
    University of Florida                 University of Texas
  Gainesville, Florida 32611             Austin, Texas 78712
         U.S.A.                               U.S.A.

This paper presents routing techniques for rearrangeable
interconnection networks used in SIMD (Single Instruction
Multiple Data) and MIMD (Multiple Instruction Multiple Data)
environments. A graphic model is first developed to derive
the data structure for routing techniques. It is shown that
the data structure thus derived is good for the routing in
interconnection networks constructed of switching elements of
arbitrary size on contrast to other routing algorithms published
in the literature. Our approach requires much less work memory
and provides synchronous and asynchronous routings on the same
data structure. A simulation model is proposed and analyzed to
observe the routing and system behavior in both synchronous and
asynchronous environments.

INDEX TERMS - parallel processing, interconnection network,
routing algorithms, simulation model.

## I.  INTRODUCTION

This paper investigates routing techniques for rearrangeable interconnection networks which are potentially useful for the interconnection strategy of parallel/
distributed processing systems. In a parallel/distributed processing system, an
interconnection network is favorably used to facilitate a mixed-mode operation of
SIMD, multiple SIMD and MIMD. In the SIMD environment, parallel algorithmic processes usually need simultaneous one-to-one connections (or permutation) between
processors. The permutation connections are established synchronously. Many interconnection networks have been proposed for permutation connections [8]. However,
these proposed interconnection networks cannot realize every permutation in a
single pass. In the multiple SIMD environment, the interconnection network must
be partitioned so that each partition can serve the need of the SIMD permutations.
Siegel [9] and associates have done useful work on the partition of these networks
mentioned in [8]. Nevertheless, the size of each partition has to be equal to a
power of two. On the other hand, in the MIMD environment, connection requests are
likely to occur dynamically and asynchronously. In regard to this stochastic property, we would like to have an interconnection network which can provide a connection path for every connection request no matter what the current status of the
interconnection network is. A crossbar switch can certainly fulfill these prescribed needs: one-pass realization of arbitrary permutation, multiple SIMD
machines of a arbitrary size, and the nonblocking requirement for asynchronous
requests. However, the cost of a crossbar switch grows as $N^2$, where N is the number of input (or output) lines. Rearrangeable networks [1] can also fulfill these
needs for the mixed-mode operation and yet its cost grows as N log N. But, one
main issue concerning the use of the rearrangeable networks is the limitation induced by backtracking routing algorithms.

Many routing algorithms have been developed for the control of rearrangeable networks. Opferman and Tsao-Wu [2] developed a looping algorithm to control a class

of rearrangeable networks with $2^n$ input (or output) lines (where n is an integer). Anderson [3] extended the looping algorithm for the network with $2^t \cdot n_t$ input lines (where t and $n_t$ are both integers). However, Anderson's extension work requires a working memory of size $(2^t \cdot n_t)$ X $(2^t \cdot n_t)$. To control rearrangeable networks with an arbitrary size, Neiman [4], Ramanujam [5], and Hall [6] provided different algorithms which are all backtracking in nature. These routing algorithms need large working memory and require long processing time for backtracking. In order to fulfill constraint of computer systems, better routing techniques should be sought. In addition to the lack of a better routing technique, there appears no algorithm which takes the needs of asynchronous routing into consideration.

In this paper, we develop both synchronous and asynchronous routing techniques for rearrangeable interconnection networks. In Section II, we present a graph model to describe general routing for the rearrangeable interconnection networks. Efficient implementations of the algorithms are illustrated and discussed. In Section III, we use the same data structure derived from the graph model to study strategies for asynchronous operations. Simulation models and the results of analysis are discussed in Section IV.

## II. A GRAPH MODEL FOR ROUTING

A rearrangeable interconnection network can generally be expressed recursively by a three-stage Clos network as shown in Figure 1. Each box in Figure 1 represents

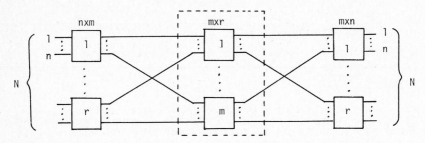

Figure 1:  A Three Stage Rearrangeable (m≥n) Clos Network.

a switching element which can be further defined. We will present graph algorithms and their implementations for three different sizes of the switch elements. Their complexities are also discussed.

### A). 2x2 switching elements

The routing algorithm for interconnection networks using 2x2 switching elements has been proposed and studied by several research groups [2,3]. The ideas are all similar to each other and can be demonstrated by a graph representation. Figure 2 shows a graph representation for a sample permutation, $P = \begin{pmatrix} 0 & 1 & 2 & 3 & 4 & 5 & 6 & 7 \\ 3 & 7 & 4 & 0 & 2 & 6 & 1 & 5 \end{pmatrix}$.

The permutation P is to be achieved by the interconnection network shown in Figure 3. The < or > in Figure 2 denotes a switch and the lines across the two sets of numbers denotes the desired connections. We observe in Figure 3 that a and b are independent subnetworks. Therefore, in order to connect a pair of terminals (one from the left hand side, one from the right hand side), they must be switched either both to a or both to b. This property indicates that the routing can be done by labelling the graph alternately. A terminal labelled a or b will be switched to the subnetworks a or b respectively. The labelling is shown in Figure 2. Since we always have an even number of paths in such a permutation graph, a non-conflict labelling is always possible. Applying the labelling to the graph we obtain two independent subgraphs as shown in Figure 4. Figures 4(a) and 4(b) are

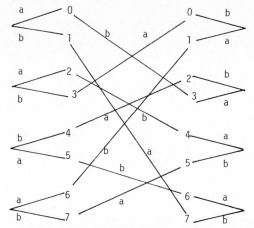

Figure 2:  Graph Representation for a Permutation.

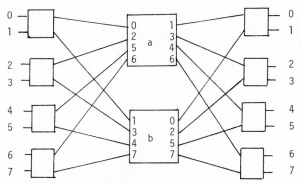

Figure 3:  A Permutation Network Using 2x2 Switching Elements.

graph representations of permutations which should be realized in subnetworks (a) and (b), respectively.  The same algorithm can be used iteratively for the subnetworks.  The algorithm can be implemented by using an array of $O(n)$ cells where N is the network size.  Figure 5 shows the array representation of the graph algorithm shown previously.  The entries in the cells represent the pointers (con-

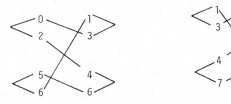

Figure 4.  (a) a-subnetwork.                    (b) b-subnetwork.

|  | left |  |  | right |  |
|---|---|---|---|---|---|
| 0 | 3a |  | 3b | 0 |  |
| 1 | 7b |  | 6a | 1 |  |
| 2 | 4a |  | 4b | 2 |  |
| 3 | 0b |  | 0a | 3 |  |
| 4 | 2b |  | 2a | 4 |  |
| 5 | 6a |  | 7b | 5 |  |
| 6 | 1a |  | 5a | 6 |  |
| 7 | 5b |  | 1b | 7 |  |

Figure 5:  An Array Representation of the Graph Algorithm.

nections) to the other side.  a and b are assigned alternately to each side, similarly to the graph method.  The time complexity is of O(N) for each iteration and O(N log N) to finalize the permutation.

B).  $2^t \times 2^t$ switching elements.

The labelling in the graph algorithm indicates that each connected pair must have the same label and that all inputs to the same switching element must be labelled distinctively.  We observe that in the case of $2^t \times 2^t$ switching elements, one can traverse and label a graph by using only two labels.  This process essentially partitions the graph into two $2^{t-1} \times 2^{t-1}$ subgraphs.  The same procedure can be applied by using different labels for each subgraph.  This repetitive process will finally lead to some 2 x 2 subgraphs which we have an algorithm to solve.  We give an example of a permutation,

$$P = \begin{pmatrix} 0 & 1 & 2 & 3 & 4 & 5 & 6 & 7 & 8 & 9 & 10 & 11 & 12 & 13 & 14 & 15 \\ 7 & 9 & 4 & 10 & 15 & 1 & 0 & 5 & 8 & 12 & 3 & 13 & 2 & 14 & 6 & 11 \end{pmatrix}$$

which is to be achieved by a rearrangeable network with 4 x 4 switching elements as shown in Figure 6.

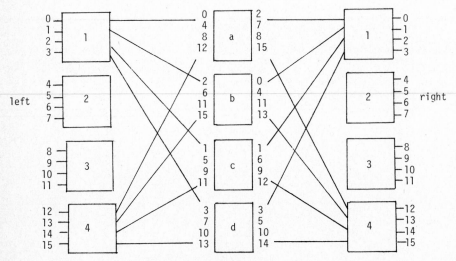

Figure 6:  A Rearrangeable Interconnection Network Constructed of $2^2 \times 2^2$ Switching Elements.

The graph (in Figure 7) which represents the desired permutation is labelled with B and W alternately as in the 2 x 2 case. It can be seen that each $2^2 \times 2^2$ switch box will have exactly two B's and two W's. By combining all the B's and W's we obtain two 2 x 2 subgraphs as shown in Figure 8.

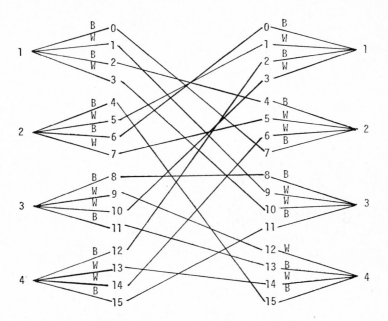

Figure 7:  Labelling of a Base 4 x 4 Network.

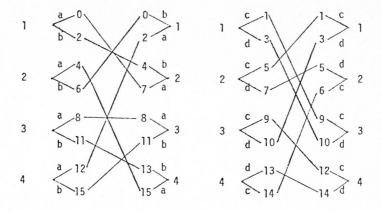

Figure 8:  (a). subgraph labelled B.        (b) subgraph labelled W.

Subgraph (a) is labelled with a and b.  Subgraph (b) is labelled with c and d.
The final routing is shown in the center stage in Figure 6.

To implement the partitioning of the $2^t \times 2^t$ graph as described, we use the matrix structure shown in Figure 9.

| B 7 (0) | W 9 (1) | B 4 (2) | W 10 (3) |
|---|---|---|---|
| B 15 (4) | W 1 (5) | B 0 (6) | W 5 (7) |
| B 8 (8) | W 12 (9) | W 3 (10) | B 13 (11) |
| B 2 (12) | W 14 (13) | W 6 (14) | B 11 (15) |

(a).  left to right

| B 6 (0) | W 5 (1) | B 12 (2) | W 10 (3) |
|---|---|---|---|
| B 2 (4) | W 7 (5) | W 14 (6) | B 0 (7) |
| B 8 (8) | W 1 (9) | W 3 (10) | B 15 (11) |
| W 9 (12) | B 11 (13) | W 13 (14) | B 4 (15) |

(b).  right to left

Figure 9:  Matrix Structure

In Figure 9, table (a) represents the connections from left to right while table (b) represent the connections from right to left. Each row in the tables denotes the inputs to a switching element.  The entries in the tables establish links for connections between the two sides. The algorithm is to visit each entry in the two tables and to mark them with B or W alternately. For example, if we mark entry $0^7$ of (a) with B then we have to mark entry $7^0$ of (b) with B.  The following step is to choose an arbitrary entry (such as $6^{14}$) in the same row of entry $7^0$ and mark it with W (and therefore $14^6$ with W). Repeat the same process until every entry is marked, we will have partitioned the 4 x 4 tables into 2 x 4 tables which are equivalent to the 2 x 2 routing problems.  The result is shown in Figure 10.

| 7 (0) | 4 (2) | 9 (1) | 10 (3) |
|---|---|---|---|
| 15 (4) | 0 (6) | 1 (5) | 5 (7) |
| 8 (8) | 13 (11) | 12 (9) | 3 (10) |
| 2 (12) | 11 (15) | 14 (13) | 6 (14) |

| 6 (0) | 12 (2) | 5 (1) | 10 (3) |
|---|---|---|---|
| 2 (4) | 0 (7) | 7 (5) | 14 (6) |
| 8 (8) | 15 (11) | 1 (9) | 3 (10) |
| 11 (13) | 4 (15) | 9 (12) | 13 (14) |

Figure 10:  Routing Result for the permutation shown in Figure 8.

The storage complexity is $O(N)$ and the time complexity for each stage is $O(N \log 2^t) = O(Nt)$.

C).  Switching elements of arbitrary size.

From the previous example, we see that it is convenient to denote an arbitrary permutation by use of a table.  For example, table (a) in Figure 9 is a permutation.  Each row in the table represents a set (i.e., inputs to a switching element). The routing algorithm can be rephrased in the following way.  We can re-arrange the entries in a row since they are in a same set. To achieve the connections for any permutation, we can simply rearrange the entries in the rows such that all the entries in a column are in different sets. This is basically the selection of SDR's (system distinct representatives) in Hall's theorem [6]. To illustrate this, we use a 5 x 5 example. Table (a) in Figure 11 represent a permutation. Since {0 1 2 3 4}, {5 6 7 8 9}, ..., and {20 21 22 23 24} are sets, we assign numbers 1 through 5 for these sets. Using these numbers we obtain a simpler table (b) in Figure 11. By rearranging the entries in the row direction we have table (c) in which every column contains distinct numbers, table (d) shows the final routing derived from table (c). A backtracking algorithm can be easily

| 24 | 15 | 22 | 5 | 23 |
|---|---|---|---|---|
| 7 | 14 | 2 | 21 | 9 |
| 1 | 0 | 13 | 4 | 10 |
| 8 | 12 | 6 | 18 | 19 |
| 20 | 3 | 17 | 11 | 16 |

(a)

| 5 | 4 | 5 | 2 | 5 |
|---|---|---|---|---|
| 2 | 3 | 1 | 5 | 2 |
| 1 | 1 | 3 | 1 | 3 |
| 2 | 3 | 2 | 4 | 4 |
| 5 | 1 | 4 | 3 | 4 |

(b)

| 4 | 5 | 5 | 2 | 5 |
|---|---|---|---|---|
| 3 | 2 | 1 | 5 | 2 |
| 1 | 1 | 3 | 1 | 3 |
| 2 | 3 | 2 | 4 | 4 |
| 5 | 4 | 4 | 3 | 1 |

(c)

| 15 | 24 | 22 | 5 | 23 |
|---|---|---|---|---|
| 14 | 7 | 2 | 21 | 9 |
| 1 | 0 | 13 | 4 | 10 |
| 8 | 12 | 6 | 18 | 19 |
| 20 | 16 | 17 | 11 | 3 |

(d)

Figure 11.

implemented for the rearrangement of the tables. The routing by using such a data structure can also be done heuristically. Note that the data structure derived needs a working memory of size O(N) which is considerably smaller than the one used in other approaches. Furthermore, the data structure is good for a network of arbitrary size while other routing algorithms are restricted to a special network size. The data structure is also convenient in developing asynchronous routing strategies which are considered in the next section.

## III. ASYNCHRONOUS ROUTING

In MIMD environment, the routing algorithm should be designed in the way that the blocking probability in adding a new connection without rearranging existing connections should be maintained as low as possible. It is observed [7] that by using the heavily loaded part of the network where possible, the lightly loaded part is more likely to have free paths available to cope with connection requests which might otherwise have been blocked. This principle, called packing, is known to give a reduction in blocking probability compared with random routing. However, since connections terminate asynchronously, there will frequently be free paths in the most used part which could handle some existing connections in the lightly

loaded part.  A call repacking scheme [7] in which rearrangement of existing connections is done each time a connection terminates can reduce blocking probability
further.  Results obtained in the previous section can be used to describe the
principles of call packing and call repacking.

In the previous section we have shown that a data structure as shown in Figure 11
can be used to implement synchronous routings. The asynchronous routing principles
of call packing and call repacking is equivalent to packing entries in as few columns as possible under the SDR restriction.  This will leave as many free entries
as possible for new connection requests. An example similar to the one depicted in
Figure 11 is shown in Figure 12.  In Figure 12(a), 14 existing connections appear.
The corresponding SDR notation is shown in Figure 12(b). If we leave connections
as the way appearing in Figure 12(a) or (b), we cannot add all new connections
without rearranging existing connections.  For example, we cannot add a connection
from input 21 to output 3.  Now if we pack entries as shown in Figure 12(c), then
we are able to add any new connection without rearranging existing connections.
The algorithm for the packing is similar to the one for selecting SDR.

| 15 | 24 |    | 5  |    |
|----|----|----|----|----|
|    | 14 | 2  |    | 9  |
| 1  | 0  |    | 4  | 10 |
| 8  |    |    |    |    |
| 20 |    | 17 |    | 16 |

(a) →

| 4 | 5 |   |   | 2 |   |
|---|---|---|---|---|---|
|   | 3 | 1 |   | 2 |   |
| 1 | 1 |   |   | 1 | 3 |
| 2 |   |   |   |   |   |
| 5 |   | 4 |   | 4 |   |

(b) →

| 4 | 5 |   |   | 2 |   |
|---|---|---|---|---|---|
| 3 | 2 | 1 |   |   |   |
| 1 | 1 | 3 | 1 |   |   |
| 2 |   |   |   |   |   |
| 5 | 4 | 4 |   |   |   |

(c)

Figure 12:  An Asynchronous Example.

A Simulation study [7] has shown that there is a positive result in using call repacking policy for telecommunication. However, the constraint and the environment
of multiple-processor systems are somewhat different. Extensive study, modeling,
and simulating the three-stage rearrangeable network under different system constraints and environments is justified. The data structure just described and its
possible advantageous implementations will make the study more realistic. In the
next section, a simulation model is proposed and some results are discussed.

IV. SIMULATION ANALYSIS

We have shown a graph routing algorithm for a class of rearrangeable interconnection networks in both synchronous and asynchronous environment. The implementation
of the algorithm uses two matrices of size N. Each element in the matrices represents a connection link which can be used for traversing the graph and thus allows
us to partition a graph or to select SDR's in a rearrangeable network. When an arbitrary permutation in a three-stage rearrangeable network is represented by a
matrix data structure (as shown in the example in Figure 11-b), the routing pro-
glem can be rephrased as a rearrangement of the data entries in the row directions
such that there is no duplicate entry in the column direction. Each row and column
correspond to the switch boxes in the left and center stages of the newtwork respectively. The numbers in the matrix denote the switch boxes in the right hand
side stage. Our simulation model is based on such a data structure.

We assume that each connection request to the network is generated independently
with exponential interarrival time distribution in the asynchronous environment.
The service time of a connection is also assumed exponential. The packing process
is performed during an arrival (connection request) and the repacking process is
done at the time of a departure (disconnection request). Since there are at most
N requests and the network is capable of servicing all N requests with proper rearrangement, the model can be regarded as a variation of finite-population-N-server

queueing system. We can describe the overall system in terms of the state transition diagram as shown in Figure 13. A state is defined as the existing number of connections in the network. It is further classified as one of the normal states, packing states, or repacking states. For brevity only the transitions to and from state $i$ are shown in the state transition diagram. The parameters $\lambda_i$, $\mu_i$ and $\gamma_i$

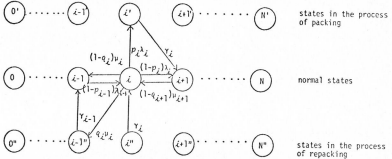

Figure 13: The State Transition Diagram

are mean rates of connection, disconnection, and rearrangement respectively. $P_i$ is the probability that a new connection request will be blocked at state $i$. $q_i$ is the probability that a repacking is needed upon a disconnection at state $i$. $\lambda_i$ and $\mu_i$ are external and their values depend only on $i$. $\gamma_i$ is a function of $i$ and the routing algorithm. $P_i$ and $q_i$ are dependent on the state of the network and the packing/repacking policies. $\gamma_i$, $P_i$, and $q_i$ can be estimated by simulation studies.

Some simulation results are obtained to observe the functionalities of $\gamma$, $p$, and $q$. The matrix data structure is used for simulation in both synchronous permutation and asynchronous interconnections. In the synchronous case, a permutation is generated randomly and stored in the matrix. Each column in the matric is checked and any duplicate is removed by interchanging entries in the same row. When such an interchange cannot be achieved, an interchange in another row is performed. This kind of interchange in a different row is referred to as the forced interchange. This implies that rearrangement in another switch box of the network is required. Table 1 shows the results for 1000 permutations using a CDC cyber 73 system. The time complexity of the routing is approximately in the order of $O(N^c)$ where $1<c<2$. The average forced interchange is low when N is relatively small.

| Network Size | | CPU sec. | average number of interchanges | average number of forced interchanges |
|---|---|---|---|---|
| N | $n=\sqrt{N}$ | | | |
| 25 | 5 | 5.6 | 5.95 | .60 |
| 100 | 10 | 60.0 | 51.83 | 15.52 |
| 225 | 15 | 273.1 | 176.60 | 65.79 |
| 400 | 20 | 829.5 | *Note: CPU time estimated in | |
| 625 | 25 | 2019.7 | these two cases. | |

Table I: Simulation Results for the Synchronous Algorithm.

A similar simulation in which some asynchronous operations are incorporated, is performed to study the packing effect and the blocking probability in asynchronous environment. In this simulation, individual connections are done one at a time. Each connection is set to the available entry in the leftmost column when there is no conflict (duplicate in the same column). This simple packing strategy leaves as many free columns as possible for other immediate connections without blocking. If a conflict exist then an interchange, or even further a forced interchange, is tested until the connection is successfully made. This process is a rearrangement of the partially connected network. Table II shows the results of the simulation with only asynchronous connections and packing.

| Network size | | CPU Time sec. | First forced interchange | Maximum # of interchange | Average # of interchange | Maximum # of forced interchange | Average # of forced interchange | Permutations without interchange |
|---|---|---|---|---|---|---|---|---|
| N | $\sqrt{N}$ | | | | | | | |
| 25 | 5 | 5.8 | 9 | 5 | 2.6 | 4 | 1.3 | 223 |
| 100 | 10 | 34.6 | 30 | 14 | 18.8 | 13 | 11.9 | 0 |
| 225 | 15 | 103.6 | 100 | 22 | 48.6 | 21 | 33.7 | 0 |
| 400 | 20 | 222.8 | 193 | 30 | 91.8 | 29 | 67.3 | 0 |
| 625 | 25 | 405.9 | 345 | 42 | 147.4 | 41 | 111.8 | 0 |

Table II:   Simulation Results for the Asynchronous Algorithm.
(1000 permutations)

Since there is no disconnection in the simulation, the algorithm performs permutations as the synchronous algorithms does. However, the time complexity shows improvement since some intelligence (the simple packing policy) is built into the algorithm to optimize the free columns. This packing strategy is also expected to reduce the blocking probability. The statistics of the average number of interchanges in Table II is clearly related to the blocking probability of the system. Another simulation which gives the average number of interchanges, and therefore the blocking probabilities, as a function of the load of the network is analyzed and plotted for three network size in Figure 14. It shows that blocking generally starts to occur when the network is half loaded and reaches the peak when the load is approximately $\sqrt{N}$ X ($\sqrt{N}$-1) connections. These results will be useful in evaluating the asynchronous interconnections in the MIMD environment.

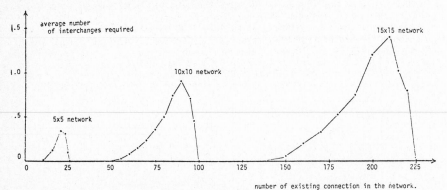

Figure 14:   Blocking vs System Load in Three Network Sizes.

V.  CONCLUSIONS

Compared to blocking-type interconnection networks, the rearrangeable interconnection network has advantages in several aspects since it can realize every arbitrary permutation in one pass; can partition a multiple-processor system into subsystems of arbitrary size; and can provide multiple paths for an input-output pair which are important for reliability. However, currently existing routing algorithms for the rearrangeable network need a work memory of impractical size, restrict their functions to a network of special size, and consume much time in back-tracking. This paper has shown a graph routing algorithm for the rearrangeable interconnection network. The algorithm can be implemented on a data structure which uses small amount of memory and is good for a network of arbitrary size. The small amount of work memory used in the algorithm suggests that associative processing is feasible and can be used to speed up the routing step. A heuristic method can be worked out to partially avoid the back-tracking. Back-tracking seems to represent a less serious problem since the routing for realizing frequently used permutations of parallel processing in the rearrangeable network can be handled in a special way. Asynchronous routing can also be implemented on the same data structure. Different routing strategies of packing and repacking can easily be implemented. A simulation model of the rearrangeable network is proposed to evaluate different routing strategies for asynchronous operations. Our simulation results show promise. Further simulation study is planned.

References

[1] V.E. Benes, "Optimal rearrangeable multistage connection networks," B.S.T.J., 43, part 2, July 1964, pp. 1641-1656.
[2] D.C. Opferman and N.T. Tsao-Wu, "On a class of rearrangeable switching networks," B.S.T.J., 50, May-June 1971, pp. 1579-1618.
[3] S. Andersen, "The looping algorithm extended to base $2^t$ rearrangeable switching networks," IEEE Trans. on Commun. Vol. COM-25, No. 10, October 1977, pp. 1057-1063.
[4] N.T. Tsao-Wu, "On Neiman's algorithm for the control of rearrangeable switching networks," IEEE Trans. on Commun., Vol. COM-22, No. 6, June 1974, pp. 737-742.
[5] H.R. Ramanujam, "Decomposition of permutation networks," IEEE Trans. on Comput., July 1973, pp. 639-643.
[6] M. Hall, Jr., "An algorithm for distinct representatives," Mathematical Notes, Vol. 63, 1956, pp. 716-717.
[7] M. Ackroyd, "Call repacking in connecting networks," IEEE Trans. on Commun., Vol. COM-27, No. 3, March 1979, pp. 589-591.
[8] C. Wu and T. Feng, "On a class of multistage interconnection networks," IEEE Trans. on Computers, August 1980.
[9] H.J. Siegel and S.D. Smith, "An interconnection network for multimicroprocessor emulator systems," Proc. 1st International Conference on Distributed Computing Systems, 1979, pp. 772-782.

Performance of Data Communication Systems
and their Applications, G. Pujolle (ed.)
© North-Holland Publishing Company, 1981

ROUTING PRINCIPLES FOR THE EIGHTIES : ARE EXPERIENCE AND THEORY SUFFICIENT
TO SETTLE FOR DISTRIBUTED AND ADAPTATIVE ROUTING ?

Michel Ossola

SESA
30, quai de Dion Bouton
92806 Puteaux
FRANCE

ABSTRACT

Routing functions and algorithms have been a major research
and experiment area for more than a decade, especially in
packet switching networks. Theoretical results and actual
implementation of commercial networks tend to converge
towards, at least, some basic principles.

Basic principles include the fact that distributed and
adaptative routing is advantageous and feasible, even in large
packet switching networks.

In this paper we try to distinguish which routing principles
could be agreed from theoretical results and experience, for
packet switching networks, and to what degree they can applied
to other networks. In addition the influence of the various
environments and services is discussed.

## I. INTRODUCTION

The importance of routing functions in message and packet switching networks has
been recognized for more than a decade, see for example [1, 2, 12, 13]. This
importance has been stressed even more when ARPANET has been designed and
implemented, since the real parameters, factors, and pitfalls of packet switching
were being discovered.

Obviously, today, every designer knows that routing and flow control principles of
a packet switched network are important issues with strong influence on the
characteristics of the service provided to users : delay, throughput, availability, stability, and fairness.

Thus, technical and commercial reasons have spurred a large amount of research and
implementation but the task of classification and taxonomy of routing functions is
not simple [2, 12, 13, 14].

The analysis of optimal, or at least good, routing functions remains an active
research domain where theoretical results are not always implementable at
reasonable cost.

The success of CCITT Recommendations related to packet switching, basically X.25
and related Recommendations X.3, X.28, X.29, X.75, X.121 and X.180, has also
largely changed the research environment into a fully industrial environment. The
purpose of this paper is to show that the main characteristics of modern routing
functions for packet-switching networks are known now from theory and experience
and that these characteristics can be used for other types of networks.

A short history of theoretical results and experience is provides in Section II in

35

order to extract the major points, distinguish the various environments and stress problems.

In section III, a set of routing principles is proposed for packet switching in various environments; the use of these principles for other types of networks is discussed.

## II. SHORT HISTORY OF ROUTING PRINCIPLES

### II.1  Experience and examples

Routing principles have always being discussed for classical message switching and circuit switching, but, after the early works of Baran [12] and NPL [24] the subject has really become a major design issue with the ARPANET, and the history of advanced routing functions is largely intertwined with packet switching history. The history of packet switching is very well summarized by Roberts [25] and Kleinrock [26]; a general survey of routing techniques is provided in [9] with some examples of actual implementations. However recent theoretical results, recent experiment and new needs should be taken into account. If we go back to original ARPANET routing, noted ARPA 69 in the following for brevity, the first main point was that routing should be distributed and adaptative versus centralized.

Purely centralized routing was, explicitly or implicitly, said to present all disadvantages:
- a central system is vulnerable or expensive if it has to be duplicated to alleviate the vulnerability aspect;
- traffic directed to the central system in order to optimize the routing would be concentrated in one area of the network, and if the amount of routing traffic is lowered in order to not disturb user traffic, optimization is not responsive enough to quick changes of the network;
- .with the same level of optimization a central algorithm is much more expensive in processing power than a distributed computation.

As a matter of fact some of these arguments were really expressed after the original choice and as many literary arguments could be developed on the other side:
- a serious network needs at least some central management system which can easily include central routing functions since the processing load is low in average,
- the traffic directed to this central function should not be so important since only major changes are interesting and not short term variations,
- it is simpler to test and to follow the behaviour of the whole network.

The ARPANET bet for routing was very appealing to the majority of designers, but if the rationale and goals were agreed, future problems were clear. Reassembly and store and forward deadlocks have been anticipated at first reading of [1].

Possible oscillations and divergence from optimality were also anticipated on examples of rather small networks. Fairness characteristics were also an issue. Other principles for distributed and adaptative routing were considered [17], in particular for EIN:
- use many good routes from a given originating node to every destination node in order to minimize delay and avoid possible oscillations;
- broadcast to every node a major reason of delay change;
- find a way to exchange updates quickly in the network, each node having a picture of the dynamic topology to every other node.

The detailed implementation of the last point remained to be worked out, in particular with symbolic addressing (the address of a user system is not directly related to its connecting node).

In any case the pioneering work of ARPA was and remains essential; the environment was experimental then, potentially encompassing private, civilian or defence network. However all the constraints of a public service were not satisfied (e.g., operation, billing, ...).

Various designs were initiated in the early seventies to provide a packet switching service in different ways.

The experimental network of the French PTT (RCP) and the experimental network CYCLADES are interesting on various grounds. RCP [28] used a virtual circuit establishment phase before any data transfer, which permitted a fixed route during the data transfer phase.

The fixed route characteristic suppressed many of difficulties of the ARPANET design:
- hop by hop flow control of individual virtual circuits is very safe and permits a designer to control closely stability and fairness of service.

The CIGALE network [29] of CYCLADES took a radically different approach: only individual packets, called datagrams were accepted and delivered by the sub-network not necessarily in the order sent. Clearly, various deadlocks of the original ARPANET design could not occur and issues were shifted to flow and congestion control; eventually routing functions were based on ARPA 69 principles.

The European Informatics Network [19] also supported the datagram service and permitted international internetworking experiments. Two options were developped in order to study the behaviour of service, with or without end-to-end flow control between nodes; routing functions were based on initial ARPA version, including improvements up to 1974, and some extensions. All these experimental networks have based routing functions largely on the ARPA 69 initial design, except for RCP which was the testbed of a public service offering virtual circuit. After wide recognition of the advantages of packet-switching technology, CCITT issued draft Recommendation X.25 for a virtual circuit service by October 1975. It was followed by companion Recommendations: X.3, X.28 and X.29 to support simple asynchronous terminals, X.75 for internetworking and X.121 for the worldwide numbering plan. The standardization process was highly desirable since various PTTs had announced, as soon as 1973, the opening of public and tariffed packet switching service.

## II.2. TRANSPAC

The routing choices for TRANSPAC, the French public network opened in fall of 1978, are an outgrowth of those tested in RCP [18, 27]:

- a path is fixed for the whole duration of a virtual call at call set up time;
- routing functions are performed by the nodes in combination with a central function hosted by a network management center (NMC) (duplicated);
- a link cost notion is based on various resource utilization measures (line and buffer utilisation);
- link cost variations, as viewed from the nodes, are reported to the NMC when the cost cross a small number of thresholds with an hysteresis mechanism;
- the NMC calculates for each node i the best path to all destinations j and informs i of changes when necessary;
- at call set up each node determines from its called party address and tables associated with the numbering plan a target node (in general the connecting node of the called party) and deduces from local cost of permitted links, and global information provided by the NMC, the current best outgoing link; each node along the path executes the same process.

Thus, the following characteristics must be stressed:
- numbering plan is symbolic;
- changes of paths occur only when noticeable variations occur, basically the updating process is event driven;
- many routes can be used simultaneously between a pair of nodes at a given time;
- the load of the central function remains low;

- the number and settings of thresholds provide tuning mechanisms.

Currently, with many thousands of users, routing functions have met initial objectives.
One should note that some choices depend on the environment and current service: the network is designed for extensions to a large number of users, so all links between nodes include at least two wideband lines, this largely suppresses the arguments against a fixed route during a call. A central function is naturally available with sufficient processing power.

II.3.  Other types of networks

Classical telephone exchanges use very often the following principles:
- for a given destination a trunk is used as long as it is not blocked or has not reached a threshold of occupancy;
- otherwise a small number of predetermined overflow trunks are tried.

Variations on the same principles, including fixed maximum percentages of traffic attributed to overflow trunks are current with stored program controlled exchanges. Two examples from defence environments are sketched to show that very different principles may be used, at least in rather small networks.

For the first network, all exchanges include an analog device which directly receives load information form each trunk; when an exchange processes a call, a simple input from the device provides the best route.

In the second example, a call is broadcasted to all neighbours and the called party, which can register itself dynamically in any exchange, is reached in any case if at least one route exists from the originating exchange. It is interesting to compare this call broadcasting to Baran's original studies on the flooding principle for data.

Message switching networks were in fact, consciously or not, integrating a packet switching function. This has been integrated in message switches themselves or supported by a separate subnetwork. Then the same rationale applied for routing in packet switching networks can be used largely also for message switching.

Some systems try to integrate packet and circuit switching, routing for the two competing services raises new problems for the choice of a common objective function [11].

II.4.  Theoretical analysis summary

Research and theoretical analysis have been and remain active. Various results can be applied for distributed or centralized control, but distributed and adaptative routing control is the principally studied principle. The whole packet-switching service is modelled as a multicommodity transportation network problem [13,31] which has been largely addressed in operations research.

The traditional objective function, to be minimized, is the average transit delay; sometimes additional separate objective are taken into account and, more generally, a cost notion is defined, largely based on delay.

Routing analytical results can be used either during the network design phase as a part of general problems, e.g. the Flow Assignment problem [13,32], or they can be used to minimize the chosen cost during the operational process of routing packets.

One should remark that practical constraints (processing power, line overhead, various failures) render operational routing more difficult since various algorithms are too expensive or too slow to implement. However analytical results are essential to give direction for actual implementations.

The various practical aspects of operational routing also render difficult the comparison of different sets of routing mechanisms, since it is very often difficult to show that one set is strictly superior to the other in any real condition: some mechanisms are superior for quasi steady traffic but react poorly to exceptional events.

Theoretical analysis tackled the following problems:
- minimization of delay under various assumptions of traffic and rate of convergence towards the optimum [13, 16, 32, 33, 35, 36, 37];
- loop avoidance or suppression [9, 34];
- oscillations avoidance or suppression;
- cost of implementation of various algorithms in memory size and processing power;
- shortest path computations with various metrics;
- choice of measurement variables and data to be exchanges [16, 33, 35].

Many other references can be found in the references provided here.

Some important results seem settled now:
- asynchronous updates are essential for quick reactions to major changes in the network;
- algorithms using only one route between a pair of nodes cannot be optimal if traffic matrix varies [32], in addition they can lend to oscillations [4, 16]; then many good routes should be preferred;
- various algorithms converging towards optimality, under certains assumptions, have been described;
- if loops are not suppressed by the fixed path implementation for virtual circuit service, some algorithms prevent loop building [9, 34].

## III.  CURRENT AND FUTURE REQUIREMENTS

### III.1.  Recent developments

After the long experience of initial routing mechanisms for the ARPANET, there have been major changes of principles and implementation recently. These changes and their rationale are published [6, 7, 8] and details are provided in BBN reports [3, 4, 5].

The new set of functions called ARPA 79 for brevity, displays the following set of characteristics:
- it remains distributed and adaptative;
- it is based on asynchronous updates unlike to ARPA 69;
- each node acquires the topology and costs of links of the whole network, all nodes have a complete and consistent view of the network;
- propagation of the delay information in the network is done by a flooding mechanism;
- a single best route to each destination is calculated by each node.

Reported experiments show that the defaults of ARPA 69 have been practically suppressed.

However, transient loops may exist and oscillations are theoretically possible (refer to the very interesting study of Bertsekas in [4]).

The implementation aspects of ARPA 79 show that memory cost, processing cost and line overheads are acceptable, even for large networks.

Transient loops may not be a major issue, but many good routes could be used to approach more closely the minimum delay objective and diminish the possibility of oscillations.

From theoretical view points, various recent papers present new or improved results: [9] specifies a failsafe algorithm to construct and maintain routing tables such that looping is prevented, [16] presents a new algorithm with a linear rate of convergence, [33] presents improvements to the convergence of the Flow Deviation method.

## III.2.  Services, environment, objectives

The current status of needs and services must be reassessed at this point.

Packet switching is now widely recognized as a major technique for data transmission and evolves in a fully industrial and commercial environment. This is largely due to the success of CCITT Recommendations. The 1976 version of X.25 specified only "pre-established virtual circuit", the 1980 version includes two facilities to fulfill the need for "short transaction": the fast select facility and datagrams [22]. In addition a fast transmission facility could be standardized. Recent ISO documents also show the same trend to include "connectionless transmissions" for level 4 and level 5 protocols [39].

The net result of recent standards, or trends of standards, is that short transactions between user systems could take place without preliminary logical establishment at any level of protocol. The real need for a short transaction service has always been there, especially for some private networks, if not for the majority of users of public networks. This need must be taken into account in current and future routing mechanisms; one should note that the fixed path principle is not ruled out if many paths are established dynamically between any origin-destination pair of nodes.

Private networks display basically the same requirements as public networks; then the majority of new private networks use CCITT Recommendations as main specifications.

For the defence environment, packet switching has already been used in many networks, new networks follow generally standardization from CCITT and ISO.
The needs for the short transaction service and for a strictly distributed and adaptative routing are often expressed, especially for tactical networks.

To summarize, the packet switching technique fulfills the requirements of many public, private and defence networks. The short transaction service is needed, especially for some private and defence networks. Distributed and adaptative routing is mandatory for some defence networks.

The size of network clearly has a large practical importance for the implementation of routing mechanisms, currently networks of few nodes to many hundreds are requested or anticipated; implementation must then remain feasible for large networks.

Modern packet switches are based on multimicroprocessor systems which may include a subsystem dedicated to control of the whole configuration [20]. In this case issues of processing overheads and memory needed are largely simplified.

## III.3.  Routing functional components and principles

The various functional components of routing must be distinguished to discuss principles. Naming, addressing and numbering plan issues should be clearly separated from actual routing functions. Currently, the use of symbolic addresses is mandatory for many networks. The size of some networks may lead to use of "regions". This last point, however, may have an influence on routing mechanisms and efficiency since some implementations may hide link status of remote nodes.

The following functional components are needed currently:
1. a measurement process of network parameters related to the cost function chosen;
2. an information dissemination process;
3. a data base for network status;
4. a translation mechanism from measured data to routing information;
5. a forwarding process.

Given the advantages of distributed and adaptative routing and ARPA 79 results, these basic principles can be used now, even for rather large networks. For networks including several hundred nodes some compromise between efficiency in exceptional cases and overhead may have to be chosen. The main parameter of cost function is delay; however, the throughput class notion in X.25, a probable delay class facility in X.25 and the cost of call processing have to be taken into account. The measurement of delay must be precise enough but averaged over a sufficient period in order to filter quick variations. The events triggering information exchange between nodes should be rare enough for theoretical and practical reasons. Various theoretical analyses necessitate the permanent measurement of first or second derivative of delays; a threshold mechanism with hysteresis seems good enough [18] and more practical currently.

A quick dissemination process is necessary, especially for exceptional events like failures; the flooding mechanism used in ARPA 79 is interesting in this respect.

With quick updates each node can constitute and maintain a data base on network status for all links, all data bases becoming consistent in a small time. The case of very large networks may imply network partition.

In order to minimize delay and prevent possible oscillations many good routes should be used for any pair of nodes. It remains to be studied whether loop-free algorithms can exhibit the same practical and theoretical advantages of other routings where loops can occur. A practical insurance that loops are limited in time can be sufficient. Clearly, the fixed path principle for the pre-established virtual circuit service leaves the problem of loop detection and prevention to the call set-up phase, it can be solved rather easily by tracing the call. The combination of local information and exchanged data to build tables for the forwarding process is practical matter.

Symbolic addressing, large network sizes and adaptability to changes, practically imply a two stage forwarding process: from tables associated with the numbering plan a target node (or region if needed) is deduced, then an outgoing link is deduced from tables reflecting the optimization of routing. The same process is repeated in each node until the delivery of data packet to the destination for the short transaction service, or until the path is fixed for the basic virtual circuit service (the fixed path is not mandatory but has many advantages).

Some complementary objectives are also important. Resilience to errors and failures is important. Permanent checking of routing programs and tables must be done in some ways which may depend on principles used and detailed implementation choices. In addition a fall-back routing may have to be actuated in exceptional cases - the shortest path, measured in hops, is a good practical candidate.

Multiconnection of user systems to more than one network node is sometimes required when very high availability of access is needed.

One should note that these cases are rare since multiconnection to a node is already provided and modern nodes can display very high availability. Then multiconnection to different nodes is actually superior if the links to different nodes have strictly no common part; this need appears mainly in the defence environment and for some private networks.

Assuming the use of the fixed path principle for virtual circuit service, load sharing can be globally guided by tables associated with the numbering plan which translates a called party address into a target node, automatic back-up between the different links can be done via a call transfer facility which is bound to be offered in X.25 networks.

In addition, by including the links connecting the multiconnected users into the routing information exchange used for internal links, a good path can be chosen without a priori load spread nor back-up mechanism. This last solution has obviously an additional cost since some access links will appear as additional internal links for routing components of the nodes.

Internetworking, national or international, raises various issues for routing. Currently, the majority of internetworking is done via a unique gateway or gateway halves (see the STE function in [23]) between a pair of networks.

In this case routing for internetwork transmission does not raise any additional problem to the internal routing principles of each network. But geographic conditions, availability concerns for civilian networks and vulnerability concerns for defence networks will justify the use of several gateways between a pair of networks, in various cases.

One can see that this problem is very similar to the multiconnection of users and can be solved in the same way. In the most general case gateways of network A with network B have to report to A the cost of links to B as if network B was a node of network A. It is unlikely that two networks have the same routing information exchanges, then, a gateway of network A will not transmit routing information from A to B but will report to A the cost of links to B.

The previous principles permit a designer to satisfy the objectives of routing:
- minimize a cost function largely based on delay;
- contribute to fairness and stability of service;
- dynamic acquisition of network topology;
- resilience to various failures;
- quick adaptation to major changes;
- enable some tuning to be done by network operators;
- prevent or suppress long term loops if they are possible.

This is currently true for networks of, say one hundred nodes, while very large networks need some further work.

### III.4. Future requirements

A routing algorithm for telephone networks with programmed exchanges is presented in [15], it is centralized. One can remark that distributed and adaptative routing, including the use of non-local information, could be used for these types of networks with the same intrisic advantages as when applied to packet switching nodes; this is rarely the case in telephone exchanges. The only major difference is the cost notion to be minimized.

Routing for an hybrid system [11] has been mentionned, it could be enhanced by the same evolution which has lead from ARPA 69 to ARPA 79; the main question is the future of this type of systems given new trends. Two trends may largely influence medium term future and the next decades: vocoders and Integrated (Services) Digital Network (ISDN or IDN) projects.

When vocoders will be available at low cost and with good quality, the circuit switching principle could disappear since the packet switching principle is superior over a large range of parameters [21].

The quality and cost of vocoders is currently highly debated for the medium term. And the debate between proponents of packet switching for speech and proponents of circuit switching, whatever the speed of coding, is far from being finished. Results in [21] show that, at least for private networks, local or not, packet switching for data and speech, may be cost effective in the medium term. The specific of speech packets have some influence on routing principles, but the majority of principles for data packet can be kept. The importance of small variations of delay may lead to modified cost functions and forwarding process.

In IDN or ISDN environment, routing is involved at two levels:
- routing of signalling information;
- routing for cuircuit switching.

As for current programmed telephone exchanges, routing can be based on what has been proposed for packet switching, except that a different cost function must be used for circuit switching.

Signalling information is bound to conform to common channel signalling system N° 7 or improved versions [38]; whatever the details of protocols, the real need is actually a short transaction packet switching application. "Semaphore" channels, which can be separated or not according to the type of signalling applications, constitute in fact a reserved network of channels where the Signalling Transfer Points (STP) may have the function of packet switches. This integrated packet switching application could largely use the routing principles proposed for traditional packet switching, especially inside a network of STPs.

Whatever happen for speech per packet in various environments and terms, the packet switching function is needed and routing principles designed for data packet switching can largely be re-used.

IV.  CONCLUSION

After a brief summary of experience and theoretical results we have proposed a set of principles for routing in packet switching networks. The main principle is that purely distributed and adaptative routing can be used safely now, even if mixed policies between local and central functions were sufficient in various networks. The same basic principles could be used in other types of networks provided that various adaptations are done for the choice of cost function and for very large networks. It is conjectured that a routing algorithm can be designed with the following properties:
- nodes will need to know only their neighbours, unlike ARPA 79;
- basically the same properties proven in [9] will hold;
- a given destination may appear in many nodes.

REFERENCES

[1]   F.E. Heart, R.E. Kahn, S.M. Ornstein, W.R. Crowther, and D.D. Walden, "The interface message processor for the ARPA computer network", in AFIPS Conf. Proc. 36, pp 551-567, June 1970.
[2]   J.M. Mc Quillan, "Adaptative routing algorithms for distributed computer networks", BBN Rep. 2831, May 1974.
[3]   J.M. Mc Quillan, I. Richer, E.C. Rosen, "ARPANET routing algorithm improvements", BBN Rep. 3803, April 1978.
[4]   J.M. Mc Quillan, I. Richer, E.C. Rosen and D.F. Bertsekas, "ARPANET routing algorithm improvements", BBN Rep. 3940, October 1978.
[5]   E.C. Rosen, J.G. Herman, I. Richer, and J.M. Mc Quillan "The updating protocol algorithm improvements", BBN Report 4088, March 1979.
[6]   E.C. Rosen, "The updating protocol of ARPANET's new routing algorithm", Computer Networks VOL. 4. N° 1, February 1980.
[7]   J.M. Mc Quillan, I. Richer, E.C. Rosen, "The new routing algorithm for the ARPANET", IEEE Trans on Com., VOL. COM 28, N° 5, May 1980.
[8]   J.M. Mc Quillan, I. Richer, E.C. Rosen, "An overview of the new routing algorithm for the ARPANET," Proceedings of the sixth Data Communication Symposium, Pacific Grove, California, November 1979.
[9]   P.M. Merlin, A. Segall, "A failsafe distributed routing protocol", IEEE Trans on Com. VOL. Com 27, N° 9, September 1979.
[10]  M. Schwartz, Computer Communication Network Design and Analysis. Englewood Cliffs, NJ : Prentice Hall, 1977.
[11]  M. Gerla, D. Mason, "Distributed routing in hybrid packet and circuit data networks", IEEE COMPCOM 78F, pp 125-131.
[12]  P. Baran et al., "On distributed Communications, vols. I-XI". RAND Corporation Research Documents, August 1964.
[13]  L. Kleinrock, Communication Nets : Stochastic Message Flow and Delay. New-York : Mc Graw-Hill, 1964. Reprinted by Dover Publications, 1972.
[14]  H. Rudin, "On routing and Delta-routing": A taxonomy and performance

comparison of techniques for packet-switched networks", IEEE Trans. Com. VOL. COM-24, January 1976.

[15] E. Szybicki, A.E. Bean, "Advanced traffic routing in local telephone networks : performance of proposed call routing algorithms", International Teletraffic Congress 9. Torremolinos 1979.

[16] D.P. Bertsekas, "A class of optimal routing algorithms for communication networks", in Proc. 5th ICCC, Atlanta, 27-30 October 1980.

[17] Discussions G. Louït, M. Ossola 71-73.

[18] J.M. Simon, A. Danet, "Contrôle des ressources et principes du routage dans le réseau Transpac", in Proc., Int. Symp. Flow Control in Comput. Networks, Versailles, France, February 1979, J.L. Grangé & M. Gien, Eds. Amsterdam : North-Holland, pp. 33-34.

[19] F. Poncet & C.S. Repton, "The EIN Communications sub-network : Principles and practice", in Proc. 3rd ICCC, Toronto, Ont. Canada, August 1976, pp. 523-531.

[20] SESA commercial brochure "DPS 25 packet switching".

[21] I. Gitman, H. Frank, "Economic analysis of integrated voice and data networks : A case study, "IEEE trans on Com., Vol. COM-28, N° 4, April 1980.

[22] CCITT VIIth Plenary Assembly, Doc. N° 7, SG VII Contribution N° 489, "Recommendation X.25".

[23] CCITT VIIth Plenary Assembly, Doc. N° 10, SG VII Contribution N° 492, "Recommendation X.75".

[24] D.W. Davies, K.A. Bartlett, R.A. Scantelbury & P.T. Wilkinson, "A digital communications network for computers giving rapid response at remote terminals", "ACM Sym. Operating Systems Problems" October 1967.

[25] L.G. Roberts, "The evolution of packet switching", in Proc. IEEE, Vol. 66, N° 11, November 1978.

[26] L. Kleinrock, "Principles and lessons in packet communications", in Proc. IEEE, Vol. 66, N° 11, November 1978.

[27] SESA internal document 8150/LN 200 72, "Algorithme de routage sur le réseau TRANSPAC".

[28] R.F. Despres, "A packet network with graceful satured operation", in Proc. ICCC, Washington DC, pp. 345-451, October 1972.

[29] L. Pouzin "Presentation and major design aspects of the CYCLADES network", in third Data Communication Symp., Tampa, FL, pp. 80-85, November 1973.

[30] CCITT Editor on fast transmission, "Fast transmission facility", CCITT SG VII, TD N° 103 revised, 7-15 February 1980.

[31] CCITT VIIth Plenary Assembly, Doc. N° 11, SG VII Contribution n° 493, "Recommendations X.80-X.180".

[32] L. Fratta, M. Gerla & L. Kleinrock, "The flow deviation method : An approach to store and forward communication network design", Networks, Vol. 3. New-York : Wiley, 1973, pp. 97-133.

[33] J. Courtois & P. Semal, "Flow assignment algorithm based on the flow deviation method", in Proc. 5th ICC, Atlanta, 27-30 October 1980.

[34] W. Naylor, "A loop free adaptative routing algorithm for packet switching network", in Proc. 4th Data Communications Symp., Quebec City, Canada, pp. 7.9-7.14, October 1975.

[35] R.G. Gallager, "A minimum delay routing algorithm using distributed computation", IEEE Trans on Com. Vol. COM-25, N° 1, January 1977.

[36] D.G. Cantor, M. Gerla, "Optimal routing in packet switched computer networks", IEEE Trans on Com., Vol. G-23, 1974, pp. 1062-1069.

[37] M. Schwartz, C.K. Cheung, "The gradient projection algorithm for multiple routing in message-switched networks", IEEE Trans. on Com., COM-24, N° 4, April 1976, pp. 449-456.

[38] CCITT VIIth Plenary Assembly, Doc. N° 18, SG XI Contribution N° 393, "Specifications of CCITT common channel signalling system N° 7".

[39] ISO DP 7498, "Data processing - Open systems interconnection - Basic reference model", 3 December 1980.
ISO 97/16 N566, "Report of the ad-hoc group on connectionless data transmission", November 1980.

Performance of Data Communication Systems
and their Applications, G. Pujolle (ed.)
© North-Holland Publishing Company, 1981

# DISTRIBUTED MINIMAL SPANNING TREE ALGORITHMS

## D. Stott Parker, Jr.

## Behrokh Samadi

### UCLA Computer Science Department
### Boelter Hall
### Los Angeles, CA 90024

Computer networks frequently require some kind of mechanism for broadcasting messages, *i.e.*, a means of sending one message to all nodes. Simply sending a copy of the message to every node, or sending a copy along every link in the network, will suffice. However, if we wish to minimize cost, a far more efficient method of broadcasting is to let the message simply 'fan-out' along the edges of a *minimum spanning tree*, a tree subgraph of the network which connects all nodes and has minimum total length.

In this paper we describe several distributed algorithms for finding minimum spanning trees. The algorithms work under a variety of network models and cost measures. The performances of the algorithms are compared, and their tradeoffs discussed.

## 1. Introduction

With increasing progress in the development of multiprocessor systems and computer networks, the need has developed for new systems functions which take advantage of, or enhance, the network environment. Examples include routing of messages, maintenance of network statistics, and setting up closed user groups (treating a subnetwork as a logically separate network). A commonly needed function is a *broadcasting* mechanism, a means for sending a message from one site to all sites in the network (or some collection of sites). A process at one site can notify all other sites of the availability or status of important resources, request status information from all sites, and so forth.

Several ways for implementing broadcasting suggest themselves immediately. We can route one copy of the broadcast message to every other node, or along every link in the network. However these methods are much less efficient than simply having the message be 'fanned out' along some tree that spans the network. We view the node originating the message as the root of the tree, and as the message arrives at each subsequent node it is propagated to all of its descendants (*i.e.*, along all links except the incoming link).

Now, assume that each link in the network has some associated *cost* reflecting, say, the expense of sending a message across it, and that the cost of transmitting messages is determined by the sum of the costs of these links. Then the best tree for efficient broadcasting from any node $x$ will be a *minimum spanning tree (MST)*. A minimum spanning tree is a tree subnetwork which is incident upon all nodes and has minimum cost.

Interesting surveys of broadcast techniques may be found in [4,14]. The minimum spanning tree has other uses in computer networks as well. To some extent it can be used as a communications path in *'closed user groups'*, a subset of nodes in the network which is closed to outside traffic and becomes a logical network on its own. More generally, it may be used as a *multicast* path. (A multicast message is transmitted to a specified subset of nodes.)

In many networks, cost may be measured by total *delay* in delivering a message. In this case, a shortest path tree for $x$, or something like it, may be the best broadcast path from $x$ [4,14]. However, the MST may still be interesting as a broadcast mechanism, since it minimizes the total load put on the network by a broadcast (it puts load where delay is least). This can lead to better network utilization. In addition, regardless of form of the cost, it turns out that reasonably good *'virtual rings'* connecting nodes in a cycle can be obtained through constructing MSTs [6]. This ring can be used, for example, to provide a simple sequencing method to avoid deadlock among processes in distributed database applications.

At any rate, we are thus led to the problem of finding minimum spanning trees in a computer network.

Due to increased potential reliability, load sharing, and performance under network changes, interest in distributed algorithms has grown. This interest can only grow as networks become larger and more complex. However for some tasks no distributed algorithm will perform better than a centralized one. That is, in some cases it is more cost-effective simply to send all relevant data to one site, do whatever computation is needed, and then send back the answer. We describe below several distributed algorithms, give bounds on their performance, and compare their tradeoffs.

We consider here only the problem of distributively constructing a MST 'from scratch'. Note that this problem is interesting mainly in networks where costs are fluctuating, since otherwise a MST may be found statically. It may be interesting, then, to examine algorithms which modify an existing tree as costs change, *i.e.*, *adapt* to cost fluctuations. Several new adaptive algorithms are discussed in [9].

The paper is organized as follows. Section 2 describes network models assumed by the algorithms discussed here. Section 3 reviews previous work on MST algorithms, both centralized and distributed. Section 4 then presents a new distributed algorithm linked tightly to the Union-Find algorithm. (An appendix gives a detailed description of this algorithm.) Finally, in Section 5 we discuss the performance of the algorithms, illustrating tradeoffs between message complexity and concurrency (speed).

## 2. Network Models

We regard a computer network as a connected undirected graph. Each node of the graph is an independent processor which interacts with its neighbors through messages. The edges of the graph correspond to the communication links of the network. We distinguish the following two models:

1. **Link model** [7,1]:
   In this model each node knows only
   (a)  its identity and the identities of its neighbor nodes, and the links on which they are adjacent
   (b)  the costs of these links

In particular individual nodes are not aware of the total number of nodes in the network.

2. **Source-destination model** [4,6,14]:
   In this model a routing subsystem provides each node $x$ with
   (a)  its identity and the identities of its neighbor nodes, and the links on which they are adjacent
   (b)  a table giving the cost of the cheapest path from $x$ to any other node $y$ in the network, and the identity of the neighbor node (on this path) via whom messages to $y$ should be routed.

Such tables are typical in extant network routing systems [11].

In both models, 'cost' can be a function of link traffic, capacity, reliability or any other network performance measure. We assume that costs of links between neighboring nodes are known exactly, and both nodes on the link agree on a consistent value. In the source-destination model, however, the costs for non-neighbor nodes do *not* necessarily meet this condition: they are just current estimates of cost. *Costs may fluctuate,* possibly even during the execution of our algorithms. If we assume costs will not fluctuate, much of the usefulness of having a distributed algorithm is put in question.

In either network model, we assume that *costs are unique*. This is important, for it provides a way to guarantee that a distributed MST algorithm will work. A consequence of assuming unique costs is that the MST is unique. Without unique costs, it is difficult to design distributed algorithms which correctly construct trees in a network containing a cycle of equi-cost links: by symmetry, no node executing the algorithm will break the cycle unless all nodes break the cycle. This symmetry must be removed somehow. Cost uniqueness seems at first a strong requirement, but actually may be implemented quite easily. One may transform non-unique costs into unique ones by appending to the cost the identities of the nodes at the ends of the corresponding link or path.

We assume that *messages arrive in sequence* across all paths, in either model. The two models count messages somewhat differently: in the link model, a single message is counted for each transfer across a link. In the source-destination model, a single message is counted for each source-to-destination transfer, although such a transfer may span multiple links.

## 3. Existing MST Construction Algorithms

There are a number of MST construction algorithms, both centralized and distributed. By 'centralized' algorithms we mean those which do not attempt distributed processing. Such algorithms execute on a network by collecting all cost information at a single node, and subsequently disseminating a solution.

## 3.1. Centralized Algorithms

Many efficient centralized algorithms for MST construction exist. The two classical algorithms are those of Kruskal and Prim-Dijkstra.

Kruskal [8] initially sorts the link costs and, starting from the smallest, adds successive links to an incident subtree whenever doing so does not form a cycle. The algorithm actually develops several subtrees simultaneously, combining them whenever possible. The algorithm takes at most $O(m \log n)$ time to complete.

The algorithm developed by Prim [10] and independently by Dijkstra [5] expands a single subtree and adds links gradually until the tree is formed. This algorithm also takes worst case time $O(m \log n)$ to construct the MST, when suitably implemented.

Yao [15] improves on the above time bounds by first partitioning the incident edges of each node into $k$ equal sets such that edges in the $i^{th}$ set have a smaller or equal cost than those of any set of higher index. Taking $k$ to be $\log n$ and using the partitions he develops an algorithm which takes time $O(m \log \log n)$ to complete.

Cheriton and Tarjan [2] give a good survey of MST algorithms and discuss implementation aspects. They employ the Union-Find algorithm [13] discussed below in Section 4.1 to produce fast MST algorithms for both the sparse and dense graph cases. Among other things, they point out that all existing MST algorithms follow the same basic paradigm:

> At any point of the execution one has constructed a set of disjoint *fragments,* trees which are contained in the network. (Each fragment initially consists of an isolated node.) One selects a fragment $F$ and finds its *cheapest outgoing link* $(x,y)$, a link connecting it with a different fragment $F'$. The fragments $F$ and $F'$ are then replaced in our set with the fragment formed by merging $F$, $F'$, and $(x,y)$. This is repeated until the set contains a single fragment, which is a MST.

The differences in the algorithms lie in the way fragments are selected; rapid algorithms result if the fragments are kept roughly equal in size.

## 3.2. Distributed Algorithms

Dalal [3] presents two algorithms to be used for constructing MSTs. The first is static in the sense that it does not adapt to the network changes. A clear description of the algorithm and a proof of its correctness may be found in [14,§4.1]. The second algorithm is adaptive to change and dynamically converts an old MST into a new one when costs fluctuate or network topology changes. Dalal does not discuss the communication costs of the algorithms.

Spira [12], and later Gallager, Humblet and Spira [7] modified Dalal's static algorithm. Their algorithm is an improvement over Dalal's algorithm in that it requires fewer messages in the worst case, and these messages are significantly smaller (Dalal's algorithm passes descriptions of the entire MST). The algorithm is quite intricate and ingenious in its savings on messages; we sketch its organization here.

This algorithm follows the paradigm above, but here each fragment possesses a *core,* a central link whose incident nodes control its operation, and is assigned a *level number,* an artificial number basically reflecting the size of the fragment. Each node starts at level zero when 'woken up' through receipt of its first message, or through external stimulus. It then connects immediately to its nearest neighbor node; the link joining these nodes becomes a core.

Thenceforth, fragments find their cheapest outgoing link and report its cost to the neighbor node within the fragment. Determining whether a link is outgoing is not trivial. The cores broadcast a fragment identifier when they request outgoing link information, and intuitively a link can be tested to see if it is outgoing simply by testing the identifier on the other side. However, many nodes may have an out-of-date identifier. This problem is resolved by also broadcasting a level number for the current fragment, and waiting to respond to an 'outgoing link' test until the level number of the testing fragment is not larger. Thus level numbers serve to guarantee up-to-date fragment information.

The 'outgoing link' reports converge toward the core of the fragment, being merged on the way. Ultimately the two adjacent core nodes exchange reports, determine the cheapest outgoing link $(x,y)$, and send a message to connect along this link to a neighboring fragment. If both fragments attempt to connect across $(x,y)$, it is made the new core for the combined fragment.

There are two other situations in which level numbers come into play. First, in the case where only one fragment desires to connect across $(x,y)$, Gallager *et al.* permit it to connect only if its level number is smaller than its neighbor's. In this case the core of the smaller level fragment is dissolved, and the fragment is notified that a new core may be found across $(x,y)$.

Second, two fragments of level $L$ connect only if they are each other's closest fragment. The link connecting the fragments becomes the core. The level of the resulting larger fragment is set to be $L+1$. Thus a fragment of level $n$ is guaranteed to contain at least $2^n$ nodes.

The algorithm takes at most $2m + 5n \log n$ messages to complete, and each message carries little information.

Chang [1] presents an MST algorithm which follows his general 'echo algorithm' scheme. In this scheme a node initially broadcasts a signal to all its adjacent nodes. The signal carries different information for different applications. Any node which receives the signal for the first time notes from which neighbor it came and retransmits the signal to its other neighbor nodes (possibly after processing the information). When a node receives the signal for the second time or has no other outgoing links, it immediately sends an echo signal back on the same link. Each node eventually receives echoes from all links on which it transmitted, and when all such echoes have accumulated it itself transmits an echo on the link over which it had first received the forwarding signal. Echo signals are hence echoed to the initiating node.

To construct the MST, echo signals deliver required information to the nodes on the way to the initiator. The nodes process the information and only retransmit that which could be used by the nodes of higher level. The information consists of an edge (link) set which forms an MST within the subgraph traversed so far by the echo. A node initiating an echo sends only the identity of the link the echo is transmitted on, as an edge set. A node receiving echoes combines their edge sets and finds the corresponding vertex (node) set. The node subsequently performs the Kruskal algorithm and obtains an MST based on that information. It then emits an echo which carries the edge set consisting of the MST edges and the edge over which the echo is transmitted. This process is carried out at every node until the initiator produces the final MST.

The algorithm requires $O(m)$ messages to construct the MST where each message carries at most $O(n)$ edge descriptors.

## 4. A Distributed MST Algorithm

Unlike the distributed algorithms presented in Section 3.2, the algorithm described in this section works with the source-destination network model of Section 2. In several respects the algorithm resembles that of Dalal, and of Gallager, Humblet and Spira, but has been designed to take advantage of some of the routing information of the source-destination model. In addition, the Union-Find (UF) algorithm [13] is used to minimize the number of transmitted messages.

### 4.1. Union-Find Algorithm

The UF algorithm carries out an intermixed sequence of two operations $FIND(x)$ and $UNION(A,B,C)$ on a collection of disjoint sets. These sets initially contain singletons. The operations are defined as follows:

$FIND(x)$:        Finds the name of the set which contains $x$.

$UNION(A,B,C)$:Performs the union of two sets $A$ and $B$, naming the resulting set $C$.

Each set is represented as a tree, the root of which contains the set name. Each node except the root represents an element of the set and has a pointer to its parent node. In order to carry out the $FIND(x)$ operation, pointers from node $x$ are followed to the root of the tree. To carry out $UNION(A,B,C)$, one of the roots $A$ or $B$ is made to point to the other and hence become a subtree. The name of the resulting tree is changed to $C$.

To optimize the above routines, two extra rules are defined:

(a)    The collapsing rule
       All pointers traversed in finding the set name (root) in a $FIND(x)$ operation are updated to point directly to the root. This reduces the number of node traversals in future $FIND(x)$ operations.

(b)    The weighted union rule
       When executing $UNION(A,B,C)$, the smaller of the two trees $A$ and $B$ (in terms of number of nodes) is chosen to become a subtree of the other. This rule preserves the balance of the tree to some extent.

The following bounds have been derived on the time $t(\mu,\nu)$ to carry out $\mu$ FINDs and $\nu-1$ UNIONs [13].

With neither the collapsing nor the weighted union rule,

$$k_1 \mu\nu \;\leqslant\; t(\mu,\nu) \;\leqslant\; k_2 \mu\nu$$

where $k_1$ and $k_2$ are positive constants.

Implementing only the weighted union rule,

$$k_1 \, \mu \, \log \nu \;\; \leqslant \;\; t(\mu,\nu) \;\; \leqslant \;\; k_2 \, \mu \, \log \nu$$

With only the collapsing rule,

$$t(\mu,\nu) \;\; \leqslant \;\; k\mu \; max( \, 1, \, \log(\nu^2/\mu)/\log(2\mu/\nu) \, )$$

Finally using both rules, we get the following bounds on the time:

$$k_1 \, \mu \, \alpha(\mu,\nu) \;\; \leqslant \;\; t(\mu,\nu) \;\; \leqslant \;\; k_2 \, \mu \, \alpha(\mu,\nu)$$

where $\alpha$ is the functional inverse of Ackermann's function and has the following property:

$$\alpha(\nu,\nu) \;\; \leqslant \;\; 3 \qquad \text{for } all \; \nu < \; 2^{2^{\cdots^2}} \Bigg\} \; 65537 \;\; twos.$$

## 4.2. Description of the MST Algorithm(s)

Initially all nodes are assumed asleep. At some point one or more of them is awakened by a signal, and initializes the algorithm. The algorithm consists of a basic loop in which each node processes a message whenever one has been received, and otherwise attempts to connect to another and form a larger fragment.

Every fragment has a *core node* which carries an *ftab,* some tabular information about the fragment. The ftab lists the identifiers and distances of all nodes adjacent to, but not in, the fragment.

After reference to the ftab, each core finds the node closest to its fragment. It subsequently sends a message requesting a connection to that node. The node receiving the request will retransmit the message to its core if not itself a core. This retransmission continues successively until finally the core receives the signal. The reason for this retransmission is that not all nodes have up-to-date information regarding the identity of the core in their fragment.

Once the latter core is reached, the cores can determine who will join the other. The core of the joining fragment then transmits its ftab to the other core, and subsequently the two form a single larger fragment. Only those nodes which have participated in the two cores' communication now have current information on the core identity. This process continues until only a single fragment remains.

Many different approaches may be taken to decide how fragments merge. In one, the fragment which has the higher identity value joins the second fragment. In another the fragment with the smaller number of nodes forms a subtree of the larger, with ties resolved as in the first approach. Below we consider the implementation of each of these methods, and investigate their performance.

Our basic algorithm is reminiscent of Dalal's static algorithm [3]. The differences are:

1.  A different network model (the source-destination model) has been considered. This is significant only insofar as messages are assumed to be routed, in one step, from any source to any destination node.

2.  Our algorithm draws on concepts of the UF algorithm, and implements the weighted union and collapsing rules for better performance.

## 4.3. Routines

The algorithm assumes that each node has several variables:

(a)  A node identifier *(nid).*

(b)  The identifier of the node considered as the core of its fragment *(coreid).* This information may be out of date.

(c)  A 'routing table', giving adjacent nodes and their distances. (Note that we only require information about immediately adjacent nodes, less than is provided by the source-destination model.)

(d)  Finally, if the node is the core of a fragment, it contains the updated version of ftab.

*Main procedure*

Initially one or more nodes will receive a signal and consequently invoke the construct_MST routine. The routine initializes the construction environment and enters a loop which repeatedly (1) processes a message, if one has been received, by invoking the appropriate routine below, or (2) otherwise attempts to connect to a nearest neighbor fragment by sending a $CONNECT(a,b,c,d)$ message. Here $a$ is the nid of the originating node, $(b,c)$ is the minimum outgoing link from $a$'s fragment, and $d$ is the node who has most recently handled the message (the message must be passed from node to node until it reaches the core of the other fragment). Note that we are assuming that all distances are unique so a unique minimum outgoing link always exists.

### process_CONNECT

This procedure is executed when a $CONNECT$ message is received. (The node starts the main procedure if asleep when this message arrives.) A node checks first to see whether it is the destination core. If not the core, it relays the $CONNECT$ message to its coreid. If it is the core, it responds with an $ACCEPT(a,b,c,d)$ provided it is not busy (involved in a connection with a different fragment). Here, just as in the $CONNECT$ message, $a$ and $d$ are the destination and source identities and $(b,c)$ is the link which will connect the two fragments. The $ACCEPT$ message will traverse the same path that the matching $CONNECT$ message has traversed, and will update the coreids of the nodes along the path.

The weighted union rule may be implemented here, at some cost to concurrency. Fragment sizes are compared, and if the receiving core's fragment is smaller, it connects to the other fragment via a $MERGE$ message. Otherwise it becomes 'drowsy' and waits for the other's ftab.

### process_ACCEPT

When an $ACCEPT(a,b,c,d,newcore)$ message is received, a node first updates its coreid to be $newcore$ and then checks the destination address, $a$. The message will be relayed to the next node on the path created by the connect routine if nid is not $a$. Otherwise, node $a$ checks whether it is $newcore$, $i.e.$, it is the new core for the fragment. If not, it will send its ftab to $newcore$ with a $MERGE$ message and hence connect to that fragment. If it is, it becomes 'drowsy' and avoids its next $CONNECT$ion until it receives the other node's ftab. This will avoid unnecessary retransmission of the ftab which can occur if node $a$ subsequently $MERGE$s with some other fragment before the ftab from this earlier fragment arrives.

This routine basically implements the collapsing rule of the UF algorithm.

### process_MERGE

Once the ftab is received, the process_MERGE routine connects the two fragments by merging their information. The new ftab contains a list of the nodes in the fragment, and a list of all outgoing links. (Many links of the respective ftabs may be found, in merging, to connect the two fragments. These links are removed.) The node is removed from the drowsy state, and may seek new connections.

As in the other algorithms, it is not difficult here to show that the algorithm cannot deadlock, assuming that costs do not fluctuate during its execution. In order to do so, it would need a cycle of nodes waiting upon one another's completion, either in drowsy or connecting state. It is easily seen that this cannot arise with a pair of nodes; nor can it happen with more than 2 nodes, since doing so would imply a cycle in the MST.

## 5. Performance Comparisons

In this section we outline the tradeoffs of the distributed algorithms and compare their performance. Two performance measures, expressed in terms of the number of nodes $n$ and the number of links $m$ in the network, are significant. The *time to completion* of an algorithm expresses the time needed to find a MST. Timing is usually hard to measure in distributed algorithms, for it depends on the number and order of nodes starting the algorithm, processor speeds, network configuration etc. We will examine the number of *steps* required for completion, where a step is a single time slot in which any nodes so desiring may transmit a message. For the sake of analysis, computation time is viewed as negligible, and nodes transmit messages at the earliest possible step. Another measure is the *message complexity,* defined as either the number of messages, or the total number of bits in messages, transmitted in executing the algorithm.

One problem with distributed algorithms is that the degree of concurrency often depends heavily on which node starts the operation; [7] show that in some cases the algorithm can perform quite sequentially. One way to tackle this problem is to make all nodes start executing the algorithm almost simultaneously, but this requires the broadcasting of a 'wakeup' message to all nodes. It seems quite reasonable for this problem to require a 'wakeup' message of some kind, if for no other reason than to get all nodes to 'freeze' their cost values and obtain a mutually consistent view of the network. If network costs are fluctuating, failure to obtain consistent views can lead to *deadlocks.*

Another concern in a dynamic environment is determining *when* a distributed algorithm should be invoked. This issue has not been investigated, except insofar as to note that invocation is required when the network changes topologically. When only cost changes are involved, determining when to invoke a procedure which reestablishes a 'global' property is difficult. Some partial results for MSTs appear in [9].

We now outline the algorithm costs for both versions in terms of number of transmitted messages.

Without the weighted union implementation, in the worst case, the number of traversed tree links in the UF algorithm for $O(n)$ finds and $O(n)$ unions is of $O(n \log n)$ [13]. This number is equivalent to the number of transmitted *CONNECT* and *ACCEPT* messages. With every ftab transfer, one link of the MST is formed. Hence $O(n)$ ftab transfers (*MERGE*s) messages are required. We also require $O(n)$ *FINISH* messages.

The total number of transmitted messages is therefore of $O(n \log n)$ when the weighted union method of merging is not used.

When the weighted union rule is used in the routine above, at most $O(n \, \alpha(n,n))$ *CONNECT* and *ACCEPT* messages are transmitted. Again, $O(n)$ ftab transfers and *FINISH* messages are required. Recall the function $\alpha$ is bounded above by 3 for any reasonable $n$. Thus this version of the algorithm uses a number of messages essentially linear in the number of nodes. The worst case running time is $\Omega(n)$, and clearly $O(n \, \alpha(n,n))$.

The algorithm of Gallager *et al.* in Section 3 takes $O(m + n \log n)$ messages to construct the tree. However, the messages are significantly smaller ($O(\log n)$ instead of $O(n^2 \log n)$ bits/message), and only traverse single links in the network. In addition, the message-passing load is well distributed throughout the network. The algorithm is extremely miserly in its use of messages, and this leads to long running times of $O(n^2)$ if there is no wakeup broadcast, and $O(n \log n)$ worst-case otherwise.

The Chang algorithm is rather simple and is possibly quite fast. It requires $O(m)$ messages and completes in time proportional to the diameter of the network. Unfortunately each message carries $O(n)$ entries, an extremely large amount of information in the echo phase.

In each of these algorithms there is an interesting tradeoff of message complexity for concurrency. These tradeoffs are manifested in each stage of the construction: in starting the algorithm, there is a tradeoff in the expense of initial wakeup messages against the higher concurrency they would gain. In finding minimal outgoing edges, one trades speed of information gathering for size of messages. Although it is clear that algorithms which strive to keep spanning subtrees as balanced as possible during the construction minimize both messages and time, it is still an interesting open problem to determine exactly how structure of algorithms and network models lead to differences in performance.

**References**

[1]  Chang, E.J. ,"Decentralized Algorithms in Distributed Systems", Ph.D. Dissertation, Dept. of Computer Science, University of Toronto, 1979.

[2]  Cheriton, D. & Tarjan, R.E. , "Finding Minimum Spanning Trees", SIAM J. Comput. Vol 5., No. 4, Dec 1976, pp. 724-742.

[3]  Dalal, Y., "Broadcast Protocols in Packet Switched Computer Networks", Ph.D. Dissertation, Tech. Rept. No. 128, Digital Systems Laboratory, Dept. of Electrical Engineering, Stanford University, April 1977.

[4]  Dalal, Y. & Metcalfe, R.E., "Reverse Path Forwarding of Broadcast Packets", CACM 21:12, December 1978, pp. 1040-1048.

[5]  Dijkstra, E.W., "A Note on Two Problems in Connection with Graphs", Numerische Mathematik 1, 1959, pp. 269-271.

[6]  Gerla, M., Grnarov, A. & Parker, D.S., "Distributed Traveling Salesman Algorithms for Distributed Database Operation", Proc. ACM Pacific '80 Conf. on Distributed Processing, San Francisco, Nov. 1980, pp. 61-67.

[7]  Gallager, R., Humblet, P. & Spira, P., "A Distributed Algorithm for Minimum Weight Spanning Trees", Technical Report LIDS-P-906A, MIT Lab. for Information and Decision Systems, Oct. 1979.

[8]  Kruskal, J.B. Jr., "On the Shortest Spanning Subtree of a Graph and the Traveling Salesman Problem", Proc. Amer. Math. Society, 7, 1956, pp. 48-50.

[9]  Parker, D.S. & Samadi, B., "Adaptive Distributed Minimal Spanning Tree Algorithms", Proc. IEEE Symposium on Reliability in Distributed Software and Database Systems, Pittsburgh, PA, July 1981.

[10]  Prim, R.C. ,"Shortest Connection Networks and some Generalizations", Bell System Tech. J., 1957, pp. 1389-1401.

[11]  Schwartz, M. & Stern, T.E., "Routing Techniques Used in Computer Communication Networks", IEEE Trans. Comm., COM-28:4, April 1980, pp. 539-552.

[12]  Spira, P., "Communication Complexity of Distributed Minimal Spanning Tree Algorithms", Proceedings 2nd. Berkeley Conf. on Dist. Data Management and Computer Networks, June 1977.

[13]  Tarjan, R.E., "Efficiency of a Good but not Linear Set Union Algorithm", JACM, Vol. 22, No. 2, April 75, pp. 215-225.

[14]  Wall, D.W., "Mechanisms for Broadcast and Selective Broadcast", Tech. Rept. No. 190, Ph.D. Dissertation, Computer Systems Laboratory, Dept. of Electrical Engineering, Stanford University, June 1980.

[15]  Yao, A.C., "An O(E log log V) Algorithm for Finding Minimum Spanning Trees", Information Processing Letters, Vol.4, No. 1, Sep. 75, pp. 21-23.

**Appendix**

Below is a detailed description of the MST construction algorithm(s) of Section 4. Note that nodes can be in exactly one of the following states: asleep, awake, connecting, or drowsy. Nodes detect the receipt of messages by repeatedly polling a FIFO queue. The algorithm is executed asynchronously by each node; it is invoked by receipt of first CONNECT message, or an external stimulus. Code in *italics* implements the weighted union rule, and may be omitted.

```
procedure construct_MST;
begin
        state := awake;          /* Initially every node has state=asleep */
        coreid := nid;           /* ... and is the core of its own fragment. */
        connectset := ∅;              /* We have sent no CONNECT messages */
        mstneighbors := ∅;       /* We are not connected to any other nodes */
        fsize := 1;              /* one node in fragment */
        fill in ftab from routing tables;  /* distances made unique */
        while  state ≠ asleep  do
                if  queue is not empty  then
                        remove first message M from queue;
                        case  type(M)  in
                                (CONNECT):   process_CONNECT,
                                (ACCEPT):    process_ACCEPT,
                                (MERGE):     process_MERGE,
                                (FINISH):    process_FINISH
                        esac
                elif  state ≠ drowsy  then
                        if  all nodes are in this fragment  then
                                process_FINISH(∅)
                        else
                                state := connecting;
                                find the cheapest outgoing link (b,c);
                                if  nid=b  then
                                        mstneighbors := mstneighbors ∪ {c};
                                        send CONNECT(nid,b,c,nid,fsize) to c;
                                else
                                        send CONNECT(nid,b,c,nid,fsize) to b;
                                fi;
                                connectset := connectset ∪ {(nid,b,c,nid)}
                        fi
                fi
        od;              /* end of main procedure body */


procedure process_MERGE(a,f,size);
begin
        state := awake;          /* we are no longer connecting */
        merge f with ftab;
        fsize := fsize + size
end process_MERGE;


procedure process_FINISH(a);
begin                    /* broadcast FINISH */
        forall x in mstneighbors - {a}
                do  send FINISH(nid) to x  od;
        state := asleep          /* halt MST construction */
end process_FINISH;
```

```
procedure process_CONNECT(a,b,c,d,size);
begin
        if b=nid then /* the smallest outgoing link leaves this node */
                mstneighbors := mstneighbors ∪ {c};
                send CONNECT(a,b,c,nid,size) to c;
                connectset := connectset ∪ {(a,b,c,nid)};
        else    /* we are on the path between the two connecting cores */
                if c=nid then mstneighbors := mstneighbors ∪ {b} fi;
                if coreid ≠ nid then /* we must relay message to core */
                        connectset := connectset ∪ {(a,b,c,d)};
                        send CONNECT(a,b,c,nid,size) to coreid
                else    /* we are the core, respond to CONNECT if not busy */
                        if state ≠ connecting  or
                           (nid,c,b,−) is in connectset
                        then
                                if (a < nid  and size = fsize )
                                              or  (size > fsize)
                                    then   coreid := a  fi;
                                send ACCEPT(a,b,c,nid,coreid,fsize) to d;
                                if coreid = a then
                                        send MERGE(nid,ftab,fsize) to a;
                                        state := drowsy
                                fi
                        else
                                put CONNECT message at end of queue
                        fi
                fi
        fi
end process_CONNECT;



procedure process_ACCEPT(a,b,c,d,newcore,size);
begin
        coreid := newcore;     /* update our coreid information */
        if a ≠ nid then        /* we have not reached originating core yet, keep forwarding */
                find the element (a,b,c,x) in connectset;
                delete that element;
                send ACCEPT(a,b,c,d,newcore,size) to x;
        else                   /* we are the originating core, complete the connection */
                if newcore ≠ nid then
                        send MERGE(nid,ftab,fsize) to newcore;
                        state := drowsy
                fi
        fi
end process_ACCEPT;



end construct_MST;
```

This research was supported by ONR Grant N00014-79-C-0866.

Performance of Data Communication Systems
and their Applications, G. Pujolle (ed.)
© North-Holland Publishing Company, 1981

BUFFER BEHAVIOR IN AN INTEGRATED DIGITAL
VOICE-DATA SYSTEM FOR ERLANG ARRIVALS

H.B. KEKRE, M. KHALID AND A.V. REDDI
Computer Centre
Indian Institute of Technology
Powai, Bombay
INDIA

The store-and-forward buffer design problem in an
integrated digital voice-data system is modelled and
analyzed as a multiserver queueing model with Erlang
arrival process and randomly interrupted service.
A closed expression for the Erlang arrival process
is presented directly in terms of characters by
converting stage arrival process into character
arrival process. An iterative algorithm is developed
for exact and approximate solution of finite buffer
state equations. Even though, the approximate
solution slightly overestimates the buffer capacity
it consumes less computational time. Finally, the
buffer behaviour in terms of overflow probability
and average queueing delay is studied for different
values of traffic intensity and buffer length and
the computed values are portrayed in the graphs.

INTRODUCTION

Communication systems starting from telegraph and telephones have
entered the era of Computer Communication Systems. The growing economic, social and political requirements coupled with the technological advances are leading to the development of large information
processing time shared systems and data bases. The invention of
sophisticated powerful switching computers is the spirit behind the
integration of communication and computer technologies into a common
technology called computer communications. As a result cost effective computer communication networks are proliferating to provide
accession of data bases at various information centres to each host
computer in the network.

Packet switching technology [1,2] achieves the effective sharing of
expensive communication resources for the performance and cost optimization. This technique for the transmission of data is now being
introduced in the field of speech communication [3]. It is expected
that this will lead to the integration of data and speech messages[4]
over a common computer communication network. In this paper integrated speech data-system is evolved for full channel capacity utilization, the analysis and design of a model store-and-forward buffer
for asynchronous data interpolation (ADI) in speech gaps is carried
out.

PROBLEM FORMULATION

It has been observed through the study of speech pattern [5] that the utilization of a telephone channel is around 40 % only, because of the occurrence of silence periods in speech. To cater to the rapidly increasing demand for communication facility asynchronous interpolation of non-real time data in speech gaps is suggested. The transmission of data in speech gaps through ADI technique, improves the channel utilization to almost 100 percent at higher loads. All it needs is the incorporation of a store-and-forward buffer for the storage of data messages and a switching mechanism at the nodes of the communication network. The store-and-forward buffer handles statistical peaks in random messages. Whereas, the switching mechanism detects the occurrence of gaps in speech and allocates the channel during speech gaps to the waiting data messages. Since the data from the buffer is transmitted at random points of time for random durations, it is said that the data is asynchronously interpolated in speech gaps. The random availability of the finite capacity communication channel together with the random nature of the input data traffic causes queue formation in the buffer. Consequently, the data message is delayed. The buffer design and its performance evaluation in such store-and-forward system for data communication where the channel capacity is being shared, is one of the most important aspects in computer communication networks design. Queueing models [6,7,8,9] are developed as a tool for the analysis of such a buffer at a node. The integrated speech data system of Fig.1 with synchronous time division multiplexing (STDM) for a large number of speech sources and Erlang arrival process data messages is modelled as a discrete time multiserver queueing system with Erlang input traffic and server interruption described by a binomial process.

Chu [10] has analyzed a multiserver queueing model for Poisson arrival process and continuous synchronous servers. Tzafestas [11] has extended it for the Erlang arrival process. Kekre and Saxena [12] have studied queueing model with finite buffer Poisson arrivals and multiple synchronous outputs. Assuming negative exponential service time distribution Kotaiah and Slater [13] have studied infinite buffer two-server Poisson queues with two types of customers. Bhat and Fisher [14] have discussed a general multi-channel system. Georganas [15] has suggested a buffered system with multiple output channels subjected to geometrically distributed interruptions. However, the explicit solution of the buffer state equations has not been possible due to the multiple dependance of buffer content states. Gauss elimination method [10,11] and the supplementary variable technique [13] have been used for the purpose. When the number of channels is large, simple approximations [14] have been suggested. In this paper an iteration algorithm has been developed for the solution of state equations.

In the earlier studies of the buffer performance with Erlang arrival process, the buffer state equations were written in terms of stages rather than characters. The solution of state equations in terms of stages is not possible in a closed form even for a single server case [16]. The consideration of a multiplexer queueing system, further complicates the solution procedure [11]. In this paper the buffer state equations are written directly in terms of characters by converting stage arrival process into character arrival process. An iterative algorithm is developed for the solution of these equations. The expressions for probability generating function of the buffer content process and the average number of characters in the queue are given.

## MODEL DESCRIPTION

The system considered for the present multiserver queueing model is the store-and-forward buffer of an integrated digital voice-data system shown in Fig.1. The transmission channel is shared by N unbuffered synchronously time division multiplexed speech sources and non-real time data stored in the buffer. The digital voice has no buffering facilities and has the priority for the transmission over the data to prevent the degradation of speech quality. The two registers of size N each record the status of the fixed assigned time slots of each user in a frame and monitor this information to the CPU. The CPU thus knowing the number of idle slots in a frame operates two registers and the buffer at the clocking epoch. As a result characters equal to or less than the number of idle slots subject to its availability are taken out from the buffer by the server and the CPU asynchronously interpolates them in the idle slots. The clocking interval equals the frame duration and is taken as one unit of service-time. The scheme suggested in Fig.1 is feasible in view of the advances in digital switching and signalling. The integration of voice and data over a common channel is discrete possibility in the near future. Tsuda et. al. [17] have discussed the development of a packetized voice/data terminal to be used in digital network.

## DATA ARRIVAL AND SERVICE PROCESSES

The data arrival process, X is Erlang distributed data character inter-arrivals with Erlang parameter, r and mean, $\lambda_e$ characters per service-interval and is assumed to be renewed at each service-interval. Each character is further assumed to be delivered in r stages. Physical arrival of a character takes place at the end of rth stage. Durations of all stages are independent identical random variables having exponential density function with average equal to $1/r$ of the average character-inter-arrival time. The occurrence of stage-renewal points can therefore be given by poisson process. The probability, $\phi_n$ of n stages completed during a service-interval is given by

$$\phi_n = \frac{(r\lambda_e)^n}{n!} \exp(-r\lambda_e), \text{ for } n = 0,1,2,\ldots \infty \quad \ldots (1)$$

The probability, $\Theta_i$ of i characters arriving in a service-interval is

$$\Theta_i = \sum_{j=ri}^{r(i+1)-1} \phi_j, \text{ for } i = 0,1,2,\ldots \infty \quad \ldots (2)$$

Then the average character arrival rate per service-interval, $\lambda$ is given by

$$\lambda = E\{X\} = \sum_{i=0}^{\infty} i\Theta_i \quad \ldots (3)$$

The characters from the finite buffer of length, $L > N$, are served by N randomly interrupted slots. Each slot is independently available with a probability, $P_{s1}$ during a service-interval. Therefore, the number of servers, $S^s$ available in a service-interval forms a binomial process with probability mass function, $p_{sn}$ given by

$$p_{sn} \triangleq \text{Prob}(S=n) = \binom{N}{n}P_{s1}^n(1-P_{s1})^{N-n},$$
$$\text{for } n = 0,1,\ldots, N \quad \ldots (4)$$

The average number of slots available in a service-interval, $S_{av}$ is

$$S_{av} = E\{S\} = N\,P_{sl} \qquad \qquad \cdots \ (5)$$

Therefore, the average data character arrivals or average offered load, $\lambda$ is

$$\lambda = \rho\,S_{av} \qquad \qquad \cdots \ (6)$$

where $\rho$ is traffic intensity.

Having in hand, the average offered load, $\lambda$ from equation (6) the character arrival probability, $\theta_i$ is obtained from equation (2) needed in the computation of buffer state probability by arbitrarily choosing $\lambda_e$ to satisfy the equation (3).

BUFFER STATE EQUATIONS

The buffer state equations are written by splitting the period between the end points of adjacent service-intervals into parts as given below.

    i) the period between the time epochs just before and after the character removal instant, and

    ii) the period between the starting and end points of the current service-interval.

Let $P_i(j)$ and $Q_i(j)$ represent the probability of i characters present in the buffer of length, L at the end and start of the jth service-interval respectively. $Q_i(j)$ can be represented in terms of $P_i(j-1)$ and the probability of server availability, $p_{sn}$ and is given by

$$Q_i(j) = \begin{cases} \displaystyle\sum_{m=0}^{N} P_m(j-1) \sum_{n=m}^{N} p_{sn} & , \ \text{for } i = 0 \\[4mm] \displaystyle\sum_{n=0}^{N} P_{n+1}(j-1)p_{sn} & , \ \text{for } i = 1,2,\ldots,L\text{-}N \\[4mm] \displaystyle\sum_{n=0}^{L-1} P_{n+1}(j-1)p_{sn} & , \ \text{for } i = L\text{-}N+2,\ldots,L \end{cases} \qquad \cdots \ (7)$$

whenever the queue attains steady state (i.e. $Q_i(j) = Q_i(j-1) = Q_i$, $P_i(j) = P_i(j-1) = P_i$), the equation (7) can be written as

$$Q_i = \begin{cases} \displaystyle\sum_{m=0}^{N} P_m \sum_{n=m}^{N} p_{sn} & , \ \text{for } i = 0 \\[4mm] \displaystyle\sum_{n=0}^{N} P_{n+i}\,p_{sn} & , \ \text{for } i = 1,2,\ldots,L\text{-}N \\[4mm] \displaystyle\sum_{n=0}^{L-i} P_{n+i}\,p_{sn} & , \ \text{for } i = L\text{-}N+1,\ L\text{-}N+2,\ldots,L \end{cases} \qquad \cdots \ (8)$$

But $P_i(j)$ depends upon $Q_i(j)$ and the character arrival probability, $\Theta_k$. The steady state relationship is

$$
P_i = \begin{cases} \displaystyle\sum_{j=0}^{i} Q_j\,\Theta_{i-j} & , \text{ for } i = 0,1,2,\ldots,L-1 \\[2em] \displaystyle\sum_{j=0}^{L-1} Q_j\,(1- \sum_{n=0}^{L-j-1} \Theta_n) + Q_L & , \text{ for } i = L \end{cases} \qquad \ldots \text{(9)}
$$

The equations (8) and (9) along with normalization

$$
\sum_{i=0}^{L} Q_i = \sum_{i=0}^{L} P_i = 1 \qquad \ldots \text{(10)}
$$

completely describe the queueing system.

ITERATIVE ALGORITHM

The buffer state equations (8) and (9) described the nature of inter relationship between $P_i$ and $Q_i$ ($i = 0,1,\ldots,L$) and so, knowing any one of the two sets, the other set can be computed. Conceptually, $Q_o$ tends towards its upper limit 1 whereas $P_o$ tends towards its lower limit $\Theta_o$ as the number of slots, N increases. Based on this intuition the initial choice is

$$
Q_i = \begin{cases} 1 & , \text{ for } i = 0 \\ 0 & , \text{ for } i \neq 0 \end{cases} \qquad \ldots \text{(11)}
$$

for the iterative algorithm described below.

Step 1 : Use the initial choice given by equation (11) in equation (9) to get

$$
P_i = \begin{cases} \Theta_i & , \text{ for } i = 0,1,2,\ldots,L-1 \\[1.5em] 1 - \displaystyle\sum_{j=0}^{L-1} \Theta_j & , \text{ for } i = L \end{cases} \qquad \ldots \text{(12)}
$$

Step 2 : Update $Q_i$ ($i = 0,1,2,\ldots,L$) by using $P_i$ obtained from equation (12) in accordance with equation (8).

Step 3 : Using $Q_i$ ($i = 0,1,2,\ldots,L$) obtained in step 2, update $P_i$ in accordance with equation (9).

Step 4 : Repeat steps 2 and 3 till the solution converges to its limit.

It is to be noted that the initial choice given by equation (11) is closer to its actual values for large number of servers. Therefore, suitability of the iterative algorithm is more for multiserver system with large N. It is also very important to note that the above given iterative algorithm is to be restarted all over again, for every value of L, which needs more computational resources. To overcome it, an alternative approach is suggested with which the finite buffer is analyzed.

INFINITE BUFFER STATE PROBABILITY GENERATING FUNCTION

Let $\hat{Q}_i$ and $\hat{P}_i$ $(i = 0,1,2,\ldots,\infty)$ be the probability of $i$ characters being present in the infinite buffer at the start and end of a service-interval respectively. The steady state equations describing the interplay between $\hat{Q}_i$ and $\hat{P}_i$ are

$$\hat{Q}_i = \begin{cases} \sum_{m=0}^{N} \hat{P}_m \sum_{n=m}^{N} p_{sn} & , \quad \text{for } i = 0 \\ \\ \sum_{n=0}^{N} \hat{P}_{n+i} p_{sn} & , \quad \text{for } i = 1,2,\ldots,\infty \end{cases} \qquad \ldots (13)$$

$$\hat{P}_i = \sum_{j=0}^{i} \hat{Q}_j \theta_{i-j} \qquad , \quad \text{for } i = 0,1,2,\ldots,\infty \qquad \ldots (14)$$

The probability generating function, $\hat{Q}(Z)$, of the buffer content process at the start of a service-interval is

$$\hat{Q}(Z) \triangleq \sum_{i=0}^{\infty} \hat{Q}_i z^i$$

$$= \hat{P}(Z) \sum_{i=0}^{N} p_{si} Z^{-i} + \sum_{k=1}^{N} (1-z^{-k}) \sum_{i=k}^{N} p_{si} P_{i-k} \qquad \ldots (15)$$

where $\hat{P}(Z)$ is the probability generating function of the buffer content process at the end of a service-interval and is given by

$$\hat{P}(Z) \triangleq \sum_{i=0}^{\infty} \hat{P}_i z^i = \frac{\theta(Z) \sum_{i=1}^{N} p_{si} \sum_{k=0}^{i-1} \hat{P}_k (1-z^{-i}z^k)}{1-\theta(Z)\sum_{i=0}^{N} p_{si} z^{-i}} \qquad \ldots (16)$$

where $\theta(Z) = \sum_{i=0}^{\infty} \theta_i z^i$ $\qquad \ldots (17)$

From normalization conditions

$$\hat{P}(Z)|_{Z=1} = \sum_{i=0}^{\infty} \hat{P}_i = 1 , \quad \hat{Q}(Z)|_{Z=1} = \sum_{i=0}^{\infty} \hat{Q}_i = 1 , \qquad \ldots (18)$$

one can get

$$\sum_{j=0}^{N-1} \hat{P}_j \sum_{i=j+1}^{N} (i-j) p_{si} = \sum_{i=0}^{N} p_{si} - \theta'(1) \qquad \ldots (19)$$

The equations (13) and (14) are solved for $\hat{Q}_i$ and $\hat{P}_i$ using previously developed iterative algorithm. Let

$$Q_i = k_q \hat{Q}_i \quad \text{for } i = 0,1,\ldots,L \qquad \ldots (20)$$

where $k_q$ is a normalizing constant. Substituting equation (20) in (10) one gets

$$k_q = 1 \Big/ \sum_{j=0}^{L} \hat{Q}_j \qquad \ldots (21)$$

Merging equations (20) and (21),

$$Q_i = \hat{Q}_i \bigg/ \sum_{j=0}^{L} \hat{Q}_j \quad , \quad \text{for } i = 0,1,\dots,L \qquad \qquad \dots (22)$$

Similarly

$$P_i = \hat{P}_i \bigg/ \sum_{j=0}^{L} \hat{P}_j \quad , \quad \text{for } i = 0,1,\dots,L \qquad \qquad \dots (23)$$

Therefore, the previously developed iterative algorithm is used only once to get $\hat{Q}_i$ and $\hat{P}_i$. Once the values of $\hat{Q}_i$ and $\hat{P}_i$ are calculated the values of $Q_i$ and $P_i$ are obtained for any value of L using equations (22) and (23). This leads to saving of large amount of computational time. The probability of infinite buffer states obtained as above is used to calculate a close estimate of the state probability of buffer of any size. Thus the set of state equations are to be solved only once.

BUFFER OVERFLOW PROBABILITY AND QUEUEING DELAY

Let, $\beta$ be the number of characters served from the buffer in a **service-internal**. It is a function of buffer states and number of servers available and thus its probability mass function, $p_\beta(n)$ is

$$p_\beta(n) \triangleq \text{Prob } (\beta=n) = P_n \sum_{i=n}^{N} p_{si} + P_{sn} \sum_{i=n+1}^{L} P_i \ ,$$

$$\text{for } n = 0,1,\dots,N. \qquad \dots (24)$$

The average throughput, $\bar{\beta}$ is

$$\bar{\beta} \triangleq E\{\beta\} = \sum_{n=0}^{N} n \ p_\beta(n) \qquad \qquad \dots (25)$$

The server capacity being N characters per service-interval, the server utilization factor, $\eta$ is

$$\eta = \bar{\beta}/N \qquad \qquad \dots (26)$$

A character arriving at an instant when the buffer is full to its capacity does not find place in it and is said to have overflown from the system. The overflow probability is the fraction of loss of characters due to overflow from the buffer because of its limited capacity. Therefore using equations (6) and (25), the overflow probability, $P_{of}$ is

$$P_{of} = 1 - (\bar{\beta}/\lambda) \qquad \qquad \dots (27)$$

Since the stage average and time average are the same only under Poisson arrival condition, the equations (25), (26) and (27) holds good only when $r = 1$ and for all other values of $r > 1$, the $\bar{\beta}$, $\eta$ and $P_{of}$ represents only approximate values.

A character entering the buffer faces the queue already present prior to its turn for service. During its turn of service, it experiences delay due to synchronous server as well. The total delay experienced by a character is derived as follows.

The average queue length at the end of a service interval, $Q_e$ is

$$Q_e = \sum_{i=0}^{L} i \ P_i \ \text{characters} \qquad \qquad \dots (28)$$

As L tends to infinity, the equation (16) gives

$$Q_e = \sum_{i=0}^{\infty} i \hat{P}_i = [\frac{d\hat{P}(Z)}{dZ}]_{Z=1}$$

$$= \frac{\sum_{i=1}^{N} p_{si} \sum_{k=0}^{i-1} (i-k)\hat{P}_k \{\theta''(1) - \theta'(1) (2\theta'(1) + i-k+1) + \sum_{j=0}^{N} j \, p_{sj}(j-i+k) \}}{2 \{ \sum_{i=0}^{N} i \, p_{si} - \theta'(1) \}^2} \qquad \ldots \text{(29)}$$

where $\theta'(1) = \lambda$         ... (30)

and $\theta''(1) \sum_{i=0}^{\infty} i(i-1)\theta_i$        ... (31)

and the average queue length, $Q_s$ at the start of the service interval is,

$$Q_s = Q_e - \lambda \qquad \ldots \text{(32)}$$

The average queue length, $Q_a$ that a character finds already present on its arrival is the average of $Q_e$ and $Q_s$ and is given by

$$Q_a = Q_e - 0.5\lambda \qquad \ldots \text{(33)}$$

The waiting time of the character, $W_1$ due to the queue already present is

$$W_1 = Q_a / \bar{P} \text{ unit service-time} \qquad \ldots \text{(34)}$$

Assuming the arrival instant of the character in a service-interval to be uniform random variable, the character waiting time, $W_2$ during its term for service due to synchronous nature of service is half unit service-interval.

Finally, the average queueing delay, $Q_t$ exprienced by the character is the sum of $W_1$ and $W_2$ and is

$$Q_t = \frac{\sum_{i=0}^{I} i \, P_i - 0.5\lambda}{\bar{\beta}} + 0.5 \text{ unit service times} \qquad \ldots \text{(35)}$$

The average queue length, $Q_c$ experienced by the data character arrival is given by

$$Q_c = Q_t \bar{P} \text{ characters} \qquad \ldots \text{(36)}$$

EXAMPLE

To illustrate the application of the model, we have considered an integrated digital voice data system as shown in Fig.1. Twenty four voice sources are synchronously multiplexed (STDM) and the data is interpolated in the speech gaps. The state of the fixed assigned time slots in a frame depends upon the speech source pattern. Brady [5] has given the average durations of the talkspurt and pause as 1.366 and 1.802 seconds respectively. The steady state probability of the slot being busy, $P_{sl}$ is obtained from reference [18] as

$$P_{sl} = 0.5688 \qquad \qquad \cdots \quad (37)$$

Using this probability and number of speech sources $N = 24$ the buffer behavior for different values of traffic intensity and buffer length is studied. The overflow probability and queueing delay are portrayed on graphs as shown in Fig.2 - Fig.5.

DISCUSSION AND CONCLUSION

An $Er/D/n$ queueing model with number of servers n having binomial distribution is proposed. The number of servers, n, varies between 0 and 24 where 24 is the total number of voice channels in STDM. Using this queueing model the performance of a store-and-forward buffer in an integrated speech/data system is studied. The analysis of the buffer in terms of characters directly rather than stages and the assumption that the arrival process is renewed at each service-interval greatly simplifies the solution procedure. An iterative algorithm for the evaluation of the buffer content state probability is presented. Explicit expression for probability generating function and average queueing length are deduced.

According to figures 2 and 3, the overflow probability, $P_{of}$ decreases with buffer length, L for a given traffic intensity, $\rho$ and Erlang parameter, r and it also decreases with r for a given $\rho$ and L . The figure 4 shows that the buffer length, L increases with the traffic intensity, $\rho$ , for a given value of the degree of Erlang distribution, r and specified overflow probability, $P_{of}$. In figure 5, the average queueing delay increases with the traffic intensity for a specified overflow probability, $P_{of}$ and Erlang parameter, r. The effect of increasing Erlang parameter r is to reduce the overflow probability and thus the buffer length requirement is reduced. However there is not much appreciable change in overflow probability for Erlang parameter beyond r = 3. Decrease of average queueing delay with increase of r is almost nil below the traffic intensity, $\rho = 0.5$. It is also observed that by computing few values of overflow probabilities and average queueing delays using exact solution for specified values of traffic intensity and buffer length and comparing those with approximate solution shows that the difference is very small. The difference between the delays is also negligible. It is also observed that in both the cases the computational **time** required for the convergence is more and more as $\rho$ increases and it is much more higher in the case of exact method than the other. This leads us to the conclusion that approximate solution is not only superior on the basis of computing time requirement but also more reliable as it slightly overestimates the buffer length. The model is directly applicable to Poisson arrival process for Erlang parameter r = 1.

The present system is feasible because of advances in the area of digital switching and signaling. The integration of voice and data on a common communication channel is a distinct possibility in the near future. Therefore, the proposed queueing model is of practical significance.

REFERENCES

[1]  Roberts, L.G., The evolution of packet switching, Proc. IEEE, 66 (1978) 1307-1313.

[2]  Kleinrock, L., Principles and lessons in packet communications, Proc. IEEE, 66 (1978) 1320-1329.

[3] Gold, B., Digital speech networks, Proc. IEEE, 65 (1977)1636-1658.

[4] Ross, M.J., Tabbot, A.C., and Waite, J.A., Design approaches and performance criteria for integrated voice/data switching, Proc. IEEE, 65 (1977) 1283-1295.

[5] Brady, P.T., A statistical analysis of on-off patterns in 16 conversations, BSTJ, 47 (1968) 73-91.

[6] Kekre, H.B., and Saxena, C.L., An on-off single server queueing model with finite waiting room and its application to computer communications, Comput. and Elect. Engg., 4 (1977) 309-321.

[7] Kekre, H.B., and Saxena, C.L., Finite buffer behavior with Poisson arrivals and random server interruptions,IEEE Trans.Comm., 26 (1978) 470-474.

[8] Kekre, H.B., Saxena, C.L., and Khalid, M., Buffer behavior for mixed arrivals and single server with random interruptions,IEEE Trans. Comm., 28 (1980) 59-64.

[9] Kekre, H.B., and Khalid M., Buffer design in a closed form with hybrid input and random server interruptions, IEE Proc., E., CRSP, Part E, 127 (1980) 448-455.

[10] Chu, W.W., Buffer behavior for Poisson arrivals and multiple synchronous constant outputs,IEEE Trans. Comput., 19(1970) 530-534.

[11] Tzafestas, S.G., Buffer length for Erlang arrivals and multiple synchronous regular removals, Electronics letters, 7(1971) 176-178.

[12] Kekre, H.B., and Saxena, C.L.,A finite waiting room queueing model with server having Markovian interruptions and its application to computer communications, comput. and Elect. Engg.,5 (1978) 51-65.

[13] Yotiah, T.C.T., and Slater, N.B., On two server Poisson queues with two types of customers, Operational Research, 21 (1973) 597-603.

[14] Bhat, U.N., and Fisher, M.J., Multichannel queueing systems with heterogeneous classes of arrivals, Naval Research Logistics Quarterly, 23 (1976) 271-282.

[15] Georganas, N.D., Buffer behavior with Poisson arrivals and bulk geometric service, IEEE Trans. Comm., 24 (1976) 938-940.

[16] Kekre, H.B., and Saxena, C.L., Simulation model of buffer behavior for data multiplexing with Erlang arrivals in analog speech, Comput. and Elect. Engg., 5 (1978) 321-333.

[17] Tsuda, T., Hattori, S., Yatsuboshi, R., and Yamauchi, Y., An approach to multi-service subscriber loop system using packetized voice/data terminals, IEEE Trans. Comm., 27 (1979) 1112-1117.

[18] Kekre, H.B., Saxena, C.L., and Srivastava, H.M., A two state Markov model of speech in conversation and its application to computer communication systems, Comput. and Elect. Engg., 4 (1977) 133-141.

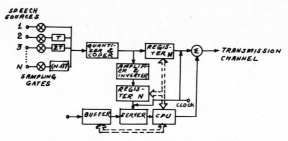

FIG·1 INTEGRATED DIGITAL VOICE-DATA SYSTEM.

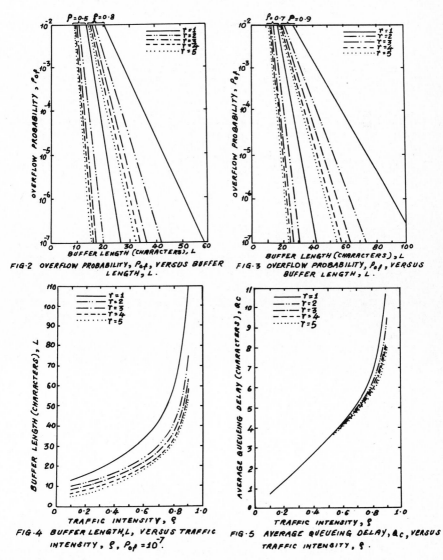

FIG·2 OVERFLOW PROBABILITY, $P_{of}$, VERSUS BUFFER LENGTH, L.

FIG·3 OVERFLOW PROBABILITY, $P_{of}$, VERSUS BUFFER LENGTH, L.

FIG·4 BUFFER LENGTH, L, VERSUS TRAFFIC INTENSITY, $\varrho$, $P_{of} = 10^{-7}$.

FIG·5 AVERAGE QUEUEING DELAY, $Q_C$, VERSUS TRAFFIC INTENSITY, $\varrho$.

Performance of Data Communication Systems
and their Applications, G. Pujolle (ed.)
© North-Holland Publishing Company, 1981

# ADMISSION DELAYS ON VIRTUAL ROUTES WITH WINDOW FLOW CONTROL

Martin Reiser

IBM Zurich Research Laboratory
8803 Rüschlikon
Switzerland

To date, virtual routes (or virtual circuits) with window
flow control have been modeled as loss systems. This has
led to a good representation of transit network performance
measures (e.g., total throughput) but has not yielded results on admission delays. We give a queueing analysis of
these admission delays, based on decomposition. Simple
models yielding to an effective computational evaluation
are the result. Using our model, we give a rule for optimum window size including admission delays. In this case,
for the optimal window we have $K_O = 2L$ (L = length of route)
which contrasts with the results found for the loss model:
$K_O = L$.

## INTRODUCTION

After initial performance-evaluation work focused mainly on the problem of routing,
we have recently witnessed increased interest in flow control [1-10]. One flow-
control protocol which enjoys great popularity due to its simple implementation is
the *window protocol*. Many existing networks and architectures use this protocol
(e.g., ARPANET [11], X.25 [12], SNA [13-14], GMDNET [15], etc.).

The basis for window control is the virtual connection, i.e., an end-to-end protocol which establishes a protected point-to-point connection. We need to distinguish *user flow control* (i.e., to match source-sink rates) and *network flow control* (i.e., to protect the transit network from overload and congestion). We use
the term *virtual route* for a network flow-control protocol (as opposed to the virtual circuit, for example, which is a user protocol). With *explicit route*, we denote a series of links used by a virtual route. An example of an architecture
which embodies flow control through windows and virtual routes is given by SNA
[7, 14]. Note that SNA also knows user flow control which is termed pacing and
constitutes part of the session.

M. Reiser modeled a network with various virtual routes employing window flow control by means of a queueing network model with *multiple closed chains* [3, 16].
However, the closed-chain approach required the assumption of a *loss system*, i.e.,
messages which arrive when the virtual route blocks admission to the transit network are lost. Contrarily, real data networks are all *wait systems*, i.e., messages
not admitted are queued at the first network node. It is the object of this paper
to give an analysis of this admission queueing process.

The virtual route introduces *blocking* into the queueing analysis, a phenomenon difficult to reflect in an exact model. We therefore use the method of *decomposition*.
We first solve the transit network assuming saturated load for all possible window
assignments (this can be done with the method described in [3]). Then we model

67

each virtual route individually, replacing the network with a "Northon equivalent server" [17]. This method was first used by Schwartz [6] who establishes its validity through extensive simulation.

The significance of our result is twofold. Firstly, we give a method to evaluate admission delays once a network is configured with routes and (static) windows. This method adds to the set of tools used in network-design problems. Secondly, we use the model to discuss window assignments which optimize end-to-end power (power is defined as throughput-delay ratio). Previous work with loss systems yielded an optimum window $K_O = L$. We show that if admission delays are considered in the power definition, the optimum window equals twice the number of hops, i.e., $K_O = 2L$. This value should be used in practice.

THE MODEL

In this section, we shall derive models for the admission delays onto virtual routes with *sliding-window flow-control* mechanism. The basic model is portrayed in Figure 1. Traffic originates from a set of terminals, say, which are controlled by a remote control unit (called TIP in the ARPA network, Cluster Controller in SNA). This control unit enables the terminals through poll commands, and schedules traffic through the transit network. Terminals are assigned to a virtual route which connects the terminal controller with a host through the transit network. The virtual route dispatches traffic onto an explicit route assumed to be fixed. The virtual route employs a sliding window which can be described as follows. A pool of K permits is kept by the sending end of the virtual route. As a message enters, it obtains a permit and is dispatched. The permit is removed from the pool. If no permit is available, the message waits (the virtual route is said to be blocked). As messages arrive at the destination node, acknowledgements are returned to the sender. We assume that each message is individually acknowledged and that acknowledgements are transmitted with higher priority than messages. As acknowledgements arrive at the source node, permits are returned to the send pool. Evidently, the total number of messages and permits is at all times fixed to K. Thus, we can model the virtual route as a *closed queueing network* (a closed chain in the case of mesh topology). Figure 2 shows the basic queueing model.

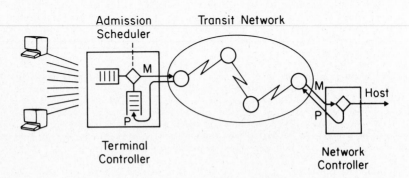

Figure 1
Conceptual Model of a Virtual and Explicit Route

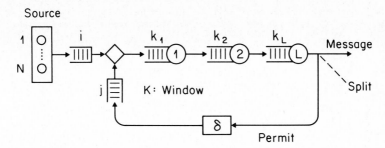

Figure 2
Queueing Model of the Virtual Route.  The Decision Box lets a Message proceed when
$j > 0$, i.e., $i \rightarrow i - 1$, $j \rightarrow j - 1$, $k_1 \rightarrow k_1 + 1$

We define: K: window size; N: number of sources (terminals); i: number of messages waiting for permits; K: number of messages in transit; $j = K - k$: number
of permits; $\lambda$: arrival rate (all terminals busy); $\tau_\ell$: mean transmission time
over channel $\ell(\ell = 1, 2, \ldots L)$; $\delta$: delay of acknowledgements over return channel;
$\gamma$: throughput of virtual route.  In order to solve the model, we postulate message
independence and exponential message-length distribution (see [6] for a recent
discussion of independence).  The virtual route introduces blocking, a phenomenon
hard to model in queueing networks.  To reduce the state space, we use the decomposition method for closed networks [17].  We decompose the system into virtual
route and explicit route (i.e., the links linking source and destination).  Figure
3 shows the decomposed system.  In the virtual-route model, the explicit route is
represented by a queue-dependent server whose rate is $\gamma(k)$, the throughput of the
explicit route with k messages in transit.

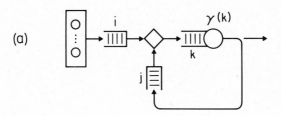

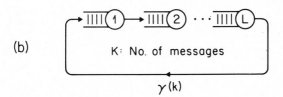

Figure 3
Decomposition into: (a) Virtual-Route Model, and (b) Explicit Route Model

The rate function $\gamma(k)$ is easily solved using mean-value analysis [18]. For the case of a balanced explicit route with unit mean transmission times, (i.e., $\tau_1 = \tau_2 = \ldots = \tau_L = 1$) and with negligible delay for the acknowledgements ($\delta = 0$), we find a simple explicit solution, viz.,

$$\lambda(k) = \frac{k}{k + L - 1} \quad . \tag{1}$$

## Loss system

The simplest model for the virtual route is a Poisson source which is instantly turned off as the number of permits drops to zero ($j = 0$). Alternatively, we may assume that the source is not turned off, but messages which do not find a permit available are lost from the system. Under this assumption, the virtual route is modeled by a simple closed chain. It allows for an exact solution through mean-value analysis [18], however, it does not yield results for admission delays. Throughput, transit delays and blocking probabilities are the only available performance measures. Reiser introduced the loss model in [3]. It was also used by Schwartz [6, 10].

## Finite-source model with negligible polling time

We assume that the source is comprised of $N$ terminals polled by the controller. Each terminal generates messages with rate $\lambda_0 = \lambda/N$. Alternatively, $\lambda_0^{-1}$ is the mean message-generation time (also called "think time"). After the message has been generated by the operator (hit of enter key), it is held in the terminal's buffer awaiting the next poll from the controller. When the poll arrives, the message gets transmitted. We assume negligible poll and local transmission times. This is a realistic assumption in the case of control units connected to terminals by coaxial local links. Whenever the number of permits drops to zero ($j = 0$), polling ceases. Messages are still being created, but once the buffer is ready for transmission (enter key hit), the terminal locks and the message-generation process stops, to be restarted only once the message has been removed. In this system, we notice that the queue $i$ is actually in the terminal's buffers, not in the controller's memory. When permits arrive, polling is resumed. It is necessary to define the dialogue mode of the terminal more precisely. Even though polling is resumed in some applications, a terminal may be allowed to start new traffic generation only after a reply from the host has been received. If this is the case, end-to-end protocols (called Data Flow Control in SNA [13]) heavily interfere with the virtual-route performance. Since we are interested in virtual-route performance proper, we assume that terminals generate new messages whenever they get polled. Such behavior is observed, for example, in data-entry applications.

With these assumptions, we observe the following relations among the state variables: $j > 0 \rightarrow i = 0$ and $i > 0 \rightarrow j = 0$. The arrival rate for the states ($j = 0$, $i = 0, 1, \ldots, N$) has the form

$$\lambda(i) = (N - i)\lambda_0 = \lambda(1 - i/N) \quad . \tag{2}$$

The result is closely related to the M/M/$\infty$ queue with state-dependent arrival and service rates, [19], namely,

$$\pi'(m) = \frac{\lambda'(1)\lambda'(2)\ldots\lambda'(m)}{\gamma'(1)\gamma'(2)\ldots\gamma'(m)} \qquad m = 0, 1, \ldots K + N \tag{3}$$

$$g = \sum_{m=0}^{K+N} \pi'(m) \tag{4}$$

$$\bar{k} = \sum_{k=1}^{K} k\pi'(k) \tag{5}$$

$$\bar{i} = \sum_{i=1}^{N} i\pi'(K + i) \quad , \tag{6}$$

where $\lambda'(j) = [\lambda$ if $j \leq K$, $(N + K - j)\lambda_0$ otherwise] and $\gamma'(j) = [\gamma(j)$ if $j \leq K$, $\gamma(K)$ otherwise].

In our model, $\lambda$ is the total message arrival rate of all N terminals if blocking does not occur. With window protocol, however, the throughput $\gamma$ is generally less than the offered load $\lambda$, viz.,

$$\gamma = \lambda_0(N - \bar{i}) \quad . \tag{7}$$

The mean admission delay is

$$\bar{d}_A = \bar{i}/\gamma \quad . \tag{8}$$

## Poisson source

Here we assume that traffic is generated by a Poisson source of rate $\lambda$. Messages arrive at the control unit, and are dispatched instantly if permits are available. Otherwise, they are queued in the controller's memory and served in order of arrivals as permits return. Thus, the Poisson source is more like a processor than a set of terminals. Its solution is analogous to that of the finite-source model above.

## DISCUSSION

Kleinrock's original open queueing model for data networks [20] led to program packages for the optimal design of networks (capacity assignment, concentrator placement, etc.). Recent analysis of window flow control in meshed topology [3] provides an additional tool which helps to design (static) windows such that the buffer constraints of the network are not exceeded, while throughput remains high. Our analysis adds a third stage: a method to evaluate admission delays created by virtual routes. These delays can be estimated with a simple and computationally trivial method. The resulting admission delays can be checked against the objectives, and the design process iterated if objectives are not.

## Numerical examples

Our model has too many parameters to discuss all their combinations. Therefore, we make the assumptions of a homogeneously loaded explicit route of three hops, i.e., $L = 3$ and $\tau_1 = \tau_2 = \tau_3 = 1$. We also neglect permit delay times ($\delta = 0$).

First, we wish to compare loss-and-wait models. Their throughput characteristics are given in Figure 4. It is obvious how the lost messages result in markedly lower load and correspondingly lower throughput $\gamma$. The loss model is clearly way off compared with the wait model.

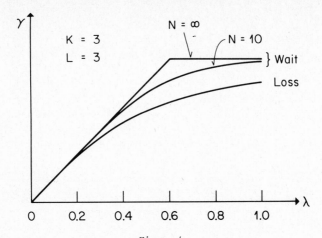

Figure 4
Throughput ($\gamma$) vs. Load ($\lambda$) Characteristics for Loss and Wait System

Finite-source congestion (N = 10) is compared with an infinite source (or Poisson source) in Figure 5. Throughput $\gamma$, admission delay $d_A$ and transit delay $d_T$ for a system with ten sources (N = 10) are shown in Figure 6 as a function of offered load $\lambda$ rather than throughput $\gamma$ as before. We see how the throughput is limited to a value below its maximum ($\gamma_{max}$ = 1) through the window protocol. The maximum throughput for a given window k is $\gamma(k)$ defined by Eq. (1).

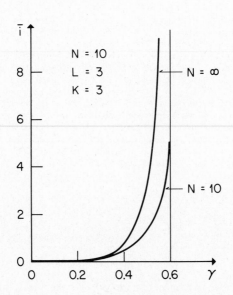

Figure 5
Comparison of Backlog Resulting from a Poisson Source and a Finite Source (N = 10)

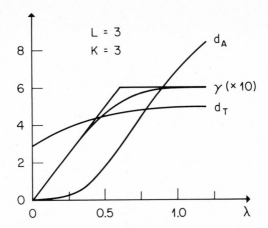

Figure 6

Admission Delay $d_A$, Transit Delay $d_T$ and Throughput $\gamma$ Plotted against the Load $\lambda$ for the Finite-Source Case (N = 10)

#### End-to-end power of the virtual route

The power of a queueing system is defined as [5, 21]

$$P = \frac{\gamma}{d} = \frac{\gamma^2}{\bar{n}} , \qquad (9)$$

where $\gamma$ denotes throughput, $d$ delay, and $\bar{n}$ mean queue size. The power measure assigns a numerical value to the well-known throughput-delay trade-off exhibited by queueing systems. It is useful as an objective function in optimization problems. Take the M/M/1 queueing system with processing rate normalized to $\mu = 1$. Then it is easy to see that $\gamma = \lambda$, and the power is given by $P = \lambda(1 - \lambda)$ which is maximized for $\lambda_0 = 1/2$.

Several authors used power to optimize the window of a virtual route [4, 5, 6, 21]. It is not difficult to carry out the calculation in the case of homogeneously loaded explicit routes for the loss system [6]. The results being

$$K_0 = L \qquad \text{if } \lambda = 1 , \qquad (10)$$

$$K_0 = L - 1 \qquad \text{if } \lambda = \infty , \qquad (11)$$

where $K_0$ is the window optimizing the power measure. To use the power to adjust the source of a waiting system to the virtual route by maximizing the admission power, i.e., $\max\{P_A = \gamma^2/\bar{i}^2\}$ suggests itself. The result, however, is $\lambda \to 0$ since the admission delay approaches zero faster than the throughput. This result is useless. Therefore, let us consider the *virtual-route power* (VR power) defined as

$$P = \gamma^2/(\bar{i} + \bar{k}) . \qquad (12)$$

This measure includes admission and transmission delays. Figure 7(a) gives the VR power as a function of offered traffic for the case of a finite source with N = 10 and L = 3. Figure 7(b) depicts the diagram $P_0 = \max_\lambda\{P(\lambda)\}$ vs. the window size K.

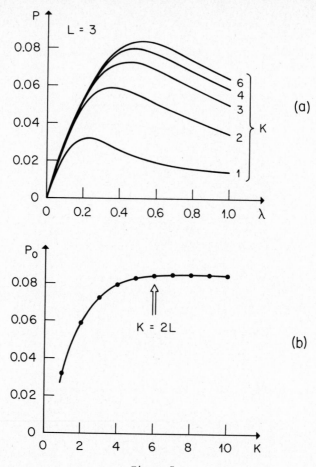

Figure 7
Power Curves for Finite Source (N = 10). $P_O$ is defined as $\max_\lambda\{P(\lambda)\}$.

From this data, we can draw a few interesting conclusions. First, we observe that the graph $P_O$ vs. K is monotonically increasing. Thus, the virtual route has no distinct window which maximizes the VR power, as was the case with the loss model. From the virtual-route point of view, the larger the window the better. This is not surprising. However, the network need is a window as small as possible in order to minimize congestion. A compromise can be defined at the "knee" of the curve $P_O$ vs. K. The data of Figure 7 augmented by many more cases which were solved provides the following interesting results:

  - The "knee" of the curve $P_O$ vs. K is located at the window size $K_O = 2L$. Thus, a window yielding near-maximum VR power is given by $K_O = 2L$.
  - The optimum power $P_O$ is achieved at the load $\lambda = 0.5$ (units such that $\tau_\ell = 1$, $\ell = 1, 2, \ldots L$).

This result contrasts with earlier results [6] which give the window minimizing VR power for the loss model as $K_0 = L - 1$. We cannot minimize VR power, but arrive at a good compromise between the network and the virtual-route point of view at $K_0 = 2L$ which compares to $K_0 = L - 1$ for the loss model. The value $K_0 = 2L$ was suggested by Deaton [7] on other heuristic grounds.

A final comment. The value $\lambda = 0.5$ for optimal VR power is the same as for the M/M/1 system. This is not surprising on the grounds that the value $(i + k)$ behaves like the M/M/1 queue with $\rho = \lambda/\gamma(K)$ as the offered rate approaches saturation.

## Generalizations

So far, we have deliberately excluded interference from end-to-end delays to isolate the delay component originating from the virtual routes. However, it is not difficult to consider the effect of such end-to-end delays on the virtual-route performance. We assume that a terminal gets polled only when permits are in the send pool, but that once a message is sent the terminal has to wait for a reply from the host (even though it may get polled in the interim). This mode of conversation is called "half-duplex flip-flop" [22]. Its queueing model is given in Figure 8. It can easily be solved with standard methods [16, 18].

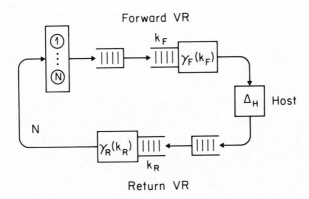

Figure 8
Model for "Half-Duplex Flip-Flop" Terminals

It is also possible to model systems where several virtual routes share a common explicit route. A multichain model results.

REFERENCES

[1] Grangé I.L. and Gien M. (eds.), Flow control in computer networks, Proc. Intl. Symp. on Flow Control in Computer Networks, Versailles, France, (North-Holland, Amsterdam, 1979).

[2] Lam S.S. and Lien Y.L., An Experimental Study of the Congestion Control of Packet Communication Networks, Technical Report TR 142, Univ. of Texas at Austin, Austin, Texas, (March 1980).

[3]  Reiser M., A queueing network analysis of computer communication networks with
     window flow control, IEEE Trans. Commun. COM-27 (1979) 1199-1209.
[4]  Kumar K.B., Optimum End-to-End Flow Control in Networks, IBM Research Report,
     RC 7949, Yorktown Heights, N.Y. (1979).
[5]  Giessler A., Hänle J., König A. and Pade E., Free buffer allocation - An in-
     vestigation by simulation, Computer Networks 1 (1978) 191-204.
[6]  Schwartz M., Performance Analysis of the SNA Virtual-Route Pacing Control,
     IBM Research Report RC 8490, Yorktown Heights, N.Y. (1980).
[7]  Deaton G. and Franse D., A computer network flow-control study, in: Proc.
     Fourth ICCC, Kyoto, Japan (1979).
[8]  Kleinrock L., On flow control in computer networks, in: Proc. ICC'78, 27.2.1-
     27.2.5 (1978).
[9]  Lam S.S. and Reiser M., Congestion control of store-and-forward networks by
     input buffer limits - An analysis, IEEE Trans. Commun. COM-27 (1979) 127-134.
[10] Schwartz M. and Saad S., Analysis of congestion control techniques in com-
     puter communication networks, in: Proc. Intl. Symp. on Flow Control in Com-
     puter Networks, Versailles, France (North-Holland, Amsterdam, 1979) 113-130.
[11] Opderbeck H. and Kleinrock L., The influence of control procedures on the
     performance of packet-switched networks, in: Proc. National Telecommunica-
     tions Conference, San Diego, Calif., (1974).
[12] IBM Europe, Technical Improvements to CCITT Recommendation X.25, submission
     to Study Group VII (Oct. 1978).
[13] IBM Corp., Systems Network Architecture, General Information, GA 27-3102-0
     (Jan. 1975).
[14] Atkins J., Path control: The transport network of SNA, IEEE Trans. Commun.
     COM-28 (April 1980) 527-538.
[15] Raubold E., The GMD Network; Goals and Structure, European Symp. on Large-
     Scale Computer Networks, Seeheim, Germany, (Oct. 1975).
[16] Reiser M. and Kobayshi H., Queueing networks with multiple closed chains:
     Theory and computational algorithms, IBM J. Res. Develop. 19 (1975) 285-294.
[17] Chandy K.M., Herzog U. and Woo L.S., Parametric analysis of queueing net-
     works, IBM J. Res. Develop. 19 (1975) 43-49.
[18] Reiser M. and Lavenberg S.S., Mean-value analysis of closed multichain queue-
     ing networks, J. ACM 27, (April 1980) 313-322.
[19] Kleinrock L., Queueing systems, vol. I: Theory (Wiley-Interscience, New York,
     1975).
[20] Kleinrock L., Queueing systems, vol. II: Computer applications, (Wiley-Inter-
     science, New York, 1976).
[21] Kleinrock L., Power and deterministic rules of thumb for probabilistic prob-
     lems in computer communications, in: ICCC'79 Conference Record,
     (Boston, 1979) 43.1.1-43.1.10.
[22] Cypser R.J., Communications architecture for distributed systems, (Addison
     Wesley, Reading, MA, 1978).

Performance of Data Communication Systems
and their Applications, G. Pujolle (ed.)
© North-Holland Publishing Company, 1981

THE EXPRESS-NET: A LOCAL AREA COMMUNICATION
NETWORK INTEGRATING VOICE AND DATA *

L. Fratta $^{+}$ , F. Borgonovo $^{+}$ and F.A. Tobagi $^{++}$

The EXPRESS-NET is a local area communication newtork based
on the Unidirectional Broadcast System (UBS) architecture.
The EXPRESS Access protocol used by the stations connected
to the bus is a distributed algorithm and has its origins
in the conflict-free Round Robin (RR) access scheme recently proposed for the UBS architecture [1]. A round robin
type scheme itself, the EXPRESS access protocol is more ef
ficient than RR in that the time required to switch from
one active user to the next in a round is of the order of
carrier detection time, and is independent of the end-to-
end network propagation delay. Moreover, some features of
the EXPRESS-NET make it particularly suitable for the in -
tegration of voice and data. A simple VOICE/DATA EXPRESS
protocol is described which allows us to meet the bandwidth
requirement and maximum packet delay constraint for voice
communication at all times, while guaranteeing a minimum
bandwidth requirement for data traffic.

INTRODUCTION

A great deal of discussion can be seen in the recent literature regarding local
networks and their applicability to many of today's local area communications needs.
These needs have primarily consisted of data communication applications, such as
computer-to-computer data traffic, terminal-to-computer data traffic, and the like.
More recently, a new line of thought has been apparent. It is the desire to inte -
grate voice communication on local data networks. The reason for this is three-
fold: (i) voice is an office communication application just as computer data, fac-
simile, etc.; (ii) recent advances in vocoder technology have shown that digitized
speech constitutes a digital communication application which is within the capabili
ties of local area data networks; and (iii) today's local network architectures,
especially the broadcast bus type, offer very elegant solutions to the local com -
munications problem, from both the point of view of simplicity in topology and device interconnection, and the point of view of flexibility in satisfying growth
and variability in the environment.

While existing solutions are elegant, they are not without their limitations in
performance. Some of these limitations arise as the characteristics of the environ
ment and data traffic requirements being supported by these solutions deviate from

* This work was supported by the United States Defence Advanced Research Projects
Agency under Contract No. MDA 903-79-X-0201, Order No. A03717, monitored by the
Office of Naval Research; and the Italian Council for National Research under Contract C-NET No. 104520/97/8007745. The order of authors is arbitrary and does not
imply any difference in contributions.

$^{+}$ Istituto di Elettrotecnica ed Elettronica, Politecnico di Milano, 20133 Milano
Italy.

$^{++}$ Dept. of Electrical Engineering, Stanford University, Stanford,California 94305.

those assumed in the original design. Examples of such characteristics are: packet length distribution, packet generation pattern, channel data rate, delay require - ments, geographical area to be spanned, etc. In [2] the performance of Bidirect - ional Broadcast System (BBS) architecture based on Carrier Sense Multiple Access with Collision Detection (CSMA-CD) [3, 4] as exemplified by ETHERNET [5] and of the Unidirectional Broadcast System (UBS) architecture with the Round Robin (RR) access algorithm [1] are analyzed. It is shown that both these schemes suffer of an overhead per packet transmission which is dependent on the ratio $\frac{\tau W}{B}$, where $\tau$

denotes the end-to-end delay defined as the time from the starting of a transmis- sion to the starting of reception between the extreme users, W denotes the channel bandwidth (bits/sec.) and B denotes the number of bits per packet (assumed to be of fixed size). The results obtained in [2] are summarized in Fig. 1 where the max

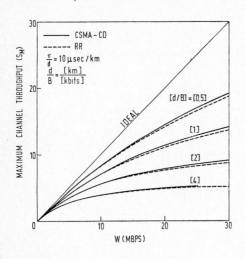

imum throughput $S_M$ is plotted as func tion of W for various values of the ratio d/B, being d the length of the cable between the extreme users. These results show that the effort required to push the technology to higher channel bandwidth with the hope to achieve a network throughput proportional to the channel speed is unfortunately rewarded by only a marginal improvement.

The aim of this paper is to present the EXPRESS-NET as an alternative which is also based on the UBS con - cept and utilizes an access protocol, the EXPRESS access protocol, which has its origin in the RR access pro- tocol. The EXPRESS-NET, however, is performance-wise more efficient than the existing schemes, and overcomes many of their limitations. Moreover, it is shown to be particularly suit able for the integration of voice

Fig. 1

*Maximum channel throughput $S_M$ versus channel bandwidth W.*

and data applications. We briefly describe a simple VOICE/DATA EXPRESS protocol which allows to meet the bandwidth requirement and maximum packet delay constraint for voice communication at all times, while guaranteeing a minimum bandwidth requirement for data traffic. These requirements are satisfied by blocking requests for voice communication which exceed a maximum allowable number, where this maximum number is easily given as a funcion of the vocoder's rate and the minimum data bandwidth requirement.

## THE EXPRESS-NET

Just as with BBS, UBS consists of a single bus to which all users are connected. Transmitting taps however are such that the transmitted signals are forced to pro- pagate in only one direction, attenuating heavily the signals in the opposite direc tion. Broadcast communication is then achieved by various means, such as folding the cable, or repeating all signals on a separate channel (or frequency) in the re verse direction, so that signals transmitted by any user reach all other users on the reverse path. Thus the system may be considered as consisting of two channels: the *outbound channel* which all users access in order to transmit, and the *inbound channel* which users access in order to read the transmitted information. In ad - dition to the transmitting capability on the outbound channel, users can sense ac- tivity on that channel in a way similar to that required in other channel sensing systems such as CSMA [1].

The EXPRESS-NET is a unidirectional broadcast system with a round-robin type access scheme. Its objective is to minimize the overhead incurred in accessing the chan - nel and thus to utilize more efficiently the channel bandwidth even when packet transmission times are short and cable distances are long. Basically, the idea is the following: contrary to the RR algorithm [1] where the time reference used in determining the right of way is the End of Carrier on the inbound channel(EOC(IN)), in the EXPRESS access protocol, the algorithm uses EOC on the outbound channel (EOC(OUT)). The mechanism used in determining access right (described below) to users in a given round is thus made independent of the propagation delay, decreas ing thegaps between consecutive transmissions to values on the same order of magni tude as the time needed to detect carrier. Secondly, the idle time separating two consecutive rounds is kept as small as a round trip propagation delay. We now give the details of operations.

Let the boolean function $c(t, OUT)$ be defined as

$$c(t,OUT)= \begin{cases} 0 & \text{if carrier is detected absent on the outbound channel at time } t \\ 1 & \text{if carrier is detected present on the outbound channel at time } t \end{cases}$$

$c(t,OUT)$ signals the presence or the absence of the carrier with a delay of $t_d$ sec., where $t_d$ is the time required to detect carrier on the channel. EOC(OUT) is said to occur when $c(t,OUT)$ undertakes a transition from 1 to 0.

Tap: The tap on the outbound channel is of the unidirectional type and it also has the capability to sense carrier on the upstream side of the tap. The tap on the in bound channel is a read only tap; it has the capability of sensing carrier, and re ceiving transmission units.

Transmission unit (TU): A transmission unit consists of a preamble followed by the information packet itself. The preamble is for synchronization purposes at the re- ceivers. It is sufficiently long for the receivers to detect presence of the unit, and then to synchronize with bit and packet boundaries.

Basic mechanism to transmit transmission units: We assume that stations are num - bered sequentially S1, S2, S3 etc. following the direction of the traffic flow on the outbound channel. A station which senses the outbound channel busy, waits for EOC(OUT). Immediately following the detection of EOC(OUT) it starts transmission of its unit. Simultaneously, it senses carrier on the outbound channel. If carrier is detected (which may happen in the first $t_d$ sec. of the transmission, and which means that a station with a lower index has also started transmission following detection of EOC(OUT)) the station immediately aborts its current transmission. Otherwise, it completes its transmission. All ready stations which detect EOC(OUT) act as described above. The only station to complete transmission is the one with the lowest index, among those ready stations which were able to detect EOC(OUT). Clearly, during and following the transmission of its TU, a station will sense the outbound channel idle, and therefore will encounter no EOC(OUT), and will not be able to transmit another TU, in the current round. Note that the possible overlap among several transmission units is limited to the first $t_d$ sec. of these trans - missions. It is assumed that the loss of the first $t_d$ sec. of the preamble of the nonaborted transmission, will not jeopardize the synchronization process at the receivers. According to the above basic mechanism two consecutive transmission units are separated by a gap of duration $t_d$ sec. (the time necessary to detect EOC(OUT)).

The succession of transmission units transmitted in the same round is called a train. A train can be seen by a station on the outbound channel only as long as the TU's in it are being transmitted by stations with lower indices. A train ge - nerated on the outbound channel is entirely seen by all stations on the inbound channel. Since there is a gap of duration $t_d$ sec. between consecutive TU's, the detection of presence of a train on the inbound channel can be best achieved by defining the new function

$$TRAIN(t,IN) = c(t-t_d,IN) + c(t,IN)$$

where $c(t,IN)$ is defined in just the same way as for $c(t,OUT)$. Clearly,

$$TRAIN(t,IN) = \begin{cases} 1 \text{ as long as a train is in progress} \\ 0 \text{ otherwise} \end{cases}$$

The transition $TRAIN(t,IN):1{\to}0$ defines the event end of train $(EOT(IN))$.

## On the topology of the EXPRESS-Net

After the last T.U. in a train has completed transmission, we need a mechanism to restart a new train of transmission units. Clearly, it is essential that access right be given to the ready station with the lowest index. One may use a mechanism similar to algorithm RR itself. That is, as soon as EOT(IN) is detected, ready stations transmit a burst, monitor the outbound channel for an appropriate period and then transmit or inhibit transmission depending on whether carrier was absent or present during this period. However, in order to keep the time gap as small as possible one should be able to have the event used as reference (namely EOT(IN)) visit the receivers in the same order as the stations' indices (which is also the order in which they can transmit). This is achieved if the inbound channel (to which receivers are connected) is such that signals on it are made to propagate in the same direction as on the outbound channel.

Thus we consider the network topology to comprise, an outbound channel and an in-bound channel assumed parallel on which signals propagate in the same direction (i.e. visiting stations in the same order), and a connection between the outbound channel and the inbound channel to broadcast all outbound signals on the inbound channel. The propagation delay along the connection $\tau_c$ is anywhere between 0 sec. and $\tau$ sec., where $\tau$ is the end-to-end propagation delay on the outbound (or in - bound) channel, depending on the geographical distribution of the users and the way the inbound and outbound channels are connecting them. The minimum of 0 sec., is observed if the inbound and outbound channels have a circular shape (or, more generally speaking the stations with the lowest and highest indices are colocated!) as illustrated in Fig.2a . The maximum of $\tau$ sec. is observed if the connection cable is made parallel to the inbound and outbound channels (Fig. 2.b ). The propagation delay between the outbound tap and inbound tap for all stations is equal to $\tau + \tau_c$.

The major feature of this topology rests on the fact that, when the inbound channel is made exactly parallel to the outbound channel, the event EOT(IN) utilized by all stations as the syncronizing event to start a new train, will reach any station exactly at the same time as the carrier on the outbound channel due to a possible transmission by a station with a lower index, and this helps resolve the overlap of several transmissions just in the same manner as the resolution obtained in the basic mechanism for transmitting TU's. This mechan - ism again allows the ready station with lowest index to complete transmission of its TU, and following that the new train will take its normal course. The time gap between two consecutive trains defined as the time between the end of the last TU and the beginning of the first TU of the subsequent train is now equal $\tau+\tau_c+2t_d$ sec. (see Fig. 3). It is worthwhile to note here that this topology also brings impro vements to the original RR access algor - ithm [1, 2].

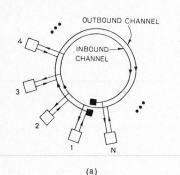

(a)

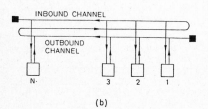

(b)

Fig. 2
*Examples of EXPRESS-NET topologies.*

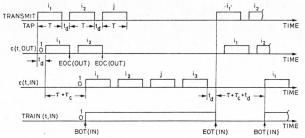

Fig. 3

*Signals and events as observed at station $j$, assuming that stations with indices $i_1 < i_2 < j < i_3$ are nonidle.*

## The cold-start procedure, and keeping the EXPRESS-Net "ALIVE"

The above algorithm and mechanisms are valid only if there always are events to which actions are synchronized, namely EOC(OUT) and EOT(IN). This assumes that at all times some station is ready, and therefore trains contain at least one TU and are separated by gaps of fixed duration ($\tau + \tau_c + 2t_d$). When this is not the case, the idle time on the inbound channel exceeds $\tau + \tau_c + 2t_d$ sec. A station which becomes ready at time $t_0$ such that (i) TRAIN ($t_0$, OUT)=0 (thus no EOC(OUT) to synchronize action to) and (ii) TRAIN(t,IN)=c(t;IN)=0 during the entire period of time $[t_0, t_0 + \tau + \tau_c + t_d]$ (thus indicating that no EOT(IN) will be detected), has to undertake the so-called cold-start procedure. This procedure must be designed such that if executed by several stations becoming ready under these conditions, it leads to a single synchronizing event to be used as a time reference, followed then by an orderly conflict-free operation of the network.

The simple one proposed here consists of the following. Once it has determined that a cold-start procedure is needed, a station transmits continuously an unmodulated carrier (called PILOT) until BOT(IN), defined as the transition TRAIN(t,IN):$0 \rightarrow 1$, is detected. At this time transmission of the pilot is aborted. The station then waits for EOT(IN) (consisting of end of the pilot) and uses that event as the synchronizing event. (Of course, an alternative could be to use the BOC(IN) due to the pilot as the synchronizing event). It is perfectly possible that pilots transmitted by several users overlap in time. This will cause no problem. Note that as long as pilots are aborted as soon as BOT(IN) is detected, it is guaranteed that the resulting PILOT as observed on the inbound channel is of length $\tau + \tau_c + t_d$ sec. Following its end, there will be the normal gap of size $\tau + \tau_c + 2t_d$ before a TU follows (Of course, using BOC(IN) as the synchronizing event, this gap is absent).

Assume that no station is ready when EOT(IN) is detected. The network is then said to go empty. The first station to become ready when the network is empty, spends $\tau + \tau_c + t_d$ sec. to determine the empty condition, after which it starts transmission of the pilot. Then it takes between $\tau_c + t_d$ and $\tau + \tau_c + t_d$ seconds before it detects BOT(IN) (The minimum $\tau_c + t_d$ is observed if the station in question is the lowest index station, and the highest index station happened to become ready exactly at the same time). Regardless of which is the case following BOT(IN), a pilot of length $\tau + \tau_c + t_d$ sec. is observed, on the inbound channel, followed by the gap of $\tau + \tau_c + 2t_d$ sec. and then the transmission unit. Therefore in this situation, the time between the moment at which the first station becomes ready in an empty network and the next EOT(IN) is between $2\tau + 3\tau_c + 4t_d$ and $3(\tau + \tau_c) + 4t_d$ sec. In other word this is the time needed to start a new round and compares to $\tau + \tau_c + 2t_d$ which is the time needed when the network is alive. Fig. 4 shows the timing of the cold start procedure when only one station becomes ready.

To avoid the cold-start operation each time the network goes empty one needs to guarantee that, as long as some stations may still become ready in the future, synchronizing events, namely EOT(IN), are created artificially by all such stations. More precisely, we consider a station to be in one of two states: DEAD or ALIVE.

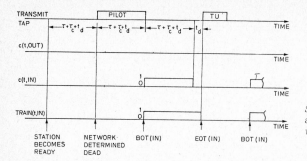

Fig. 4

*Signals and events as ob -
served at station j undertaking a cold-start.*

A station in the ALIVE state has responsibility to perpetuate the existence of the synchronizing event EOT(IN) for as long as it remains in that state. To accomplish this, each time EOT(IN) is detected, the station transmits a short burst of un - modulated carrier, of duration sufficiently long to be very reliably detected (at least $t_d$ sec.). Such a burst is called LOCOMOTIVE. If the train were to be empty (no ready stations when EOT(IN) is detected), now the LOCOMOTIVE constitutes the TRAIN, and EOT(IN) is guaranteed to take place. Clearly, if some station which is ALIVE is also ready, then immediately following the LOCOMOTIVE, it initiates trans mission of its TU and follows the transmission mechanism giving access right to the lowest index. The network is said to be ALIVE if at least one station in the network is ALIVE, otherwise it is said to be DEAD. A station is said to be in the DEAD state if it is not engaging in keeping the network ALIVE, and therefore is prohibited from transmitting any TU. To be able to transmit, a station has to be- come ALIVE.

For a DEAD station to become ALIVE, it must first determine whether the network is ALIVE or not. Letting t denote the time at which a dead station whishes to become ALIVE, the network is determined ALIVE if a train is detected on the inbound chan- nel anytime in the interval $[t, t+\tau+\tau_c+t_d]$. Otherwise, it is determined DEAD. If the network is determined ALIVE, then the station simply switches to the ALIVE state and acts accordingly. Otherwise, it executes the cold-start procedure, fol- lowing which it becomes ALIVE.

A station which is ALIVE can be either READY or NOT READY at any moment. This is determined by the state of its transmit buffer, empty or nonempty. To that effect, we define a function TB(t,X) for station X as

$$TB(t,X) = \begin{cases} 0 \text{ if its transmit buffer is empty} \\ 1 \text{ if its transmit buffer is nonempty} \end{cases}$$

An ALIVE station which becomes ready does not have to wait for EOT(IN) to under - take the attempts to transmit its packet. In fact, if an outbound train is observ ed, the station synchronizes transmissions with EOC(OUT). If, however, at the time it becomes ready, no train is observed on the outbound channel, then EOT(IN) is the synchronizing event.

THE EXPRESS ACCESS PROTOCOL

We have defined above c(t,OUt), c(t,IN), TRAIN(t,IN), TB(t,X), BOT(IN), EOT(IN), EOC(IN) and EOC(OUT). We now define CTX as the event corresponding to the comple- tion of transmission of the current TU, given that such a transmission has been initiated. We also define TIME-OUT($\alpha$) as the event corresponding to the completion of a period of time of duration $\alpha$, starting the clock at the time when waiting for the event is initiated. From the above discussion, we may define PILOT as a con - tinuous unmodulated carrier, and LOCOMOTIVE as an unmodulated carrier of duration $t_d$.

## The EXPRESS Access Protocol

We consider that initially station X is in the DEAD state. Upon command (for bring ing the station to the state ALIVE and eventually for transmission of data), the following basic algorithm is executed.

Step 1. [Check whether the Express-Net is ALIVE or not. If it is, then proceed with Step.2, otherwise undertake the "cold-start" procedure and then proceed with Step.2]. If TRAIN(t,IN)=1, then the Express-Net is already ALIVE, go to step 2. Otherwise wait for the first of the following two events: BOT (IN) or TIME-OUT $(\tau+\tau_c+t_d)$. If BOT(IN) occurs first, then again it means that the Express-Net is ALIVE; go to step 2. If, on the contrary, TIME-OUT $(\tau+\tau_c+t_d)$ occurs first, then it means the Express-Net is not ALIVE, and station X must undertake the "cold-start" procedure. Immediately at the oc currence of TIME-OUT $(\tau+\tau_c+t_d)$, the station initiates the transmission of a PILOT and maintains transmitting it until it detects BOT(IN), at which time it aborts transmission of PILOT and proceeds with step 2.

Step 2. Wait for the first of the following two events: EOC(OUT) and EOT(IN). If EOC(OUT) occurs first then go to step 4. Otherwise go to step 3.

Step 3. [A new train has to be started] X transmits LOCOMOTIVE, and go to step 4.

Step 4. [Determine state of station X. If X is ready attempt transmission of packet] If TB(t,X)=0 go to step 2.
Otherwise initiate transmission of packet. If $t_d$ sec. later c(t,OUT)=1 (meaning it is not X's turn), then abort transmission and go to step 2. Otherwise, complete transmission of the packet and go to step 2.

The flow chart of the basic algorithm is represented in Fig. 5.

## Performance of the EXPRESS-Access Protocol

The maximum throughput is evaluated as the ratio between the time in a train spent for data transmission and the minimum time between two consecutive trains, and is given by

$$S_M = \frac{MT}{M(T+t_d)+\tau+\tau_c+2t_d} \tag{1}$$

which shows that for the practical values of M, $\tau$, $\tau_c$ and $t_d$ encountered in local networks the maximum throughput is nearly one.

## INTEGRATING VOICE AND DATA ON THE EXPRESS-NET
## Voice Traffic Characteristics and Requirements

Assume vocoders digitize voice at some constant rate. Bits are grouped into packets which then are transmitted via the network to the destination voice decoder. To achieve interactive speech and smooth playback operation, it is important to keep the end-to-end delay for each bit of information (from the time the bit is generated at the vocoder until it is received at the destination decoder), within tight bounds. Two components of delay are identified: the packet formation delay and the network delay. The sum must not exceed the maximum allowed in order for all bits to satisfy the delay requirement of speech.

The interesting feature of round robin schemes with finite number of stations is that the delay incurred in transmission of a packet is always finite and bounded from above. This renders it particularly attractive for packet voice, which we examine now in more detail.

Let $W_v$ be the bandwidth required per voice user (i.e., the vocoder rate in bits/sec), and $D_v$ the maximum delay allowed for any bit of digitalized voice (not including the propagation delay). Let $B_v$ denote the number of bits per voice packet consisting of the two components: $B_v^{(1)}$ which encompasses all overhead bits (preamble, packet header and checksum) and $B_v^{(2)}$, the information bits. Let $t_g$ be the time required to form a packet (it is also the packet intergeneration time for a vocoder) and $T_v$ the

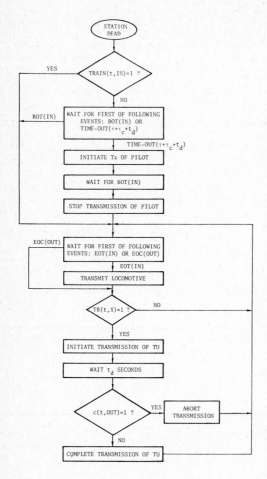

**Fig. 5**
*Flow chart for the EXPRESS Access Protocol.*

transmission time of a voice packet on the channel (of band - width W). We clearly have

$$t_g = \frac{B_v^{(2)}}{W_v} \quad \text{and} \quad T_v = \frac{B_v}{W} \qquad (2)$$

We model each voice user by a D/G/1 queue where packet arrivals are deterministic, occuring every $t_g$ sec. Let $D_n$ denote the network packet service time. It is the time from when the packet reaches the head of the queue, until it is successfully transmitted. Clearly we must have

$$t_g \geq D_n \qquad (3)$$

for bandwidth constraint, or stab ility conditions for the D/G/1 queue.

Let M denote the number of active voice sources. Assuming all queues non-empty, a train is of length $M(T_v+t_d)+\tau+\tau_c+2t_d$. The service time distribution of a packet can be bounded by a deterministic one, with the service time equal to a maximum train length. That is, we now consider our queues to be (pessimistically) represented by D/D/1, where the interarrival time is $t_g$ and the service time is $D_n=M(T_v+t_d)+\tau+\tau_c+2t_d$. Under these considerations, provided that the queue size is initially 0, the waiting time of a packet is 0 and its total delay is $D_n$. The max - imum delay requirement for a voice bit is now written as

$$t_g+D_n \leq D_v. \qquad (4)$$

The two above constraints lead to the maximum M when we choose $t_g=D_n=\dfrac{D_v}{2}$ . Accordingly, we have the optimum packet size given by

$$B_v^{(2)} = \frac{D_v W_v}{2} \qquad (5)$$

and the maximum number of voice users allowed at any one time given by

$$M_{max} = \frac{D_v/2-(\tau+\tau_c+2t_d)}{B_v/W + t_d} \qquad (6)$$

Neglecting $\tau+\tau_c+2t_d$ with comparison to $D_v$, and $t_d$ with comparison to $T_v$, we get the simple expression

$$M_{max} = \frac{D_v W}{2B_v} = \frac{D_v W}{2B_v^{(1)} + D_v W_v} \qquad (7)$$

We note that as long as $M \leq M_{max}$, it is guaranteed that the train lengths never exceed M transmission units, the network packet service time never exceeds the maximum determined above, i.e., $D_n = M_{max}(T_v+t_d)+\tau+\tau_c+2t_d$ and consequently no queueing delays are incurred (the queue size at all users remains $\leq 1$), and the total delay constraint for all voice bits is always satisfied.

## Integrating Voice and Data

The principal constraints we have to satisfy here are: the delay constraint on voice packets and a minimum bandwidth requirement for data. Although we do not impose a delay constraint on data packets, it is important to provide the bandwidth "reserved" for data on as continuous a basis as possible, and to fairly allocate that bandwidth to data users. Furthermore, we require that the protocols be dynamic in allocating the bandwidth to voice and data applications, allowing data users (or background traffic) to gracefully steal the bandwidth which is unused by voice. To accomplish these objectives, we consider two types of trains, voice train (VT) and data train (DT). Trains are always alternating between the two types, and stations transmit their packets on the train of the corresponding type. To satisfy the delay constraint for voice packets, it is important not only to limit the number of voice communications to a maximum, but also to limit the data trains to a certain maximum length.

Let $W_d$ be the minimum data bandwidth required. Assume that data trains are limited to a maximum length L. The effect that the existence of data trains on the calculations of optimum M is just to increase the overhead (safety gap = $\tau+\tau_c+2t_d$) by $L+\tau+\tau_c+2t_d$. The maximum M is then given by

$$M_{max} = \frac{D_v/2-2(\tau+\tau_c+2t_d)-L}{B_v/W + t_d} \tag{8}$$

where L is easily determined in function of $W_d$, and data packet length characteristics. For example, if data packets are of fixed length, say $B_d = B_d^{(1)} + B_d^{(2)}$ bits/packet, where $B_d^{(1)}$ accounts for packet overhead and $B_d^{(2)}$ for information bits equation (8) reduces to

$$M_{max} = \frac{D_v(W-W_d\frac{B_d}{B_d^{(1)}})}{2B_v^{(1)}+D_vW_v} \tag{9}$$

Remark 1. It is important to limit data trains to the maximum length L, even if the number of active voice users is smaller than $M_{max}$. Otherwise, there can be situations where the packet delay for a voice packet exceeds $D_v$. This particularly takes place if, during the data train, a number of new voice users become ready, some of which incur an initial delay longer than the maximum allowed $D_v$.

Remark 2. Since a data train may not contain the TU's of all ready stations, it is important that the next data round resumes where the previous data train has ended. This is easily accomplished by the inclusion of the DORMANT/ACTIVE states for data users in the same ways as in [1]. To switch from the DORMANT and ACTIVE state, data users have to monitor the length of data trains on the inbound channel; they switch to the ACTIVE state whenever the data train length has not reached its maximum limit L.

## The Voice/Data EXPRESS Protocol

To implement alternation between the two types of trains, a station maintains a flag $\phi$ which gets complemented at each EOT(IN). We use the convention $\phi=0$ for a data train and $\phi=1$ for a voice train. Now we face the problem of having a station initialize $\phi$ when it becomes ALIVE. The simplest way is as follows. If the network is found DEAD, then, following the pilot, initialize $\phi$ such that the first train is of the voice type. If the network is found ALIVE, then monitor the inbound channel until either a valid packet is observed or the network has gone dead. In the first eventuality, the type of train is derived from the type of packet observed, and $\phi$ is initialized accordingly. In the second case, the station undertakes a cold-start

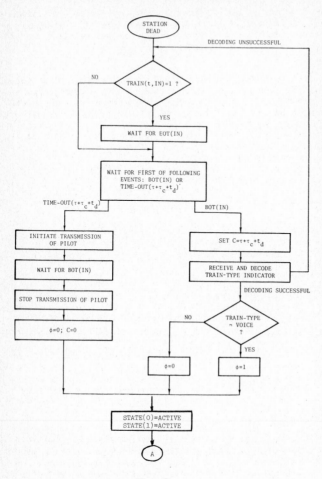

and the initialization of φ is independent of past history. Note that as long as the network is determined ALIVE, a station may not become ALIVE until it has observed a valid packet transmission; all empty trains are ignored. If it is highly likely that long successions of empty trains occur, the above mechanism may induce a high initial delay before the station becomes ALIVE. This can be overcome by including explicit information in the LOCOMOTIVE which indicates the type of train. That is the LOCOMOTIVE becomes now a train-type indicator (TI) packet. This packet can be transmitted (and an attempt to do so is undertaken) by all ALIVE stations in the network, regardless of the type of packets they intend to transmit, following EOT(IN). Clearly only one transmission of the TI packet is accomplished (by the station in the ALIVE state with the lowest index). With this mechanism, a station wishing to become ALIVE in a network determined ALIVE waits for BOT(IN) following which it receives and decodes the TI packet, and initializes the flag φ accord-

Fig. 6a

*Flow chart for the initialization portion of the VOICE/DATA EXPRESS algorithm.*

ingly. The use of the TI packet increases the overhead caused by the LOCOMOTIVE from $t_d$ to the transmission time of the TI packet. This extra overhead has small impact on protocol performance which are still approximated by the equation given previously.

A different alternative is to require that each station insert one bit power encoding in the LOCOMOTIVE itself in such a way that, in case of disagreement among the ALIVE stations, the train indicator will result of the voice type. For example $t_d$ sec. power on for voice type and $t_d$ sec. power off for data type.

It has been shown that in order to satisfy the delay constraints on voice packets it is necessary to limit the number of phone calls to check whether a new phone call can be accepted or not. The decision is based on the number of calls already set up which can be measured simply observing the length of the previous voice-train.

Although the algorithm presented by the flow charts in Fig. 6a and b considers only two types of trains, the concepts can be applied to any larger number.

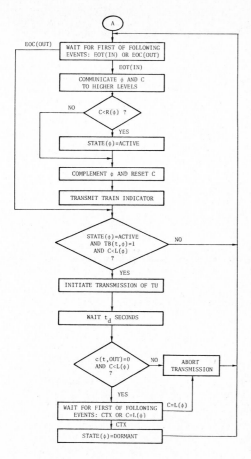

Fig. 6a shows the part of the algorithm which is executed, upon command from higher levels, to bring a station to the ALIVE State. The second part of the flow chart (Fig. 6b) shows only the core operations performed by an ALIVE station, which are needed to decide when a specific TU can be transmitted. In particular a DORMANT/ACTIVE state is associated to a station with regard to each specific type of train (STATE ($\phi$)).

STATE ($\phi$) is switched to DORMANT after a completion of TU transmission and it will return to ACTIVE when the length of the corresponding train is smaller than $L(\phi)$, the max length of train of type ($\phi$).

When it is required that a station be always ACTIVE, as for instance for voice transmission, the switching to ACTIVE at each train is guaranteed by setting $L(\phi)$ greater than the max allowed train length. The measure of the train lenght is performed by the clock C which is reset at each EOT(IN) and it is compared with $R(\phi)=L(\phi)+\tau+\tau_c+t_d$ to check for DORMANT/ACTIVE transition.

The transfer of the values of C and $\phi$ to higher level at occurrence of each EOT(IN) is needed in order to enable this level to implement any desired flow control as for instance acceptance or rejection of a new phone call.

The transmission of train indicator which has not been detailed in the flow chart, has to be performed according to which one of the two techniques previously discussed has been chosen.

## Fig. 6b

*Flow chart for the portion of the VOICE/DATA EXPRESS algorithm executed by a station in the ALIVE state.*

All the previous analysis has been carried out assuming that the integration of different types of traffic is obtained by using different types of trains and requiring that each type of traffic will use only the corresponding type of train. A possible different approach is to allow mixing of different types of traffic on the same train. In this case no need exists to transmit train indicators having only one kind of train. However it is required that each station measures not only the length of the current train but also the time in the train already utilized by each type of traffic. The first one is needed to control for the global train length and the other to control that the bandwidth taken by each traffic does not exceed the maximum value allowed. In this approach, in order to fulfill the delay requirements for voice traffic it is easy to see that the global amount of data transmitted in a train has to be limited to L/2. Note however that this limitation does not affect the overall efficiency of the system nor the bandwidth assigned to data. Due to the difficulty foreseen in implementing this approach, we adopted in this paper and the flowcharts presented the scheme consisting of different types of trains.

CONCLUSIONS

We have proposed and analyzed the EXPRESS-NET which is a local area communication network based on the Unidirectional Broadcast System architecture. The EXPRESS Access Protocol used by all stations connected to the bus is a distributed algorithm which provides a confict-free multiple access.  It is essentially a Round Robin scheme in which the time to switch from one active user to the next in a round is of the order of the carrier detection time, thus achieving performances which are indepedent of the end-to-end network propagation delay. This feature represents the major improvement of this protocol with respect to other existing ones such as CSMA-CD [3, 4] or Round Robin [1] and makes it very suitable for local networks in which, because of very high speed channel or very long end-to-end delay or very small packet size, the propagation delay is a large fraction of or is even bigger than the packet transmission time. Furthermore we have shown that this protocol is particularly suitable for transmission of packetized voice as it is able to guarantee a bounded transmission delay for each packet. Its adapta - bility to any kind of traffic has been also proved and a possible way to integrate voice and data has been detailed. The EXPRESS Access Protocol seems to be most suitable for local networks supporting office automation application where a large amount of voice is integrated with data.

REFERENCES

[1] F.A. Tobagi and R. Rom "Efficient Round-Robin and Priority Schemes in Uni - directional Broadcast Systems" IFIP-WG 6.4 Local Area Networks Zurich Work - shop, August 1980.

[2] F.A. Tobagi, F. Borgonovo and L. Fratta "The Express-Net: A local Area Communication Network Integrating Voice and Data", submitted for publication to the IEEE Transactions on Communications.

[3] L. Kleinrock and F.A. Tobagi "Packet Switching in Radio Channels: Part I - Carrier Sense Multiple Access Models and their Throughput Delay Characteristics", IEEE Transactions on Communications, Vol. COM-25, Dec. 1975.

[4] F.A. Tobagi and V.B. Hunt "Performance Analysis of Carrier Sense Multiple Access with Collision Detection", Computer Networks, Vol. 4, n. 5, Oct. 1980.

[5] R.M. Metcalfe and D.R. Boggs "ETHERNET: Distributed Packet Switching for Local Computer Networks", CACM, Vol. 19, n. 7, July 1976.

Performance of Data Communication Systems
and their Applications, G. Pujolle (ed.)
© North-Holland Publishing Company, 1981

RESEAU LOCAL POLYVALENT PAR FIBRE OPTIQUE

William F. GIOZZA
Département de Génie Electrique
Université Fédérale de la Paraiba
Campina Grande-Brésil

Gérard NOGUEZ
Institut de Programmation
Université de PARIS VI
PARIS-FRANCE

Les réseaux à diffusion de paquets de type Ethernet ont ancré
l'idée du "câble" de transmission qui parcourt tout un bâtiment, et sur lequel tous les utilisateurs peuvent se raccorder.
Cet article décrit un "câble" de ce type, mais dont les fondements diffèrent de ceux des réseaux locaux à diffusion de paquets. La notion de canal remplace l'algorithme de diffusion,
afin de pouvoir garantir un débit constant aux utilisateurs
qui le désirent. Le "câble" est partagé temporellement en deux
types de service de base : liaisons point-à-point en "full-
duplex" et canaux partageables à très haut débit. L'implantation de mécanismes de jeton câblé permet de partager les canaux à très haut débit. Enfin, les fibres optiques remplacent
les câbles coaxiaux afin de rendre possible la transmission
de données à très haut débit et à faible taux d'erreurs.

I - INTRODUCTION

Dix ans après la démonstration par Corning Glass de la première fibre optique à
20 dB/km d'atténuation, on peut oser affirmer, sans excès d'optimisme, que l'utilisation des fibres optiques comme support de transmission devient, aujourd'hui, un
atout considérable pour les nouveaux systèmes de transmission qui exigeront, de
plus en plus, la transmission de données à très haut débit et à faible taux d'erreurs. Les avances technologiques des années 70 ont permis d'envisager pour l'avenir l'utilisation de fibres optiques dont l'atténuation est inférieure à 1 dB/km
et dont le produit bande passante-distance est de l'ordre de 100 GHz-km [1].
Ce qui est le plus important pour les applications, c'est qu'à l'heure actuelle,
on produit et on commercialise couramment des fibres ayant une atténuation inférieure à 5 dB/km, tout en utilisant des émetteurs/récepteurs optiques (LED's et
photodiodes pin par exemple) fiables et économiques. En outre, plusieurs résultats
d'études sur le coût projeté des systèmes par fibre optique, indiquent que les fibres offrent, face aux moyens de transmission traditionnels, des avantages économiques pour les débits supérieurs à 8 Mbits/s [1].

Les réseaux locaux feront certainement partie des nouveaux systèmes de transmission, pour lesquels des communications fiables à très haut débit sur des distances
moyennes sont nécessaires, en vue d'une distribution de la puissance de calcul des
gros ordinateurs et du partage des ressources communes aux utilisateurs locaux [2].
Divers réseaux locaux, utilisant des fibres optiques comme support de transmission
ont déjà été proposés, soit dans un point de vue expérimental, soit dans un point
de vue pratique [3, 4, 5]. Ils diffèrent selon la configuration et le débit, c'est-
à-dire, selon les applications envisagées et les technologies employées.

Dans cet article nous poposons un réseau local polyvalent par fibre optique à
10 M bits/s[1], entièrement réalisé du point de vue matériel, avec des technologies
assez courantes sur le marché. Les réseau locaux à diffusion de paquets du type

Ethernet [6,7] ont ancré l'idée du "câble" de transmission qui parcourt tout un
bâtiment, ou groupe de bâtiments, et sur lequel tous les utilisateurs peuvent se
raccorder. Nous présentons un "câble" de ce type, mais dont les fondements diffèrent de ceux des réseaux locaux à diffusion de paquets. L'algorithme de diffusion
est remplacé par la notion de canal (multiplexé temporellement) dans une trame
synchrone. Cette notion de canal garantit un débit constant aux utilisateurs qui
le désirent. Le "câble" (trame synchrone est partagé temporellement entre deux
types de services de base : liaisons point-à-point en "full-duplex" et canaux à
très haut débits partageables. Les liaisons point-à-point en full-duplex servent
à deux types d'utilisateurs du réseau : utilisateurs synchrones et utilisateurs
asynchrones. Des mécanismes de jeton câblé comparables à ceux du système DCS [8]
contrôlent l'accès aux canaux à très haut débit. Dans les sections qui suivent
nous décrivons la structure physique et logique de ce réseau local, les caractéristiques de la réalisation expérimentale et nous essayons d'exposer les contraintes imposées par l'emploi des fibres optiques comme support de transmission.


II - CARACTERISTIQUES DU SYSTEME

II. 1 Configuration

La configuration du réseau polyvalent proposé est celle d'une boucle active unidi-
rectionnelle représentée sur la figure 1. Deux éléments constitutifs, outre la
fibre et les utilisateurs, apparaissent :

- un mécanisme qui assure la synchronisation de la boucle, qu'on appelle
  "synchronisateur de boucle" (SB) ;
- des stations qu'on appelle "modem-utilisateur" (MU), qui constituent les
  noeuds de la boucle et permettent l'accès des utilisateurs au réseau.

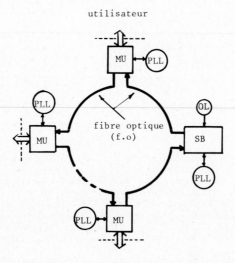

Figure 1   Configuration du réseau polyvalent

La boucle (ou le "câble")est composée, du point de vue logique, d'une trame de bits synchrone. Etant donné que la boucle est active (contrainte imposée par l'utilisation des fibres optiques), chaque noeud, y compris le SB, est responsable de la synchronisation de la liaison au niveau du bit. Le SB, qui est le principal responsable des fonctions de synchronisation, se charge du synchronisme au niveau des trames, en utilisant pour cela des registres-tampon. Ce tampon assure un temps de parcours logique de la boucle indépendant de la distance. Le SB se charge aussi des fonctions d'initialisation et de gestion de la boucle. Les MU, outre leur responsabilité dans la synchronisation de la boucle, permettent aux utilisateurs l'écriture et la lecture sur la boucle à des endroits prédéfinis de chaque trame. La base de temps du réseau est fournie par l'oscillateur local (OL) du SB. L'horloge est délivrée aux utilisateurs du réseau (MU) avec les données, par le biais de la modulation en bande de base. A chaque noeud de la boucle, c'est-à-dire à chaque MU (ou à la réception du SB), l'horloge est récupérée par l'intermédiaire d'une PLL ("Phase-Lock-Loop") qui compose la "base de temps locale" du MU (ou la base de temps à la réception du SB).

## II.2 - Système de Modulation

Le système de modulation choisi est la modulation en bande de base biphase différentielle [8] . Parmi les caractéristiques de ce système de modulation (ou codage) en bande de base on peut remarquer :

- l'absence de composante continue dans le spectre des fréquences ;
- la présence de l'information sur le rythme des données (horloge).

L'absence de composante continue est une contrainte imposée par l'ensemble coupleur opto-électronique/fibre optique ; tandis que l'information sur le rythme des données permet la récupération de l'horloge qui sert à la synchronisation des tâches de réception et d'émission des données, à chaque noeud de la boucle. La simplicité des circuits de codage et de décodage, ainsi que les caractéristiques des fibres, telles que large bande passante et faible taux d'erreurs, font que la modulation biphase différentielle est la plus adaptée au réseau. La redondance d'information qui provient de ce type de codage peut être utilisée, comme on le verra plus tard dans cet article, pour envoyer l'information de début de trame.

## II.3 - Multiplexage Temporel du "câble"

L'utilisation des trames synchrones sur la boucle ("câble") assure un débit constant aux utilisateurs qui en ont besoin. En outre, elle évite les silences et les frais généraux de synchronisation de la liaison, associés aux réseaux du type diffusion de paquets. Elle assure une régularité parfaite dans l'utilisation du moyen de transmission.

La trame est composée de bits que les canaux d'information ou de contrôle utilisent selon des règles établies. La trame est délimitée par une marque de début de trame au niveau du bit. Cette marque correspond à une violation de la règle de codage du biphase différentiel, traduite par l'absence d'une transition d'horloge (figure 2). Le synchronisme du système de décodage et de récupération de l'horloge choisi exige que le bit de donnée qui suit l'absence de transition d'horloge, soit un "1" logique. Ce bit est donc associé à la marque de début de trame comme canal de synchronisation. L'adressage des canaux se fait par comptage à partir du canal de synchronisation. Outre ce canal de synchronisation, il existe un canal (ou des canaux comme on verra plus tard) de jeton, lui-aussi équivalent à un bit sur la trame. D'autres bits (canaux) peuvent être affectés à des tâches de contrôle supplémentaires afin d'augmenter la fiabilité, par exemple, dans le cas de perte de jeton. Les bits correspondants aux canaux d'information sont partagés parmi les trois types d'utilisateurs : champ synchrone, champ asynchrone et champ des canaux à très haut débit.

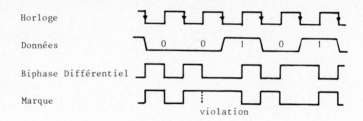

Figure 2  Marque de début de trame.

La longueur de la trame est définie, en principe, par un compromis entre les distances parcourues par le réseau et la taille du tampon du SB. Les utilisateurs
peuvent, eux aussi, influencer ce choix, en fonction de la disponibilité des oscil-
lateurs locaux et des caractéristiques de vitesse des canaux de base. Deux exemples de trame sont présentés dans la figure 3.

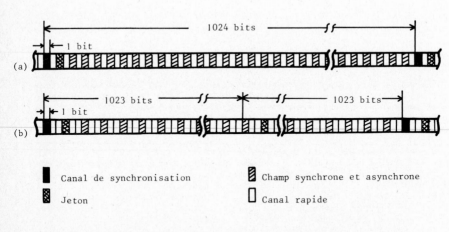

Figure 3  (a) trame de 1024 bits ( canal rapide 1 bit  sur 2 )
            (b) trame de 1023 bits ( canal rapide 2 bits sur 3 ).

III - DESCRIPTION DES COMPOSANTS DU SYSTEME

III.1 - Emetteur et récepteur

Puisque les caractéristiques de transmission sont les mêmes, les parties émettrices et réceptrices du SB et des MU sont à peu près identiques. La seule différence à remarquer est que, du côté de l'émetteur du SB, l'horloge et les signaux de contrôle sont délivrés à partir d'un oscillateur local ; tandis que pour les MU, la "base de temps locale", constituée par une PLL, est commune aux parties émettrice et réceptrice. Dans la figure 4, on présente les diagrammes en blocs des émetteurs et des récepteurs utilisés dans le réseau polyvalent. L'émetteur est composé de trois grands blocs :

- Module émetteur optique : composé d'un comparateur/convertisseur et d'un coupleur opto-électronique. L'ensemble comparateur/convertisseur adapte le signal pseudo-biphase différentiel au niveau de commande du coupleur opto-électronique qui, de son côté, se charge de la conversion électro-optique sur la fibre.

- Codeur : c'est le bloc chargé de coder les données selon les règles du codage biphase différentiel et de les délivrer, après, à l'émetteur optique. Il se charge aussi de la reconstitution de la marque de début de trame à partir d'une commande délivrée par le générateur de marque.

- Générateur de marque : ce bloc se charge de délivrer au codeur les signaux de commande permettant la reconstitution de la marque de début de trame. Ce générateur reçoit des signaux de contrôle à partir d'un compteur qui, dans le cas des MU, est commun à l'émission et à la réception. Le SB possède un compteur propre à l'émission et un autre compteur propre à la réception.

Le récepteur est composé de quatre grands blocs :

- Module récepteur optique : composé d'un coupleur opto-électronique, d'un amplificateur et d'un comparateur/convertisseur. Le coupleur opto-électronique se charge de la conversion opto-électronique sur la fibre. L'ensemble amplificateur et comparateur/convertisseur se charge d'adapter les signaux électriques pour la démodulation.

- Décodeur : c'est le bloc chargé de reconnaître les données et l'information de l'horloge à partir du signal reçu du module récepteur optique. Ce signal est un signal "on-off" dont les transitions sont équivalentes à celles du signal biphase différentiel transmis sur la fibre. Il faut donc qu'il reconnaisse les transitions significatives correspondantes aux données et à l'information de l'horloge. Le signal reçu du module récepteur optique est dérivé par un dérivateur digital qui fournit les commandes au système de démodulation. Ce système de démodulation utilise des lignes à retard de précision. Il reconnait les données et délivre au détecteur de marque un signal correspondant aux transitions de l'horloge. Les données récupérées sont tamponnées à l'aide d'un registre à décalage discret, afin de permettre leur synchronisation avec la marque de début de trame.

- Détecteur de marque : Il a pour charge de reconnaître la marque de début de trame à partir du signal délivré par le décodeur et de fournir le signal de référence, correspondant à l'information de l'horloge, à la PLL. La marque récupérée sert à initialiser les organes de traitement de données.

- PLL ("Phase-Lock-Loop") : C'est la base de temps des MU et la base de temps à la réception du SB.

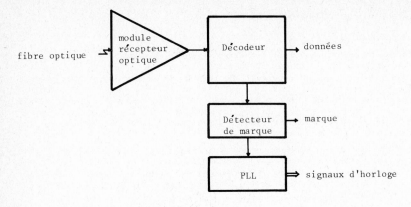

(a) Récepteur

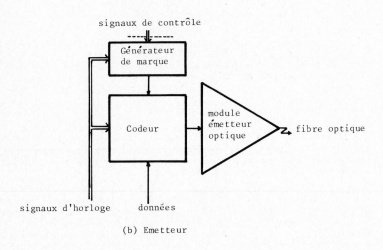

(b) Emetteur

Figure 4 (a) Récepteur, (b) Emetteur.

III.2 - <u>Synchronisateur de boucle</u>

Le synchronisateur de boucle (SB) se charge fondamentalement de la synchronisation
de la boucle au niveau des trames. Fonctionnant à la fois comme fin et début de
boucle, le SB doit assurer la synchronisation des trames émises avec celles reçues
sur la boucle. Pour autant, le SB introduit un retard, complémentaire à celui de
la propagation sur la boucle, par l'intermédiaire d'un tampon. Le retard total est
donc quantifié à un nombre entier de trames. Pour n'avoir qu'une seule trame physique sur la boucle (simplicité des contrôles) on quantifie le retard total à une
trame. La taille du tampon est donc associée à la longueur de la trame qui doit,
pour sa part, tenir compte des caractéristiques envisagées pour le réseau, telles

que les distances, les types et les nombres d'utilisateurs, etc... Le tampon assure donc un temps de parcours logique de la boucle, pour chaque utilisateur, constant et équivalent à celui de deux trames. Le fonctionnement du tampon qui assure
la synchronisation de la boucle au niveau des trames est décrit dans la figure 5.

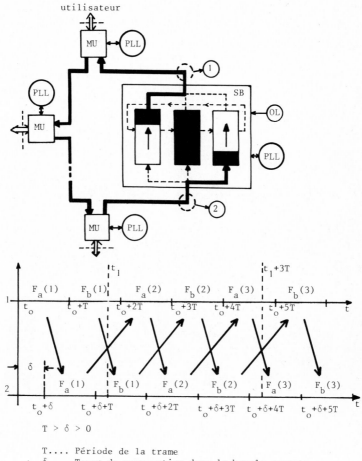

T.... Période de la trame
δ.... Temps de propagation dans la boucle ouverte
$F_{a,b}$. Trames

Figure **5** Synchronisation des trames

L'état des registres-tampon sur cette figure correspond aux instants $t_1 + k\,3T$
($k = 0,1,2,...$) représentés par des lignes pointillées dans le diagramme de temps.
Par exemple, à l'instant $t_1$ le registre-tampon à gauche commence à envoyer les derniers bits de la trame $F_b(1)$, celui à droite vient d'être rempli par les premiers
bits de la trame $F_b(1)$ tandis que le registre-tampon du milieu est plein de la

trame $F_a(2)$ et attend l'instant $t_o + 2T$ pour commencer à l'envoyer. Les lignes

pointillées dans le bloc SB indiquent le sens d'opération des registres-tampon,
soit à l'émission, soit à la réception des trames.

Le diagramme en blocs du SB est présenté sur la figure 6. Il se compose de quatre
organes principaux : l'émetteur, le récepteur, le tampon et l'unité d'initialisation. L'émetteur est chargé des fonctions de modulation des trames, lues sur le
tampon ou l'unité d'initialisation, y compris la génération de la marque de début
de trame. Il délivre aussi les signaux de contrôle de lecture sur le tampon, à partir des signaux fournis par le compteur d'émission ajouté à l'unité d'émission.
Le récepteur, de son côté, se charge des fonctions de démodulation des trames reçues de la fibre, de la récupération de l'horloge et de la marque de début de trame. Il délivre au tampon les trames reçues et les signaux fournis par le compteur
de réception ajouté à l'unité de réception auparavant présentée. Le tampon mémo-
rise les trames reçues ; tandis que l'unité d'initialisation assure la synchronisation des opérations d'écriture et de lecture sur les mémoires-tampon. Pendant la
période d'initialisation, l'unité d'initialisation se charge automatiquement ou
sous commande externe, de l'émission et du contrôle des trames d'initialisation.
L'écriture sur le tampon est contrôlée, à partir des signaux délivrés par le récepteur, par un démultiplexeur de trames. L'horloge est fournie par la PLL du récepteur. La lecture sur le tampon est pour sa part contrôlée, à partir des signaux
délivrés par l'émetteur, par un multiplexeur de trames. L'horloge est fournie par
l'oscillateur local.

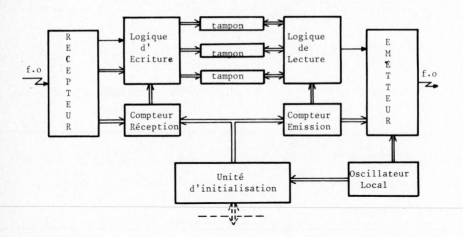

Figure **6** - Diagramme en blocs du Synchronisateur de Boucle (SB)

III.3 - <u>Modem - Utilisateur</u>

Les modem-utilisateur (MU) sont les stations qui permettent l'accès des utilisateurs au réseau. Puisque la boucle est active, chaque MU correspond à un noeud de
la boucle, responsable donc des fonctions de synchronisation de la liaison, lors
des conversions opto-électriques et vice-versa. Les MU sont composés fondamentalement d'un émetteur, d'un récepteur et d'une unité d'interface avec l'utilisateur.
Son diagramme en blocs est présenté sur la figure 7. L'émetteur et le récepteur
accomplissent les mêmes fonctions auparavant définies. Ici, étant donné que l'hor-

loge est commune aux parties émission et réception, il n'y a qu'un compteur qui délivre les commandes aux deux fonctions. Les données sont reçues du MU précédent
(ou du SB) dans la boucle et sont réémises vers le prochain MU (ou SB) dans la boucle par le support de transmission. L'unité d'interface permet à l'utilisateur la
lecture et l'écriture sur la boucle pour les deux services proposés aux utilisateurs du réseau : liaison point-à-point full-duplex et canaux rapides à accès con-
trôlé par des mécanismes de jeton câblé.

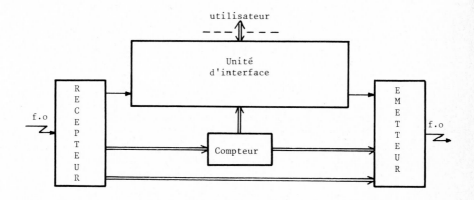

Figure **7** - Diagramme en blocs des Modem-Utilisateur (MU).

Deux types d'utilisateurs, donc de MU, sont proposés pour le service point-à-point
en full-duplex :

- Modem-Utilisateur Synchrone (MUS), où un canal(1 bit/trame)est choisi sur
  un champ de canaux de la trame, dit champ synchrone, à l'aide d'une table
  de distribution programmable ;

- Modem-Utilisateur Asynchrone (MUA), où un canal est composé par un ensemble de bits uniformément distribués sur le champ asynchrone de la trame.
  Dans le cas du réseau expérimental, un canal asynchrone de 19200 bauds
  occupe 32 bits/trame (16 échantillonnages pour chaque "bit" asynchrone).

Le protocole d'échanges avec les utilisateurs, dans les MUS et les MUA, suivent
les recommandations du CCITT (avis V.28 et V.24). Le réseau présente une transparence aux données délivrées par les utilisateurs. Dans le cas des MUA, c'est le
balayage des bits uniformément distribués sur la trame qui assure cette transparence ou quasi transparence.

Les canaux à très haut débit sont asservis par des modems qu'on appelle Modem-Utilisateur Rapide (MUR). Outre les caractéristiques des MU précédentes (émission,
réception, accès à la trame par multiplexage temporelle, etc...), les MUR se ca-
ractérisent par l'unité de contrôle de jeton câblé qui permet le partage des canaux à très haut débit. La lecture et l'écriture sur la trame sont synchrones, l'
horloge étant délivrée à l'utilisateur par le MUR. Cette partie partagée du réseau
(champ des canaux à très haut débit) peut être utilisée comme un seul canal rapide
partagé à très haut débit, ou comme plusieurs canaux rapides partagés parmi divers
groupes d'utilisateurs partenaires. Pour chaque canal rapide, existe un jeton câblé qui correspond à un bit sur la trame (canal de contrôle). La prise de jeton
donne à l'utilisateur l'accès à l'écriture sur le canal rapide. Chaque MUR a la

responsabilité de remettre le jeton à sa place après l'utilisation du canal rapide.
Les conflits de prise de jeton sont éliminés implicitement par la non-transparence
de la boucle. Le protocole d'échanges du MUR avec l'utilisateur correspond simplement à une demande-à-émettre (réquisition du jeton) de la part de l'utilisateur et
à une réponse prêt-à-émettre (jeton pris) du côté du MUR. L'horloge est fournie
par le MUR.


IV - PRINCIPALES APPLICATIONS

Le réseau décrit a été conçu comme un "câble", c'est-à-dire comme un moyen d'échange polyvalent. Ce câble peut aussi bien supporter des liaisons point-à-point que
des liaisons multipoints. De plus, les hauts débits-fiables-de transmission permettent de supporter des nouvelles fonctions, en particulier le déport de ressources
matérielles.


IV.1 - Liaisons point-à-point

Comme le réseau est constitué d'une boucle active, chacun des deux partenaires
"coupe" le canal de la liaison point-à-point. De cette façon, la liaison est bidirectionnelle ("full-duplex"). Ces liaisons garantissent la régularité du débit,
suivant les normes CCITT.


IV.2 - Liaisons multipoints

Comme la boucle est active, chaque partenaire peut facilement :

    - se mettre à l'écoute d'un canal synchrone,

    - retransmettre ce canal,

    - ou bien émettre de l'information sur ce canal synchrone.

Ces possibilités permettent d'implanter, sans modification, les protocoles de types HDLC. La première solution consiste à allouer un canal au primaire et un autre
canal à tous les secondaires. Les conflits d'accès à ce dernier canal sont réglés
par le protocole HDLC lui-même. La limitation du débit n'est pas due au réseau
mais aux logiciels de gestion des protocoles HDLC. Une seconde solution consiste
à utiliser un seul canal de plus fort débit. Un jeton est alors nécessaire pour
régler les conflits d'accès entre, d'une part, le primaire et, d'autre part, l'ensemble des secondaires. L'utilisation d'un seul canal sur une structure de boucle
soulève, de plus, un problème d'adressage. Un message émis par un partenaire revient en effet à ce partenaire, lequel a la charge de "couper" le canal, afin d'é-
viter une circulation permanente du message. Comme les adresses sont uniquement
celles des secondaires, un message émis par un secondaire lui reviendra et sera
alors interprété comme un message, issu du primaire, à destination de ce secondaire.
Une solution consiste à affecter deux adresses à chaque secondaire : l'une pour
l'émission et l'autre pour la réception. La seconde solution - mono-canal avec
jeton - est rentable pour les hauts débits (par exemple 1 M bit s/s). L'utilisation des protocoles HDLC permet d'implanter des structures de réseaux existantes.
Aucun nouveau logiciel ou matériel n'est nécessaire.


IV. 3 - Déport de ressources matérielles

Les canaux fiables à très haut débit (par exemple 6,5 M Bits/s) permettent de déporter des fonctions considérées jusqu'alors comme locales. C'est le cas des disques. Le réseau permet d'écouler l'information à la vitesse de la ressource. Le
mécanisme de jeton permet de résoudre les conflits au plus bas niveau. Le mécanisme de déportation le plus raisonnable est alors le suivant :

    - un canal, à débit moyen et dont l'accès est contrôlé par un jeton, permet
      d'écouler les requêtes et les accusés de réception ;

- un canal à très haut débit, sans jeton, permet d'écouler des "paquets de données". Les conflits sont réglés par les utilisateurs à l'aide de l'autre canal.

Un tel mécanisme permet de simuler des ressources locales en "temps réel". Si la ressource réelle centralisée a un temps d'accès réduit (par exemple, disque à multi-têtes), plusieurs requêtes peuvent être satisfaites dans un temps égal au temps d'accès de la ressource simulée. Ainsi, par exemple, un disque "Winchester", couplé à un canal à 6,5 M bits/s, permet d'émuler dix disques souples et, ceci, sans dégradation des performances attribuées à un véritable disque souple.

Couplé à un mécanisme de prêt de supports d'information (par exemple, "La Discothèque" [10] ), le déport des ressources matérielles est un principe de distribution non négligeable :

- son rendement est excellent ;
- sa mise en oeuvre n'implique pas une modification des systèmes opératoires ("OS"). Seuls les moniteurs d'entrée/sortie doivent être ré-écrits ;
- sa mise en oeuvre est indépendante de la ressource à déporter, elle dépend uniquement du débit. Cette mise en oeuvre est grandement facilitée par la garantie de régularité des débits (les réseaux à diffusion n'offrent pas cette garantie).

Le déport de disques souples, émulés par un disque "Winchester", est en cours de réalisation sur le réseau prototype décrit.

## V - RESEAU EXPERIMENTAL

Les modules opto-électroniques (émetteur/récepteur) ont été fournis par le LEP (Philips-France) dans le cadre d'une coopération pour le développement d'un modem pour communication optique point-à-point [ 11] . Le système de modulation a été caractérisé sur ce modem, confirmant les caractéristiques attendues : taux d'erreurs non corrigées inférieur à $10^{-9}$ pour des distances jusqu'à 1km. Le tableau 1 présente les principales caractéristiques des composants du système optique.

Les caractéristiques de base du réseau expérimental sont les suivantes :

- rapidité de modulation : 19,6 M bauds
- débit binaire : 9,8 M bits/s
- longueur de la trame : 1023 ou 1024 bits
- temps de bit : $\sim$ 100 ns
- canaux synchrones : 9,6 K bits/s
- canaux asynchrones : 19,2 K bauds
- canal rapide : 6, 5 M bits/s ou 5 M bits/s

La technologie de circuits intégrés employée est celle du TTL Schottky. La réalisation du SB a consommé environ 65 CI's de petite et moyenne échelle, assez courant dans le marché et à un prix accessible. Pour le tampon, sont utilisées trois mémoires RAM bipolaires de 1K ayant un temps d'accès inférieur à 50 ns. Le MUS et le MUA ont été réalisés à l'aide d'environ 35 circuits intégrés pour chacun. Le MUR augmente ce chiffre, 46, à cause de ses tâches de traitement plus élaborées. La puissance de consommation typique du SB est de l'ordre de 20 Watts, tandis que pour le MU elle est de l'ordre de 10 Watts.

## VI - CONCLUSION

Le principe de trames synchrones sur une boucle optique offre aux utilisateurs locaux un moyen de transmission de l'information à débit régulier, de très grande capacité et d'une grande fiabilité et efficacité. La simplicité dans la réalisation des stations ainsi que la souplesse des protocoles d'accès constituent des avantages non négligeables pour ce type de réseau à très haut débit. Des nouvelles fonctions comme, par exemple, le déport de ressources matérielles peuvent être envisagées sur ce réseau grâce à la régularité des débits.

Les principes de conception peuvent être conservés pour des débits supérieurs à 10 Mbits/s, à condition de choisir des techniques d'implantation matérielles plus performantes telles que, par exemple, des fibres à gradient d'indice, des diodes laser, des photodiodes à avalanche et la technologie de circuits intégrés ECL. Cette extension est réalisable d'une part, parce que les protocoles d'accès sont intégrés matériellement (i.e."câblés"), et d'autre part grâce au principe d' émission permanente dans une boucle de trames multiplexées.

Le choix du débit à 10 Mbits/s prend en compte la disponibilité à l'heure actuelle des technologies courantes sur le marché, soit du point de vue de la réalisation du réseau lui-même, soit du point de vue du matériel et du logiciel envisagés comme utilisateur du réseau. Les contraintes classiques des boucles actives, d'ailleurs comme de tout système décentralisé, non hiérarchisé au niveau matériel, peuvent être prises en compte de façon classique. Les techniques de sécurité doivent être choisies en fonction des besoins. En particulier, la fiabilité (taux d'erreurs) dans la transmission de l'information peut être de l'ordre de celle d'un bus de gros ordinateur. Le jeton peut être protégé contre les erreurs aléatoires, à des niveaux encore plus fiables, par le codage et, la perte de jeton limitée dans le temps par un système de supervision dans le synchronisateur de boucle. Une politique d'entretien matériel adaptée au réseau peut assurer un niveau de pannes convenable.

---

1. Support de transmission

   Fibre optique  QSF 200 A de Quartz & Silice
   Multimode à saut d'indice
   Produit bande passante. distance : 25 MHz.km
   Affaiblissement : 5 dB/km
   Ouverture numérique : 0,40 (théorique)/0,27

---

2. Module émetteur optique

   LED OF 843 de RTC
   Longueur d'onde : 830 nm
   Puissance injectée : 25 µW
   Bande passante : $\sim$ 35 MHz
   Ouverture numérique : 0,17

---

3. Module récepteur optique

   Diode PIN OF 844 de RTC
   Bande passante : 1 KHz - 25 MHz
   Seuil de réception : - 35 dBm typique pour $10^{-9}$
                                de taux d'erreurs
   Ouverture numérique : 0,18

---

4. Connecteurs

   Type RFO de RADIALL
   Pertes de connection : 9,5 dB ("LED-fibre")
                          2 dB ("fibre-PIN")

---

Table 1 : Caractéristiques du support de transmission.

VII - REFERENCES

1. Giallorenzi, T.G. "Optical Communications Research and Technology : Fiber Optics" Proc. IEEE, Vol.66, N°7, Juillet 1978.

2. Clark, et co-auteurs "An Introduction to Local Area Networks" Proc. IEEE, Vol.66, N°11, Novembre 1978.

3. Rawson, E.G. et Metcalfe, R.M. "Fibernet : Multimode Optical Fibers for Local Computer Networks" IEEE Trans. on Comm., Vol. Com.26, N° 7, Juillet 1978.

4. Ikeda, K. et co-auteurs. "Computer Network Coupled by 100 MBPS Optical Fiber Ring Bus - System Planning and Ring Bus Subsystem Description" Fall. Compcon, Septembre 1980.

5. Gelenbe, E. et co-auteurs "Réseau Local à Diffusion de Paquets sur Fibre Optique : Le système XANTOS". Document LRI, Université d'Orsay, Novembre 1979.

6. Metcalfe, R.M. et Boggs, D.R. "Ethernet : distributed packet switching for local computer networks" Communication of the ACM, 19(7)395, Juillet 1976.

7. Crane, R.C. et Taft, E.A. "Practical Considerations in Ethernet Local Network Design" Hawaï International Conference on System Sciences. Janvier 1980.

8. Farber, D.J. et co-auteurs "The Distributed Computing System" Compcon 73, Février 1973.

9. Macchi, C. et Guilbert, J.F. "Téléinformatique" Dunod, 1979.

10. Riad, H. et Stec.J. "La Discothèque : Système Distribué de Prêt de Supports Virtuels d'Information" Rapport interne, Institut de Programmation, Université de Paris VI, Février 1981.

11. Noguez, G. et Trécourt, D. "Transmissions Digitales sur Fibre Optique" Photon 80, Paris, France.

(1)  Ce réseau est réalisé dans le cadre de coopération suivant :

- ATP CNRS
- Contrat Philips CTI-LEP / Institut de Programmation
- Accord C.A.P.E.S / C.O.F.E.C.U.B. (Brésil/France).

Performance of Data Communication Systems
and their Applications, G. Pujolle (ed.)
© North-Holland Publishing Company, 1981

COMPARATIVE INFORMATION RATE
ADVANTAGES OF ALTERNATIVE
DEEP SPACE COMMUNICATION SYSTEMS

Robert F. Rice

Jet Propulsion Laboratory
Pasadena, CA., U.S.A.

This paper addresses a specific communication system problem
which has particularly characterized planetary exploration but
which also appears in other applications. The results provide
a new means of comparing the efficiency of various communication systems which are required to transmit both imaging and a
typically error sensitive class of data called general science/
engineering (gse) over a Gaussian channel. The approach
jointly treats the imaging and gse transmission problems, allowing comparisons of systems which include various channel coding and data compression alternatives. Actual system comparisons include an "Advanced Imaging Communication System "
(AICS) which exhibits the rather significant potential advantages of sophisticated data compression coupled with powerful
yet practical channel coding.

## I. INTRODUCTION

This paper addresses a specific communication system problem which has characterized planetary exploration but which also appears in other applications. We provide
a new means of comparing the efficiency of various communication systems which are
required to transmit both imaging and a typically error sensitive class of data
called general science/engineering (gse) over a Gaussian channel (the usual space
channel, no bandwidth limitations). This approach jointly treats the imaging and gse
transmission problems and allows comparisons of systems which include various channel coding and data compression alternatives. Using this technique, specific comparisons of five alternative communication systems are provided, graphically displaying the sometimes huge performance differences that can exist between systems. For
example, under certain conditions, the most sophisticated system (AICS, Ref. 1)
would offer more than two orders of magnitude increase in imaging information rate
compared to a single channel uncoded, uncompressed system while maintaining the
same gse data rate in both systems (for the same antenna and transmitter power).
The selected five systems probably span the full range of potential performance available today for communicating imaging and gse over the classic space channel. The
relative performance of other systems not treated here can be obtained by simple
derivations using the same techniques or in many cases simply by parameter
substitution.

### The Error Rate Disparity

Clearly, a communication system which must transmit more than one form of data must
satisfy the minimum transmission error rate requirements of all the data. Performance
comparisons of various systems to accomplish this task must account for these constraints. This is precisely the situation considered here. Generally speaking, gse
data can be classified as strictly error sensitive data although there may be slight
differences in the error vulnerability of various types. Imaging data, on the other
hand, may or may not be error sensitive depending on the method of image

representation. The effect of transmission errors on uncompressed or subsampled imaging tends to be significantly less than compressed imaging (or gse) for many techniques, particularly adaptive algorithms. However, certain image transform techniques have roughly an equal susceptibility to errors as uncompressed imaging. In either case a measure of system performance must account for the fact that the error requirements of all data must be simultaneously satisfied.

## Systems Considered, Method of Comparison

The systems selected for comparison here represent an evolution of communication systems developed for planetary missions. The first four systems represent steps in that evolution (not chronological) based on the assumption that imaging data would be uncompressed (except for simple subsampling) and gse data would be either nonexistent or at least always a small percentage of the total information rate. In that sense a comparison of systems 1-4 demonstrates distinct step-by-step improvements in efficiency. Part of the motivation of this paper is to display the relative efficiencies of these systems to transmit both uncompressed imaging and gse data.

Certainly there are variations to systems 1-4 and modifications which include various compression algorithms. It is a straightforward matter to present comparisons of such systems by use of the approaches developed here. However, we elect to demonstrate the potential advantages of data compression by providing comparisons with system 5. System 5, called an "Advanced Imaging Communication System" (AICS) in Ref. 1, is the result of an end-to-end system design aimed at transmitting all forms of data efficiently and includes advanced channel coding and adaptive data compression techniques. Comparisons with system 5 should indicate roughly the maximum gains that are presently available from data compression.

Method of comparison. Each of the first four systems will be separately viewed as "baseline systems." It is assumed in all cases that the channel parameters of each system are selected so that the minimum error rate requirements for all data are simultaneously satisfied. The gse transmission rate will be fixed in all systems as a fraction of the total information rate in the selected baseline. Then, the imaging information rate available in the baseline will be compared with that available in each other system. This is illustrated in Fig. 1. An improvement in imaging information rate by $\beta$ in any system means roughly the ability to transmit $\beta$ times as many images with the equivalent information content as those transmitted in the baseline.

## II. SYSTEM COMPARISONS

Each of the systems considered will be introduced while treating system 1 as a baseline system (that is, the system to compare others to). The necessary performance curves for various channel options can be found in Refs. 1-4. In all cases presented here we will assume PSK modulation and ideal coherent receiver operation.

## System Descriptions: System 1 as Baseline

System 1 is simply the familiar "uncoded channel" as diagrammed in Fig. 2.

Assuming this is the baseline system, gse data rate is fixed at an average rate of r bits/sec where $r/\alpha = f$ and $\alpha$ is the total available bit rate over the channel. Then $R_{B_1} = \alpha - r$ is the imaging information rate available in the baseline system 1.

Assuming we fix antenna size, transmitter power, etc., $\alpha$ is determined solely by the allowed probability of error, $P_e$. The error sensitive gse data confines this choice to be low. For comparison purposes we will use $P_e = 10^{-5}$. The exact choice will have little impact on the end results and $10^{-5}$ has in practice been an acceptable value. This operating point is obtained at a signal-to-noise ratio of roughly 9.7 db.

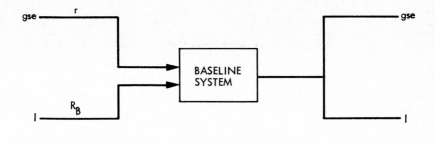

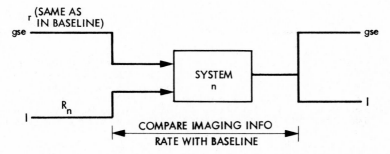

$$\frac{r}{r + R_B} = f = \text{GSE FRACTION OF TOTAL INFORMATION RATE IN BASELINE}$$

$$\frac{R_n}{R_B} = \text{IMAGING RATE ADVANTAGE OF SYSTEM n: A FUNCTION OF f}$$

Fig. 1.  Method of System Comparisons

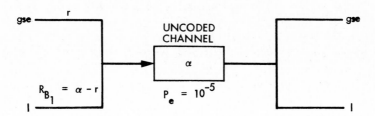

Fig. 2.  System 1, Uncoded Channel

<u>System 2: Uncoded/Golay</u>. This system is diagrammed in Fig. 3.

As shown in the figure, Golay block coding is applied to gse data before transmission over an uncoded channel.[5]  This is held fixed at the same rate as the baseline system, r.  The Golay decoder corrects errors made in transmission over the "inner" uncoded channel.  r parity bits are required for each r information bits.  Uncompressed imaging is transmitted directly over the uncoded channel.

Because of the additional protection of gse data, the uncoded channel in this system may be operated at higher error rates and hence higher transmission rates.  Specifically, transmission rate on the uncoded channel portion may be increased provided

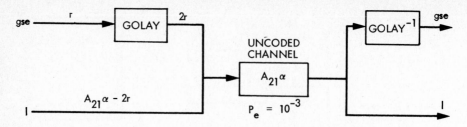

Fig. 3.  System 2 (Uncoded/Golay) vs. Uncoded Baseline

that the net gse error rate is around $10^{-5}$ or less and uncompressed or subsampled imaging is not substantially degraded.  To meet this objective bit error rate requirements for imaging have historically been $P_e \leq 5 \times 10^{-3}$.

This gse constrained operating point for the inner uncoded channel occurs in the range of $5 \times 10^{-3}$ to $10^{-3}$.  We will assume a $P_e = 10^{-3}$ in the graphical examples. From uncoded channel performance curves the $P_e = 10^{-3}$ operating point occurs at roughly 6.8 db.  This satisfies the requirements for imaging noted above.  Thus the uncoded channel in system 2 may be operated at 2.9 db above that in system 1 or at a rate which is $A_{21} \approx 1.95$ times that in system 1.  Operating points substantially above this point would rapidly damage gse data.  This leaves an imaging rate of $R_2 = A_{21}\alpha - 2r$ in system 2.

Note that for the channels over which imaging data passes $A_{ij} = 1/A_{ji}$ will henceforth denote the rate improvement factor of system i over system j.

System 3:  Convolutional/Viterbi.  A block diagram of system 3 is shown in Fig. 4. System 3 looks much like the baseline system except that all data is first coded by a convolutional coder, and then decoded using Viterbi decoders.  There are many variations that may fit different mission situations.  For the purpose of presenting graphical results here we will assume the same principal code used on the Voyager missions to Jupiter and Saturn, a constraint $K = 7$, $v = 2$ code with 3 bits of receiver quantization.  Graphs for other options can easily be obtained by modifying input parameters.  From the $K = 7$, $v = 2$ performance curves under ideal receiver operating conditions, $A_{31} \approx 3.09$, when $P_e = 10^{-5}$.

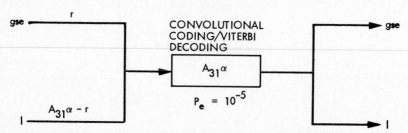

Fig. 4.  System 3 (Conv/Viterbi) vs. Uncoded Baseline

System 4, Voyager.  A block diagram of system 4 appears in Fig. 5.

This system configuration is basically the Voyager communication system (also called the Jupiter/Saturn communication system in Refs. 1 and 2).  It looks much like system 2, Uncoded/Golay, except that the inner channel is the more powerful convolutional/Viterbi.[5]

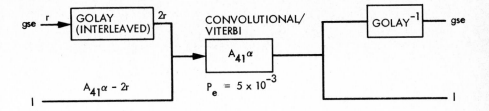

Fig. 5. System 4 (Conv/Viterbi-Golay) vs. Uncoded Baseline

We will assume that the inner channel can be operated at up to a $P_e = 5 \times 10^{-3}$ while maintaining an adequately low $P_e$ on gse data. Again it is unimportant to worry about precise operating points. The main differences between systems is much more significant. Using the $K = 7$, $\nu = 2$ performance curves we have $A_{41}\alpha \approx 5.5$ leaving $A_{41}\alpha - 2r$ to imaging.

System 5, AICS. The last system has been called "Advanced Imaging Communication System." A full description can be found in Ref. 1. Particular details on the channel coding aspects may be found in Refs. 2-4 and 6. A block diagram appears in Fig. 6.

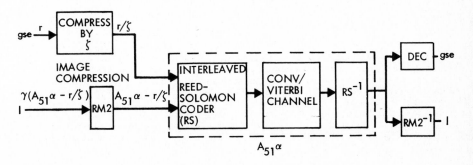

Fig. 6. System 5 (AICS) vs. Uncoded Baseline

In this system all data passes through an interleaved Reed-Solomon coder before entering the same Voyager convolutional/Viterbi channel. The net result, virtually error-free data can be communicated at rates up to very nearly that at which the convolutional/Viterbi channel alone obtains a $5 \times 10^{-3}$ error rate. That is, $A_{51} \approx A_{41}$.

With this kind of channel, there is no problem with communicating error sensitive data. In Fig. 6, we have assumed that gse data is compressed by some factor $\zeta$ without any loss in true information. This appears quite feasible and in any event $\zeta$ should be a system parameter even if we set it equal to 1. In the graphical results the case of $\zeta = 1$ or 2 will be included.

The imaging data compression assumed in called RM2[1] and was basically developed for monochromatic images. It is an extremely adaptive algorithm which gives the user and mission designer extensive flexibility. Any compression factor can be selected for any image.

RM2 was evaluated for flyby missions by imaging scientists in Ref. 7 and in a more recent study for the NASA End-to-End Data System who concluded that it offered an information rate advantage in the range of 4-6 compared to the alternatives of no compression or subsampling. Comparisons of RM2 with other monochromic algorithms can be found in Ref. 8. Adaptive cosine curves were mislabeled as adaptive Fourier in that document. For other missions which could make full use of the adaptive character of RM2, the upper range might be more like 10:1.[9] Then $\gamma$ in Fig. 6 refers to the effective increase in the number of pictures of roughly the same quality or information content that would be obtained using RM2 on monochromatic images compared to what is presently done, an uncompressed digital representation with or without direct PCM or subsampling.

If registered color bands were available, then higher compression factors (for the same fidelity) should be possible either with RM2 (and some small increase in operations) or more directly using the CCA algorithm [10]-[12] developed specifically for multispectral images.

Referring back to the diagram in Fig. 6 we see that $\gamma(A_{51}\alpha - r/\zeta)$ is the imaging information rate for AICS.

## Derivation of Imaging Rate Advantages

For each system just described we wish to obtain a more useful form of the ratio $R_n/R_B$ given in Fig. 1. This requires no more than basic algebra. We will illustrate the procedure here for AICS only. Equations for all systems, including different baseline choices are given in Table 1.

### Table 1. Equations for Computing Imaging Rate Advantages

| Assumed Baseline System | Imaging Rate Advantage Factor Above Baseline | | | | |
|---|---|---|---|---|---|
| | System 1 Uncoded | System 2 Uncoded Golay | System 3 Conv/ Viterbi | System 4 Conv/Viterbi- Golay | System 5 AICS |
| System 1 Uncoded | $\cdot 1$ | $\dfrac{A_{21}-2f}{1-f}$ | $\dfrac{A_{31}-f}{1-f}$ | $\dfrac{A_{41}-2f}{1-f}$ | $\dfrac{\gamma(A_{51}-f/\zeta)}{1-f}$ |
| System 2 Uncoded/ Golay | $\dfrac{A_{12}-f(1-A_{12})}{1-f}$ | $1$ | $\dfrac{A_{32}-f(1-A_{32})}{1-f}$ | $\dfrac{A_{42}-f(2-A_{42})}{1-f}$ | $\dfrac{\gamma[A_{52}-f(1/\zeta-A_{52})]}{1-f}$ |
| System 3 Conv/ Viterbi | $\dfrac{A_{13}-f}{1-f}$ | $\dfrac{A_{23}-2f}{1-f}$ | $1$ | $\dfrac{A_{43}-2f}{1-f}$ | $\dfrac{\gamma(A_{53}-f/\zeta)}{1-f}$ |
| System 4 Conv/ Viterbi- Golay | $\dfrac{A_{14}-f(1-A_{14})}{1-f}$ | $\dfrac{A_{24}-f(2-A_{24})}{1-f}$ | $\dfrac{A_{34}-f(1-A_{34})}{1-f}$ | $1$ | $\dfrac{\gamma[A_{54}-f(1/\zeta-A_{54})]}{1-f}$ |

- gse data rate held fixed in all systems as fraction f of total information rate in Baseline System.
- $A_{ij} = 1/A_{ji}$ = Rate Advantage in operating imaging channel of system i over imaging channel of system j (see Figs. 2-6).

From Figs. 1 and 2 we have

$$f = r/\alpha \qquad (1)$$

$$R_B = \alpha - r = r(1 - f)/f \qquad (2)$$

Then from Fig. 6

$$R_5 = \gamma(A_{51}\alpha - r/\zeta)$$

$$= \gamma(A_{51}\frac{r}{f} - r/\zeta) \qquad (3)$$

$$= \frac{\gamma(A_{51} - f/\zeta)}{1 - f} R_B$$

The same approach can be followed for other systems. Similarly, picking a new base-line is no more complicated. The only difference is to now let $\alpha$ be the "imaging channel" rate for the selected baseline. Imaging channel refers to those channel ele-ments over which imaging data passes. It does not exclude gse data.

Equations for Computing Imaging Rate Advantages

The necessary equations are shown in Table 1. Note that the rate factor $A_{ij} = 1/A_{ji}$ now more generally refers to the increase in transmission rate of the imaging channel of system i over that of system j. Observe that the f=0 condition is really a discon-tinuity point for some of the systems because gse requirements would not constrain channel operating points. This fact is not included in Table 1 or subsequent graphs.

A complete listing of the $A_{ij}$ used here is given in Table 2.

Table 2. Tabulation of the $A_{ij}$

| System Number | | Imaging Channel Rate Improvement Factor $A_{ij}$ | | | | |
|---|---|---|---|---|---|---|
| | | j | | | | |
| | | 1 | 2 | 3 | 4 | 5 |
| i | 1 | 1.0 | 0.51 | 0.32 | 0.18 | 0.19 |
| | 2 | 1.95 | 1.0 | 0.63 | 0.35 | 0.38 |
| | 3 | 3.09 | 1.58 | 1.0 | 0.56 | 0.60 |
| | 4 | 5.50 | 2.82 | 1.78 | 1.0 | 1.07 |
| | 5 | 4.90 | 2.50 | 1.59 | 0.88 | 1.0 |

Graphical Results

Plots of the equations in Table 1 are shown in Figs. 7-10 using f as a parameter. Included is a separate graph of RS/Viterbi which is AICS with $\gamma = 1$, $\zeta = 1$.

Example 1. Suppose that the uncoded channel (system 1) was considered the base-line communication system. Upon sizing up the power, antenna, etc., it was

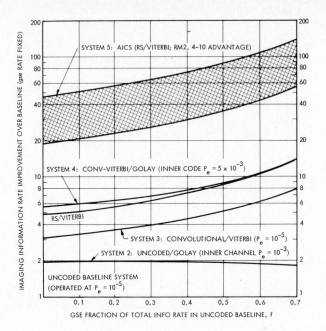

Fig. 7. System 1 Baseline: Uncoded

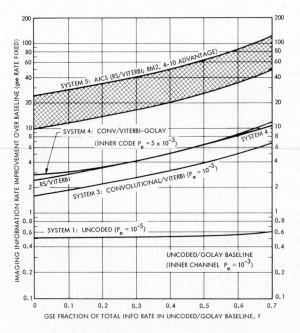

Fig. 8. System 2 Baseline: Uncoded/Golay

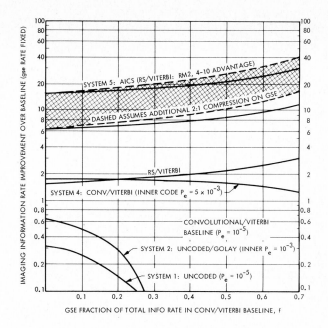

Fig. 9.  System 3 Baseline:  Conv/Viterbi

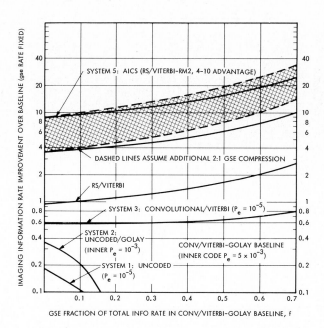

Fig. 10.  System 4 Baseline:  Conv/Viterbi-Golay

concluded that 1 kilobit/sec was available at the required $P_e = 10^{-5}$. Science instruments required at least $r = 500$ b/sec to be reasonable, leaving 500 b/sec for imaging. Then

$$f = \frac{500}{1000} = 0.5, \; R_B = 500 \tag{4}$$

The graphs in Fig. 7 compare the relative amount of imaging information rate with the $R_B = 500$ in the baseline under the constraint that the gse data rate is the same (500 here) in all systems. From Fig. 7 with $f = 0.5$ we see the following imaging information rate advantages in Table 3.

Table 3. Imaging Rate Advantages, Example 1

| System | Approximate Factor, $R_n/R_B$ | Imaging Information Rate (bits/sec) |
|---|---|---|
| Uncoded/Golay | 1.9 | 950 |
| Convolutional/Viterbi | 4.5 | 2250 |
| Conv/Viterbi-Golay | 8.6 | 4300 |
| RS/Viterbi | 9.0 | 4500 |
| AICS | 37 to 90 | 18500 to 45000 |

Given AICS and 18500 bits/sec or more of imaging instead of 500 it is likely that the allocation to gse data would increase since it would constitute now less than 3% of the total.

Example 2 . Now start with a more powerful baseline system, the Voyager communication system. Assume that the available data rate for imaging and gse (at acceptable error rates) is 5 KB/sec. This is similar to the situation which would be faced if X-band failed near Saturn during the actual Voyager mission. Let $f = 0.5$ again so that the gse data rate is $r = 2500$ b/sec. Using Fig. 10 we see that if we assume no gse data compression, AICS offers an imaging rate advantage of between 6.5 and 16 (16250 and 40000 bits/sec respectively). If in addition we assume a not unreasonable additional 2:1 gse compression, the rate advantage factors increase to between 8 and 20 (20000 and 50000 bits/sec respectively).

Discussion

The graphical results illustrate the significant performance differences between several alternative systems for communicating imaging and gse over the classic Gaussian space channel with no bandwidth limitations. These results and the approach in obtaining them will hopefully be useful in addressing some of the possible tradeoffs for future space missions as well as other applications.

ACKNOWLEDGMENT

The research described in this paper was carried out by the Information Processing Research Group of the Jet Propulsion Laboratory, California Institute of Technology, and was sponsored by the National Aeronautics and Space Administration under contract NAS7-100.

REFERENCES

1. R.F. Rice, "An Advanced Imaging Communication System for Planetary Exploration," Vol. 66 SPIE Seminar Proceedings, Aug. 21-22, 1975, pp. 70-89.

2. R.F. Rice, "Channel Coding and Data Compression System Considerations for Efficient Communication of Planetary Imaging Data," Chapter 4, Technical Memorandum 33-695. Jet Propulsion Laboratory, Pasadena, CA, June 15, 1974.

3. J.P. Odenwalder, "Concatenated Reed-Solomon/Viterbi Channel Coding for Advanced Planetary Missions: Analysis, Simulations and Tests," submitted to Jet Propulsion Laboratory by Linkabit Corp., San Diego, CA, Final Rep., Contract 953866, Dec. 1, 1974.

4. K.Y. Liu and K. T. Woo, "The Effects of Tracking Phase Error on the Performance of the Concatenated Reed-Solomon Viterbi Channel Coding System," Proceedings of the 1980 National Telecommunications Conference," Houston, Texas, Nov. 30, 1980.

5. L.D. Baumert and R. J. McEliece, "A Golay-Viterbi Concatenated Coding Scheme for MJS'77'," JPL Technical Report 32-1526, Vol. XVIII, pp. 76-84, Dec. 1973.

6. R.F. Rice, "Potential End-to-End Imaging Information Rate Advantages of Various Alternative Communication Systems," JPL Publication 78-52, June 15, 1978.

7. J. Cutts and L. Lebofsky, "Evaluation of the RM2 Image Data Compression Technique for Outer Planet Missions with the Pioneer Spacecraft," submitted to Jet Propulsion Laboratory by Planetary Science Institute, Pasadena, CA, Final Rep., Contract 954152, Nov. 1975.

8. R.F. Rice, "RM2: rms Error Comparisons," Technical Memorandum 33-804, Jet Propulsion Laboratory, Pasadena, CA., Sept. 15, 1976.

9. R.F. Rice, "A Concept for Dynamic Control of RPV Information System Parameters," Proceedings of the 1978 Military Electronics Exposition, Anaheim, CA., Nov. 1978.

10. E.E. Hilbert, "Joint Classification and Data Compression of Multi-Dimensional Information Sources - Applications to ERTS," Internat. Conf. on Commun., Vol. II, Session 27, pp. 6-11, June 1975.

11. E.E. Hilbert, "Joint Pattern Recognition/Data Compression Concept for ERTS Multi-Spectral Imaging," SPIE Seminar Proceedings, Vol. 66, pp. 122-137, Aug. 1975.

12. E.E. Hilbert, "A Joint Clustering/Data Compression Concept," Doctoral Dissertation, Dept. of Elec. Eng., Univ. of Southern Calif., Los Angeles, CA., May, 1975.

Performance of Data Communication Systems
and their Applications, G. Pujolle (ed.)
© North-Holland Publishing Company, 1981

A ONE-COEFFICIENT ACCELERATED-SPEED EQUALIZER
FOR CHANNELS WITH PHASE AND GAIN FLUCTUATIONS

EGALISEUR RAPIDE A UN SEUL COEFFICIENT POUR LIGNES
AFFECTEES DE GIGUE DE PHASE ET DE GAIN

E. EWEDA[*]   O. MACCHI[**]

[*] Military Technical College, LE CAIRE (Egypte)
[**]LABORATOIRE DES SIGNAUX ET SYSTEMES, C.N.R.S.-E.S.E.
Plateau du Moulon, 91190 - GIF SUR YVETTE, France.

ABSTRACT :  The presence of phase and/or gain rapid fluctuations in addition to intersymbol interferences (ISI) in data transmission channels causes an increase in the error rate. To reduce it, a new and simple solution is presented in this  paper, which can serve for both phase and gain corrections.
It uses a one coefficient equalizer (OCE) following the ISI
adaptive equalizer; the complex coefficient of the OCE  is
adapted according to the steepest descent algorithm. Because of the simplify of the OCE algorithm, it can be repeated many times during each baud interval. We have investigated the effect of this repetition with the help of computer simulations. For signal to noise ratios (SNR) higher
than 25 dB, the repetition makes the OCE able to track faster and larger gain and/or phase fluctuations. For example
at a bit rate of 9600 b/s with baud frequency 2400 Hz, a
phase jitter of 30° peak-to-peak with the frequency 150 Hz
in addition to a 5 Hz frequency offset can be tracked with
bit error rate less than $10^{-4}$ by an OCE using 5 repetitions
while it is impossible to track such rapid fluctuations
with an OCE without repetition. For SNR smaller than 20 dB,
the output of the repeated algorithm is more noisy and consequently the error rate increases. This drawback is reduced by properly low - pass filtering the output of the algorithm. The repetition neither adds technical complexity,
nor puts a limitation on the speed, especially when the
arithmetic units are used in time-sharing with other parts
of the receiver.

I - INTRODUCTION

It is well-known that, for the purpose of data transmission, ISI and phase fluctuations are the major drawbacks of telephone lines.Since carrier recovery can never
be perfect, the phase of the receiver local oscillator is not exactly that of the
actual carrier wave at the input of the receiver. The difference $\phi_k$ between both
fluctuates, k representing the index of emitted data.

Many authors have studied the joint problem of ISI suppression [1] and phase-tracking (or equivalently carrier-recovery), in data-transmission channels. In particular Kobayashi [2], Falconer [3], Magee [4] and Desblache [5-6] have investigated various receiver structures where both phase-tracking and ISI suppression (and
possibly time-recovery) are adjusted on the basis of the estimated data (among
other variables). Other important contributions include Ungerboeck's phase tracking method [7]. All these systems share the feature that an explicit phase estimation is performed. On the other hand, we have presented in a previous work [8-11]
a system for ISI suppression and phase-tracking composed of and adaptive ISI equalizer followed by a one-coefficient adaptive equalizer (OCE) placed immediately

before the decision circuit delivering the estimated data. This system is suitable for correction of rapide phase fluctuations although it performs no explicit phase estimation. Moreover, the OCE can serve also for gain correction which is necessary when the channel suffers from fading. It provides an alternative to the use of an automatic gain control (AGC), and is more efficient in the case of rapid gain fluctuations.

In the case of pure phase fluctuations, it may seem wasteful a priori to use in the OCE a complex coefficient that is designed for both gain-and-phase fluctuations. However, the performances of the OCE are essentially those of a discrete phase locked loop (DPLL) such as that of [3]. The detailed comparison can be found in [11]. In this work we describe a simple method for increasing the efficiency of the OCE, that is the range of fluctuation frequencies that can be tracked. The idea is to repeat several times, during a single baud interval, the iterative algorithm used for adapting the coefficient of the OCE. Although no extra-information is added, this will make the final value of the OCE's coefficient closer to the optimum one, provided the additive noise, possibly including the residual ISI after the ISI equalizer, is not large. This procedure, called repeated OCE (ROCE) is investigated and discussed in the following on many examples which all resort to data transmission on telephone lines at 9600 bit/s with various types of rapid phase and/or gain fluctuations. The ROCE has the same spirit as the cyclic equalization proposed in [13]. However the ROCE accelerates the speed in both the learning and emitting periods, while the cyclic equalization procedure is by no means extendable to the emitting period. In the latter, the data themselves are cyclicly repeated, thus unproper to information transmission, while in the former the repetition concerns the algorithm only, the data being useful information-bearing ones.

II - THE CHANNEL MODEL AND THE OCE.

Consider the transmission of a sequence $a_k$ of data drawn independently out of a finite alphabet, over a channel suffering from fluctuations in the gain $A_k$ (real and positive) and/or in the phase $\phi_k$ (real), both having rapid variations with the time t=kT, where T is the time interval between two successive data. We assume that the channel is not affected by linear distortion or equivalently that it is perfectly equalized by the receiver. Then, a good model for the information bearing signal at the OCE is :

$$x_k = a_k \ e^{j\phi k} \ A_k + n_k \ , \ j = \sqrt{-1} \ , \tag{1}$$

where $n_k$ is the additive noise sample at t=kT. Equation (1) holds when the data signal modulates the amplitude and phase of a carrier wave and when the received signal is demodulated with two quadrature carriers (for instance QASK and PSK). Then $x_k$, $a_k$ and $n_k$ are complex, the components of $n_k$ being the noises in each quadrature demodulation channel, while $\phi_k$ is the mismatching of carrier recovery. In other cases such as baseband transmission and single side-band modulation with synchronous demodulation ($\phi_k$=0) $a_k$, $x_k$ and $n_k$ are real quantities. If the channel is not perfectly equalized, then $n_k$ includes the residual ISI at the output of the ISI equalizer. A reasonably good model for the components of $n_k$ is given by two independent stationary sequences of independent Gaussian random variables with zero mean.

A typical receiver with an OCE is depicted in fig. 1. The OCE is made of a multiplier that multiplies $x_k$ by an adaptive coefficient $g_k$ to give the sample $y_k$ on which is based the decision $\hat{a}_k$ concerning the data $a_k$. That is

$$y_k = g_k \ x_k ,$$ (2)

$$\hat{a}_k = \text{Decision} \ (y_k) ;$$ (3)

equation (2) can be viewed as the gain correction and the carrier-recovery part of the system , while (3) expresses the non-linear deterministic treatment that gives the estimated data. The OCE is adjusted according to the standard stochastic gradient algorithm [1]- [2] :

$$g_{k+1} = g_k + \lambda(\hat{a}_k - y_k) \ x_k^*$$ (4)

where $\lambda$ is a positive step-size, and where $x_k^*$ denotes the complex conjugate of $x_k$. This algorithm has been designed to follow the value $\tilde{g}_k = E(a_k \ x_k^*)/E(|x_k|^2)$ that minimizes $E(|g \ x_k - a_k|^2)$ at time kT. Assuming, as is usually the case, that the noise and data are uncorrelated and denoting the power of the data by $a^2$ and that of the noise by $b^2$, we get from (1),

$$\tilde{g}_k = \frac{e^{-j\phi_k}}{A_k} \ (1 + \frac{1}{SNR} \cdot \frac{1}{A_k^2})^{-1}, \ SNR \triangleq a^2/b^2.$$ (5)

It has been shown [11] that in case of pure phase fluctuations ($\phi_k$ varies but $A_k$ remains constant) the autoadaptive algorithm (2), (3) and (4), together with the algorithm that governs the ISI equalizer describe a good adaptive data receiver, i.e. $g_k$ is reasonably close to $\tilde{g}_k$ and the error rate is admissible provided $\lambda$ is well chosen. These results can be easily extended to the cases of gain fluctuations.

III - THE REPEATED ONE-COEFFICIENT EQUALIZER.

In order to introduce the ROCE, let us consider the case of no noise and of negligible error rate. Then from (5) and (1) we have :

$$\tilde{g}_k = \frac{e^{-j\phi_k}}{A_k} = a_k/x_k = \hat{a}_k/x_k.$$ (6)

Therefore, in order to reach optimality, we should find some means to set $g_k$ to the ratio $\hat{a}_k/x_k$. This ratio is not available at time kT, where $x_k$ is to be processed, since $\hat{a}_k$ cannot be delivered before $g_k$ is available. However, the ratio $\hat{a}_{k-1}/x_{k-1}$ is very close to (6) if the variation of $\phi_k$ and $A_k$ during one baud interval is not significant i.e. if

$$FT << 1$$ (7)

where F is highest frequency component in the phase or gain fluctuations.

In words, when the noise is small and when no decision error happens, the rotation of the measured $x_{k-1}$ with respect to the estimated data $\hat{a}_{k-1}$ gives the value of $\phi_{k-1}$ that will be accepted as best estimate for $\phi_k$. Similarly for $A_k$. Therefore, without any extra information, within one baud interval, the optimal value of the OCE coefficient can be reached.

Unfortunately, rapide and accurate dividers are not yet available. However, the division can be closely approximated by the use of adders and multipliers only. Indeed, if we repeat M-1 times the algorithm (4) during one baud interval according to the system

$$g_{k,1} = g_{k-1} + \lambda(\hat{a}_{k-1} - g_{k-1} x_{k-1}) x^*_{k-1}$$

$$g_{k,2} = g_{k,1} + \lambda(\hat{a}_{k-1} - g_{k,1} x_{k-1}) x^*_{k-1}$$

$$g_{k,M} = g_{k,M-1} + \lambda(\hat{a}_{k-1} - g_{k,M-1} x_{k-1}) x^*_{k-1}$$ (8a)

$$g_k = g_{k,M} \, ,$$ (8b)

we shall decrease iteratively the error $|g_k x_{k-1} - \hat{a}_{k-1}|^2$ to zero, and then the coefficient $g_k$ will get very close to the optimum value (6) provided $\lambda$ is smaller than $2/|x_{k-1}|^2$, which is always fulfilled in the applications. The system (8) can be rewritten in the form

$$g_k = C_k g_{k-1} + (1-C_k) \frac{\hat{a}_{k-1}}{x_{k-1}} \; ; \; C_k \triangleq (1-\lambda|x_{k-1}|^2)^M \, .$$ (9)

The adaptation algorithm (8) or (9), together with equation (2) and (3) describes the ROCE that is discussed hereafter.

At first look, and OCE with larger $\lambda$ can replace a ROCE, provided the quantities $C_k$ are the same in the two systems. However, the possibility of having the same value for $C_k$ in both systems relies heavily on the fact that $|x_{k-1}|^2$ is constant with time k. This is only true in the case of PSK modulation, and no gain fluctuations. In the usual case of phase-amplitude modulation, the possibility of having the same value for $C_k$ in the ROCE and OCE depends on whether or not

$$\lambda M|x_{k-1}|^2 \ll 1 \, .$$ (10)

When (10) holds then the ROCE is actually equivalent to an OCE with step-size $\lambda M$. However this corresponds to the case of slow and weak gain and/or phase fluctuations.

As far as we are concerned with severe fluctuations, M and $\lambda$ do not satisfy $M\lambda|x_k|^2 \ll 1$; $M\lambda|x_k|^2$ may even be much greater than unity. In such cases an OCE with larger $\lambda$ cannot replace a ROCE. On (9) we see that $C_k$ should be kept enough small so that $g_k$ can follow $\frac{\hat{a}_{k-1}}{x_{k-1}}$. In the cases of phase-amplitude modulation, $|a_k|^2$ and consequently $|x_k|^2$ fluctuates and it is impossible in the OCE to keep a small value of $C_k$ for all values of $|a_k|^2$. However, this is possible in the ROCE by choosing $\lambda$ such that $|1-\lambda L_1|$ and $|1-\lambda L_2|$ are both smaller than unity and M sufficiently large, $L_1$ and $L_2$ being the upper and lower bounds of $|x_k|^2$. The choice of $\lambda$ and M must ensure that the maximum frequency present in $\tilde{g}_k = A_k^{-1} e^{-j\phi_k}$, denote it by $F_{max}$, is smaller than the -3dB frequency $F_c(|x_k|^2)$ of the system (9) for all values of $|x_k|^2$. It can be easily seen that $F_c(|x_k|^2)$, if it exists, is given by

$$F_c(|x_k|^2) = \frac{1}{2\pi T} \text{ Arc cos } [2 - \cosh \{\ln C_{k+1}\}] \, .$$ (11)

It is sufficient to choose $\lambda$ and M such that $F_c(L_1) \geq F_{max}$ and $F_c(L_2) \geq F_{max}$ to ensure that $F_c(|x_k|^2) \geq F_{max}$ for all values of $|x_k|2$.

Now, what is the effect of the repetition on the probability of decision errors ? In the channels with high SNR the algorithm (8) of the ROCE reaches a nearly perfect cancellation of the phase-gain fluctuations. These fluctuations, when severe are the main source of decision errors. Consequently, the better cancellation of these fluctuations ensured by the ROCE is associated with a reduction in the probability of error. This is confirmed by figure 2 showing the performances of the OCE and ROCE with M=6, evaluated with the help of computer simulation. It deals with a channel suffering from 30° peak-to-peak, 150 Hz sinusoïdal phase jitter plus a frequency shift of 5 Hz, the bit rate being 9600 bit/s  and the baud frequency being 2400 Hz. The SNR in the channel is 30 dB. This ROCE ensures  an error free decision over a period of $10^4$ bits for $0.3 \leq \lambda \leq 1$ while the minimum number of erroneous bits is 37 for the OCE, reached with $\lambda = 0.9$.

In practice, the ROCE and ISI equalizer and possibly other devices will use the arithmetic units in time sharing. The number of arithmetic operations needed for the ISI equalizer is much higher than that needed for either the OCE or the ROCE and the maximum baud rate will not be significantly changed if the OCE is replaced by a ROCE. Moreover, the repetition adds no technical complexity (increase of the size of memory) as it is performed recursively.

It should be mentioned that the OCE and the ROCE are more robust and simple than the algorithms adjusted to the specific statistical properties of the fluctuation processes [5], [7]. The OCE and ROCE don't need any non-linear estimation algorithm (phase estimation or power estimation). Moreover the power regulation offered by the OCE (and ROCE) is much faster than in the convetional AGC based on power estimation. Indeed, in the decision-directed algorithm of the OCE the gain is adjusted every baud interval, whereas in conventional AGC the receiver has to average the power over a relatively large number of baud intervals to estimate the channel gain.

## IV - THE EFFECT OF NOISE ON THE ROCE, AND ITS REDUCTION BY SMOOTHING.

We have seen in the previous section that the ROCE can track severe and rapid fluctuations of the gain and/or phase, more efficiently than the OCE, at a high SNR such as 30 dB. In the case of smaller SNR (e.g. 20 dB) this is no longer true. Let us consider the case of extremely rapid fluctuations where we choose $\lambda$ and M such that $(1-\lambda|x_{k-1}|^2)^M$ is negligibly small. Then $g_k$ will follow the value $\hat{a}_{k-1}/x_{k-1}$ independently of $g_{k-1}$. But, according to (1), this is not the optimum value of the equalizer coefficient, given by (5), even if $\hat{a}_{k-1} = a_{k-1}$; $\hat{a}_{k-1}/x_{k-1}$ can even be more distant from the optimum than is the coefficient of the OCE. This phenomenon is enhanced when $g_k$ of the ROCE is shifted to an incorrect value due to an error in $\hat{a}_{k-1}$. On the other hand, the weak dependence of $g_k$ on $g_{k-1}$ in the ROCE, enables it to get rid of an erroneous $g_k$ once a correct decision has been done.

If a correct decision is made at step k-1 corresponding to a noise sample $n_{k-1}$ much smaller in magnitude than $a_{k-1} A_{k-1}$, then

$$g_{k,M} \approx \frac{e^{-j\phi_{k-1}}}{A_{k-1}} - \frac{n_{k-1}}{a_{k-1}} \cdot \frac{e^{-2j\phi_{k-1}}}{A_{k-1}^2} . \tag{12}$$

On the other hand, according to (5), the optimum value is

$$\tilde{g}_k \approx \frac{e^{-j\phi_k}}{A_k} - \frac{b^2}{a^2} \frac{e^{-j\phi_k}}{A_k^3} \approx \frac{e^{-j\phi_{k-1}}}{A_{k-1}} , \tag{13}$$

which holds because of (7) and for relatively large SNR ($\geq 15$ dB). Thus

$$g_{k,M} = \tilde{g}_k + b_k, \quad b_k \simeq -\frac{n_{k-1}}{a_{k-1}} \cdot \frac{e^{-2j\phi_{k-1}}}{A^2_{k-1}} . \tag{14}$$

In (14), $b_k$ is the noisy part of the ROCE gain. If the successive sample $n_k$ are zero-mean, uncorrelated, then the samples $b_k$ are also uncorrelated. Thus they have a flat spectrum over the Nyquist frequency range $[\frac{-1}{2T}, \frac{1}{2T}]$. However, even in the cases of extremely rapid fluctuations, the spectrum of $\tilde{g}_k$ is not flat. Hence a low pass filtering (smoothing) of the coefficient $g_{k,M}$ will usually result in reducing $b_k$ more than in limiting the speed of the ROCE. Ideally the bandwith B of the smoothing filter $\mathcal{B}$ should be set close to the value $F_{max}$. In an actual implementation the ROCE will be designed with a frequency $F_c$ greater than any expected $F_{max}$ and B will be set to the average value $F_{max}$. In most cases B is less than $F_c$ and the power of $b_k$ will be reduced approximatively by the factor $B/F_c$. The ROCE with low pass filtering $\mathcal{B}$ indicated in dotted lines is illustrated in fig. 3.

The previous analysis is based on the error-free assumption. The behaviour of the OCE, ROCE with and without smoothing in the presence of errors cannot be theoretically analyzed. It is reached through simulation hereafter.

It should be remarked that a better suppression of $b_k$ can be achieved if $\phi_k$ (and/or $A_k$) is the sum of sine waves. In that case, a good smoothing filter $\mathcal{B}$ is made of a set of narrow-band filters tuned at the powerful harmonics in $e^{-j\phi_k}$ (and/or $A_k^{-1}$). A similar procedure is used in [5], [6] for predicting $\phi_k$. However this is reached at a greated price of complexity, and cannot work when the fluctuations have smooth spectrum instead of peaks.

## V - COMPUTER SIMULATIONS.

We have studied, with the help of computer simulations, the performance of algorithm (8) for the cases M = 1, 3, 6 and the effect of smoothing $g_{k,M}$ in the cases M = 3, 6. Thus five systems have been investigated : $S_1$(M=1); $S_3$(M=3, no smoothing) $S_6$(M=6, no smoothing); $S_3^S$(M=3 with smoothing) and $S_6^S$(M=6 with smoothing).

Our purpose was to find an equalizer that can work for a large variety of channels with high SNR (e.g. 30 dB) and rapide gain-phase fluctuations or with smaller SNR (e.g. 20 dB) and slower fluctuations. For the former class the smoothing is not favourable while it is favourable for the latter. As a compromise we have introduced a weak smoothing that improves the performance for the second class without a great degradation for the first one. Taking into account the technical simplicity, we considered the smoothing filter

$$g_{k+1} = \frac{1}{2}(g_k + g_{k+1,M}). \tag{15}$$

The amplitude characteristic of this filter is shown in figure 4 with the spectrum of $b_k$ and of $g_k$ for one of the channels of the second class mention ed above. The - 3 dB frequency of the filter (15) is 0,25/2T while the maximum frequency $F_{max}$ contained in $g_k$ for the second class of investigated channels is 0,0416/2T. We have assumed sinusoïdal variations for the gain and sinusoïdal variations plus frequency shift for the phase :

$$\phi_k = \alpha \sin 2\pi \ kF_\phi T + 2\pi k\Delta f.T + \phi_o \ , \tag{16}$$

$$A_k = \frac{1+\delta}{2} + \frac{1-\delta}{2} \sin 2\pi k \ F_A T \ . \tag{17}$$

All cases deal with data transmission over a telephone line at 9600 bit/s, T is $\frac{1}{2400}$ s in cases of complex $a_k$ and $\frac{1}{4800}$ s in cases of real $a_k$ . The phase fluctuation frequency $F_\phi$ is taken as a multiple of that of the mains (50 Hz, 100 Hz, 150 Hz), as it is in practice. From the cases considered, the following four are presented because of their good representativity.

Case A : $2\alpha$ = 15°; $\delta$ = 0 dB; $F_\phi T$ = 1/48; $\Delta f$ = 0; SNR = 20 dB.

Case B : $2\alpha$ = 30°; $\delta$ = 0 dB; $F_\phi T$ = 1/16; $\Delta f$ = 0; SNR = 30 dB.

Case C : $2\alpha$ = 0 ; $\delta$ =-9 dB; $F_A T$ = 1/48; $\Delta f$ = 0; SNR = 30 dB.

Case D : $2\alpha$ = 30°; $\delta$ =-3 dB; $F_\phi T$ = 1/24; $F_A T$ = 1/26.7; $\Delta f.T$ = 1/1200; SNR = 30 dB.

In the cases of phase fluctuations ($\alpha \neq$ 0 and/or $\Delta f \neq$ 0) with or without fading, the $a_k \triangleq a_k' + ja_k''$ are complex. We have modeled the sequences $a_k'$ and $a_k''$ by independent sequences of independent random variables that assume the values $-3/\sqrt{10}$, $-1/\sqrt{10}$, $1/\sqrt{10}$, $3/\sqrt{10}$ with the same probability ($E\{|a_k^2|\}$= 1). In this case each complex symbol $a_k$ is used to encode a group of 4 bits according to a Gray code in the complex plane. A similar model, with $E\{a_k^2\}$ = 1, is used in the cases of pure fading ($\alpha$ = 0, $\Delta f$ = 0). In any case, the ISI equalization and sampler timing are assumed to be perfect.

We have compared the performance of algorithm (8) for different values of M, in terms of the number n of erroneous bits over a period of $10^4$ bits. To each channel we have assigned a number $n_{max}$ of erroneous bits that should not be exceeded. The more severe the channel impairments, the greater the value assigned to $n_{max}$. To the channels A, B, C and D the numbers $n_{max}$ = 0, 15, 39 and 7 have been respectively assigned. A given system is declared acceptable if there exists a non-empty, fixed range of $\lambda$ over which $n_{max}$ is not exceeded for any channel. We search for an acceptable system.

The results are plotted in fig. 5 that shows n for the five equalizers $S_1, \ldots, S_6^s$ for each one of the cases A, B, C and D.

For the cases B, C, and D where $\phi_k$ and/or $A_k$ are severe and SNR is high, the algorithms with repetition, as expected, have the best performances. For example, the use of 5 repetitions makes it possible to reduce n to 0 (resp. 19) in the case B (resp. C), while the minimum value attainable with the OCE is 2 (resp. 479). This improvement due to the repetition for the channels with severe $\phi_k$ and/or $A_k$ is also stressed by fig. 2.

For the more noisy cases such as A the curves show how the performance deteriorates with the repetition. They also show, as explained in IV, how the introduction of smoothing gives a significant improvement.

Generally, the algorithms with 5 repetitions have better performances than those with 2 for SNR > 25 dB. However, the difference is not large except in the extreme cases of large and rapid fluctuations as B, C and D. The only equalizer in which $n_{max}$ is not exceeded for any channel is that with M = 6, $\lambda$= 0.9 and smoothing. Thus $S_6^s$ will be declared acceptable. This means that, when it is not known apriorily what type of channel is dealt with, we recommend to use a ROCE with large M, to track the possible severe fluctuations, and a slight smoothing, to give it some resistance against the noise.

It should be remarked that we have conducted an experiment on the OCE and ROCE without smoothing. The results of that experiment have excellent agreement with those obtained by the simulations. The experimental results are not included in fig. 5 to make it more readable. This agreement is stressed out by another example in fig. 6.

VI - CONCLUSION.

The ROCE presented in this work is intended for tracking rapid and large fluctuations in the phase and/or gain of data transmission channels. If the SNR is high (SNR $\gtrsim$ 25 dB) then the step-size $\lambda$ of the algorithm and the number of the repetitions(M-1)can be determined, as explained in section III, to track the most rapid fluctuations expected. If the SNR is smaller than 20 dB or if it is not apriorily known, then the ROCE with a slight smoothing as that introduced is section V is recommended. Finally, we mention that the ROCE is not more complicated than the OCE as the repetition of the algorithm is performed recursively. Moreover there is no limitation on the baud frequency introduced by the ROCE when, as usually done in practice, the arithmetic units are used in time sharing with the ISI equalizer.

REFERENCES

[1]  R.W. LUCKY, J. SALZ, E.J. WELDON : Principles of data communications. New-York : Mc Graw-Hill (1968).

[2]  H. KOBAYASHI : "Simultaneous adaptive estimation and decision algorithm for carrier modulated data transmission systems". IEEE Trans. Comm., COM 19, pp. 268-280 (June 1971).

[3]  D.D. FALCONER : "Analysis of a gradient algorithm for simultaneous passband equalization and carrier phase recovery", BSTJ, 55, pp. 409-428, (1976).

[4]  F.R. MAGEE : "Simultaneous phase tracking and detection in data transmission over noisy dispersive channels", IEEE Trans. on Comm., pp. 712-715, (1977).

[5]  A. DESBLACHE, T.E. STERN, P. THIRION : "Filtre de phase". French Patent n° 7430001 (August 30, 1974).

[6]  A. DESBLACHE : "Traitement numérique du signal appliqué aux transmissions de données". Thèse d'Etat. Nice (Juin 1979).

[7]  G. UNGERBOECK : "New applications for the Viterbi algorithm : carrier phase tracking in synchronous data transmission systems", Nat. Telecomm. Conf. pp. 734-738 (1974).

[8]  M. LEVY and O. MACCHI : "Auto-adaptive phase jitter and intersymbol interference suppression for data transmission receivers", Nat. Telecomm. Conf., Dallas, IEEE catalog n° 76CH1149-4 CSCB, Vol. III, p. 45-2, 1-3, (Nov. 76).

[9]  M. LEVY and O. MACCHI : "Egaliseur de gigue", 6ème Colloque GRETSI sur le traitement du signal et ses applications; Nice. Records printed by Thomson-CSF,Colloque GRETSI, B.P. n° 93, 06802 CAGNES S/MER (France),(April 1977).

[10] O. MACCHI, M. LEVY, C. MACCHI : "Perfectionnement aux systèmes de transmission de données". French Patent n° 76 17156 (June 4, 1976) and First addition certificate n° 77 33960 (November 10, 1977).

[11] M. LEVY : "Elimination conjointe des interférences intersymboles et des écarts de phase dans les systèmes de transmission de données". Thèse d'Ingénieur-Docteur, Orsay,(July 1977).

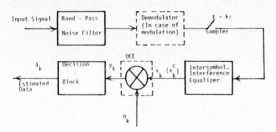

Fig. 1: A typical data transmission receiver with an OCE.

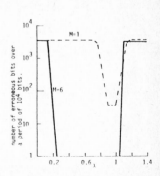

Fig. 2: Comparison of the number of erroneous bits (over a period of $10^4$ bits) for systems equipped with an OCE and a ROCE.

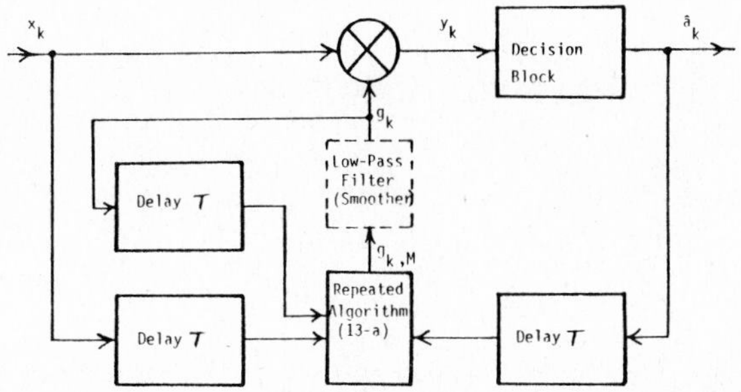

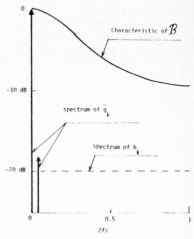

Fig. 3: The repeated one-coefficient equalizer.

Fig. 4: The spectrum of $b_k$ and $\tilde{g}_k$ and the characteristic of the smoothing filter.

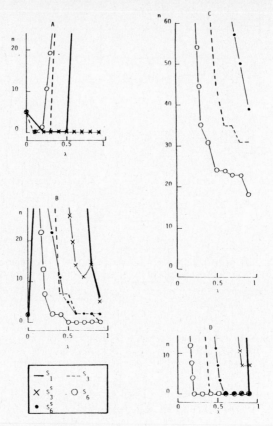

Fig. 5: Computer simulation results

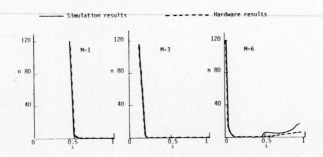

Fig. 6: Comparion between the simulation and hardware results in a case of:
$\alpha = 0$, $\Delta f = 0$, $\delta = -6$ dB, $F_A T = 1/48$ and SNR = 25 dB.

Performance of Data Communication Systems
and their Applications, G. Pujolle (ed.)
© North-Holland Publishing Company, 1981

"ON THE PERFORMANCE EVALUATION OF SIMULCAST RADIO NETWORKS"

Dr. Hugo dePedro

Strategic Systems Division
GTE Products Corp.
189 "B" Street
Needham Heights, MA  02194

A method to evaluate and compare the performance of various
coding schemes implemented in a broadcast simulcast network
is presented.  The performance of various error correcting
codes is evaluated in terms of the time required to transmit
a fixed length message across the network.  Orthogonal codes,
Hadamard codes and concatinated codes using concatenated
dual-k codes in conjunction with one of the above codes were
considered.  It is shown that a large improvement in
performance is achieved using an appropriate coding scheme.

I.   INTRODUCTION

In its simplest form, simulcast propagates messages through a network in a
broadcasting mode with receivers situated farther and farther away from the
originator participating in the message transmission until they have all
transmitted the message.  The terminal having a message to transmit must first
access the network; this is necessary so that other terminals will be
receiving its message when it transmits and nobody else will be transmitting
at the same time.  The message may be generated at any time.  This results in
a random time delay before the message can be transmitted by the terminal
depending on the particular multiple access scheme.  Upon transmission, a
certain number of terminals in the network receive the message correctly.
The number of terminals receiving the message will depend on several factors:
modulation and coding technique used, particular noise conditions during
transmission time, the presence of jamming and interference and the
geographical placement of the transmitter and other terminals.  All of these
factors will determine how wide an area is covered by the first transmission.
A terminal that has correctly received the message and validated its authenticity
will then immediately retransmit it in the next time slot.  Geographically
separated transmitters will then send the same message, covering a wider area
than the first transmission has covered and acting as relays for stations
situated farther away, as shown in Figure 1.

The main idea of simulcast then is that communication links are not pre-
established, but are set up when the transmission is made.  For a dense
enough network where many terminals exist and for a wide enough transmission
range, simulcast provides great reliability of message throughput.  The
network is insensitive to the loss of individual links, which may occur due
to terminal destruction or malfunction or particularly bad channel conditions.
This flexibility provides the network with high survivability and low
vulnerability to jamming.

The simulcast network connectivity is very flexible, since links are
established during transmission.  A disadvantage of this technique is that
only one message at a time can exist in the channel being monitored by the

receiving stations.  When a station transmits a message, all stations within
its propagation radius must be monitoring that channel in order to receive
and repeat the message.  Since the stations operate in a half-duplex mode,
the protocol should be such that no messages are expected when a station is
transmitting.

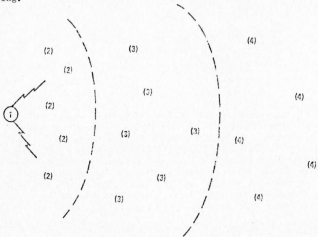

Figure 1  Simulcast Concept

One of the most important characteristics of a simulcast network is its high
survivability.  This high survivability is provided by the fact that the
network does not depend on pre-established links to route a message to its
destination.  The message will take all paths within the radius of propagation of the transmission.  If this radius of propagation is large enough
to reach a substantial number of radio terminals, the probability of message
reception by at least one of these terminals is very high.

The success of the simulcast concept, then, depends on maintaining a large
enough radius of propagation.  Unfortunately, when more than one terminal
sends on the same channel, there is mutual signal interference at the
receiver due to different propagation distances and frequency instabilities at
the transmitters, resulting in signal fading.  This reduces the nominal signal
propagation distance.  There are powerful channel and message coding techniques
that may be used to successfully combat the effects of fading signals.  This
paper describes the performance of some codes in a simulcast channel and a
method of selecting the optimum coding strategy.

## 2.  DEFINTIONS AND ASSUMPTIONS

Define $T_{tot}$, the total duration of a simulcast transmission, as the product
of a single message transmission time, $T_M$, times the number of times K,
the message is transmitted via simulcast,

$$T_{tot} = KT_M$$

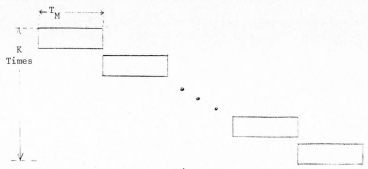

Figure 2
Message Transmission Through the Network

The message information size, N, will be taken to be 75 bits. The probability
of message error, $P_{mess}$, will be fixed to be equal to $10^{-3}$. With

$$P_{mess} \approx NP_{bit}, \text{ we get}$$

$$P_{bit} = 1.33 \times 10^{-5}$$

The channel bandwidth B required for transmission, $B = \dfrac{1}{T_p}$, will be kept

constant by fixing the transmitted pulse duration $T_p$.

The received signal power will be assumed to be inversely proportional to the
square of the distance to the transmitter. This free-space assumption is
used in this example although other functions of signal power with distance
may be used. Additive white gaussian noise is assumed throughout this paper.

2.1  TRANSMISSION TIME CALCULATION

An expression for the total message transmission time, $T_{tot}$, is now
determined. Assume that L pulses are transmitted per message of size N bits.
Then

$$L \frac{E_p}{N_o} = N \frac{E_b}{N_o}$$

and with

$$E_p = ST_p$$

where S is the signal pulse power, $T_p$ the pulse duration, and $E_p$ the pulse
energy,

$$\frac{LST_p}{N_o} = \frac{NE_b}{N_o}$$

or

$$S = \frac{N\,N_o}{LT_p} = \frac{E_b}{N_o}$$

Let $\left(\dfrac{E_b}{N_o}\right)_r$ be the required energy contrast ratio for a given code to produce a $P_b = 1.33 \times 10^{-5}$

Then define

$$S_r = \frac{N_o\,N}{LT_p}\left(\frac{E_b}{N_o}\right)_r$$

where $S_r$ is the required received signal power. The signal power varies as the inverse of the square of the distance. With C a given constant,

$$S_r = \frac{C}{R_r^2}$$

or

$$R_r = \sqrt{\frac{C}{S_r}}$$

$R_r$ will be the maximum distance the receiver can be from a transmitter and still satify the required probability of bit error.

Let M be the maximum distance required to cross the network. Then, it will take K simulcast repetitions of the message to cover the network, where

$$K = \frac{M}{R_r}$$

or

$$K = \frac{M}{\sqrt{C}}\sqrt{S_r}$$

Let

$$T_M = L_1\,T_p$$

Again, $T_M$ is the duration of a message transmission and $T_p$ is the duration of a pulse transmission. Therefore $L_1$ is the number of pulse durations per message. Note that L, the number of pulses actually transmitted per message, may be less than $L_1$.

Then, with $T_{tot}$ the total duration of a simulcast message transmission,

$$T_{tot} = KT_M$$

$$= \left( \frac{M}{\sqrt{C}} \sqrt{S_r} \right) L_1 T_p$$

$$= \frac{M}{\sqrt{C}} T_p L_1 \sqrt{\frac{N N_o}{L T_p} \left( \frac{E_b}{N_o} \right)_r}$$

or

$$T_{tot} \propto \sqrt{\frac{L_1^2}{L} \left( \frac{E_b}{N_o} \right)_r} = Q$$

All constants except $L$, $L_1$ and $\left( E_b/N_o \right)_r$ will be common to all codes used. The parameter $Q$ is a quality parameter that may be used to compare different codes. The total transmission time will be directly proportional to $Q$ for each code.

## 3. CODE EVALUATION

In this section, the parameter $Q$ will be evaluated for selected codes. The channel model used in the calculations is that of a Rayleigh fading channel, which seems appropriate for a simulcast transmission in which transmitters interfere with each other producing signal fading. It will be assumed, as a worst case, that all transmissions, including the first, are fading.

For reference, $Q$ is evaluated for uncoded binary pulse position modulation. A time frame consists of two slots of duration $T_p$. For every information bit a pulse is sent either in the first or the second slot according to the bit value being a zero or a one. Then for $N = 75$, $L_1 = 150$ and $L = 75$. From probability of error curves, $\left( \frac{E_b}{N_o} \right)_r = 49$ dB for $P_b = 1.33 \times 10^{-5}$.

Then

$$Q = \sqrt{\frac{L_1^2}{L} \left( \frac{E_b}{N_o} \right)_r} = 4880.$$

## 3.1 ORTHOGONAL CODES

Reference (1) gives the performance of several orthogonal, Hadamard and concatenated codes in a fading channel. Those curves will be used to evaluate $\left( \frac{E_b}{N_o} \right)_r$ for each code.

Orthogonal codes are denoted as $0 (n,k)$ which means that for every k bits, one of n subchannels may be selected for transmission. For every k information bits D pulses are sent in D of n slots.

The parameter D is called the diversity of the code and equals $D = \frac{n}{2^k}$.

Notice that M-ary FSK, multiple repetitions and multichip per bit coding schemes are examples of orthogonal codes.

Table I gives the results of the calculations for several orthogonal codes. Of these codes, the code that results in minimum transmission time is the orthogonal code of diversity 6.

Table I   Orthogonal Code Performance

| O(n,k) | D | L | $L_1$ | $\left(E_b/N_o\right)_r$ (dB) | Q |
|--------|---|-----|-------|------------------------------|-----|
| O(8,2) | 2 | 75 | 300 | 27.8 | 850 |
| O(16,2) | 4 | 150 | 600 | 19.4 | 457 |
| O(24,2) | 6 | 225 | 900 | 17.1 | 430 |
| O(32,2) | 8 | 300 | 1200 | 16.1 | 442 |
| O(72,3) | 9 | 225 | 1800 | 14.5 | 637 |
| O(96,3) | 12 | 300 | 2400 | 14 | 694 |

## 3.2   HADAMARD CODES

Hadamard Codes are interesting because maximum likelihood detectors (matched filters) can be used at the receiver. Figure 3 shows the code structure. Hadamard codes are denoted H (n,k). For every k information bits, n/2 pulses are sent in n time slots. For the case where each pulse is repeated i times we denote the codes by $H_i$ (n,k).

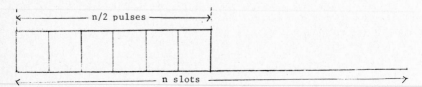

Figure 3   Hadamard Code Structure

Table II shows the result of the calculations. The values of Q are lower for these codes than for orthogonal codes indicating that Hadamard codes perform better.

Table II  Hadamard Code Performance

| $H_i(n,k)$ | $L$ | $L_1$ | $\left(E_B/N_o\right)_r$ (dB) | $Q$ |
|---|---|---|---|---|
| H(20,5) | 150 | 300 | 19 | 218 |
| $H_2$ (20,5) | 300 | 600 | 16 | 218 |
| H(48,6) | 312 | 624 | 15 | 199 |
| $H_2$(36,6) | 468 | 936 | 14.6 | 232 |
| $H_2$(48,6) | 624 | 1248 | 14.4 | 262 |
| $H_4$(36,6) | 936 | 1872 | 14.4 | 321 |

Note:  $H_i$ (n,k) indicates that the coded transmission is repeated i times.

## 3.3  CONCATENATED CODES

If the information bits are encoded with one code and then the output is again encoded with another code, the codes are said to be concatenated.

Convolutional dual-k rate 1/2 codes are concatenated with either orthogonal or Hadamard codes for this example. The results are shown in Table III. It is shown that best performance is obtained by using a dual-5 code with a Hadamard (20,5) code. The value of Q is 138 which results in a reduction in transmission time by a factor of 35 over uncoded binary PPM performance.

Table III  Concatenated Code Performance

| | $L$ | $L_1$ | $\left(E_b/N_o\right)_r$ (dB) | $Q$ |
|---|---|---|---|---|
| Dual-2,0(4,2) | 75 | 300 | 17 | 245 |
| Dual-2,0(8,2) | 150 | 600 | 13.5 | 232 |
| Dual-3,0(24,3) | 150 | 1200 | 11.2 | 356 |
| Dual-4,0(64,4) | 152 | 2432 | 10 | 624 |
| Dual-5, H(20,5) | 300 | 600 | 12 | 138 |
| Dual-6, H(36,6) | 468 | 936 | 11.5 | 163 |

## 4.0  SUMMARY AND CONCLUSIONS

This paper has presented a method to evaluate and compare the performance of various coding schemes implemented in a broadcast simulcast network.

In order to present a meaningful comparison, the channel bandwidth required
for transmission has been fixed for all transmission schemes.

The performance of the various codes is evaluated in terms of the relative
time required to transmit a fixed length message across the network by
using each of the coding schemes.  This relative time is directly proportional
to a quality factor, Q, which is expressed in terms of the overhead required
by each code, including the code rate and the degree of diversity, and the
signal to noise ratio required by the code to satisfy a given probability
of message error.

The channel is modeled as a Rayleigh fading channel, which is appropriate
for a simulcast transmission discipline in which multiple signals interfere
with each other.  Therefore, it may be expected that powerful codes and
diversity schemes will provide substantial gains in performance.

Indeed this is the case.  It is shown that the best orthogonal code
considered reduces total message transmission time by a factor of 11.  This
means that, if it takes 10 seconds to simulcast a message using binary FSK
in a particular network, it would take less than a second if an orthogonal
code is used, in spite of the code overhead.

Hadamard codes perform better than orthogonal codes, mainly because maximum
likelihood decoding allows the use of less overhead for a given probability
of message error.  Hadamard codes outperform orthogonal codes by reducing
transmission time by a factor of two.

The use of convolutional codes is introduced in a concatenated coding
scheme.  These codes are more complex and the performance gains obtained
over Hadamard codes would not justify their use.  It is shown that the
best concatenated code is roughly equivalent in performance to the best
Hadamard code.

In conclusion, it may be said that error correcting coding is definitely
required in a simulcast network.  A large degree of improvement is realized
with coding schemes of moderate complexity but a point of diminishing
returns is reached, beyond which the increased hardware complexity may
not be justified by the performance gains.

## REFERENCE

(1)  J. Proakis, I. Rahman, "Performance of Concatenated Dual-k Codes on a
     Rayleigh Fading Channel with a Bandwidth Constraint", IEEE
     Transactions on Communications, Vol. COM-27, No. 5, May 1979, pp
     801-806.

Performance of Data Communication Systems
and their Applications, G. Pujolle (ed.)
© North-Holland Publishing Company, 1981

DATA COMMUNICATIONS AS A NEW SERVICE
OF THE TELECOMMUNICATION NETWORK

V.Sinković, M.Tkalić, E.Šehović

Zagreb University, Faculty of Electrical Engineering -
Telecommunications Institute
41000 Zagreb, Unska 3, Yugoslavia

A model of voice and data integration in the channel switching network with common loop concentrator is described.
Assuming the distributed concentrator design, the traffic
analysis is discussed. Some conclusions for the implementation
of the proposed ISDN model within the Yugoslav telecommunication
network are derived.

## 1. INTRODUCTION

The classical concept of systems derived from matter and energy has in the course
of development been replaced by models combining three elements: matter, energy,
information. For the behaviour of telecommunication systems the information element is of decisive importance. The information system is defined as an organized
set of distributed automata interconnected with information channels. Systems
capable of enhancing their self-organization in time are studied and technical
implementation problems discussed.

The integrated digital communication network is defined as an information system
which, on the basis of standardized digital signal formats, allows for: technological integration within the electronic domain, integration of transmission, switching and processing in the time-space domain and finally service integration
relying on a common primary network and the development of switched secondary networks towards integrated communications. The implementation of the integrated digital communication network is the objective of the present stage in telecommunications development [1].

## 2. USER DEMANDS AND SERVICE INTEGRATION

It has become evident that secondary telephone networks will eventually develop
into a digital 64 kbit/sec channel switching network and that all other services
will be integrated into this future network. Growth predictions are difficult to
make, particularly in periods of technological changes. In the present stage of
telephone network development it is not easy to define the volume and properties

of future services and thus network adaptability acquires vital importance. It is,
however, expected that the next period too will be dominated by telephone traffic
with a relatively small number of facilities and a lower contribution of other
services to total network information flow. The additional increase of user requirements will be considered a consequence of introducing new functional user classes, demanding primarily the services of information systems integrated into the
public communications network. These services mark the next stage in network development /2/.

The user regards the network as his own information system, required to provide
the following:
- establish connection for speech communication; in addition to some other telephone services it is achieved by extending the dial of the digital telephone
  terminal;
- establish communication paths towards connected data systems; service extension
  is in this case dependent on the existence of data bases, facsimiles, videotexts,
  etc;
- extend service control in the network by introducing special centres and increasing basic terminal capabilities;
- establich connections with other secondary data networks after having achieved
  compatibility of standards between channel and packet switching networks.

The problems associated with the influence of service integration on the basic
network characteristics, user-network interfacing and signalling, development of
transmission media within the user area, and other questions of interlinking have
to be solved before users can be connected to the integrated digital network. It
follows that access to a 64 kbit/s network need not be provided for all users;
some of them /alarm services, meters, supervision, remote control, data transmis-
sion/ will operate at lower speeds. However, on network level no user information
switching is expected outside the 64 kbit/s range.

In addition to the integration methods resulting from former network development
/allocation of semi-permanent paths to a service or their alternative use for two
or more services/ the call-by-call paths are now used on the user level simultaneously for two or more services of the same or even different speeds. The above
mentioned problems call for a new approach to user-network connection, revealing
the need for more extensive research    . The possibilities for service integration differ largely,    this resulting in different lines of development towards the integrated services network. Not withstanding the fact that 1980 marks
the end of the decade devoted to large-scale research during which thoroughly
elaborated recommendations for the definition of basic network parameters were
issued by the CCITT, investigation of digital network parameters will continue
to figure prominently among the efforts aimed at further telecommunications

growth. For on a number of questions there is still no general agreement in opinion. Far from questioning the objectives, the existing differences in opinion, which are the consequence of both tradition and lack of models, can be reduced to different estimates of the necessity and justifiability of various rates of change. The need for preparing a common basis upon which to carry out the international digital network standardization has made it imperative for each country to define its own line of development towards the integrated services digital network.

The main direction of further telecommunications development is characterized by the following:
- speech communication will always prevail and the introduction of new services must not interfere with the development of telephony;
- the secondary telephone network is developing towards the integrated digital 64 kbit/s channel switching networks; the integration of other services into this network is expected in the course of its development towards the integrated services digital network /ISDN/;
- the flexibility requirement should ensure continuous introduction of new services /some of which have not been fully defined so far/ with the purpose of creating such adaptive possibilities in the network for it to be able to meet future user demands;
- it should be borne in mind that further development towards the ISDN will continue within the large analog telephone network and in the presence of existing secondary networks providing various services;
- investigations of functional connection between user area und communication network follow the commonality requirement;
- service integration results in the introduction of special-purpose communication centres into the network which makes it necessary to define user access to these centres.

## 3. STARTING POINTS FOR COMMUNICATION MODEL CORRECTION

In the previous periods network design was based on the probability characteristics of traffic models: statistical balance, Poisson distribution, uncertainty of events, exponential service distribution. The need for correcting statistical models was among other things /random process irregularity, information source dependence, statistical flow unbalance, unhomogeneous information source distribution/ brought about by the following phenomena associated with communication network growth:
- traffic demand predictions have become unreliable; user mobility and his demands for various communication types are rapidly growing;
- there has been an increase in telecommunication service type and volume; information volume and transmission speeds are increasing;
- the increased data volume passing through the network disturbs both the random traffic distribution and the former characteristics of communication paths in

the network;
- call interdependence is on the increase;
- consistent application of automatic information flow routing disturbs random
  traffic distributions in various network parts and levels;
- analysis of independent system and subsystem behaviour has increased in complexity and the problems associated with information delay analysis have become more
  serious;
- the formerly defined hierarchy and present topology considerably differ; the
  cable network has been significantly extended, satellite communications are in
  service, mobile telephony and maritime services are integrated, the number of
  PCM transmission paths is rapidly growing;
- the number of SPC switching centres is increasing, accompanied by corresponding
  widening of possibilities for adaptive call processing; the difference between
  standard and emergency routing procedures is built into the network;
- CCS systems ensuring the introduction of new services and a more rapid integration of existing ones are undergoing standardization.

The basic type of communication - speech - has been selected to serve as starting
point for standardization of digital communication network parameters. Such an
approach was taken for two reasons. Communications of the man-to-man type are,
for deeply human reasons, at the very top of the priority scale in the network,
all the characteristics of the dialogue being maintained by minimal information
delay. The second reason is related to the fact that the telephone network, the
largest secondary network judging by the number of terminals, links and traffic,
is experiencing a rapid growth. The basic parameters of the primary network PCM
transmission media, the basic switching and processing standards within corresponding SPC secondary networks and the basic characteristics of the  CCS control
network can be implemented by means of the above approach.

Modern communication network development started with the shift from centralized
star structures to decentralized tree structures continuing towards distributed
mesh structures with built-in loops. There are two basic lines of development:
evolution of the existing network and construction of networks with ISDN parameters.

In the course of its development, the integrated digital communication network
will acquire packet switching in addition to channel switching in a wide range of
information speeds, packet lengths and their arrival times. The methodology  of
further parameter development is defined by the hypothetical reference path and
matrix model for optimal parameter selection. The optimality criterion is determined by the generalized service quality criterion. Model selection depends on
design requirements for the primary PCM communication network, CCS control network
and secondary SPC communication networks. The selected model must provide solutions

to the following global cathegories: topology design, capacity allocation, traffic control and routing.

Starting from the present state of telecommunications development with the objective of improving our own practices, we have embarked on the test of integrating speech and data within a single network beginning with the user level. The various possibilities of new technologies which are built in the existing network were taken into account.

4. DATA SUBSYSTEM AS A "CLOSED USER GROUP" OF THE ISDN

4.1. Network Model

The network model under study is shown in Fig. 1. Switching nodes, constructed according to CCITT recommendations, ensure 64 kbit/s channel switching in time-space coordinates /s, t/. The nodes are interconnected by PCM links of the primary or secondary multiplex /2.048 or 8.448 M bit/s/. The user region is connected to the network via two levels of digital loops /secondary 8.448 M bit/s and primary 2.048 M bit/s loops/. User terminals are linked to the primary loop through the time-space concentrator /2/, resulting in distributed concentration.

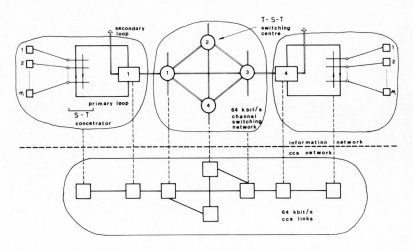

FIG. I

The entire control is effected solely by a network of processor systems linked through a CCITT No. 7 signalling system.

Let us assume now that user A in region 11 wants to put through a call to user B in region 34. First of all, this requires the establishment of a 64 kbit/s digital connection in time-space coordinates between regions 11 and 34 through the controlling  network after which user messages can be allocated to the connection on the concentrator level, one octet every 125 $\mu$s, which is the speed of a standard IDN channel. If terminal speed corresponds to channel capacity is fully utilized. Hower, if terminal speed is < 64 kbit/s, the channel is not maximally occupied. In that case additional multiplexing by the envelope method is performed, signalling information on it being transmitted by the CCS network. In this way the channel capacity not utilized because of low terminal speed is made available for other users. No new channel has to be  provided for other 64 kbit/s users of region  11  wanting a connection with users from region  34  as long as the capacity of the existing channel has not been exhausted. Their messages are allocated to the existing channel by multiplexing until its capacity has been exhausted, the control information being transmitted through the CCS network. The same principle may be employed also for star-connected concentrator networks, however at the expense of some of the advantages offered by dynamic capacity redistribution.

## 4.2. Implementation Principles for the Proposed Model

Having described the network model, we can now proceed to the  discussion of the principles of its implementation, paying special attention to problems associated with user connection, concetrator-exchange and exchange-exchange communication as also switching within the exchange. All these problems will be viewed in the light of multicomponent flows occurring in the network.

### 4.2.1. User Connection to the Network

The concentrator shown in Fig. 1 represents a vital component of the proposed ISDN model. Since users can be connected in loop or star, we will consider both possibilities.

In a loop structure based on a 2.048 M bit PCM multiplex, a frame consisting of 30 information /$TS_i$; i 1, 2, ... 15, 17, ..., 31/ one framing  /$TS_o$/ and one signalling /$TS_{16}$/ time-slot covers all users. Since a concentration  procedure is involved, the number of users considerably exceeds the number of information time--slots. The discipline required for  $TS_i$  occupation and loop control are effected by outband signalling in a 64 kbit $TS_{16}$. Signalling based on the HDLC principle ensures optimal solutions owing to both the wide possibilities of the procedure itself and compatibility with other areas of its application. Provided that the PCM frame has been synchronized and $TS_{16}$ detected, the A-field from the HDLC-frame, /this frame is transmitted in $TS_{16}$!/ allows for the identification of up to 256 users. Since there is only one concentrator in the loop, commands and responses exchanged between the  $j^{th}$  user and the concentrator will bear the address of the  $j^{th}$ user. Furtheromore, since the signalling blocks of all users form a multipoint connection with regard to the $TS_{16}$-channel, the polling technique should be employed. The CCS-format frame is not suitable at this network level, for neither the C-field nor the P/F bit are declared. According to some of the CCS principles, the signalling information preceded by the identifier of the corresponding $TS_i$ and possibly of the data subchannel within the $TS_i$ /a field similar to the Circuit Identification Code in the Signalling unit label/ will be transmitted through the I-field. This organization makes it possible for all information channels to be completely freed from user-concentrator signalling /regardless of whether a telephone, data or some other subscriber is involved/, thus setting apart information time-slots $TS_i$ for "useful" transmission. After the signalling procedures have been completed, control units of both sides posess sufficient information to perform the allocation of octets to particular time-slots. For telephone subscribers with digitalized 64 kbit/s speech signals the connection problem would be solved in this way. Data subscribers, however, impose some additional preprocessing.

The cyclic structure of the PCM frame and the proposed loop organization require the 64 kbit/s to be a multiple of all input data transmission rates, for only in this way can data octets fit into time-slots. Hawever, standardized rates of 600, 2400, 4800, 9600 and 48000 bit/s cannot be completely accomodated by the 64 kbit--carrier. The problem may be solved either by deviating from the standard, which would enhance internetworking complexity, or by artificially increasing source rates. Opting for the latter solution, we applied the 6+2 envelope generating principle . A 33% increase in source rates will result in 800, 3200, 6400, 12800 and 64000 kbit/s envelope inputs to the loop, which can be interleaved in $TS_i$s.

The two additional bits to the six information ones /F and S bit/ are generated and positioned in the same way as within "genuine" envelopes. Having adjusted the rates to the 64 kbit-carrier, we have secured the necessary conditions for data channel multiplexing at concentrator output and further transfer to the network through the PCM links. In the case of data users operating at 64 kbit/s /new data user class?/ all these measures would be superfluous; the generated octets would be treated as coded speech samples.

After discussing concentrator functions with regard to users, whereby it has been noticed that loop organization allows simple local subscriber connections, a few words remain to be said about its network oriented functions.

Let us return briefly to the network shown in Fig. 1. The concentrator acts as source or sink of 64 kbit/s channels being built into 2.048 M bit/s PCM links and transmitted and switched in the network. For this reason the concentrator should allow loop signalling transposition into Signalling system No. 7 and, when lower rate data are transmitted, the complete multiplexing procedure according to the CCITT Recommendation X.50. A 64 kbit/s PCM channel seized for data transfer

cannot be used for speech transmission; concentrator /and exchange/ control units
must provide it economically with low rate data channels.

At the end of this discussion of digital loops, a few words will be said about the
relationship between the proposed model and the emerging ideas concerning the ISDN
implementation    . The suggested partitioning of a $64 + \Delta$ kbit/s loop bit rate:

$64$ kbit/s  -  voice or data as required

$2-8$ kbit/s  -  signalling

$n_1$ kbit/s  -  low bit rate data

$n_2$ kbit/s  -  telemetry

$n_3$ kbit/s  -  alignment and framing

very probably represents a complete solution and a long-term objective. The specific features of our telecommunication network, the possibility of a relatively
simple implementation of the model /to a great extent it relies on  existing solu-
tions/ and the need for comparative analyses have determined the direction of our
research programme.

Star connection of users will be briefly discrussed at the end of this survey.
In that case service integration is performed economically from the concentrator
upwards, $64$ kbit/s concentrator outputs being allocated, before entering the PCM
link, to speech channels or data multiplexes    . Services are separated from the
concentrator downwards, which means that the data subsystem must employ, at these
levels, all standard procedures designed for public data networks /DTE/DCE interfaces, envelope generation, inband signalling/. In principle, it would be possible
to integrate services down to the terminal user even in this configuration. However, it is generaly agreed that for this purpose the loop offers a much more efficient solution.

### 4.2.2. Communication Between Network Nodes

On the basis of what has been said it is evident that all communication processes
between concentrators end exchanges or between exchanges - in a word, between
network nodes - to a great extent depend on digital telephone network procedures.
Once established, the $64$ kbit/s path connecting terminal  points /in this model:
concentrators/ behaves as a temporarily leased line for data channels. All control
processes are performed within the CCS network. It is important to note that some
data circuits in the data multiplex can be permanently allocated to particular
services, for instance to packet transmission. /This requires the implementation
of packet switching modules in the exchanges and X.25 inputs to the network./

### 4.2.3. Switching Within the Exchange

Leaving apart any detailed discussion concerning new conceptions of switching procedures in exchanges    , it is sufficient to say for our present purpose that

they are characterized by modular organization and universal application. In other words, the presented model will not collide with future solutions.

4.3. Traffic Analysis

When analysing the proposed ISDN model, we start from the assumption that there are k different terminal classes within the user region which can be grouped in s groups having similar traffic characteristics. Assuming a Markov's communication model /Fig. 2/, the average amount of generated information for any terminal of the $k^{th}$ class is approximately

$$H_k^{(1)} \doteq \frac{p_{21}^k}{p_{21}^k + p_{12}^k} v_k T_k = A_k v_k T_k \quad \textit{/erl·bit/} \qquad 1$$

where $p_{21}^k$ is the probability of transition from the IDLE to the BUSY state, $p_{12}^k$ the probability of transition from the BUSY to the IDLE state, $v_k$ terminal transmission rate, $T_k$ average communication duration and $A_k$ average traffic intensity per terminal. The pauses between characters, messages, etc. within a single communication have not been taken into account.

If, for instance, a terminal operating at 100 bit/s requires 3 communications per hour with the average duration of ten minutes in the busy hour, then the average amount of information is 5 kbits. Further, if there are $n_k$ terminals operating independently within a class, then the total information amount generated by the whole group of terminals can be expressed as:

$$H_k = n_k A_k v_k T_k \quad \textit{/erl·bit/} \qquad 2$$

Provided that the analysis is performed for the busy hour, the traffic amount can be expressed as $A = \lambda_k T_k$, where $\lambda_k$ is the average number of communications per second. If $v_k T_k = 1/\mu_k$ is the average duration of communication, then the effective information flow generated by a group of terminals is given by the following expression:

$$f_k = n_k \lambda_k / \mu_k \qquad 3$$

When the entire user region is taken into account, the total information flow entering the concentrator loop amounts to:

$$f = \sum_k f_k \qquad 4$$

Assuming the described network model and the distributed concentrator design, traffic analysis of the user region can be performed. The distributed concentrator covering a given user region is regarded as a switching system with full availability. One and the same user may possess several terminals of various classes /rates/ but he can use only one at a time. The total information flow generated in the region under disc ussion is expressed in relation /4/.

Assuming that in each 32-channel system 30 channels are used for information transmission, the total loop capacity offered by the configuration with two systems per region will be  C = 3840 kbit/s /Fig.3/.

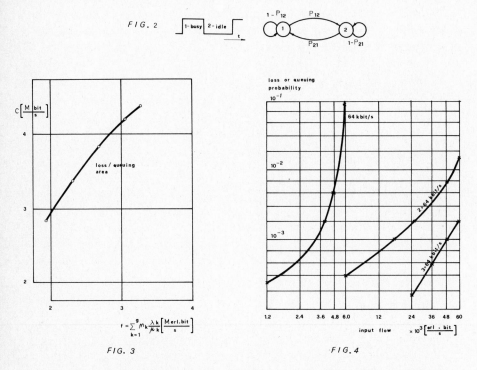

*FIG. 2*

FIG. 3

FIG. 4

A simulation was performed for the above model under the following assumptions: information unit generation for terminals belonging to the same class is an independent Pisson process of $\lambda_k$ intensity and $1/\mu_k$ average information unit length with an exponential probability function. The M/M/1 queuing system was employed subject to the condition that the queue is empty. The results obtained are shown in Fig. 4.

When the distributed concentrator covers only telephone traffic, the relation /4/ is transformed into  $f = \lambda / \mu$ , which has been analysed in /2/.

In the case of combined telephone and data traffic with the above described multiplexing possibilities, the connection established by 64 kbit/s channel switching can accomodate lower rate requirements. If the connection becomes overloaded, a new 64 kbit/s channel is established in the same direction, this doubling the capacity. A simulation was performed for the described data multiplexing procedure

in a 64 kbit/s digital channel under the assumption that information units generated in terminals follow Poisson's law and that their length is exponentially
distributed. The queuing or loss probability values obtained for the input flow
ranging between $0.6 \cdot 10^3$ and $60 \cdot 10^3$ bit erl/s for 1 x 64 kbit/s, 2 x 64 kbit/s
and 3 x 64 kbit/s are shown in Fig. 6.

## 5. CONCLUSION

While discussing the feasibility of the gradual implementation of the proposed
ISDN model within the Yugoslav telecommunication network, the following elements
were considered:

1. the existing telecommunication network is mainly analog with a small number of
   SPC switching systems and completely separated services;
2. AXE and AXB systems produced by "Nikola Tesla" Zagreb in cooperation with "LM
   Ericsson" Stockholm provide an excellent technological basis for future network
   development;
3. this technological basis should be used for service updating during the transi-
   tional stages in ISDN development;
4. the digital transmission media should be intensively developed;
5. areas containing a controlling CCS network will be further extended;
6. network areas with 64 kbit/s digital channel switching and CCS control will be
   extended;
7. source information integration for various services will be performed in the
   periphery, the signalling being restricted to the CCS network.

This is only a rough sketch of the tasks awaiting us in the next period. More detailed answers to all technical and economic questions related to gradual ISDN
implementation in Yugoslavia will have to be sought in the period from 1981-1985.
It will be completely taken up by work on the project entitled "Telecommunications"
whose major objective is the optimal gradual implementation of the ISDN under do-
mestic conditions.

REFERENCES:
1. V.Sinković, M.Tkalić, E.Šehović, S.Rajilić: "Step-by-Step Implementation of
   the Integrated Digital Network", VI International Switching Symposium ISS 79,
   Paris 1979, 13A6, pp. 123-128.
2. V.Sinković, M.Tkalić, E.Šehović, M.Kos, S.Šarić: "Suburban Area Telecommunication Network Planning", NETWORKS 80, Telecommunication networks planning,
   Paris 1980, Session XIV, pp. 348-355.

Performance of Data Communication Systems
and their Applications, G. Pujolle (ed.)
© North-Holland Publishing Company, 1981

USER—ORIENTED DATA COMMUNICATION
PERFORMANCE PARAMETERS

Dana S. Grubb*
and
Marshall D. Abrams

Institute for Computer Sciences and Technology
National Bureau of Standards
Washington, D. C., U.S.A.

and

Neal B. Seitz

National Telecommunications and Information Administration
Boulder, Colorado, U.S.A.

This paper is a discussion of a newly developed set of
parameters that define data communication performance
from an end user viewpoint and in system independent
terms. The parameters are the subject of a proposed
American National Standard. Where possible, actual text
from the proposed standard is used.

## 1. Introduction

There is a need for data communication performance parameters that permit the
user to specify the information flow rate, delay, accuracy, and reliability required by the user. Parameters such as bit rate and retransmission rate are only
indirectly useful to the user, who is concerned with the transfer of information
(not raw bit rates) and residual error rates (not errors occurring within and
corrected by the data communication system).

The user can avoid costly over-design by specifying exactly what is needed;
reduce costs by comparing various data communication services (including widely
varied types of service); and determine how well the selected service satisfies
the requirements only if there are appropriate user-oriented parameters and if
those parameters are applied to the interface between the user and the data communication system. The parameters defined in this paper are designed to accomplish that purpose. They are intended to be applied universally to any digital
data communication system regardless of the control protocol or network topology
used.

The parameters are the subject of a proposed American National Standard developed
by X3S3 Task Group 5 and contained in its working document X3S35/125 [1]. The
parameters are related to a similar set of parameters contained in Interim
Federal Standard 1033 [2] [3] [4].

---

*This paper is a contribution of the National Bureau of Standards, not subject to
copyright in the United States.

## 2. Concepts

Defining data communication performance parameters at the interface to the end user is a concept that necessitates definition of several terms.

End User: the user of data communications may be an application program in a computer, a device medium (for example, punched paper cards in a remote job entry terminal), or a human operator at a terminal.

Data Communication System: the data communication system (hereinafter called system) comprises all functional and physical elements between the interfaces with the end users. The system element that interfaces with the end user may be a data terminal equipment (DTE), or a telecommunication access method (the computer program that serves as a first point of contact for application programs requiring data communication service).

### 2.1 User/System Interface

The proposed standard applies to the interface between the end user and the system, though it can also be applied to other interfaces within the system. There are three general types of user/system interfaces, each corresponding to a particular type of end user. When the end user is a human terminal operator, the user/system interface is the physical interface between the operator and the data terminal. When the end user is a device medium, the user/system interface is the physical interface between the medium and the data terminal. When the end user is an application program, the user/system interface is the functional interface between that program and the local telecommunication access method or its equivalent.

### 2.2 User and Overhead Information

Performance is defined in terms of user pairs. When there are more than two users, representative user pairs are used. User information consists of all digital information that is intended to cross both of the user/system interfaces. The user information bits are those bits used for the binary representation of the user information transferred from the source user to the system, or from the system to a destination user. When user information is transferred to (from) the system as non-binary symbols (for example, operator keyboard entries) user information is defined to be the bits used to initially (finally) encode (decode) these symbols.

Overhead information consists of all digital information other than user information. Examples of overhead information are parity and start-stop bits; enquiry and acknowledgment characters; and off-hook and on-hook signals.

### 2.3 Interface Events

Any discrete transfer of information across a user/system interface is called an interface event. Such events can occur in a variety of ways. Typical events at the operator/terminal interface are manual keystrokes and the printing or displaying of received characters. Typical events at the application program/access method interface are the issuance of operating system calls, co-routine calls, inter-process communications, and setting and clearing of flags.

For the purpose of defining the time of occurrence of interface events, information is defined to have been transferred from a user to the system when two conditions have been met: 1) the information is physically present within the receiving (system) facilities; and 2) the system has been authorized to send or, in

the case of overhead information, process that information. Similarly, information is defined to have been transferred from the system to a user when two conditions have been met: 1) the information is physically present within the receiving (user) facilities; and 2) the user has been notified that the information
is available for use. When the user/system interface is within a computer,
transfers can occur either by the movement of computer words or by buffer re-
allocation (transfer of buffer "ownership").

## 2.4 Data Communication Session

A data communication session is a sequence of user/system interactions (interface
events) by which data communication service is provided in a particular instance.
Performance is normally specified in the context of a data communication session
in order to clearly set the conditions under which the specified values apply.

The nature and sequence of events that occur during a data communication session
are system dependent. In general, a session begins with an interface event that
commits at least one user to attempt communication. It includes all subsequent
events that occur as a result of, or depend for their intended effect on, that
initial event. It ends with an event that permits the user to initiate a new access attempt. Data communication sessions are divided into two general categories: 1) circuit-oriented, where users must be committed to the session
before the transfer of the user information can begin; and 2) message-oriented,
where user information transfer can begin with only one of the two users (the
source of user information) in the committed state. The circuit-oriented category includes both virtual circuit and physical circuit-switched services. The
message-oriented category includes both datagram and message-switched services.

## 3. Primary Functions

This section defines the specific data communication functions whose performance
is described in the standard. The beginnings and endings of the primary functions are defined in terms of general, system-independent reference events rather
than in terms of system-specific interface signals.

## 3.1 Access Function

The access function includes those activities that the user and the system must
accomplish in order for the system to accept source user information for transfer
to a destination. The access function begins upon issuance of an access request
signal or its implied equivalent at the interface between a user and the system.
It ends when the first bit of source user information is input to the system
after access request. An access request may be issued either by a user or by the
system. There is only one access function per session.

## 3.2 User Information Transfer Function

The user information transfer function includes those activities that the system
and the users must accomplish (after completing access) in order to transfer user
information from the source user through the system to the destination user. The
function begins when the first bit of source user information is input to the
system after access request. The function ends when the last disengagement request in that session is issued. In cases where full duplex is used, each user
is both a source and a destination user.

The user information bit transfer function (hereinafter, bit transfer function)
begins, for any source user information bit, when the bit has been input to the

system and the system has been authorized to begin its transmission.  The function ends on transfer of the corresponding bit from the system to the destination user.

The user information block tranfer function (hereinafter, block transfer function) begins, for any source user information block, when the block has been input to the system and the system has been authorized to begin its transmission. The function ends on completion of transfer of the corresponding block from the system to the destination user.

### 3.3 Disengagement Function

There is a disengagement function associated with each participant in a session. Thus, there are at least two disengagement functions associated with each session.  Each disengagement function begins on issuance of a disengagement request. The function ends, for each end user, when 1) disengagement has been requested for that end user; and 2) that end user is able to initiate a new access attempt. In many systems there is a disengagement confirmation signal.  In cases where no disengagement confirmation signal is issued by the system, the user must issue a new access request to confirm disengagement.

### 4.  Primary Parameters

The primary parameters are specific measures of speed, accuracy, and reliability associated with the three primary functions; access, user information transfer, and disengagement.  The primary parameters are shown on Table 1 and in the rectangular boxes on the Figures.

PRIMARY PARAMETERS                                              ANCILLARY PARAMETERS

| FUNCTION | PERFORMANCE CRITERION | | | PERFORMANCE TIME ALLOCATION |
|----------|-------|----------|-------------|-------------|
|          | SPEED | ACCURACY | RELIABILITY |             |
| ACCESS | ACCESS TIME | INCORRECT ACCESS PROBABILITY | ACCESS DENIAL PROBABILITY<br><br>ACCESS OUTAGE PROBABILITY | USER FRACTION OF ACCESS TIME |
| USER INFORMATION TRANSFER | BLOCK TRANSFER TIME | BIT MISDELIVERY PROB.<br>BIT ERROR PROBABILITY<br>EXTRA BIT PROBABILITY | BIT LOSS PROBABILITY | USER FRACTION OF BLOCK TRANSFER TIME |
| | | BLOCK MISDELIVERY PROB.<br>BLOCK ERROR PROBABILITY<br>EXTRA BLOCK PROBABILITY | BLOCK LOSS PROBABILITY | |
| | USER INFORMATION BIT TRANSFER RATE | TRANSFER DENIAL PROBABILITY | | USER FRACTION OF INPUT/OUTPUT TIME |
| DISENGAGEMENT | DISENGAGEMENT TIME | DISENGAGEMENT DENIAL PROBABILITY | | USER FRACTION OF DISENGAGEMENT TIME |

Table 1

The primary parameters are developed in two steps.  First, a set of possible outcomes are developed for each function.  Second, rate, delay and/or probability parameters are defined relative to each possible outcome.  The outcomes are the possible end results that may occur on an attempt to perform these functions.

The parameters are developed using the average of many consecutive attempts. The parameter values are based on a reduced sample that excludes failures attributed to a user.

## 4.1 Access Parameters (See Figure 1.)

### 4.1.1 Access Time

Access Time is the average value of elapsed time between the start of an access attempt and successful access. Elapsed time values are calculated only on access attempts that result in successful access. The successful access outcome is indicated when at least one bit of source user information is input to the system within the specified maximum access time (i.e., before access timeout). In the case of circuit-oriented data communication sessions, there is the additional requirement that the intended non-originating user must have been contacted and committed to the data communication session prior to the start of user information transfer.

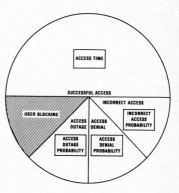

Figure 1.   Access

### 4.1.2 Incorrect Access Probability

Incorrect Access Probability is the ratio of total access attempts that result in incorrect access to total access attempts included in the reduced access sample. Incorrect Access is essentially the case of a "wrong number". It occurs when the system establishes a physical or virtual circuit connection to a user other than the one intended by the data communication session originator, and then does not correct the error before the start of user information transfer. Incorrect Access can only occur in circuit-oriented data communication sessions. An incorrect access due to the user (e.g., dialing a wrong number) is excluded from system performance measurement.

### 4.1.3 Access Denial Probability

Access Denial Probability is the ratio of total access attempts that result in access denial to total access attempts included in the reduced access sample. Access denial (also termed system blocking) can occur in two ways: a) the system issues a blocking signal to the originating user during the access period; or b) the system delays excessively in responding to user actions during the access period, with the result that user information transfer is not initiated before access timeout. Access denial is distinguished from access outage by the issuance of some form of active response by the system during the access performance period. An access attempt can also fail as a result of user blocking. Such failures are excluded from system performance measurement. Access timeout is specified to occur whenever the duration of an individual access attempt exceeds three times the value of Access Time which the user has specified.

### 4.1.4 Access Outage Probability

Access Outage Probability is the ratio of total access attempts that result in access outage to total access attempts included in the reduced access sample. Access outage is distinguished from access denial by the fact that the system fails to issue any active interface signal during the access performance period.

4.2 User Information Transfer Parameters

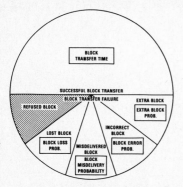
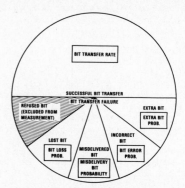

User Information Block Transfer          User Information Bit Transfer

Figure 2                                 Figure 3

### 4.2.1 Block Transfer Time

Block Transfer Time is the average value of elapsed time between the start of a block transfer attempt and successful block transfer. Elapsed time values are calculated only on blocks that are successfully transferred. Successful block transfer is identified by the occurrence of the successful bit transfer outcome for all bits in the transferred block.

### 4.2.2 Bit Error Probability

Bit Error Probability is the ratio of total incorrect bits to total successfully delivered bits. The incorrect bit outcome is declared when a bit is transferred from the source user to the intended destination user within the maximum transfer time allowed for the associated block, but the delivered bit is incorrect in content. (That is, a "one" becomes a "zero" or vice versa.)

### 4.2.3 Block Error Probability

Block Error Probability is the ratio of total incorrect blocks to total successfully delivered blocks. The incorrect block outcome is declared when one or more bits in a block are incorrect bits; or when some, but not all, of the bits in a block are lost bits or extra bits.

### 4.2.4 Bit Misdelivery Probability

Bit Misdelivery Probability is the ratio of total misdelivered bits to total bits transferred between a specified source and destination. The misdelivered bit outcome is declared when a bit is transferred from a source user to an unintended destination user. The bit may be correct or incorrect.

### 4.2.5 Block Misdelivery Probability

Block Misdelivery Probability is the ratio of total misdelivered blocks to total blocks transferred between a specified source and destination. The misdelivered block outcome is identified by the occurrence of the misdelivered bit outcome for any or all bits in a transferred block.

### 4.2.6 Extra Bit Probability

Extra Bit Probability is the ratio of total extra bits to total bits received by a particular destination user. The extra bit outcome is declared when a bit is received by a particular destination user, and the bit was not output by the source user participating in that data communication session. Extra bits are frequently duplicates of previously transferred bits occurring as a result of system timing errors or retransmission protocol failures.

### 4.2.7 Extra Block Probability

Extra Block Probability is the ratio of total extra blocks to total received blocks. The extra block outcome is identified by the occurrence of the extra bit outcome for all bits in a received block.

### 4.2.8 Bit Loss Probability

Bit Loss Probability is the ratio of total lost bits to total transmitted bits. The lost bit outcome is declared when a bit output by a source user is lost by the system. A bit transfer attempt can also fail as a result of nonperformance or excessive delay on the part of a user. Such outcomes, termed refused bits, are excluded from system performance measurement.

### 4.2.9 Block Loss Probability

Block Loss Probability is the ratio of total lost blocks to total transmitted blocks. The lost block outcome is identified by the occurrence of lost bit outcomes for all bits in a transmitted block. Block transfer timeout occurs whenever the duration of an individual block transfer period exceeds three time the value of Block Transfer Time that the user has specified. A block transfer attempt can also fail as a result of nonperformance or excessive delay on the part of a user. Such outcomes, termed refused blocks, are excluded from system performance measurement.

### 4.2.10 User Information Bit Transfer Rate

User Information Bit Transfer Rate is the total number of successful bit transfer outcomes in a transfer sample divided by the input/output time for that sample. The input/output time for a transfer sample is the larger of the input time or the output time for that sample. The sample input time begins when the sample (defined in 4.2.11) begins and ends when either: (1) all bits in the sample have been input to the system, and the system has been authorized to transmit them; or (2) sample input/output timeout occurs. The sample output time begins when the first user information bit in the sample is delivered by the system to the destination user. It ends when either (1) the last bit of user information in the sample is delivered to the destination user; or (2) sample input/output timeout occurs.

A sample input/output timeout occurs (i.e., a transfer sample is declared a failure for performance assessment purposes) whenever the duration of an individual sample input or output period exceeds three times the specified average input/output time. Either the input or the output of a transfer sample may be

delayed excessively by user nonperformance.  Such failures are excluded from system performance measurement.

## 4.2.11 Transfer Denial Probability

Transfer Denial Probability is a measure that  includes both  system  outages  and those instances
where system  performance  is  unacceptably  poor.
See  Figure  4.  In determining whether the performance of a data communication system is above  the
threshold of acceptability, it is necessary to observe enough bit transfer outcomes to ensure  reasonable  confidence  in  the  measured performance
values.  A unit of observations called a  transfer
sample is defined to satisfy this requirement.

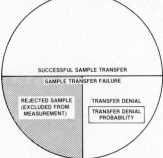

Figure 4. Sample Transfer

A transfer sample (which is not itself a parameter) is a selected observation  of
user  information transfer performance between a specified source and destination
user.  It begins upon start of a randomly chosen user information block  at  the
source  user interface and continues until a given number of consecutive user information bit transfer outcomes has been  determined.  The  number  of  bits  is
selected  to provide estimates of the values for four supported parameters having
a relative precision of 50 percent of the specified value and with  a  confidence
level of 90 percent [5] [6].

Transfer Denial Probability is the ratio of  total  transfer  denials  to  total
transfer samples.  Transfer denial occurs whenever the performance for the sample
is worse than the threshold of acceptability for any of four  supported  transfer
parameters.   The  four supported parameters are: Bit Error Probability; Bit Loss
Probability; Extra Bit Probability; and User Information Bit Transfer Rate.

The transfer denial threshold for each of the three bit transfer  failure  probabilities  is  defined  by taking the fourth root of the specified values.  In the
case of User Information Bit Transfer Rate, the threshold is defined as one-third
of the specified rate.  These values are somewhat arbitrary.  They were chosen to
represent a level of performance below which the service is unusable.

## 4.3 Disengagement Parameters

Figure 5  summarizes  the  possible  disengegement
outcomes  and the associated disengagement parameters.  There is a separate disengagement  function
associated  with  each end user.  The outcomes are
determined separately for each function,  and  the
outcomes  for  all  users  in a data communication
session are weighted equally  in  determining  the
disengagement parameter values.

## 4.3.1 Disengagement Time

Disengagement Time is the average value of elapsed
time  between the start of a disengagement attempt
at a particular user/system interface and successful disengagement at that interface.

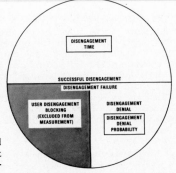

Figure 5.   Disengagement

Elapsed time values are calculated only on disengagement attempts that result in successful disengagement. The successful disengagement outcome is indicated in one of two ways: (1) by the occurrence of a disengagement confirmation signal within the specified maximum disengagement time (in systems that provide such a signal); or (2) by the fact that the user is able to initiate a new access within the specified maximum disengagement time (in systems that do not provide such a signal).

### 4.3.2 Disengagement Denial Probability

Disengagement Denial Probability is the ratio of total disengagement attempts that result in disengagement denial to total disengagement attempts included in the reduced disengagement sample. The disengagement denial outcome is indicated in one of two ways: (1) by the absence of a disengagement confirmation signal within the disengagement timeout period (in systems that provide such a signal); or (2) by the inability of the user to initiate a new access within the specified disengagement timeout period (in systems that do not provide such a signal). Disengagement timeout occurs whenever the duration of an individual disengagement attempt exceeds three times the specified value of the parameter Disengagement Time.

## 5. Ancillary Parameters

An important characteristic of the primary communication functions is that they require user participation. That is, their successful completion depends on intermediate activities which must be performed by a user. The ancillary parameters provide a method of specifying the influence of user delays on the primary rate and delay parameter values. The ancillary parameters are developed by dividing the overall performance time for an associated primary function into subintervals, each corresponding to a period of user or system responsibility. Each ancillary parameter expresses the average proportion of the total primary function performance time that is attributable to user delay.

### 5.1 User Fraction of Access Time

The User Fraction of Access Time is the ratio of the average access time for which the user is responsible to the average total access time, measured over a series of successful access attempts.

### 5.2 User Fraction of Block Transfer Time

The User Fraction of Block Transfer Time is the ratio of the average block transfer time for which the user is responsbile to the average total block transfer time, measured over a series of successful block transfer attempts.

### 5.3 User Fraction of Input/Output Time

The User Fraction of Input/Output Time is the ratio of the average user input/output time to the average total input/output time for a transfer sample, measured over a series of successful transfer samples. The user input/output time for a transfer sample is that portion of the sample input/output time for which the user is responsible.

5.4 User Fraction of Disengagement Time

The User Fraction of Disengagement Time is the ratio of the average disengagement time for which the user is responsible to the average total disengagement time, measured over a series of successful disengagement attempts.

## 6. Measurements

This proposed standard defines a set of parameters, but does not define the measurement methodology. A later ANSI standard is planned for the measurement methodology.

Work is already in progress in support of the measurement standard. This work includes the development of the necessary data collection and data analysis programs for use in applying the parameters in measuring the performance of the ARPANET.

## 7. Conclusions

The parameters discussed offer the data communication user an opportunity to specify needs in user-oriented, system-independent terms. The proposed parameters may be used to specify and compare data communication services and, when the measurement methodology is available, to measure the service received.

## References

[1] User-Oriented Data Communication Performance Parameters, Proposed American National Standard X3S35/125, American National Standards Institute Task Group X3S35, December 31, 1980.

[2] Interim Federal Standard 001033, General Services Administration, May 1, 1979.

[3] Interim Federal Standard 1033 Reference Manual, Seitz, N. B., NTIA Report 80-55, National Telecommunications and Information Administration, December 1980.

[4] Digital Communication Performance Parameters for Proposed Federal Federal Standard 1033, Volumes 1 and 2, NTIA-Report 78-4, U. S. U.S. Department of Commerce, May 1978.

[5] Confidence Limits for Digital Error Rates from Dependent Transmissions, Crow, E. L. and Miles, M. J., Office of Telecommunications Report 77-118, U. S. Department of Commerce Laboratories, Boulder, CO 80303, 1977.

[6] Statistical Methods for Estimating Time and Rate Parameters of Digital Communications Systems, Crow, E. L., National Telecommunications and Information Administration Report 79-21, U. S. Dept. of Commerce Laboratories, Boulder, CO 80303, 1977.

[7] Criteria for the Performance Evaluation of Data Communication Services for Computer Networks, Grubb, D. S. and Cotton, I. W., National Bureau of Standards Technical Note 882, National Bureau of Standards, Washington, D. C., 20234, 1975.

Performance of Data Communication Systems
and their Applications, G. Pujolle (ed.)
© North-Holland Publishing Company, 1981

# SOME PROBLEMS WHICH ARISE IMPLEMENTING X.29
# PROTOCOL IN A MAINFRAME

G ANDREONI

CREI-Politecnico di Milano
Pza L da Vinci, 7
Milan, ITALY

This paper deals with some problems relating
to pratical aspects of the cooperation between
user and process for which the solution may be a
difficult task if the only support is the set of
protocols defined in ESP20 recommendations. These
problems are presented in relation to an
implementation working in a very large mainframe,
with excellent support by the local Operating
System.

## INTRODUCTION

During April 80, after the official opening to public service
of EURONET, in order to allow access to the mainframe used for our
experimental work via the PAD facilities, a software module
implementing the X 29 protocol was implemented on top of the already
working X 25 interface. Such a module acts as an interface between
all the services made available by the Operating System and the end
user , as seen through the network.

This paper deals with several problems faced in this
implementation that occur on both sides when service machines are
put on networks, some at Host and some related to limits in the
ESP20 bis recommendations [1](X.3, X.28, X.29 as implemented in
EURONET). They are considered in relation to recent proposals for
layered architecture, which could provide a better environment for
their solution.

## PRIVACY DURING AUTHENTIFICATION PHASE

The X.28, as implemented in EURONET, has the capability of
ensuring a good degree of privacy for the Network User Identi-
fier(NUI), if the terminal acts in full-duplex modality (Echo
facility ON in the PAD): the NUI is not echoed when the proper field
separator is used.

This is not a general case because user could prefer to work in
half-duplex modality without the echo facility in the PAD: the delay
between the depress of a key and the printing of the corresponding
character may seriously disturb the operator and the little increase
in the error control performed does not justify it; the attempt,
made by several hosts, to force users to adopt the full duplex
modality setting the corresponding parameter immediately after the
connection is not fair.

Once the connection phase is completed, the end user has to deal with a similar authentication phase before being allowed access to the desired service. This phase is not considered by ESP20 specifications and each service provider tries to ensure privacy often with the same procedure applied to users directly connected. As a result, several different modalities are used, and some of them are less effective when used through the Packet Switched Network(PSN) than for directly connected users; some are completely inefficent in the new environment.

An example of the first case is a system in which the standard procedure consists of preparing a printed field on which the password has to be overwritten. Then 3 more strings of suitable symbols are overwritten. The connection to that system via EURONET is realized with a black box inserted between the system and the network. This black box inserts a form effector ( Carriage Return and Line Feed characters) between the two sequences of symbols. As a consequence this modality becomes less effective in providing privacy.

An example of the second case  is  the mainframe considered for our implementation. The number of form effectors which ensure the disappearing of the password on top of the screen in the scroll mode screen terminals normally used in direct connections, only has the effect of somehow underlining the password in typewriter terminals connected via the PSN.

A possible solution for this problem can be found in the capability of reading  and modifying parameters inside the PAD ("Read parameter(s)" and  "Set parameter(s)" control messages in X29 specifications). To ensure the same degree of privacy as the one provided by the network for the NUI, the echo facility could be disabled before, or immediatly after, the request for password. It has to be restored to the previous value after the reception of a valid password.  This  procedure, implemented in our mainframe, has the same limit as the one for NUI: it may be effective only for terminals working in full duplex modality.

The implementation of this procedure requires the identification of the authentification phase of the service provider; this is reasonably simple at the opening of the connection, because this phase  normally is preliminary to any other exchange of messages with the process involved. Nevertheless it is necessary to identify the answer to a wrong password, to repeat the same procedure or to close down the connection in the simplest implementation. There is the same need if another "interactive job" may be opened after the conclusion of the first one,using the same connection. The term "interactive job" is used here to indicate the work done with a service provider starting with an authentification phase ("Password" or "Logon") and ending with the indication of the willingness to terminate it ("Logoff", "Quit", "Term"...).

Another possible solution, if the interactive job has the same duration as the connection, is the use of the User Data Field (UDF)

in the call request packet. When the content of the usable part of
this field is entered in the X.28 procedure, the field is treated as
the NUI: if the proper separator is used, these data as well are not
echoed to the terminal. Unfortunately this field is often used by
EURONET's Hosts for the activation or the selection of the desired
processor, a function which does not require privacy at all.

A sufficient degree of uniformity and privacy in the
authentification phase is a highly desirable service, even if not
essential. The ESP20bis provides it only for the NUI, which is
concerned with the cost of the transmission service, and this cost
is usually only a fraction of the global cost of access to data
bases or other services. Protocols should provide the identification
of the authentication phase, and manage it. Local interface would be
able to ensure privacy according to the physical terminal features.

## IMPACT OF BLOCKING DURING DATA TRANSFER ON THE TRANSMISSION COST

The X.29 recommendation does not specify how the data packets
have to be filled by the host: this phase is completely transparent
and the user cannot control the way in which data are transmitted,
even if he could have to pay an extra cost for it.

### Transmission from PAD to Host

The modality and the time at which a packet is sent by the PAD
to the host is under the control of the end user. They are influenced by the terminal in use and by the process accessed. In many
cases the string of characters representing a single command (to the
process) or an answer is placed in a single packet and sent to the
host at the occurrence of some known forwarding condition.

### Transmission from the host

The number of characters generated by the process is often
greater than the one previously considered. Furthermore the way in
which these characters are placed into packets and forwarded to the
PAD is matter of local implementation. For example, in our
implementation the interface to the process in use provided by the
Operating System acts in such a way as to deliver the message line
by line. The simplest way to send it to the end user is to put each
line, completed with a form effector, in the data field of one
packet.

A more sophisticated way is to completely fill the data field
of each packet with several lines, or part of line, separated by
form effector, before sending it. An additional information is
needed to implement this blocking: a forwarding condition for the
last (generally incompletely filled) packet in a sequence. This
condition may be based on the expiration of a timeout, or, better,
on the "exchange of turn" between process and user. The "Exchange
of turn" is the transition between these two phases: one, when the
process is computing or generating an output, and the other when it
is in idle state, waiting for input from the user, and viceversa.

Effects on the cost

The blocking of several lines in each packet does not only affect the number of packets, and consequently the level of utilisation of the physical line between the host and the network. If the charge applied is not based on the number of data characters, but on the integer number of blocks of octets (segments of 64 octects or fraction in EURONET), the use of blocking will change significantly the cost of communication. Table 1 reports the number of packets and the related cost in number of segments for the traffic recorded between our implementation and EURONET in the period 2 Feb - 6 Feb 1981, and the corresponding one computed for a non-blocked solution. Most of the traffic was generated by access to general purpose processes (Compilers, editor , utilities, games...). A small amount was created by access to a data base as STI traffic (Scientific Technical Information). Other traffic (Outgoing X.29 calls, experimental non X.29) is not recorded here.

Fig.1 shows the different distribution in the length of lines and packets when the blocking is performed and the amount of packets with the maximum length (2 segments) gives the reason for the convenience of the blocked solution if only the communication cost is considered

Final consideration on the cost

The better performance in term of cost for the use of the network has been achieved with some complications in the module implementing the X.29 protocol. Furthermore the correct identification of the "exchange of turn" at the interface with the Operating System was not an immediate task.

A more complicated module means not only a greater developement time (2 man-months for the first release and 4 additional man-months for our 2nd release with blocking); it will also affect the cost of running such a module, in terms of CPU time and buffers consumption. Both parameters are relevant in our implementation, because all modules implementing X.25 and X.29 protocols are resident in the mainframe. In these conditions the convenience of the two solutions

|          | RECORDED (Blocked) | | COMPUTED | |
|----------|---------|----------|---------|----------|
|          | PACKETS | SEGMENTS | PACKETS | SEGMENTS |
| FROM PAD | 958     | 965      | 958     | 965      |
| TO  PAD  | 2208    | 3579     | 5909    | 6526     |
| TOTAL    | 3166    | 4544     | 6867    | 7491     |

Table 1: on the left the number of packets recorded during the period 2-6 Feb 1981 and the related cost (in segments of 64 octects). On the right the corresponding figures computed for a non blocked solution for the same traffic.

has to be considered case by case, taking into account the tarifs applied by the public carrier and by the computing centre. A separate layer in charge of this problem should provide a better enviroment for the implementation of these protocols and releave higher level protocols from any concern on the modalities with which a reliable and cost effective transport service is performed.

EXCHANGE OF TURN BETWEEN USER AND PROCESS

The data channel provided by an X.25 Virtual Circuit, and used by ESP20 protocols, works in two way simultaneous modality: thus, both the user and the process are authorized to send data at every moment without restriction due to the traffic in the other direction. On the contrary applications usually work is two way alternate: only one of the two interlocutors has the right to send data messages at a given time. This may be cause some problems to

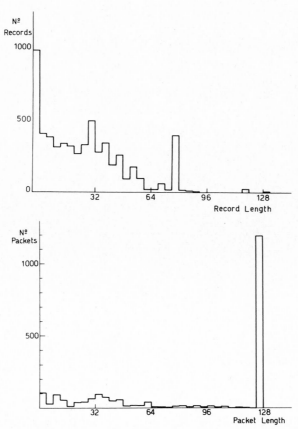

Fig.1 These hystograms show the distribution in the lenght of packets without blocking(upper) and when blocking is performed using the "Exchange of turn" information as forwarding condition for incomplete packets.

the user because if the identification of the exchange of turn is
not easy, the network will not prevent the delivery of messages at
the wrong time.

Service provided by ESP20bis.
         The only service that ESP20 provides is the capability of
protecting user against non-desired messages from the network ,
setting the corresponding parameter in the PAD. The service provider
has no possibility of preventing the user sending messages at the
wrong time.  In this situation the exchange of turn must be handled
directly by the process, or by the interface to it provided by the
Operating System of the host.

Degree of service which can be provided
         The simplest approach to this problem is to do nothing, and
leave the problem to the process. This means that the process has to
communicate to the user the exchange of turn sending  a suitable
string of characters. But in our mainframe most processes do not
provide such a service because the Operating System, when an input
is requested by the process, takes care to translate this change of
status into a "solicit" character presented at the user terminal. So
an acceptable solution could be a similar character sent through the
network to the end user. A negotiation of the character chosen
should be supported, to  avoid possible confusion if used with
different meaning by a specific process.

         Then another problem has to be solved: what to do with the
messages sent by the user at the wrong time, using the two way
simultaneous capability of the X.25 channel. This message can be:
         1.Queued for later processing
         2.Discarded
         3.Discarded with the emission of a diagnostic to the user

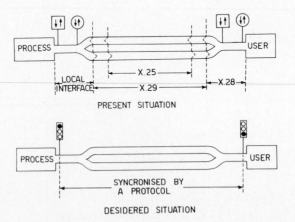

PRESENT SITUATION

DESIDERED SITUATION

Fig.2 In the present situation the exchange of turn is managed directly from the
process and the end-user, while the communication path is not involved. A better
service could be provided if an adequate protocol could inform the end user of
the willingness of the process to receive data.

The better solution appears to be the third one with some complications for the X.29 module.

Finally let us mention the possibility of forcing the exchange of turn for the user, which can be achieved only if adequately supported by the Operating System in the mainframe. Otherwise the use of the Reset procedure by the user for this purpose is subordinated to the capability of identifying the exchange of turn: it is necessary to know which is the last message to be discarded after which the completion of the operation has to be notifyed.

The ordered exchange of data is relevant for an effective use of a generic process and it should be supported by an adequate protocol when the process is accessed through a PSN. Fig.2 shows the present situation and the desired one, in which the exchange of turn involves the data channel as well, and an adequate protocol supports exception conditions.

RECONNECTION AFTER NETWORK FAILURE

Rather than the connection establishment procedure, which can require few seconds,one of the most disturbing things for a user after a disconnection due to a network failure is the need to proceed through the identification phase of the host, which may not be so simple, and the effort to recover the situation with a minimal amount of losses.

Reconnection call

We have considered the possibility of adopting, also for our implementation of X.29, a reconnection procedure with the capability of restarting the work after a short failure in the connection.

In order to be able to identify the two partners in the reconnection call, a sort of mutual identification has to be provided for the process and for the user. We have not seen any pratical solution for this problem. An exchange of references at the set up of every new call is essential to the general solution of this problem, and this is not provided by the ESP20 protocols.

CONCLUSIONS

The problems examined in this paper may be ascribed to the fact that recommendations ESP20bis are capable of solving mainly the communication part of the interaction between user and service provider. In order to realize an effective cooperation between them some other functions should exist, even if they may be considered not essential for the communication. Some of these services may be somehow realized on the basis of the features offered by ESP20, but the engineering task could be much easier and the service provided in a more effective way if they could be grouped in a layered structure.

In the ISO reference model for Open System Interconnection

(OSI) [2], such aspects  refers to the functions in the upper four layers. Infact the problems faced in our implementation could be better solved considering th following suggestions:

- Extend protocols to support entry of authentification information with suitable privacy in display (overprinting, no echo, or whichever modality may better fit the real terminal peculiarity. In OSI this extension should be included in application protocol.

- Consider augmenting host terminal output software to block output into full packets. In OSI the need for blocking to reduce cost has been already pointed out.  Layer 5, Session, has all the information needed to perform it.

- Extend procedure to support Two-Way-Alternate exchange of data. In OSI current proposal for Session service already provides such a procedure.

- Develop reconnection procedure to simplify recovery after connection failures. Class 3 in current proposal for Transport protocol has this capability in OSI, even if the detailed procedure has not yet been defined.

It is highly desirable that international standards for protocols could be defined in the next future for all this layers because this is the real solution for  problems as the ones here described.


REFERENCES

[1] EQUIPE PROJET-Réseau pour EURONET : "ESP 20 bis: support of asynchronous terminals" - CTR 184-2 Issue 2 - Aug 1977.

[2] ISO : "Data processing - Open System Interconnection - Basic Reference Model" - ISO/TC97/SC16 N537 Revised, Nov 1980.

Performance of Data Communication Systems
and their Applications, G. Pujolle (ed.)
© North-Holland Publishing Company, 1981

RETINA - UNE EXPERIENCE DE RESEAU MULTICONSTRUCTEURS
BASE SUR L'ARCHITECTURE ISO

Nicolas Nahas et Charles R. Parisot

Electricité de France - Gaz de France
21, rue Joseph Bara
92132 Issy-les-Moulineaux, France

Le REseau TéléInformatique NAtional RETINA est le nouveau réseau mis en place par Electricité de France et
Gaz de France pour relier ses divers équipements informatiques. Son architecture est conforme à celle du modèle normalisé par l'ISO. En se basant sur l'expérience
RETINA, cette communication se propose d'aborder les
différentes solutions de raccordement des équipements
informatiques proposés par les constructeurs dans le
cadre de leur propre architecture, avec une architecture et des protocoles normalisés. Une classification
de ces solutions est élaborée en se basant sur les concepts du modèle ISO d'interconnexion des systèmes
ouverts.

1 - INTRODUCTION

La nécessité pour un réseau informatique d'autoriser les communications entre
des ordinateurs et des terminaux hétérogènes est naturellement apparue dès que
les parcs informatiques ont atteint une taille importante, ce qui fut le cas à
EDF-GDF dès la fin des années 60. L'étude d'un nouveau réseau adapté à un environnement multiconstructeurs a débuté en 1972, époque où la normalisation in-
ternationale se limitait à quelques travaux autour d'HDLC ; EDF-GDF a donc été
conduit à définir sa propre architecture [1],[2],[3].

Ces travaux ont abouti en 1976 a la publication par EDF-GDF d'une série de
normes portant sur l'architecture et les protocoles des niveaux de transport
de RETINA. En 1980 ces normes ont été complétées par celles des niveaux supérieurs (session, présentation et application) pour les échanges de fichiers,
de jobs et de restitutions ainsi que par des protocoles de session et de présentation pour les terminaux conversationnels.

Cet effort de normalisation interne, qui a précédé celui qui se déroule actuellement à l'ISO [5], a conduit EDF-GDF a envisager les problèmes de raccordements d'ordinateurs hétérogènes, dans des conditions similaires à celles que
provoquera l'apparition de normes internationales.

Après une brève présentation des principes d'architecture de RETINA et de
l'état actuel du réseau, l'adaptation des équipements de traitements est abordée pour les échanges batch, puis pour les échanges conversationnels.

2 - PRESENTATION GENERALE DE RETINA

2.1. Architecture et protocoles de RETINA

L'architecture de RETINA est structurée suivant un modèle en couches ou les
fonctions "réseau" liées au transport et au traitement sont clairement séparées (figure 1), [1].

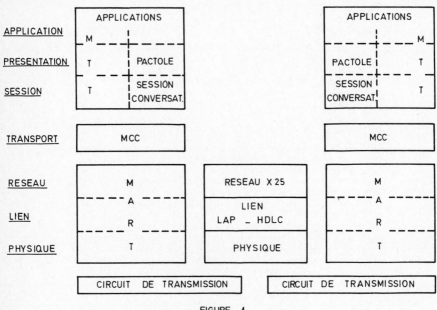

FIGURE 1
L'ARCHITECTURE DE RETINA

Les protocoles des niveaux "physique" et "lien" sont assurés par la procédure
LAP définie dans la recommandation X25 du CCITT [6]. Au niveau "réseau" le
protocole "paquet" d'X25 est complété pour fournir un service réseau indépendant du moyen de communication utilisé (TRANSPAC ou lignes louées). Ces protocoles de niveau réseau sont définis dans la norme MART [8]. Un protocole de
transport défini par la norme MCC [7] utilise les services de MART pour fournir un service de transport complet et identique à celui défini actuellement
par l'ISO. Ce protocole MCC assure des fonctions de multiplexage, de contrôle
de flux, de récupération des incidents réseau (réinitialisation ou libération
des circuits virtuels) et de surveillance des connexions de transport.

En ce qui concerne les protocoles des niveaux supérieurs, RETINA a opté pour
deux voies distinctes suivant qu'il s'agit des échanges batch ou conversationnel. Dans chacun de ces domaines aussi bien le sens des fonctionnalités session que les types de présentation utilisés sont en effet très différents.

Les protocoles assurant les transferts de trains, c'est-à-dire de lots de données, de travaux, de restitutions ou de fichiers, ont été conçus comme un ensemble cohérent. La norme MTT [9] définit les trois niveaux session, présentation et application. Le niveau session assure l'établissement de la session
vers le destinataire du train avec échange des paramètres et options du transfert (points de reprises par exemple) puis le transfert jusqu'à ce qu'il soit
terminé et que le récepteur garantisse la sauvegarde du train. Au niveau présentation, seules des données ayant une organisation séquentielle sont prises

en compte. Au niveau application, on distingue différents serveurs : soumission de travaux, transfert de données pour mise à jour de fichiers, édition de restitutions, création de fichiers.

Sur le plan des échanges conversationnels un effort de standardisation est actuellement en cours à EDF-GDF. Un protocole de session conversationnelle et un protocole de présentation nommé "PACTOLE" sont en cours d'implantation. Ils permettront une banalisation des terminaux beaucoup plus large que celle qui est actuellement en service sur RETINA : les écrans-claviers peuvent déjà se connecter au sous-système transactionnel de leur choix que ce soit CICS sur un central IBM, ou TDS sur un central CII-HB.

## 2.2. Situation du Réseau

RETINA est appelé à se substituer aux divers réseaux qui ont été exploités par EDF-GDF depuis la fin des années 60 [1]. Les premières mises en service ont eu lieu au début de 1978 et ont été limitées à une quinzaine de sites équipés de satellites batch (SEMS Mitra) (figure 2) et de centres de traitement (IBM 370/148 et 168), ces sites étant reliés par TRANSPAC et des lignes louées.

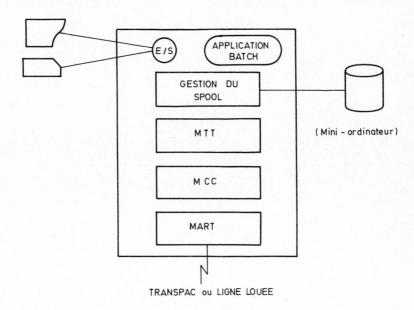

FIGURE 2

PRODUIT SATELLITE BATCH

En 1980 s'est amorcée la phase de généralisation, qui a porté à une quarantaine le nombre de sites utilisant RETINA (figure 3).

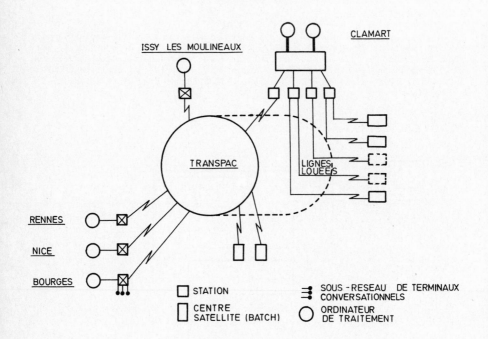

FIGURE 3

RETINA FIN 1980

Au cours de 1981 et de 1982 ce mouvement se poursuivra pour atteindre en 1983 un réseau interconnectant environ 200 ordinateurs (IBM 3033, 3031, 4341, 4331 ; CII-HB DPS 8, DPS 7, DPS 6) et mini-ordinateurs (SEMS Mitra, CII-HB Mini 6) ainsi que plus de 4000 terminaux conversationnels (figure 4). Le volume des données échangées sur RETINA sera alors de l'ordre de 7 milliards d'octets par mois.

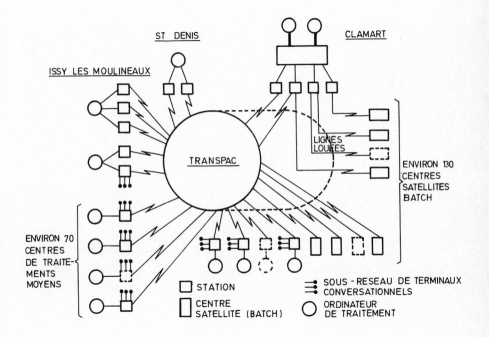

FIGURE 4

RETINA HORIZON 1983

Les ordinateurs de moyenne ou de forte puissance sont raccordés à RETINA par
l'intermédiaire d'une "station" (figure 5) réalisée sur un mini-ordinateur
(CII-HB Mini 6 ou SEMS Mitra) qui gère les protocoles de transport (MCC) et de
réseau (MART) ainsi que toutes les adaptations nécessaires à l'accès aux centraux et au support d'un sous-réseau de terminaux conversationnels.

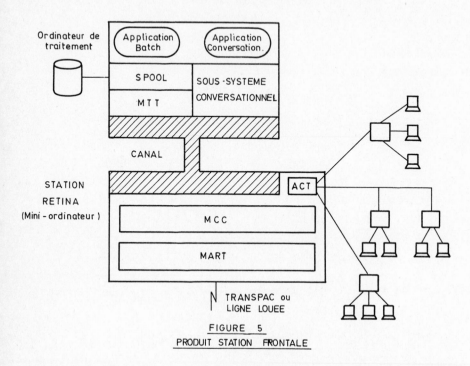

FIGURE 5
PRODUIT STATION FRONTALE

3 - PRINCIPE D'APPROCHE DU PROBLEME DE RACCORDEMENT DES SYSTEMES CENTRAUX

Le problème de la constitution de réseaux informatiques est en fait celui de
l'interconnexion de différents équipements informatiques et c'est sur cette
base que l'ISO s'est posé le problème de la normalisation de l'interconnexion
des systèmes ouverts ; ceci a conduit dans une première étape à définir un
modèle d'architecture. Ce modèle décrit la visibilité que chaque système a de
ceux avec lesquels il communique. La notion de système y est définie de manière très large (figure 6) et peut varier d'un équipement pris isolément à un
large ensemble d'équipements reliés entre eux par des moyens et des méthodes
très spécifiques formant ainsi un ensemble "fermé".

Dans cette communication, il est fait appel aux concepts de ce modèle à 7 niveaux de l'ISO pour décrire d'un côté l'équipement "constructeur" et d'un autre le réseau normalisé. Sous le terme réseau normalisé nous entendrons le
réseau RETINA dans le contexte EDF-GDF actuel, ou, dans l'avenir, tout réseau
ouvert au sens des normes et des protocoles ISO. Sous le terme architecture
"constructeur" nous désignerons la structure et le comportement des équipements tels qu'ils sont actuellement fournis par les constructeurs et que leur
hétérogénéité interdit d'interconnecter.

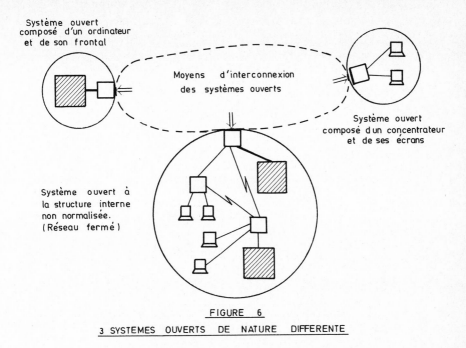

**FIGURE   6**

**3 SYSTEMES  OUVERTS   DE  NATURE   DIFFERENTE**

4 - RACCORDEMENT DES SYSTEMES CENTRAUX DANS LE CAS DES ECHANGES BATCH

4.1. Evolution des échanges batch

Un phénomène passant relativement inaperçu dans l'évolution qui se produit actuellement dans le cadre des échanges batch est la disparition du terminal lourd conventionnel ou "remote batch". Ce type de terminal très esclave de l'ordinateur dont il dépend perd tout son sens dans des réseaux organisés de façon très décentralisée. De plus, il est économiquement concevable de réaliser ce type de fonction "terminal lourd" à base d'un petit ordinateur de traitement général dont les applications gèreront uniquement les entrées/sorties. Cette remarque conduit à n'envisager les échanges batch que d'ordinateur à ordinateur et à considérer comme un ensemble cohérent les transferts qu'ils soient de travaux, de fichiers, de restitutions ou de lots de données.

Ce type de "nouveau terminal lourd" est, dans le cadre de RETINA, réalisé sur des équipements du type mini-ordinateur. La gestion des protocoles réseau (7 niveaux) est en général facilement intégrée sous le logiciel standard du constructeur.

En ce qui concerne les ordinateurs de moyenne ou forte puissance leur structure exige que l'accès au réseau fasse appel à un ordinateur frontal ou station, pour supporter la gestion des protocoles des niveaux réseau et transport. Ce cas sera envisagé en détail par la suite aussi bien au niveau de la gestion des protocoles de haut niveau que de celui de la connexion de la station à l'ordinateur de traitement.

4.2. Gestion des protocoles de haut niveau

La gestion des niveaux session, présentation et application chargés des transferts batch doit être effectuée dans l'ordinateur de traitement afin de garantir une gestion correcte des reprises, des sauvegardes et de l'accès aux systèmes de spooling ou de gestion de fichiers. L'intégration de la gestion de ces
protocoles normalisés sous un système d'exploitation standard ne pose en général pas de problèmes insurmontables, bien que l'accès aux sous-systèmes batch
(soumission de travaux, extraction des restitutions) soit assez délicat.

4.3. Connexion de la station avec l'ordinateur de traitement

Le raccordement d'un ordinateur de traitement de moyenne ou de forte puissance
à un réseau normalisé exigera de résoudre le problème de son interconnexion
avec une station. Deux grands modes sont en général utilisés :
- le mode "émulation" d'un sous-ensemble d'une unité supportée par le constructeur du central. Cette solution a le mérite de permettre l'utilisation des
méthodes d'accès standard de l'ordinateur de traitement.
- le mode "spécifique" qui consiste à développer dans le central une méthode
d'accès spécifique pour communiquer avec la station. Cette approche se justi-
fie bien dans le cas de raccordement canal à canal car elle permet d'atteindre
des niveaux de performance très élevés.

Ces deux voies sont utilisées dans RETINA avec des connexions de type canal à
canal. Il est cependant à remarquer que le mode émulation avec des connexions
de type "télécommunication" est aussi possible : il avait été retenu lors des
premiers démarrages sur RETINA.

Par la suite, nous examinerons plus en détail le cas du mode de connexion "émulation" qui seul, pose réellement le problème d'interconnexion de l'architecture et des protocoles du constructeur avec ceux du réseau normalisé, le mode
"spécifique" détournant le problème (figure 7).

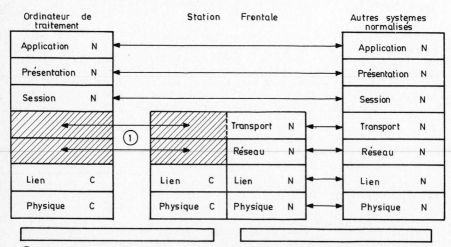

FIGURE 7

RACCORDEMENT BATCH EN MODE SPECIFIQUE

Sur le plan de l'architecture, les raccordements entre centraux et stations conduisent à dégrader les niveaux de l'architecture du constructeur en utilisant la session constructeur comme une connexion de niveau réseau reliant les deux équipements (figure 8). A ceci l'on peut voir deux raisons principales : la première concerne la souplesse d'implémentation et d'exploitation obtenue par l'utilisation de ressources fixes, la seconde provient du choix d'émuler des unités dont les fonctionnalités aux niveaux transport et session sont très réduites.

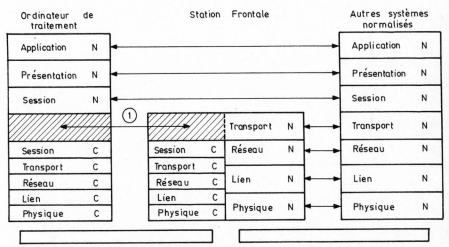

① Protocole local d'extension des connexions de transport par multiplexage sur une session constructeur dégradée au niveau connexion réseau.

FIGURE     8

RACCORDEMENT  BATCH  EN  MODE  EMULE

Cette situation de dégradation du niveau session est aussi admise par certains constructeurs qui l'ont retenue comme moyen standard et ouvert de support de l'interface d'accès aux réseaux publics en X25. Dans ce cas la session est dégradée au niveau du circuit virtuel et toute la gestion des niveaux supérieurs de protocoles (transport, session, présentation et application) est reportée au niveau de l'ordinateur de traitement (figure 9).

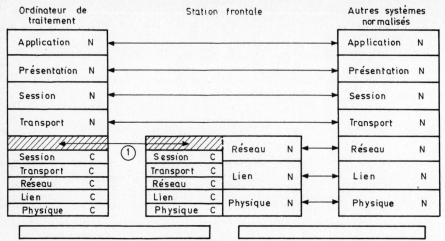

1. Protocole local d'extension des circuits virtuels permettant leur gestion à partir de l'ordinateur de traitement.

FIGURE 9

RACCORDEMENT PAR LE SUPPORT EN STANDARD DE LA GESTION DE
X25 DANS LA STATION FRONTALE DU CONSTRUCTEUR

Il parait vraisemblable que cette situation de sous-utilisation des produits standard n'évoluera pas tant que la normalisation des protocoles de haut niveau pour les échanges batch n'aura pas débouché sur le plan international. En effet il est très difficile, voire impossible d'effectuer des conversions de protocoles à ce niveau ; seule l'utilisation de la bonne vieille technique du "store and forward" serait à la limite envisageable au niveau d'un "gateaway" entre deux réseaux, mais certainement pas au niveau de chaque ordinateur de traitement.

5 - RACCORDEMENT DES SYSTEMES CENTRAUX DANS LE CAS DES ECHANGES CONVERSA-
TIONNELS

5.1. Evolution des échanges conversationnels

Cette évolution a permis de franchir successivement plusieurs étapes : le terminal conversationnel, d'abord prisonnier d'une application s'est ensuite ouvert à l'ensemble des sous-systèmes de l'ordinateur auquel il était connecté, puis une ouverture encore plus large est maintenant possible dans la mesure où le terminal conversationnel peut avoir accès à un ensemble d'ordinateurs de traitement interconnectés par un réseau. Cette banalisation complète conduit à ce que les terminaux ne soient plus raccordés à un ordinateur de traitement mais au réseau lui-même. De même les sous-systèmes conversationnels doivent de leur côté être accessibles à partir du réseau.

Contrairement à la situation dans laquelle on se trouve pour les échanges batch, il est possible et même fortement souhaitable d'utiliser les sous-systèmes conversationnels standard des constructeurs, compte-tenu des investissements qu'ils représentent. Dans la suite, la question du raccordement au réseau normalisé des sous-systèmes conversationnels standard des constructeurs sera abordée en distinguant les problèmes qui se posent au niveau session et au niveau présentation. Nous serons aussi amenés à effectuer une distinction parmi les sous-systèmes conversationnels, entre les sous-systèmes transactionnels (tels que CICS chez IBM ou TDS chez CII-HB) et les sous-systèmes interactifs (par exemple TSO chez IBM ou IOF chez CII-HB). En effet les sous-systèmes interactifs constituent un produit fermé alors que les sous-systèmes transactionnels constituent une structure d'accueil aux applications utilisateur et sont donc plus ouverts aux adaptations réseau éventuelles.

5.2. Gestion du protocole session

L'utilisation de sous-systèmes conversationnels standard impose en général de les associer avec une méthode d'accès standard. Pour dialoguer avec ces produits il est donc nécessaire de respecter le protocole de session du constructeur. Deux voies sont envisageables pour répondre à ce problème de raccordement au niveau session.

- Dégradation de la session constructeur.
Cette solution n'est possible que dans le cas des sous-systèmes transactionnels car elle consiste à gérer le protocole de session normalisé par un programme d'application du sous-système. La session constructeur est alors dégradée en connexion de niveau transport (figure 10). Cette solution est actuellement en exploitation dans RETINA pour le raccordement des sous-systèmes transactionnels CICS et TDS.

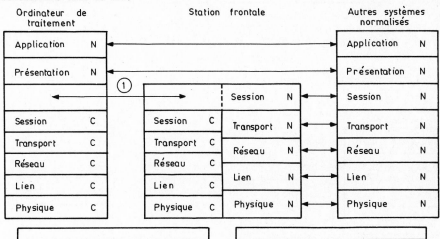

① Protocole local d'extension des sessions normalisées dont la gestion dans l'ordinateur de traitement est assurée sous le moniteur transactionnel.

FIGURE 10

RACCORDEMENT CONVERSATIONNEL - DEGRADATION DE LA SESSION CONSTRUCTEUR EN CONNEXION DE TRANSPORT

- Traduction de session.
Cette solution consiste à traduire le protocole session du constructeur dans le protocole session normalisé. Au niveau des services de base de la session conversationnelle cette traduction est envisageable, toutefois certains services très particuliers comme les reprises ou le "bracket" doivent souvent être

ignorés. La fonction de traduction de la session peut être effectuée soit dans l'ordinateur de traitement grâce à l'usage de session constructeur locale, soit dans la station frontale (figure 11).

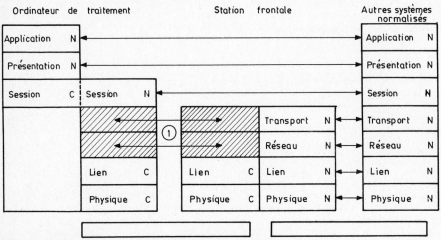

(1) Protocoles locaux d'extension des connexions de transport . Seuls les niveaux lien et physique du constructeur sont utilisés (régles des échanges sur le canal).

RACCORDEMENT CONVERSATIONNEL — TRADUCTION DE SESSION DANS L'ORDINATEUR DE TRAITEMENT

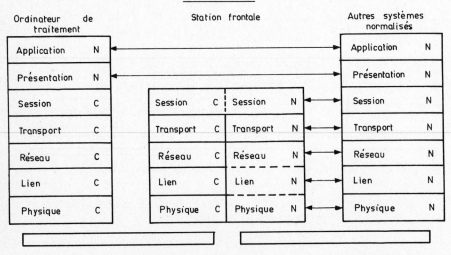

RACCORDEMENT CONVERSATIONNEL — TRADUCTION DE SESSION DANS LA STATION

FIGURE 11

La connexion de la station frontale à l'ordinateur de traitement peut comme dans le cas des échanges batch être envisagée suivant deux modes, le mode "émulation" qui encourage plutôt une traduction de session au niveau de la station frontale, ou le mode "spécifique" conduisant à une traduction de session réalisée au niveau de l'ordinateur de traitement. Ces deux modes de connexion font actuellement l'objet d'études dans le cadre de la prise en compte sur RETINA des sous-systèmes conversationnels.

## 5.3. Gestion du protocole de présentation

La prise en compte de protocoles de présentation normalisés est certainement le problème le plus délicat posé par le raccordement des sous-systèmes conversationnels ; ce problème se pose en termes très différents suivant qu'il s'agit de sous-systèmes transactionnels ou interactifs.

- Cas des sous-systèmes transactionnels.
C'est certainement le cas le plus simple dans la mesure où le but de ce type de sous-système est d'accueillir des applications utilisateurs et que les services de présentation qui sont offerts en standard sont optionnels. Il est donc tout à fait possible d'offrir aux applications des primitives de gestion du protocole de présentation normalisé, protocole auquel le sous-système transactionnel sera transparent. Il est intéressant de remarquer que la maîtrise de ces primitives de présentation permet du même coup de résoudre une partie du problème de la portabilité des programmes d'application entre ordinateurs de traitement hétérogènes.

- Cas des sous-systèmes interactifs.
Pour ces sous-systèmes il n'est en général pas possible ou réaliste de modifier les fonctions de présentation traitées en interne. On est donc conduit à envisager une traduction entre le protocole de présentation constructeur et le protocole de présentation normalisé. Une telle traduction est en général très complexe, c'est pourquoi la solution particulière retenue dans RETINA se base sur un protocole de présentation de type IBM 3270 qui est le seul offert actuellement par plusieurs constructeurs.

## 5.4. Conclusion

En ce qui concerne le raccordement des sous-systèmes conversationnels à un réseau normalisé un certain nombre d'alternatives sont donc envisageables aussi bien pour le raccordement de la station frontale que pour la gestion du niveau session. Cependant c'est au niveau présentation que la situation est la plus complexe en particulier pour les sous-systèmes interactifs. Ceci révèle combien l'élaboration d'un protocole de présentation normalisé par l'ISO pour les terminaux conversationnels est un objectif urgent.

BIBLIOGRAPHIE

[1] RETINA. REseau TéléInformatique NAtional. Brochure bleue publiée par EDF-GDF 4ème trimestre 1980. Groupe d'Etudes de Transmission, 21, rue Joseph Bara, B.P. 34, 92132 Issy-les-Moulineaux.

[2] Gornet, J.F., Lacroix, M.J., Parisot, C., Nahas, N. et Pillon, F. Studies and experiments for a multipurpose data transmission network. ICCC 1976 Toronto.

[3] Chesneau, C., Nahas, N. et Vassort, P., Les applications de télétraitement à travers TRANSPAC, Convention Informatique 1976, Paris.

[4] Chesneau, C., Parisot, C., Pillon, F. et Vassort, P., Normalisation des fonctions de communication à travers un réseau de transmission de données à commutation de paquets à Electricité de France et Gaz de France, Computer Network Protocols, Université de Liège, 1978.

[5] Data Processing-Open System interconnection-Basic Reference Model, ISO TC 97 Sous-Comité 16 Proposition de Standard ISO/DP 7498.

[6] Recommandation X25 publiée par le CCITT, Novembre 1976.

[7] Protocoles de Communication, Norme EDF-GDF HN Z 66-S-02, Groupe d'Etudes de Transmission, 21, rue Joseph Bara, B.P. 34, 92132 Issy-les-Moulineaux.

[8] Modules d'Accès au Réseau Transpac, Norme EDF-GDF HN Z 66-S-03, Groupe d'Etudes de Transmission, 21, rue Joseph Bara, B.P. 34, 92132 Issy-les-Moulineaux.

[9] Module de Transfert de Trains, Norme EDF-GDF HN Z 66-S-04, Groupe d'Etudes de Transmission, 21, rue Joseph Bara, B.P. 34, 92132 Issy-les-Moulineaux.

Performance of Data Communication Systems
and their Applications, G. Pujolle (ed.)
© North-Holland Publishing Company, 1981

# AN APPROACH TO ANALYSIS AND OPTIMIZATION
## ON LINE REQUEST SERVICE DISCIPLINE
## IN A COMMUNICATION SUBNET NODE

B. Lanowska,  J. Lewoc

Computer  Center
Technical University of Wroclaw
Poland

Computer Center of Wroclaw Technical University is
involved in realization and development of an
interuniversity computer network MSK. One of the
major tasks within project was to develop and
implement X-25 communication subnet node. An approach to analysis and optimization of one detailed solutions in the node is presented.

## INTRODUCTION

A major problem to be solved by a designer of any communication
subnet node is that of data transfer delay in the node. The need of
node design optimization for a criterion in terms of transfer delay
time is widely recognised: minimization of transfer delay expected
value being probably the most frequent specific criterion [5].

In this paper, another approach is presented. As a primary measure
of node operation quality, the maximum possible transfer delay
time is assumed. Briefly, we may say that such operating measure
should be more useful for evaluation of operating quality in maximum node load (traffic) conditions and enable for the node designer
to guarantee that some definite service quality will be ensured for
each request. Basing on this characteristic one may attempt to
optimize network design solutions so that the maximum possible
transfer delay in the overall network is minimized.

The paper presents some propositions referring to optimization of
node software pieces deciding of service discipline for requests
obtained from individual communication links (lines). The discipline applied in the first version of communication subnet node software worked out for the interuniversity computer network (MSK) is
described. Some competitive solution which, in the author's opinion,
may result in less values of the maximum possible transfer delay
time are also specified.

## PRIMARY CHARACTERISTIC OF COMMUNICATION SUBNET NODE

In Literature on computer networks (eg. [12] , [3] , [4] , [5]), there
are described studies on individual design problems such as: buffer
management, routing methods process scheduling, different characteristic being studied for different problems. Usually, problems
are formulated and, eventually, solved in a probabilistic manner
and the most frequent optimization cryteria are expected values of
sum random variables in the steady state. Examples of such random
variables may be transfer delays, queue lengths, core usage factors,
line loads, etc.

We feel such approach needs to be changed. It seems vital that a
common primary characteristic is defined for all individual problems and any optimization of individual solutions is performed on
a common cryterion. In other case, results obtained from individual
studies may be inconsistent and their practical usefulness to be
doubty.

As the primary characteristic of a computer network node we propose
the maximum packet transfer delay which may occur for a packet  1
flowing through the node. More precise definition is the following:

Def. 1. The maximum packet transfer delay, T, is supremum of time
        interval lengths from the instant that the last octet of a
        data frame arrives to the node from a source neighbour to
        the instant that the last octet of a resulting data frame
        transmitted to the destination neighbour leaves the node.

To be more formal, let us introduce some additional explanations:

Let N be the set of node neighbours, ie. DTE's or other nodes connected to the node via line adapters and communication links;

let $i \in N$ be the index of the source neighbour transmitting to the
node data frames $k \in 1,2,\ldots$

let $j(k,i) \in N$ or, for simplicity, $j \in N$  be the index of destination
neighbour defined by the source neighbour i and the data frame number k (ie. the index of the neighbour to which a data frame generated by the node from the frame k received from the neighbour i is
to be transmitted),

let $\tau_{li}^{k} \geqslant 0$ be the instant that the first octet of data frame  k
transmitted by the neighbour i arrives the node, and let $\tau_{ij}^{k,i} \geqslant 0$ be
the instant that the last octet of the resultant data frame is
transmitted by the node to the neighbour j.

The set of $\tau_{li}^{k}$ described by distributions of time  intervals
between arrival of sequential data frames from the neighbours $i \in N$
forms the basic input process for the node. Let us call the random
variable

$$\theta_{ik} = \tau_{ij}^{k,i} - \tau_{li}^{k}$$

the packet transfer delay. Now we can formulate definition 1 formally.

Def. 2. The maximum packet transfer delay is defined as:

$$T = \sup_{\substack{i \in N \\ k \in \{1,2,\ldots\}}} \theta_{ik}$$

We require that T is of a finite value. This implies that distributions of for each $i \in N$, the random variable  $\theta_{ik}$ is concentrated on
a finite time interval $\langle 0, T_i \rangle$  $T_i \leqslant T$ or, more generally, $\langle S_i, T_i \rangle$
$0 \leqslant S_i \leqslant T_i \leqslant T$. In this way, we formulate the basic condition for
real-time operation of the node. If the above postulate is not met,
there will be possible realization of the random variable  $\theta_{ik}$ ex-
ceeding any finite bound; the condition is known as time      "saturation" of the node.

As the basic cryterion for optimization of any individual solutions of the node we propose minimum of T.

## MATHEMATICAL MODEL OF COMMUNICATION SUBNET NODE

We describe a communication subnet node as the system:

$$\mathcal{S} = (\mathcal{S}, [\tau_i], \mathcal{T}, \{\mathcal{T}_i\}, \prec, [\mu_k], \{\mathcal{R}_k\})$$

1. $\mathcal{S} = \{S_1,\ldots,S_N,S_{N+1}, \ldots S_M\}$ is a set of sources generating requests for node service. The sources $S_1,\ldots,S_N$ which generate requests for service independly of operation of the node will be called primary sources, while the sources $S_{N+1}, \ldots, S_M$ which produce requests for service resulting from node operation will be called secondary sources. A simple example of secondary sources are line adapter transmitters producing requests for service, i.e. interrupts, after the node initiates output transfers.

2. $[\tau_i] = [\tau_1,\ldots,\tau_N]$ is a 1xm matrix defining distributions of time between subsequent requests from the primary sources.

3. $\mathcal{T} = \{T_1,\ldots,T_n\}$ is the set of processes that can be run in the mode.

4. $\{\mathcal{T}_i\} = \{\{T_{l_1}(i),\ldots, T_{l_r}(i)\} \subset T\}$, $i \in \{1,\ldots,M\}$

is the set consisting of the maximum sets of processes to be run after arrival of requests from individual sources of requests.

Note: usually, for a request from source $i \in \{1,\ldots,M\}$ some subset of $\mathcal{T}_i$ is be run.

5. $\prec$ identifies antireflexive partial order relation defined on and specifying procedence constraints. $T_p \prec T_q$ means that process $T_q$ can not be started before process $T_p$ is completed.

6. $\mu_k = \mu_1,\ldots,\mu_n$ is a 1xn matrix defining distributions of $T_k$ process execution time, $k \in \{1,\ldots,r\}$

7. $\mathcal{R}_k = [R_1(T_k),\ldots, R_s(T_k)]$, $1 \leqslant k \leqslant n$

defines quantity of $R_m$ type of resource required during execution time of process $T_k$, where $1 \leqslant m \leqslant s$. A typical example of resource required for execution of various processes are data buffers.

The basic real-time operation constraints are introduced by demanding that some initial processes $T_{l_1}(i),\ldots,T_{l_m}(i)$ (usually the first process $T_{l_1(i)}$ initiated by the k-th request from source $S_i$ are completed before (k+1)-th request arrives from this source. This is similar to the problem of deadline scheduling described eg. in [6]. Some real-time operation constraints are implied by $\{\mathcal{R}_k\}$ since lack of resource required by any process $T_{l_k(i)}$ results in, obviously, inadequate service of the request from source $S_i$, that initiated the process.

To study the model, we draw flow diagrams combining requests for service, software modules of the node involved in service of the

requests, processes initiated and resources required. We try to find
the realizations of the primary input process described by $[\tau_i]$
which result in maximum values of $\theta_{ik}$. On this basis, we try to
evaluate T versus the maximum number of virtual calls and permanent
connections that can be held in the node.

## AN APPROACH TO OPTIMIZATION OF SPECIFIC NODE DESIGN SOLUTIONS

For the organization of the node software and basing on flow diagrams mentioned above, we evaluate T from formula 1:

$$T = \sum_{i \in N} ( \sum_{k=1}^{r(i)} \mu_{1k(i)}^* ) + \sum_{j \in M} t_j^* + \sum_{i \in M} ( \sum_{k=1}^{r(i)} \mu_{1k}^* i ) + A \qquad (1)$$

where:

$N$ is the set of primary sources indices, requests from which
result in maximum value of $\theta_{ik}$,

$\mu_{1k(i)}^*$ is realization of $\mu_{1k}(i)$ resulting in maximum value of $\theta_{ik}$

$M$ is the set of indices of secondary which are operated as a
result of requests from sources $\{S_i\}$, $i \in N$

$t_j^*, j \in M$ is frame transfer time to line j

A  is processor time spent at priority level above PR3 during
T.

Specific design solutions are of influence on some $\mu_{1k}^*(i)$ in (1).
Therefore, we assume the other terms to be constant and try to express the $\mu_{1k}^*(i)$ involved as a function of some parameters and
/or to compare $\mu_{1k}^*(i)$ values  competitive solutions and to find the
parameter values and/or solutions resulting in minimum T.


## OPTIMIZATION OF REQUEST SERVICE DISCIPLINE - PROBLEM FORMULATION

For the purpose of this paper, the system will be limited to software directly defining the way of service of requests arriving from
communication lines. The state of the system may be defined as
follows:

$$S = \{ F, F_0, F_1, \mathcal{F}, \tau_{IN}, \tau_{OUT}, r \} \qquad (2)$$

where:

1. $F = \{ F_1, \ldots, F_N, F_{N+1}, \ldots, F_M \}$ $\qquad (3)$

Individual elements of this set are called specific semaphores. They
are meant in the sense of Dijkstra's semaphores [7] and, in our specific case of the communication subnet node, we have:

$F_i = \{a\}$ - where a set is the number of requests from primary source $S_i$
$i \in N$   (ie. line adapter receiver), waiting for service in the input
queue, and $N = \{1, 2, \ldots, N\}$ is the set of primary request
source indices.

$F_j = \{b\}$ where b is the number of requests from secondary source $S_j$
$j \in \mathcal{M}$ (ie. line adapter transmitter, waiting for service in
the output queue, and $\mathcal{M} = \{N+1, N+2,...,M\}$ is the set of secondary request source indices.

As described more detaily in [8], modified P and V operations are
executed on the specific semaphores. The operation P increases an
involved specific semaphore of one at the instant that a frame terminating request is served by a line adapter transmitter or receiver
driver operating at the priority level PR 6 . The operation V decreases the semaphore just before initiating service (at PR3) of the
data frame waiting in the output or input queue, respectively.

2. $\mathbb{F}_o = \sum_{i=1}^{N} F_i$ \hfill (4)

$\mathbb{F}_o$ is the general semaphore informing of requests waiting in the
input queues. The general semaphore is used in order to decrease
overhead necessary for the node to reveal specific semaphores of
not-zero values and initiate service at PR3.

3. $\mathbb{F}_1 = \sum_{j=N+1}^{M} F_j$ \hfill (5)

$\mathbb{F}_1$ is the general semaphore informing of requests waiting in the
output queues.

4. $\mathcal{F}$ is the global two-state semaphore set after any general semaphore is increased and reset when starting of searching for a not-
-zero general semaphore $\mathbb{F}_k$ at PR3. In the first version of node
software $k \in \{0,1,2\}$ where $\mathbb{F}_o$ and $\mathbb{F}_1$ are defined here above, and
$\mathbb{F}_2$ is the general semaphore increased of 1 after each second is sensed by the line clock driver at PR6. The global semaphore is used to
decrease the length of critical section [7] connected with synchronization of processes using the general and specific semaphores.

5. $\tau_{IN} = \{[\tau_{1_1}^1, \tau_{1_1}^2, ..., \tau_{1_1}^{k_1}], ..., [\tau_{1_N}^1, \tau_{1_N}^2, ..., \tau_{1_N}^{k_N}]\}$ \hfill (6)

where: $\tau_{1_i}^m$ , $i \in N$, $m \in \{1,...,k\}$ is the instant thet the frame terminating request is received from source $S_i$ by the line dri-
ver receiver at PR6; m being the sequential number of the
frame in the i-th input queue and $k_i$ - the capacity of the
i-th input queue.

6. $\tau_{out} = \{[\tau_{1_{N+1}}^1, ..., \tau_{1_{N+1}}^{k_{N+1}}], ..., [\tau_{1_M}^1, ..., \tau_{1_M}^{k_M}]\}$ \hfill (7)

where: $\tau_{1_j}^m$ , $j \in M$, $m \in \{1,...,k_j\}$ is the instant that the request

from secondary source $S_j$ informming that the frame terminating byte has been transmitted into communication line j is
sensed by the line adapter transmitter driver at PR6, m
being the sequential number of the frame in the j-th output queue and k - the capacity of the j-th output queue.

7. $r = \{[r_{1_1}^1, \ldots, r_{1_1}^{k_1}], \ldots, [r_{1_N}^1, \ldots, r_{1_N}^{k_N}]\}$ (8)

where

$$\prod_{i \in N} r_{1_i}^m = \begin{cases} 1 \text{ if the m-th frame from } S_i \text{ is an information frame } [5] \\ 0 \text{ if the m-th frame from } S_i \text{ is not an information frame.} \end{cases}$$ (9)

$m \in \{1, \ldots, k_i\}$

This set makes it possible to pick up input requests requiring simplified service ie. that without the need to run through the packet level (level 3 [1] layer in node software.

Let   $\mathcal{D} = \{D_1, \ldots, D_p, \ldots, D_1\}$ (10)

will be a set of allowable line request service disciplines ie. those ensuring that the real-time operation constraints specified above are met.

We look for an optimum discipline $D^*$ such that

$$T(D^*) = \min_{D^* \in \mathcal{D}} T(D)$$ (11)

As discussed above we reduce the problem to analysis of $T^p$ ie. the share in T of processes on which $D^p$ is of influence.
In the aftergoing discussion, we shall define any element of set as a set of decissions [9] characterizing this service discipline, so that:

$$D_p = [d_1^p, \ldots, d_r^p, \ldots, d_n^p]$$ (12)

Each of elements $d_r$, $r \in \{1, \ldots, n\}$ is a decission undertaken basing on testing of the corresponding element of the set defining the system state $\$$.

LINE REQUEST SERVICE DISCIPLINE IN THE FIRST VERSION OF MSK NODE SOFTWARE

The model for studying the behaviour of the system $\$$, realized in the first version of the communication subnet node for MSK is shown in Figure 1.
System state is defined by:

$$\$ = \{F, \mathbb{F}_0, \mathbb{F}_1, \mathcal{F}\}$$ (13)

The implemented request service discipline consists of decisions

$$D_p = [d_1^p, d_2^p, d_3^p] \qquad p \in \{1, \ldots, n\}$$ (14)

where  $d_1^p$ is the decision undertaken upon values of elements in the set of general semaphores, ie. $\mathbb{F}_0 \cup \mathbb{F}_1 \cup \mathbb{F}_2$,

$d_2^p$ is the decision undertaken upon values of components of vector $F_i$, $i \in N$ ie. specific semaphores for the input queues, and

$d_3^f$ is the decision undertaken upon values of components of vector $F_j$, $j \in M$, ie. specific semaphores for the output queues.

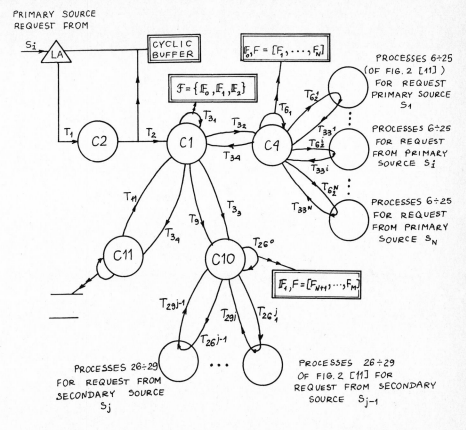

PRIMARY SOURCE
REQUEST FROM

Notes:

    C1, C2 ...  — PROGRAM MODULES

    $T_1, T_2$ ...  — PROCESSES

Figure 1

Specific data frame flow diagram referring to semaphores

This is seen in Figure 2. The system under investigation operates at PR3. The decision undertaken upon the global semaphore, $\mathcal{F}$ , is not shown since it is implied by other software consideration and common to all $D_p$, $p \in \{1,\dots,n\}$ under study.

The decision undertaken upon values of elements in the set of genneral semaphores $\mathbb{F}_0 \cup \mathbb{F}_1 \cup \mathbb{F}_2$, $d_1^p$ is realized by performing the operation $V$ sequentially for each general semaphore. It means, that the non preemptive, head-of-line discipline scheduling [6] is assumed for these semaphores. This is justified by simplicity of programming.

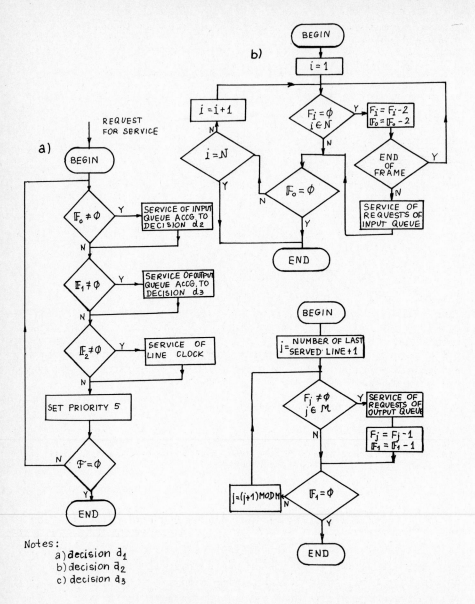

Notes:
  a) decision $d_1$
  b) decision $d_2$
  c) decision $d_3$

Figure 2
Undertaking decisions $d_1, d_2, d_3$ depending on system state $

The decision $d_2^p$ undertaken upon values of specific semaphores for
the input queues is made by performing the operation V on sequential
semaphores $F_i$, $i \in \{1,\ldots,N\}$. We start with i = 1 and if the request

served did not inform of a received frame, we try to execute the
operation V again for the same i. In this way, we can rapidly dis-
card "idle" requests produced by a line adapter when disturbances occur in the communication line served by it and/or inhibit interrupts
from a faulty adapter. After any request informing of a frame received is served, a test is made on the general semaphore $\mathbb{F}_o$. If zero,
we go to procedure for decision $d_3^p$, thus eliminating idle V operations upon zero values specific semaphores $F_i, i \in \{1,...,N\}$. If not,
we increase i of 1 and repeat the above procedure until $i > N$. This
means, that we scan the specific semaphores for the input queue only
once (to say nothing of the special case of idle requests) and proceed to testing of the specific semaphores $F_j, j \in \{N+1,...,M\}$ even
if some input queues are not empty.
We assumed this solution in order to limit time delays in responding
to requests from line adapter transmitters, $S_j, j \in \{N+1,...,M\}$, in the
case of intensive traffic through the node, and consenquently, to
enable releasing of data buffers necessary for subsequent frames of
data.

The decission $d_3^p$ is undertaken by executing the operation V on semaphores $F_j, j \in \{N+1,...,M\}$. We start with the line j being the next line in $\mathcal{M}$ after that which has been served lastly and perform the operation V on $F_j$ until $F_j = 0$. Then we test $\mathbb{F}_1$ and if not zero, increase
j modulo $(M-N)$ and processes $F_j$, etc.

Thus, we serve all requests from the secondary sources $S_j$,
$j \in \{N+1,...,M\}$ prior serving any other requests from the primary sources $S_i, i \in \{1,...,N\}$. As discussed in [11] this does not result in serious problems et the node input, since transfer even of the shortest possible frame can not be completed during processing all normal-
state interrupts from line adapter transmitters.

EVALUATION OF ASSUMED SOLUTION

If the data flow model Figure 1 is interpreted as an activity network [10] in which the graph nodes are $C1, C2,...$ and graphs arcs
represent activity durations, then in dependence on the decision undertaken time,

$$\Theta_{ik} = \tau_{l_j}^{k,i} - \tau_{l_i}^{k}$$

will be the sum of respective durations of individual activities
along the path through the graph, representing service of the request from the i-th source, $i \in \{1,...,N\}$. The primary characteristic
of the node, T, given by (10) will be treated as the sum of durations
of individual activities along the critical path (that of the longest overall duration) of the graph, representing service of a request from source $S_i$ in the worst case. Therefore, if we look for an
optimum service discipline, we are to select the one for which the
critical path is of minimum duration.
The value of T is defined by:

$$T = \sum_{i=1}^{N} \left( \sum_{k=1}^{r(i)} \mu_{1_{k(i)}}^{*} \right) + \sum_{j=N+1}^{M} t_j^{*} + \sum_{i=N+1}^{M} \left( \sum_{k=1}^{r(i)} \mu_{1_{k(i)}}^{*} \right) + A \qquad (15)$$

where $\mu_{1_{k(i)}}^{*}, i \in \{1,...,M\}$ is a realization of completion time of process $T_{l_k(i)}$ resulting in reaching T by $\theta_{ik}$.

As stated before, we are interested in minimizing the share of processes dependent on the service discipline in T, ie. in minimizing

$$T^p = \sum_{i=1}^{N} ( \sum_{k \in \mathcal{R}(i)} \mu^*_{l_k(i)} ) + \sum_{i=N+1}^{M} ( \sum_{k \in \mathcal{R}(i)} \mu^*_{l_k(i)} ) \tag{16}$$

where $p \in \{0, 1, \dots\}$ is the index of the service discipline, 0 being reserved for that implemented in the first version of the MSK subnet node, and
$\mathcal{R}(i)$ is the set of processes connected with the discipline under investigation.

The value of T for first version of the node is $T^* \cong 880$ ms.
The expression

$$\mu^p = \frac{T^p}{T^*}, \quad i \in \{0, 1, \dots\} \tag{17}$$

makes it possible to evaluate influence of individual discipline $D_p$ upon T.

As we plan to use the first version of the node for up to 6 communications lines, we have N=6 and M=12. Any input queue may include up to 7 information frames. This number is limited by the LAPB protocol window and by the fact, that we are not interested in studying the frame retransmission mechanism: we are to ensure for the node not to operate this mechanism and if it is operated due to any transmission error, realizations of $\theta_{ik}$ will not reach T (since subsequent information frames are simply discarded).

From this, Figure 1 and analysis of the first version of MSK subnet node software, we have:

$$T^o \leqslant 7 \cdot 6 \sum_{k=6}^{33} \mu^*_{l_k} + 7 \cdot 6 \sum_{k=26}^{29} \mu^*_{l_k} \cong 7 \cdot 6 \cdot 5,2 \text{ ms} = 218 \text{ ms} \tag{18}$$

And

$$\mu^o = \frac{T^o}{T^*} = \frac{218}{880} = 25\% \tag{19}$$

## DISCUSSION OF SOME COMPETITIVE SERVICE DISCIPLINES

The FIFS (first in first served) discipline may be realized by studying the elements of sets $\tau_{IN}(6)$ and $\tau_{out}(7)$. The instants that any frame transmission are completed are recorded by the line adapter (receiver or transmitter) drivers involved and, therefore, are available for processes at PR3.
The FIFS discipline, $D_1$ minimizes individual realizations of $\theta_{ik}$ and, therefore, may decrease T when compared with $D_o$. Nevertheless, till the moment we have not studied this problem in more detail and when performing rough, worst case analysis, we may easily present input process realization resulting $T^1$ similar to $T^o$, and even somewhat higher, since we have to perform additional comparison of

$$\tau_{l_i}^k, \quad i \in \{1, \dots, M\}, \quad k \in \{1, 2, \dots\}$$

On the base of approximate evaluation of code required for implementing $D_1$, we have:

$$T^1 \cong 250 \text{ ms} \tag{20}$$

and

$$\mu^1 = 28 \% \tag{21}$$

Thus

$$\frac{T^1 - T^0}{T^*} = \mu^1 - \mu^0 \cong 3 \% \tag{22}$$

From (22) we may suspect that influence of service discipline upon T is rather inconsiderable and, perhaps, some secondary cryteria may be defined for optimization of this software solution. Nevertheless, we feel the problem need farther studies which are in progress.
A single software modification may result in another doscipline taking into account type of frame served $(D_2)$: we may insert the folloving procedure after serving request m from source $S_i$ , $i \in \{1,...,N\}$ :

**if** $r_{1i}^m = 0$ **go to** **Procedure** **V** **on** **F** **alse** **go to** **Test** $\mathbb{F}_0$-

In such a way, we can serve the information frame in the input queue just after serving any proceeding non-information frames in this queue. Therefore, we eliminate the need for non-information frames to wait in such cases for service till requests from other sources tested and, eventually, served.
Of course, we increase $\theta_{ik}$ for requests from other $i \in \{1,...,N\}$, but not too much since processing of not-information frames needs, in general, less processor time then processing of information frames (the level 3 layer is not to be operated).
Influence of this subsequent service disciplines needs further their studies.

Another discipline which is worthwhile considering seems to be the head-of-line one. In this case we are to execute the operation V on $F_i$ till $F_i = 0$, ie. till the instant that all requests from source $S_i$, $i \in \{1,...,N\}$ are served, and then go to test on $\mathbb{F}_0$ and so on, as discussed with reference to Figure 1.
This discipline may decrease overhead connected with processing of semaphores but, of course, gives some priviledge to first line.
Perhaps, it could be useful if prognosed traffic in some communication lines is more intensive than that in other lines.


CONCLUSIONS

The maximum packet transfer delay, T, seems to be an adequate primary characteristic for the node. Optimization of individual node design solutions for minimum T should be a good approach to improvement of the node.
Analysis of the above discussed and other acceptable competitive solutions, performed in the way outlayed in this paper, should enable us to answer the following questions:
- Which of acceptable competitive solution results in minimum value of the primary characteristic T?
- What relative benefits in terms of T may be achieved?

To answer the questions, detail theoretical and experimental studies are requised. Nevertheless, we may suspect that the request service discipline is of minor influence on T and that some additional optimization criteria may be defined for this problem.

# REFERENCES

[1 ] CCIT, Revised Recommendation X.25, Preface and Level 3, (COM
VII No. 384-E, August 1979).

[2 ] Heart, F.E. et al., The interface message processor for ARPA
Computer Networks, in: AFIPS Conference Proceedings, 1970.

[3 ] Davies, D.W., Barber, D.L.A., Communication Networks for Computers (John Woley and Sons, New York, 1973).

[4 ] Seidler, I., Analiza i optymalizacja sieci łączności dla syste-
mów teleinformatycznych (WNT, Warszawa, 1978).

[5 ] Kleinrock, L., Queueing Systems (John Wiley and Sons, New York,
1976).

[6 ] Coffman, E.G., Ir., Computer and Job-Shop Scheduling Theory
(John Wiley and Sons, New York, 1976).

[7 ] Shaw, A.C., The Logical Design of Operating Systems (Prentice
Hall, USA, 1974).

[8 ] Lewoc, J., Koordynator węzła podsieci komunikacyjnej, Scientific Papers of the Computer Center of Wrocław Technical University, Series Studies and Research (Ianuary 1981).

[9 ] Lindgren, B.W., Elements of Decission Theory (The MacMillan Co.,
New York, 1971).

[10] Deo, N., Graph theory with applications to engineering and
computers science (Prentice Hall, USA, 1974).

[11] Bieleninik, E., Evaluation of Maximum Possible Number of Logical Connections for a Communication Subnet Node, Computer Centre, Technical University of Wroclaw (April 1981).

Performance of Data Communication Systems
and their Applications, G. Pujolle (ed.)
© North-Holland Publishing Company, 1981

UN MODELE POUR ETUDIER LES PERFORMANCES DE DEUX PRODUITS SNA :
LES SOUS-SYSTEMES D'APPLICATION IMS ET CICS

Vincent DINH VAN TOAN

IBM-FRANCE
1, place Jean-Baptiste Clément
93164 NOISY LE GRAND CEDEX

Il existe dans IMS plusieurs disciplines de priorité dont
les principales sont : la priorité de traitement et la priorité de sélection. Deux modèles sont proposés dans cet article pour étudier ces deux types de priorité.

SNA  : Systems Network Architecture
IMS  : Information Management System
CICS : Customer Information Control System


INTRODUCTION

Un travail traité dans un ordinateur peut monopoliser longtemps l'Unité Centrale
(UC) au détriment d'autres travaux. Il est possible d'éviter cette situation en
instituant un ordre de priorité : donner par exemple une haute priorité aux travaux qui immobilisent moins l'UC et une faible priorité à ceux qui consomment beaucoup de temps UC. L'instauration des priorités fournit ainsi un moyen d'éviter les
blocages, donc de régulariser les flots de travaux à travers les différentes ressources.

Il y a deux sortes de priorités : la priorité de traitement ("dispatching priority") et la priorité de sélection ("scheduling priority"). Le sous-système IMS a
été choisi pour illustrer ces deux types de priorités. Cet article est consacré à
l'analyse de IMS et de CICS qui lui est similaire.

BREF APERÇU DES CARACTERISTIQUES DE IMS/VS

*IMS/VS, un sous-système d'application SNA*

IMS/VS [16] a pour objectif d'aider les programmes d'application "batch" et "on-
line" à travailler facilement sur des données organisées en une structure hiérar-
chisée. Il fournit un support pour créer, consulter et maintenir les bases de données à l'aide du langage DL/1. Il peut lancer des programmes d'application appelés
par une tâche en batch ou par un message venant d'un terminal. Différents langages
de-programmation sont admis : ASSEMBLER, COBOL, PL1.
Sa capacité de gérer des programmes d'application vaut à IMS/VS le nom de sous-
système d'application ; ce terme désigne un logiciel conçu pour fournir un support
spécial à une classe de programmes d'application. Il est aussi devenu un produit
SNA grâce à l'incorporation dans sa structure des fonctions de contrôle orientées
télétraitement et réalisées d'après les concepts d'architecture unifiée de réseaux
énoncés dans SNA [5][7].

*Le système DB/DC de IMS/VS*

Les deux parties les plus importantes de IMS/VS sont :

- "Data Base (DB) System", chargé de gérer les bases de données ;
- "Data Communication (DC) feature", chargé de communiquer avec le réseau.

Ces deux composantes forment le "Data Base/Data Communication System" (DB/DC). Dans cet article nous nous intéressons aux caractéristiques du système DB/DC qui concourent à l'évolution d'un modèle de files d'attente.

IMS/VS occupe plusieurs régions du Systeme d'Exploitation (SE). Pour les exécutions en télétraitement ("on line execution"), IMS/VS nécessite une région dite "région de contrôle" ("control region") et plusieurs régions dites "régions dependantes" ("dependent regions") ; ces dernières sont destinées à traiter des applications. La région de contrôle gère les bases de données utilisées par les applications dans les régions dépendantes. Elle est également responsable de la sélection des transactions à traiter dans les régions dépendantes.

*La priorité de traitement ("dispatching priority")*

La mémoire (réelle ou virtuelle) d'un ordinateur est divisée en un nombre limité de zones appelées des régions ou des partitions du SE. Chaque région traite une seule application chaque fois. Le SE crée pour chaque région un bloc de contrôle que nous appelons une tâche pour simplifier le langage. Elle sert à représenter le travail à faire dans cette région, en l'occurrence la transaction à traiter dans une région dépendante. La tâche demande au superviseur (c'est la partie du SE qui est responsable de la gestion des tâches), l'accès à l'UC et aux unités d'E/S. L'ordre dans lequel le superviseur attribue ces ressources aux différentes tâches constitue la priorité de traitement ("dispatching priority"). Cet ordre dépend des priorités affectées aux régions. Une tâche a la même priorité que la région à laquelle elle est associée. La priorité de traitement est préemptive pour l'UC, et FIFO (quelque fois non-préemptive) pour les E/S.

*La priorité de sélection ("scheduling priority")*

Une fois qu'une transaction est initialisée dans une région dépendante, celle-ci la fait traiter jusqu'au bout. Ce n'est qu'à la fin du traitement que la région de contrôle lui assigne une autre transaction à traiter. L'ordre d'admission des transactions dans une région, désigné par "scheduling priority", est celui d'une priorité simple (non-préemptive). Les transactions sont sélectionnées d'après un certain nombre de paramètres dont les principaux sont décrits ci-après.

Une trasaction est une entité qui représente une application, c'est-à-dire un travail à faire par un processeur de télétraitement. Les données du travail sont contenues dans un message d'entrée, les résultats du travail constituent un message de sortie (ou message de réponse). Chaque transaction provoque l'exécution d'un ou de plusieurs modules de programme. Dans IMS/VS, une transaction est matérialisée par un bloc de contrôle qui contient notamment :

- un "code transaction" spécifique à l'application que représente la transaction ; il constitue le type de la transaction, par exemple : type "interrogation", type "mise à jour" de comptes bancaires ;
- une classe de traitement, qui est utilisée pour la sélection de la transaction dans une région en vue de son traitement, exemple classe A ;
- un niveau courant de priorité de sélection.

Chaque message d'entrée porte un "code transaction" pour indiquer à quel type de transaction il est destiné. Les messages sont placés dans des files d'entrée d'après le code transaction (une file par type de transaction). Les messages de sortie sont placés dans des files associées aux terminaux.

Les programmes d'application sont liés aux transactions : à chaque type de transaction est associé un programme.

Les régions dépendantes sont dédiées à des classes de transactions déterminées. Une région peut traiter plusieurs classes ; l'ordre dans lequel les classes sont définies pour une région constitue l'ordre de priorité des classes dans cette région.

En vue de la sélection des transactions à traiter, celles-ci sont groupées par classe de traitement, à l'intérieur de chaque classe elles sont choisies d'après leurs priorités courantes.

## LES MODELES

La description précédente de IMS/VS fait ressortir deux niveaux de ressources, donc deux niveaux de files d'attente.

Les ressources de premier niveau sont constituées par les unités directement impliquées dans le traitement des transactions (ou des tâches) à savoir l'UC et les unités d'E/S. Avant qu'une transaction soit autorisée à utiliser ces ressources élémentaires, il faut d'abord qu'elle obtienne une région. Les régions forment donc des ressources de deuxième niveau.

Chaque niveau de ressources donne lieu à un modèle de files d'attente ; au premier niveau correspond un modèle de "dispatching priority", au second un modèle de "scheduling priority".

### *Modèle de "dispatching priority"*

Une fois initialisée dans une région, chaque transaction lance plusieurs accès-disques et réclame plusieurs fois l'UC. Elle parcourt plusieurs cycles fermés entre l'UC et la batterie de disques. Le traitement des transactions peut donc être représenté par un modèle de serveur central [3][9][15] avec plusieurs classes de priorité : chaque transaction a la priorité de la région qu'elle occupe. Il y a une transaction par région, donc par classe de priorité. Dès qu'une transaction quitte la région, une autre y est admise ; ce remplacement est représenté par la boucle ABC sur la figure 1.

Les interruptions d'E/S ont un caractère aléatoire et se traitent uniquement dans l'UC. Elles peuvent être représentées par un flot de Poisson à travers l'UC. Ce flot ouvert a une priorité plus grande que les flots fermés des transactions traitées dans les régions dépendantes.

### *Modèle de "scheduling priority"*

Ce modèle est constitué par des régions et des messages. Il est raisonnable d'admettre que les files de messages d'entrée sont alimentés par des flots de Poisson. En effet, les applications de IMS (ou de CICS) sont généralement ouvertes à des centaines d'usagers (parmi lesquels il peut y avoir des ordinateurs). Une file d'entrée reçoit des messages provenant d'un grand nombre de terminaux ; de plus, ces messages traversent un réseau de communications en empruntant des itinéraires différents. Ainsi, l'arrivée dans une file d'entrée a un caractère aléatoire et peut être estimée par une loi de Poisson.

Le modèle de serveur central décrit précédemment, sert à évaluer la durée d'un cycle de chaque priorité. La durée de traitement d'une transaction est le produit de la durée d'un cycle par le nombre de cycles faits par la transaction. C'est le temps de service de la région quand elle traite ce type de transaction.

## LES SOLUTIONS

### *Modèle de "dispatching priority"*

Comme il a été mentionné plus haut, c'est un modèle de serveur central. Cette appellation a été introduite par Buzen [3]. Mais les réseaux fermés de files d'attente à services exponentiels avaient été étudiés par Gordon et Newell [12] dont les travaux constituent une extension de ceux de Jackson [13].

Les résultats les plus intéressants, dans l'étude des réseaux de files d'attente, sont obtenus par les travaux de Baskett, Chandy, Muntz et Palacios [2]. Ils conduisent au théorème généralement connu sous le nom de théorème de BCMP. On trouve également une présentation de ces travaux dans [10][11]. Nous nous proposons d'utiliser le théorème de BCMP pour calculer la durée moyenne d'un cycle dans le modèle de serveur central. Nous en déduirons ensuite la durée d'un cycle moyen dans chaque priorité. Cette valeur sera enfin réajustée pour tenir compte de l'influence des interruptions d'E/S.

### *Application du théorème de BCMP*

Un exposé sur ce théorème n'est pas nécessaire. Rappelons seulement qu'il donne la

distribution des longueurs de file d'attente, à l'état stable, dans un réseau à plusieurs classes de clients et que cette distribution a la forme produit.
Les hypothèses adoptées pour le modèle sont :

- le temps de service résultant dans l'UC a une distribution exponentielle ;
- le nombre de disques est largement supérieur au nombre de transactions actives ; celui-ci est au maximum égal au nombre de régions (au maximum une transaction par région).

L'hypothèse du service exponentiel a été adoptée par plusieurs auteurs, par exemple par Chiu, Dumont et Wood [4] quand ils mettaient au point un modèle de réseau fermé pour étudier le système 360/75 de l'Université de Californie, Santa Barbara (UCSB). C'étaient les mesures sur machine conduites par Chiu qui les ont amenés à faire cette approximation. L'UC sera représentée dans notre modèle par une station de type 1.
Notre deuxième hypothèse est le reflet de la réalité : dans les systèmes DB/DC les bases de données occupent toujours une grande quantité de disques, une vingtaine d'unités ou plus, tandis que le nombre de régions dépassent rarement une dizaine.
Cette observation nous amène à modéliser le pool de disques par une station de type 3. Cette représentation élimine la nécessité d'admettre que les temps de service-disque sont exponentiellement distribués ; dans la réalité, ce sont des lois d'Erlang d'ordre élevé (supérieur à 10).
Les notations utilisées dans les formules sont :

$i$    : indice station ; $i = 1, 2$ ;
$r$    : indice classe ; $r = 1, 2, \ldots, R$ ;
$e_{ir}$  : fréquence relative de visite des transactions de classe $r$ à la station $i$ ;
$\mu_i$  : taux de service de la station $i$ ;
$\mu_{ir}$ : taux de service de la station $i$ pour la classe $r$ ;
$p_{ijr}$ : probabilité de passage d'une transaction de classe $r$ de la station $i$ à la station $j$ ; les transactions ne changent pas de classe ;
$n_i$  : nombre de transactions dans la station $i$ ;
$n_{ir}$ : nombre de transactions de classe $r$ dans la station $i$ ;
$N$   : nombre total de transactions dans le réseau

Sur la figure 1, on a immédiatement :

$$(1) \qquad e_{2r}/e_{1r} = p_{1\,2r} = p_r$$

Désignons l'état S du réseau par $(y_1, y_2)$ avec $y_i = (n_{i1}, n_{i2}, \ldots, n_{ir}, \ldots, n_{iR})$.

Le théorème de BCMP permet d'écrire la distribution marginale :

$$(2) \qquad P(S = (y_1, y_2)) = C \cdot g_1(y_1) \cdot g_2(y_2)$$

Pour la station 1. de type 1 :

$$(3) \qquad g_1(y_1) = n_1! \; (\mu_1^{-1})^{n_1} \prod_{r=1}^{R} \frac{1}{n_{1r}!} \, (e_{1r})^{n_{1r}}$$

Pour la station 2, de type 3 :

$$(4) \qquad g_2(y_2) = \prod_{r=1}^{R} \frac{1}{n_{2r}!} \, (e_{2r} \, \mu_{2r}^{-1})^{n_{2r}}$$

Il u a une seule transaction par classe :

$$n_{ir} = 1 \; ; \; R = N.$$

Soient $R_1$ et $R_2$ deux ensembles complémentaires, $R_1$ contient $n_1$ transactions dans la station 1 et $R_2$ contient $n_2 = N-n_1$ transactions dans la station 2. Si les $n_1$ clients sont par exemple de classes $(1, 2, \ldots, n_1)$, les $n_2$ clients seront de classes $(n_1+1, n_1+2, \ldots, N)$. Désignons par $1_i$ le client de classe $i$ :

$$(5) \qquad g_1(y_1) = n_1! \; (\mu_1^{-1})^{n_1} \prod_{r \in R_1} (e_{1r})$$

$$(6) \qquad g_2(y_2) = \underset{r \in R_2}{\Pi}(e_{2r}\,\mu_{2r}^{-1}) = \underset{r \in R_2}{\Pi}(p_r\,e_{1r}\,\mu_{2r}^{-1})$$

$$P((y_1 = 1_1, 1_2, \ldots, 1_{n_1}),\ (y_2 = 1_{n_1+1}, 1_{n_1+2}, \ldots, 1_N))$$

$$(7) \qquad = (C \overset{R}{\underset{r=1}{\Pi}} e_{1r})\, n_1!\,(\mu_1^{-1})^{n_1} \underset{r \in R_2}{\Pi}(p_r\,\mu_{2r}^{-1})$$

Le terme $C' = C \underset{r \in R_1}{\Pi} e_{1r} \underset{r \in R_2}{\Pi} e_{1r} = C \overset{R}{\underset{r=1}{\Pi}} e_{1r}$ est une constante de normalisation.

Soit $E_2$ l'ensemble des états dans lesquels il y a $n_2 = N-n_1$ transactions dans la station 2. Faisant la sommation de (7) sur tous les états pour éliminer la distinction entre classe :

$$P(n_1, N-n_1) = \underset{E_2}{\Sigma} P(y_1, y_2)$$

$$(8) \qquad n_1!(\mu_1^{-1})^{n_1} \underset{E_2}{\Sigma} \underset{r \in R_2}{\Pi}(p_r\,\mu_{2r}^{-1}) \ / \ \overset{N}{\underset{n_1=0}{\Sigma}} [n_1!(\mu_1^{-1})^{n_1} \underset{E_2}{\Sigma} \underset{r \in R_2}{\Pi}(p_r\,\mu_{2r}^{-1})]$$

Tous les temps de service-disque ont la même moyenne et la même distribution ; par exemple, la longueur des enregistrements est en général fixe ; elle peut avoir par exemple la taille d'une page, celle d'une demi-piste ou d'une piste sur disque

$$\mu_{2r}^{-1} = \mu_2^{-1}\ .$$

L'équation (8) devient, en écrivant $\underset{r \in R_2}{\Pi}(\mu_2^{-1}) = (\mu_2^{-1})^{N-n_1}$

$$(9) \qquad P(n_1, N-n_1) = n_1!(\mu_2/\mu_1)^{n_1} \underset{E_2}{\Sigma}(\underset{r \in R_2}{\Pi} p_r) \ / \ \overset{N}{\underset{n_1=0}{\Sigma}} [n_1!\,(\mu_2/\mu_1)^{n_1} \underset{E_2}{\Sigma}(\underset{r \in R_2}{\Pi} p_r)]$$

Si toutes les transactions ont la même probabilité de passage $p_r = p$, le terme $\underset{E_2}{\Sigma}(\underset{r \in R_2}{\Pi} p_r)$ devient, en remplaçant $n_2$ par $N-n_1$ :

$$\underset{E_2}{\Sigma}(\underset{r \in R_2}{\Pi} p) = C_{n_2}^N\,p^{n_2} = \frac{N!}{n_1!(N-n_1)!}\,p^{N-n_1}$$

Par ailleurs, $n_2$ n'a qu'un état possible par valeur de $n_1$ ; la distribution jointe $P(n_1, N-n_1)$ est égale à la distribution marginale $P(n_1)$. On aura donc :

$$(10) \qquad P(n_1) = P(n_2 = N-n_1) = P(n_1, N-n_1) = P(0)\,\frac{N!}{(N-n_1)!}\left(\frac{p^{-1}\mu_2}{\mu_1}\right)^{n_1}$$

avec

$$(11) \qquad P(0)^{-1} = \overset{N}{\underset{n_1=0}{\Sigma}}\frac{N!}{(N-n_1)!}\left(\frac{p^{-1}\mu_2}{\mu_1}\right)^{n_1}$$

Nous allons faire comme dans [3] [9] [15] et supprimer la boucle "feed back" de l'UC. ($p_r=1$).
Les distributions deviennent :

$$(12) \qquad P(n_1) = P(n_2 = N-n_1) = P(0)\,\frac{N!}{(N-n_1)!}\left(\frac{\mu_2}{\mu_1}\right)^{n_1}$$

$$(13) \qquad P(0)^{-1} = \overset{N}{\underset{n_1=0}{\Sigma}}\frac{N!}{(N-n_1)!}\left(\frac{\mu_2}{\mu_1}\right)^{n_1}\ .$$

La longueur moyenne de la file d'attente dans l'UC est, avec $\rho = \mu_2/\mu_1$ :

$$E(n_1) = \bar{n}_1 = \overset{N}{\underset{n_1=1}{\Sigma}} n_1 P(n_1) = P(0)\overset{N}{\underset{n_1=1}{\Sigma}}\frac{N!}{(N-n_1)!}\,n_1\,\rho^{n_1}$$

Après calculs on obtient :

$$(14) \qquad \bar{n}_1 = N - \frac{1 - P(o)}{\rho}$$

et

$$(15) \qquad \bar{n}_2 = N - n_1 = \frac{1 - P(o)}{\rho}$$

Soient $TR_i(N)$ les temps moyens de réponse dans les deux stations quand il y a N transactions dans le système. Appliquons LIttle :

$$U_1 = 1 - P(o) \ ; \ \text{(taux d'utilisation de l'UC)}$$

$$(16) \qquad TR_1(N) = \frac{\bar{n}_1}{U_1 \mu_1} = \frac{N}{\mu_1[1 - P(o)]} - \frac{1}{\mu_1 \rho} \ ; \quad TR_2(N) = \frac{\bar{n}_2}{U_1 \mu_1} = \mu_2^{-1}$$

La durée moyenne d'un cycle, quand N transactions sont dans le système, est :

$$(17) \qquad T(N) = TR_1(N) + TR_2(N) = \frac{N}{U_1 \mu_1} = \frac{N}{\mu_1[1 - P(o)]}$$

*Les classes de priorité*

Soient : $C(j)$　　la durée moyenne d'un cycle de la priorité j
　　　　　$U_1(j)$　l'utilisation de l'UC par la priorité j
　　　　　$n(j)$　　le nombre de transactions de priorité j

Le taux de service ou le taux d'arrivée de la classe j dans l'UC est $\mu_1 U_1(j)$. Appliquons Little :

$$[\mu_1 U_1(j)] \ C(j) = n(j) \quad ; \quad \mu_1 U_1(j) = \frac{n(j)}{C(j)}$$

L'utilisation totale de l'UC est la somme des $U_1(j)$ :

$$(18) \qquad \mu_1 U_1 = \mu_1 \sum_{j=1}^{K} U_1(j) = \sum_{j=1}^{K} \frac{n(j)}{C(j)}$$

K étant le nombre de classes de priorité. Avec :

$$\sum_{j=1}^{K} n(j) = N \ ; \ n(j) = 1 \ ; \ K = N$$

on obtient d'après (17) :

$$(19) \qquad \mu_1 U_1 = \sum_{j=1}^{N} \frac{1}{C(j)} = \frac{N}{T(N)}$$

La priorité étant préemptive dans l'UC et le pool de disques ayant une grande capacité en E/S, les K premières priorités sont indépendantes des (N-K) priorités inférieures. On a finalement :

$$(20) \qquad \sum_{j=1}^{K} \frac{1}{C(j)} = \frac{K}{T(K)}$$

La formule de récurrence suivante permet de calculer les $C(j)$ :

$$(21) \qquad \frac{1}{C(k)} = \frac{K}{T(K)} - \frac{K-1}{T(K-1)} \qquad \text{pour } K = 1, \ C(1) = T(1).$$

*Influence des interruptions d'E/S*

Les interruptions d'E/S constituent un flot de Poisson ouvert ayant la plus haute priosité. Soit

$$\rho_0 = \lambda_0 \mu_0^{-1}$$

le taux d'occupation qu'elles produisent dans l'UC ; $(\lambda_0 t)$ étant le paramètre de la loi de Poisson, $\mu_0^{-1}$ le temps moyen de traitement d'une interruption.
L'unité centrale doit impérativement réserver aux interruptions une fraction égale

à $\rho_0$ de son temps disponible. Le reste est consacré aux autres transactions. On peut dire qu'elle traite ces dernières à la vitesse de $(1-\rho_0)$ seconde. Les durées d'exécution des transactions sont donc allongées dans la proportion de $1/(1-\rho_0)$ du temps normal. Nous considérons donc un serveur équivalent ayant un temps moyen de service égal à $\mu_1^{-1}/(1-\rho_0)$.

## Modèle de "scheduling priority"

Le modèle général que nous proposons pour étudier la priorité de sélection est composé de file M/G/1 avec des priorités non préemptives.
On peut considérer pour la modélisation que chaque région a une file d'attente dans laquelle les messages vont se placer d'après un ordre de priorité déterminé. Les processus d'arrivée sont supposés être des processus de Poisson. Soient :

$X_i$ : le temps de service de la priorité i ;

$X_i(t)$ : la distribution de probabilité de $X_i$ ;

$\bar{X}_i$ : la valeur moyenne de $X_i$ ;

$\overline{X_i^2}$ : le moment d'ordre 2 de $X_i$ ;

$Var(X_i)$ : la variance de $X_i$ ;

$\lambda_i$ : le taux d'arrivée de priorité i ;

$\rho_i = \lambda_i \bar{X}_i$ : le taux d'utilisation du serveur produit par la priorité i ;

$\sigma_j = \sum_{K=1}^{j} \rho_K$ : le taux d'utilisation du serveur produit par les j premières priorités ;

$P$ : le nombre total de priorités dans le modèle.

Le temps moyen d'attente de la priorité i, quand il y a P priorités au total, est [6] :

$$(22) \qquad \bar{W}_i = \sum_{K=1}^{P} \lambda_K \overline{X_K^2} / 2(1-\sigma_{i-1})(1-\sigma_i)$$

Deux calculs sont nécessaires, l'un pour déterminer les flots des dérivations quand un flot d'entrée se subdivise en plusieurs branches, l'autre pour évaluer les moments d'ordre 2 des temps de service des régions.

## Les flots dérivés

On a l'habitude de grouper dans une même région les classes qui utilisent la même base de données. Mais si le taux d'arrivée d'une classe est trop élevé pour une région, on fera traiter la même classe par d'autres régions pour décharger la première. Les messages de cette classe se dirigent donc vers plusieurs destinations. On peut admettre que le flot d'entrée dans chaque région est un flot de Poisson. Chaque région constitue donc une file M/G/1 avec des priorités non préemptives. L'intensité moyenne de chaque flot dérivé est proportionnelle à la disponibilité de la région qui le reçoit. Ce résultat est obtenu en ramenant le problème de partage des flots au problème de répartition des machines en panne : les régions sont assimilées à des réparateurs et les instants d'arrivée des messages dans le flot principal sont les instants où surviennent les pannes. Les réparateurs les prennent en charge selon leur disponibilité. Les temps de service des régions sont les délais de réparation. Les fins de service ont lieu comme les pannes de façon aléatoire. Considérons un exemple avec deux régions et six classes. On peut supposer sans nuire à la généralité que chaque classe comporte un seul type de transaction, donc une seule file d'attente des messages. Envisageons deux cas de répartition :

Cas 1 : Région P1 : cl. A,B,C ; Région P2 : cl. D,E,A ; Région P3 : cl. F,A,C.

Soient $\rho_X$ le taux d'utilisation dû à la classe X, et $\rho_{Xn}$ le flot dérivé de $\rho_X$ se dirigeant vers la région $P_n$. On a

$$\rho_A = \rho_{A1} + \rho_{A2} + \rho_{A3}$$
$$\rho_C = \rho_{C1} + \rho_{C3}$$

Les disponibilités des régions P1, P2 et P3 pour la classe A sont respectivement : 1, $1-(\rho_D+\rho_E)$ et $1-\rho_F$. Celles des régions P1 et P3 pour la classe C sont respectivement : $1-(\rho_{A1}+\rho_B)$ et $1-(\rho_F+\rho_{A3})$. Les équations suivantes expriment que $\rho_{Xn}$ est proportionnel à la disponibilité de la région n pour la classe X :

$$\frac{\rho_A}{1} = \frac{\rho_2}{1-(\rho_D+\rho_E)} = \frac{\rho_{A3}}{1-\rho_F}$$

$$\frac{\rho_{C1}}{1-(\rho_{A1}+\rho_B)} = \frac{\rho_{C3}}{1-(\rho_F+\rho_{A3})}$$

Les inconnues sont $\rho_{A1}, \rho_{A2}, \rho_{C1}$ ; les valeurs de $\rho_X$ sont connues ; on écrit :

$$\frac{\rho_{A1}}{1} = \frac{\rho_{A2}}{1-\rho_D+\rho_E} = \frac{\rho_{A3}}{1-\rho_F} = \frac{\rho_A}{3-(\rho_D+\rho_E+\rho_F)}$$

$$\frac{\rho_{C1}}{1-(\rho_{A1}+\rho_B)} = \frac{\rho_{C3}}{1-(\rho_F+\rho_{A3})} = \frac{\rho_C}{2-(\rho_{A1}+\rho_B+\rho_F+\rho_{A3})}$$

De ces relations, on tire successivement $\rho_{A1}, \rho_{A2}, \rho_{A3}$ puis $\rho_{C1}, \rho_{C3}$.

Cas 2 : Supposons que l'on permute dans P3 les priorités des classes F et C : Région P3 : classes, C,A,F.

La répartition des classes dans les régions P1 et P2 reste inchangée :

$$\frac{\rho_{A1}}{1} = \frac{\rho_{A2}}{1-(\rho_D+\rho_E)} = \frac{\rho_{A3}}{1-\rho_{C3}} = \frac{\rho_A}{3-(\rho_D+\rho_E+\rho_{C3})}$$

$$\frac{\rho_{C1}}{1-(\rho_{A1}+\rho_B)} = \frac{\rho_{C3}}{1} = \frac{\rho_C}{2-(\rho_{A1}+\rho_B)}$$

En posant $x = \rho_{A1}$, on aboutira à l'équation :

$$x = \frac{\rho_A(2-x-\rho_B)}{(3-\rho_D-\rho_E)(2-x-\rho_B)-\rho_C}$$

C'est une équation de 2ème degré en x.

Ces exemples montrent qu'un flot qui se subdivise en n branches donne lieu à (n-1) équations à (n-1) inconnues. Donc, il existe toujours une solution.

*Les moments d'ordre 2 des temps de service des régions*

Il faut d'abord calculer les moments d'ordre 2 des durées des cycles dans le modèle de serveur central avec priorités. Dans [1] Avi-Itzhak et Heyman traitent le cas d'une seule classe de travaux entrant dans un modèle de serveur central. Ils proposent une solution approchée dans laquelle ils font l'hypothèse que la durée entre deux sorties de travaux est exponentiellement distribuée. Les entrées des travaux étant estimées par une loi de Poisson, le nombre de travaux présents dans le système constitue un processus de naissance et de mort, bien que la fin des travaux ne forme pas un vrai processus de décès.
Comme cette approximation, on peut aussi admettre que le flot d'entrée dans l'UC (flot d'arrivée de nouveaux travaux mélangé au flot de rebouclage) est un flot de Poisson. Cette hypothèse est évidemment fausse. Pujolle et Soula [17] ont en effet démontré que dans une file exponentielle, ni le flot de rebouclage, ni le flot d'entrée n'est un flot de Poisson. A plus forte raison, quand on introduit une station de service (la batterie de disques) dans le flot de rebouclage, ces deux flots ne seront pas poissonniens. Mais l'hypothèse d'un flot de Poisson permettre d'es-

timer facilement les moments des temps de séjour de l'UC à partir de la relation :

(23) $\qquad Y_i^*(S) = X_i^*[S+\lambda'_{i-1}-\lambda'_{i-1}Z'^*_{i-1}(S)]$

(24) $\qquad E(Y_i) = \bar{Y}_i = \dfrac{\bar{X}_i}{1-\sigma_{i-1}}$

(25) $\qquad E(Y_i^2) = \overline{Y_i^2} = \dfrac{\overline{X_i^2}}{(1-\sigma_{i-1})^2} + \bar{X}_i \dfrac{\lambda'_{i-1}\overline{X'^2_{i-1}}}{(1-\sigma_{i-1})^3}$

Dans ces formules :

$X_i(t)$ : distribution de probabilité de $X_i$, temps de service de la priorité i ;

$Y_i(t)$ : distribution de probabilité de $Y_i$, durée de séjour de la priorité i dans l'UC ;

$X_i^*(S)$ : transformée de Laplace de $X_i(t)$ ;

$Y_i^*(S)$ : transformée de Laplace de $Y_i(t)$ ;

$\lambda'_j$ : taux d'arrivée d'une classe équivalente à la réunion des j premières priorités ;

$\sigma_j$ : taux d'utilisation de la classe équivalente ;

$Z'^*_j(S)$ : transformée de Laplace de la "busy period" de la classe équivalente.

Une autre approximation est nécessaire pour continuer les calculs : nous supposons que le temps d'attente devant l'UC est exponentiellement distribué. D'après Kingman [14] , cette approximation n'est valable que pour les trafics chargés. Nous formulons cette hypothèse quelle que soit l'intensité du trafic, afin de pouvoir estimer le moment d'ordre 2 du temps d'attente. Le temps moyen d'attente s'obtient en enlevant les temps moyens de séjour UC et disque de la durée moyenne d'un cycle.
La durée d'un cycle comprend un délai de séjour dans l'UC, un temps de service-disque et un temps d'attente UC. Les trois distributions sont considérées commes indépendantes (ceci est exact pour les temps de service UC et disque, c'est une approximation en ce qui concerne le temps d'attente UC). La somme des variances de ces temps est la variance du cycle (la distribution du temps de service disque étant une loi d'Erlang d'ordre élevé, supérieur à 10, ce temps peut être considéré comme constant).
Une transaction effectue $N_C$ cycles avant de quitter la région. La durée d'un cycle est indépendante des durées des cycles précédents. La moyenne, la variance et le moment d'ordre 2 du temps de séjour de la transaction dans la région se calculeront sans difficulté. Ce temps constitue le temps de service de la région. Le temps d'attente pour obtenir la région se calcule à partir de la formule (22).
On peut calculer le temps de service d'une région en tenant compte de la probabilité p qui est celle qu'une transaction fasse un cycle supplémentaire ; (1-p) est la probabilité qu'elle quitte la région.
Soient :
W : le temps d'attente devant l'UC;
Y : le temps de séjour dans l'UC ;
Z : le temps de service disque ;
V : le temps de service de la région
W(t),Y(t),Z(t),V(t) : les distributions de probabilités de W,Y,Z,V ;

$W^*(S),Y^*(S),Z^*(S),V^*(S)$ : les transformées de Laplace de ces distributions.

On a la relation :

(26) $\qquad V^*(S) = (1-p)W^*(S).Y^*(S).1/[1-pZ^*(S)W^*(S)Y^*(S)]$

D'où l'on tire le temps moyen :

(27) $\qquad E(V) = \bar{V} = \bar{W}+\bar{Y}+p\bar{Z} /[1-p]$

et le deuxième moment

$$(28) \quad E(V^2) = \overline{V^2} = \frac{\overline{W^2} + \overline{Y^2} + p\overline{Z^2}}{1-p} + \frac{2(1+p)\overline{W}\,\overline{Y} + 4p(\overline{W}\,\overline{Z} + \overline{Y}\,\overline{Z})}{(1-p)^2} + \frac{2p[(\overline{W})^2 + (\overline{Y})^2 + p(\overline{Z})^2]}{(1-p)^2}$$

Le premier terme de (28) est très faible (2 à 3 %) par rapport aux deux derniers pour p voisine de 1. La méthode suivie pour estimer $\overline{Y^2}$ et $\overline{W^2}$ a donc peu d'importance. On peut écrire quand p est proche de 1 :

$$E_1(t_R^2) \simeq 2\left[\frac{2\overline{W}\,\overline{Y} + 2\,p\overline{Z}(\overline{W}+\overline{Y})}{(1-p)^2}\right] + 2\left[\frac{(\overline{W})^2 + (\overline{Y})^2 + p^2(\overline{Z})^2}{(1-p)^2}\right] \simeq 2\left(\frac{\overline{W}+\overline{Y}+p\overline{Z}}{1-p}\right)^2 = 2E_i^2(t_R).$$

Ce résultat permet d'énoncer que la distribution de la durée de traitement d'une transaction dans le processeur tend vers une loi exponentielle quand elle fait beaucoup d'E/S (au delà de 15 accès). Cette propriété est très intéressante pour le praticien, car elle lui permet de simplifier ses calculs.

*Exemple numérique*

Les valeurs suivantes sont celles mesurées sur un système IMS/VS : Nombre de transactions traitées :
- 12116 transactions en 1 heure 09 minutes.
Chaque transaction déroule en moyenne 235.000 instructions et fait 17 E/S dont 15 sur la base de données ; celle-ci occupe 33 disques ; le temps moyen d'un accès est 40 ms. Les mesures indiquent que 95% des accès se font sans délai (temps d'attente nul).
Le traitement d'une interruption coûte 2500 instructions, chaque E/S donne lieu à une interruption.
La vitesse de l'UC est de 2 MIPS (2 milions d'instructions par seconde). A partir de ces données, on détermine :
- fréquence d'entrée : 12116/69×60 $\simeq$ 3 transactions par seconde
- taux d'utilisation de l'UC dû aux interruptions : $\rho_0$ = 17 E/S×3×2500/2.10^6 =0,064
- temps UC par transaction : 235.000/2.10^6 = 0,1175 sec = 117,5 ms
- temps UC par cycle (17 E/S = 17 cycles) : 117,5/17 = 6,90 ms
- temps de service UC par cycle sur une Unité Centrale équivalente :
  6,90/1-$\rho_0$ = 6,90/1-0,064 : 7,37 ms.

D'où

$$\mu_1^{-1} = 7{,}37 \text{ ms} \; ; \; \mu_2^{-1} = 40 \text{ ms} \; ; \; \rho = \mu_2/\mu_1 = 0{,}184$$

Le tableau T1 donne pour 8 régions les valeurs de $P(o), n_1, n_2, U_1, U_2, T(N)$ et $C(j)$ ; $U_2 = n_2/33$ est le taux d'utilisation d'un disque.

|  | N | | | | | | | |
|---|---|---|---|---|---|---|---|---|
|  | 1 | 2 | 3 | 4 | 5 | 6 | 7 | 10 |
| $P(o)$ | 0,845 | 0,696 | 0,558 | 0,431 | 0,319 | 0,224 | 0,148 | 0,029 |
| $n_1$ | 0,158 | 0,353 | 0,603 | 0,910 | 1,300 | 1,780 | 2,371 | 4,72 |
| $n_2$ | 0,842 | 1,647 | 2,397 | 3,090 | 3,700 | 4,220 | 4,629 | 5,28 |
| $U_1$ | 0,155 | 0,304 | 0,442 | 0,569 | 0,681 | 0,776 | 0,852 | 0,971 |
| $U_2$ | 0,026 | 0,050 | 0,073 | 0,094 | 0,112 | 0,128 | 0,140 | 0,160 |
| $T(N)$ | 47,36 | 48,50 | 49,95 | 51,74 | 54,04 | 56,92 | 60,49 | 75,86 |
| $C(j)$ | 47,36 | 49,69 | 53,13 | 57,97 | 65,72 | 77,64 | 96,99 | 307,69 |
| $\frac{U_1'}{U_1} = \frac{U_2'}{U_2}$ |  |  | 0,847 | 0,663 | 0,552 | 0,485 | 0,440 | 0,388 |
| $N_{RA}$ |  |  | 2,54 | 2,65 | 2,76 | 2,91 | 3,08 | 3,88 |
| $\lambda_{MAX}$ | 1,24 | 2,43 | 3,54 | 4,53 | 5,43 | 6,18 | 6,81 | 7,74 |

TABLEAU 1

Les variations de $T(N)$ et $C(j)$ sont représentées sur la figure 2. On peut faire quelques commentaires. Le taux moyen d'utilisation de l'UC est, avec une fréquence d'arrivée de 3 transactions par seconde :

$$U'_1 = 7,37 \text{ ms} \times 17 \times \frac{3}{1000} = 0,376.$$

Le Tableau T1 montre que 3 régions sont nécessaires.

Le rapport $U'_1 / U'_1 = U'_2 / U_2$ représente le pourcentage de capacité consommée ; la réserve de puissance est $1 - U'_1 / U_1$. ($U'_2 = 40 \text{ ms} \times 17 \times \frac{3}{1000} \times \frac{1}{33} = 0,062$).

Le nombre moyen de régions actives est : $N_{RA} = N \, U'_1 / U_1$.

Le nombre maximal de transactions traitées a pour valeur : $\lambda_{MAX} = 3 \, U_1 / U'_1$.

Ces résultats sont indiqués dans le tableau T1. Remarquons que $\lambda_{MAX}$ croît lentement à partir de sept régions.

On adopte couramment un coefficient de pointe égal à 1,5 : la charge à l'heure de pointe est 1,5 fois la charge moyenne de la journée ; la charge aux jours de pointe est 1,5 fois la charge des joursnormaux. D'où :
- charge à l'heure de pointe : $3 \times 1,5 = 4,5$ transactions par seconde
- charge à l'heure de pointe d'un jour de pointe : $3 \times 1,5 \times 1,5 = 6,75$ transactions par seconde.

Le Tableau T1 indique qu'il faut au moins 4 à 5 régions aux heures de pointe (pour 4,5 transactions/sec) et 7 à 8 régions aux heures de pointe pendant une journée de pointe. Le taux d'utilisation de l'UC dans ce dernier cas est :

$$0,376 \times 1,5 \times 1,5 = 0,846.$$

En admettant qu'on peut accepter un long temps de réponse résultant de la création de 10 régions, le système peut supporter un accroissement de charge de $0,972/0,846 = 1,15$, soit 15 %.

Supposons que le taux de croissance prévu par les usagers du système est de 20 % par an ; il faudra faire installer une UC plus rapide dans 6 mois si l'on veut écouler le trafic de pointe dans le délai prévu. Pendant le trafic normal l'UC peut traiter d'autres travaux moins prioritaires et demandant de préférence moins d'E/S ; les fichiers qu'ils utilisent doivent être rattachés à d'autres canaux que ceux réservés à la base de données.

CONCLUSION

Il faut remarquer que les modèles présentés dans cet article ne sont que des modèles approchés et de ce fait sont destinés à l'usage des praticiens à qui ils pourraient être utiles. Cet article vise un autre but, celui d'exposer le problème des priorités tel qu'il existe dans certains systèmes. Les solutions plus élégantes, basées sur des fondements mathématiques plus solides, sont évidemment très attendues. La formulation d'un modèle qui traite globalement les deux types de priorités, la priorité de sélection et la priorité de traitement, sera certes difficile et conduira vraisemblablement à des équations complexes. Mais il existe certainement d'autres approches meilleures que celle préconisée ici, même si l'on se contente de solutions approchées.
Pour terminer, il est nécessaire de préciser que d'autres disciplines de "scheduling priority" de IMS/VS ne sont pas abordées dans cet article.

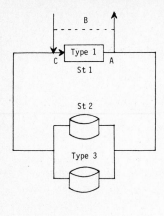

Figure 1

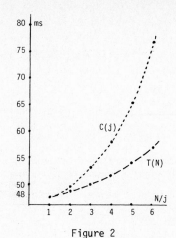

Figure 2

REFERENCES :

[1] Avi-Itzhak, B., Heyman, D.P., Approximate queueing model for multiprogramming computer systems, Oper. Research 21 n° 6 (1973) 1212-1230.
[2] Baskett, F.K., Chandy, M., Muntz R.R., Palacios, F., Open, closed and mixed networks of queues with different classes of customers, Journal of ACM 22 n° 2 (1975) 248-260.
[3] Buzen, J., Queueing network models of multiprogramming, Ph. D. thesis, Division of Engineering and Applied Science, Harvard University, Cambridge, Mass. (1971).
[4] Chiu, W., Dumont, D., Wood, R., Performance analysis of multiprogrammed computer system, IBM Journal of Research and Development 19 n° 3 (1975) 263-271.
[5] Cyspser, R.J., Communications architecture for distributed systems (Addison Wesley publishing company 1978).
[6] Dinh, V., Théorie élémentaire des files d'attente, Cours de l'Ecole Supérieure d'Electricité.
[7] Fayden, J.H., Cullum, P.G., Hobgood, W.S., Systems network architecture, IBM Systems Journal 15 n° 1 (1976) 4-80.
[8] Fry, J.P., Sibley, E.H., Evolution of data management systems, ACM Computing Survey 8 n° 1 (1976) 7-42.
[9] Gaver, D.P., Shelder, G.S., Processor utilization in multiprogramming systems via diffusion approximations, Oper. Research 21 (1973) 569-576.
[10] Gelenbe, E., Muntz, R.R., Probabilistic models of computer systems - Part I, Acta Informatica 7 (Springer Verlag, 1976) 35-60.
[11] Gelenbe, E., Réseaux de files d'attente (Editions Hommes et Techniques, 1980).
[12] Gordon, W.J., Newell, G.F., Closed queueing systems with exponeltial servers, Oper. Research 15 (1967) 254-265.
[13] Jackson, J.R., Jobshop like queueing systems, Management Science 10 n° 1 (1963)
[14] Kingman, J.F.C., On queue in heavy traffic, Royal Statistical Society series B 24 (1962) 383-392.
[15] Lewis, P.A.W., Shelder, G.S., A cyclic queue model of system overhead in multiprogrammed computer systems, Journal of ACM 18 n° 2 (1971) 199-220.
[16] McGee, W.C., Information management system, IBM Syst. Journ. 16 n° 2 (1977) 84-168.
[17] Pujolle, G., Soula, C., A study of flows in queueing networks and an approximation method for solution, Performance of computer systems, M. Arato, A. Butrimenko, E. Gelenbe (Eds) (North Holland publishing company, 1979).

Performance of Data Communication Systems
and their Applications, G. Pujolle (ed.)
© North-Holland Publishing Company, 1981

# Multiple Resource Systems Maximum Mean Throughput Analysis

*E. Arthurs*
*B. W. Stuck*

Bell Laboratories
Murray Hill, New Jersey 07974

## ABSTRACT

There are two fundamental methods for improving the traffic handling capabilities of digital systems:

- speed--making sure that each subsystem executes its work as quickly as possible

- concurrency--attempting to have as many tasks executed in parallel as possible

In this report we focus on the second avenue, concurrency. We present a state description or model of transaction processing that requires different resources at different stages of execution. We then attempt to analyze the best possible concurrency that can be obtained, for a given transaction mix and a given complement of resources. In the approach used here, a linear programming problem must be solved. The result is the maximum mean throughput rate of completing work in the system. Examples given to show the power of the approach include

- performance impact due to transaction requiring serial and concurrently shared resources

- multiple processor and multiple memory interference

- link level flow control over local networks or over space satellite links

## 1. Introduction

At the heart of modern digital systems is the issue of allocation of *finite* sets of resources among competing tasks. This is a vital factor in determining the traffic handling characteristics of any such system. Here we present a popularization of one technique for calculating the maximum mean throughput rate of completing work in systems where jobs require multiple different types of resources at each stage of execution. The approach developed here was suggested by measurements on actual systems, and indeed one of its merits is that it can in many cases be directly related to actual data on actual systems. The method has undoubtedly been used by workers in the field for years, in one guise or another; the first reference in the open literature that we can find is due to Omahen(1977). Our goal here is to point out the power and potential wide applicability of this approach, nothing more.

The abstraction we deal with here is as follows. Different types of jobs are executed on a given system; we will fix the mix or fraction of each type of job that is executed, and vary the total mean arrival rate of jobs. Each job consists of one or more stages of execution which we call a task. Each task requires multiple resources for its execution; we will specify the mean amount of each type of resource required for each type of task. A final ingredient is the policy for allocating resources: resources can be used serially, or shared (e.g., reentrant code shared by several tasks in a common area of memory, or a processor multiplexed amongst several tasks). Given all of these ingredients, our goal is to calculate the largest possible mean rate of completing work as a function of the job mix, mean resources consumed at each stage of execution, and scheduling policy.

Two ideas are at the foundations of this work: the notion of *state* of the system, along with the notion of the fraction of time, averaged over a suitably long time interval, that the system spends in each state, and the second notion due to Little (1961) that the mean number in the system must equal the mean arrival rate of work multiplied by the mean time in system, for each type of transaction. These two ideas allow us to attempt to calculate the *maximum mean throughput rate* of completing work by posing this calculation as a linear programming problem, which is a problem that has been dealt with elsewhere and at length.

There are two fundamental methods for improving the performance of a given system, speed (reducing the execution time of a task) and concurrency or parallelism (executing more than one task simultaneously); the approach presented here is a systematic exposition of how to exploit concurrency in digital systems.

In order to allow this report to have as wide an audience as possible, we will begin with a motivating example, move on to a precise statement of the model and problem and its solution, and then dwell on several examples at length to show the power of this approach. The precise problem statement and its solution can be skipped by those so inclined. We stress that the area of delay characteristics for multiple resource systems executing several types of transactions will require much more work than is at hand at present; cf the amount of work required to obtain even the simplest characterization of delay for special simplified problems (Omahen, 1977).

We begin our study with an example, a system consisting of two processors, one memory partition, and two peripheral processors each of which can access two auxiliary storage units. We assume there are N tasks present at time zero, and they require T time units to be completely executed. The state of system is given by

[1]    one processor active

[2]    one peripheral processor busy doing input

[3]    one peripheral processor busy doing output

[4]    two peripheral processors busy, one doing input and one doing output

[5]    one peripheral processor busy doing input and the processor busy

[6]    one peripheral processor busy doing output and the main processor busy

We denote by $F(K)$ the fraction of time, over the interval of duration T, that the system is in state $K=1,...,6$. We see that the fraction of time the system is in *one* of these states must sum to unity:

$$\sum_{K=1}^{6} F(K) = 1$$

Furthermore, by definition, we see that

$$0 \le F(K) \le 1 \qquad K=1,...,6$$

The mean throughput rate of completing work, denoted by $\lambda$, is given by

$$\lambda = \frac{N}{T} \quad transactions/unit\ time$$

Finally, we use Little's Law. The mean number of tasks in the system in the input phase are given by

$$\lambda\ TINPUT = mean\ number\ in\ input$$

where *TINPUT* is the mean time required to execute an input phase of a task with no contention. On the other hand, states 2, 4, and 5 are the only states involving input, and since only one task can be in memory, we see

$$\lambda\ TINPUT = F(2) + F(4) + F(5)$$

To do output, only states 3, 4, and 6 are involved, and we see

$$\lambda\ TOUTPUT = F(3) + F(4) + F(6)$$

where *TOUTPUT* is the mean time required for the output phase of a task with no contention. Finally, for processing, only states 1, 5, and 6 are involved, and so

$$\lambda\ TPROC = F(1) + F(5) + F(6)$$

where *TPROC* is the mean time required for the processing phase of a task with no contention. Finally, our goal is to maximize the mean throughput rate, by varying the fraction of time spent in various states, subject to all of the above constraints:

$$\max_{F(K),K=1,...,6} \lambda = maximum\ mean\ throughput\ rate$$

This is posed as a *linear programming problem* (Dantzig, 1963) because this class of problems is amenable to algorithmic methods for approximating numerical solutions involving thousands of states and constraints. This type of problem is stated as

$$maximize\ (C(1)X(1)+...+C(N)X(N))$$

subject to

$$A(1,J)X(J) + \cdots + A(J,N) = B(J) \quad J=1,...,M$$

$$A(1,J)X(1) + \cdots + A(J,N)X(N) \le B(J) \quad J=M+11,...,N$$

where $C(1),...,C(N))$ are costs associated with the various $X(J)$ and

$$0 \le X(J) \quad J=1,...,N$$

By inspection of the above equations for our simple illustrative model, we see that

$$\lambda \le \min\left[\frac{1}{TPROC}, \frac{1}{TINPUT}, \frac{1}{TOUTPUT}\right]$$

These are single resource maximum mean throughput rate upper bounds. On the other hand, if we add the three inequalities gotten by Little's Law, we find

$$1 + F(4) + F(5) + F(6) = \lambda(TINPUT + TOUTPUT + TPROC)$$

In order to maximize the mean throughput rate, we must schedule work so that

$$F(4) + F(5) + F(6) = 1 \quad \rightarrow \lambda = \frac{2}{TPROC + TINPUT + TOUTPUT}$$

Combining all of this, we see

$$\lambda \le \min\left[\frac{1}{TPROC}, \frac{2}{TPROC + TINPUT + TOUTPUT}\right]$$

This can be rewritten as

$$\lambda \le \frac{1}{\frac{1}{2}max[TPROC + max(TPROC,TINPUT + TOUTPUT)]}$$

As a check on this, suppose that

$$TPROC \ge TINPUT + TOUTPUT$$

and hence

$$\lambda = \frac{1}{TPROC}$$

If we substitute into the three relationships from Little's Law, we find

$$F(2) + F(4) + F(5) = \frac{TINPUT}{TPROC}$$

$$F(3) + F(4) + F(5) = \frac{TOUTPUT}{TPROC}$$

$$F(1) + F(5) + F(6) = 1$$

The last equation implies that

$$F(2) = F(3) = F(4) = 0$$

and hence that

$$F(5) = \frac{TINPUT}{TPROC} \quad F(6) = \frac{TOUTPUT}{TPROC}$$

$$F(1) = 1 - \frac{TINPUT + TOUTPUT}{TPROC}$$

What is this condition? It says that we should schedule work on the system to maximize the mean throughput rate such that the fraction of time the processor is busy is unity, i.e., the processor is completely busy. Furthermore, we should schedule work according to the time required without contention to do input, output, and processing, according to the above percentages. This is a very powerful technique, and has many implications. For example, if we measure a system and find out that we are not scheduling work in this way, we might change the scheduler.

We leave the other case,

$$maximum\ mean\ throughput\ rate = \frac{2}{TINPUT + TOUTPUT + TPROC}$$

$$TPROC \le TINPUT + TOUTPUT$$

as an exercise for the reader, to fix ideas.

## 2. Description of Model

The ingredients in the general model are as follows:

- I--the number of resource types
- *RES*--the available resource vector--$(RES(1),...,RES(I))$ (both physical and logical resources are included here)
- J--the number of job classes
- $F(K)$--the fraction of jobs that are type $K=1,...,J$
- L--the number of types of job steps
- *TRES*$(K) = (TRES(1,K),...,TRES(I,K))$--the vector of resources for each type of job step
- $TPROC(K),K=1,...,L$--the mean time to finish job K
- $NSTEP(K,M);K=1,...,J;M=1,...,L$--the mean number of steps of type K that are in job step M
- *NMIX*--the number of feasible mixes
- $KMIX(R,M);R=1,...,NMIX;M=1,...,L$--the number of type M job steps in mix R

Finally, we must describe how resource I can be scheduled. For example, it can be serially used, or multiplexed among a set of tasks, or a combination of these two. We describe this via the function $SCHED(R,K)$, which involves the mix $R$ and the job step $K$:

$$\sum_{K=1}^{L} SCHED(R,K)KMIX((K,R)TRES(Q,K) \le RES(Q) \quad \text{for all } R,Q$$

We denote by $F(STATE)$ the fraction of time the system is in a given state, denoted $STATE$. We wish to maximize the mean throughput rate, subject to

- the fraction of time the system is in any state sums to unity
- the fraction of time the system is in a given state is lower bounded by zero and upper bounded by one
- Little's law for the mean number in system for each transaction type

$$\sum_{K=1}^{M} F(K)KRES(I,K)SCHED(R,K) = \lambda \sum_{K=1}^{J} F(K)NRES(K,R)T(K) \quad R=1,...,L$$

The proof of this assertion is two fold (Dantzig, 1963): first, a variety of techniques can be used to convert this formulation to a linear programming formulation, and second, existence of at least one solution follows, because the fraction of time the system is in any one state must lie between zero and one, and the solution space is finite and bounded.

This can now be handled via linear programming packages that are widely available to explore quantitatively the consequences of different design choices.

At the crux of the analysis is the assertion that the mean number of jobs in the system divided by the maximum number of jobs in the system equals the mean time in system of a job divided by the maximum time in system of a job (Conway, Maxwell, Miller, p. 16, 1967), and is independent of

- the number, kind, or arrangement of resources in any way
- the nature of the jobs, their routing over the machines, their processing times, or any *a priori* knowledge of processing time
- other activities of the processors, such as the execution of other jobs before, during, and after the arrival of a given set of jobs
- the resource allocation policy

To see why this is so, we assume that all jobs are present at time zero, and that these jobs are executed and leave the system at time epochs denoted by $C_1, C_2,..., C_N$ and so forth, i.e., at each of these epochs one job leaves. Since the number of jobs in the system changes value at only N+1 points in time, we see that the integral of the number of jobs in the system is given by

$$\int_{0}^{C_N} \tilde{N}(t)dt = NC_1 + (N-1)(C_2 - C_1) + \cdots + [N - (N-1)][C_N - C_{N-1}] = \sum_{k=1}^{N} C_K$$

The ratio of the average number of jobs in the system divided by the maximum number of jobs in the system equals the ratio of the mean time in system to the maximum time in system:

$$\frac{\sum_{K=1}^{N} C_K}{C_N} = N \frac{E(C)}{C_N} \rightarrow \frac{E(N)}{N} = \frac{E(C)}{C_N}$$

which was what was claimed above.

It is unknown at present what gain (if any) is to be had by adopting the full flexibility inherent in mulplexing a set of resources amongst a set of tasks via a policy *SCHED*(.,.) Put differently, the benefit in using scheduling policies other than serially reusable ones for a given resource have not been quantified within the framework presented here. It may well be that there is **no** advantage to using multiplexing strategies other than to run one job at a time in order to maximize the mean throughput rate; on the other hand, this may significantly impact the delay statistics of a job!

Finally, the enumeration of all system states is a matter requiring combinatorial and algebraic analysis. Preliminary indications are that straightforward enumeration techniques may not be feasible for reasons of storage and computation cost.

### 3. One Processor and One Disk

The first example is a system that handles transactions submitted from terminals or other computers elsewhere. Each transaction requires some processing, then some disk access time, then some more processing, then some more disk access time, and so forth, until the transaction is finished. Each job requires a mean amount of *TPROC* and *TDISK* time on the processor and disk respectively. The system state is to a pair (I,J) where I denotes the number of jobs either queued or running on the processor, and J denotes the number of jobs either queued or making use of the disk. From Little's Law, we see that the mean number of tasks on the processor is equal to the mean arrival time multiplied by the mean time spent using the processor:

$$\sum_{I}\sum_{J} I \; F(I,J) = \lambda TPROC$$

Similarly, the mean number of tasks on the disk is equal to the mean arrival rate multiplied by the mean time spent using the disk:

$$\sum_{I}\sum_{J} J \; F(I,J) = \lambda TDISK$$

Finally, we must be in some state:

$$\sum_{I}\sum_{J} F(I,J) = 1$$

Since neither the processor nor the disk can be used by more than one transaction at a time, we see that the allowable states are simply (0,0), (1,0), and (0,1):

$$F(1,0) + F(1,1) = \lambda TPROC \quad\quad F(0,1) + F(1,1) = \lambda TDISK$$

Two scheduling policies come to mind: either run a transaction to completion, so called *single thread* execution, before letting the next transaction start execution, or multiplex the processor and disk amongst transactions. For the first case, the state (1,1) is not allowed, and we see

$$F(1,0) = \lambda TPROC \quad\quad F(0,1) = \lambda TDISK \quad\quad F(1,0) + F(0,1) = 1$$

Combining all this, we see

$$\lambda_{single \; thread} = \frac{1}{TPROC + TDISK}$$

If we allow multiplexing of the processor and disk amongst transactions, then the state (1,1) will maximize the mean throughput rate, and we should spend zero time in the states (1,0) and (0,1):

$$\lambda_{multiplexing} = \frac{1}{max(TPROC,TDISK)}$$

The ratio of the these two maximum mean throughput rates is an indication of the gain due to scheduling:

$$\frac{\lambda_{multiplexing}}{\lambda_{single\ thread}} = \frac{TPROC + TDISK}{max\,(TPROC,TDISK)} \leq 2$$

This gain can be at most two, no matter what *TPROC* or *TDISK* are! This is also called the *degree of multiprogramming* and the two cases we have examined are degree of multiprogramming one and two, for single thread and multiplexing operation, respectively.

The reader is encouraged to extend this analysis to multiple processors and multiple disks in order to gain some appreciation for the power of this analytic technique.

### 4. Serially Reusable versus Concurrently Shared Resources

In many applications, some resources must be used serially, one task at a time, and others can be shared simultaneously or in parallel with many tasks. An example of this is a single processor that executes two sets of programs, one set comprising an operating system, the second set comprising application programs. The operating system must necessarily do certain so called house keeping tasks serially (e.g., controlling access to tables and files), while other tasks can in principal be done in parallel. For application programs executing on OS/360, typically 40% of the processor time was found to be devoted to serially reusable resources, and with a great deal of effort this might be reduced to 20% of the processor time (Amdahl, 1967). This suggests that identical multiple processor configurations with one processor devoted to serial tasks and P devoted to the parallel tasks might find little benefit in going to more than four processors handling parallel work under the most optimistic of scenarios. Furthermore, since the serial tasks are a fundamental bottleneck, every effort should be made to make these execute as quickly as possible.

Here is a somewhat more quantitative approach to these intuitive notions. A job consists of two tasks. The first task must be done using a serially reusable resource (e.g., a critical region of the system), and will execute in time *TSER*. The second task can be done concurrently, and requires *TCON* units of time to be executed. We might think of the serial portion being the work associated with classifying a task, readying it for subsequent execution, while the second portion might involve execution using a read only storage for example.

We assume there are P processors total for our resource vector. The system states are given by an ordered pair, with the first index denoting the number in execution and requiring the serially reusable resource, while the second index denotes the number in execution and required the shared resource:

- $(0,K), K = 0, 1, ..., P$ --no task requiring the serially reusable resource, and up to P tasks using the shared resource
- $(1,K), K = 0, 1, ..., P\text{-}1$ --one task requiring the serially reusable resource, and up to P-1 tasks using the shared resource

The mean number of tasks in execution and requiring the serially reusable resource is given by

$$\sum_{K=0}^{P-1} F(1,K) = \lambda TSER$$

while the mean number of tasks in execution and requiring the shared resource is given by

$$\sum_{K=1}^{P-1} \frac{K}{P} [F(1,K) + F(0,K)] + F(0,P) = \lambda \frac{TCON}{P}$$

We note the obvious upper bound

$$\lambda_{max} \leq min\left[\frac{1}{TSER}, \frac{P}{TSER + TCON}\right]$$

From the problem definition, some reflection shows that if and only if

$$\frac{TCON}{TSER} + 1 \leq P$$

then the serially reusable resource will be a bottleneck, always busy, so

$$\sum_{K=0}^{P-1} F(1,K) = 11$$

and thus we see

$$\lambda_{max} = \frac{1}{TSER} \qquad P \geq \frac{TCON}{TSER} + 1$$

For the other case, the shared resource is the bottleneck, and

$$\lambda = \frac{P}{TSER + TCON} \qquad P < \frac{TCON}{TSER} + 1$$

and so we summarize:

$$\lambda_{max} = \begin{cases} \dfrac{P}{TSER + TCON} & P \le \dfrac{TCON}{TSER} + 1 \\[2ex] \dfrac{1}{TSER} & P > \dfrac{TCON}{TSER} + 1 \end{cases}$$

with this plotted in Figure 1.

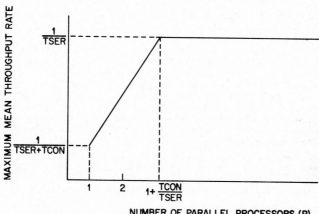

Figure 1

## 5. Multiple Processor and Multiple Memory Interactions

We now discuss one example in great detail, to illustrate the power and utility of this technique.

### 5.1 Two Processors and Two Memory Partitions

Two types of jobs must be executed by a system. Each type of job involves loading the job into memory and then executing it. We have two processors and M bytes of memory. One type of job, called *small*, requires (M/2) bytes of memory and is executed without contention in *TS* time units on one processor. The other type of job, called *big*, requires M bytes of memory, and is executed without contention in *TB* time units on one processor. N jobs total are present at time zero, with *FS* and *FB* denoting the fraction of small and big jobs in the mix. There are three system states:

[1]  one small job in main memory

[2]  one big job in main memory

[3]  two small jobs in main memory

The fraction of time the system is in these states is given by $F(K), K=1,2,3$. The constraints are

$$F(1) + F(2) + F(3) = 1$$
$$0 \le F(K) \le 1 \quad K=1,2,3$$

Finally, we must use Little's Law. The mean number of small jobs in the system is given by

$$F(1) + 2 F(3) = \lambda FS \times TS$$

The mean number of big jobs in the system is given by

$$F(2) = \lambda FB \times TB$$

If we simply add up these last two equations, we see

$$1 + F(3) = \lambda(FS \times TS + FB \times TB)$$

and hence to maximize $\lambda$ we must maximize $F(3)$. We can do this by choosing $F(1) = 0$ and thus we find

$$F(2) = \lambda FB \times TB$$

$$F(3) = \tfrac{1}{2}\lambda FS \times TS$$

and finally

$$\text{maximum mean throughput rate} = \frac{1}{\tfrac{1}{2}FS \times TS + FB \times TB}$$

Two scheduling rules will achieve this maximum mean throughput rate:

- Run two small jobs at highest priority, one big job at next highest priority, one small job at lowest priority
- Run one big job at highest priority, two small jobs at next highest priority, one small job at lowest priority

The delay characteristics for these two policies could be radically different. For example, if the small jobs run much faster than the big jobs, then running the big jobs at highest priority will force the small jobs to be delayed for possibly quite long time intervals, while the reverse priority ordering will allow the small jobs to run quickly while the long jobs (which take a long time anyway) will be delayed. which involved two processors and two memory partitions. We wish to see the impact on the maximum mean throughput rate as we add memory partitions and processors.

### 5.2 Three Memory Partitions and Two Processors

The total resource vector $RES$ is given by

$$RES = [number\ of\ processors, number\ of\ memory\ partitions] = [2,3]$$

The resources required by the big and small jobs are

$$RES(BIG) = [1,2] \quad RES(SMALL) = [1,1]$$

The states the system can be in are summarized in the table below:

| System State Space | | |
|---|---|---|
| Index | Small | Big |
| 0 | 0 | 0 |
| 1 | 1 | 0 |
| 2 | 2 | 0 |
| 3 | 3 | 0 |
| 4 | 0 | 1 |
| 5 | 1 | 1 |

We denote by $F(K)$ the fraction of time, averaged over a suitably long time interval, that the system is in each of these states, with the constraints that

$$\sum_{K=0}^{5} F(K) = 1 \quad 0 \leq F(K) \leq 1 \quad K = 0,1,2,3,4,5$$

Using Little's Law, we see that the mean number of small jobs in the system is

$$\lambda \times FS \times TS = F(1) + 2F(2) + 2F(3) + F(5)$$

while the mean number of big jobs in the system is

$$\lambda \times FB \times TB = F(4) + F(5)$$

In order to maximize $\lambda$, we should maximize $F(5)$. We guess how to do this by assuming $F(3)=0$ and then check its' consequences for self consistency:

$$\lambda \times FB \times TB = F(4) \quad \rightarrow$$

$$\lambda \times FS \times TS = F(1) + 2F(2) + 2F(3) + \lambda \times FB \times TB$$

We next assume that $F(1)=0$ guessing that this state will be highly unlikely (zero probability!) under heavy loading:

$$\lambda \times (FS \times TS - FB \times TB) = 2F(2) + 2F(3)$$

Now we see that there are basically two states:

- States 2,3--both processors busy with two small jobs
- State 4--both processors busy with one big and one small job

The fraction of time we are in these two macrostates must sum to unity. If $FS \times TS$ is smaller than $FB \times TB$ then we see the fraction of time we are in the state of both processors running two small jobs must be lower bounded by zero, and hence

$$maximum \ mean \ throughput \ rate = \frac{1}{FB \times TB} \qquad F(4) = 1 \qquad FS \times TS < FB \times TB$$

On the other hand, if $FS \times TS$ is bigger than $FB \times TB$ then the maximum mean throughput rate is given by

$$maximum \ mean \ throughput \ rate = \frac{2}{FS \times TS - FB \times TB} \qquad F(2) + F(3) = 1$$

provided

$$FS \times TS > FB \times TB$$

Combining all this, we see that

$$maximum \ mean \ throughput \ rate = \frac{1}{FB \times TB + (1/2)max(0, FS \times TS - FB \times TB)}$$

Note that the maximum mean throughput rate depends on the scheduling policy! This is different than a single resource system, where if each job requires a mean of $TPROC$ time units then the maximum mean throughput rate is simply $1/TPROC$. The policy for achieving this maximum mean throughput rate is to always run one big job if its available and fill in the rest with small jobs.

### 5.3 Three Memory Partitions and Three Processors

The modification to three memory partitions and three partitions is now straightforward. The table below summarizes the system state space:

| System State Space | | |
|---|---|---|
| **Index** | **Small** | **Big** |
| 0 | 0 | 0 |
| 1 | 1 | 0 |
| 2 | 2 | 0 |
| 3 | 3 | 0 |
| 4 | 0 | 1 |
| 5 | 1 | 1 |

Using Little's Law, we see the mean number of small jobs in the system is

$$\lambda \times FS \times TS = F(1) + 2F(2) + 3F(3) + F(5)$$

while the mean number of big jobs in the system is

$$\lambda \times FB \times TB = F(4) + F(5)$$

Anticipating our solution, we guess $F(1) = F(2) = F(4) = 0$ and see if this is self consistent:

$$\lambda \times FB \times TB = F(5) \qquad F(4) = 0$$

$$\lambda \times FS \times TS = 3F(3) + F(5) \qquad F(1) = F(2) = F(4)$$

Proceeding as above, we see

$$maximum \ mean \ throughput \ rate = \frac{1}{FB \times TB + (1/3)max(0, FS \times TS - 2 \times FB \times TB)}$$

Again, the maximum mean throughput rate is load dependent, and the policy achieving this maximum is to run one large one when available and fill in with whatever small jobs are left.

Note that if $FS \times TS < FB \times TB$ then adding more processors need not help. On the other hand, if the converse is true, then the maximum mean throughput rate increases by $(3/2)$!

## 6. Link Level Flow Control

We wish to illustrate the flexibility of this technique in a very common situation, assessing flow control strategies for a data link. The first case is actually the quantification of a notion known in the processor design area as overlapped fetch and execution of instructions, while the general problem dealt with here is that of pipelining or executing a transaction on a successive chain of processors.

### 6.1 Zero Link Propagation Delay

We begin with the case where the link propagation is assumed zero; this will be met in practice if the time required by the transmitter and receiver separately to process a message are much greater than the time for a message to propagate from the transmitter to the receiver or vice versa.

The resources are a transmitter, a receiver, and a buffer capable of holding M messages. Hence, the resource vector is given by

$$RES = [\ number\ of\ transmitters,\ number\ of\ receivers,\ number\ of\ buffers\ ] = [1\ 1\ M\ ]$$

We assume there is one type of message. A message is first processed at the transmitter, then buffered for subsequent processing by the receiver. Hence the resource vector associated with the transmitter side is given by:

$$RESOURCES\,(TRANSMITTER) = [1\ 0\ 1]$$

while for the receiver side this is given by

$$RESOURCES\,(RECEIVER) = [0\ 1\ 1]$$

The mean processing times for the transmitter and receiver are $TRANS$ and $REC$ respectively. The feasible states are four: either none or one at the transmitter and receiver. More formally, if we let (i,j) denote the ordered pair with $i=0,1$ denoting the number in the transmission phase and $j=0,1$ in the reception phase, then we see that

$$F(0,0) + F(1,0) + F(0,1) + F(1,1) = 1$$

where $F(i,j)$ is the fraction of time the system is in state (i,j), averaged over a suitably long time interval. The mean number in the transmitter phase is given by

$$\lambda\ TRANS = F(1,0) + F(1,1)$$

while the mean number in the receiver phase is given by

$$\lambda\ REC = F(0,1) + F(1,1)$$

The utilization of the transmitter is simply the fraction of time it is busy:

$$transmitter\ utilization = F(1,0) + F(1,1)$$

while the utilization of the receiver is given by

$$receiver\ utilization = F(0,1) + F(1,1)$$

We are now ready to solve the particular problem at hand.

For a single buffer, $M=1$, we see $F(1,1)=0$, and hence

$$\lambda = \frac{1}{TRANS + REC}$$

For two or more buffers, $M>1$, we see that to maximize the mean throughput rate, we must maximize $F(1,1)$. If we examine the extreme points, $F(1,0)=0$ and $F(0,1)=0$, it is straightforward to see that

$$\lambda = \min\left[\frac{1}{TRANS}\ ,\ \frac{1}{REC}\right]$$

We now summarize:

a.  For one buffer at the receiver

$$maximum\ mean\ throughput\ rate = \frac{1}{TRANS + REC}$$

b.  For two buffers at the receiver

$$maximum\ mean\ throughput\ rate = \frac{1}{max\,(TRANS,REC)}$$

c.  For infinite buffering at the receiver

$$maximum\ mean\ throughput\ rate\ = \frac{1}{max\,(TRANS,REC)}$$

For the case of equal processing at the transmitter and receiver, going from single to double buffering can double the maximum mean throughput rate, while going to infinite buffering gains nothing relative to double buffering in terms of maximum mean throughput rate.

For the case of a factor of ten speed mismatch in the transmitter and/or receiver, we see that going from single to double buffering can increase the maximum mean throughput rate by (11/10) or ten per cent, while going from double to infinite buffering results in the same net gain.

The reader is encouraged to extend these notions to allow for multiple transaction types, e.g., control and data messages with a fixed mix or proportion of each type but with different processing time requirements. The impact of dedicating buffers to each type versus sharing a common pool of buffers can also be addressed in a straightforward manner.

### 6.2 Nonzero Link Propagation Delay

Either the transmitter, the receiver, or the link (i.e., the propagation time between the transmitter-receiver pair) may be a bottleneck. The propagation time between the transmitter and receiver is not a fundamental bottleneck, because we can overcome this bottleneck by clever use of concurrency or scheduling by choosing a larger and larger high water mark, i.e., more and more buffering. On the other hand, the time required by the transmitter and by the receiver to process a message are in fact fundamental bottlenecks that no amount of concurrency or scheduling can surmount. The fundamental cycle that will describe the maximum mean throughput rate of messages is that the transmitter must process H-1 messages while the rest of the system handles one message (over the transmitter to receiver link, receiver processing, and an acknowledgement via the receiver to transmitter link).

$$(H-1)\ TRANS\ \geq\ TRANS-REC + REC + REC-TRANS$$

where $TRANS-REC$ and $REC-TRANS$ are the link propagation times from the transmitter to receiver and receiver to transmitter, respectively. When H is chosen sufficiently large that this is true, then

$$maximum\ mean\ throughput\ rate\ = \frac{1}{max\,(TRANS,REC)}$$

When this condition is not satisfied, the maximum mean throughput rate must increase linearly with the window or high water mark, i.e., the amount of buffering available is the limiting bottleneck. Note that this allows for different propagation delays (e.g., by satellite versus by land) over different directions. Figure 2 plots the maximum mean throughput rate versus the high water mark or window: two regimes are evident, one region when the maximum mean throughput rate grows linearly in the window size and the link is the bottleneck, and the other region when the maximum mean throughput rate is constant or independent of window size, and the transmitter or receiver is the bottleneck.

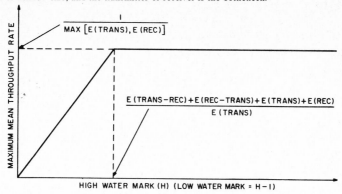

SINGLE LINK FLOW CONTROL

Figure 2

Performance of Data Communication Systems
and their Applications, G. Pujolle (ed.)
© North-Holland Publishing Company, 1981


# AN OPERATING SYSTEM FOR A MICROCOMPUTER NETWORK


G. Neumann

*Forschungsinstitut für Funk und Mathematik
5307 Wachtberg-Werthhoven, Germany


A microcomputer network is presented which consists of
loosely-coupled multiprocessor nodes to support communicating sequential processes working at a task. Each node of the
network is controlled by a local operating system with local
authority only. The local operating system is conceived
to permit parallel access of local processors to system routines. In this way high efficiency of parallel computation is
extended from process level to system level. The local operating systems manage the communication of parallel processes
in the network without using global variables or a common storage for the exchange of messages. As a tool for efficient communication of a process with several partner processes the multiple communication is introduced.


## I.    INTRODUCTION

The FFM* microcomputer network MICON is an experimental, local, loosely-coupled
network. Its intention is to expand applications in the wide area  of industrial
process control, which is so far dominated by central computers, to distributed
computing.As MICON is a research project for structural problems of such networks
it is neutral with respect to applications. As a unitized construction, each
node of MICON is built up from only a few building blocks (node elements). Depending on the application each node will be provided with a different number of
memories and of processors of different types. These are connected by the internal bus of their node. The connection of nodes in the network is accomplished by
processors of type coupling processor. A coupling processor differs from a conventional processor in that it has access to the internal busses of two nodes (a detailed description will be given in section II). Therefore MICON can be easily
extended by adding further nodes to the network. The number of nodes and their
interconnection (chain, ring, star, or other networks) can be arbitrarily
chosen (figure 1).

MICON had been built to support communicating sequential processes working at a
common task. The distribution of these processes in the network enables a high
parallelity and efficiency of process computation. According to the division of
the network into functionally autonomous nodes the network operating system is
divided into identical local operating systems (LOS) without a central controller. So the physical distribution of the network has its counterpart in the
logical distribution of the operating software (terms used are defined in /1/ ).
Each node is controlled by a LOS with local authority only. Process scheduling
and interprocess communication are handled autonomously by each LOS. The identity of the LOSs supports an easy extension of the network. At first, during the
bootstrap phase of a node, one of the local processors determines the local
physical equipment and notes it in identically pre-defined LOS lists. After that
start phase there is no hierarchy concerning local processors. In contrast to

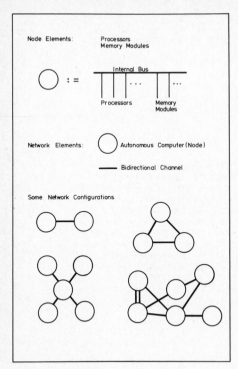

Figure 1
Structure of MICON

the FFM multi-computer network /2/ ,
a forerunner of MICON, where only
one distinguished processor could
work at the operating system the LOS
permits all of the local processors
not only the parallel processing of
user processes but also parallel
processing of the LOS itself. How the
parallel access of several processors onto the LOS determines its
construction is the object of this
paper.
In section II the hardware of MICON
is briefly introduced as far as it
is necessary for the understanding
of the following sections. The
operating software is described in
section III. Process scheduling
and the protection of operational
lists against multiple access of
several processors are discussed.
As the MICON software is message-
oriented, section IV exclusively
deals with the communication between
processes. The symmetric and asymmetric communication and the telegram communication are described.
For an efficient communication of
one process with several partner processes the multiple communication
is introduced.

## II.   HARDWARE OF MICON

The hardware of MICON permits parallel processing of the nodes in the network
and of the processors in each node. Each node can selectively be provided with
up to 16 (16-bit) processors and memory modules which define a local common
memory with a maximal address width of 16 bits. The processors had been built
from microprogrammable microprocessor slices of the AMD 2900 type /3/. According
to the microprogram /4/ a processor can be used as

                    conventional processor or
                    I/O-Controller or
                    processor with a private memory or
                    coupling processor.

Conventional processors have only one port to the internal bus which is used to
access data and instructions from the local memory.
Each processor of the three other types is equipped with two ports. The first
port enables it to use the internal bus in a manner similar to conventional
processors. But the second port has a number of connection possibilities
(figure 2):

a) to an I/O - device or
b) to a private memory or
c) to the internal bus of another node.

An appropriate microprogram for the first type creates an intelligent I/O -
device. The second type leads to a considerable increase in the speed of
processing when the private memory contains instructions and/or data which are
used for a special function. A further benefit is a decrease of bus contention
and thus an increase of the overall efficiency of the node. However, in MICON
these types are of limited importance compared to the third type, the coupling
processor.

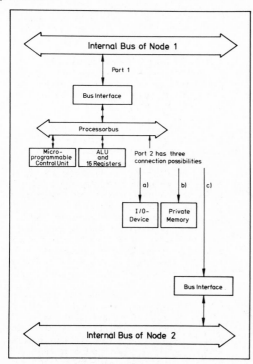

Figure 2
Structure of a MICON Prozessor

During interrupt processing a coupling processor is used by the LOS
as a coupler and otherwise as a
conventional processor. A coupling
processor accepts interrupts from
processors of the two nodes which
it connects. Interrupts are accepted instantly and are processed
sequentially. First the interrupts
from processors in that node
are processed where the coupling
processor is physically plugged
in. Subsequently the interrupts
from processors of the other
node are processed. The fairness
in severing pending interrupts
is guaranteed by the microprogram.
During interrupt processing, the
coupling processor can transport
data from the common memory of
one node via the two internal
busses to the common memory of
the other node. In addition,
the coupling processor has the
ability to switch its control to
the other port to perform management functions in the other
node. The coupling processor returns from interrupt processing if
all of the interrupts had been processed which were queued up from
processors of both nodes. Then the
coupling processor works as a conventional processor in that node
where it is physically plugged.

The functional behaviour of processors can be changed by a software switch, provided that the selected function is supported by hardware and firmware. For example, after a failure of the second port of a coupling processor it can still
be used as a conventional processor.
All processors in a node are connected to the internal parallel bus via a micro-
programmed bus interface. These bus interfaces take care of the bus control by
a handshake procedure. In this way fairness is guaranteed in serving the processors. Simultaneous bus requests from several processors will lead to a bus access
of one of the processors according to the daisy-chain method /5/. A special microprogram command permits the processor to access the internal bus exclusively for
a sequence of read and write operations from and to the local common memory.
In this way processors can lock the internal bus for processing this sequence.
This access method is used by a processor when working at a critical program part
(for example, see the REQUEST and RELEASE commands in the next section).

An increasing number of processors accessing the internal bus leads to a growing number of memory conflicts and a larger bus contention which limits the efficiency of the node. Detailed measurements at the FFM multi-computer network /2/ gave close insight to the bus contention problem under several typical conditions /6/. This led to the decision to extend the standard instruction set with some special powerful instructions which avoid cyclic calls of primitive instructions and therefore relieve the internal bus.


III.   THE LOCAL OPERATING SYSTEM

The software environment of MICON:
Figure 3 shows the software environment of MICON. The devices represent the interface to the outer world. Device I/O is controlled by processes which are called device monitors (DM). The I/O information is sent as messages through the network. As these limited resources of the network are controlled by resource monitors, a global resource manager in the network is not necessary.

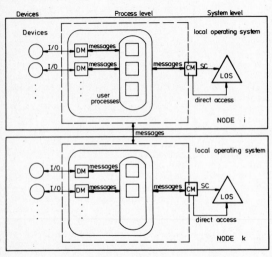

The process level contains the processes in the network. During the lifetime of a process it owns a fixed partition of the local common memory. Each process has a unique name within the network. The system level contains the LOSs. The main tasks of them are local process scheduling and process communication. An exceptional position in each LOS is taken by the control monitor (CM). On the one side, it accepts messages from processes. At that instant the control monitor behaves as a process: it requests the LOS by a system call (SC) for communication. On the other side, for execution of orders, which are encoded in these messages, the control monitor needs direct access to the LOS routines. The control monitor performs the following system utilities for processes in the network:

Figure 3
Software Environment of MICON

1) Load, initialize, and start/suspend a process
2) Start a process
3) Terminate a process
4) Change the priority of a process
5) Load and start a LOS in an adjacent node.


The execution of one of these system services can result in further communications with other processes in the network. For example, the first service listed above implies further communications between the control monitor and the disk monitor which is responsible for disk management. The disk monitor fetches the instruction code and the data of the new process from the process library and sends them as messages to the control monitor. The control monitor loads the new process into a partition of the local common memory and updates the LOS lists.

Structure of LOS:
Figure 4 shows the logical structure of a LOS. The partition of
the LOS in different tasks enabled
a modular construction of the LOS
software. The advantages of the
modularity have been extensively
described by Brinch Hansen /7/.
The LOS consists of simple clearly
defined software modules with minimal interfaces to other modules
(black arrows). All of the modules,
with the exception of the LOS lists,
contain instruction code. This code
is written reentrant, as the modules
can be used simultaneously by several
local processors. The transition from
process level to system level can be
done by each processor independent
from other processors. A system call
of a process causes the corresponding
processor to save all of the registers into the process control block
(figure 5). Then the register set of
the processor is free. The processor
jumps to the LOS routine for "identification of system calls" (see figure
4) and tries to fulfill the system
work for the process. If the system
service could be instantly performed
by the processor, it returns to process computation by loading the process control block back into its
registers. These transitions are
schematically shown in figure 6 for
"process S". If the service could
not be instantly performed by the
processor, the corresponding process scheduling is presented in figure 6 at the example of "process R".
Besides, figure 6 shows the process
scheduling of two communicating processes which corresponds to figure
12 and will be explained in the next
section.
Process states:
Process states and their transitions
are shown in figure 7a. The state
"suspended" was introduced to stop a
process after its loading into the
network. Because each communication
attempt of a process with a non-exis-
ting partner process will lead to the
termination of the calling process,
a set of communicating processes can
start working only when all the processes needed for the communications
are loaded and are known to the system.
This technique is a practicable way for
sets of processes which are loaded

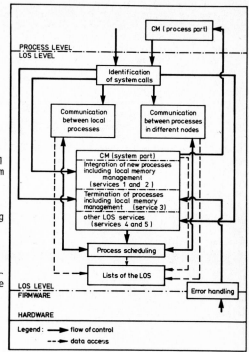

Figure 4
Structure of a Local Operating System

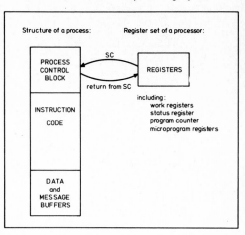

Figure 5
Structure of a Process

once and then will run for a long time. A process cannot force the state "suspended" for another process of the set. Waiting periods for a process can be achieved in another way by waiting for synchronization belonging to a communication.  During lifetime of a set of sequential communicating processes, each process can take the state "ready for processing", or "active", or " blocked" (terms defined in /8/ ). The state "blocked" is characterized in that the process waits for an event, i.e. for the synchronization with a partner process. A processor can be withdrawn from a process by preemption. This is possible only if

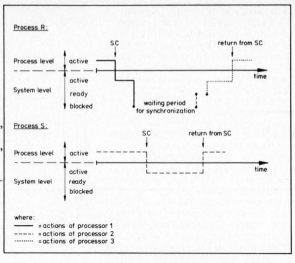

Figure 6
Process Scheduling for two Communicating Processes (an example)

1) the processor is busy on process level or
2) the processor is busy in the LOS (for the process) and passes one of the checkpoints where its registers are in a neutral state.

Protection of LOS lists against multiple access: The management of each LOS requires a modul which reflects the actual state of the node. This module consists of the LOS lists. The use of system routines by several processors trying to access simultaneously the LOS lists requires the protection of these lists against multiple access. This protection is guaranteed by the REQUEST and RELEASE instructions /4/ (figure 8) which enclose each instruction code working at the LOS lists. These instructions were efficiently implemented in the microprogram.  The simultaneous request of several processors to work at a LOS list leads to the interlinkage of them according to FIFO (figure 9). The execution of the REQUEST instruction can result in a suspension of the processor (for processor states see figure 7b). In contrast to the processor state "idle" where the processor is

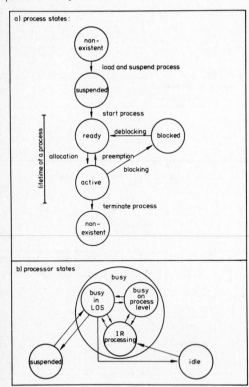

Figure 7
Process States and Processor States

detached from the process, here the
processor remains bounded to the
process. The matching process has
to wait, but its state remains "active".  On account of appraisable
small waiting periods for the processor suspension, it is not profitable
to engage the processor with another
process.  Therefore no system costs
for process management arise. Moreover, the suspension of a processor
avoids the continuous test of the
entry condition. In this way the
number of memory conflicts and bus
contentions is decreased.
The LOS lists:
In order to shorten the processor
suspension period because of a
REQUEST, the protected instruction
code should be passed through quickly.
This is accomplished:
1) by using LOS lists with only short
   items (units).  Ordinarily the
   program working on such a list
   is also short.
2) by partition of LOS lists into sublists /9/ . Thus the protected instruction code is partitioned, too.
   A processor is suspended only if
   another processor has locked the
   same sublist.
The PROCESS SCHEDULING LIST satisfies
criterion 1.  This list is arranged
according to the priority of processes in a node. It consists of 32
units (this is an arbitrarily chosen
maximum number of processes in each
node of MICON). Each of them contains the following information:
1) The priority of the process.
   This information determines unit
   position within the list.
2) The memory address of the process.

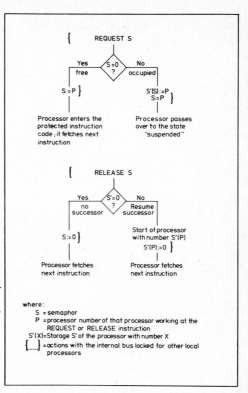

Figure 8
Instructions for Mutual Exclusion
of Processors from Protected
Instruction Code

Inside each node a process is uniquely defined by its address in common memory.  The user defined name would increase unit length.
3) The state of the process, an address of a LOS routine, and the address of
   the actual message buffer of the process. If the state of a process becomes
   "blocked", a LOS routine must be specified which is processed when the
   "active" state is reached again. The knowledge of the address of the actual
   message buffer is necessary for the execution of such a LOS routine.
A processor looking for a ready process in the PROCESS SCHEDULING LIST uses the
instruction shown in figure 10a. Of course, for an other list organization a
similar instruction could be implemented.  The search strategy, which is implic-
itely included in this instruction, guarantees that the unit with a ready process
is found which is nearest to the list beginning, i.e. which contains the ready
process of highest priority. The informations in that unit are sufficient for
the processor to continue the process. The "SLW" instruction can be used for
both, the search for a process with definite state and highest priority (where:
W = pattern for the state), and the search for a definite process (where: W =
memory address of the process). In this way for process scheduling only one list
is needed. A state transition of a process is noted by changing only one unit in

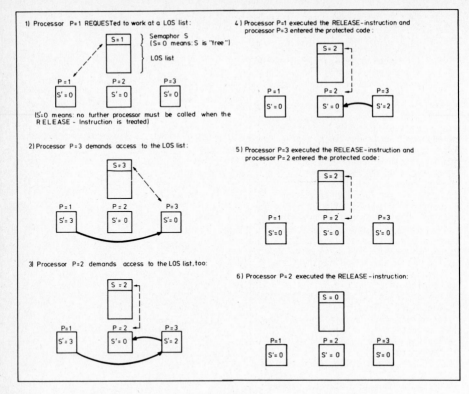

Figure 9
Illustrative Example for the Protection of a LOS List

one list. Management costs are therefore minimal. An exception with higher costs are the initialization or termination of a process or an operator demanded change of priority. Then the list must be sorted again according to the priority of the processes.

The COMMUNICATION LIST for local processes was constructed taking criterion 2 into consideration. This list is used for both, the survey of the processes existing in a node, and the control of communication between processes. These different functions imply the partition into sublists. Each of the 32 units of this list contains:
1) The user defined name and the memory address of a process.
   The memory address is coordinated with the user defined name. The first one identifies a process within the node, and the name defines a process within the network. The user defined name of a process is utilized for the communication in the network.
2) Process-specific information (for example: priority, length of the process in memory).
3) A pointer to a sublist, the synchronization list.
   Each unit has a synchronization list which can be accessed via the unit. A process which is ready for communication informs the partner process by inserting a message into its synchronization list. A detailed description of the synchronization list is left to the next section.

```
a) Search in a list for a given word:  SLW (AL,Z,N,M,W,R)
      begin
        I:=Z; R:=N;
   L:   if Mem(AL+I)= W then R:=AL+I-Z
                     else begin
                          I:=I+M; R:=R-1;
                          if R > 0 the go to L end
      end


b) Search in a list for a given pattern: SLE (AL,Z,N,M,AP,L,R)
      begin
        I:=Z; J:=0; R:=N;
   L:   if Mem(AL+I+J) = Mem(AP+J) then
                          if J=L then R:=AL+I-Z
                                 else begin J:=J+1; go to L end
                          else begin
                              I:=I+M; R:=R-1;
                              if R > 0 then begin J:=0; go to L end
      end
```

Where
```
I,J = auxiliary variables             Mem(X)= content of memory location X
AL  = address of the list             AP = address of the pattern
N   = number of units of the list     L  = length of the pattern
M   = length of each unit             R  = result: R=0 if the pattern/word
Z   = position of the entry in each        was not found, otherwise R contains
      unit                                 the address of the unit where it
W   = word                                 was found
```

Figure 10
Firmware Implementation of Instructions for the Search in LOS Lists

The search of a definite process in this list is done using the instructions shown in figure 10.

The LOS also manages lists containing the hardware equipment of the node. Since hardware modules of a node can only be activated via these lists, it becomes easy for the software to disconnect faulty modules. These modules are cancelled from the corresponding list.


IV. COMMUNICATION

MICON was conceived for parallel computation of user tasks divided into parallel asynchronous processes. The goal, the solution of the task, requires a mechanism for the processes to exchange their computation results, i.e. to communicate. The synchronization and communication of two processes is guaranteed by the operating system and does not depend on the relative position of the processes within the network. Both are event-driven.

Language constructs for the communication of parallel processes have been discussed in detail (/10/,/11/,/12/,/13/). Implementation designs of these constructs must be cognizant of the fact that the efficiency of interprocess communication strongly influences the efficiency of the distributed network. The benefit of parallelism which is obtained by distributing the processes into the nodes can easily be ruined by the management costs of the operating system for the communi-

cation. This was the reason for rejecting global variables for  synchronization
which were suggested in the form of eventcounts /14/ (to realize a broadcast
network). Synchronization would be shifted from system level to process level
and would require further system costs. Moreover communication channels of the
network would be heavily loaded by messages for updating the global variables.
Therefore interprocess communication in MICON is performed without using global
variables or a common buffer for messages. The LOSs are designed to support
interprocess communication independent of unforeseeable delays or fault situations in the network.

At a given instant, a process can communicate with only one other process, its
communication partner. An exception is the multiple communication which is explained later. The processes transmit their communication requests to their LOSs
by system calls. Each process makes a process-internal message buffer available
to the LOS. This internal buffer is used  for storage of messages which are to
be sent or which have been received. Each buffer consists of a message control
block which is composed of the sender's name, the receiver's name, a message
sequence number, and the length of the message. All activities between system
calls of communication partners and the command following the system call in
the processes are managed by the LOSs. After the end of a faultless communication
the message buffer of the receiver contains the message.

Standard communication offered by the MICON system software:
Like the FFM multi-computer network /2/, the MICON software has three types of
communications (figure 11):
1) The symmetric communication which is similar to the message concept proposed
   by Hoare /10/. Both, the sender and receiver know each other when holding a
   private conversation.
2) The asymmetric communication which is similar to the rendezvous concept
   adopted for ADA /13/. The receiver does not know the name of the sender and
   accepts a communication with that sender announcing itself first. If the
   receiver is equipped with a pattern for the name of potential senders, it can
   choose a sender according to that pattern. Asymmetric communication is the
   precondition for implementation of monitors at the process level.
3) The telegram communication is marked by the absence of synchronization between
   sender and receiver. Corresponding to the mail box concept the sender process
   transmits a one word telegram into a pre-defined buffer of the receiver. A
   telegram communication is used for the fast transmission of actual data.
Figure 11a presents the phases of a system protocol for symmetric communication.
The communication phase is preceded by the synchronization phase. The processor
handling the system call of process R induces the transmission of a synchronization message to the synchronization list of process S. This synchronization
message contains:
1) The name of process R. This name enables process S to select the actual
   synchronization message from others which might have been received from
   other processes.
2) The number of the node where process R is resident. This information permits
   selection of a transmission channel for the message.
3) The length of the message buffer which is available at process R. The LOS
   checks this value by comparing it with the corresponding value of process S.
4) The address of the message buffer of process R. This information enables a
   direct interprocess transmission of the message.
5) A rendezvous flag. This rendezvous flag characterizes the message type (message announcement, synchronization message, message, acknowledgement).
During the communication phase, the processor, which handles the system call of
process S, induces the direct transmission of the message from the message buffer
of process S to that of process R. Process R is informed about the arrival of
the message by a rendezvous flag which is set in its synchronization list. If
desired by the communication partners an acknowledgement phase follows. So the
user determines whether protection (with acknowledgement) or efficiency (without

acknowledgement) of the communication is preferred.

The asymmetric communication is based on the protocol of the symmetric variant. As the receiver is open to communicate with different senders a sender must announce itself to the receiver by transmitting a message announcement into the synchronization list of the receiver (figure 11b). Then the protocol of the symmetric communication is adopted.

Each arrow of figure 11 a/b includes both, the transmission of data and the process scheduling of the target process. Figure 12 shows the process scheduling during communication for a simple example, the symmetric communication (without acknowledgement) between partner processes in the same node (see also figure 6). The two situations presented are unique because of the mutual exclusion of sender and receiver from the synchronization list. If communication partners are located in different nodes, one of the coupling processors is activated (by interrupt) for the transport of the message. If this coupling processor is directly connected to the node of the target process it will also execute the process scheduling. Otherwise the message is stored in the neighbouring node and another coupling processor is activated. To avoid expensive waiting periods for the processor which activated the first coupling processor, it accepts other work.

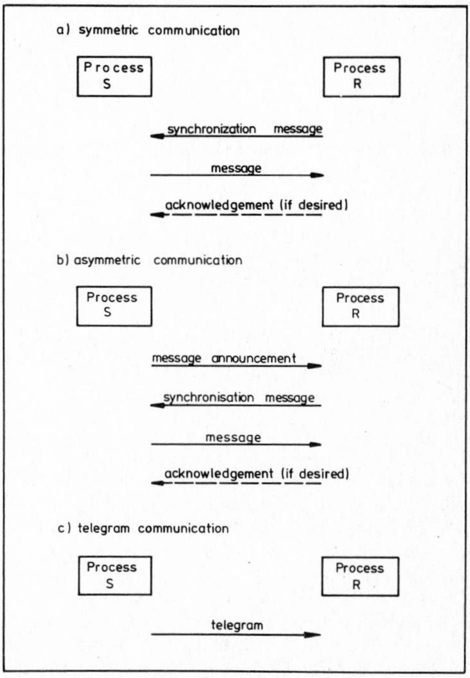

Figure 11
End-to-End Protocols for the
Standard Communications
between two Processes each
(S=Sender, R=Receiver)

Multiple communication:
The synchronization between two processes can lead to a considerable waiting period for one of them. If this process must subsequently execute further communications with other processes, these waiting periods add up. Moreover, these other processes might also wait (figure 13a). Under the following conditions the multiple communication permits a process to simultaneously handle communications with more than one partner and to shorten waiting periods (figure 13b):

1) Multiple communication is exclusively used if the sequence of processing communications is arbitrary. Messages sent or received during a multiple communication must be independent, i.e. the contents of messages which are to be received must not be precondition for messages which are to be sent.

2) The partners of a process using multiple communication must be different. Otherwise problems arise in assigning messages to the correct message buffers. The processor, which handles the system call of process A for a multiple communication, processes each single communication as far as possible. Process A is blocked and detached from the processor if none of the single communications can be continued. Then the transition of process A from state "blocked" to "ready" is determined by the partner processes. The system call of process A is finished

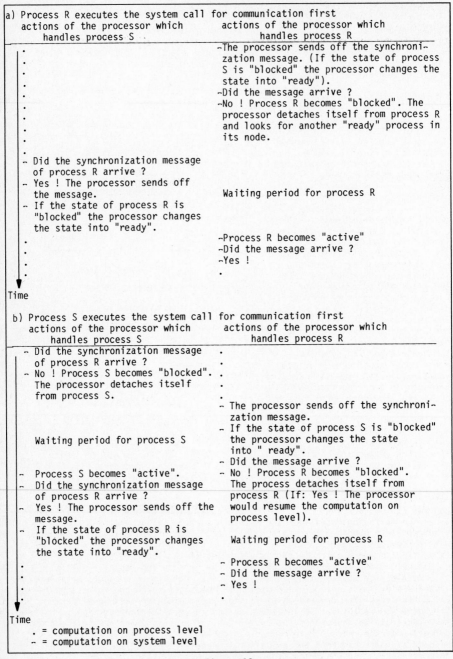

Figure 12
Process Scheduling during Communication

only when each single communication is completed. So the multiple communication introduces a linkage of standard communications according to the logical "and" operation.

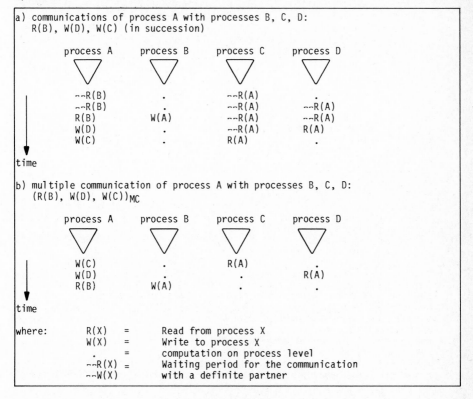

a) communications of process A with processes B, C, D:
   R(B), W(D), W(C) (in succession)

|  | process A | process B | process C | process D |
|---|---|---|---|---|
|  | ~~R(B) | . | ~~R(A) | . |
|  | ~~R(B) | . | ~~R(A) | ~~R(A) |
|  | R(B) | W(A) | ~~R(A) | ~~R(A) |
|  | W(D) | . | ~~R(A) | R(A) |
|  | W(C) | . | R(A) | . |

time

b) multiple communication of process A with processes B, C, D:
   (R(B), W(D), W(C))$_{MC}$

|  | process A | process B | process C | process D |
|---|---|---|---|---|
|  | W(C) | . | R(A) | . |
|  | W(D) | . | . | R(A) |
|  | R(B) | W(A) | . | . |

time

where:    R(X)  =    Read from process X
          W(X)  =    Write to process X
          .     =    computation on process level
          ~~R(X) =   Waiting period for the communication
          ~~W(X)     with a definite partner

Figure 13
Efficiency of Multiple Communication shown at the Example of Several
Communicating Processes

Handling of communication errors:
Exceptions during a communication are caused by hardware transmission errors or by software errors in the user processes. Transmission errors induce the LOSs to repeat the communication. If the next communication attempt will cause the same error, both partner processes are terminated. Software errors in processes are: 1) the length of corresponding message buffers of the two communicating
          processes are incompatible
      2) the partner process is non-existent.
These errors will lead to the immediate termination of the participant processes. Then these processes are marked in the process scheduling list by the state "ready" and an address of a routine for error termination. In the course of the error termination the synchronization list is inspected: other processes which announced themselves for a communication are also terminated. If these processes reside in another node of the network, a termination message is sent to the corresponding control monitor. Future communication partners of a terminating process will be found in a list of the process control block which is defined at compile

time. In this way the termination of only one process of a set of communicating
processes can result in the termination of the set. Of course, system monitors
cannot be terminated. The user is informed about the termination of each process.

Thus, exceptions during a communication are handled by the LOSs alone. Exception
handlers of the participant processes are not addressed. Such exception handlers
would mostly try to repeat a communication. In this way, persistent errors would
lead to a programmed infinite loop.


## V.   CONCLUSION

MICON was built up using the experiences and extensive measurements with the
FFM multi-computer network. The operating system was completely redesigned and
contains the following innovations:
1) The parallelism of computation is extended from the process level to the
   system level. The processors of each node are allowed to use the routines of
   their local operating system simultaneously.
2) An efficient mechanism to guarantee exclusive access of a processor to protected instruction code is introduced. Processors waiting to access protected
   code are linked together according to FIFO.
   The suspension period of processors waiting to work on a LOS list is shortened
   by an appropriate construction of the lists, i.e. the system lists are kept
   short or are divided into sublists.
3) The efficiency of a computer network is essentially influenced by system costs
   for the interprocess communication. The aim was to keep these costs small.
   Only one message is used for the synchronization and one for the communication.
   Time measurements concerning the execution of a system call for communication
   /6/ showed that system costs are propotional to the distance to the partner
   process in the network and to the number of communication protocol arrows.
4) Multiple communication permits the communication of a process with several
   partner processes simultaneously. Waiting periods which result during successive communications of a process with its partners are reduced in this way.
As MICON is conceived as an experimental system the operating system will be
subject to changes and improvements. This is especially true for the routing of
messages in the network.  At present, experience with a deterministic routing
policy has been obtained on the FFM multi-computer network /2/. In the future,
an adaptive routing policy will be implemented and tested for efficiency.

Parallel with that, MICON will serve as an experimental tool for research on
fault tolerance. The concept of distribution of the resources in the network and
the absence of central controllers on all levels is the starting point for fault
tolerance. The correct functional behaviour of the network is maintained, when
single modules of a node or complete nodes fail. The operating system is constructed so as to permit the implementation of routines for reconfiguration without
high expense.

ACKNOWLEDGMENT
The author wishes to thank W. Grünewald and H. von Issendorff for valuable discussions. The colleagues at Werthhoven, especially those mentioned in the references,
had an active part in the construction of the network. Not mentioned and therefore
introduced here are W. Jansen, E. Kossack and L. Rössing. To all of them the
author is indebted.

REFERENCES

/1/ Jones, A.K. and Schwarz, P., Experiences using multiprocessor systems – a status report, Computing Surveys 12 (1980)121–165.

/2/ von Issendorff, H. and Grünewald, W., An adaptable network for functional distributed systems, in: Proceedings of 7th annual Symposium on Computer Architecture (La Baule, France, 1980).

/3/ Langer, W., Ein mikroprogrammierbarer Prozessor für Mehrrechnersysteme, FFM–Werthhoven, Germany (1981).

/4/ Grünewald, W., Haak, N., Langer, W., Skupin, U., MUMI Prozessor Befehls- handbuch (FFM–Bericht Nr. 306, Werthhoven, Germany, 1981).

/5/ Kittmann, K., Ein dezentraler Systembus als Baustein für Mikrorechner- Netze, FFM–Werthhoven, Germany (1981).

/6/ Neumann, G., Ackermann, R., Grünewald W., Messungen zum Kommunikationsauf- wand für Prozesse in einem lokalen Rechnernetz: Erfahrungen aus einer Imple- mentation, in: Nehmer, J., Implementierungssprachen für nichtsequentielle Programmsysteme (German Chapter of the ACM, Bericht 7, 1981).

/7/ Per Brinch Hansen, The architecture of concurrent programs (Prentice Hall, New Jersey, 1977).

/8/ Wettstein, H., Aufbau und Struktur von Betriebssystemen (Hanser Verlag, München–Wien, 1978).

/9/ Nehmer, J., Dispatcher–Elementarfunktionen für symmetrische Mehrprozessor- Datenverarbeitungssysteme, Interner Bericht der Gesellschaft Kernforschung, Karlsruhe/Germany (1973).

/10/ Hoare, C.A.R., Communicating Sequential Processes, Com. ACM 21 (Aug. 1978) 666–677.

/11/ Per Brinch Hansen, Distributed processes: a concurrent programming concept, Com. ACM 21 (Nov. 1978) 934–941.

/12/ Silberschatz, A., Communication and synchronization in distributed systems, IEEE Trans. Software Engineering SE–5 (Nov. 1979) 542–546.

/13/ Ichbiah, J. et al., Rationale for the Design of the ADA Programming Language, ACM Sigplan Notices 14 (June 1979).

/14/ Bullis, K., Franta, W., Implementation of eventcounts in a broadcast net- work, Computer Network 4 (1980) 57–69.

Performance of Data Communication Systems
and their Applications, G. Pujolle (ed.)
© North-Holland Publishing Company, 1981

DISTRIBUTED PROCESSING IN A NUCLEAR
DATA ACQUISITION SYSTEM

Antonino   Anzalone, Francesco Giustolisi, Giuseppe Scollo

Istituto Nazionale di Fisica Nucleare
Laboratorio Nazionale del Sud
Catania
Italia

Aim of this report is to present the first applications of
distributed processing made at the Laboratorio Nazionale
del Sud (LNS), one of three national laboratories of the
Istituto Nazionale di Fisica Nucleare (INFN), where a 13
MeV Tandem Accelerator is going to be installed.
The paper describes a small system, named SINGLE, already
tested and implemented, and gives some draft notes on the
design choices of a larger system, named MONDAN, to be implemented within the end of this year.


INTRODUCTION

In the domain of nuclear physics experiments the technological evolution enforces
more and more pressing requirements to the capabilities of the involved computing
resources. Very high rate of raw data acquisition, on line processing and visualization of spectra, fast collection of large amounts of data onto mass storage devices, user friendly interface: this brief summary of the typical requirements can
be satisfied only by means of a clean separation of functions to be performed - in
a parallel processing environment - by systems, interconnected through adequate
communication lines, providing a coordinated processing of the information.

With regard to the tasks of the computing system devoted to the collection and analysis of the experimental data, the experiments can be grouped in the following
classes:
1) experiments on many uncorrelated parameters: often they are called "single experiments";
2) experiments on many correlated parameters: usually they are called "multiparameter experiments";
3) experiments on many parameters, some correlated and some others not: frequently
   these are called "mixed experiments".

The classification above is useful to the computing system designer, since experiments of the same class require a similar approach to almost all the problems of
data acquisition, on line processing and collection on mass storage devices: single
experiments usually ask for a completely on line processing of the experimental
data, whilst multiparameter experiments usually ask for both partial on line processing of the experimental data - for the purpose of user control and setup of
the experiment - and a complete, "hystorical", collection of the raw data onto mass
storage for the purpose of subsequent, off line, more complex processing and eva-

luation of the experimental results.

The first class of experiments requires a very high counting rate of the system, but low computational complexity; the second class shows opposite characteristics. The experiments of the third class are, in this, similar to those of the second one, but with much higher input rate.

The system SINGLE deals only with the first class of experiments, whilst the system MONDAN is designed to match with the more complex requirements of the second and third class, but allowing single experiments as well.

HARDWARE CONFIGURATION

The most relevant features of the hardware configuration of the data acquisition system in course of installation at LNS are:
- the CAMAC standardization [1], that regulates the interfacing between the computing system and the instrumentation charged with the task of producing the input data;
- the heterogeneity of the computing resources that, variously linked together, build up the system;
- the choice of the fastest instrumentation, as available on the market, to build up the part of the system delimited by the detectors, on one side, and the CAMAC Dataway, on the other side.

The hardware configuration is shown in Figure 1.

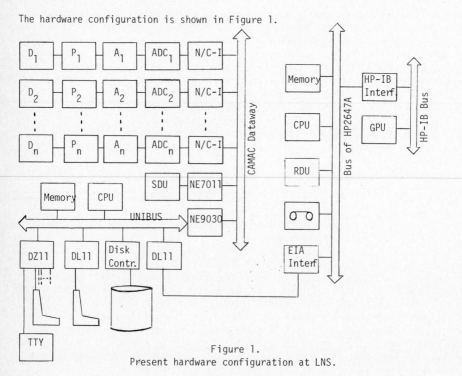

Figure 1.
Present hardware configuration at LNS.

An analog signal, coming from a detector $D_i$, after stepping through the preamplifier $P_i$ and the amplifier $A_i$, is converted by the Analog to Digital Converter $ADC_i$: for the latter, the ADC Laben Models 8115 and 8116 have been chosen, which convert the signal into 4K and 8K output channels, respectively (i.e. that show 12 and 13 output bits, respectively). These ADC's operate under NIM standard rules: each of them goes into CAMAC by means of an appropriate NIM to CAMAC interface, so that it can be seen to be on the CAMAC instrumentation crate by the acquisition system.

Most valuable features of these ADC's are:
- low integral non-linearity: 0.05% and 0.04% for the 8115 and 8116 respectively;
- low differential non-linearity: 0.2% for both models;
- low conversion time, independent on the signal amplitude: about 4.5 $\mu$s and 9.2 $\mu$s for the 8115 and 8116 respectively.

A Storage Display Unit (SDU), Tektronix Model 603, is also interfaced to the CAMAC Dataway: the interface (Nuclear Enterprises Mod. 7011) incorporates two 10-bits Digital to Analog Converters, so that each point of a 1024X1024 array can be addressed, thus allowing - for the size of the SDU - for high level of detail, beyond the scope of resolution of the human eye.

In addition to this basic instrumentation, a large variety of instrumentation will find room in the CAMAC crates, depending on the user needs. The CAMAC system is linked to an "acquisition computer", presently a PDP 11/34A, by means of a main crate controller Nuclear Enterprises Model 9030, which lodges the interface for the computer bus. This controller can accomodate for a variety of computer interfaces, so increasing the global flexibility of the system.

The PDP 11 configuration includes 256 KB of main memory, 2 disk units of 5 MB each, an asynchronous buffered multiplexer for 8 communication lines operating in EIA RS 232C, 2 independent single interfaces for communication lines operating in the same standard, the VDU consolle (VT100), an additional VDU (Tesak) and a teletype (LA120) of 180 cps of speed, a paper tape reader/puncher and a DMA interface.

The PDP can "speak", through one of the asynchronous lines at 9600 bps, with an intelligent terminal HP2647A, oriented to graphics data processing and visualization. This computer features: 32 KB of memory for graphics data and 9 KB for alphanumeric data, programmability in Basic (64 KB for program and interpreter), 220 KB of magnetic tape storage, visualization "raster scan", 64 KB of ROM holding the firmware for internal management and utilities, besides a good variety of I/O interfaces. Furthermore, it is connected to a graphic printer HP7310A, in order to allow the on line hard-copy of what is visualized on the screen.

Hitherto the already installed hardware has been described. Before the end of this year the system will include also the following machines:
- a fast magnetic tape double unit for the PDP;
- an independent data acquisition and machine control system, based on a microprocessor LSI-11: this system will be equipped with 32 KB of main memory and 512 KB of mass storage (floppy disks); its software will be developped on the PDP, that is furnished with all the necessary software development utilities;
- an independent data acquisition system for single experiments, Le Croy 3500, equipped with graphics VDU, floppy disks, communication interfaces and direct CAMAC coupling facility;

- a 32-bit word computer VAX-11/780, intended mainly for off line data analysis
  and experiment databases management (but also for on line data acquisition, when
  the maximum input rate is mandatory); this system will be equipped with 2 MB of
  main memory, 2 disk units of 67 MB each, a magnetic tape unit, floating point
  processor and battery back-up.


THE SYSTEM SINGLE

SINGLE is a distributed system, implemented at LNS on two computers - the PDP and
the HP - which performs the following tasks:
- real-time data acquisition, in CAMAC, for single experiments, and spectra computation, by the PDP;
- on line spectra visualization both on the CAMAC interfaced SDU, handled by the
  PDP, and on the raster-scan graphics display unit (RDU) of the HP, handled by
  the latter;
- RDU spectra manipulation (scaling, zoom, etc.), hard-copy on the graphic printer
  unit (GPU) and permanent storage on the HP magnetic tape;
- user-friendly interfacing on the HP's console, that acts as system console.

The SINGLE architecture is shown in Figure 2.

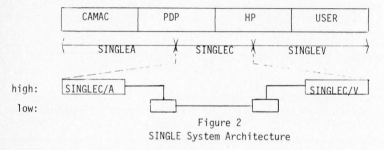

Figure 2
SINGLE System Architecture

It consists of three main subsystems:
1) a communication subsystem, named SINGLEC, implemented on both computers in order to allow their cooperation: at the application level this is regulated by the
protocol SINGLEP - "ad hoc" defined - that ensures the correct and coordinated execution of their respective functions;
2) an acquisition subsystem, named SINGLEA, running on the PDP, that performs all
the control and management functions pertinent to the CAMAC interfaced instrumentation and, moreover, builds the spectra in memory;
3) a visualization subsystem, named SINGLEV, running on the HP, that performs the
RDU spectra presentation, manipulation, hard-copy and tape storing and, last not
least, implements the user interface.
The most relevant features of each subsystem will be detailed in the sequel.

THE COMMUNICATION SUBSYSTEM

The meaning of the terms "interlocutor", "message", "command", "text", "message
procedure", "protocol", used in the sequel, is the one defined in the "Second Theory of Colloquies" by Le Moli [2]. The SINGLEC architecture is layered in two levels
of colloquy [3]: a "low" level, which deals with message transmission, reception

and error control, and a "high" level whose functions are defined by the message semantics. In the "Open Systems Interconnection" (OSI) terminology of ISO [4] these two levels correspond to the "Link Layer" and "Application Layer", respectively: the first Osi layer is here constituted by the EIA RS 232C standard, whilst the intermediate layers, between Link and Application, are substantially absent.

The message format consists of two fields always present:
'MI' : message identifier
'ML' : message length
and of a third field, present only within messages carrying text:
'MP' : message parameters.
'MI'+'ML' size ranges from 2 through 3 bytes, 'MP' size ranges from 0 through 2048 bytes.
At the low level a preliminary decision has been taken about the information code: to use as alphabet a subset of the ISO-5 7-bits code such that only printable codes would be exchanged; this decision eliminates a lot of problems due to hardware uncompatibility between heterogeneous systems [5],[6]. Subsequently, in order to minimize the overhead due to this decision, that would have been considerable mostly for the transmission of long blocks of numerical data, a radix-64 representation has been adopted for numerical data, named RAD64, whose alphabet consists of the 7-bits progressive binary strings from 0110000 (digit 0) through 1101111 (digit 63): this alphabet satisfies the above mentioned constraint about the printability of the ISO-5 codes exchanged on the line.

For the error control function performed at the low level of colloquy, the character parity control has been considered satisfactory, due to the small distances at stake: both positive and negative acknowledgements are used, to get the maximum level of security.
Two reception buffers are permanently allocated to the low level, whose size is 2048 bytes in the HP and 16 bytes in the PDP: this asymmetry reflects the difference of roles between the two computers, as long messages are sent only from the PDP to the HP.

At the high level of colloquy, the application level, the protocol SINGLEP regulates the correct and coordinated operation of the application subsystems SINGLEA and SINGLEV. Two distinct and related message dictionaries are defined, one for each direction of transmission: they are listed in Tab. la, for the direction from PDP to HP, and Tab. lb, for the reverse direction.

Each interlocutor's message procedure can be described by means of a state diagram representing its behaviour as a Finite State Machine (FSM): given a set of states, the state diagram represents the set of rules that establish the state transition and possible output message production corresponding to each meaningful couple (old state,input) of the FSM. For the message procedure of the interlocutor SINGLEC/A, running on the PDP, the following set of states is defined:
SAI: Initial State, SAN: Acquisition On, SAF: Acquisition Off.
An analogous set of states is defined for the message procedure of the interlocutor SINGLEC/V, running on the HP:
SVI: Initial State, SVN: Acquisition On, SVF: Acquisition Off.

Each of these interlocutors does not "run alone" on its machine, but is properly interfaced with the subsystem that uses it as a tool to cooperate: this means that

| message name | MI | ML | semantics and MP |
|---|---|---|---|
| SCC | '4' | '2k+2' | Set CAMAC configuration: k is the number of ADC's on line; for h=1,...,k it is: MP(h)='0' if the h-th ADC has 4K channels, MP(h)='1' if the h-th ADC has 8K channels, MP(k+h)='CAMACstation number' of the interface of the h-th ADC. |
| BAT | '3' | '5' | Time spent in acquisition, at the moment of acquisition break MP(1::3)='time' in seconds. |
| EAT | '6' | '2' | Acquisition break due to timeout expiration |
| EAV | '5' | '9' | Acquisition break due to channel overflow MP(1)='identifier' of the ADC that resulted in overflow, MP(2::4)='channel' in overflow, MP(5::7)='time' spent in acquisition. |
| CEX | '9' | '5' | CAMAC X Error: MP(1)='CAMAC station number' MP(2)='CAMACsubaddr.' MP(3)='CAMACfunction' |
| YSF | '7' | '7' | Spectrum parameters: MP(1::2)='scaled Y-maximum value' MP(3::5)='Y-scale factor'. |
| BDD | '8' | 'n' | Block of Y-data for visualization; the ML field is two bytes long:it is 3 n 2051 MP(1::2)='Y(1)' MP(3::4)='Y(2)' ................. MP(2m-1::2m)='Y(m)' ................. |

Tab. 1a: Output message dictionary of SINGLEC/A message procedure(1)

| message name | MI | ML | semantics and MP |
|---|---|---|---|
| ACC | '6' | '2' | Ask for CAMAC configuration. |
| SA | '1' | '3' | Start Acquisition, no timeout MP(1)="C":clear spectra memory, MP(1)="N":do not clear spectra memory; |
|  | '1' | '6' | Start Acquisition with a timeout MP(1) : as above, MP(2::4):'timeout' in seconds. |
| BA | '2' | '2' | Break Acquisition. |
| RA | '3' | '2' | Resume Acquisition with the same timeout,if any (to be restarted if expired); |
|  | '3' | '5' | Resume Acquisition with a new timeout MP(1::3)='timeout' in seconds. |
| HA | '4' | '2' | Halt Acquisition. |
| SDD[C] | '5' | '8' | Spectrum Data onDisplay CAMAC, one curve Full Scale: MP(1)="C"; |
|  | '5' | '13' | Spectra Data on Display CAMAC, two curves Half Scale: MP(1)="D"; |
| SDD[H] | '5' | '8' | Spectrum Data onDisplay HP: MP(1)="H"; |
| SDD[G] | '5' | '8' | Spectrum Data onDisplay HP, and Resume Acquisition immediately (set parallel processing). |

For all SDD messages the following parameters are specified:
MP(2)= 'identifier' of the ADC whose spectrum is requested,
MP(3::5)= 'first channel' corresponding to X=1 in the display,
MP(6)= 'compression factor' that is X-scale factor.
For SDD[C] in which two curves are requested(MP(1)="D"),parameters MP(7::11) have the same meaning,orderly, as MP(2::6), but they refer to the second curve

Tab. 1b: Output message dictionary of SINGLEC/V message procedure(1)

state transitions can be enforced not only by remote input message reception, but also by significant occurrences in the subsystem "user of the interlocutor".These occurrences generate commands that must be taken into account as local inputs to the FSM describing the message procedure, thus completing the input dictionary of the FSM itself. Tables 2a and 2b contain the list of local inputs to the FSM of SINGLEC/A and SINGLEC/V, respectively.

| TE | Timeout Expiration |
|----|--------------------|
| CO | Channel Overflow   |
| CX | CAMAC X Error      |

| UO  | User On                          |
|-----|----------------------------------|
| US  | User Start                       |
| UB  | User Break                       |
| UR  | User Resume                      |
| UVC | User Visualization on SDU        |
| UVH | User Visualization on RDU        |
| UVG | User Visualization on RDU and    |
|     | immediate Resume                 |
| UH  | User Halt                        |

Tab. 2a: Local input dictionary of  
       SINGLEC/A message procedure

Tab. 2b: Local input dictionary of  
       SINGLEC/V message procedure

The state diagrams of the two FSM's are represented in Figures 3a,3b, with the following notations:
- each state is represented by its name closed into a circle;
- each state transition is represented by an arrow, on the right side of which the relevant input is indicated by its name (for clarity, if it is a local input its name is enclosed in angle brackets);
- if, besides the state transition, an output message is produced, its name follows the name of the input, separated by the symbol "/"; if, rather than one output message, a sequence of output messages is produced, the names of the messages in the sequence are orderly indicated, separated by the symbol "/";
- a state transition can occur after a multiple message exchange: for the sake of simplicity the intermediate states are not included in the set of states defined above; they are just indicated by the symbol ":" in the state diagram;
- a state transition can take place under different conditions: these are indicated in the state diagram separated by the symbol "or".

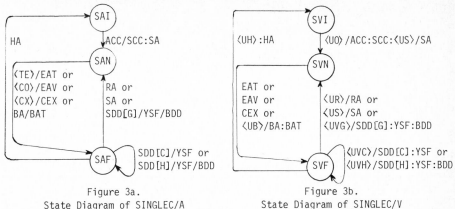

Figure 3a.  
State Diagram of SINGLEC/A

Figure 3b.  
State Diagram of SINGLEC/V

The SINGLEP protocol, so far described, allows parallel execution of acquisition on the PDP and visualization on the HP; this possibility is in act after the following state transitions:

SAF → SAN , under condition SDD[G]/YSF/BDD, in SINGLEC/A
SVF → SVN , under condition ⟨UVG⟩/SDD[G]:YSF:BDD, in SINGLEC/V.

With other words, after a break of the acquisition (due to user command or to events like a user-specified timeout expiration, or a channel overflow, or a 'X' CAMAC error indication) the user can ask for the visualization of some spectrum on the HP, with immediate resume of the acquisition: thus he can issue on the HP local commands - e.g. "zoom" of a portion of the spectrum, graphic printout, tape storage, etc. - while acquisition is going on.

THE ACQUISITION SUBSYSTEM

In a typical single experiment the pure acquisition system is charged of a few simple operations: getting the conversion results, discarding the invalid ones, incrementing the memory address reserved to the "event" (i.e. the couple (ADC, valid conversion result)), suspending and resuming the acquisition on user- or system-specified conditions, allowing the on line visualization of the spectra corresponding to the ADC's.

At this point the basic user need is to achieve the maximum input rate allowed by the available resources: the typical solution is based upon the definition of a privileged process, memory-locked, that captures and serves the interrupts of interest [7]; in this way the best performance can be obtained, observing the constraint of software compatibility with the manufacturer's Operating System. This constraint is not mandatory in a dedicated resources environment: the authors have developped a loader that disables the manufacturer's Operating System and loads into memory a new "system" generated on disk. All the software for the PDP at LNS that will implement autonomous systems will make use of this loader.

An effective input rate of 7 kHz has been measured: this figure can be compared with the correspondent value of 1 kHz obtained in the implementation of a software interface for CAMAC [8], running on a PDP 11/34 under RT-11.

No special purpose hardware - such as, e.g., Direct Memory Increment (DMI) - was available for the purpose of fast spectra computation: this means that all the process of event classification and memory address construction is in charge of the software. With regard to this constraint, and to the characteristics of the CAMAC-interfaced instrumentation installed at LNS (see above), the system SINGLEA shows the following features:
- off line reconfiguration of the CAMAC system: the parameters of the instrumentation (e.g. number of ADC's, CAMAC addresses, etc.) are known by SINGLEA by means of a properly formatted CAMAC-data file, defined and linked at system generation time; an indirect command file [9], named CAMCON, drives the SINGLEA generation; though CAMCON is tailored to the system SINGLEA, its block diagram - shown in Figure 4 - is completely general and can be used for any CAMAC system definition;
- control and management, through proper CAMAC interfacing, of a number of $n_4$ ADC's Laben 8115 and $n_8$ ADC's Laben 8116, such that $n_4 + 2n_8 \leqslant 19$;
- spectra computation in memory, with a capacity of 24 bits/event;
- control and management of the CAMAC-interfaced SDU, with one Full Scale or two

Half Scale spectra visualization: the latter allows a fast spectra comparison:
- definition of the duration of each acquisition run: the maximum timeout is 262,144 seconds;
- channel overflow management;
- optimization of the CAMAC interrupt service time, under the constraint of a full utilization of the available memory (that means direct management of the base registers by the CAMAC interrupt service process).

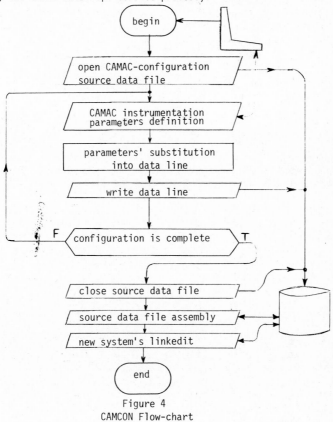

Figure 4
CAMCON Flow-chart

## THE VISUALIZATION SUBSYSTEM

The design goal of the SINGLEV specifications definition can be condensed in the following words: the implementation of an user-friendly interface tailored to allow him(her) to see "all of what" the system can do , without having to know "anything of how" the system does it.

The experimenter gets the experiment control by means of commands and, when required, assignation of values to command parameters. At any time he (she) can ask for the "menu" of available commands. If parameters are associated to the selected command, the system solicits the user for their value assignation. Syntax errors as well as incorrect parameter value assignations trap to User Error Diagnose and

Recovery, that signals the error and asks for a correct command or parameter value
input.
As already said, two visualization units are available to the experimenter: the
CAMAC-interfaced SDU is managed by the PDP only when acquisition is suspended;this
choice has been made in order to avoid affecting the acquisition rate of the disturb of SDU service time. SDU usage is intended for fast, qualitative control of
the experiment and quick detection of anomalies as well. The main resource for
visualization is the RDU of the HP: the powerful graphics capabilities of this
system can be fully exploited by the user while the acquisition goes on.


DRAFT DESIGN OF THE SYSTEM MONDAN

MONDAN stands for "Modular Online Nuclear Data Acquisition Network". In this application domain, main reason for networking is the possibility of setting up a reasonably complex system that should be flexible enough to allow a quick allocation of
the appropriate resources needed by the experimenter.

Five computers, as shown in Figure 5, are involved in this first design of the system, each of them having specific functions, briefly summarized in the sequel.

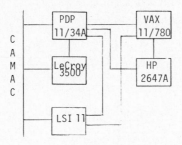

Figure 5
MONDAN Network

LeCroy 3500 is a specialized system devoted to single experiments: 130 kHz is the
achievable event count rate(2).As such,this system is designed to work alone. Two
reasons make convenient putting it on line on the network: first, the possibility
of transfer of files, containing the results of experiments, to larger file systems and databases on line; second, the possibility of coordinating LeCroy's operation with the acquisition of another computer in those mixed experiments which
statically distinguish the sources of uncorrelated spectra from the sources of
correlated ones.

LSI 11 is foreseen to play two different roles, depending on the experiment setup.
Generally it can drive CAMAC-interfaced control and visualization instrumentation
(the SDU mentioned above, stepping motor controllers, etc.). The other role is to
act as first acquisition computer in multiparameter experiments, the second being
the PDP: as will be discussed below, a bufferization of the input data allows to
increase the throughput from CAMAC to mass storage.

The PDP is the heart of the network. For multiparameter and mixed experiments it
has the main task of storing the raw data onto mass storage for subsequent analy-

sis: it can get the data either directly from CAMAC or through a fast parallel connection with the LSI (40 KBps). Data will be moved onto disk one track (5 KW) per
write operation, in order to optimize rotational latency. If the data come from
LSI, a bufferization of the same size would maximize the total throughput.

The visualization is again entrusted to the HP: for correlated spectra only a fraction (10% or less, depending on the acquisition rate) of the input data have to be
routed to the HP for visualization, when acquisition is online. The HP will be
used also for the graphic output of offline processing performed on the VAX.

The latter is designated for both all the off line analysis tasks and the maintenance of the databases relevant to the experimental results. The raw data collected
by the PDP will be transferred onto the VAX file system. Exceptionally, when the
acquisition rate requires faster processing capabilities, the VAX can replace the
PDP in the latter's role. The user interface will run on the LeCroy for single experiments, on the HP for the other cases.


CONCLUSIONS

The first LNS applications of distributed processing for nuclear data acquisition
have been presented in this paper, with a double hope: first, to show how concepts
and ideas arisen in the computer networking field can be fruitfully applied to this
class of applications and, second, to sound how far the meaning of "computer networking" changes when the computers are charged of providing specialized classes
of functions, instead of general purpose computing power; the second point is for
an open discussion.


ACKNOWLEDGEMENTS

The authors are grateful to S. Alfonzetti for his fruitful suggestions about the
description of the protocol SINGLEP.

NOTES

(1) The following notations are adopted: 'n' means RAD64 code of integer n, "X"
    means ISO-5 code of character X.
(2) This figure can be achieved only when the special LeCroy 3512 ADC's are used:
    in fact each of these ADC's is provided with 1Kx24 bit memory and DMA/DMI tran-
    sfer to LeCroy 3500's memory; the data acquisition by other ADC's takes place
    by following usual standard CAMAC readout, at a maximum rate of 2.75 kHz.

REFERENCES

[1] EUR 4100, CAMAC: A modular instrumentation system for data handling (1972),and
    EUR 4600, CAMAC: Organization of Multi-Crate Systems (1972)
[2] Le Moli, G., The second Theory of Colloquies, submitted to Computer Networks
    (1980)
[3] Le Moli, G., On networking, in: Schoemaker, S. (ed.), Computer Networks and Si-
    mulation (North-Holland, Amsterdam, 1978)
[4] ISO/TC97/SC16, Open System Interconnection, Version 4, N227 (August 1979)

[5] Barber, D.L.A., New protocols for intelligent systems, INWG General Note 190, Teddington,UK (February 1979)

[6] Barber, D.L.A., "You don't know me, but..." , INWG General Note 191, Teddington,UK (February, 1979)

[7] Lycklama, H. and Bayer, D.L., The MERT Operating System, Bell System Technical Journal 6 (1978) 2049-2086

[8] Anghinolfi, M. and Masulli, F., Software di base per la gestione di un CAMAC da minicomputer, INFN/BE-81/5, Genova (1981)

[9] D.E.C., RSX-11M/M-PLUS MCR Operations Manual,Ch. 5 (Digital Equipment Corporation, Maynard, Massachusetts,June 1979)

Performance of Data Communication Systems
and their Applications, G. Pujolle (ed.)
© North-Holland Publishing Company, 1981

# BASIC CONCEPTS OF THE QUALITY
# OF TRANSPORT SERVICE MONITORING
# IN AN INTER-UNIVERSITY COMPUTER NETWORK

Jerzy A. Barchański
Tomasz Muehleisen
Institute of Engineering Cybernetics
Technical University of Wrocław
Wrocław, Poland

Services to be provided by the transport layer of
an inter-university computer network under construction in Poland are introduced and basic principles of the monitoring of their quality presented. As a sequel, some parameters characterizing
the quality of the transport services are proposed.
Software measurement tools are reviewed and their
applicability for the transport layer monitoring
analysed. Finally, it is shown how to evaluate practically the quality of service parameters.

INTRODUCTION

The problems presented in the paper concern the quality of service
monitoring of the transport layer in a first Polish inter-university
computer network under design [1] and result from our previous, more
general research [2]. The transport services in the network are based
upon the X.25 protocol provided by the network control layer and hence we shall confine our attention to the connected-oriented services
only. Those services can be segmented into three groups, each associated with one of the three phases of a transport connection's existance: the establishment phase, the data transfer phase and the termination phase.
The establishment services group consists of the following services:

    a/ transport connection establishment,
    b/ class of service negotiation.

The data transfer services group consists of:

    a/ transport-service-data-units transfer,
    b/ expedited-transport-service-data-units transfer,

c/ error notification,

d/ purge.

The termination services group consists of one service: transport connection termination.

## PRINCIPLES OF TRANSPORT LAYER QUALITY OF SERVICE MONITORING

Transport users are capable of establishing, maintaining and terminating transport connections by means of a transport protocol which
supports simultaneous operation of many transport connections between
two entities known as transport stations. For this reason, we project
the notion of the quality of service from the layer as a whole to the
individual connections supported by the both entities.

For each connection, we shall identify its current quality of service as a set of current values of some quality of service parameters
evaluated by means of a monitoring function. Additionally, we shall
identify a class of service, i.e. a requested quality of service, as
a set of boundary values for the parameters, as chosen by the user
/i.e. the session layer/ at the connection establishment time. Different classes of service are intended to cover the transport service requirements of the various types of traffic generated by the session entities /e.g. batch type of traffic, real-time type of traffic,
etc./. The selected class of service should be maintained throughout
the life-time of the transport connection; in other words, any failure to maintain the agreed class of service on any given connection
will necessarily terminate the existance of that connection.

From the above it results that, in order to maintain a requested quality of service, a control function should exist, capable of comparing the current /i.e. monitored/ and the requested /i.e. negotiated/
qualities of service on each transport connection. If, for a connection, the former falls below the latter, the control function requests
the transport layer to terminate that particular connection. Since
transport connections are established upon network connections, the
terminated connection can be re-established by choosing such network
connections that give more chances of maintaining the requested quality of service. Figure 1 illustrates the above considerations. It
should be noted that the actual location of the control and monitoring module can be different from those depicted, without any impact
on the presented principle.

The practical utilization of the above considerations is justified
by the fact that in the inter-university network the network control

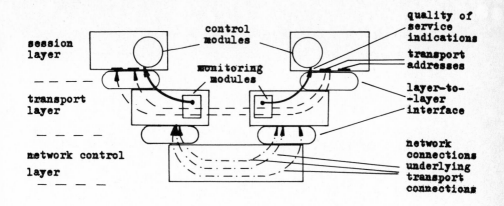

Figure 1
Monitoring Module and Control Module
for Transport Layer

layer will provide the X.25 service making use of the switched virtual and permanent virtual circuits [4]. Prospective establishment
of transport connections upon network connections by performing N:1,
1:N or just 1:1 mapping /the first two referred to as "upward" and
"downward" multiplexing, respectively/ can result in a variety of
classes of service and cost ranges provided by the individual transport connections. The indication of a current value of the quality of
service and the previously registered quality indications /averaged
over a period of time/ enable the layer to choose most cost-effective
connections. Hence, by means of the feedback loop a local /i.e. one-
-level/ improvement of performance can practically be achieved.

QUALITY OF SERVICE PARAMETERS

A proper choice of the quality of service parameters is a fundamental problem, both for networks in early design stages and for those
already oparational. The question what aspects of their either predicted or real behaviour will be cognizable depends heavily on the
chosen set of parameters.

In compliance with the Open Systems Architecture's philosophy the
parameters should be relevant to all the consecutive phases of the
transport connection operation. Taking this into account, we propose
the following set of the quality of service parameters [3] :

/i/ for the connection establishment phase:

  connection set-up delay

  connectability

/ii/ for the data transfer phase:

  mean /maximum/ throughput

  transit delay

  residual error rate

  availability

/iii/ for the connection termination phase:

  connection termination delay.

The above set of parameters is sufficient to give a many-sided insight into the quality of service provided by the individual transport connections. Out of this parameter base some quality of service parameters can be selected for the on-line monitoring /e.g. throughput, residual error rate/.

The insight into the quality of service of the transport connections would not be complete without the cost factor. Knowledge of costs involved in the operation of every transport connection enables the session layer to choose such connections for which a given class of service can be achieved at minimum cost, or in short, for which the services are most cost-effective.

Since in the inter-university network the packet-switched network will provide the X.25 service, the costs of the transport connections will be dependent on the costs of the network connections underlying those transport connections [3], whereas the costs of the X.25-type connections will be established by the owner of the packet-switched network, i.e. the Post Office Authority. The actual cost of utilization of the network connections depends on such factors as: connection's throughput or capacity, residual error rate, length /geographical and/or topological/ and many others. The charges may not, however, take into account the above factors at all, reflecting only a network policy of the authority. In any case, the costs of the network connections will be known once the packet-switched network is operational.

MEASUREMENT TECHNIQUES AND TOOLS

Monitoring systems or monitors in short can be regarded as practical means for carrying out measurement experiments on both single computer systems and multi-computer networks. Their classification is as follows:

    /i/ hardware monitors,
    /ii/ software monitors,
    /iii/ hybrid, i.e. hardware/software monitors.

Hardware monitoring is a measurement technique utilizing stricktly
a hardware system or a computer system which is completely separate
from the object network. The level of intelligence of a hardware monitor is dependent on the level of self-control which the monitor has.
While the most simple monitors are controlled manually by human inter-
vention, the most intelligent of them have capability of being run
under minicomputer control. Their main advantages are: minimal or no
impact on the network behaviour, high operation speed and network-to-
-network portability while the disadvantages include: high manufactu-
ring cost and low degree of versatility.

Software monitoring is a measurement technique utilizing programs designed to execute and to make use of the resources available on the
object computer. Among a number of classes of software monitors, the
performance monitors are of special interest for the quality monitoring. They are designed to collect data characterizing operation of
a network from the user point of view. Their advantages are as follows: easy implementation, low cost, versatility and high degree of
intelligence which can be overshadowed by their gratest disadvantage - impact on the network operation. However, a careful design of
measurements can reduce this impact satisfactorily.

Taking into account the above considerations, we propose that the measurements of the quality of service parameters in our inter-university network should be carried out exclusively by software techniques.
The techniques utilize a number of measurement tools which are presented in the reference [5]. Those tools have been applied to the
packet-switched communications network /i.e. the network control
layer/ only, and we shall herein review them with particular regard
to their applicability for measurements of the transport layer.

In a most general sense, the measurement tools can be segmented into
three groups:

    /i/ observation tools,
    /ii/ analysis tools,
    /iii/ special-purpose tools.

The observation tools are used for direct data measurements and can
be further classified into:

/i/ snap-shot observation,
/ii/ trace observation,
/iii/ accumulated observation,
/iv/ status reports.

Snap-shot observation consists in the data gathering in the communications sub-network at some pre-determined instants of time. This tool can not be applied directly to the monitoring of the transport-layer quality of service. It can, however, be used for determining an instanteous state of the transport layer resources. In particular, it can be used for measurement of the current number of the existing transport connections and the number of free buffers.

Trace observation is utilized for examining the packet route as it crosses the communications sub-network. As the transport layer protocol supports the end-to-end connections, the trace observation can be used by extending its scope beyond the communications sub-network to host computers and/or their front-ends. With this approach, so called time-stamps can be applied for determination of all the component values of the transport connection's delay by time-stamping a measurement packet as it travels accros the transport connection. It should be noted, that the component delays can be calculated from the differences between the time-stamps in the same packet, while throughput from the differences between corresponding time-stamps in successive packets [6].

Accumulated observation is a measurement tool for gathering data characterizing activity of the communications sub-network in an interval of time. This tool can be applied for the monitoring of the transport layer and the following data should be gathered:
  - number of sent and received transport-data units,
  - number of sent and received acknowledgements,
  - time instants of sending transport-data units,
  - time instants of receiving acknowledgements,
  - number of retransmissions,
  - number of error notifications and others.
The above parameters will be used for evaluating the quality of service for the transport connections. The accumulated observation can also result in some histograms characterizing the transport layer operation.

Status reports allow in the communications sub-network to monitor the operational state of its nodes and their line adaptors. The application of the status reports is not directly connected with the quality of service evaluation. It can, however, reveal the real causes of the quality of service degradation in the transport layer.

The above presented methods are applicable for gathering of the measurement data only. As a general rule, those data will have to be further processed and to serve this purpose, analysis tools are applied. Two methods can be distinguished:

/i/ on-line analysis,
/ii/ off-line analysis.

The usefulness of one or the another of the above methods depends, generally speaking, on the degree of impact the analysis results have on an improvement of the current network behaviour.

Special-purpose tools are applicable for experimental measurements in the network. As an example we can mention the artificial traffic generators, useful for throughput evaluation in the transport-layer context.

In conclusion, for the current evaluation of majority of the quality of transport service parameters the application of the accumulated observation and on-line analysis is sufficient. However, the other tools can also be applied in order to gain a more complete insight into the operational state of the transport layer resources.

EVALUATION OF QUALITY OF SERVICE PARAMETERS

In the following, we shall present some hints for practical evaluation of the quality of transport service parameters, as defined in [3].

Connection set-up delay can be evaluated from the differences between the time instant when the session layer issues a SET CONNECTION /or equivalent/ command and the time instant when the information is received from the network control layer that all the network connections underlying this particular transport connections have been established. The appropriate time instants are easily observable and, if stored over a period of time, the average set-up delay of this particular connection or of all the transport connections /"double average"/ can be calculated.

Connectability can be evaluated by monitoring successes and failures to establish a particular transport connection. The component parameters can be measured from an establishment/termination module within a prospective transport station. This module will be equipped with

a timer and its task is to control the time of the connection establishment activities. When this time is excessive /i.e. greater than
a specified time-out/, a failure to establish the transport connection can be recorded.

Connection termination delay can be evaluated from the differences
between the time instant when the session layer issues a TERMINATE
/or equivalent/ command and the time instant when the information is
received from the network control layer that it has terminated all
the network connections underlying this transport connection. Similarly with the set-up delay evaluation, in order to evaluate average
termination delays the appropriate time instants have to be stored
over a period of time.

Throughput can be evaluated by monitoring the number of acknowledged
transport-data units in a time period. To avoid ambiguity an arbitrary observation point should be chosen, e.g. the input buffer. Additionally for each data unit its size should be memorized /if not uni-
form/ in order to express throughput in bits/sec. The throughput thus
evaluated is commonly reffered to as "net throughput". The observation time period should be considerably long, so that mean throughput
can be reflected. In order to determine the maximum throughput, the
artificial traffic generators should be used for creating as many
"fake" transport-data units as the communications sub-network can accept.

It should be noted that the above considerations are related to
throughput evaluation in the networks in which each system is equipped with a monitoring module. If this is not the case, the throughput can be evaluated by utilization of special measurement packets
or normal data packets with especially interpretable measurement data. When using such packets, the time instants of leaving the transport stations should be recorded in an appropriate field and the value of throughput can be calculated from the time differences in consecutive packets.

Transit delay can be evaluated from the difference of the time instant when a transport-data unit is received at its destination and
the time instant when it is sent from its source. It should be noted,
however, that for practical measurement experiments both the source
and destination transport station clocks would have to be synchronized which is, by no means, an easy problem. For this reason, it is
more convenient to measure so-called round-trip delay or the time
difference between sending a packet and receiving an acknowledgement

that the packet has reached its destination without any information loss. If the measurements are carried out exclusively by a software monitor within a network, the one-way delay can be evaluated from the difference between appropriate time-stamps of the same measurement packet.

Residual error rate, availability can both be evaluated in a straight-forward fashion by recording number of error notifications and un-transmitted data units, respectively.

The above remarks on the practical evaluation of the proposed quali-ty of service parameters can serve as guidelines for the design of the measurement tools to be utilized in the transport-station moni-toring module. It should be noted that, if each system in the net-work has a monitoring module of its own, the utilization of the mea-surement packets or especially interpretable data packets is not re-quired. Those packets will be needed for other purpose such as aggre-gating the mass measurement data at memory buffers of an off-line analysis centre.

FINAL REMARKS

The measurement program presented in our paper can only be introdu-ced in an outline, mainly due to early stages of the inter-universi-ty network development. In the course of the measurement software development, the measurement program will probably have to be modi-fied and once the network is operational, the monitor should be up-graded to accomodate yet another monitoring services. Prior to any prospective extentions to the monitoring services, it should be rea-lized that excessive measurements can cause severe degradation of the network services and that - due to the introduced artifact - the measurement data themselves can be severely corrupted.

The next remark concerns the possibility of controlling the transport layer quality of service by means of a "short" feedback loop. This possibility is implied in the ISO document [7] and is undoubtedly an attractive proposal for a local /i.e. one-level/ improvement of the network behaviour. Nevertheless, we suggest that the quality control mechanism should be included in the network at some further stages and in the meantime the measurement data should be sent to a measure-ment centre for off-line analyses. Our suggestion is more obvious when it is realized that at the beginning the 1:1 mapping of the transport connections into the network connections will only be performed, re-

sulting in more-or-less equal qualities of service for every transport connection. Once differences between them begin to appear /by
introduction of the multiplexing rules/, the quality of service control mechanism should be included in the network.

REFERENCES:

[1]  Barchański, J.A., Bazewicz, M., A preliminary project of an
     inter-university computer network, Technical University of
     Wrocław, Institute of Engineering Cybernetics, Report 12/79,
     November 1978 /in Polish/.

[2]  Barchański, J.A., Muehleisen, T., Quality of service monito-
     ring of the Open Systems Architecture transport layer, in
     Proc. Conf. Operating Systems Theory, Visegrad, Hungary, Fe-
     bruary 1980.

[3]  Barchański, J.A., Muehleisen, T., Basic concepts of trans-
     port service monitoring in an inter-university computer net-
     work, Technical University of Wrocław, Institute of Engine-
     ering Cybernetics, Report PRE/4/81, February 1981.

[4]  Bilski, E., Budzianowski, L., Muehleisen, T., Sorokin, E.,
     Wietrzych, J., Żabnieński, W., A FEP for the inter-univer-
     sity network - design aspects, Technical University of Wroc-
     ław, Institute of Engineering Cybernetics, Report SPR/11/79,
     October 1979 /in Polish/.

[5]  Cole, G.D., Computer network measurements: techniques and
     experiments, University of California, Eng. Report No. UCLA-
     -ENG-7165, 1971.

[6]  Bennet, C.J., Hinchley, A.J., Measurements of transmission
     control protocol, in Proc. Workshop on Computer Network Pro-
     tocols, Liege, Belgium, February 1978.

[7]  Reference Model of Open Systems Architecture, version 4 as of
     June 1979, ISO/TC97/SC16N227/.

Performance of Data Communication Systems
and their Applications, G. Pujolle (ed.)
© North-Holland Publishing Company, 1981

## PALM'S MACHINE INTERFERENCE MODEL ALIAS
## ERLANG'S LOSS SYSTEM

Villy Baek Iversen

The Institute of Mathematical Statistics
and Operations Research
The Technical University of Denmark
DK-2800 Lyngby - Denmark

This paper interprets Palm's machine interference
model as a loss system. For the case of a single repairman it is equivalent to Erlang's loss system; for
multiple repairmen it is equivalent to a more general loss system. This interpretation allows a direct
transfer of numerous results from Erlang's loss system
to the machine interference model. This holds good of
numerical methods, validity, economic optimization,
generalizations, etc. For exponential distributed repair times the model is insensitive to the distribution
of the operating times. This is the background for the
successful applications of the machine interference
model, which is analogous with the success of teletraffic theory. The paper both presents the state-of-the-
art and widens this in several ways.

ERLANG'S LOSS SYSTEM (Erlang, 1917 [4])

We consider a service system composed of n full available servers
(trunks). Customers arrive in accordance with a Poisson process (intensity $\lambda$). Customers arriving when all servers are busy are lost
("lost calls cleared") (fig. 1). The holding-time distribution is
assumed to be (negative-) exponential (intensity $\mu$). The system is
assumed to be in a state of statistical equilibrium.

The state-transition diagram of this system is shown in fig. 2.

Erlang (1917) calculated the state probabilities of this system [4]:

$$p(i) = \frac{\dfrac{A^i}{i!}}{1 + A + \dfrac{A^2}{2!} + \cdots\cdots + \dfrac{A^n}{n!}} \tag{1}$$

where

$$A = \lambda/\mu \tag{2}$$

is the offered traffic. This is a truncated Poisson distribution.
Since the arrival process is a Poisson process with a constant intensity (unrelated to the state of the system), the time congestion E
(the proportion of time all servers are busy) is equal to the call
congestion B (the proportion of calls which are lost) (E = B =
$E_{1,n}(A)$):

$$E_{1,n}(A) = \frac{\dfrac{A^n}{n!}}{1 + A + \dfrac{A^2}{2!} + \cdots + \dfrac{A^n}{n!}} \tag{3}$$

This is Erlang's famous B-formula (Erlang's first formula, Erlang's loss formula).

The carried traffic A' is $A' = A \cdot [1 - E_{1,n}(A)]$ $\qquad$ (4)

The lost traffic is: $A'' = A \cdot E_{1,n}(A)$ $\qquad$ (5)

The increase (improvement) in carried traffic, when adding one server, is:

$$F_{1,n}(A) = A[E_{1,n}(A) - E_{1,n+1}(A)] \tag{6}$$

$F_{1,n}(A)$ is called the improvement function. The traffic carried per server is as follows:

Random hunting:

$$a = \frac{A'}{n} = \frac{A[1 - E_{1,n}(A)]}{n} \tag{7}$$

Sequential hunting: the i'th server carries the traffic $a_i$:

$$a_i = A[E_{1,i-1}(A) - E_{1,i}(A)] = F_{1,i-1}(A) \tag{8}$$

Numerical values of Erlang's B-formula are obtained by the following recurrence formula, which is very accurate.

$$E_{1,n}(A) = \frac{A \cdot E_{1,n-1}(A)}{n + A \cdot E_{1,n-1}(A)}, \quad E_{1,0}(A) = 1 \tag{9}$$

This recurrence formula has been known since the days of Erlang. We also have accurate methods for the numerical calculation of the inverses (A as a function of (E,n) and n as a function of (E,A); n may be a real number. [6], [10]. A lot of tables comprising Erlang's B-formula has been published, e.g. [11].

Erlang's B-formula is valid for any holding-time distribution [2], [3], [17]. It has been the subject of numerous papers, and it has been generalized in many different ways (e.g. [5], [8]).

PALM'S MACHINE INTERFERENCE MODEL - ONE REPAIR-MAN

Let us consider n terminals connected to a computer system with one single server (fig. 3). In Palm's formulation the terminals were automatic machines, and the computer system was a repair-man taking care of the machines. We want to calculate the optimal number of machines per repair-man. For the present being we shall keep to Palm's formulation.

A machine is either (fig. 4) (a) operating, (b) waiting for the repair-man, or (c) being serviced by the repair-man. The repair-man is either (a) working or (b) idle. We assume the operating times of a machine are exponential distributed (rate $\mu$), and that the service

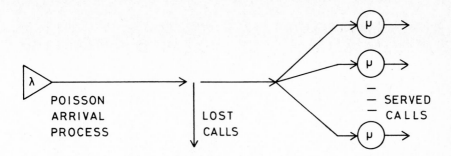

Figure 1: Erlang's classical model of a loss system.

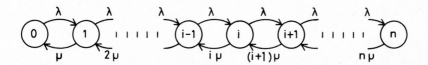

Figure 2: State-transition diagram of Erlang's loss system and Palm's machine interference model.

times of the repair-man also are exponential distributed (rate $\lambda$).

We define the state of the considered system to be the number of operating machines. Then the state-transition diagram is given by fig. 2, which also was the state-transition diagram for Erlang's loss system!! (This has been noticed by Takács [18], but the consequences have not been taken). As Erlang's loss system and Palm's machine interference model have the same state-transition diagram, they are basically identical. It is only two different interpretations of the same mathematical structure.

Palm's machine interference model can be interpreted in the following way: when the repair-man is working, he generates jobs to the n machines according to a Poisson process (intensity $\lambda$). When all n machines are busy, he is in fact idle, but we may just as well assume, he generates jobs which are lost. In this way we notice the analogy to Erlang's loss system.

We are now able to transfer the conprehensive amount of information on Erlang's loss system to Palm's machine interference problem. We notice that the offered traffic still is

$$A = \frac{\lambda}{\mu} \tag{10}$$

(1/A) is called the service factor (Palm's definition). The state probabilities of the system (fig. 3) is given by (1), where i now is the number of operating machines. Especially we have

$$P\{\text{repair-man idle}\} = P\{n\} = E_{1,n}(A) \tag{11}$$

This is the average of the total time per unit time when all the n machines are operating. We then get the average number of machines

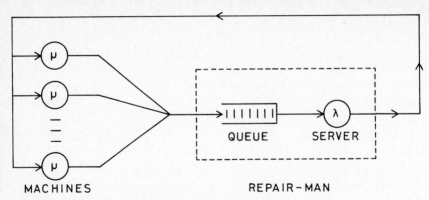

Figure 3: Palm's machine interference model.

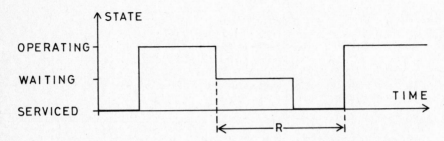

Figure 4: Palm's machine interference model. A machine is either
          operating, waiting for the repair-man, or being serviced
          by the repair-man. The response time R is equal to the
          waiting time plus the service time.

being serviced $n_s$:

$$n_s = 1 - E_{1,n}(A) \qquad\qquad\qquad (12)$$

The average number of operating machines $n_o$ corresponds to the carried traffic:

$$n_o = A[1 - E_{1,n}(A)] \qquad\qquad\qquad (13)$$

Then the average number of idle machines $n_d$ becomes

$$n_d = n - n_s - n_o \qquad\qquad\qquad (14)$$

In accordance with Palm [15] we thus get for one machine:

$$\text{operating time per time unit} \quad = o = \frac{n_o}{n} \qquad\qquad (15)$$

$$\text{service time per time unit} \quad = s = \frac{n_s}{n} \qquad\qquad (16)$$

$$\text{waiting time per time unit} \quad = d = \frac{n_d}{n} \qquad\qquad (17)$$

The average response time R (waiting time + service time) is obtained
by applying Little's formula ($L = \lambda \cdot W$) to (a) the operating machines,

(b) the queue, and (c) the repair-man. $\lambda$ is the same for these three systems:

$$\lambda = \frac{1/\mu}{n_o} = \frac{w}{n_d} = \frac{1/\lambda}{n_s} = \frac{R}{n_d + n_s} \tag{18}$$

where w is the average waiting time for obtaining the repair-man. Substituting (12) into (18) gives

$$R = \frac{n_d + n_s}{n_s} \cdot \frac{1}{\lambda} = \frac{n - n_o}{n_s} \cdot \frac{1}{\lambda}$$

$$R = \frac{n}{\lambda [1 - E_{1,n}(A)]} - \frac{1}{\mu} \tag{19}$$

because $n_s \cdot \lambda = n_o \cdot \mu$ (18). The mean waiting time becomes

$$w = R - \frac{1}{\lambda} \tag{20}$$

If the arrival process is a Poisson process, then Erlang's loss system is valid for any holding time distribution. Therefore, if the service time of the repair-man is exponential distributed, then Palm's machine interference model (mean values) is insensitive to the distribution of the operating times.

Little's formula (18) is valid for any time distribution. For a single server queue we always have (12). Thus, if we take into account that $E_{1,n}(A)$ depends upon the distribution of the service time of the repair-man, then (19) & (20) are valid for any time distribution. This has been noticed by e.g. Kobayashi [13].

All numerical calculations of Palm's machine interference model should of course be based upon (9) and upon the methods given in [6], [10] for the inverses.


HISTORICAL NOTES

Even though Conny Palm had been working for many years within the field of loss systems, he did not notice the equivalence with Erlang's loss system. During the same year (1947), as Palm published the above-mentioned work [15], he also published a book of tables of Erlang's B-formula using the recurrence formula (9). Nevertheless, in the second part of his work on machine interference he recommends a method of numerical calculation which is based upon the calculation of the individual terms ($A^i/i!$) of the denominator of formula (3). This is an inaccurate method, which is only usable for very small values of A and n.

On the basis of his experience within the field of loss systems Conny Palm argued that the machine interference model is insensitive to the distribution of the service times, whereas exponential distributed operating times are of critical importance. These erroneous statements have been referred and repeated by numerous authors - they have even been supported by numerical simulations!!! In fact, we have just noticed that it is the other way about. The critical matter is the Poisson departure process from the repair-man.

ECONOMIC CONSIDERATIONS: ERLANG'S LOSS SYSTEM

In the following we consider two different ways for optimization of the above-mentioned model. The first method, Moe's principle, has obtained widespread applications within the field of teletraffic. The second method was applied by Conny Palm to the machine interference model for which it is still applied.

Moe's principle [11] is applied for optimizing loss systems (trunk groups) in telephony. The expenses for servers are assumed to be a linear function of the number of servers:

$$c_n = c_0 + c \cdot n \tag{21}$$

Furthermore, there is a loss of revenue due to lost traffic:

$$c_a = g \cdot A \cdot E_{1,n}(A) \tag{22}$$

where g is the revenue per carried erlang. Hence for a given number of servers the total cost are

$$C_n = g \cdot A \cdot E_{1,n}(A) + c_0 + c \cdot n \tag{23}$$

This function is to be minimized with respect to n. The optimal value is denoted by $n_0$:

$$C_{n_0-1} > C_{n_0} \leq C_{n_0+1} \tag{24}$$

or by using (6):

$$F_{1,n_0-1}(A) > F_B \geq F_{1,n_0}(A) \tag{25}$$

where

$$F_B = \frac{c}{g} = \frac{\text{cost per server}}{\text{income per erlang}} \tag{26}$$

The improvement function $F_{1,n}(A)$ (6) has been tabulated (e.g. [11]). This method maximizes the profit. An example is given in fig. 5. Notice that the solution is independent of $c_0$.


ECONOMIC CONSIDERATIONS: PALM'S MACHINE INTERFERENCE MODEL

Conny Palm [15] minimizes the unit cost of the product manufactured.

He assumes the following cost functions:

$Q_0$ = unit cost of the manufactured product
$Q_o$ = cost per unit time for an operating machine
$Q_s$ = cost per unit time for a machine being serviced
$Q_d$ = cost per unit time for a machine waiting for service
$Q_a$ = cost per unit time for the repair-man.

When a repair-man takes care of n machines, we get the following cost per unit of time per machine (15), (16), (17):

$$o \cdot Q_o + s \cdot Q_s + d \cdot Q_d + \frac{1}{n} Q_a \tag{27}$$

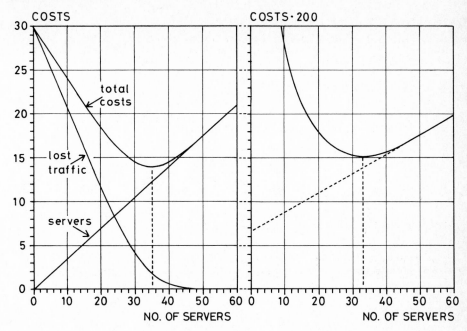

Figure 5: Erlang's loss system. The cost function (23) for $F_B$ = 0,35 (g = unit of cost) as a function of the number of machines. A = 30 erlang.

Figure 6: Palm's machine interference model. The cost function (34) for V = 1/30 and A = 30 as a function of the number of machines.

During the same time unit we produce the quantity o. The cost of this quantity is then $o \cdot Q_0$ and equals (27). We assume the repair-man is idle during the time when there is no machine to service.

Defining $\quad V = Q_d/Q_a$ $\hspace{7cm}$ (28)

and (18) $\quad A = \dfrac{o}{s} \; (= \dfrac{\lambda}{\mu})$ $\hspace{6cm}$ (29)

we get from (27) $Q_0 = Q_o + \dfrac{1}{A} \cdot Q_s + Q_a \cdot \dfrac{V \cdot d + \frac{1}{n}}{o}$ $\hspace{3cm}$ (30)

For different values of n only d and o are varying. A minimum of $Q_0$ is thus equal to the minimum of

$$R_n = \dfrac{V \cdot d + \frac{1}{n}}{o}$$ $\hspace{6cm}$ (31)

This is the result of Palm. By means of (12)-(17) we may rewrite (31) as follows:

$$R_n = \dfrac{V \cdot \dfrac{n_d}{n} + \dfrac{1}{n}}{\dfrac{n_o}{n}} = \dfrac{V\{n - [1 - E_{1,n}(A)](1+A)\} + 1}{A[1 - E_{1,n}(A)]}$$ $\hspace{2cm}$ (32)

$$R_n = \frac{V \cdot n + 1}{A[1 - E_{1,n}(A)]} + \text{constant} \qquad (33)$$

A minimum of $Q_0$ is thus equal to the minimum of

$$\frac{V \cdot n + 1}{A[1 - E_{1,n}(A)]} \qquad (34)$$

The numerator is similar to (21), whereas the denominator is the traffic carried. An example is given in fig. 6.

We have applied two different criteria for optimizing the same system. We notice that Moe's principle maximizes the total profit, whereas Palm's model minimizes the unit cost of the manufactured product. Both criteria are relevant and may be combined to a more general criteria.


GENERALIZATIONS OF THE SINGLE REPAIR-MAN MODEL

As one example of applying results from Erlang's loss system we may study a system, where the machines (in telephony trunks) have individual operating time distributions [5].

As another example we may consider a loss system with sequential hunting (8). This corresponds to giving priority to the machines in Palm's model. As the service times are exponentially distributed, this is valid for all preemptive queueing disciplines. For this case the usage of the machines are given by (8).

If the output process of the repair-man is a Poisson process, then the arrival process to the repair-man is also a Poisson process, because the operating times correspond to a random displacement. Therefore, the machine interference model will be valid for an arbitrary operating time distribution in the following cases (results known from the theory of queueing networks): the repair-man is working as a

        a)   M/G/1 processor sharing model

        b)   M/G/1 Last in-first out preemptive resume model

        c)   M/G/$\infty$ model

        d)   M/M/n model

d) will be considered from a different point of view in the following.

The only condition put upon the operating times is that they are independent observations from a stationary distribution. This distribution may be generated in a more complex way (e.g. the Central server model).

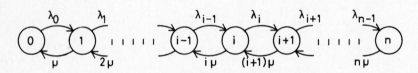

Figure 7: State-transition diagram for a general loss system; a special case is the multiple repair-man model.

PALM'S MACHINE INTERFERENCE MODEL - MULTIPLE REPAIR-MEN

We consider a model having m repair-men, each servicing a machine at rate $\lambda$. Under the assumption of exponential service and operating times this model is defined by the state-transition diagram shown in fig. 7, where the state, as before, is defined as the number of operating machines, and where

$$\lambda_i = \begin{cases} m\lambda, & 0 \le i \le n-m \\ (n-i)\lambda, & n-m \le i \le n \end{cases} \tag{35}$$

This system (fig. 7) is equivalent to a general loss system, where the arrival intensity is state-dependent and the n servers are homogeneous (all have the same mean operating time = $1/\mu$). By means of some recent results for Cox distributions [7] this loss system can easily be shown to be independent of the operating time distribution [9]. Therefore, the multiple repair-men model is also independent of the operating time distribution. (This has been proved in [1]).

Under the assumption of statistical equilibrium the state probabilities become:

$$P(i) = \frac{\lambda_0 \cdot \lambda_1 \cdot \lambda_2 \cdot \ldots \cdot \lambda_{i-1}}{i! \mu^i} \cdot P(0) \tag{36}$$

where $P(0)$ in obtained from

$$\sum_{i=0}^{n} P(i) = 1 \tag{37}$$

CONCLUDING REMARKS

By the equivalence to loss systems we have thrown light upon the validity of Palm's machine interference model, a field which has been the subject of much confusion. Furthermore, we have shown how the model can be generalized in several ways.

The basic result is that the state probabilities are independent of the distribution of the operating times of the machines when the service (repair) times are exponential distributed; this also holds good for multiple repair-men. Thus the mean values of the system are also independent of the operating time distribution.

As for the waiting time distribution this is a Cox distribution, which for exponential operating times is given in [16]. For non-exponential operating times it is necessary to study the state probabilities at machine arrival epochs. If these (call averages) are identical to those of the time averages with one machine removed, then the waiting time distribution is also independent of the operating time distribution. This is being studied at the moment.

Finally, the theory of reversible processes seems to be of great potential use in this field. In [12] the single repair-man model is dealt with in an elegant way.

ACKNOWLEDGEMENTS

Anonymous referees have given useful references. The paper has been typed by Kirsten R. Nielsen.

REFERENCES

[ 1]   Bunday, B.D. and Scraton, R.E., The G/M/r machine interference
       model, European Journal of Operational Research 4(1980) 399-
       402.
[ 2]   Cohen, J.W., On Erlang's Formula for the Loss System M/G/k,
       Eighth International Teletraffic Congress, paper 124, Melbourne
       1976. 6 pp.
[ 3]   Cohen, J.W., Sensitivity and Intensensitivity, Delft Progr.
       Rep., 5(1980) pp. 159-173.
[ 4]   Erlang, A.K., Løsning af nogle Problemer fra Sandsynligheds-
       regningen af Betydning for de automatiske Telefoncentraler,
       Elektroteknikeren 13(1917) 5-25. English version: Solution of
       some Problems in the Theory of Probabilities of Significance in
       Automatic Telephone Exchanges, P.O. Elect. Engrs. J. 10(1918)
       189. Also published in: Brockmeyer, E., Halstrøm, H.L. and
       Jensen, Arne, The Life and Works of A.K. Erlang, pp. 138-155
       (Copenhagen, 1948).
[ 5]   Fakinos, D., The M/G/k Blocking System with Heterogeneous Ser-
       vers, J. Opl. Res. Soc. 31 (1980) 919-927.
[ 6]   Farmer, R.F. and Kaufman, I., On The Numerical Evaluation of
       Some Basic Traffic Formulae, Networks 8(1978) 153-186.
[ 7]   Hordijk, A. and Schassberger, R., Weak Convergence of Genera-
       lized Semi-Markov Processes. Institute of Applied Mathematics
       and Computer Science, University of Leiden, The Netherlands.
       Report 77-8, revision February 1979 (original version 1975).
       35 pp.
[ 8]   Iversen, V.B., The A-Formula, Teleteknik (English edition)
       25(1980) 64-80.
[ 9]   Iversen, V.B., A Generalized Loss System, IMSOR, Technical
       University of Denmark, 1981.
[10]   Iversen, V.B. and Nielsen, K.R., Numerical Evaluation of Er-
       lang's Formulae on HP41C/TI-59. IMSOR, Technical University
       of Denmark, 1981.
[11]   Jensen, Arne, Moe's Principle - An econometric investigation
       intended as an aid in dimensioning and managing telephone plant.
       Theory and Tables. (Copenhagen, 1950). 165 pp.
[12]   Kelly, F.P., Reversibility and Stochastic Networks. (J. Wiley
       & Sons, 1979), 230 pp.
[13]   Kobayashi, H., Modeling and Analysis - An Introduction to
       System Performance, Evaluation Methodology (Addison-Wesley,
       1978), 446 pp.
[14]   Moe, K., Driftskontrol og Betjeningsøkonomi ved Centraltjenes-
       ten, pp. 41-49 in Kjøbenhavns Telefon 1881-1931 (Copenhagen,
       1931, in Danish). Also published in English: The Development
       of Telephonic Communication in Copenhagen 1881-1931, Ingeniør-
       videnskabelige skrifter A, no. 32 (Copenhagen, 1932), p. 142.
[15]   Palm, C., Arbetskraftens fördelning vid betjäning av automat-
       maskiner. Industritidningen Norden, 1947, pp. 75-80, 90-94 och
       119-123 English version: The Assignment of Workers in Servicing
       Machines, The Journal of Industrial Engineering 9(1958) 28-42.
[16]   Sekino, A., Response Time Distribution of Multiprogrammed
       Time-Shared Computer Systems, in Proceedings of the 6th Annual
       Princeton Conference on Information Sciences and Systems, pp.
       613-619, 1972.
[17]   Sevast'yanov, B.A., An Ergodic Theorem for Markov Processes and
       its Application to Telephone Systems with Refusals, Theory of
       Probability and its Applications 2(1957) 104-112.
[18]   Takács, L., Introduction to Theory of Queues. (Oxford Univer-
       sity Press, 1962). 268 pp.

Performance of Data Communication Systems
and their Applications, G. Pujolle (ed.)
© North-Holland Publishing Company, 1981

MARKOV RENEWAL PROCESSES IN MODELLING
BINARY COMMUNICATION CHANNELS

Ioan Duma
Department of Electronic and Telecommunications,
Polythecnical Institute, Bucharest, Romania.
Gheorghiţă Zbăganu
Centre of Mathematical Statistics, Bucharest, Romania.

In this paper two models for the occurence of errors
in digital communication channels, models related to
Markov reneval processes (MRP), are presented. The
first model is a Fritchman-type model with semi-
Markovian evolution of channel states. The error-free
run and error-cluster distributions are derived. In the
second- a Muntner-Wolf-type model-the channel is represented as a sequence of renewal processes governed by a
general MRP. The proposed models include many of
earlier models as special cases.

INTRODUCTION

The mathematical models for digital channels are required for characterizing the statistical dependences observed between errors in
the real communication channels. They are useful in evaluation of
different error control techniques in data transmission systems.

There are three main categories of models:
a) Finite-state Markov chain models suggested by Gilbert[7] ,
Fritchman [9] .
b) Renewal models (in which the gaps are supposed to be independent
and identically distributed). See Elliot [8]  , Adoul, Fritchman and
Kanal [10]   .
c) Nonrenewal models such as Muntner-Wolf model [4] and Markov gap
model proposed by Haddad et al. [12]   .

Data analysis shows [10] that finite-state Markov chain models are
unsuitable to describe certain kinds of real channel behaviour.
Haddad et al. [12] demonstrated that renewal assumption is not valid
for troposcatter and VHF channels.

The assumptions made on the process which governs the choice of
renewal processes, although facilitating the parameter selection are
perhaps too restrictive[4],[6].

In this paper we consider two models related to Markov renewal processes which extend many known ones. In Section II the Markov renewal processes are defined. In Section III Fritchman-type models with
semi-markovian evolution of channel-states are presented. In section
IV we extend the Muntner-Wolf model.

261

## II. MARKOV RENEWAL PROCESSES

Let $(\Omega, \mathcal{F}, P)$ be a probability space. Let $S=\{1,2,\ldots,N\}$. We consider a random vector $(J_n, T_n): \Omega \longrightarrow S \times R_+$ $(n=0,1,\ldots)$ with $T_0 \equiv 0$ and suppose it to be a special case of a two-dimensional Markov chain in the sense that

$$P(J_{n+1}=j, T_{n+1} \leqq t | J_0, J_1, \ldots, J_n, T_0, \ldots, T_n) = P(J_{n+1}=j, T_{n+1} \leqq t | J_n, T_n) =$$
$$= Q_{J_n,j}(t-T_n) \tag{1}$$

In that case we shall say that the chain is induced by the matrix Q. If the matrix Q satisfies the properties :

a) $Q_{ij}(t)=0$ if $t \leqq 0$ for every i,j in S;

b) $\sum_{j \in S} Q_{ij}(\infty) = 1$ for every i in S;

c) the map $t \longrightarrow Q_{ij}(t)$ is nondecreasing and right continuous;

then we shall call it a semimarkov matrix over S. A two-dimensional Markov chain induced by a semimarkov matrix Q will be called in the sequel a Markov renewal prosess induced by Q and will be abbreviated to MRP.

A MRP has the following properties (see [3] )

1) $(J_n)_n$ is a Markov chain having the transition matrix $p_{ij}= Q_{ij}(\infty)$;

2) Let $X_n := T_n - T_{n-1}$ be the sojourn time in the state entered at the time $T_{n-1}$ and $X_0=0$. Then the distribution of the sojourn time in the state i is given by:

$$P(X_n \leqq t | J_0, J_1, \ldots, J_{n-1}=i) = \sum_{j \in S} Q_{ij}(t) := W_i(t) \tag{2}$$

3) Let $\quad F_{ij}(t) = \begin{cases} Q_{ij}(t)/p_{ij} & \text{if } p_{ij} > 0 \\ 1_{[1,\infty)}(t) & \text{if } p_{ij} = 0 \end{cases}$

where $1_{[1,\infty)}$ takes the value 1 on $[1, \infty)$ and 0 otherwise. Then the following equalities hold:

$$P(X_n \leqq t | J_0, J_1, \ldots, J_{n-1}=i, J_n=j) = P(X_n \leqq t | J_{n-1}=i, J_n=j) = F_{ij}(t) \tag{3}$$

$$P(X_{n_1} \leqq t_1, \ldots, X_{n_k} \leqq t_k | J_0=i_0, J_1=i_1, \ldots) = \prod_{j=1,k} F_{i_{n_j-1}, i_{n_j}}(t_j) \tag{4}$$

We remark that (4) means that $X_{n_1}, \ldots, X_{n_k}$ are independent given the states $J_0, J_1, \ldots$ .

Let $N(t) := \sup\{ n \geqq 0 | T_n \leqq t\}$ and $N_j(t)$ be the number of times that $J_k=j$ for $0 < k \leqq N(t)$. Let $Z_t := J_{N(t)}$. Then Z is called a semi-Markov process determined by $(N,I,Q)$, where $I=(a_1, \ldots, a_N)$ is the vector of the initial probabilities; such a process will be abbreviated to SMP.

The discrete-time SMP is defined ( [5] ) when t is a positive integer by the transition matrix $P=(p_{ij})_{i,j \in S}$ where

$$p_{ij}=P(J_n=j | J_{n-1}=i) \tag{5}$$

and by the distributions

$$f_{ij}(t) := P(X_n=t | J_{n-1}=i, J_n=j) . \tag{6}$$

In this case the distribution of the sojourn time in the state i is

$$w_i(t):=P(X_n=t \mid J_{n-1}=i)= \sum_{j=1,N} p_{ij}f_{ij}(t) \qquad (7)$$

whatever be the next state.

Another way to construct a SMP is to start with the distributions

$$q_{ij}(t)=P(J_n=j \mid X_n=t,J_{n-1}=i) \qquad (8)$$

and

$$w_i(t)=:P(X_n=t \mid J_{n-1}=i) \qquad (9)$$

Finally, a last procedure to construct a discrete SMP is to use the "core matrix" $C=(c_{ij}(t))_{i,j \in S}$ (see [5] ) where

$$c_{ij}(t)=P(J_n=j,X_n=t \mid J_{n-1}=i) \qquad (10)$$

Clearly,

$$\sum_{j \in S} c_{ij}(t)=w_i(t) \text{ and } c_{ij}(t)=p_{ij}f_{ij}(t)=w_i(t)q_{ij}(t) \qquad (11)$$

If $N=1$ the MRP becomes a renewal process. In general the succesive times $T_n$ at which a fixed state k is entered describe a renewal process (possibly delayed - see [3] ).

If $Q_{ij}(t) = p_{ij}1_{[1,\infty)}(t)$, the n the SMP becomes a Markov chain..

In the theory of MRP and SMP a main role is played by the probabilities

$$P_{ij}(t):= \begin{cases} P(Z_t=j \mid Z_0=i) & \text{if } t \geq 0 \\ 0 & \text{otherwise} \end{cases}$$

and

$$G_{ij}(t):= \begin{cases} P(N_j(t)>0 \mid Z_0=i) & \text{if } t \geq 0 \\ 0 & \text{otherwise .} \end{cases}$$

The states i and j are said to communicate iff $G_{ij}(\infty)>0$ and $G_{ji}(\infty)>0$. The MRP is called irreducible iff all the states communicate. The state i is called recurrent iff $G_{ii}(\infty)=1$; otherwise it is called transient. For a MRP the state i is recurrent (transient) iff it is the same in the Markov chain $J_n$(see [1] ).

We shall consider in the sequel only irreducible and recurrent MRP (i.e. all the states are recurrent).

We shall need in the following sections the probabilities $P_{ij}(t)$. It was shown ( [5] ) that

$$P_{ij}(t)= \delta_{ij}(1-W_i(t))+ \sum_{k \in S} \sum_{n=1,t} c_{ik}(n)P_{kj}(t-n) \qquad (12)$$

Let $m_i = \int_0^\infty tdW_i(t)$ ; $m_{ij}:= \int_0^\infty tdF_{ij}(t)$ ; $\mu_{ij}= \int_0^\infty tdG_{ij}(t)$

Suppose that all these quantities are finite. Then ( [1] ) there exists a stationary distribution $\pi =( \pi_1,\ldots,\pi_N)$ such that $\pi P=\pi$ .

We define:

$V^+(t,.)=T_{N(t)+1}-t$  - the time until the next jump occurs;

$J^+(t)$   $=J_{N(t)+1}$    - the next state              ;

$Z_t$    $=J_{N(t)}$ .

Let

$R_{jk}^{(i)}(x,t):=P(Z_t=j,J^+(t)=k,V^+(t)\leqq x \mid Z_0=i)$ .                    (13)

If $Q_{ij}(t)$ are lattice distributions of span 1, the asymptotic behavior of (13) is given by:

$$\lim_{t\to\infty} R_{jk}^{(i)}(x,t)=\mu_{jj}^{-1}p_{jk}\sum_{n=0}^{[x]+1}(1-F_{jk}(n))$$                    (14)

where [x] is the largest integer less than x . Similarly,

$$\lim_{t\to\infty} P(Z_t=j,V^+(t)\leqq x|Z_0=i) = (\sum \pi_k m_k)^{-1}\pi_j\sum_{n=0}^{[x]+1}(1-W_j(n))$$     (15)

and

$$\lim P_{ij}(t) =(\sum_k m_k\pi_k)^{-1}m_j\pi_j=m_j/\mu_{jj}.$$                    (16)

The proof of the above estimations is given in [2] .

We extend a little our definition of a MRP, admitting that $T_0\leqq 0$ and that the first transition is governed by another semimarkov matrix $\bar{Q}$ ,i.e. $\bar{Q}_{ij}(t)=P(J_1=j,T_1\leqq t \mid J_0=i)$. Such an object will be called a delayed MRP, induced by $(Q,\bar{Q})$.

If $\bar{Q}_{ij}(t) = p_{ij}(\sum_{n=0}^{[t]-1}(1-F_{jk}(n)))/m_j$  and the initial distribution is $a_j=m_j/\mu_{jj}$ for every j from S, then we have:

$P(Z_t=i,J_{N(t)+1}=j,T_{N(t)+1}\leqq t+x)= \lim_{n\to\infty} R_{ij}^{(k)}(x,n)$, i.e. it does not

depend on t neither on k. In this case we say, that the delayed MRP is stationary and its corresponding SMP is stationary. The first core-matrix which appears will be denoted with $\bar{C}$.

If $X_n$ is a sequence of i.i.d. random variables with $X_0=0$, the sequence $T_n=X_1+\ldots+X_n$ is called a renewal process. It is not difficult to see that a MRP with N=1 is a renewal process.

III. FRITCHMAN-TYPE ADDITIVE COMMUNICATION CHANNELS.

Let A be a finite set called alphabet, I the set of integers and $A^I$ the space of the sequences $(\ldots,x_{-1},x_0,x_1,\ldots)$ with $x_i\in A$, $i\in I$. The set $[a_m,\ldots,a_{m+n-1}] = \{x\in A^I \mid x_i=a_i,\ m\leqq i<m+n$ is called a n--dimensional block. Let $\mathcal{F}_A$ be the $\sigma$-algebra on $A^I$ generated by all the blocks.

A communication channel is a transition probability $\nu$ from $(A^I,\mathcal{F}_A)$

to $(B^I, \mathcal{F}_B)$ where A is the input alphabet and B is the output one. Denote it by $(A, \upsilon, B)$. The channel $(A, \upsilon, A)$ is an additive channel (cf. [11] ) iff :

a) The input-output alphabet A is a commutative group denoted additively;

b) There exists a probalility p on $\mathcal{F}_A$ such that for every $x, y \in A^I$ and $t \geqq s$ the equality $\upsilon_x( [y_s, \ldots, y_t] ) = p( [y_s - x_s, \ldots, y_t - x_t] )$ holds. If $y_s - x_s$ and $x_s$ are independent random variables (given the probability p) then the channel is said to be symmetric. If $A = GF(2)$ then the channel is a binary additive channel.

We shall consider in this section a binary additive symmetric communication channel.

Let $e_t := y_t - x_t$ be the difference between the output y and the input x at the moment t. We suppose that $e_t = f(Z_t)$ where Z is a stationary SMP in the sense given in Section II, and that $f(i)$ is equal to o if $i \in A$ and to 1 if $i \in B$ where A,B is a partition of the state space S.

The sequences of zeros between two successive errors are called gaps; the length of a gap is one plus the total number of zeros in the sequence between two 1's. Because Z is stationary, then $e_t$ is stationary too and we have

$$P(e_{t_1 + s} = i_1, \ldots, e_{t_k + s} = i_k) = P(e_{t_1} = i_1, \ldots, e_{t_k} = i_k)$$

Therefore the associated gap-process is stationary and all the gaps have the same distribution. That means that the notations

$$P(0^{m-1} \mid 1) := P(G_n \geqq m) \qquad (G_n \text{ is the n'th gap})$$
$$P(0^{m-1} 1 \mid 1) := P(G_n = m)$$
$$P(1^m \mid 0) := P(e_1 = 1, \ldots, e_m = 1 \mid e_0 = 0) \quad \text{(the error cluster distribution)}$$

are consistent. We compute these probabilities for the model just described above.

Using the techniques of [9] , we have :

$$P(o^m \mid 1) = (P(10^m) / P(1)) = \left( \sum_{i_0 \in B} \sum_{i_1 \in A} \ldots \sum_{i_m \in A} P(Z_0 = i_0, \ldots, Z_m = i_m) \right) / \left( \sum_{i_0 \in B} P(Z_0 = i_0) \right) =$$

$$= \frac{\sum_{i_0 \in B} \sum_{i_1 \in A} P(Z_0 = i_0, Z_1 = i_1) \sum_{i_2 \in A} \ldots \sum_{i_m \in A} P(Z_m = i_m, \ldots, Z_2 = i_2 \mid Z_0 = i_0, Z_1 = i_1)}{\sum_{i \notin B} P(Z_0 = i_0)}$$

Because
$$P(Z_0 = i_0, Z_1 = i_1 \mid i_0 \in B, i_1 \in A) = P(J_1 = i_1, J_0 = i_0, X_1 = 1 \mid i_0 \in B, i_1 \in A) =$$
$$= P(J_1 = i_1, X_1 = 1 \mid J_0 = i_0) P(J_0 = i_0), \text{ this probability is further equal to}$$
$a_{i_0} \bar{c}_{i_0 i_1}$ (1). But $i_0 \neq i_1$ implies that a jump is made at the moment 1, so that we have:
$$P(Z_m = i_m, \ldots, Z_2 = i_2 \mid Z_0 = i_0, Z = i_1) = P(J_{N(m)} = i_m, \ldots, J_{N(2)} = i_2 \mid J_0 = i_0, J_1 = i_1)$$
$$= P(Z_m = i_m, \ldots, Z_2 = i_2 \mid Z_1 = i_1) \quad \text{(because Z is a SMP)}.$$

Let us denote

$$\bar{P}_{i_1 i_m}(m-1) := \sum_{i_2 \in A} \cdots \sum_{i_{m-1} \in A} P(Z_m = i_m, \ldots, Z_2 = i_2 | Z_1 = i_1)$$

We partition the matrix C as follows:

$$C = \begin{array}{c} \\ A \\ B \end{array} \begin{array}{cc} A & B \\ \left\| \begin{array}{cc} D & E \\ F & H \end{array} \right\| \end{array}$$

According to (12) we have

$$\bar{P}_{i_1 i_m}(m-1) = \delta_{i_1 i_m}(1 - \sum_{k=1}^{m-1} w_i(k)) + \sum_{r \in A} \sum_{u=1}^{m-1} d_{i_1 r}(u) P_{rj}(m-1-u)$$

where $d_{ir}$ is the component situated on the i'th line and on the r'th column of the matrix D - the restriction of C to states belonging to A. Therefore we have:

$$a_{i_0} \bar{c}_{i_0 i_1}(1) = (\pi_{i_0} m_{i_0} P_{i_0 i_1}) / (m_{i_0} \sum_{k=1}^{N} \pi_k m_k) = (\pi_{i_0} P_{i_0 i_1}) / (\sum_{k=1}^{N} \pi_k m_k)$$

Finally,

$$P(0^m | 1) = (\sum_{i \in B} \sum_{j \in A} \sum_{k \in A} {}_i P_{ij} \bar{P}_{jk}(m-1) / (\sum_{s \in B} \pi_s m_s)$$

$P(1^m | 0)$ is analogous, changing A with B.

The results generalize Fritchman's ones ( [9] ) in the semimarkovian case.


IV.  AN EXTENSION OF MUNTNER-WOLF MODEL


Let $t_1, \ldots, t_n, \ldots$ be the moments when the errors occur in a binary additive symmetric communication channel. If $t_i - t_{i-1}$ are i.i.d. random variables $(i \geq 2)$ we say that the channel is a renewal one. Let E(t) be equal to 1 if there exists a k such that $t_k = t$ and be equal to 0 otherwise. In other words E(t) is equal to 1 iff an error occurs at the moment t. We call it the error process attached to the channel.

Consider now a family $S = \{1, \ldots, N\}$ of mutually independent renewal channels. Let $E_i(t)$ be the error process attached to the i-th channel and $p_i = P(E_i(t) = 1)$. We further assume that these probabilities do not depend on t (i.e. the channels are stationary). Let $FAC_i(t) = = P(E_i(s+t) = 1 | E_i(s) = 1)$ be the autocorrelation function of $E_i$. Let also $(J_n, T_n)$ be a delayed stationary MRP whose state space is S and $Z_t$ be its corresponding SMP. Assume that the processes $E_i(t)$ and $Z(t)$ are all independent.

In our model we make the hypothesis that the errors in the channel are given by the process $e_t = E_{Z_t}(t)$. That means the errors in the interval $[T_{n-1}, T_n)$ are generated by the renewal channel $J_{n-1}$. The choice of channels and occupation times are given by the MRP $(J_n, T_n)$.

We shall calculate the autocorrelation function of e, denoted by FAC(t). We have:

$$FAC(t) = P(e_{s+t}=1 | e_s=1) = (P(e_{s+t}=1, e_s=1))/P(e_s=1) =$$

$$= (\sum_{i \in S} P(e_{s+t}=1, e_s=1, Z_s=i))/(\sum_{i \in S} P(e_s=1, Z_s=i)) =$$

$$= (\sum_{i \in S} P(e_{s+t}=1 | e_s=1, Z_s=i) P(e_s=1 | Z_s=i) P(Z_s=i))/(\sum_{i \in S} P(e_{s+t}=1 | Z_s=i)a_i)$$

Taking into account that $Z_s=i$ implies that $e_s=E_i(s)$ and that the processes $E_i$ are independent of each other and all are independent of Z, the last expression becomes:

$$= (\sum_{i \in S} P(e_{s+t}=1 | E_i(s)=1, Z_s=i) p_i a_i)/(\sum_{i \in S} p_i a_i) \qquad (1)$$

It remains to compute:

$$P(e_{s+t}=1 | E_i(s)=1, Z_s=i) = \sum_{j \in S} P(e_{s+t}=1, Z_{s+t}=j | E_i(s)=1, Z_s=i) =$$

$$\sum_{j \in S} P(E_j(s+t)=1, Z_{s+t}=j | E_i(s)=1. Z_s=i) =$$

$$= \sum_{j \in S} P(E_j(s+t)=1 | E_i(s)=1) P(Z_{s+t}=j | Z_s=i) =$$

$$= P(E_i(s+t)=1 | E_i(s)=1) P(Z_{s+t}=i | Z_s=i) + \sum_{j \neq i} P(E_j(s+t)=1) P(Z_{s+t}=j | Z_s=i) =$$

$$= FAC_i(t) d_{ii} + \sum_{j \neq i} p_j d_{ij} \qquad (2)$$

where (observe that the SMP is delayed)

$$d_{ij} := P(Z_{s+t}=j | Z_s=i) = P(Z_t=j | Z_0=i) =$$

$$= \begin{cases} P(\bar{w}_i > t) + \sum_{m \in S} \sum_{k=1}^{t} \bar{c}_{im}(k) P_{mi}(t-k) & \text{if } j=i \\ \sum_{k=1}^{t} \sum_{m=1}^{N} \bar{c}_{im}(k) P_{mj}(t-k) & \text{if } j \neq i \end{cases}$$

and all the terms can be computed, namely:

$$P(\bar{w}_i > t) = \sum_{j=1}^{N} \sum_{s=t+1}^{\infty} \bar{c}_{ij}(s) \qquad (3)$$

and

$$\bar{c}_{ij}(t) = (p_{ij}/m_j)(1 - F_{ij}(t-1)) \qquad (4)$$

Replacing (2) into (1) we obtain finally:

$$FAC(t) = (\sum_{i \in S} (FAC_i(t) d_{ii} + \sum_{j \neq i} p_j d_{ij}) p_i a_i)/(\sum_{i \in S} p_i a_i) \qquad (5)$$

This model includes as a special case the model proposed by Muntner and Wolf ( [4] ). There, the choice of the renewal processes is governed by a degenerated delayed MRP described by the following distributions:

$$P_{ij} = \lambda_j, \quad \sum_{j=1}^{N} \,_j = 1; \quad \bar{c}_{ij}(n) = \begin{cases} \lambda_j/T & \text{for } n=1, 2, \ldots, T \\ 0 & \text{for } n > T \end{cases}$$

and

$$c_{ij}(n) = \begin{cases} \lambda_j & \text{for } n=T \\ 0 & \text{for } n \neq T \end{cases}$$

## CONCLUSIONS

The semimarkovian models of communication channels extend the three classes of models met in the literature. Their great advantage is that this surplus of generality and flexibility does not imply major computing difficulties. The present research has been directed toward the unification and generalization of the existing models. Our formulas are not much more complicated than Fritchman's ones. Their reccursive form permits the use of an electronic computer.

To establish the validity  of the model and to estimate the parameters in the real communication channels, further investigations are required.

## REFERENCES

1. R.Pyke,"Markov Renewal Processes: definitions and preliminary properties", Ann.Math.Stat.vol.32 (1961),pp 1231-1242
2. R.Pyke,"Markov Renewal Processes with finitely many states" Ann.Math.Stat.,vol 32 (1961),pp. 1243-1250
3. E.Çinlar,"Markov renewal theory",Adv.Appl.Prob.,vol.1(1969) pp. 123-187
4. M.Muntner, I.K.Wolf,"Predicted performance of error control techniques over real channels",IEEE Trans.Inform.Theory.,vol.IT-14 sept.1968,pp.640-650
5. R.A.Howard,Dynamic Probabilistic Systems",vol.II;Semi-Markov and Decision Processes,Wiley,1971.
6. I.Duma,"Modèles semi-markoviens pour les canaux numériques",An. Univ.Buc.Anul XXIX-1980,pp.37-45.
7. E.N.Gilbert,"Capacity of a burst noise channel",Bell Syst.Tech.J. vol.39,Sept.1960,pp.1253-1266.
8. E.O.Elliott,"A model of a switched telephone network for date communications",Bell.Syst.Tech.J.,vol.44,Jan.1965,pp.89-109.
9. B.D.Fritchman,"A binary channel characterization using partitioned Markov chains",IEEE Trans.Inform.Theory,vol.IT-13,Apr.1967,221-236.
10. J.P.A.Adoul,B.D.Fritchman,L.N.Kanal,"A critical statistic for channels with memory",IEEE Trans.Inform.Theory,vol.It-18,N.I., Jan.1972,pp.133-171.
11. S.Guiaşu,"Information Theory with applications",McGraw-Hill 1977.
12. A.H.Haddad,S.Tsai,B.Goldberg,G.C.Ranieri, "Markov gap models for real communication channels",IEEE Trans.Commun.,vol.COM-23, pp.1189-1197,Nov.1975.

Performance of Data Communication Systems
and their Applications, G. Pujolle (ed.)
© North-Holland Publishing Company, 1981

BOUNDS ON THE PERFORMANCE OF
MULTIPLE BUS MULTIPROCESSOR SYSTEMS

M. Ajmone Marsan
Istituto di Elettronica e Telecomunicazioni
Politecnico di Torino, Italy.

M. Gerla
Computer Science Department
University of California, Los Angeles, USA.

Markovian models for the performance analysis of a class of
multiprocessor systems are introduced. The performance index
considered is the average number of active processors, from
which a variety of other performance measures can be obtained. Exact models are shown to be impractical for even medium
size systems, because of the number of states needed for the
exact system description. Two approximate models are introduced that provide, respectively, an upper and a lower bound to
the system performance. The complexity of the approximate
models allows to study any system of reasonable size, as the
number of states increases only proportionally to the number of
processors. Results are presented for some test cases, showing
that the accuracy of the approximate models is extremely good
for a wide range of configurations.

INTRODUCTION

Tightly connected multiprocessor systems are characterized by the
presence of several processing units and one or more common memory areas,
used by the processors for the exchange of information and, possibly, the
storage of common code and data structures of non frequent use. Processors
and common memories are connected by some kind of communication system,
usually called interconnection network.

Early multiprocessor systems were developed using crossbar networks
to connect processors and memories. A widely known crossbar multiprocessor
system is C.mmp, the Carnegie Mellon multiminicomputer /1/. The performance
of crossbar multiprocessors has been widely analyzed in recent years, /2-6/.

With the availability of inexpensive microprocessors, multiprocessor
systems with a very large number of components are now becoming feasible
and cost effective. For such systems a crossbar interconnection network may
be intolerably expensive and in general it would provide a bandwidth much
higher than needed. A more attractive alternative is represented by bus-ori-
ented interconnection networks. Single or multiple bus architectures can be
used, according to the bandwidth required for the specific application.
These interconnection networks are generally called "multiple-bus" or "high-
way deficient" /6/ networks. Some papers addressing the analysis of bus
systems appeared very recently in the literature /6-8/.

This paper presents approximate models for the analysis of a class of
multiprocessor systems. The models we develop are an extension of those
considered in /2,3,5/, as we consider a reduced number of paths between

269

processors and memories, like in /6/, where different approximations were presented to solve the same problem. The advantage of the models presented here is that they can be used to numerically obtain performance indices for multiprocessor systems with a large number of processors, and that they provide upper and lower bounds on system performance.

Section 2 describes the class of multiprocessor systems considered in this study and the assumptions on their operations. Section 3 discusses exact models, and in section 4 the two approximate models are introduced. Results are presented in section 5. Section 6 concludes the paper.

THE MULTIPROCESSOR SYSTEM

The multiprocessor system considered in this paper consists of processing units that exchange informations using several external common memory modules. The connection among processing units and common memories is assured by a set of global busses.

Processing units (or Processors for short) are composed by a CPU and a private memory, connected by a private bus, and are interfaced to all global busses. The global busses are connected to all processors and common memory modules. Common memory modules can be reached using any global bus. Only one processor at a time can access a memory.

A multiprocessor system containing p processing units, m common memory modules, and b global busses is called a pxmxb system. The block diagram of a 3x3x2 system is shown in fig. 1.

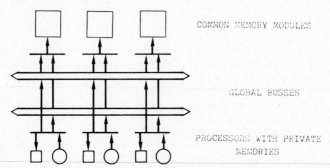

COMMON MEMORY MODULES

GLOBAL BUSSES

PROCESSORS WITH PRIVATE MEMORIES

Fig. 1   Block diagram of a 3x3x2 system.

Interference among processors is caused by the sharing of busses and common memories: when a processor has to write or read in a given common memory module, it must contend with other processors to use the shared resources; if the processor is not granted them, it queues until they are available.

Crossbar systems are obtained by providing a number of busses at least equal to the minimum between the number of processors and the number of common memories, i.e. $b = \min(m, p)$. We consider here the case in which less busses are available, i.e. $b < \min(m, p)$. Moreover we assume that the number of processors is larger than that of common memories, or equal to it, i.e. $p \geqslant m$.

This class of multiprocessor systems can be represented as a closed queueing network with p classes of customers and with passive resources /9,10/ as shown in fig. 2.

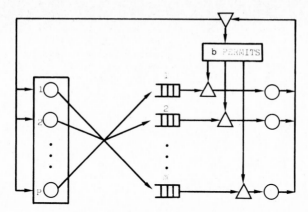

Fig. 2   Queueing network model.

When we are in the crossbar case, the effect of busses can be ignored and the queueing system has a product form solution /11/. For multiple bus systems no product form solution exists, and the exact analysis becomes rapidly cumbersome when the system size increases. It is thus convenient to resort to approximate models. Several methods can be used to obtain approximate performance indices; those introduced in this paper are derived directly from the exact Markovian representation of the system.

The assumptions we make regarding the operation of the system are similar to those found in the literature on crossbar systems.

Each processing unit is active for some time, while the CPU is executing a program that only requires accesses to its own private memory; the duration of these activity periods is an exponentially distributed random variable with the same parameter $\lambda$ for all processors. At the end of an activity period, processors generate access requests directed to a specific memory, chosen at random among the external common memory modules; each memory is requested with the same probability $1/m$. If a bus is available and the requested memory is free, the processor accesses it for an exponentially distributed period with parameter $\mu$, the same for all processors and memories. If either no bus is available or the requested memory is busy, the processor idles waiting for the necessary resources. At the end of an access the processor begins a new activity period; bus and memory are released and can be accessed by other processors. An arbitration mechanism for the assignment of the bus is assumed, that randomly chooses among the heads of the nonempty queues referencing free memory modules.

The model we consider is thus completely symmetric with respect to processors and memories. These symmetries are not necessary to obtain a Markovian model, but allow some reductions in the size of the resulting Markov chain.

The performance index we consider is the average number of active processors, called processing power and denoted by P. From this quantity it is possible to obtain many other performance measures: for instance we can evaluate the average time needed to satisfy an access request using

Little's result twice:

$$P = \lambda' \ \frac{1}{\lambda}$$

$$p - P = \lambda' \ T$$

(1)

where $\lambda'$ is the rate at which customers cycle through the network and T is the time spent in the queue and accessing the memory. Solving for T we find:

$$T = \frac{p - P}{\lambda P}$$

(2)

Other interesting quantities can be evaluated in a similar way.

EXACT MODELS

The behaviour of the multiprocessor system can be modeled using a continuous-time Markov chain whose state is defined by the 2p-tuple:

$$(m_1, s_1, m_2, s_2, \ldots, m_p, s_p)$$

(3)

where:

   $m_i$ is the memory referenced by processor i

   $s_i$ is the state of processor i

$m_i$ can take values:

   0: processor's private memory

   K: k-th common memory module

$s_i$ can take values:

   0: active

   j: queueing (j-th in queue) for module $m_i$

   -1: accessing common memory module $m_i$

The symmetries introduced in the model allow reduction of the state description, and hence the number of states in the Markov chain, using the lumping technique /12/. The resulting state description is:

$$(n_m, \ q_1, \ q_2, \ldots, \ q_m)$$

(4)

where

$n_m$ is the number of processors currently accessing a common memory

$q_1, \ldots, q_b$ are the numbers of processors queueing for the memories currently accessed, arranged in decreasing order

$q_{b+1}, \ldots, q_m$ are the numbers of processors queueing for a free memory, not accessible because no bus is available, arranged in decreasing order.

As an example, the state transition diagram of the lumped Markov chain for a 4x3x2 system is shown in fig. 3.

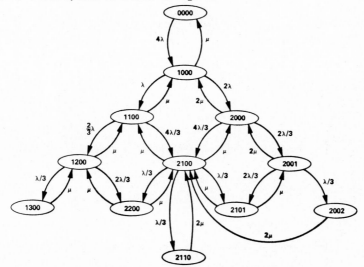

Fig. 3 State transition diagram for a 4x3x2 system.

It must be noted that an increase in the number of processors and/or memories complicates the Markov chain, whereas an increase in the number of busses tends to simplify the Markovian representation. This is due to the fact that the presence of a higher number of busses makes the system more similar to a crossbar, and thus reduces the number of possible queueing situations.

APPROXIMATE MODELS

With the application of lumping to the exact Markov chain with state definition (3), we obtain the most compact Markovian system description. If we further reduce the state information, we no longer have a transition system that satisfies the Markov property.

The two approximate models we now present are obtained reducing the state information and still assuming a Markovian behaviour on the reduced state space. An approximate model is defined by the state definition and by a method to evaluate the transition rates.

Upper bound

In order to derive an upper bound to the system performance we do not keep track of the state of each memory queue, but simply assume that all queued processors can request with uniform probability one of the memory modules that are not accessible. This implies that a queued processors can select a new memory when a bus or a memory become unblocked; we thus redistribute processors in the memory queues and tend to relieve congestion.

The state definition is

$$(n_m, n_q) \tag{5}$$

where:

$n_m$ is the number of processors in service

$n_q$ is the number of queued processors

The total number of states required to describe the operation of a pxmxb multiprocessor system, N, is:

$$N = 1 + b \{ p + (1-b) / 2 \} \tag{6}$$

The transition rates are easily obtained; from state $(i,j)$ we can only reach four states:

$$(i+1,j) \quad (i-1,j) \quad (i,j+1) \quad (i,j-1) \tag{7}$$

and, denoting by $R_{k,k\pm1}$ the transition in which k is increased (or decreased) by one we have:

$$R_{i,i+1} = (p-i-j) \; \lambda \; \frac{m-i}{m} \qquad \begin{array}{c} 0 \leq i < b \\[6pt] p-i-j > 0 \end{array}$$

$$R_{i,i-1} = \begin{cases} i \; \mu \left( \dfrac{i-1}{i} \right)^j & i < b \\[10pt] b \; \mu \left( \dfrac{b-1}{m} \right)^j & i = b \end{cases} \tag{8}$$

$$R_{j,j+1} = \begin{cases} (p-i-j) \; \dfrac{i}{m} \; \lambda & i < b, \quad p-i-j > 0 \\[10pt] (p-b-j) \; \lambda & i = b, \quad p-b-j > 0 \end{cases}$$

$$R_{j,j-1} = \begin{cases} i \; \mu \left\{ 1 - \left( \dfrac{i-1}{i} \right)^j \right\} & i < b \\[10pt] b \; \mu \left\{ 1 - \left( \dfrac{b-1}{m} \right)^j \right\} & i = b \end{cases}$$

The processing power is easily evaluated once the steady state probabilities are known; the number of active processors associated to each state is $p - n_m - n_q$.

Birth and death model (lower bound)

The most simplified approximate model we can build for the multiprocessor system, in order to estimate the average number of active processors, is a birth and death continuous time Markov chain, in which the state definition is given by the number of active processors. No information is recorded about the state of the memory queues. The transition rate from state $i$ to state $i-1$ is given by $i\lambda$; the transition rate from state $i$ to state $i+1$ is evaluated using an "averaging" technique: the number of states in the exact lumped chain with $i$ active processors is counted; the transition rates from all such states to all states with $i+1$ active processors are added; the transition rate between macrostates is estimated as the ratio of the sum of the transition rates to the number of states.

The state transition diagram of the Markov chain for a pxmxb system is shown in fig. 4, where

$$\beta_i = \frac{\sum_{j=1}^{b-1} j\, p_j(i) + b \sum_{j=0}^{i-b} \left\{ P_b(j+b)\, P_{m-b}(i-2b-j+m) \right\}}{\sum_{j=1}^{b-1} p_j(i) + \sum_{j=0}^{i-b} \left\{ P_b(j+b)\, P_{m-b}(i-2b-j+m) \right\}} \quad , \quad i > 1 \tag{9}$$

and $P_i(j)$ is the number of unordered partitions of $j$ in $i$ parts, with $i$ and $j$ integers.

Fig. 4   State transition diagram for a pxmxb system.

The processing power can now be evaluated in closed form as:

$$P = \sum_{i=1}^{p} \frac{\left(\frac{\lambda}{\mu}\right)^{p-i} \frac{p!}{(i-1)!} \prod_{k=1}^{p-i} \beta_k^{-1}}{1 + \sum_{j=0}^{p-1} \left\{ \left(\frac{\lambda}{\mu}\right)^{p-j} \frac{p!}{j!} \prod_{k=1}^{p-j} \beta_k^{-1} \right\}} \tag{10}$$

Note that no error is made in the approximation if all states with $i$ processor are equally likely.

Results obtained with this second approximation show that the estimate of the processing power it provides are smaller than the exact value. We therefore conjecture that this approximation provides a lower bound on processing power for the considered multiprocessor systems.

RESULTS

Exact and approximate results were compared by solving the exact lumped chain and the approximate ones for several multiprocessor systems. When the number of states in the exact chain becomes too large to be easily handled, we resort to a simulation program, rather than to a computer generation of the transition rate matrix.

First we present results for a 4x3x2 system, whose exact lumped chain is shown in fig. 3. The values of processing power obtained by solving the exact and the two approximate models are given in table 1, for several values of $\varrho = \lambda / \mu$.

| $\varrho$ | Processing power | | |
|---|---|---|---|
| | lower bound | exact | upper bound |
| 0.001 | 3.996 | 3.996 | 3.996 |
| 0.01 | 3.96 | 3.96 | 3.96 |
| 0.1 | 3.603 | 3.604 | 3.605 |
| 0.3 | 2.886 | 2.892 | 2.90 |
| 0.5 | 2.326 | 2.338 | 2.358 |
| 1. | 1.489 | 1.506 | 1.538 |
| 3. | 0.571 | 0.58 | 0.60 |
| 5. | 0.35 | 0.356 | 0.37 |
| 10. | 0.178 | 0.18 | 0.188 |

Table 1 - Processing power for a 4x3x2 system.

The second system we consider is a 6x4x2 multiprocessor: the exact lumped chain has in this case 37 states and is not shown. The two bounds yield chains with 12 and 7 states respectively. The values of processing power are given in table 2.

| $\varrho$ | Processing power | | |
|---|---|---|---|
| | lower bound | exact | upper bound |
| 0.001 | 5.994 | 5.994 | 5.994 |
| 0.01 | 5.94 | 5.94 | 5.94 |
| 0.1 | 5.365 | 5.386 | 5.39 |
| 0.3 | 4.07 | 4.17 | 4.2 |
| 0.5 | 3.08 | 3.19 | 3.25 |
| 1. | 1.79 | 1.86 | 1.90 |
| 3. | 0.63 | 0.65 | 0.66 |
| 5. | 0.383 | 0.393 | 0.399 |
| 10. | 0.192 | 0.197 | 0.20 |

Table 2 - Processing power for a 6x4x2 system.

The last set of results is for a 16x8x3 system. The exact solution was in this case estimated using a simulation program written in SIMULA 67 and run on a DEC-10 mainframe. Table 3 shows the values of processing power.

Note that in this case the number of busses is much smaller than the

| $\varrho$ | Processing power | | | |
|---|---|---|---|---|
| | lower bound | simulation | upper bounds | |
| 0.001 | 15.98 | 15.98 | 15.98 | 15.984 |
| 0.01 | 15.83 | 15.85 | 15.84 | 15.842 |
| 0.1 | 13.89 | 14.26 | 14.27 | 14.428 |
| 0.333 | 8.20 | 8.7 | 8.73 | 8.81 |
| 0.5 | 5.79 | 5.96 | 5.99 | 5.99 |
| 1. | 2.97 | 3.04 | 2.99 | 3.0 |
| 3. | 0.99 | 1.02 | 1.00 | 1.00 |
| 5. | 0.60 | 0.61 | 0.60 | 0.60 |
| 10. | 0.3 | 0.3 | 0.3 | 0.3 |

Table 3 - Processing power for a 16x8x3 system.

number of common memory modules: we can thus obtain a very simple upper bound to the processing power by disregarding the contention for common memories: the model is thus a closed queueing network of the machine repairman type with three exponential servers. Using queueing theory notation we can also identify this model as a M/M/3//p queue. Results are very easy to obtain because, again, we only need to solve a birth and death Markov chain. In table 3 we also give the value of the processing power as obtained with this method. Note that the approximation is very good; we expect that this is generally the case when the number of common memory modules largely exceeds that of busses.

Results show that the approximate models presented in this paper provide very tight bounds on processing power. The relative error is well below 5% in the two cases where we can compare the approximate results with the exact ones. For the 16x8x3 system the approximate results lie in the 99.9 confidence interval associated to the estimate of the processing power in the majority of cases; furthermore, the solution of the Markovian model by numerical methods requires much less CPU time than the simulation program.


CONCLUSIONS

The availability of simple models of multiprocessor systems should impact on the architectural choices in the design stage of multiprocessor systems: these models allow one to evidentiate and compare the quantitative behaviour of the different architectural solutions.

The Markovian assumption, necessary to obtain models that can be computationally solved, is seldom justified in practice; it is thus more convenient to construct approximate models whose solution is very easy to obtain, rather than solving exactly a complex Markovian model that only approximates the behaviour of the real system. This is particularly true if we can easily obtain bounds on the solution of the exact model.

In this paper two approximate Markovian models were presented, suitable for the estimation of the processing power of a class of multiple bus multiprocessor systems. The approximate models provide results that are upper and lower bounds, respectively, to the processing power as obtained using an exact Markovian model. The upper bound is intuitively justified, whereas the lower bound is only conjectured. The percentage errors introduced by the approximations are very low (generally lower than 5%), thus, for most practical purposes, they provide a very good alternative to the solution of the exact model, which is expensive to obtain when the system size increases due to the enormous number of states in the Markov Chain.

Performance indices different from processing power and better suited to particular applications can be easily obtained.

## REFERENCES

/1/    W.A. Wulf and G.C. Bell "C.mmp, a multiminiprocessor". Proceedings AFIPS 1972 Fall Joint Computer Conference.

/2/    F. Baskett and A.J. Smith "Interference in multiprocessor computer systems with interleaved memory". Communications of the ACM, June 1976, pp. 327-334

/3/    D.P. Bhandarkar "Analysys of memory interference in multiprocessors". IEEE Transactions on Computers, September 1975, pp. 897-908

/4/    C.H. Hoogendoorn "A general model for memory interference in multiprocessors". IEEE Transactions on Computers, October 1977, pp. 998-1005

/5/    A.S. Sethi and N. Deo "Interference in multiprocessor systems with localized memory access probabilities". IEEE Transactions on Computers, February 1979, pp.157-173

/6/    P.J. Willis "Derivation and comparison of multiprocessor contention measures". IEE Journal on Computers and Digital Techniques, August 1978, pp. 93-98

/7/    F. Fung and H. Torng "On the analysis of memory conflicts and bus contentions in a multiple-microprocessor system". IEEE Transactions on Computers, January 1979, pp. 28-37.

/8/    S. Hoener and W. Roeder "Efficiency of a multiprocessor system with time-shared busses". EUROMICRO Newsletter, 1977, pp. 35-42

/9/    K.M. Chandy and C.H. Sauer "Approximate methods for analyzing queueing network models of computer systems". ACM Computing Surveys, September 1978, pp. 281-317

/10/   T.W. Keller "Computer system models with passive resources". PhD Thesis, University of Texas at Austin, 1976

/11/   F. Baskett, K.M. Chandy, R.R. Muntz and J. Palacios "Open, closed and mixed networks of queues with different classes of customers". ACM Journal, April 1975 pp. 284-260

/12/   J.G. Kemeni and J.L. Shell "Finite Markov Chains". Van Nostrand Princeton, 1960

*This work was supported in part by ONR under contract N00014-79-C-0866 and by NATO.*

Performance of Data Communication Systems
and their Applications, G. Pujolle (ed.)
© North-Holland Publishing Company, 1981

SIMULATION OF AN X.25 NETWORK

PROVIDING THROUGHPUT GUARANTEES

A. Giessler, A. Jägemann, E. Mäser
Gesellschaft für Mathematik und Datenverarbeitung (GMD)
Rheinstrasse 75, 6100 Darmstadt, F.R. Germany

The problem of throughput guarantees in public packet
networks is considered and has been studied by simulation
methods.  The simulation experiments are based on a
transportation system applying a DCE-DCE end-to-end
protocol with multiplexing functions.  A summary of the
objectives of the network concept is given in the first
part of this paper describing all components which
are of interest with respect to the service aspect of
throughput guantees.  Simulation results showing the
performance characteristics of this approach are discussed in the second part of this paper.

## 1. INTRODUCTION

In this paper we discuss the problem of throughput guarantees in
public packet networks. For this purpose a hypothetical network has
been proposed [1] and simulation experiments have been done in order
to gain an understanding of the network behaviour.

So far 'guarantee for throughput' is one important, however not well-
known aspect of service quality in public packet networks which needs
some clarification. This term means that the throughput which is
requested by a user within the facility field of the X.25 call re-
guest packet [2] has to be considered as minimum and guaranteed
throughput, which may be exceeded in the case of free transportation
capacity. Other important aspects of service quality are:

- 'fairness' properties [3] or
- delay objectives [4].

The basic idea of our network proposal is that the problem of throughput guarantees can be solved by providing appropriate mechanisms of
network control involving 'static' and 'dynamic' control mechanisms
which are simply characterized by:

- Static control: Reservation of network resources
                (data routes, buffers, capacities);
- Dynamic control:Observation and control of the net-
                work traffic and resource utilization.

Both mechanisms have to be balanced in order to satisfy the requirement for service quality as well as network flexibility. We set the
following main goals for the transportation systems:

- Guaranteed service:
  All users should achieve a throughput which is at least equal to
  their requested throughput.
- High network efficiency:
  The global network throughput should be as close as possible to
  the theoretical throughput limit, especially in the case of an
  'infinite' applied load.
- Fair user service:
  Virtual calls requesting the same throughput should be served with
  the same degree of service quality independent of the actual load
  situation or of their path length.
- Independence of the network behaviour from the environment: Any
  'misbehaviour' of users should only affect their own virtual call
  and does not cause interference with other ones. Therefore, the
  network resources must be prevented from being utilized by virtual
  calls which are congested at their sinks.

The network model has already been described in [2]. We thus give
only a short characterization of the main network components in the
next section. The behaviour of the proposed transportation systems
has also been studied by simulation methods and some of the results
are presented and discussed in the second part of this paper.

## 2. NETWORK MODEL:

In [5] a summary and comparison of different network architectures
are given and the advantages and disadvantages of the so-called:

- concatenated segment approach [6];
- endpoint approach [7] and
- DCE-DCE approach [8]

are discussed. Our own model is quite similar to the mentioned DCE-
DCE approach but has the following additional and different features
(see also figure 1):

- Between all possible pairs of subnetwork nodes (all nodes in the
  network without the DTEs) exists at least one logical DCE-DCE connection called virtual line (VL).
- VLs are assumed to be permanently in the data transfer phase. Thus
  the subnetwork consists of a preallocated and completely meshed
  'VL skeleton'.
- VLs are equipped with reserved channel capacity and buffers, whose
  size is equal to the VL window size. The reservation is done at
  the network entry and exit nodes as well as at the transit nodes.
  Thus the capacities of physical channels in the subnetwork are sub-
  divided into the capacities of VLs which share common physical
  channels and also the problem of buffer deadlocks is excluded. The
  selection of VL capacities and VL routes is critical and needs
  global traffic assumptions and an VL capacity adaptation scheme[2].
  In the following this problem is ignored and we may concentrate on
  flow control problems in a 'static' network.
- VLs involve a multiplexing function. This means that each VL handles

the total traffic of several X.25 virtual calls, which are multiplexed into the considered VL and which use the same source and
destination DCE.

- The access of X.25 logical channels to the network resources is controlled by a special 'control multiplexer' component.
- X.25 logical channels are invisible within the subnetwork, and user-
specific resource allocation only takes places at the network bor-
der. The reservation includes:
  -- buffer reservation, whose size is equal to the applied X.25
     window size;
  -- capacity reservation as specified by the throughput class. Calls
     are refused  if the VL capacity would be exceeded.

Figure 1 shows the network architecture with all important network
components that also have been modelled by our simulation system.
These are:

- Source/sink
  components:
  Realized by
  random number
  generators
  producing
  different dis-
  tribution func-
  tions for
  source input
  rates, sink
  output rates
  and packet
  lengths.
- L2/L3/VL/VLT
  protocols:
  Only a simple
  version of
  these proto-
  cols has been
  modelled
  providing
  send/receive
  functions and
  flow control.
  L2,L3 and VL
  operate on a
  window mecha-
  nism, while
  the VLT func-
  tion ('VL-
  protocol'in
  transit nodes)
  only performes
  routing tasks.
  VL specific
  node-to-node
  signalling
  between tran-
  sit nodes is
  unnecessary,

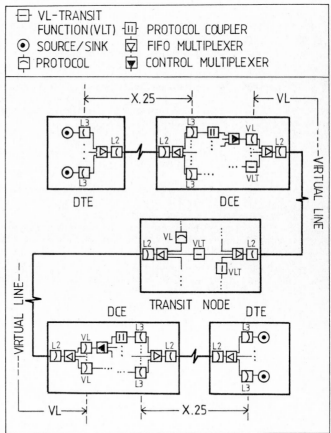

FIG. 1:    STRUCTURE OF THE TRANSPORTATION SYSTEM

because the VLT component uses separate and reserved 'cyclic'buffers
On the access lines L2 and L3 are the level 2 and 3 protocols of

X.25 [9, 10].

- Protocol coupler component:
  This unit couples the local X.25 protocol shell with the VL protocol shell and controles the X.25 input rate at the network entry
  point due to the load situation at the remote X.25 segment. Any
  rotation of the remote X.25 window is signalled across the network
  to the local protocol coupler by special VL acknowledgement packets
  which perform a similar credit mechanism as in [11].The coupler uses
  a so-called 'packet injection counter' whose value is equal to the
  remote X.25 window size. The counter is decremented when packets
  are handed over to the network. X.25 packets are only allowed to be
  injected into the subnetwork if this counter is greater than zero.
  Otherwise packets are delayed at the source DCE until credits are
  received incrementing the counter. Therfore the receive sequence
  number P (R) has an end-to-end significance in our model independent of the setting of the D-bit [10] in data packets.

- FIFO multiplexer:
  Trunk and access lines are modelled with FIFO multiplexers.

- CONTROL multiplexer:
  The control multiplexer has to control the sharing of the VL-capa-
  city between several X.25 logical channels and has to satisfy the
  following requirements:
  -- The throughput of each controlled virt. call should be equal to
     or even greater than the requested throughput. Of course this
     is only possible if certain conditions are met (input and output
     rates$\geq$ requested throughput).
  -- Free capacities should be distributed in a fair way among compe-
     ting virtual calls.
  -- Control multiplexers at different locations should cooperate in
     the sense that their local control decisions have no negative
     effect on the global network behaviour.
  -- virt. calls with different throughput classes and high or low
     priority are supported.

All the mentioned components have been modelled on a level of detail
which was necessary in order to simulate the data transfer phase and
especially the applied flow control algorithms. However the following
simplifications were made:

- processing delay is neglected;
- propagation delay is neglected;
- error-free transmission lines and
- fixed data packet length are assumed with:
  -- 128 bytes user data field and
  --   8 bytes overhead on access lines and
  --  11 bytes overhead on trunk lines;
- 'infinite' input and output rates (saturated network) are simulated. (Infinite input rate means that packets are generated by the
  source components in the DTEs whenever the L3 component is able to
  queue a new packet and infinite output rate means that packets are
  immediately accepted at receipt at their sinks).

## 3. SIMULATION EXPERIMENTS:

Before starting with the presentation of the simulation results a few
terms are defined which will be used for the interpretation of the
simulation curves.

## 3.1 TERMINOLOGY:

- Throughput request (TR) [p/sec]:
  TR is derived from the throughput class (TC) and the maximum packet length (MPL).

$$TR = 2^{TC}/MPL$$

(It should be mentioned that we have used the definition of TC given in [9]. MIAT = $TR^{-1}$ denotes the mean maximum inter-arrival time of data packets which is tolerable at the control multiplexers in order to provide throughput guarantees. Table 1 summarizes TR and MIAT for different TCs.

| TC | 5 | 6 | 7 | 8 | 9 | 10 |
|---|---|---|---|---|---|---|
| TR [p/sec] | 0.23 | 0.46 | 0.92 | 1.84 | 3.68 | 7.37 |
| MIAT [sec] | 4.40 | 2.17 | 1.09 | 0.54 | 0.27 | 0.14 |

Table 1: Throughput request and maximum inter-arrival time

- Throughput limit (TL) [p/sec]:
  TL is the maximum possible network throughput which depends on the network topology, trunk and access line capacities, VL capacities, source and sink rates of X.25 logical channels. The ratio of the simulated network throughput (ST) and TL is a measure for the efficiency (E) of the transportation system.

- Packet delay (PD) [sec]:
  PD is the elapsed time when a packet is handed over to the packet level at the source DTE and its receipt at the destination DTE. Therefore PD is the DTE-DTE end-to-end delay.

- Reservation degree (RD):
  RD is defined by the ratio of the sum of the requested throughputs on an access, trunk or virtual line and its capacity (in our simulation model we have only considered situations with $0 \le RD \le 1$).

The following terms refer to the control multiplexer:

- Control period (CP) [sec]:
  CP is the interval during which all virt. call requests should be satisfied by the control multiplexer. We assumend, that a throughput request only has to be guaranteed if it is equal to or greater than a minumum throughput threshold (MT), which can be defined as the fraction X of the controlled capacity (CC). Thus two types of network traffic can be distinguished.

  -- guaranteed traffic:  $TR \overset{>}{=} MT$
  -- unguaranteed traffic: $TR < MT$

The introduction of this threshold is necessary and plausible, because otherwise all virt. calls with TR.CP < 1 might have a too small input rate at the multiplexer and will not be able to deliver at least one packet during each control period. It is not reasonable to choose the CP parameter arbitrarily for each multiplexer. Therefore, we calculated this quantity in such a way that during the control period at least NMIN packets (NMIN$\overset{>}{=}$ 1) can be served on a subchannel whose throughput request is equal to the throughput threshold. Thus we have:

CP.MT/8MPL = NMIN or
CP = (8.MPL.NMIN)/(X.CC)$\ge$ 8.MPL/(X.CC) = 8.MPL/MT

- Relative load (RL):
  RL is the ratio of the mean multiplexer queueing delay of a virt. call and the control period. This quantity is a measure of the

'virt. call pressure' on the control multiplexer.

- Relative service delay (RSD):
  RSD is the ratio of the time interval which is actually needed to
  serve the throughput request of a virt. call and the control period.

- Relative service quality (RSQ):
  RSQ is the ratio of the simulated virt. call throughput and the
  requested throughput.

Now we have sufficient measures to study the problem of throughput
guarantees. Throughput guarantees are possible, if $RSQ \geqq 1$ and $RSD < 1$
holds for all virt. calls with $TR \geqq MT$.

## 3.2. TEST CONFIGURATIONS:

Figure 2 shows the simulated test
configurations. Configuration 1
has been used to study the effect
of different throughput classes
on the network behaviour and configuration 2 has been simulated
to demonstrate the network behaviour in dependency of the
number of hops. Both configurations are characterized by:

- configuration 1:
  Configuration 1 consists of
  two subnetwork nodes and two
  hosts connected to them. 10
  virtual calls are esta-
  blished with TC=1 up to 10
  sharing the capacity of a
  single VL.

- configuration 2:
  Configuration 2 is a 6-node
  chain subnetwork with 15 VLs
  (=6(6-1)/2) and 30 virtual
  calls (VC). In figure 2
  VLs and VCs starting from
  node 7 have only been plotted.
  All hosts are connected by two
  VCs with the same TC=8, but
  with different priorities.

Simulation runs based on other
and more complex test configurations lead to a quite similar
network behaviour like these
simple configurations. We thus
are allowed to restrict our-
selves to the easier discussion of the simulation results concerning
configurations 1 and 2

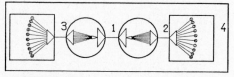

CONFIGURATION-1

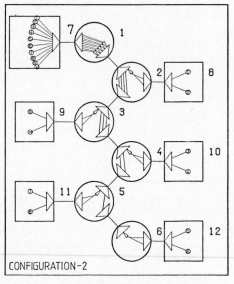

CONFIGURATION-2

FIG.2:     TEST CONFIGURATIONS

## 4. SIMULATIONS RESULTS:

The behaviour of the proposed transportation system is analyzed by a
separate discussion of the following points:

- global network throughput;
- time behaviour of the control multiplexer;
- network behaviour in dependency from:

-- the number of hops(VL path length);
-- the throughput class;
-- the X.25 window size;
-- VL window size and
-- the reservation degree;
- comparison between FIFO and CONTROL strategies.

## 4.1. VARIATION OF THE CONTROL PERIOD:

Figure 3 shows the multiplexer characteristics (RL, RSQ, RSD) of the configuration 1 for the following two cases:

Run 1: CP ≈ 60 sec (NMIN=10, X=0.01,CC=
19200 bits/sec) See curve O.
Run 2: CP ≈ 6 sec (NMIN=1, X=0.01, CC=
19200 bits/sec). See curve ¤.

In both cases trunk, access line and
VL capacities 19200 bits/sec were
tested. The throughput threshold is
MT=0.17 p/sec and therefore the guaranteed traffic consists of all virtual channels with TC≧5.

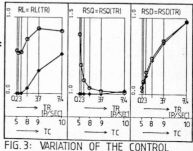

FIG.3: VARIATION OF THE CONTROL
PERIOD

The graphs show RL, RSQ and RSD as a function of TR resp. TC and indicate that:

- throughput guarantees are possible, because RSQ $\geq$ 1 and RSD < 1 for
  all simulated VCs;

- the guaranteed traffic is not effected by the variation of the CP
  over a wide range;

- The CP has a lower limit, below which the virt. calls have no chance
  to buid-up a high enough load. The curves show that NMIN=1 and X=
  0.01 define such a limit.

## 4.2. HIGH AND LOW PRIORITIES:

The effect of high and low priority
packets on the network behaviour has
been observed testing a modified configuration 1 with 10 more virtual
calls of high priority and also with
TC=1 up to 10. In addition all capacities have been doubled and NMIN=20
and X=0.01 have been assumed yielding
CP≈60 sec. Figure 4 illustrates the
service characteristics (RL, RSQ, RD)
of the control multiplexer for:

- high priority virtual calls (see
  curve O) and
- low priority virtual calls (see
  curve ¤).

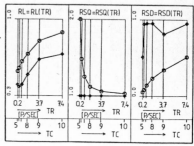

FIG.4: HIGH AND LOW PRIORITIES

The results of run 3 demonstrate that
- throughput guarantees are possible for both types of traffic;
- low priority virt. calls are served only after all requests of high
  priority virt. calls are satisfied;
- free network capacity is utilized by high priority virtual calls

## 4.3. GLOBAL NETWORK BEHAVIOUR:

The global network throughput of the three discussed simulation runs is compared in table 2 with the throughput limit and the throughput request. Obviously the goal for throughput guarantees and high network efficiency is met. About 90% of the theoretical throughput limit is achieved.

| simulation run | TL [p/sec] | TR [p/sec] | ST [p/sec] | RSQ | E |
|---|---|---|---|---|---|
| 1 | 34.53 | 29.44 | 31.46 | 1.07 | 0.91 |
| 2 | 34.53 | 29.44 | 31.26 | 1.06 | 0.91 |
| 3 | 69.06 | 58.88 | 63.28 | 1.08 | 0.92 |

Table 2: Global network behaviour

## 4.4. VARIATION OF THE X.25 WINDOW SIZE:

Next we looked at the influence of the X.25 window size on the network behaviour. The results, shown in figures 5 and 6, are produced by simulation experiments done with the configuration 1 and the simulation parameters of run 3. Window sizes 1 (curve O), 3 (curve Δ) and 5 curve ¤) are compared and the following dependencies have been plotted:
- the virtual call   throughput versus the throughput request (left picture in figure 5);
- the mean packet delay versus the maximum mean inter-arrival time; (right picture in figure 5);
- histograms of the packet delay distribution (figure 6).

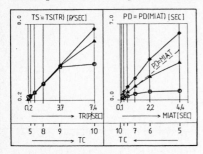

FIG.5:  VARIATION OF THE X.25 WINDOW SIZE

It turns out that:
- window sizes lower than 4 cause throughput degradation of the highest throughput class;
- packet transmission tends to be more bursty, when the window size is increased;
- the maximum of the packet delay distribution is near the correlated MIAT value.

## 4.5. 'FAIR' SERVICE:

The simulation results have demonstrated that throughput guarantees are possible. An open question is how free capacities are distributed among competing virtual calls.

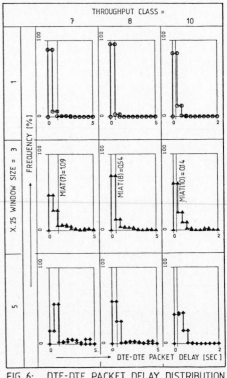

FIG. 6:   DTE-DTE PACKET DELAY DISTRIBUTION

This question can be answered if we replace the RSQ-curves in figure 4 by (RSQ-1). TR, which gives the surplus throughput. The final results in table 3 confirm our network goal for fair service, because free capacities are equally distributed to competing virt. calls.

| | TR [p/sec] | 0.23 | 0.46 | 0.92 | 1.84 | 3.68 | 7.37 |
|---|---|---|---|---|---|---|---|
| HIGH PRIO. | RSQ | 2.00 | 1.48 | 1.25 | 1.12 | 1.06 | 1.03 |
| | (RSQ-1) .TR | 0.23 | 0.22 | 0.23 | 0.22 | 0.22 | 0.22 |
| LOW PRIO. | RSQ | 1.00 | 1.00 | 1.00 | 1.00 | 1.00 | 1.00 |
| | (RSQ-1) .TR | 0.00 | 0.00 | 0.00 | 0.00 | 0.00 | 0.00 |

Table 3: Surplus throughput of virtual calls

## 4.6. TIME BEHAVIOUR:

In figures 7 and 8 the time-behaviour of the control multiplexer is shown during one control period. The curves (window size 1/curve O, window size 3/ curve △, window size 5/ curve ▫) present some of the previously discussed aspects and the following dependencies are plotted:

- Fig. 7: RSQ versus simulation time for TC=5, 8 and 10 as well as for high (left pictures) and low (right pictures) priorities (overlapping curves are indicated by ✳);

- Fig. 8: RSD.CP versus TR for high (left picture) and low (right picture) priorities.

Obviously different throughput classes as well as priorities can be supported by the transportation system. The window size has a limiting effect on the service quality of higher throughput classes for small window sizes.

## 4.7. COMPARISON BETWEEN FIFO AND CONTROL ALGORITHMS:

Some general observations can be made about the throughput and the mean packet delay (DTE-DTE delay) if we compare the CONTROL-strategy with the FIFO strategy. For this purpose the configuration 1 has been simulated (parameters like in run 3) without controlling the access of virtual calls to the VL capacity. Simple FIFO multiplexer components have been used instead of control multiplexers and the obtained results are compared with the results of simulation run 3. Table 4 and figure 9 point out the advantages of the control mechanism concerning throughput guarantees.

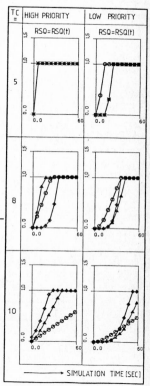

FIG.7:  TIME BEHAVIOUR

| multiplexer algorithm | sufficient support of priorities | sufficient support of throughput classes | guaranteed service |
|---|---|---|---|
| FIFO | NO | NO | NO |
| CONTROL | YES | YES | YES |

Table 4: Comparison between FIFO and CONTROL multiplexer

## 4.8. VARIATION OF THE VL PATH LENGTH:

Finally the effect of the number of hops on the network behaviour is discussed. Simulation results, which were achieve when the configuration 2 has been tested, have shown that the network behaviour becomes independent of the VL-path-length, if the VL-window size is chosen proportional to the VL-path-length. In order to minimize the amount of reserved buffers we first determined the minimal VL-window size, which will achieve the desired behaviour. It turned out, that a VL-window size=2.VL path-length is sufficient, since for greater values the trunk capacities have become the throughput limiting factor. The histograms in figure 10 show the observed mean buffer utilization of VLs for the VL window size= 1., 2., 3. VL-path-length. Next we observed the network behaviour for different trunk capacities (or reservation degrees).Two cases were tested:

| reservation degree | case 1 | case 2 |
|---|---|---|
| trunk lines | 0.96-1.00 | 0.30-0.68 |
| access lines | 0.74 | 0.74 |
| VLs | 0.98 | 0.98 |

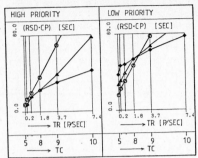

FIG.8: SERVICE DELAY VS. THROUGHPUT REQUEST

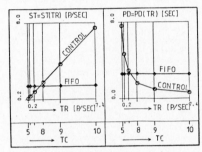

FIG.9: COMPARISON BETWEEN FIFO AND CONTROL MULTIPLEXERS

The results are compared in fig. 11, 12, 13 and table 5.

- In figure 11 the throughput of virtual calls is plotted as a function of the number of hops (case1/curve ¤;case 2/ curve O).

- In figure 12 the relative service quality is given in dependency of the number of hops (case 1/left picture; case 2/ right picture) for high (curve O) and low (curve ¤) priority.

- In figure 13 the DTE-DTE packet delay distribution is shown for the VL path lengths=1, 3 and 5 (case 1/curve ¤) case 2/curve O).

- Table 5 summarizes the mean VL packet delay.

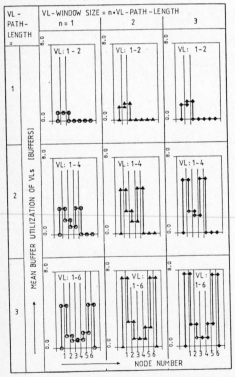

FIG.10: MEAN BUFFER UTILIZATION OF VLs

| VL-path length | | 1 | 2 | 3 | 4 | 5 |
|---|---|---|---|---|---|---|
| delay | case 1 | 2.02 | 1.83 | 1.82 | 2.08 | 2.17 |
| [sec] | case 2 | 2.05 | 2.01 | 2.03 | 2.03 | 2.00 |

Table 5: Mean VL packet delay

As can be seen, the reservation degree has an important effect on the network behaviour and the main network goals - throughput guarantees, utilization of free capacities, fair service and independence of the VL path length - can be met, if the reservation degree is limited.

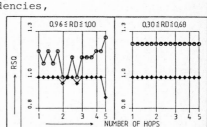

FIG.11: THROUGHPUT VS. NUMBER OF HOPS

CONCLUSIONS:

In this paper the aspect of service quality for packet switched networks has been discussed. For this purpose a network model has been proposed considering the main goals for - fair,qualified and efficient service. The behaviour of the hypothetical network has been studied by simulation methods observing various dependencies, like:

- reservation degree;
- number of hops;
- window size;
- throughput class and
- priority.

The achieved results have demonstrated that the network model meets its major goals and especially that throughput guarantees are possible even under high load situations.

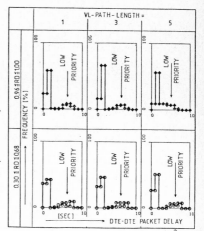

FIG.12: RELATIVE SERVICE QUALITY VS. NUMBER OF HOPS

REFERENCES:

[1] A. Giessler: J. Hänle: Jendra: 'Leistungsmerkmale des Dienstes - virtuelle Verbindungen - in einem öffentlichen Packet-vermittlungsnetz und Entwurf des dazugehörigen Transportsystems', study by FTZ Fernmeldetechnisches Zentralamt, Darmstadt, FRG,1977

[2] A. Giessler: 'Throughput Guarantee in X.25 Networks', Flow Control in Computer Networks, Noth Holland, 1979

[3] J.M. Jaffe: 'A Decentralized, "Optimal" Multiple-User, Flow Control Algorithm', ICCC, Atlanta, Oct. 1980

[4] D. Sproule: M. Unsoy: 'Transit Delay Objectives for the Datapac Network',ICCC,Atlanta, Oct. 1980

[5] G.R. Grossmann: A.Hinchley: C.A. Sunshine: 'Issues in International Public Data Networking',Computer Network 3, North Holannd, 1979

FIG.13: DTE-DTE PACKET DELAY DISTRIBUTION

[6] J. Peterson:
'Remarks on the Implementation of the Packet Level Protocols of Public Packet Switching Networks',Computer Network Protocols, Liege, 1978

[7] C.A. Sunshine:
'Current Trends in Computer Network Interconnection', Proc. European Computing Congress, London May 1978, Online Conferences Ltd. Uxbridge

[8] P.M. Cashin:
'Datapac Network Protocols', ICCC, Toronto, Aug. 1976

[9] CCITT:
'Recommendation X.25', Orange Book, Vol. VIII.2,Geneva, 1977

[10] CCITT:
'Draft Revised CCITT Recommendation X.25', CCITT Study Group VII Meeting, Geneva, 1980

[11] R. Magoon: D. Twyver:
Networks', Flow Control in Computer Networks, North Holland, 1979

Performance of Data Communication Systems
and their Applications, G. Pujolle (ed.)
© North-Holland Publishing Company, 1981

INFLUENCE DU DEGRE D'ANTICIPATION
SUR LES PERFORMANCES DE LA
PROCEDURE H.D.L.C.

Dominique SERET

Institut de Programmation
Université Pierre & Marie Curie
4, Place Jussieu
75230 PARIS CEDEX 05

Laboratoire des Signaux et Systèmes
Ecole Supérieure d'Electricité
Plateau du Moulon
91190 GIF S/YVETTE

RESUME

Le but de notre article est d'analyser les performances de la procédure HDLC
et en particulier l'influence du degré d'anticipation sur ces performances. En
effet dans cette procédure l'émetteur peut transmettre plusieurs trames consécu-
tives sans attendre d'accusé de réception. Le nombre de trames qu'il peut ainsi
émettre est limité. Cette limite (taille de la fenêtre) va influer sur le débit
maximal utile de la liaison. Nous étudions le taux maximal d'utilisation de la
liaison en fonction de la taille de la fenêtre à l'aide d'un modèle markovien fini.
Nous montrons qu'un modèle avec une fenêtre infinie donne une bonne approximation
du modèle précédent. Nous étudions sur ce modèle l'influence du taux d'erreurs dû
à la ligne et nous comparons les deux modes de retransmission existant dans la
procédure : le rejet et le rejet sélectif. Des résultats de simulation nous
permettent de valider l'approximation par un modèle à fenêtre infinie.

INTRODUCTION

Dans les réseaux d'ordinateurs, le niveau "contrôle de la liaison", niveau 2 du
modèle ISO pour l'architecture des systèmes ouverts, contient de nombreuses fonctions telles : adressage, numérotage de trames, contrôle d'erreurs, contrôle de
flux. A ce niveau, l'ISO a défini une procédure de contrôle de liaison HDLC
(High level Data Link Control procedure) [1][2].
Le but de notre article est d'analyser les performances de cette procédure et en
particulier l'influence du degré d'anticipation sur ces performances. De nombreux
articles sur l'évaluation des performances des procédures [3]-[9] sont parus ces
dernières années. Ils utilisent des modèles à files d'attente, des chaînes de
Markov ou des automates probabilistes. Il est difficile de prendre en compte tous
les paramètres qui limitent les performances de ces procédures [10]. Certains
articles négligent les erreurs dues à la ligne, d'autres le délai de propagation,
les trames de service... Ici nous construisons un modèle markovien fini ou infini
pour évaluer l'influence du degré d'anticipation sur une liaison bidirectionnelle
simultanée. Nous supposons que le délai de propagation est négligeable devant la
longueur des trames et nous étudions l'efficacité des deux modes de retransmission:
le rejet et le rejet sélectif. Les simulations nous permettent de valider les
résultats du modèle infini et donc de le considérer comme un excellent outil pour
obtenir une bonne approximation du comportement de deux stations HDLC.

PROCEDURE HDLC ENTRE DEUX STATIONS $S_1$ ET $S_2$

Nous considérons deux stations $S_1$ et $S_2$ reliées entre elles par une liaison bidirectionnelle exploitée avec la procédure HDLC. Nous supposons que chaque station
a une suite infinie de trames à transmettre à l'autre station. La liaison est
caractérisée par un certain délai de propagation et nous considérons que les délais
(overhead) matériels et logiciels dûs à chaque station comme inclus dans ce délai
de propagation. Nous étudions le cas où le délai de propagation est petit devant
la longueur des trames et nous l'incluons alors dans celle-ci. La transmission est
bidirectionnelle simultanée. Dès qu'une station a émis une trame, elle en conserve

une copie dans une file d'attente jusqu'à la réception d'un accusé de réception positif concernant cette trame. Soit $F_1$ (resp. $F_2$) la file d'attente dans la station $S_1$ (resp. $S_2$).
Ces deux files ont une capacité limitée respectivement à $N_1$ et $N_2$ trames. Lorsque la file $F_1$ est pleine, la station $S_1$ doit interrompre sa transmission de trames vers la station $S_2$, ce qui limite donc l'utilisation de la liaison.

Chaque trame émise contient un accusé de réception relatif aux trames précédemment reçues. Cet accusé de réception ne peut être pris en compte qu'après la réception complète de la trame et sa vérification (calcul du FCS et test du numéro N(S) en séquence). Cet accusé de réception porte sur un certain nombre de trames seulement et non sur toutes celles contenues dans la file d'attente comme le montre la figure 1. Sur l'exemple de cette figure, à l'instant $t_1$, la file $F_2$ contient une trame (la trame 0 de $S_2$ vers $S_1$), elle est acquittée par la trame 2 de $S_1$. A l'instant $t_2$, la file $F_1$ contient 3 trames (trames 0 à 2 de $S_1$ vers $S_2$), la trame 1 de $S_2$ ne peut acquitter que la première d'entre elles.

## MODELISATION DE LA PROCEDURE

Nous considérons tout d'abord la liaison comme parfaite c'est-à-dire sans erreurs de transmission.

### Définition du diagramme d'états :

Nous modélisons la procédure par un diagramme d'états illustré par la figure 2 (dans le cas où les deux files $F_1$ et $F_2$ sont limitées à $N_1 = N_2 = 6$ trames). La procédure se trouve dans l'état $(k, 1, i, j)$ où l'on a :
$\qquad$ i trames dans la file $F_1$, $i \leqslant N_1$
$\qquad$ j trames dans la file $F_2$, $j \leqslant N_2$

La station $S_1$ transmet la trame numérotée $i + 1$. Si cette trame se termine la première, elle peut acquitter les k premières trames en attente dans $F_2$. De même la station $S_2$ transmet la trame numérotée $j + 1$ qui si elle se termine la première peut acquitter les l premières trames en attente dans $F_1$. Nous avons donc $k \leqslant j$ et $l \leqslant i$.

Les seuls états possibles de la procédure sont :
. $(k, 0, 0, j)$ et par symétrie $(0, k, j, 0)$ dont un exemple est illustré par la figure 3a.
. $(j, 0, 1, j)$ et par symétrie $(0, j, j, 1)$ dont un exemple est illustré par la figure 3b.
. $(k, 1, 1, j)$ avec $k = j$ où $j-1$ et par symétrie $(1, k, j, 1)$ dont un exemple est illustré par les figures 3c et 3d.

Nous supposons que les trames émises sont de longueur aléatoire, suivant des lois exponentielles de paramètres respectifs $\lambda_1$ et $\lambda_2$. Appelons $\pi_1$ la probabilité que la trame issue de $S_1$ se termine avant celle issue de $S_2$. La propriété d'oubli de la loi exponentielle nous permet d'écrire :

$$(1) \quad \pi_1 = \frac{\lambda_1}{\lambda_1 + \lambda_2}$$

De même la probabilité que la trame issue de $S_2$ se termine la première vaut

$$(2) \quad \pi_2 = \frac{\lambda_2}{\lambda_1 + \lambda_2}$$

On peut remarquer que les états $(j, 1, 1, j)$, $j = 1,..,N_2$ sont issus de situation où la station $S_2$ est bloquée. Le cas particulier $j = N_2$ laisse à nouveau un état bloqué pour la station $S_2$.

D'une façon générale les transitions d'états de la procédure sont les suivantes :

$$(3) \qquad (k,1,i,j) \underset{\pi_2}{\overset{\pi_1}{\rightleftarrows}} \begin{array}{l} (j-k,\ 1,\ i+1,\ j-k) \\[4pt] (k,\ i-1,\ i-1,\ j+1) \end{array}$$

avec $\begin{cases} j = 1,\ldots,\ N_2-1 \\ i = 0 \text{ ou } 1 \end{cases}$ $\quad \begin{array}{l} k = 0,\ldots,\ j \\ 1 = 0,\ldots,\ i \end{array}$

et
avec $\begin{cases} i = 1,\ldots,\ N-1 \\ j = 0 \text{ ou } 1 \end{cases}$ $\quad \begin{array}{l} 1 = 0,\ldots,\ i \\ k = 0,\ldots,\ j \end{array}$

Les cas particuliers $j = N_2$ et $i = N_1$ donnent :

$$(4) \qquad \begin{array}{ll} (k,0,0,N_2) \xrightarrow{1} (N_2-k,1,1,N_2-k) & k = 0,\ldots,N_2-1 \\ (0,1,N_1,0) \xrightarrow{1} (1,\ N_1-1,\ N_1-1,1) & 1 = 0,\ldots,N_1-1 \\ (N_2-1,1,1,N_2) \xrightarrow{1} (1,2,2,1) & \\ (N_2,1,1,N_2) \xrightarrow{1} (0,2,2,0) & \\ (1,N_1-1,N_1,1) \xrightarrow{1} (2,1,1,2) & \\ (1,N_1,N_1,1) \xrightarrow{1} (2,0,0,2) & \end{array}$$

Notons enfin que les transitions d'états de la procédure définies en (3) donnent deux fois celles obtenues à partir de l'état $(1,1,1,1)$.

Etude du modèle :

Lorsque la procédure arrive dans l'état $(k,1,i,j)$ elle y reste un temps qui est exponentiellement distribué avec une moyenne $(\lambda_1 + \lambda_2)^{-1}$ puisque c'est le plus court de deux temps de transmission exponentiellement distribués avec des moyennes $\lambda_1^{-1}$ et $\lambda_2^{-1}$.

Nous pouvons alors écrire les équations de transition de la chaîne de Markov défi-nie par le diagramme précédent. Les équations générales sont :

$$(5) \quad \begin{cases} (\lambda_1 + \lambda_2) \ P(k,0,0,j+1) = \lambda_2 \ P(k,0,0,j) \\ \qquad\qquad j=2,\ldots,N_2-2 \quad k=0,\ldots,j-3 \\ (\lambda_1 + \lambda_2) \ P(0,1,i+1,0) = \lambda_1 \ P(0,1,i,0) \\ \qquad\qquad i=2,\ldots,N_1-2 \quad 1=0,\ldots,i-3 \end{cases}$$

$$(6) \quad \begin{cases} (\lambda_1 + \lambda_2) \ P(j,0,1,j) = \overset{N_2-j-1}{\underset{k=0}{\Sigma}} \ \lambda_1 \ P(k,0,0,k+j) \\ \qquad\qquad\qquad\qquad\qquad\qquad j = 1,\ldots,N_2-1 \\ (\lambda_1 + \lambda_2) \ P(0,i,i,1) = \overset{N_1-i-1}{\underset{1=0}{\Sigma}} \ \lambda_2 \ P(0,i,i+1,0) \\ \qquad\qquad\qquad\qquad\qquad\qquad i = 1,\ldots,N_1-1 \end{cases}$$

$$(7) \quad \begin{cases} (\lambda_1 + \lambda_2) \ P(j-1,1,1,j) = \lambda_2 \ P(j-1,0,1,j-1) \\ \qquad\qquad\qquad\qquad\qquad\qquad j = 2,\ldots,N_2-1 \\ (\lambda_1 + \lambda_2) \ P(1,i-1,i,1) = \lambda_1 \ P(0,i-1,i-1,1) \\ \qquad\qquad\qquad\qquad\qquad\qquad i = 2,\ldots,N_1-1 \end{cases}$$

Il reste de nombreuses autres équations correspondant aux états bloqués ($j=N$, $i=N$) et aux états qui en sont issus. Nous ne les écrirons pas toutes ici, le système d'équations obtenu est complexe. Sa résolution est longue et fastidieuse. Notons que le calcul de la probabilité que la station soit bloquée donne :

$$P(S_2 \text{ bloquée}) = P(N_2-1,1,1,N_2) + P(N_2,1,1,N_2)$$

$$(8) \qquad\qquad\qquad + \overset{N_2-1}{\underset{k=0}{\Sigma}} \ P(k,0,0,N_2)$$

Dans le cas d'un trafic symétrique ($\lambda_1 = \lambda_2$) et avec le même degré d'anticipation ($N_1 = N_2 = N$) nous obtenons :

(9)
$$P(\text{blocage}) = \frac{(N+1)2^{N+1} - 4N-1}{2^{2N+2} + (2N-11)2^N - 3(N-5)}, \quad N \geqslant 2$$

Ceci nous permet de calculer le taux d'utilisation de la liaison c'est-à-dire la probabilité que la liaison soit occupée :

(10)    $\tau = 1 - P(\text{blocage})$

Les résultats numériques sont donnés par la figure 4 où l'on voit un taux d'utilisation de 90 % est obtenu pour N = 5.

MODELE SIMPLIFIE

Le modèle précédent étant relativement complexe à résoudre, nous avons cherché à comparer les résultats obtenus avec le modèle où l'on suppose la taille de la fenêtre infinie. Le diagramme obtenu dans ce cas est beaucoup plus simple, il est illustré par la figure 5.

De nombreux états n'existent plus par rapport au diagramme de la figure 2. Ce sont tous les états (j11j) (et(1ii1)), (k00j) avec k=j et j-1 (et(0li0) avec l=i et i-1) et enfin (1011) (et(0111)).

Notons $p_{jk}$ la probabilité de l'état (k,0,0,j) avec $j \geqslant 2$ et $k \leqslant j-2$, $q_j$ la probabilité de l'état (j,0,1,j) avec $j \geqslant 2$, $r_j$ la probabilité de l'état (j-1,1,1,j) avec $j \geqslant 2$. Notons enfin $P_{il}$, $Q_i$, $R_i$ (avec des majuscules) les probabilités des états symétriques.

Les équations du système sont :

(11)
$$\begin{cases}
(\lambda_1 + \lambda_2) \quad p_{20} = \lambda_2 \sum_{1=2}^{\infty} Q_j \; ; \; (\lambda_1 + \lambda_2)P_{20} = \lambda_1 \sum_{k=2}^{\infty} q_k. \\[2mm]
(\lambda_1 + \lambda_2) \quad p_{jk} = \lambda_2 \; p_{j-1,k} \quad ; \; (\lambda_1 + \lambda_2)P_{il} = \lambda_1 \; P_{i-1,1}. \\[1mm]
\quad j \geqslant 3 \text{ et } k=0,\dots,j-3 \qquad ; \quad i \geqslant 3 \text{ et } l=0,\dots,i-3. \\[1mm]
(\lambda_1 + \lambda_2) \quad P_{j,j-2} = \lambda_2 \; r_{j-1}, \, j \geqslant 3 \; ; \\[1mm]
\qquad\qquad (\lambda_1 + \lambda_2) \; P_{i,i-2} = \lambda_2 \; R_{i-1}, \, i \geqslant 3. \\[1mm]
(\lambda_1 + \lambda_2) \quad q_j = \lambda_1 \sum_{k=0}^{\infty} p_{j+k,k} \, , \, j \geqslant 2 \; ; \\[1mm]
\qquad\qquad (\lambda_1 + \lambda_2) \; Q_i = \lambda_2 \sum_{1=0}^{\infty} P_{i+1,1}, \, i \geqslant 2. \\[1mm]
(\lambda_1 + \lambda_2) \quad r_2 = \lambda_2 \sum_{i=2}^{\infty} R_i \quad ; \quad (\lambda_1 + \lambda_2) \; R_2 = \lambda_1 \sum_{j=2}^{\infty} r_j. \\[1mm]
(\lambda_1 + \lambda_2) \quad r_j = \lambda_2 q_{j-1}, \quad j \geqslant 3 \; ; (\lambda_1 + \lambda_2) \; R_i = \lambda_2 \; Q_{i-1}, \, i \geqslant 3.
\end{cases}$$

La résolution de ce système est longue mais aisée, la solution en est remarquable :

(12) et
$$\begin{cases}
p_{jk} = q_j = r_j = \dfrac{\lambda_1^2 \, \lambda_2^{\,j}}{(\lambda_1 + \lambda_2)^{j+2}} \qquad j \geqslant 2, \; k \leqslant j-2. \\[4mm]
P_{il} = Q_i = R_i = \dfrac{\lambda_2^2 \, \lambda_2^{\,i}}{(\lambda_1 + \lambda_2)^{i+2}} \qquad i \geqslant 2, \; 1 \leqslant i-2.
\end{cases}$$

Les probabilités des différents états ne dépendent que du nombre de trames en attente et non du nombre de trames acquittables.

Nous pouvons calculer à chaque station le nombre moyen de trames en attente : (resp. $\bar{n}_1$ et $\bar{n}_2$)

$$(13) \qquad \bar{n}_1 = 2 \frac{\lambda_1}{\lambda_2} \qquad\qquad et \quad \bar{n}_2 = 2 \frac{\lambda_1}{\lambda_2}$$

De même la probabilité qu'il y ait dans une file au moins N trames en attente vaut :

$$Prob \ (F_1 \geqslant N) = \lambda_2^N . \frac{\lambda_2 + (N+1) \ \lambda_1}{(\lambda_1 + \lambda_2)^{N+1}}$$

$$(14)$$

$$Prob \ (F_2 \geqslant N) = \lambda_1^N . \frac{\lambda_1 + (N+1) \ \lambda_2}{(\lambda_1 + \lambda_2)^{N+1}}$$

Ces deux probabilités sont à comparer avec la probabilité de blocage d'une station lorsque le degré d'anticipation est limité à N. Dans le cas particulier du trafic symétrique entre les deux stations nous trouvons :

$$(15) \qquad Prob \ (F_1 \geqslant N) = Prob \ (F_2 \geqslant N) = \frac{N+2}{2^{N+1}}$$

Le tableau 6 nous donne les valeurs numériques de cette probabilité en la comparant à la valeur de (9) :

| N | File limitée Prob($F_1$=N) | File infinie Prob($F_1 \geqslant$ N) |
|---|---|---|
| 3 | 0,3125 | 0,2297 |
| 4 | 0,1875 | 0,1461 |
| 5 | 0,1094 | 0,0893 |
| 6 | 0,0625 | 0,0527 |
| 7 | 0,0352 | 0,0306 |
| 8 | 0,0195 | 0,0173 |

Tableau 6 : Comparaison des deux modèles.

Plus N est grand et plus la valeur $P(F_1 \geqslant N)$ du modèle infini est voisine de celle obtenue dans le modèle fini du paragraphe III. Nous garderons les valeurs calculées en (12), (13), (14) dans le reste de cette étude.

Si la file $F_1$ est limitée à $N_1$ trames nous pouvons approximer le taux d'utilisation de la liaison dans le sens $S_1$ vers $S_2$ par :

$$(16) \qquad \tau_1 = 1 - Prob(F_1 \geqslant N_1)$$

D'où nous déduisons le débit maximal utile $\mathcal{D}_1$ de la liaison dans le sens $S_1$ vers $S_2$ :

$$(17) \qquad \mathcal{D}_1 = \tau_1 . D$$

où D est le débit nominal de la ligne. La figure 7 illustre le débit maximal utile pour plusieurs valeurs du rapport et plusieurs valeurs des fenêtres $N_1$ et $N_2$.

Le nombre moyen de trames acquittables se calcule aisèment. Notons le $\bar{m}_1$ (resp.$\bar{m}_2$)

pour la file $F_1$ (resp. $F_2$). Nous obtenons avec le résultat (12) :

$$(18) \qquad \bar{m}_1 = \frac{\lambda_1}{\lambda_2} \qquad\qquad \text{et} \quad \bar{m}_2 = \frac{\lambda_2}{\lambda_1}$$

Il est intéressant de noter qu'en moyenne une trame reçue acquitte la moitié des trames qui étaient en attente.

INFLUENCE DU TAUX D'ERREURS DU A LA LIGNE

Nous avons caclulé au paragraphe précédent un débit maximal utile en tenant compte du fait qu'une station pouvait être bloquée, en attente d'acquittement. Nous avons supposé que toutes les trames étaient transmises correctement. Lorsque la ligne introduit des erreurs, certaines trames peuvent être erronées (et donc ignorées du récepteur). Elles nécessiteront une ou plusieurs retransmissions jusqu'à la transmission correcte. Nous allons calculer le débit efficace de la liaison c'est-à-dire faire le rapport entre le nombre de trames utiles (correctement transmises) et le nombre total de trames réellement transmises.

Soit $\tau_e$ le taux d'erreurs sur les éléments binaires. La probabilité $\alpha$ qu'une trame de longueur L soit correcte est :

$$(19) \qquad \alpha = (1-\tau_e)^L$$

Nous supposerons que toutes les trames issues de $S_1$ ont la même probabilité d'être correctes :

$$(20) \qquad \alpha_1 = (1-\tau_e)^{\lambda_1^{-1}}$$

et de même pour $S_2$ $\qquad \alpha_2 = (1-\tau_e)^{\lambda_2^{-1}}$

La procédure HDLC possède deux modes de retransmission : - le rejet qui nécessite la retransmission de toutes les trames depuis celle qui est erronée (il y aura donc des trames correctes à retransmettre).
$\qquad\qquad\qquad\qquad\qquad\qquad\qquad\qquad\qquad$ - le rejet sélectif
qui nécessite la retransmission spéciale de la trame erronée.
Nous étudions les deux modes l'un après l'autre.

Cas du rejet

Supposons qu'il y a j trames dans la file $F_2$ dont k sont acquittables. Sur ces k trames si le rang de la première trame erronée est $1 + i$ ($1 \leqslant k$) il y aura les k-1 dernières trames à retransmettre. La probabilité d'un tel événement est $a_{1k}$ avec

$$(21) \qquad \begin{cases} a_{1k} = \alpha_2^1 (1-\alpha_2) & 0 \leqslant 1 < k \\[2mm] a_{kk} = \alpha_2^k \end{cases}$$

Le calcul du nombre moyen de trames utiles $\bar{u}_2$ parmi les trames acquittables donne

$$(22) \qquad \bar{u}_2 = \sum_{j=2}^{\infty} \left[ \sum_{k=0}^{j-2} \left( \sum_{1=0}^{k} 1 a_{1k} \right) p_{jk} + \sum_{1=0}^{j} 1 a_{1j} \, q_j + \sum_{1=0}^{j-1} 1 a_{1_{j-1}} r_j + \alpha_2 \, R_j \right]$$

soit en posant $\rho = \frac{\lambda_1}{\lambda_2}$

$$(23) \qquad \bar{u}_2 = \frac{\alpha_2}{1 + \rho - \alpha_2}(1 - \frac{\alpha_2}{(1+\rho-\alpha_2)(1+\rho)^2}\frac{\rho^2}{})$$

De même nous pouvons calculer $\bar{u}_1$ en remplaçant $\rho$ par $\rho^{-1}$ et $\alpha_2$ par $\alpha_1$ dans (23).

Le débit efficace de la liaison dans le sens $S_2$ vers $S_1$ est donc

$$(24) \qquad De_1^{REJ} = \mathcal{D}_1\frac{\bar{u}_1}{\bar{m}_1}$$

et dans le sens $S_1$ vers $S_2$

$$(25) \qquad De_2^{REJ} = \mathcal{D}_2\frac{\bar{u}_2}{\bar{m}_2}$$

La figure 8 illustre l'influence du taux d'erreur sur le débit efficace de la liaison. Nous avons choisi des valeurs $\tau_e$ allant de $10^{-3}$ à $10^{-5}$.

## Cas du rejet sélectif

Plaçons nous dans la même situation que précédemment: il y a j trames dans la file $F_2$ dont k sont acquittables. Sur ces k trames, seules les trames erronées seront à retransmettre. La probabilité $b_{1k}$ qu'il y en ait l correctes vaut cette fois :

$$(26) \qquad b_{1k} = \binom{k}{1} \alpha_2^1 \ (1-\alpha_2)^{k-1} \qquad 0 \leqslant 1 \leqslant k$$

$$(27) \qquad \bar{v}_2 = \frac{\alpha_2}{\rho(1+\rho-\alpha_2)} \ (\rho + (1- \alpha_2)(1 + \frac{\rho^2}{(1+\rho)^2}))$$

Le débit efficace se calcule de la même façon qu'au paragraphe précédent :

$$(28) \qquad De_1^{SREJ} = \mathcal{D}_1.\frac{\bar{v}_1}{\bar{m}_1} \qquad et \qquad De_2^{SREJ} = \mathcal{D}_2.\frac{\bar{v}_2}{\bar{m}_2}$$

La figure 9 illustre dans les mêmes conditions que la figure 8 l'influence du taux d'erreur sur le débit efficace.

Notons que le débit efficace est toujours meilleur si on utilise le rejet sélectif (SREJ) à la place du rejet (REJ), il reste au récepteur à remettre les trames dans l'ordre pour retrouver la suite logique de trames envoyées par l'émetteur. Remarquons enfin que nous avons calculé le débit efficace en trames utiles, nous aurions pu l'exprimer en bits utiles en exprimant le rapport entre les bits d'informations transmis et les bits d'enveloppe de trames (fanion, adresse, commande, contrôle d'erreur). De plus nous avons négligé le temps nécessaire à la transmission des accusés de réception négatifs soit REJ et SREJ.

Dans les deux cas, le débit efficace total est maximal lorsque les trames sont de même longueur pour les 2 stations ($\lambda_1= \lambda_2$). Pour le rejet, ce maximum vaut 3500 bit/s dans les deux sens de transmission soit un rendement de 73 % lorsque le taux d'erreur vaut $10^{-5}$ et que la longueur moyenne des trames est 1000 bits.

Notons que cette longueur correspond par exemple à la taille standard des paquets circulant dans le réseau Transpac : 128 octets [11]. Pour le rejet sélectif dans les mêmes conditions on obtient un rendement de 96 %. La différence entre les

modes de retransmission est d'autant plus sensible que la liaison est mauvaise :
pour un taux d'erreurs de $10^{-3}$ le rendement est doublé par l'utilisation du rejet
sélectif (il passe de 20 % à 41 %). Par contre le temps consacré par la station
réceptrice à la gestion des trames reçues à considérablement augmenté puisque 60%
des trames sont erronées et arrivent donc dans le désordre.

Dans le paragraphe suivant nous allons présenter des résultats de simulation qui
nous permettent de comparer les deux modèles des paragraphes III et IV.

RESULTATS DE SIMULATION

La simulation du comportement de deux stations $S_1$ et $S_2$ s'échangeant des trames
selon la procédure HDLC est simple à réaliser. Nous avons considéré le cas du
trafic symétrique et nous avons comparé les deux modèles : fenêtre finie et
fenêtre infinie. Sur chaque simulation nous avons mesuré le nombre de trames en
attente dans les files $F_1$ et $F_2$, le temps moyen d'attente dans ces mêmes files,
le taux de blocage lorsque les files sont pleines. Les résultats sont illustrés
par le tableau 10 et les courbes de la figure 11.

Toutes ces simulations faites avec une fenêtre finie variant entre 2 et 8 montrent
que l'approximation par un modèle à fenêtre infinie est excellente dès N vaut 4.

CONCLUSION

Nous avons étudié dans cet article les performances de la procédure HDLC et en
particulier l'influence du degré d'anticipation sur ces performances. Nous avons
fait l'hypothèse que les deux stations avaient une suite infinie de trames à se
transmettre.

Nous avons supposé que lalongueur des trames était exponentiellement distribuée
et nous avons construit un modèle markovien du comportement de chaque station dans
le cas où le degré d'anticipation est limité. Nous avons comparé ce modèle à un
second modèle sans limite d'anticipation et montré sur des calculs théoriques et
à l'aide de simulations que l'approximation par un modèle à fenêtre infinie était
excellente.

Nous avons examiné les deux modes de retransmission existant dans la procédure
HDLC pour corriger les erreurs : le rejet et le rejet sélectif.

Nous avons calculé l'efficacité de ces deux rejets pour mettre en évidence
l'influence du taux d'erreur dû à la ligne.

Les performances de la procédure peuvent donc être évaluées par un modèle
markovien infini lorsque le délai de propagation est bref par rapport à la longueur des trames émises et reçues. Ce modèle donne une excellente approximation
(dès que le degré d'anticipation dépasse 3) pour de nombreuses quantités caractéristiques du comportement de chacune des deux stations (le nombre de trames en
attente, le nombre de trames que pourra acquitter la prochaine trame reçue, le
nombre de trames utilement transmises, le temps d'attente nécessaire pour recevoir
un accusé de réception...) Il permet de juger quantitativement l'influence du
degré d'anticipation et du taux d'erreur sur l'efficacité de la procédure HDLC.

REFERENCES BIBLIOGRAPHIQUES

[1]    Data Communication - High Level data link control procedures - Frame
       structure. International Standard ISO 3309.

[2]    HDLC - Proposed balanced class of procedures. Doc. ISO/TC 97/506-1444.

[3]   K.C. TRAYNHAM, R.F. STEEN "SDLC and BSC on satellite links : a performance comparison",Ass. Comput. Mach. Comput. Commun. Rev. vol. 7 pp 3-14, Oct 1977.

[4]   E. GELENBE, J. LABETOULLE, G. PUJOLLE "Performance evaluation of the protocol HDLC". Proc. Symp. Computer Networks Protocols, Liège, Belgique, 13-15 fév. 1978, A. Danthine Ed. North Holland.

[5]   J. LABETOULLE, G. PUJOLLE "Modelling and performance evaluation of the protocol HDLC" Proc. Symp. Flow Control in Comput. Networks, Versailles, France, 12-14 fév. 1979. J.L. Grangé, M. Gien Eds. North Holland.

[6]   W. BUX, H.L. TRUONG "A queueing model for HDLC controlled data links", Proc. Int. Symp. Flow Control in Comput. Networks, Versailles, France, 12-14 fév. 1979. J.L. Grangé, M. Gien Eds, North Holland.

[7]   L.W. YU, J.C. MAJITHIA "An analysis of one direction of window mechanism" I.E.E.E. Trans. on Comm. vol. COM-27, pp. 778-788, 1979.

[8]   D. TOWSLEY, J.K. WOLF "On the statistical analysis of queue lengths and waiting times for statistical multiplexers with ARQ retransmission schemes" I.E.E.E. Trans. on Comm. vol COM-27, pp. 393-402, 1979.

[9]   W. BUX, K. KUMMERLE, J.L. TRUONG "Balanced HDLC procedures : a performance analysis" I.E.E.E. Trans. on comm. vol. COM-28 pp. 1889-1898, 1980.

[10]  D. DROMARD, D. SERET "Performances réelles d'une liaison télématique" Actes du Congrès international sur la conception des systèmes télématiques, Nice, France, 2-5 juin 1981.

[11]  Transpac, "Spécifications techniques d'utilisation du réseau" Manuel de référence, sept. 1977 avec mise à jour périodique.

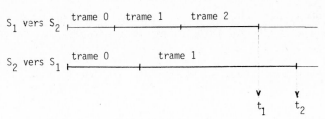

Figure 1. Exemple de transmission.

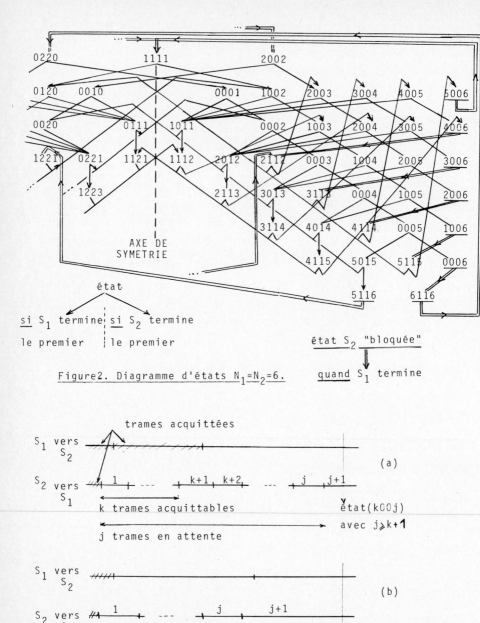

Figure2. Diagramme d'états $N_1=N_2=6$.

Figure3. Détail des différents états.

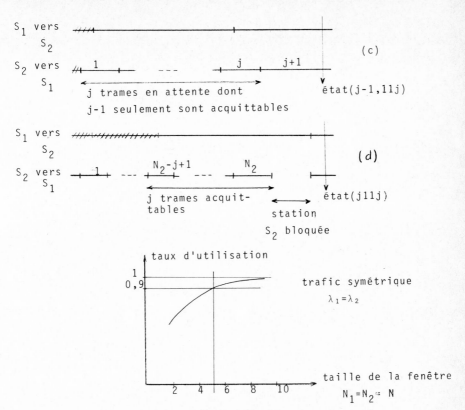

Figure 4. Taux d'utilisation en fonction de la
taille de la fenêtre.

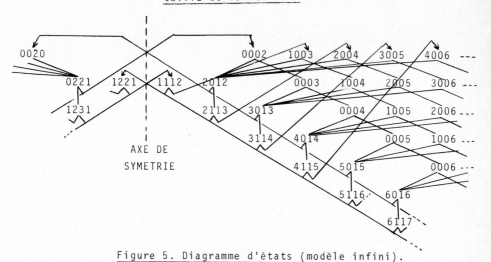

Figure 5. Diagramme d'états (modèle infini).

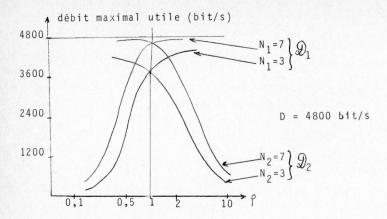

Figure 7. Débit maximal utile.

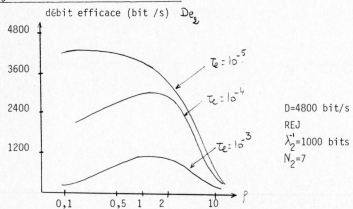

Figure 8. Débit efficace en fonction du taux d'erreurs.

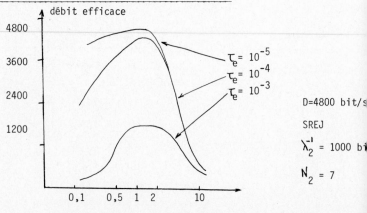

Figure 9. Débit efficace en fonction du taux d'erreurs.

| N | Prob($F_1$=N) |
|---|---|
| 3 | 0,26 ± 0,03 |
| 4 | 0,20 ± 0,03 |
| 5 | 0,10 ± 0,02 |
| 6 | 0,05 ± 0,02 |
| 7 | 0,031 ± 0,005 |
| 8 | 0,017 ± 0,005 |

Tableau 10. Modèle à fenêtre finie
Probabilité de blocage.

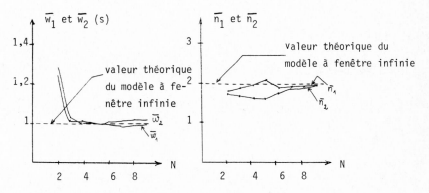

Figure 11. Temps moyen d'attente et nombre de trames en attente en fonction de la taille de la fenêtre . D= 4800 bit/s $\lambda_1^{-1} = \lambda_2^{-1}$ = 2400 bits.

Performance of Data Communication Systems
and their Applications, G. Pujolle (ed.)
© North-Holland Publishing Company, 1981

## PREVENTION OF STORE-AND-FORWARD DEADLOCK ON A
## MICROPROCESSOR NETWORK

David Gelernter

Department of Computer Science
State University of New York at Stony Brook
Stony Brook, New York
U.S.A.

Store-and-forward deadlock (SFD) occurs in a packet-switched computer
network when, among some cycle of packets buffered by the communication system, each packet in the cycle waits for the use
of the buffer now occupied by the next packet in the cycle. An
SFD-prevention technique is described that is significantly less
obtrusive than previous algorithms with respect to packet routing,
buffer-pool partitioning and buffer-pool sizes. The integrated
microprocessor network in the context of which the work was performed, and the implementation now under construction, are described.

## 1. INTRODUCTION

Store-and-forward deadlock (SFD) occurs in packet-switching computer networks when
some group of packets exists in the network communication system such that among
this group, no packet has arrived at its destination and none can make a next
hop towards its destination. The simplest case of SFD is direct SFD in which,
given two adjacent nodes $N_i$ and $N_j$, $N_i$'s packet buffers are full of packets destined for $N_j$, and $N_j$'s buffers are full of packets for $N_i$; as a result, no packet can move. In more complex SFD's, a cycle of nodes is involved. Each node in
the cycle holds packets bound for the next node in the cycle. If $N_i$, $N_j$ and $N_k$
are three consecutive nodes in a deadlocked cycle, $N_j$'s buffers need not be
completely filled with packets bound for $N_k$; deadlock only requires that all
buffers on $N_j$ in which packets waiting on $N_i$ may legally be buffered be full of
packets bound for $N_k$.

Several algorithms for prevention of SFD on networks of arbitrary topology are
known, and they will be considered in two groups.

1. The "structured buffer pool technique" is described by Raubold and Haenle[1];
it is discussed by Giessler et. al.[2] and by Gerla and Kleinrock[3] in their survey
of flow control techniques. This technique requires that every node's buffer
pool be divided into classes, a 0-hop class, 1-hop class and so on through a
K-hop class, where K is the length of the longest path in the network. The
buffers of the i-hop class may hold only those packets that are i hops or more
removed from their node of origin. Thus, a packet that is h hops from its source
node may be buffered in any j-class such that $j \leq h$. Toueg and Ullman[4] discuss
variants of this scheme and converse schemes (the forward count and forward state
algorithms) in which admission to buffer classes is based on distance to destination rather than distance from source.

2. Merlin and Schweitzer[5] discuss a generalization of the structured pool technique. Their algorithm requires the construction of a directed acyclic buffer
graph. The nodes of the graph are buffers, and there may be an edge between two
nodes if they represent buffers that are located on one processor or on adjacent
processors. Every permissable packet route must correspond to some path in the
directed graph. A packet may hop from buffer $b_1$ to buffer $b_2$ only if the edge

305

$b_1 \rightarrow b_2$ is part of the graph. (This restriction may be relaxed when the network is not congested.) Gelernter and Bertapelle[6] discuss a scheme that is in a sense the converse of Merlin and Schweitzer's. It requires the construction, not of an acyclic buffer graph, but of a set of buffer cycles containing all permissible packet routes. This algorithm relies for deadlock prevention not on an acyclic collection of paths, but on a priority protocol that insures that every cycle must contain at all times at least one empty buffer.

All of these techniques prevent SFD, each at some cost in flexibility and efficiency of packet handling by the communication system. Obviously SFD-prevention must be paid for somehow, but the costs imposed by the techniques above are troublesome. An ideal SFD-prevention algorithm would have the following properties.

a. Packet routing is unrestricted. Ideally, the communication system should be free to construct packet routes dynamically without interference from the SFD-prevention algorithm. The algorithms in group (1) above do not impose routing restrictions, except for the forward-count and forward-state techniques[4]. These require that the length of a packet's route be declared beforehand; the route may be constructed dynamically, but must not exceed the pre-declared length. In the group (2) algorithms, a packet's next hop must follow an edge in the buffer graph (in the Merlin and Schweitzer scheme) or--a more severe restriction--the unique next edge in the buffer cycle. In both cases, the restriction may be relaxed when the network is not congested. The severity of the restriction in the buffer graph scheme depends on the elaborateness and completeness of the graph constructed.

b. The number of buffers each node is required to provide is independent of the size of the network. This requirement is particularly important for networks of microcomputers that may be enlarged regularly and may ultimately grow very large. The group (1) schemes require a buffer pool on each node that contains strictly more buffers than the length of the longest path in the network. If communication, then, is permitted between any two network nodes, buffer pools must grow with network diameter. The pools required by the group (2) algorithms vary in size from node to node and are topology dependent, but may in general grow with network size.

c. Minimal partitioning is imposed on buffer pools. The number of times that a packet seeking entrance to some node's buffer pool is refused admission despite there being empty buffers somewhere in the pool should be minimal. Congestion and flow control may make some degree of pool partitioning necessary or desirable, but the amount of partitioning required simply for SFD-prevention should be as small as possible. The group (1) schemes impose explicit[1] or implicit[4] pool partitioning as described above. The group (2) schemes partition pools explicitly on the basis of their position in the acyclic buffer graph or in some buffer cycle. Note that minimal partitioning is desirable so that pools may be used efficiently and delivery times be minimized, but also so that heavily-used packet-switching software be no more complex than necessary.

The algorithm described below has desirable properties (a), (b) and (c) above. It imposes new costs in return. The costs it imposes, however, are unconventional and make this scheme not strictly comparable to the other SFD-prevention techniques. Specifically, the new algorithm
i. imposes no a priori routing restrictions.
ii. Requires a pool size per node that is independent of network size. No more than two buffers on most nodes and one on the rest are required to insure SFD-freedom.
iii. Imposes no buffer-pool partitioning.
The costs of the new technique are these:
i. Under certain circumstances, packets are forcibly re-routed around potential deadlocks.

ii. One arbitrarily-chosen node is required to accept within finite time any packet seeking entrance to its buffer pool, even if this requires its erasing some packet. This means in effect that one node will have a pool that is substantially larger than the pools on other nodes (to minimize instances of such deliberate erasure).

It will be argued that, despite its costs, the algorithm's benefits make it well worth consideration.

Section 2 describes the new algorithm; section 3 gives examples. Section 4 discusses livelock and failure. Section 5 describes the integrated micro-processor network for which the algorithm was developed, and outlines the implementation now under construction. (A formal definition of SFD, a more formal presentation of the algorithm's proof and a comparison of the logical bases of the several available SFD-prevention algorithms is found in Gelernter[7].)

## 2. THE ALGORITHM

Let any network N be represented by undirected graph G. Nodes in G correspond to processors in N; edges in G correspond to (assumed bidirectional) communication lines in N. The algorithm requires the construction of some directed graph $G_1$ with the following properties:

a. The nodes and directed edges of $G_1$ correspond to the nodes and the undirected edges of G.

b. $G_1$ is acyclic and has exactly one node with no incident incoming edges. This unique node will be called the root of $G_1$.

> The following procedure will produce a directed graph $G_1$ from an undirected graph G. First, construct a directed spanning tree T of G with root r-- all nodes are reachable from r via the edges in T. Now assign direction to all edges in G that are not part of T such that these edges together with the edges of T remain acyclic. To accompish this, edges between nodes at different distances from the root may be pointed away from the root; edges at the same distance from the root may be assigned either direction, so long as all edges at any given distance from the root remain acyclic. The result is a $G_1$ graph.

Having constructed graph $G_1$, construct the inverse graph $G_2$ by reversing the direction of all edges in $G_1$.

Now, every hop a packet makes in N corresponds to an edge either in $G_1$ or in $G_2$. A $G_1$-packet is a packet whose next hop will be over a $G_1$ edge; a $G_2$ packet is analogously defined. If a packet may wait on more than one output queue simultaneously for the use of whatever link becomes available first, then so long as it waits for the use of at least one $G_2$ link, it is a $G_2$ packet.

The $G_1$ root node (or simply the root), r, has no incoming $G_1$ edges. All packets in r are $G_1$ packets, because no $G_2$ edges leave r. The nodes without incoming edges in the $G_2$ graph (there may be one or many) are called $G_2$ roots. All packets in $G_2$ roots are $G_2$ packets, because no $G_1$ edges leave $G_2$ roots.

The deadlock-free property of the algorithm derives from the following requirement: every node must at all times contain either an empty buffer or a $G_2$ packet. This means that:

a. If a non-root node Nq, after accepting some new packet, finds that every one of its buffers is now filled with a $G_1$ packet, then some packet in Nq must be redirected and routed out over a $G_2$ edge. (That is, some packet must be trans-formed into a $G_2$ packet.)

b. The root, since it can contain no $G_2$ packets, must always have an empty buffer. Any packet waiting for admission to r must be admitted in finite time, even if this involves erasing some packet in r.

Erasure at r may be made arbitrarily rare by increasing the size of the buffer pool on r relative to buffer pools in the rest of the network.

Note that the forced redirection of packets required by (a) occurs only when all packets in a node are $G_1$ packets and therefore contending for the use of the same set of links. Such redirection generally corresponds to the forcing of some packet from a set of congested output queues to some empty queue, which may be inherently desirable. (Of course, the fact that all other packets buffered on a node are $G_1$ packets does not mean that all or any are waiting for the particular $G_1$ link that the rerouted packet would have used. On the other hand, a node is free to choose any currently-buffered packet for rerouting when rerouting is necessary, and therefore it is always possible to accomplish rerouting by transferring some packet from a relatively congested output queue to an empty output queue.)

> Implementation Note. Suppose a $G_1$ packet p arrives at node Nj from node Ni over a $G_1$ edge. Suppose further that p makes Nj full of $G_1$ packets, and thus makes a rerouting necessary. The rerouting is accomplished if p itself is chosen for rerouting, and routed back to node Ni--that is, if p is simply sent back where it came from. (The hop from Nj to Ni must be a $G_2$ hop.) But this means that, rather than accepting and rerouting p, Nj could simply have refused p to begin with. A packet like p--any $G_1$ packet arriving over a $G_1$ link--will be referred to below as a refusable packet. The algorithm does not require that refusable packets be refused, but--as an implementation point--if they are, a rerouting is avoided. Note that such an implementation imposes an implicit buffer pool partitioning (albeit a minor one), insofar as the last buffer in a pool full of $G_1$ packets is closed to a $G_1$ packet arriving over a $G_1$ link.

Note finally that if the buffer pool on r is not proportionately larger than other buffer pools, the algorithm may be regarded as implementing the following pragmatic congestion control policy: when traffic in the net is such as to make deadlock possible, excess packets are drawn to the root and eliminated. (Ordinarily of course an implementation, by specifying a large buffer pool at the root, will be designed to avoid packet deletion, not to allow it routinely for congestion control.)

Theorem. The algorithm is SFD-free.

Proof. (1) No $G_2$ packet can be deadlocked.
Suppose p is a $G_2$ packet and p is deadlocked. Let pwQ, where Q is some set of packets, mean that p is waiting for the use of buffers currently occupied by the packets in set Q. (The packets contained in Q are buffered on some node or nodes adjacent to the node on which p is buffered.) If p is deadlocked, then clearly there exists some sequence $pwQ_1wQ_2w...$ and all packets in each $Q_i$ are deadlocked. Note that if a packet is waiting for any buffer on node Nq, it is waiting for all buffers on Nq. Therefore, if $Q_i$ contains some packet buffered on node Nq, it contains all packets buffered on Nq; if Nq contains empty buffers, $Q_i$ contains the "empty packet". Now, no $Q_i$ can contain an empty packet, because if it did, the packets in set $Q_{i-1}$ would not be deadlocked, contradicting the assumption. Therefore, each $Q_i$ must contain a $G_2$ packet, since the algorithm requires each node to include either an empty buffer or a $G_2$ packet. Since each $Q_i$ contains a $G_2$ packet, some node whose buffers hold packets included in $Q_{i+1}$ must be reachable via $G_2$ from some node whose buffers hold packets included in $Q_i$. Since $G_2$ is acyclic, there must therefore exist some $Q_n$ such that all packets buffered on the root, r, are part of $Q_n$. But since by assumption r contains an empty buffer, $Q_n$ contains an empty packet and $Q_{n-1}$ is not deadlocked. $Q_{n-2}$ is therefore not deadlocked, and working backward in the sequence of waiting packet sets, it is clear that p cannot be deadlocked.

(2) No $G_1$ packet can be deadlocked.
Let p now be a $G_1$ packet. If p, again, is waiting for the use of some buffer on node Nq, it is waiting for all buffers on Nq. But since every node must contain either an empty buffer or a $G_2$ packet, p can never be deadlocked, since it must always be waiting for the use of some buffer occupied by a non-deadlocked packet. Thus no packet, whether $G_1$ or $G_2$, can be deadlocked, and the theorem is proven.

In sum, the algorithm has the following advantages:
a. There are no a priori routing restrictions.
b. Required buffer pool size is independent of the size of the network. Deadlock prevention requires $\geq 2$ buffers on non-roots and $\geq 1$ buffer on ($G_1$ or $G_2$) root nodes. (A non-root must have at least two buffers, otherwise any packet accepted would be required to be a $G_2$ packet, and no $G_1$ hops from a non-root could ever occur. A $G_2$ root requires only one buffer, since it buffers only $G_2$ packets by definition. The $G_1$ root must always include an empty buffer, and therefore requires one, but no more than one, buffer.)
c. Buffer pools are unpartitioned. Any packet may be shipped to any empty buffer (with the reservation that a given implementation may choose to refuse refusable packets).

The costs are:
a. Packets buffered in full buffer pools on nodes other than the root are subject to re-routing.
b. Packets buffered in a full buffer pool on the root are subject to deletion.

## 3.   EXAMPLES

### 3.1.   The Torus.
Fig. 1 shows a $G_1$ graph for a 6 x 6 torus, with each row and each column looping back on itself. The root is circled twice. Assuming that most packets on the torus will follow a minimum-hop route from source to destination, re-routing imposed by the algorithm is normally restricted to the following cases.

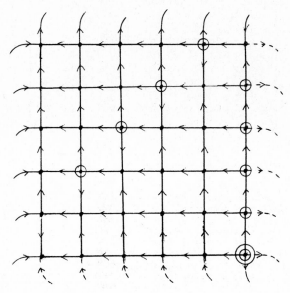

Figure 1

a. Suppose packet p is at least one horizontal and one vertical hop removed from its destination node Nd, and that p is therefore willing to make either a horizontal or a vertical hop so long as that hop brings it closer to Nd. A packet may be re-routed only if its next hop is a $G_1$ hop. Since packets like p may all potentially make their next hop over either of two adjacent links, re-routing of such packets may take place only on nodes that hold two adjacent outward-directed $G_1$ edges. But if, furthermore, the implementation chooses to refuse all refusable packets, then re-routing is possible only on nodes with <u>three</u> outward-directed $G_1$ edges; $G_1$ packets incoming over $G_1$ links will be <u>refused</u> rather than re-routed. Redirection of packets at least one horizontal and one vertical hop from their destinations may therefore take place only at the nodes circled in fig. 1.
b. Suppose packet p has arrived on an axis of its destination. Such a packet will have only one choice for its next hop. It will hop from node to node along the destination's axis until it arrives. Packets in this category may be redirected whenever their next hop is a $G_1$ hop, and this may occur on any node with at least one outgoing $G_1$ link, that is, on all nodes but $G_2$ roots. If we assume again an implementation that refuses refusable packets, redirection of such packets is restricted to nodes with at least two outgoing $G_2$ links.

Thus although, in theory, any $G_1$ packet is susceptible to re-routing on any non-root node, the regularity of the torus graph restricts re-routing to a subset of $G_1$ packets.

3.2.  An Arbitrary Graph.

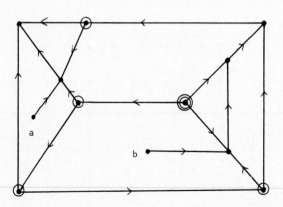

Figure 2

Fig. 2 shows a $G_1$ graph for the ARPANET of the early seventies[8]. Nodes of degree two are omitted. (ARPANET is discussed here only as an example of a realistic network graph.) The root is circled twice. Assuming an implementation that refuses refusable packets, packet re-routing may occur only at the four singly-circled nodes--the rest lack two outbound $G_1$ links. (No packet buffered on a node of degree two--the majority of nodes in this case, although they are not shown in the figure--can be re-routed.) Note that nodes of degree one (the nodes labelled a and b) have been added as supplementary roots. This is permissible. Neither will be required to delete packets, assuming 1) that packets are never forwarded through a or b, 2) that neither a nor b ever entirely fills its packet buffers with new packets.

## 4. LIVELOCK AND FAILURE

Livelock as discussed by Toueg[9] is a state in which some packet is prevented indefinitely from making its next hop because of unfavorable traffic patterns. The structured buffer pool algorithms are livelockable as follows. Suppose the distance-from-source technique is used. Node $N_i$ may be h hops from $N_q$ and $N_i$ g hops, $g<h$. Packets originating on $N_j$ and passing through $N_q$ are eligible for buffering in all k-hop buffer classes such that $k\leq h$. Packets originating on $N_i$ and passing through $N_q$ are only eligible for k-hop classes such that $k<g$. A stream of packets from $N_j$ may therefore fill all k-classes where $k<g$--all classes, in other words, for which packets from $N_i$ are eligible. But when all such classes are filled with packets from $N_j$, more packets from $N_j$ may still be admitted, although none from $N_i$ may be admitted. If a new packet from $N_j$ arrives at $N_q$ before each old packet from $N_j$ is passed along, $N_i$'s packets will never be admitted to $N_q$ and are "livelocked".

Toueg proposes a modification of the structured pool scheme that requires all packets to be time-stamped at creation, and each packet's time-stamp to be checked against the time-stamps of all other waiting packets before it is granted or refused admission to any node. The group (2) algorithm, on the other hand, are in general inherently livelock-free, because buffers are reserved for packets travelling given routes. One route's packets cannot exclude another route's. (In the directed buffer graph technique, buffers on nodes $N_a$ and $N_b$ may each feed via a directed edge into a single buffer on adjacent node $N_c$. A continuous stream of packets through $N_a$ bound for $N_c$, together with unfair scheduling on $N_c$'s part, may indefinitely exclude packets from $N_b$. But this is not livelock: $N_c$ is free at all times to admit packets from $N_b$; it simply chooses not to. In the previous example, $N_q$ was forbidden by the algorithm to admit packets originating on $N_i$.)

The algorithm given above is also livelock-free, because it imposes no buffer pool partitioning. So long as empty buffers are made available fairly to waiting packets, no waiting packet can be excluded indefinitely.

The fact that the algorithm allows packets to be forcibly re-routed makes it possible in theory for a packet to circle endlessly and never arrive at its destination, a situation akin to livelock. In practice, when some packet must be re-routed on $N_i$, any packet on $N_i$ may be chosen for re-routing. Packets that have been re-routed once may have a header bit so indicating (the "re-route bit") set on, and will be avoided when again buffered in a pool where re-routing is necessary. A node that is entirely full of once-rerouted packets might choose to delete incoming packets rather than re-route any packet a second time. (A node in this state meets the algorithm's requirements by including an empty buffer rather than a $G_2$ packet, as the root does.) Alternatively, incoming packets might be deleted only by a node full of twice-re-routed packets and so on. Given the expected infrequency of the situation, the procedure chosen is likely to be of little practical significance.

> Given the global clock posited by Toueg, the algorithm can be adapted to insure that every packet, so long as it is not deleted at the root, will eventually reach its destination, that is, that no packet will loop indefinitely. The global time at which a packet is created, concatenated with the unique id of the processor on which it is created, may serve as a packet's birthdate. Assuming that no processor can create more than one packet simultaneously, there is accordingly at all times a unique oldest packet in the net. When a packet must be chosen for re-routing, the youngest packet in the pool is chosen. Clearly, every packet must eventually either arrive, be deleted at the root, or become the unique oldest packet in the net. If the last-named occurs, then this unique oldest packet can never be re-routed and must therefore, unless it is deleted, arrive at its destination in finite time. (A header field counting the number of times a packet has been re-routed, concatenated with a serial number assigned sequentially by each processor to each packet it creates, may replace the global creation-time discussed above.)

To summarize, under the general group (1) schemes, a packet, though not deadlocked, may fail to reach its destination because of livelock; under the new
algorithm, a packet, though not deadlocked, may fail to reach its destination
because of indefinite looping or--of course--because of deletion at the root.  A
livelock-free version of the group (1) schemes is known, and as for the new
algorithm, it seems likely that heuristic techniques--a header "re-route bit" or
bits, increasing the size of the buffer pool on the root--will be sufficient to
control the problem.  In all events, the new algorithm relies on a higher-level
end-to-end protocol to detect and cause the retransmission of lost packets.  It
promises not delivery but only probable delivery of any given packet.  (This is
of course the most it could promise in any case given a system in which hardware
may fail.)

Hardware failures affect the algorithm in two cases.  1) All of some node Np's
outgoing $G_2$ links, or the nodes terminating them, fail.  2) The root fails, or
all links leading to it fail.

In case (1), Np becomes a "pseudo-root", unable to re-route packets over $G_2$ links.
It may delete excess incoming packets as the real root does, or it may initiate a
reconfiguration of the network graph.  In case (2), some node adjacent to the
root takes over the root's functions, deleting excess incoming packets for as
long as the root remains down.


5.  NOTES ON AN IMPLEMENTATION

The algorithm described above was developed for implementation on the Stony
Brook microprocessor Network[10,11] (SBN), now under construction.  SBN will be a
"network computer" in the sense that users will log on not to a given node but to
the network as a whole, jobs will move from node to node transparently and the
network will be controlled by a distributed operating system running on many
nodes simultaneously.  SBN is configured in an end-around torus of the sort
pictured in fig. 2.  Network nodes are LSI-11 microprocessors; each node interfaces directly to its four neighbors via word-parallel buffered links.  Each
node is both host and packet-switch; there are no front-end processors.

Store-and-forward deadlock has been simulated in settings that model the
ARPANET[12] and the GMDNET[2].   SFD occurs with low probability in these environments.
(ARPANET has no explicit SFD-prevention technique; GMDNET uses the structured
buffer pool method.)  But SFD prevention was considered essential on SBN for
several reasons.

a. If SBN's goals of supporting both a distributed operating system and distributed user jobs (including massively parallel user jobs) are met, packet traffic
in the network will at times be very heavy.

b. At the same time, resources for handling heavy traffic are limited.  Buffer
pools must necessarily be rather small, since each node's limited store must be
shared by system and user jobs.  Further, the torus is a highly "SFD-prone"
topology insofar as its connectivity is strongly redundant.

c. Finally, packet deadlock on SBN disables not merely a peripheral service
(the communication subnet), but the host system itself.  The network is the
host machine.

The conditions that make SFD-prevention important on SBN also increase the
importance of the favorable properties noted above.  Storage space must be
shared between the system and the users, so demands on the size of the buffer
pool, and pool-partitioning requirements that decrease the effective size of the
pool, must be minimal.  Processor-time likewise must be shared between system and
users.  Time the system spends on packet handling is lost to computing; communication software must be as simple as possible.  These requirements gave rise to
the development of the new algorithm.

The communication system for SBN is being developed in the concurrent language Modula[13].  Deadlock prevention is concentrated almost entirely in a single "re-route" routine.

Each node's communication kernel includes a node descriptor word unique to that node.  Four bits of the node descriptor word indicate the $G_1/G_2$ status of each of that node's four links.  Incoming packets are buffered and passed to an out-put-queuing routine; when an output queue is chosen, the $G_1/G_2$ status of its associated link is checked, and if necessary a counter recording total $G_1$ packets currently buffered is incremented.  If it is then discovered that all store-and-forward buffers are full of $G_1$ packets, the re-route routine is invoked.

Each packet carries a single re-route bit in its header.  The re-route routine chooses the first packet with its re-route bit off (or the last packet in the pool, if all packets have re-route bits set), and reassigns it to a $G_2$ output queue.  If no $G_2$ queues are available--always true on the root, true otherwise only in case of hardware failure--some packet is marked "deleted".

In this simplest-case initial implementation, then,
a. A single priority bit serves as the basis for re-routing choices.
b. In cases of hardware failure, no dynamic reconfiguration is attempted. Pseudo-roots delete packets as the real root does.  In addition,
c. Refusable packets are not refused.

The next-step version of the communication system will refuse refusable packets-- a simple change--but details (a) and (b) will not be changed unless observed performance makes change necessary.

Answers to open questions about the efficiency and practicality of the new algorithm will come, for our setting at least, directly from measured network performance.


ACKNOWLEDGEMENT

Thanks to Professor Arthur Bernstein for extensive advice and assistance.


REFERENCES

1.   Raubold, E. and Haenle, J, A Method of Deadlock-Free Resource Allocation
     and Flow Control in Packet Networks, in: Proc. ICCC 76 (Toronto, Aug. 1976)
     483

2.   Giessler, A., Haenle, J., Koenig, A., Pade, E., Free Buffer Allocation--An
     Investigation by Simulation, Computer Networks 2(1978) 191

3.   Kleinrock, L. and Gerla, M., Flow Control: A Comparitive Survey, IEEE
     Transactions on Communications COM-28,4(1980) 553

4.   Toueg, S. and Ullman, J., Deadlock-Free Packet Switching Networks, in:
     Proc. ACM Symposium on Theory of Comp. (1979) 89

5.   Merlin, P. and Schweitzer, P.,  Deadlock Avoidance in Store-and-Forward
     Networks--I: Store-and-Forward Deadlock, IEEE Transactions on Communications
     COM-28,3(1980) 325

6.  Gelernter, D., Bertapelle, K, General and Topology-Specific Algorithms for Prevention of Store-and-Forward Deadlock in Packet Networks, technical report, Dept. of Computer Science, State University of New York at Stony Brook (Dec. 1980)

7.  Gelernter, D., A DAG-Based Algorithm for Prevention of Store-and-Forward Deadlock in Packet Networks, to appear in IEEE Transactions on Computers

8.  Schelonka, E., Resource Sharing with Arpanet, National Telecommunications Conference 1974 Record, 1045, reprinted in: Abrams, M., Blanc, R., Cotton, I., Computer Networks: A Tutorial (IEEE, 1978) 5-19

9.  Toueg,S., Deadlock and Livelock-Free Packet-Switching Networks, in: Proc. ACM Symposium on Theory of Comp. (1980) 94

10. Bernstein, A.J. and Gelernter, D., Storing and Retrieving the Network State: a Survey and a Proposal, technical report, Dept. of Computer Science, State University of New York at Stony Brook (Oct. 1980)

11. Gelernter, D., An Integrated Microprocessor Network for Experiments in Distributed Programming, technical report, Dept. of Computer Science, State University of New York at Stony Brook (May 1981)

12. Kahn, R.E. and Crowther, W.R., A Study of the ARPA Network Design and Performance, technical report, Bolt Beranek and Newman (Aug. 1971)

13. Wirth, N., Modula: a Language for Modular Multiprogramming, Software-- Practice and Experience 7,3-35(1977) 3

Performance of Data Communication Systems
and their Applications, G. Pujolle (ed.)
© North-Holland Publishing Company, 1981

Réseau d'Echange Reconfigurable pour Contrôle de Processus Réparti

Ch. MERAUD (SAGEM 6, avenue d'Iéna PARIS 16ème)

B. MAUREL (SAT 41, rue Cantagrel PARIS 13ème

RESUME

      Ce texte expose les résultats pour la partie procédure de l'étude d'un système d'échanges ultrafiable à débit élevé.

      Ce système doit permettre la réalisation décentralisée des échanges entre les divers équipements d'un système réparti de contrôle de processus, pour l'intégration et la reconfiguration de fonctions pouvant être critiques (chimie, sidérurgie, nucléaire, distribution d'énergie ...).

      L'apparition des VLSI et des fibres (2) optiques insensibles aux perturbations électromagnétiques a conduit, pour atteindre les objectifs visés, à une solution décentralisée performante par l'incorporation d'intelligence dans un module de raccordement de type universel appelé Interface Sous-Système (ISS).

      Le principe retenu substitue au mécanisme traditionnellement programmé de gestion des échanges, un mécanisme dynamique immédiatement adapté aux modifications, et permettant une grande souplesse de synchronisation. Il fonctionne par diffusion de messages groupant des mots de 16 bits suivant une partition jouée en orchestre de chambre par l'ensemble des ISS répartis sur l'ensemble des équipements raccordés. Les ISS se synchronisent entre eux par extraction de l'horloge de l'émission en cours et se concertent périodiquement pour valider les échanges, commuter de mode éventuellement ou recouvrir les pannes.

      La gestion des échanges au niveau de chaque équipement est donc confiée à l'ISS qu'il incorpore. Celui-ci joue sa partie spécifique en interprétant les paramètres messages que l'équipementier a inscrit dans une mémoire morte. Périodiquement, ils se donnent rendez-vous pour échanger les codes cycliques élaborés par chacun d'eux à partir des informations observées sur la ligne pendant le cycle précédent. Cette phase sert à la détection, au diagnostic des pannes, à la reconfiguration et enfin à la resynchronisation et à la réinitialisation des ISS victimes d'une panne transitoire.

      Le principe substitue au mécanisme traditionnellement programmé de gestion des échanges, un mécanisme dynamique immédiatement adapté aux modifications, et permettant une grande souplesse de synchronisation.

INTRODUCTION

      Une réflexion sur l'évolution des systèmes de contrôle de processus répartis vers tout à la fois plus de performances de complexité et de sûreté de fonctionnement ; un bilan de l'expérience acquise sur les liaisons normalisées actuelles aux possibilités limitées en regard des besoins futurs ; un examen en contrepartie de l'accroissement considérable des performances de la technologie avec l'apparition des VLSI et des fibres optiques suggèrent pour atteindre les objectifs visés une orientation nouvelle pour la réalisation de la fonction de communication vers une solution répartie par l'incorporation d'intelligence dans un module universel (ISS) de raccordement incorporé à chaque équipement.

Une recherche en ce sens a été effectuée dans le cadre d'un
contrat DRET (1) par la SAGEM en collaboration avec la Société Electronique
Marcel DASSAULT. Elle a abouti en décembre 1979 à une solution basée sur l'utilisation des composants de ligne des bus normalisés actuels permettant des échanges
à 1 ou 2 MBd. Il faut insister sur la souplesse de cette solution sure et immédiatement réalisable.

La solution présentée ici en collaboration avec la SAT (2) prévoit
l'utilisation des fibres optiques pour atteindre les vitesses d'échanges de
10 MBd nécessaires dans les futurs systèmes.

Elle permettra alors :

- de simplifier la maintenance en réalisant toutes les communications digitales
  (lentes et rapides) suivant le même protocole et avec une seule famille de
  matériel (réseau de bus optiques redondés 10 MBd et un seul type de coupleur
  très intégré incorporé à chaque équipement),

- de faire survivre automatiquement la fonction de communication aux pannes et
  d'avoir un diagnostic précis facilitant la maintenance . La sécurité de fonctionnement pourrait dépasser $10^{-10}$/heure (probabilité d'une panne non passi-
  vée), et la fiabilité avant réparation pourrait atteindre compte tenu des possibilités de reconfiguration automatique $10^{-4}$ par 24 heures dans des conditions
  d'environnement sévères,

- d'incorporer des équipements en redondance pour filtrer leurs pannes et faci-
  liter les opérations de maintenance en ligne, ·

- d'effectuer avec une grande souplesse pour le matériel et le logiciel, le raccordement des équipements et les modifications de configuration et d'échanges
  du système,

- d'obtenir une datation précise des variables échangées.

Ce système de communication, vu à travers le module de raccordement ISS, fournira aux constructeurs d'équipements un moyen d'interconnexion uni-
versel facile à interfacer et dont l'intelligence incorporée libèrera les  équipements des sujétions liées aux échanges.

En ce sens, il permettra l'exécution d'échanges privés et pré-définis
entre boîtes d'un même sous-système afin d'en accroître l'interchangeabilité
d'une application à une autre.

Dans le même but, il substituera au mécanisme traditionnel de gestion
des échanges par programmation, un mécanisme dynamique non programmé immédiatement adapté aux modifications, améliorant la datation des variables et permettant une grande souplesse de synchronisation entre les équipements informatiques
du système.

Pour le maître d'oeuvre et l'équipementier, il sera accompagné d'un
moyen de gestion efficace pour l'intégration du système ou d'un sous-système
séparé en phase de développement, sous la forme d'outils logiciels d'aide à la
conception et à l'analyse permettant la vérification et l'optimisation des
échanges, la documentation de chaque édition du système et la génération des
paramètres de gestion des messages.

## DESCRIPTION GENERALE

### Composition d'une Interface Sous-Système (figure 1)

Les équipements sont interconnectés par une double liaison série multi-plexée via un interface intelligent (dit ISS Interface Sous-Système).

En plus des fonctions d'interface classiques, sa fonction est :

- d'assurer la gestion des échanges systèmes ou privés, critiques ou non, sur la liaison multiplexée,

- de permettre la synchronisation des tâches de son équipement sur l'exécution des échanges,

- de réaliser la détection et le recouvrement des erreurs de transmission et leur recouvrement par reconfiguration du bus,

- de réaliser la détection et le recouvrement de ses propres fautes, ainsi que sa mise hors service et son isolement du bus en cas de panne permanente.

### Structure matérielle du bus

Le bus est physiquement dupliqué pour survivre aux pannes. Chaque ligne est constituée de deux fibres, l'une montante, l'autre descendante.

Les dérivations sont réalisées par des coupleurs passifs transparents. En normal, chaque ISS répète l'information incidente pour que le niveau soit maintenu sur toute la ligne. En cas de panne d'un ISS, la transparence du coupleur assure la continuité de la liaison.

### Structure matérielle d'un ISS (figure 2)

Un ISS est un canal spécialisé réalisé à l'aide d'un contrôleur micro-programmé dupliqué. Une telle structure permet de détecter et de neutraliser immédiatement toute anomalie de fonctionnement pour empêcher tout comportement anarchique d'un ISS vis-à-vis du bus.

L'ISS exécute un microprogramme canal qui interprète les instructions de gestion des seuls messages intéressant l'équipement. Les instructions sont stockées dans une EPROM appartenant à l'équipement.

Il est relié aux lignes physiques du bus dupliqué par un connecteur optique et les circuits de conversion parallèle/série, modulation/démodulation, émission/réception opto-électronique qui assurent les fonctions du niveau d'interface avec la ligne.

### Informations échangées

Deux types d'informations doivent être échangées : les variables pério-diques et les variables aléatoires aux délais maxima fixés. La périodicité des émissions des variables du premier type ayant leur source dans l'équipement, du point de vue des échanges elles peuvent être traitées comme les secondes pourvu que les délais d'acheminement spécifiés soient respectés. C'est ce qui est réa-lisé en répartissant les variables sur 4 niveaux de priorité.

Gestion des redondances

        Les équipements générant des variables critiques peuvent être implantés
plusieurs fois, ce qui permet une diffusion multiple de ces variables pour
accroître leur disponibilité. A la réception, l'ISS de chaque équipement concerné
se charge du filtrage des fautes et de l'enregistrement du seul résultat juste
dans la zone de l'équipement affectée à la réception de la variable.

        Ce mécanisme favorise l'interchangeabilité en permettant l'intégration
redondante d'équipements standards dans les systèmes critiques sans leur imposer
de modifications notables.


Tolérance aux pannes et aux erreurs de transmission

        La structure interne de l'ISS assure une détection très efficace de ses
propres erreurs grâce aux choix d'une structure dupliquée/comparée.

        Les erreurs de transmission sont détectées :

- par détection d'erreurs de modulation grâce à l'emploi d'un codage
  autorythmé,

- par l'emploi d'un bit de parité par mot de 16 bits échangé,

- par l'utilisation d'un code cyclique élaboré et comparé périodiquement par
  l'ensemble des ISS.

        Lorsqu'une erreur est détectée, un basculement sur la deuxième ligne
est effectué. Ce mécanisme permet de filtrer les pannes transitoires sans dégrader le système.

        Un ISS détectant une erreur persistante dont il est la cause se met
hors service avec une sécurité élevée à cause de sa structure dupliquée.

        Afin d'éviter l'accumulation de pannes cachées sur le bus de secours,
le rôle des deux bus est périodiquement inversé afin d'être exercé par le fonctionnement normal et bénéficier d'une réparation préventive évitant la panne
double.


Gestion décentralisée de l'attribution du bus aux demandes d'émission des tâches

        La production des variables à échanger a pour source l'ensemble des
tâches réparties dans les divers équipements. Il faut ordonnancer la diffusion de
ces variables pour une consommation par le même ensemble de tâches à l'initiative
de chacune d'entre elles.

        Pour être échangées, les variables sont groupées par train de mots de
16 bits en messages à structure fixe avec un label d'en-tête et une priorité
définie à l'échelle du système. Les messages sont diffusés par les ISS de chaque
équipement à tour de rôle, et identifiés en réception grâce au label.

Le problème de l'ordonnancement des messages sur le bus est de même nature que celui de l'ordonnancement des tâches sur l'unité centrale. Celui-ci est aujourd'hui très correctement résolu dans les systèmes temps réel multitâches modernes par un mécanisme d'activation prioritaire à partir d'évènements et d'une gestion des files d'attentes des tâches prêtes sur chaque niveau de priorité. La meilleure solution consiste donc à adopter ce mécanisme pour l'ordonnancement des messages. On disposera alors d'une interface souple et facile entre les moniteurs temps réel de chaque équipement et la fonction d'échange. La solution répartie pour l'exécution de ce mécanisme consiste à faire exécuter simultanément le même algorithme par tous les ISS qui doivent donc fonctionner en synchronisme. A chaque instant, un ISS est en émission. Les autres sont alors en réception synchronisée par l'horloge des émissions en cours. Il y a donc une horloge commune à la population d'ISS à chaque instant qui suffit aux besoins de synchronisation.

### Implémentation d'une phase de contrôle périodique des échanges (figure 3)

L'ensemble des messages susceptibles d'être diffusés a été réparti à l'avance sur les 4 niveaux de priorité du système. Le niveau courant reste actif tant qu'il existe dans le système des messages en attente d'émission à ce niveau, et qu'il n'est pas apparu de messages à un niveau supérieur.

Pour décider des changements de niveau et pour les autres besoins du contrôle des échanges, un dialogue entre les ISS est nécessaire. Pour limiter les retards au minimum tout en conservant un bon rendement au bus, une fenêtre de 64 mots pour un cycle de 1024 mots échangés est réservée à ces besoins.

En début de fenêtre, chaque ISS détermine parmi 4 files de 64 bits où s'affichent les messages à émettre le niveau le plus élevé de la file non vidé. Ce niveau est inséré sur 2 bits dans un mot de contrôle. Ces mots de contrôle sont ensuite diffusés successivement par les ISS selon leur ordre d'adresse physique croissante. A la fin de ces émissions et quand la fenêtre de contrôle s'achève pour démarrer un nouveau cycle, les ISS savent :

- s'ils doivent poursuivre les échanges sur le même niveau,

- s'ils doivent commuter sur un niveau supérieur et qui doit prendre la parole (elle est prise par l'ISS d'adresse physique la plus petite à ce niveau). Dans ce cas, chaque ISS sauvegarde les pointeurs du niveau interrompu pour un retour ultérieur.

En cours de cycle et en dehors de la fenêtre de contrôle, les ISS se comportent comme un canal spécialisé entre les mémoires des équipements servis et le bus. Ils n'assurent que des opérations simples de transfert de mots à l'aide de pointeurs incrémentés à chaque pas et la mise à jour du code cyclique. Néanmoins, quand l'ISS émetteur n'a plus de messages au niveau courant, la commutation vers un successeur a lieu immédiatement. Ces commutations se font vers un autre ISS soit sur le même niveau, soit vers un niveau inférieur à partir des valeurs de pointeurs antérieurement sauvegardées. Elles ne nécessitent pratiquement pas de calcul, les paramètres de commutation ayant été déterminés pendant la dernière fenêtre de contrôle.

Critère de ventilation des messages sur les niveaux de priorité (figure 4)

        Les 4 niveaux sont les suivants :

- niveau 0 : des échanges différés (échanges longs, échanges de surveillance de routine, échanges de fond divers ...),

- niveau 1 : échanges temps réel ordinaire,

- niveau 2 : échanges temps réel urgents ou à fréquence rapide,

- niveau 3 : alarmes, etc.

        Il est clair que la souplesse du dispositif et la facilité d'évolution dépend des marges de charges.

        La figure 4 illustre le principe de répartition sur un exemple limité à 3 niveaux pour plus de clarté. En ordonnée, on classe les messages par ordre d'urgence spécifiée décroissante (courbe de droite).  On calcule (courbe de gauche) la situation de pire cas de délai d'acheminement. Celle-ci s'obtient pour les de pointes de demande, en accumulant les temps de transfert des messages supposés transmis dans l'ordre de leur classement en ordonnée. La figure montre alors le principe d'une ventilation par niveau qui ménage des marges équilibrées et maximales.


Datation fine pour le calcul des vieillissements des variables

        La solution efficace à ce besoin pour les variables qui le nécessitent consiste à transporter la date d'échantillonnage dans le message plutôt que d'accroître inutilement la fréquence d'échange par rapport à la fréquence de consommation juste nécessaire. Les tâches utilisatrices peuvent alors réactualiser spécifiquement les valeurs reçues.

        Pour celà, une heure système uniquement utilisable pour les calculs de retards est entretenue par chaque ISS à la cadence des échanges mots sur la ligne. Cette heure est transmise à chaque équipement par son ISS avec une périodicité spécifique (par exemple toutes les 0,5 ms, une fréquence trop élevée saturerait inutilement l'accès direct mémoire de l'équipement).


Synchronisation mutuelle des échanges et des tâches (figure 5)

        Les lieux de production et de consommation des variables sont des tâches hébergées dans les équipements.

        Un mécanisme souple par évènements référencés, interruption ou mise en file permet de réaliser la synchronisation mutuelle tâche-message. Ce mécanisme est le suivant :

- pour l'émission, le message préparé par une tâche est signalé "prêt" à l'ISS par positionnement d'un bit d'état dans une table de 64 bits (pour un maximum de 64 messages elligibles par équipement). Il sera diffusé au plus tôt par l'ISS en tenant compte de son niveau de priorité,

- pour la réception, les messages étant systématiquement diffusés en mode label (c'est-à-dire avec un nom dans un mot de procédure en-tête), il revient aux ISS de détecter à l'aide des paramètres inscrits dans la PROM d'adaptation de l'équipement les messages qui les concernent. L'instruction de gestion fournie sur 32 bits par l'EPROM permet à l'ISS de spécifier s'il est concerné et ce qu'il doit faire pour charger le message à sa bonne place puis insérer un numéro d'évènement avec un compte rendu d'état dans une file d'attente de l'équipement. Celui-ci exploite cette file à son rythme en activant les tâches en attente sur les évènements qu'elle contient.

## Portée d'adressage à structure de bloc emboîtés

La portée de désignation des labels fournie par les mots de procédure est structuré en 3 niveaux :

- un niveau de commande pouvant comporter 256 valeurs (dont un petit nombre seulement est utilisé),
- un niveau de labels systèmes comportant 512 valeurs,
- un niveau de labels sous-système pouvant comporter jusqu'à 128 groupes de 256 valeurs.

Chaque ISS a la vision complète des deux premiers niveaux et des valeurs d'un seul groupe sous- système auquel il appartient. Ce niveau correspond aux échanges privés entre équipements attachés à un même sous-système. Les échanges à ce niveau peuvent être librement modifiés sans produire d'interférence entre les sous-systèmes pourvu que les marges de charges soient respectées.

La structuration avec un niveau hiérarchique supplémentaire est envisageable.

Outre sa souplesse, ce dispositif limite la capacité d'adressage néces-saire au niveau de chaque ISS à 640 valeurs permettant de limiter la capacité de l'EPROM paramètres à 1 Kmots (de 32 bits).

## SURETE DE FONCTIONNEMENT

Elle s'appuie sur une très grande sécurité de détection des anomalies de fonctionnement des ISS qui exige leur réalisation par duplication du matériel et comparaison des sorties (figure 2).

Les ISS réalisent ensemble :
- la validation des échanges en fin de cycle,
- le filtrage des erreurs dû à des transitoires,
- la reconfiguration du bus ou leur auto-reconfiguration.

## Validation des échanges en fin de cycle

Au fur et à mesure des échanges, chacun des ISS élabore un code cyclique pour l'ensemble des 1024 mots du cycle.

Ce code est inséré sur 14 bits dans le mot de contrôle que chaque ISS diffuse. Le cycle est validé quand tous ces mots de contrôle sont identiques.

Les causes de pannes étant indépendantes entre les ISS, et ces derniers étant parfaitement testés par comparaison grâce à leur structure matérielle dupliquée et leur exercice continu, la validation du cycle faite par chacun d'eux, complétée par les tests de parité déjà réalisés au niveau de chaque mot échangé, est d'une sécurité pratiquement absolue.

Cette validation déverrouille l'utilisation par les tâches de l'information échangée.

## Filtrage des erreurs transitoires

En cas d'erreur constatée une première fois au cours du cycle ou lors de sa validation, le cycle est affiché en faute le mode reprise est allumé et l'ensemble des ISS bascule sur l'autre ligne (ou reste sur la même en cas de perte de la deuxième).

L'ISS de plus petite valeur d'adresse qui n'a pas fait de faute, envoie en début de cycle suivant un message d'initialisation des paramètres courants qui tient en quelques mots (heure système, configuration des ISS présents, pointeurs courants).

L'ISS en faute qui avait débrayé du cycle dès la détection de l'erreur pour attendre ce message est alors resynchronisé. Les échanges non validés maintenus par les tâches émettrices sont ensuite répétés. En cas de succès, le mode reprise est effacé.

## Reconfiguration des ISS ou du bus

Après trois tentatives infructueuses du même ISS, celui-ci s'éteint automatiquement. Ce signal allume un ISS de secours qui s'initialise suivant le même procédé. S'il n'y a pas d'ISS de secours, l'équipement disparaît des échanges sur le bus.

Quand plus d'un mot de contrôle se sépare des autres, l'erreur est mise au compte d'une panne de bus. En cas de faute persistante sur le même bus physique, celui-ci est abandonné.

## CONCLUSION

Les principes de base du protocole ont été exposés ainsi que celui sur lequel repose la sûreté de fonctionnement et pour lequel un calcul de fiabilité prévisionnelle a été réalisé.

Aujourd'hui, l'étude au niveau du système est en attente d'une progression des résultats au niveau des bus optiques. Au-delà, une maquette expérimentale pourra être réalisée.

## REFERENCES

(1) SIERRA : Système d'Intégration et d'Echanges Réparti et Reconfigurable automatiquement.
Rapport de synthèse - Février 1980 - Contrat DRET

(2) Programme "Ville câblée de Biarritz" - Maîtrise d'oeuvre SAT

(3) J.P. QUEILLE. The CESAR System : An aided design and certification system for distributed applications. The 2nd international conference on distributed computing systems PARIS France April 08-10 80

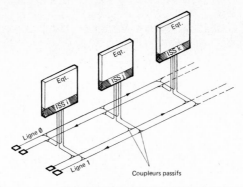

## Figure 1 — CONFIGURATION D'ENSEMBLE

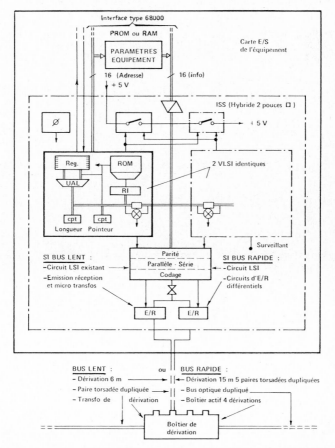

## Figure 2 — ISS REPRESENTE MONTE DANS UN EQUIPEMENT

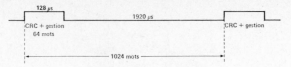

**Figure 3 — TRAME**

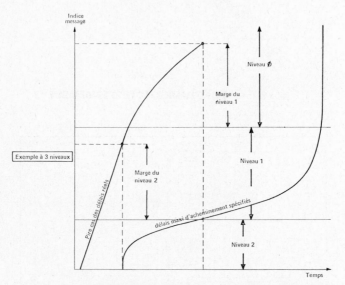

**Figure 4 — REPARTITION EN NIVEAUX DES MESSAGES**

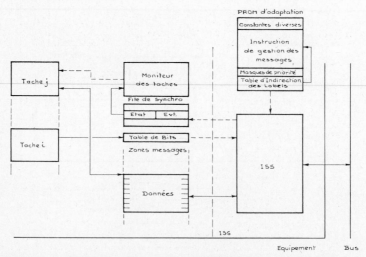

**Figure 5 — SYNCHRONISATION ENTRE L'ISS ET L'EQUIPEMENT**

Performance of Data Communication Systems
and their Applications, G. Pujolle (ed.)
© North-Holland Publishing Company, 1981

RESEAUX LOCAUX A TRES HAUT DEBIT : L'EQUIVALENT
DU CODE DE TRANSMISSION ASYNCHRONE "START-STOP"

N. M'RABET - Université de Paris VI
G. Noguez  - Université de Paris VI
D. Trécourt- Université de Paris I

Le code de transmission asynchrone "start-stop" est à l'heure
actuelle universellement utilisé pour les interconnexions de
type serie. Les contrôleurs d'émission-réception asynchrone
associés permettent de réaliser à faible coût des réseaux
locaux dont le débit est inférieur à 2 Mb/s. Ce code ne peut
être utilisé pour les transmissions à très haut débit (200 Mb/s)
car il est fondé sur un principe d'échantillonnage à n fois
(en général 16) la fréquence de transmission. Cet article
présente un code autosynchrone qui offre les mêmes avantages,
mais qui ne nécessite pas un échantillonnage à 16 fois la
fréquence de transmission. La structure des contrôleurs
d'émission-réception est décrite. La particularité la plus
"originale" du récepteur est de ne comporter aucun récupérateur
d'horloge. Les contrôleurs d'émission-récepteur de mots de 8
bits sont très simples et fiables; ils sont en cours d'intégration en technologie ECL 100K. Leur débit utile sera de 300 Mb/s.
N.B. : cette étude a été réalisée dans le cadre d'une ATP CNRS.

INTRODUCTION

La popularité du code de transmission asynchrone "start-stop" provient de sa
souplesse d'emploi et de sa facilité  de mise en oeuvre. La souplesse d'emploi
résulte de l'asynchronisme   au niveau des caractères (de 5 à 8 bits). La facilité
de mise en oeuvre provient de la récupération locale de l'horloge au niveau des
caractères. Cette récupération est resynchronisée à chaque caractére; elle est
fondée sur le principe d'échantillonnage à 16 fois la fréquence de transmission
des bits. Ce principe de récupération est facile à mettre en oeuvre, malheureu-
sement il limite d'une part la taille des caractères et d'autre part le débit de
transmission. Cette contrainte interdit l'intégration de contrôleurs asynchrones
à très haut débit.

Pour être aussi "populaire",un code de transmission à très haut débit doit comporter les caractéristiques suivantes:
        - Délimitation immédiate des caractères (dont la taille peut être
quelconque).
        - Asynchronisme au niveau des caractères : l'intervalle de temps qui
sépare l'émission de deux caractères doit être quelconque. Cette propriété est
fondamentale pour les réseaux de type"bus".
        - La récupération des données ne doit pas nécessiter des séquences de
synchronisation. Les séquences devraient en effet être répétées à chaque caractère. Les récupérations d'horloge de type "PLL" sont donc exclues.
        - Les contrôleurs associés d'émission et de réception doivent être
facilement intégrables à moyenne échelle (technologies rapides).

ALGORITHME D'ASSEMBLAGE

L'algorithme d'assemblage se résume alors à des déealages de 1 ou 2 positions d'un registre de nbits + 1 bit de parité :

| intervalle entre deux transitions de même sens | $d^-$ | $d^+$ | décalage | insertion |
|---|---|---|---|---|
| T/2 puis T/2 | 0 | 0 | 1 position | 0 |
| T   puis T | 1 | 1 | 2 positions | 11 |
| T   puis T/2 (anticipation) | 1 | 0 | 2 positions | 01 |
| T/2 puis T   (compensation) | 0 | 1 | 1 position | 1 |

Le schéma de câblage du registre d'assemblage est alors celui de la figure 4.

Un exemple de réception avec diagramme des temps est donné figure 5.

Le détecteur de marque utilise une ligne à retard de 2T/4 en plus de celle indiquée et l'ensemble du registre est "tamponné" sur la transition de fin de marque (montante dans le cas du code IP (figure 1)) en même temps que le signal "donnée-prête" monte.

Un exemple d'utilisation en remplacement d'un uart est donné figure 6.


CONCLUSION

Le code proposé offre les mêmes avantages que le code asynchrone "start-stop". De plus, il ne nécessite aucune récupération d'horloge au sens habituel, et ne possède pas de composante continue. D'un point de vue débit, la simplicité structurelle de l'émetteur et du récepteur permet de compenser le rendement moyen du code.
Ainsi, en technologie ECL, les tranmissions à 325 Mhz sont réalisables à 25°C. Pour les caractères de 16 bits utiles, les frais généraux (fixes) s'élèvent à 4 bits par caractère (parité + marque) soit 20%. Le débit utile d'information est alors de 325 x (16/20) = 260 Mb/s. Ce chiffre de 260 Mb/s est à rapprocher de celui obtenu avec un code NRZ : 650 Mb/s. Ce chiffre correspond donc à 40% du débit théorique maximum. Si le rendement n'est pas excellent, par contre il n'en est pas de même:
          -1) de l'intégration : l'émetteur et le récepteur tiennent chacun dans un boitier ECL de 24 pattes, et
          -2) de la souplesse : aucune séquence de synchronisation n'est nécessaire et n'importe quel intervalle de temps peut séparer l'émission de deux caractères. Un émetteur et un récepteur de ce type sont en cours d'intégration.

Pour ce qui est des applications de tels boîtiers, elles peuvent aller du simple remplacement d'un UART courant afin d'améliorer les performances, jusqu'àl'utilisation à la place de transmissions synchrones quand ces transmissions ne sont synchrones que pour des questions de débit, et tout spécialement dans des réseaux où le partage du lien physique nécessite de longues séquences de synchronisation à chaque changement d'émetteur.

STRUCTURE DU CODE

Pour atteindre ces objectifs, la structure suivante de code a été retenue (fig. 1):

-1) La transmission et la récupération d'horloge se fait à l'échelle d'une cellule élémentaire de 1 bit, grâce à un codage biphase différentiel. Les codes N/M (n bits d'information pour M bits transmis ) ont été exclus car ils sont trop difficiles à"récupérer". Comme une transition d'horloge est associée à chaque bit d'information, la longueur des caractères peut être quelconque.

-2) La délimitation des caractères se fait alors simplement par omission locale de la transition d'horloge; c'est le principe des marques d'enregistrement sur disque magnétique. Cette délimitation suit le caractère. Cette particularité permet d'émettre en permanence entre deux caractères. Cette possibilité est fondamentale lorsque le système de transmission ne passe pas la "composante continue".

-3) La récupération des données se fait globalement à l'échelle d'un caractère grâce à un registre d'assemblage. Ce registre à décalage est activé directement par les transitions du signal biphase. Le registre est décalé de 1 ou 2 positions en fonction du dernier"bit" de donnée reçu (cf. algorithme d'assemblage et figures 3 et 4). La viabilité de ce principe est garantie par l'insertion d'un bit de parité (paire). Cette insertion garantit la parité paire du nombre de transitions dans un caractère.

-4) La marque de fin de caractére a une durée de deux fois trois demiespériodes. Sa structure est symétrique: la durée de l'état haut égale celle de l'état bas, afin que la composante continue résultante soit nulle.

Le récupérateur de données utilise une ligne à retard de précision. Cette ligne à retard est le seul point critique du montage. Une imprécision sur sa valeur, ajoutée à la jigue, est la seule cause d'erreur à la réception. A l'exception de cette ligne à retard, le récepteur est insensible aux dérives thermiques (comprises entre 0 et 85°C).

STRUCTURE DU RECEPTEUR

La structure de l'émetteur n'est pas décrite car elle est classique. C'est la structure connue d'un émetteur biphase différentiel. Par contre, la structure du récepteur est "révolutionnaire". Elle comporte trois parties :

- un récupérateur de données (figure 3),
- un registre d'assemblage à 2 décalages possibles de (n+1) bits,
- un détecteur classique de marque.

L'assemblage des bits d'un caractère est fondé sur les propriétés du code biphase différentiel :

-1) deux transitions de même sens sont séparées de deux, trois ou quatre demies-périodes.

-2) lorsque deux transitions de sens opposé sont séparées de deux demies périodes, ces transitions sont des transitions d'horloge.

-3) avec un bit de parité, la durée totale des états hauts égale celle des états bas pour un caractère de n bits + 1 bit de parité.

-4) il en résulte que, lorsque deux transitions sont séparées de trois demies-périodes (1 longue (T) suivie d'une brève (T/2) par exemple), cette configuration est obligatoirement suivie,immédiatement ou plus tard dans le caractère, par la configuration complémentaire (1 brève (T/2) suivie d'une longue (T) ) .

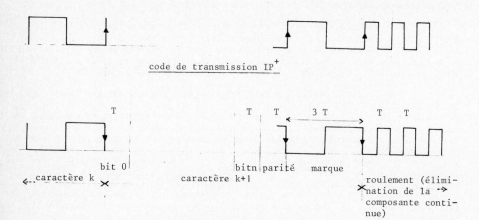

code de transmission IP$^+$

bit 0

caractère k

T　T　3 T　T　T

bitn parité　marque

caractère k+1

roulement (élimi-
nation de la
composante conti-
nue)

Code de transmission asynchrone IP$^-$

figure 1

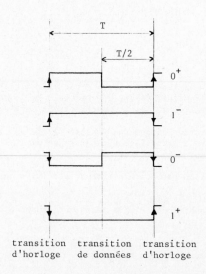

T

T/2

0$^+$

1$^-$

0$^-$

1$^+$

transition　transition　transition
d'horloge　de données　d'horloge

Code biphase différentiel

figure 2

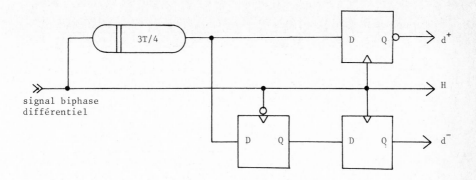

Récupération de données

figure 3

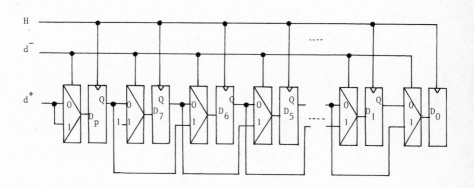

Registre d'assemblage
(code $IP^+$)

figure 4

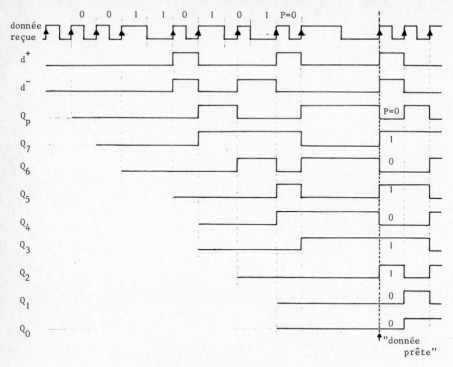

exemple de décodage d'un octet + parité

( code IP$^+$ )

figure 5

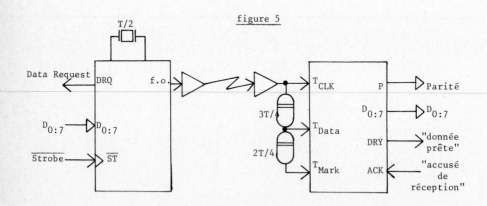

Application de base ( UART)

figure 6

Performance of Data Communication Systems
and their Applications, G. Pujolle (ed.)
© North-Holland Publishing Company, 1981

# ANALYSIS OF A FEEDBACK SCHEME FOR CONGESTION CONTROL
# IN COMPUTER NETWORKS

Parviz Kermani

IBM T.J. Watson Research Center
P.O. Box 218
Yorktown Heights, NY 10598
U.S.A.

In this paper performance of a feedback congestion control scheme is evaluated. The control mechanism is suitable for virtual circuit networks with fixed routing. By introducing a novel optimality criterion and using the Markov decision theory, the optimal control parameters are identified and the implications of using this mechanism in practical applications are discussed.

## INTRODUCTION

Flow and congestion control problems have been identified as one of the important issues in the design of computer communication networks. Networks with no control imposed on the use of their resources have been shown to exhibit a throughput-delay relation similar to contention systems [10]. That is, the throughput increases with the applied load up to some maximum (optimum) value, beyond which, due to unpredictable behavior by users and additional user-user and user-server interaction and overhead, more load causes a reduction in throughput [1]. The physical reason behind this phenomenon is that when a network is overloaded, it's resources are either wasted and not utilized for useful purposes (e.g. at congested nodes data is not accepted and retransmission occurs) or processors may be blocked (because of lack of enough resources [16]). In any case, work is not conserved and throughput degradation occurs. When this phenomenon appears in a network, it is said to be in a *congested* state.

Traditionally, *flow control* has been referred to mechanisms used to protect end-users from each other, e.g. match the speed of the sending users to the acceptance rate of the receiving user. *Congestion control*, on the other hand, has been used to refer to the tools which protect the network from users and coordinate the traffic inside a network. In this paper we are mainly concerned with congestion control issues, as such, we use flow control synonym to congestion control.

There are two classes of congestion controls: *global* versus *local*.[1] Global congestion control schemes are the ones which stop input to the network as a mean to prevent the network from reaching a congested state. This control can be achieved by limiting the number of packets which are simultaneously in the entire and/or certain region of the network. Isarithmic flow control [3] is a global control scheme whereby the total number of messages in the network are controlled and kept limited. In most *virtual circuit* (*virtual route, session*) architectured networks a variant of *window* mechanism is used for end-to-end flow control. In virtual circuit networks communication between source and destination nodes are carried out on logical channels which are set up between these nodes. Through window flow control number of messages in each logical channel is kept limited.

Local congestion controls, are the ones which are carried out by individual nodes of a network based on their own traffic data and resource utilizations. Basically, when a node is short of resources, it stops accepting any more traffic from its neighbors as well as from external sources.

---

[1]  The definition brought here may not be universally accepted. However, for the sake of discussions in this paper this classification is adequate and proper. For some other views regarding these definition interested reader is referred to [4].

In this paper a local control scheme, referred to as *feedback congestion control* (FDBKCC), is analyzed and its implications are studied. This control mechanism is suitable for virtual circuit networks with fixed routing. A variant of this control was initially proposed in [2].

The basic idea behind the feedback congestion control is to enable each node of a network to control the rate of traffic which it receives from its neighbor nodes. IN VC networks this control is imposed on virtual circuits which pass through a node to limit throughput of individual VCs out of the node.

There is a control table at each node which has $I+1$ entries, we refer to these entries by $T(i)$, $0 \leq i \leq I$. The entries are such that $T(1) < T(2) < \ .. \ < T(I)$. Associated with a virtual route, $j$, which passes through the node there is a pointer $p_j$, $0 \leq p_j \leq I$. The entry $T(p_j)$ associated with VC$j$ determines the time gap between successive messages of VC$j$ which are sent out to the next node on VC$j$'s path.

Occasionally each node sends s control messages to its neighbor nodes. The messages contains a field for each VC which leaves the neighbor node and passes through this node. Based on the resource availability at a node, the control field contains -1, 0, or 1. When a VC receives a -1 it reduces its pointer to the control table by 1, hence reducing it inter-packet gaps and increasing its output rate. A 0 results in no change and a 1 results in increasing the pointer by one and reducing the output rate. We point out that control messages can be piggy backed to out going messages to reduce the overhead.

The above mechanism is a powerful tool to divert traffic from a congested node and, more generally, from a congested region of a network. If the congestion is temporary, this control is sufficient to keep the load in nodes within a desired limit. In case of more persistent overload conditions one the following alternatives can be decided upon:

- The slowing down of traffic to the congested node is relayed, node-by-node, to the sources of the traffic and eventually throttles them.

- A global (but slower) congestion control mechanism can be triggered at the onset of a local congestion. If the congestion prolongs, the global mechanism eventually throttles the sources involved.

The first alternative, though simple, may be too slow and inefficient; it translates the local congestion to a network wide congestion (or at least along the path of affected VCs) and only then the source of traffic is throttled. The second alternative is a more plausible solution, though may be more difficult to implement.

To use such a feedback control scheme it is necessary to know

1. How the control tables should be set up and what are their contents.

2. How the value of control signals (-1,0,1) are decided upon.

Regarding 1, a table with exponential table entries is a plausible choice. Because a large pointer indicates heavy congestion on the next node, increasing the pointer by 1 should have greater effect in reducing the traffic when the pointer is large than when the pointer is small. Exponential table entries reflect this point. One can specify a control parameter $\alpha$ and set $T(i) = \alpha^i$. The question now is what is a good choice for $\alpha$?

To address point 2, one needs to define an optimality criterion, based on which control signals are evaluated. One criterion may be to maximize the nodal throughput and minimize the nodal delay. There may be other criteria which one may choose.

In this paper we analyze this feedback control scheme and study the implications of using such a mechanism. In "The Model" an analytic model based on markov decision processes is developed to study the optimal control. We use a novel optimality criteria and demonstrate, via numerical examples, its effectiveness in controlling the nodal delays. In "Numerical Examples" some numerical examples are presented and finally in "Applications and Conclusions" applications of this scheme are discussed.

We should point out that neither local, nor global congestion control is sufficient by itself as an effective control tool. In a locally congested network, a global control may be either too slow -there are some messages already accepted in the network which pass through the congested areas-, or too drastic -a local control is sufficient to temporarily deny traffic to the congested node- and causes underutilization of the network resources. On the other hand if the users who chiefly contribute to an overload are distant from the point of congestion, then local control methods require that congestion measures spread over long distances before effective measures are taken [3]. In "Applications and Conclusions" we discuss how the present scheme can be used with a previously proposed scheme in [13] to provide a local/global congestion control for networks.

## THE MODEL

In this section we develop an analytical model based on Markov decision theory to study the congestion control described in "Introduction". Our specific aim is to address the points raised in the previous section and study the implications of those issues. To this end, and to lend the model amenable to analysis, only two consecutive nodes on a communication path are considered and furthermore, control of only one VC is studied. The mechanism can be applied at each node on every VC in a network.

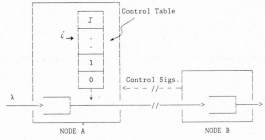

**Figure 1.** Two consecutive nodes on a communication path.

Figure 1 shows two consecutive nodes along with a VC which passes through nodes A and B, and goes to its destination. Messages that arrive at node A are sent to node B using a control table as described in "Introduction". The channel between nodes A and B is assumed to have enough capacity not to cause any bottleneck. At node B messages are queued up in front of node B's output channel; the queueing discipline is FCFS. Control messages are transmitted to node A to adjust the VC pointer to the control table. As a results of this control, the rate of message arrivals to node A, $\lambda$, may be larger than the transmission rate of messages out of node A. In a real implementation this rate change would cause a backlog to develop in node A and would trigger slowing down of traffic to this node. In our model, however, we disregard this backlog and the variation of message rate $\lambda$ to node A; we assume this node has infinite buffer capacity and the input rate stays the same.

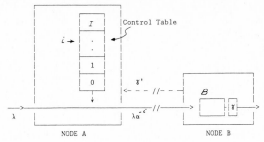

**Figure 2.** An abstract model

The analysis of the control scheme is based on the abstraction of the model as shown in Figure 2. Messages arrive with rate $\lambda$ to node (control box) A which has a table with $I+1$ entries. Entries are denoted by $T(i)$ where

$$T(i) = \alpha^{-i} \qquad 0 \le i \le I \tag{1}$$

and $\alpha > 1$ is a control factor. Associated with the control table there is a pointer; when the pointer is $i$ the transmission rate of messages out of control box A to node B is given by

$$\lambda(i) = T(i)\lambda = \alpha^{-i}\lambda \tag{2}$$

Node B has a finite number of buffers; when this buffer is full, no more messages are accepted and an arriving message is lost (the reason for a finite buffer assumption will be clear shortly). After each state change (to be defined), node B send a control signal to node A. The rate of transmission of control signal is $\gamma'$ messages/sec (usually $\gamma' > \gamma$ to account for the small size of control messages). The control message contain -1, 0 or 1. The criteria to choose the control signal is our task to find out.

To analyze the model we make the following assumptions:

1.  The output process from control box A is a Poisson process and when the pointer is $i$ the arrival rate of message to node B is $\lambda(i) = \alpha^{-i}\lambda$.

2.  When a control signal arrives at the control box the change in traffic rate out of node A is instantaneous.

3.  The distribution of transmission time of messages out of node B is exponential with mean $1/\gamma$.

4.  The distribution of transmission time of control signals from node B to the control box A is exponential with mean $1/\gamma'$.

5.  At node B there are $B$ buffers and each message occupies one, and only one, buffer. When the buffer is full arriving messages are lost.

Assumptions 1 to 2 are made to make the model amenable to analysis. The justification of assumptions 3 to 5 lies on measurement studies of existing networks [14].

With the above abstractions and assumptions, we are able to analyze the system using the Markov decision theory. The formalization of the idea follows:

**The State Space.** When there are $n$ messages at node B and the pointer is $i$, the state of the system is represented by $(n,i)$. The set of state space is denoted by $\mathscr{S}$, where

$$\mathscr{S} = \{(n,i) \mid 0 \le n \le B, 0 \le i \le I\} \tag{3}$$

**The Action Space.** The set of actions is denoted by $\mathscr{A}$ where

$$\mathscr{A} = \{-1, 0, 1\} \tag{4}$$

**The Policy Space.** A policy specifies the control signal to be sent when the system is state $(n,i)$. More precisely, by a policy $f$ we mean a decision rule that says, given the system is state $(n,i)$, the action to be taken is

$$f(n,i) \in \mathscr{A} \tag{5}$$

Because the control table has a limited number of entries, $[0,I]$, we define the boundary conditions as follows

-If $i=I$ then $f(n,I)=1$ is treated equivalently as $f(n,I)=0$.

-If $i=0$ then $f(n,0)=-1$ is treated equivalently as $f(n,0)=0$.

We are implicitly using policies that are functions of the present state of the system; policies in this class are known as *stationary policies* [19], and will be denoted by $\mathscr{F}$.

***State Transition Probabilities.*** Let

$$P_{(n,i),(m,j)}(f) \overset{\Delta}{=} \text{ transition rate from state } (n,i) \text{ to state } (m,j) \text{ when policy } f \text{ is used}$$

then

$$P_{(n,i),(m,j)}(f) = \begin{cases} \lambda(i) & \text{if } m = n+1, \ j = i \ \text{ and } \ n < B \\ \gamma & \text{if } m = n-1, \ j = i \ \text{ and } \ 0 < n \\ \gamma' & \text{if } m = n, \ j = \lfloor (I, \lceil (0, i + f(n,i))) \ \text{ and } \ j \neq i \\ 0 & \text{otherwise} \end{cases} \tag{6}$$

where $\lceil (i,j) \overset{\Delta}{=} max\{i,j\}$ and $\lfloor (i,j) \overset{\Delta}{=} min\{i,j\}$. The state transition matrix under policy $f$ is denoted by $\mathscr{P}(f)$, i.e.,

$$\mathscr{P}(f) \overset{\Delta}{=} \{P_{(n,i),(m,j)}(f)\} \tag{7}$$

The diagonal elements of $\mathscr{P}(f)$ are defined as follows:

$$P_{(n,i),(n,i)}(f) \overset{\Delta}{=} - \sum_{\substack{(m,j) \in \mathscr{P} \\ (m,j) \neq (n,i)}} P_{(n,i),(m,j)}(f)$$

*Remarks:*

1. According to Eq. (6) an action becomes effective, on the average, after $\gamma'$ second; before that, the input rate is determined by the present control table pointer.

2. Only nonzero (-1 or 1) actions are transmitted back to box A. If $f(n,i)=0$, there is no change in the control table pointer and no control signal is transmitted. In practice, however, because there may be more than one VC, a control signal is transmitted even if $f(n,i)=0$.

***Performance Criteria and The Reward Function.*** The basic performance measures in communication networks are throughput and delay. Generally problems related to communication systems are formulated as constrained optimization problems, e.g., maximize the throughput subject to some limit on the average delay. Unfortunately, Markov decision theory, as used here, does not provide for solution of constrained optimization problems. As such we have to seek for an unconstrained optimality formulation which combines the two performance measures. Examples of such formulations are *power*, defined as the weighted ratio of throughput and delay: $\Gamma^\beta/D$, [5] [15], or a linear combination of throughput and delay: $\beta\Gamma - D$, [11], [12] (where $\Gamma$ is the throughput, $D$ is the average delay and $\beta$ is a weight factor).

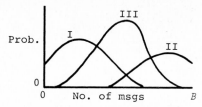

**Figure 3.** Sketches of density functions of the number of messages at the queue B.

While these formulations may seem plausible, we choose not to use them essentially because both require an extra parameter $\beta$ to be specified. As pointed out earlier, the main objective of our research is to find out how sensitive the performance of FDBKCC is to its parameters. Therefore, it behooves us to use a formulation which requires minimum number of parameters. To this end, we choose to use a performance measure which was introduced in [13]. This measure is obtained by considering the probability density function (or histogram) of the number of messages in the queue at node B. In Figure 3 we have sketched such density functions when different control policies are in effect. A density with nonzero intercept at 0 buffer occupancy, curve I, implies during some fraction of time the queue is empty and the output channel is idle and its capacity wasted. On the other hand, a nonzero intercept at buffer occupancy $B$ indicates some fraction of traffic was rejected entry to the queue, curve II. In fact, a desirable curve is a one which entirely lies within the boundary $(1,B)$, curve III.[2] One can achieve this goal by choosing a policy $f$ such that the sum $\pi_0(f) + \pi_B(f)$ is minimized, where

$$\pi_n(f) \stackrel{\Delta}{=} \text{Prob}[n \text{ messages in the queue and policy } f \text{ is used}] \tag{8}$$

With these considerations, we use $\pi_0(f) + \pi_B(f)$ as our objective function and try to minimize it (or maximize $-\pi_0(f) - \pi_B(f)$) over policies $f \epsilon \mathcal{F}$.

To translate the above objective function to the formulation of Markov decision theory, we need to define *the expected reward rate*, $q_{(n,i)}(f)$, which is the reward, or gain, achieved on the next state transition given the present state is $(n,i)$ and policy $f$ is used. It is easy to show that

$$q_{(n,i)}(f) = \begin{cases} -1 & n = 0 \text{ or } n = B, (n,i) \epsilon \mathcal{S} \text{ and } f \epsilon \mathcal{F} \\ 0 & \text{otherwise} \end{cases} \tag{9}$$

results in minimizing $\pi_0(f) + \pi_B(f)$. We also define the vector $\vec{Q}(f)$ as

$$\vec{Q}(f) \stackrel{\Delta}{=} \{q_{(n,i)}(f)\} \tag{10}$$

**Statement of The Problem.** The above formulation specifies a Markov decision process with states and transitions between them given by Eq. (3) and Eq. (6); actions and policy space given by Eq. (4) and Eq. (5); and rewards criterion given by Eq. (9). Under a stationary policy $f$, the average reward per transition is designated by vector $G(f)$,

$$\vec{G}(f) \stackrel{\Delta}{=} \{g_{(n,i)}(f)\}$$

where $g_{(n,i)}(f)$ is the long term expected reward per unit time, given that the process initially starts at state $(n,i)$ and policy $f$ is used. $G(f)$ is given by

$$\vec{G}(f) = \lim_{n \uparrow \infty} \frac{1}{(n+1)} \sum_{t=0}^{n} [\mathcal{P}(f)]^t \vec{Q}(f)$$

where $[\mathcal{P}(f)]^t$ is the $t^{\text{th}}$ power of $\mathcal{P}(f)$. Our objective is to find a stationary policy $f^*$ which maximizes each component of the expected reward per unit time, i.e.

$$\vec{G}(f^*) = \max_{f \epsilon \mathcal{F}} \{\vec{G}(f)\} \tag{11}$$

It can be shown that for a bounded reward function, when the action space and the state space are finite, that such an optimal stationary policy always exists [9] [19]. These conditions are met in the problem at hand. In Appendix A: "Optimality of the Reward Function" we show how this formulation results in maximizing $-(\pi_0(f^*) + \pi_B(f^*))$.

**Solution to The Problem.** We use the policy iteration algorithm of Howard [7] and [8] to solve the above decision problem. Briefly, the above decision model is translated to a set of linear homogeneous equations. The computation starts with an arbitrary policy and at each iteration the policy is improved. An iteration

---

[2]   We will see in "Numerical Examples" that the buffer size $B$ can be considered as a system parameter which reflects the maximum nodal delay at node B.

cycle consists of two phases. In the first phase the present policy is evaluated; this is done by solving the set of linear equations specified by the policy. In the second phase an improvement to the policy is searched. If such an improvement is possible, the improved policy replaces the old one and a new cycle starts. If no improvement is possible this last policy becomes the optimal one. In [7] it is shown that this algorithm always ends in a finite number of steps. The complexity of computation depends on the number of states and the number of recurrent chains under a policy. By using sparse matrix techniques, [6], the complexity and the storage requirement (for storing the transition matrix) can be reduced drastically. In all of our numerical experiments the iterations converges to the optimal policy in less than 5 cycles.

In the next section we present some numerical examples.

## *NUMERICAL EXAMPLES*

We start with studying the effect of the parameter $\alpha$ (the factor used in the control table) on the performance of the optimal policy. In this example the input rate $\lambda=8$ msg/sec, the transmission rate of messages out of queue B is $\gamma=4$ msg/sec, the transmission rate of control signals is $\gamma'=40$ signals/sec, the buffer limit at B is $B=10$, and the control table has 11 entries, 0 to 10 ($I=10$).

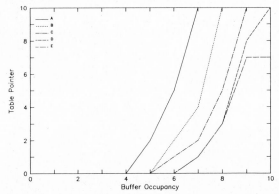

**Figure 4.**   Decision curves vs buffer occupancy for varying $\alpha$ : $\lambda=8$, $\gamma=4$, $\gamma'=40$ (msg/sec); $B=I=10$.
A: $\alpha=1.25$, B: $\alpha=1.5$, C: $\alpha=2$, D: $\alpha=3$, E: $\alpha=4$.

Figure 4 shows the optimal decision curves when $\alpha$ changes. The $X$ axis represents the number of messages in the B queue and the $Y$ axis is the control table pointer. For each $\alpha$ the action for points above its corresponding curve is -1, for points below the curve is +1, and the action for points on the curve is 0. For example consider the solid curve for $\alpha = 1.25$ and buffer occupancy n=6. This curve shows

$$f(6,i) = \begin{cases} -1 & 6 \le i \le 10 \\ 0 & i = 5 \\ +1 & 0 \le i \le 4 \end{cases}$$

i.e., when there are 6 messages in the buffer and the control table pointer is $6 \le i \le 10$ the input rate is to low and the action is -1 to lower the control table pointer and increase the input rate. On the other hand when the control table pointer is $0 \le i \le 5$ there is too much input and the action is +1 to move the control table pointer to a higher position and to decrease the input rate. Finally when the control table pointer is 6 the input rate is proper and there is no change in the pointer. Figure 4 shows that the optimal control depends on the value of $\alpha$. Intuitively for larger values of $\alpha$, increasing the control table pointer has stronger effect on decreasing the input rate that smaller values of $\alpha$. The strong dependency of the optimal action on $\alpha$ is very discouraging when one considers using this feedback control tool in a real system. Fortunately the behavior shown in Figure 5 alleviates this deficiency.

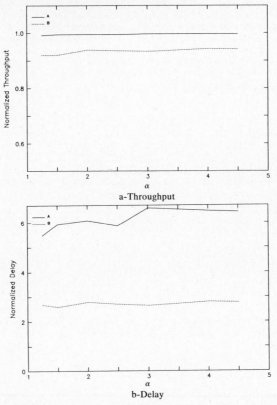

**Figure 5.**   Normalized Throughput and delay vs. $\alpha$ for different buffer limits : Parameters are the same as in Figure 4; A: $B=10$, B:   $B=5$.

Figure 5-a and Figure 5-b show the normalized throughput ($\Gamma/\gamma$, $\Gamma$ being the throughput) and the normalized delay ($D\gamma$, $D$ being the average delay), under the optimal policy as a function of $\alpha$ for two different buffer limits: $B = 5$ and $B = 10$. Consider the solid curves for $B=10$. This curves shows that under the optimal policy the throughput and delay are very insensitive to $\alpha$. As a result, one can use any value of $\alpha$ and as long as the optimal policy is followed, one is guaranteed the same level of service in terms of throughput and delay.   For a binary computer a convenient and practical choice for $\alpha$ is 2.

We now focus on the effect of another system parameter, namely $B$ the buffer limit, on the performance. First some words on the physical interpretation of $B$. One of the goals in many network implementations is to impose some limit on the end-to-end delay and guarantee some level of service. One way to achieve this is to limit the delay at each node. To this end a threshold is imposed on the queue in front of channels beyond which no message is admitted to the nodes. The buffer limit $B$ introduced here can be viewed as such a threshold. For example if the maximum nodal delay is found to be $D_{max}$, this limit will be

$$B = ceiling\{\frac{D_{max}}{1/\gamma}\}$$

where $1/\gamma$ is the average transmission time of a message out of a node and *ceiling*$\{x\}$ is the smallest integer larger than $x$.

The throughput/delay performance for $B=5$ and $B=10$ shown in Figure 5-a and -b indicate that decreasing $B$ reduces the throughout and delay; however, percentage wise, the delay is reduced much more than the throughput. In fact, through proper control, only enough messages are let in the queue to keep the channel busy and the rate of overflow minimal. This shows the plausibility of our optimality criterion. The next few figures are aimed to demonstrate this point more clearly. In these figures $\alpha=2$ is used and the other parameters are the same as above, unless otherwise indicated.

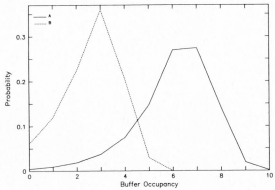

**Figure 6.**   Density of the number of messages in the queue for different buffer limits :  $\alpha=2$, all other parameters as before; A: $B=10$; B: $B=5$.

Figure 6 shows the density of the number of messages in the queue for the two values of $B$. The change in $\pi_0$ for the two values of $B$ is very negligible and the throughput for the two cases are very close to each other.

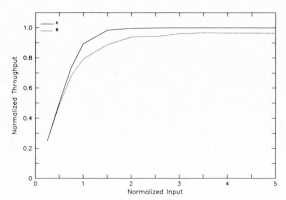

**Figure 7.**   Normalized throughput vs normalized input rate for different buffer limits :  $\alpha=2$, all other parameters as before; A: $B=10$; B: $B=5$.

In Figure 7 we show the normalized throughput ($\Gamma/\gamma$) versus normalized input ($\lambda/\gamma$) for $B=5$ and $B=10$. This figure again indicates the drop in the throughput when the buffer limit is decreased is minor. To show the effect of changing $B$ on the delay, in Figure 8 we show the normalized delay versus normalized throughput for these two buffer limits. Note that at light load the delays are almost identical; however, at heavy traffic there is a significant difference in the delays for the two choices of $B$. This figure specifically demonstrates the fact that "using buffers means delaying traffic, and there is no advantage in providing for a large amount of buffers because transit delays would unnecessarily increase manyfold"[17].

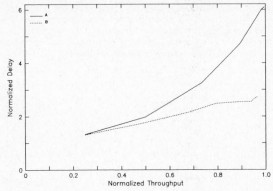

**Figure 8.** Normalized delay vs normalized throughput for different buffer limits : $\alpha = 2$, all other parameters as before; A: $B = 10$; B: $B = 5$.

As we pointed out earlier, as a results of the feedback congestion control the rate of messages out of node A may become less than the input rate of messages to this A. When node A is equipped with the same congestion control and signalling tool, it can reduce its own input rate. Therefore, another performance measure is the percentage of traffic that leave node A toward node B. Figure 9 shows the percentage throughput $(\Gamma/\lambda)$ versus normalized input $(\lambda/\gamma)$ for different buffer limits. Two points should be brought to attention here. The percentage throughput is a decreasing function of the normalized load and asymptotically reaches a lower bound (at which point the normalized throughput is 1). The other point is that changes in $B$ has minor effect on the percentage throughput.

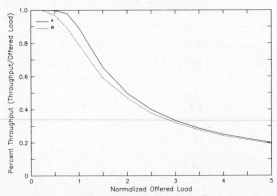

**Figure 9.** Percentage throughput vs normalized throughput for different buffer limits : $\alpha = 2$, all other parameters as before; A: $B = 10$; B: $B = 5$.

We conclude this section by pointing out that behaviors similar to the one shown above are manifested if we use *power* or *linear combination of throughput and delay* ("The Model") as our performance measures. Obviously, the absolute values of throughput and delay depend on the criterion used; however, the phenomena that under optimal policy the throughput and delay are not sensitive to $\alpha$ is true any way.

## APPLICATIONS AND CONCLUSIONS

In this paper we analyzed a feedback control scheme suitable for local congestion control in virtual circuit networks with fixed routing. Our basic goals have been to discover the implications of using such scheme in practice.

Aside from local congestion control, as we pointed out in "Numerical Examples", this mechanism can be used in networks which provide some sort of *guaranteed services* in terms of network delay. By choosing proper values for $B$ at each queue one can restrict the nodal delays to certain limits. This in turn establishes an upper bound on the network delay.

We pointed out earlier that neither local nor global congestion control is sufficient by itself as an effective control tool. The local congestion control described in this paper can be used in conjunction with the flow control scheme proposed in [13] for global flow control in computer networks. Like the present scheme, the flow control mechanism introduced in [13] is also suitable for virtual circuit networks with fixed routing, equipped with window flow control mechanism. The basic idea is to balance the input and output of data in each node of the network by throttling the *source* of traffic (note that in FDBKCC local congestion is controlled by slowing down the traffic from neighbor nodes to the congested node). Each node is capable of withholding acknowledgements belonging to the VCs which pass through it and are being transmitted from the destinations to the sources of data, hence throttling the traffic. While the effectiveness of this scheme was demonstrated in [13], this mechanism may be either too drastic and/or too slow (in view of discussion in "Introduction"). To eliminate these deficiencies one can use FDBKCC studied here in conjunction with the mechanism introduces in [13]. Doing so, when a congestion starts to develop in a node, an attempt is initiated to simultaneously throttle the sources of traffic *and* to slow down the traffic from the neighbor nodes of the troubled node. If congestion prolongs and the local control measure does not turn out to be sufficient, the global control tool becomes effective. On the other hand, if the congestion is temporary, the local congestion measure is sufficient to eliminate it and the global congestion control never comes into picture.

Our studies reveal basically two drawbacks of FDBKCC, namely

1. The dependency of the optimal control signals in a node on the control table pointer at its neighbor nodes. This is a result of system state specification, $(n,i)$.

2. The dependency of optimal control signals on the parameter $\alpha$ (Figure 4).

With respect to 1 one can provide a field in the message headers to pass the necessary information to the adjacent nodes; an approach introduces some overhead. Another alternative is a heuristic solution which does not require the value of the control table pointer to determine the optimal control signals. Research in this direction is now in progress.

The second drawback listed above may seem to be more serious. However, in view of the discussions in "Numerical Examples", especially the characteristics demonstrated in Figure 5, a value of $\alpha=2$ is a proper choice which is particularly convenient in binary computers.

## APPENDIX A- OPTIMALITY OF THE REWARD FUNCTION

In this appendix we show the reward function defined in Eq. (9) maximizes $-(\pi_0(f^*) + \pi_B(f^*))$, where $\pi_n(f^*)$ is the equilibrium probability that there are $n$ messages in the queue, Eq. (8), and $f^*$ is the optimal policy, Eq. (11). In the following, we assume under policy $f^*$ that the system has only one recurrent chain; the same argument, with minor added complexity, holds true for multichain systems.

With only one chain, it can be shown that, [7] [8]

$$g_{(n,i)}(f^*) = g^* \qquad (n,i) \in \mathscr{P}$$

Furthermore

$$g^* = \sum_{(n,i)\in \mathscr{S}} q_{(n,i)}(f^*)\pi_{(n,i)}(f^*)$$

where $\pi_{(n,i)}(f^*)$ is the equilibrium probability that under policy $f^*$ the system is in state $(n,i)$. Using $q_{(n,i)}(f^*)$ as defined in Eq. (9) we get

$$g^* = -\sum_{0\leq i\leq I} \pi_{(0,i)}(f^*) + \pi_{(B,i)}(f^*)$$

however,

$$\pi_n(f) = \sum_{0\leq i\leq I} \pi_{(n,i)}(f) \quad \text{for all } 0\leq n\leq B \text{ and } f\in \mathscr{F}$$

Therefore,

$$g^* = -(\pi_0(f^*) + \pi_B(f^*))$$

which shows under policy $f^*$, $\pi_0(f^*) + \pi_B(f^*)$ is minimized.

## REFERENCES

[1] Agnew, C.E., "Dynamic Modeling and Control of Congestion-Prone Systems," Department of Engineering-Economy Systems, Stanford University, Stanford, California, Technical Report 10, January 1974.

[2] Cabanel, J.P. *et. al.*, "Flow Control Method in The Aramis Packet Switching Network," *Nato Conf. on Packet Switching Networks*, Holland, 1975.

[3] Davies, D.W., "The Principle of Congestion Control in Packet Switching Networks," *Proc. of the 2nd ACM-IEEE Symposium on Problems of the Optimization of Data Communication*, Palo Alto, California, October 1971, pp. 46-49.

[4] Gerla, M. and L. Kleinrock, "Flow Control: A Comparative Survey," *IEEE Trans. on Commun.*, Vol. COM-28, No. 4, April 1980, pp.553-576.

[5] Giessler A., *et. al.*, "Free buffer allocation-An investigation by simulation," *Computer Networks,* Vol.2, 1978, pp.191-208.

[6] Gustavson, F.G. "Sparse Matrix Methods," *IBM Research Report*, RC 8330, June 1980.

[7] Howard, R., *Dynamic Programming and Markov Processes*, M.I.T. Press, Cambridge, Mass. 1960.

[8] Howard, R., *Dynamic Probabilistic Systems, Vol.1: Markov Models and Vol. II: Semi-Markov and Decision Processes*, Wiley, New York, 1971.

[9] Jewell, W.S., "Markov-Renewal Programming, I and II," *Operations Research*, Vol. 11, No. 6, Nov.-Dec. 1963, pp. 938-971.

[10] Kahn, R. and W. Crowther, "Flow Control in Resource Sharing Computer Networks," *IEEE Trans. on Commun.*, Vol. COM-20, June 1972.

[11] Kermani, P., "Switching and flow control techniques in computer communication networks," Ph.D. Dissertation, Computer Science Department, University of California, Los Angeles, UCLA-ENG-7802, February 1978.

[12] Kermani, P. and L. Kleinrock, "Dynamic flow control in store-and-forward computer networks," *IEEE Trans. on Commun.*, Vol. COM-28, No. 2, February 1980, pp. 263-271.

[13] Kermani, P. and K. Bharath-Kumar, "A Congestion Control Scheme for Window Flow Controlled Computer Networks," *IBM Research Report*, RC 8401, August 1980.

[14] Kleinrock, L. and W. Naylor, "On Measured Behavior of The ARPA Network," *1974 Spring Joint Computer Conf., AFIPS Conf. Proc.*, Vol. 43, Chicago, IL May 1974, pp.767-780.

[15] Kleinrock, L., "Power and Deterministic Rules of Thumb for Probabilistic Problems in Computer Communications," *Proc. Int. Conf. on Commun.*, July 1979.

[16] Opderbeck, H. and L. Kleinrock, "The Influence of Control Procedures on the Performance of Packet-Switched Networks," *Proceedings of NTC Conference*, San Diego, California, December 1974.

[17] Pouzin, L., "Flow control in data networks: Methods and tools," *Profc. of ICCC,*Toronto, Aug. 1976, pp. 467-474.

[18] Rinde, J. and A. Caisse, "Passive Flow Control Techniques for Distributed Networks," *Proc. Int. Symp. on Comp. Networks,* Versailles, France, Feb. 1979.

[19] Ross, S.M., *Applied Probability Models With Optimization Applications*, Holden-Day, San Francisco, 1970.

Performance of Data Communication Systems
and their Applications, G. Pujolle (ed.)
© North-Holland Publishing Company, 1981

AN APPROXIMATION ANALYSIS FOR CONGESTION CONTROL SCHEME
IN DISTRIBUTED PROCESSING SYSTEMS

Yutaka TAKAHASHI[*], Nobuo SHIGETA[**] and Toshiharu HASEGAWA[*]

[*] Department of Applied Mathematics and Physics
Faculty of Engineering, Kyoto University, Kyoto, Japan.
[**] Nippon Telegram and Telephone Public Corporation
Tokyo, Japan.

A composite congestion control scheme adopting isarithmic
control and input buffer limiting control is proposed and
is analyzed approximately by queueing theoretic approach
and simulation. Through testing in comparison with simulation results, our approximation method is evaluated.
Moreover another approximation method is developed for
the system with finite link buffers.

INTRODUCTION

Any system sharing resources has a finite processing capacity, so if it is highly
utilized congestion must be inevitable. But congestion causes excessive delay,
degradation of throughput and possibly, what is worse, system deadlock. System
deadlock is a situation where each component of system is blocked and gives up
operating. Flow control is a system of algorithm which prevents congestion,
and is classified into two categories, that is, routing control and congestion
control. The former is a scheme determining customer's traversable route dynamically or statically and aims at attaining maximum throughput or minimum delay.
However, this scheme is powerful only at light traffic load, and its usefulness
degrades as traffic load level becomes higher. It should be noted that routing
control prevents local congestion and pushes up the offered traffic level causing
gloval congestion, but that it does not keep a system away from congestion completely. The latter is a scheme which is devised to keep a system operating
efficiently in case some portion of offered load must be lost. It has merits,
that is, prevention from an increase of delay and a decrease of throughput,
reducing the possibility of deadlock and so on.

Congestion control schemes being used in practical situation are as follows.

(1) Local control: This scheme is used on the basis of informations concerning local traffic data and immediate neighbors' states. For example, if a stage
keeps being busy without stopping for prescribed interval, an input is rejected.
From the microscopic standpoint it may prevent local congestion, but is useless
for global congestion. What is worse, if local congestion is caused by users
remote from the congested point, it is still less effective.

(2) Central control: A whole network system is overviewed by a central controller. However this scheme introduces additional traffic in gathering informations from local users and announcing the decisions from the center. So possibly, it may not operate the system efficiently.

(3) Congestion control table scheme [1]: Congestion control table containing
the data about whole the network circulates in the network. Each user selects
the information necessary for its own decision and revises the table. This
scheme also increases loads.

(4) Hop priority technique: Each job is assigned priority according to the

number of nodes which it has passed.    Therefore the longer a job proceeds, the higher priority it has.

(5) End-to-end control [8]:  The maximum number of acceptable jobs is predetermined for each Origin-Destination pair group.   When jobs in the network are saturated to a limit with respect to some pair, incoming jobs in the same group are rejected to enter.  The stochastic behaviors of networks with this scheme are well analyzed through a closed queueing network theory.

(6) Input buffer limiting control:  External jobs and transit jobs are separated at each stage.   The former first enters input buffers where maximum possible queue length is limited to a finite level and may be rejected because of lack of holding space.   If this scheme is used without any other scheme, this is not effective.

(7) Link buffer limiting control:  At each stage, the maximum possible queue length of transit jobs or transit jobs plus accepted input jobs are restricted. So with this scheme blocking may occur.   Blocking is a phenomenon that after completion of service a transit job cannot enter the next immediate neighboring stage because there is no buffer available for it.    Blocking decreases service efficiency and causes system deadlock if it spreads over the network.    Therefore this scheme must be incorporated with other schemes.

(8) Isarithmic control [2]:  Fixed number of permits circulate according to some rule in a network.   External jobs first join an input buffer queue and catch available permits (accompanying no job) passing through source stage from the head of queue.   After receiving a permit a job is able to proceed through the network to a destination stage.

Multiple level flow controls have been studied recently.   Two-level flow control scheme is proposed [9], where a limit is set on the total number of jobs in the network and separate limits are set on the number of jobs belonging to each disjoint group of source-destination pairs.  Moreover three-level flow control scheme is given [10], where in addition to the limits of two level flow control scheme each stage blocks all the jobs from neighboring stages if a threshold is exceeded.

In the following, we propose a composite congestion control scheme, that is, isarithmic control incorporated with input buffer limiting control.  Its scheme is analyzed approximately and evaluated numerically.   Our approximate analysis is tested in comparison with extensive simulation results.   The simulation program is also verified by applying it to a model which can be analyzed exactly.   As a result, fairly good approximate stochastic behaviors of the composite scheme can be determined through our method.   Moreover the behaviors when our control scheme is applied to a network with finite link buffers are also analyzed approximately.

COMPOSITE CONGESTION CONTROL SCHEME

Isarithmic control, as first suggested by Davies [2] and Price [6], is one of the earliest attempts to control congestion by restricting the number of jobs which can be in the network system.   Our composite congestion control scheme is an isarithmic control scheme incorporating input buffer limiting and is illustrated as follows.    Each stage consists of two substages, that is, one is the link substage and the other is the input substage, as shown in Figure 1.    External jobs can join the input buffer queue at their stage of origin when the queue length before their arrival is less than the capacity of the buffer.   When an overflow takes place the overflown jobs will be rejected and lost.    From the head of the input queues, each accepted job catches a permit if one is available at the permit queue and then goes into the link buffer queue to wait to be served by a link server.    If there is no available permit at the permit queue, the accepted jobs in the input buffer must wait for permits coming to this stage.    After completion of service, the job leaves the system or moves to an immediate neighboring stage

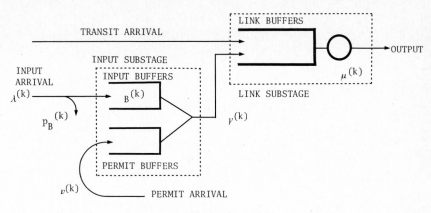

Figure 1
Configuration of Stage k

according to the predetermined probabilities.  On leaving a job at its destination stage, the permit accompanying the job goes to the permit queue at a particular stage.   Permit returning rules can return permit to the original stage of
each permit (fixed permits), to a stage at random (free permits), to the most congested stage and so on.

First, a model where the size of link buffers is not limited is treated.   As soon
as a job finds an available permit, it enters the link substage because of the
adequate capacity of the link buffers.   Therefore, either input buffer or permit
buffer at each stage is always unoccupied.

Second, an extended model where finite link buffers are provided is considered.
When the link buffer in a stage is fully occupied, any more jobs from the input
substage or immediate neighboring stages in the upstream of the stage are refused
entrance and all of the jobs in these places are kept waiting.   This phenomenon
is called blocking.   When an internal job is blocked, it interrupts its previous
server.   If blockings prevail over the system and, as a result, stages block each
other, system deadlock occurs.

APPROXIMATE ANALYSIS

The composite congestion control scheme proposed here is applied to a tandem link
with M stages as shown in Figure 2.   It represents the path taken by jobs in the
given network system.   Stochastic behaviors of this system are considered from
the standpoint of a queueing theory.   Jobs are assumed to arrive according to a
Poisson process and to be served by link servers with exponential service time.
Permits are assumed to return to their returning stages as soon as they are released from their accompanying jobs at the destination of the jobs, without loss
of time.   The following notations are defined where k denotes the stage k:

$\lambda^{(k)}$ : average external arrival rate offered to stage k

$\gamma^{(k)}$ : average external arrival rate accepted by stage k

$\nu^{(k)}$ : average arrival rate of permits at stage k

$B^{(k)}$ : input buffer size of stage k

$N^{(k)}$ : number of permits assigned to stage k

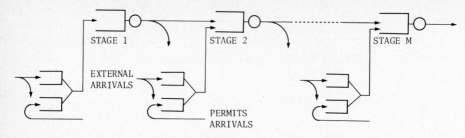

Figure 2
Tandem Link Model

$\mu^{(k)}$ : average service rate of link servers at stage k

$p_B^{(k)}$ : probability that all input buffers are occupied at stage k

$p_{ij}$ : probability that a job from stage i is destined to stage j.

When the link buffer in a stage becomes fully occupied, jobs in either or both the input substage and the upstream stage are blocked. In order to release the blocking, the blocked job should be served first. When jobs in both the upper link substage and the input substage are blocked, the job in the upper link substage should be served first.

It is almost impossible to analyze the above model exactly, even for equilibrium behaviors, and, therefore, an approximation method is introduced. our method is based on the assumption that each permit returns to a fixed stage at exponentially distributed intervals whose mean is the average delay experienced by the accompanying job. Its algorithmic description is as follows.

[STEP 1] $\nu^{(k)}$, an average arrival rate of a permit, is represented as an unknown variable.

[STEP 2] At each stage k, input buffers and permit buffers ( input substage ) are treated independently of the link facility. Let:

    p(i) : probability that the number of jobs in the input buffers minus the number of permits in the permit buffers plus N equals i.

    C(i) : expected number of different destinations of jobs when i jobs accepted by this input substage are currently on the link.

C(i) can be calculated from an O-D matrix and if M, the number of stages, is sufficiently large for i and the destinations are evenly distributed, C(i) may be replaced by i. Applying a similar method as in M / M / N with N+B different states, we have,

$$p(i) = \frac{1}{\prod\limits_{k=1}^{i} C(k)} \cdot \left(\frac{\lambda}{\nu}\right)^i \cdot p(0) \qquad\qquad (0 \le i \le N)$$

$$p(N+i) = \frac{1}{\prod\limits_{k=1}^{N} C(k)} \cdot \left(\frac{\lambda}{C(N)\nu}\right)^i \cdot \left(\frac{\lambda}{\nu}\right)^N \cdot p(0) \qquad (0 \le i \le B).$$

In addition, we obtain for p(0)

$$p(0) = \left[ \sum_{j=0}^{N} \frac{1}{\prod\limits_{k=1}^{j} C(k)} \left(\frac{\lambda}{\nu}\right)^j + \frac{1}{\prod\limits_{k=1}^{N} C(k)} \cdot \left(\frac{\lambda}{\nu}\right)^N \cdot \sum_{j=1}^{B} \left(\frac{\lambda}{C(N)\nu}\right)^j \right]^{-1} .$$

[STEP 3]   From this probability, we have

$$P_B = p(N+B)$$
$$= \frac{1}{\prod_{k=1}^{N} C(k)} \cdot \left(\frac{\lambda}{C(N)\nu}\right)^B \cdot \left(\frac{\lambda}{\nu}\right)^N \cdot p(0) \ .$$

Using this probability, an external accepted arrival rate is given as:

$$\gamma^{(k)} = \lambda^{(k)} (1 - P_B^{(k)}) \ .$$

The STEPS 1, 2 and 3 are carried out at each stage.    Hereafter, a job accepted at stage k is called a class k job.

[STEP 4]   Traffic flow rates at each stage   and  of  each  class  are  calculated through $\gamma^{(k)}$ and O-D matrix.

[STEP 5]   Let $\lambda_i^{(k)}$ equal traffic rate of class i jobs at stage k.    Average time spent in stage k, $T^{(k)}$, is given as :

$$T^{(k)} = (\mu^{(k)} - \sum_{i=1}^{M} \lambda_i^{(k)})^{-1} \ .$$

[STEP 6]   For each class i, $T_i$, average time  spent on the link from the origin to the destination stage, is calculated by O-D matrix.    $\nu^{(i)}$ is given as  a  form  of the inverse of $T_i$.    From the above procedure, $\nu^{(i)}$ is expressed by a function of $\nu^{(j)}$ $(1 \leq j \leq M, \ j \neq i)$.    So simultaneous equations with respect to $\nu^{(i)}$ $(1 \leq i \leq M)$ are established and the solution can be numerically obtained.    In this way the equilibrium behaviors for the input substage have been analyzed approximately.

As for network performance, the following characteristics are estimated.

(1) Throughput : In our model, throughput is  defined  as  the accepted input rate at each stage.    Moreover, network throughput, $\Gamma$, means  the total throughput, that is, a sum of throughput of each stage.

(2) Delay : Delay experienced by a job consists of admission delay and link delay. The former is the waiting time at the input buffers and the latter is the traverse time along the link.    Admission delay of a stage can be calculated easily by means of state probabilities of input substages.    Average link delay is approximated as:
     average link delay = [number of permits (equal to active jobs) in the link]
                         /(accepted traffic rate) ,
which is analogous to Little's formula.    Let:
     average delay = (average admission delay) + (average link delay).
And average network delay T is a weighted average of each class job's average delay by throughput.

(3) Power : An interesting performance ratio was introduced in [4], which is called power.    It compromises  two  extreme  performance  measures,  that  is, throughput and delay into the following simple measure,
     power = total throughput / average network delay
           = $\Gamma/T$

(4) Blocking probability : Network blocking probability $P_B$ is obtained by  the following relation:

$$\sum_{i=1}^{M} \lambda^{(i)} (1 - P_B) = \Gamma$$

Hereafter, the model with finite link buffers is treated.    Even if  input substage can be decomposed independently of link buffers like before, input substages cannot be described by using one dimensional state probabilities because there is a possibility that both jobs and permits may be present at input buffers.    Therefore simple approximation must be incorporated with the previous method.

Blocking in the substage is influential in the upper service facility, so the service rate at each stage decreases significantly.   Let $\mu_e^{(k)}$ denote effective service rate in consideration with service degeneracy.   It is given as follows:

$$\mu_e^{(k)} = \mu^{(k)} \cdot (1 - a^{(k-1)} \cdot p_{full}^{(k)})$$

where

$p_{full}^{(k)}$ = Prob[link buffers are filled with jobs at stage k]

$a^{(k)}$ = (transit traffic rate from stage k to stage k+1) / (traffic rate at stage k).

$a^{(k)}$ is an influencial factor from stage k+1 to stage k.   Both numerator and denominator are expressed indirectly by the unknown variables $\mu_e^{(i)}$, $\nu_e^{(i)}$ (i = 1, ···, M).   Moreover even when permits are available, jobs cannot enter link buffers because of blocking.   So this phenomenon is taken into consideration by the introduction of an effective available permit's arrival rate, $\nu_e^{(k)}$, and is given by:

$$\nu_e^{(k)} = \nu^{(k)} \cdot (1 - p_{full}).$$

Analogous to the model with infinite link buffers, we have again simultaneous equations, which can be solved numerically.


NUMERICAL RESULTS

Approximation analysis is evaluated in comparison with simulation results.   Before using simulation data, the validity of its results must be tested, then a simple two-stage model is considered.   Simulation results for this system are compared with exact ones obtained by establishing steady state balance equations.   Figures 3 and 4 show the delay and the throughput of each stage against external arrival rate, respectively.   In both of these parameters are as follows.

average external arrival rates: $\lambda^{(1)} = \lambda^{(2)} = 0.05 \sim 1.10$

average service rates: $\mu^{(1)} = \mu^{(2)} = 1.0$

link buffer sizes: $L^{(1)} = L^{(2)} = \infty$

input buffer sizes: $B^{(1)} = B^{(2)} = 1$

number of permits: $N^{(1)} = N^{(2)} = 2$

O-D matrix: $\begin{bmatrix} 0.5 & 0.5 \\ 0 & 1.0 \end{bmatrix}$

Even in such a simple model, balance equation have as many as 75 unknown variables. These results show that our simulation program is reliable and may be used to compare with approximation results in a more complex system.

Our numerical results obtained by the approximate analysis were calculated in the five-stage model in the following cases:

Case 1. unlimited link buffers, homogeneous arrivals
Case 2. unlimited link buffers, non-homogeneous arrivals
Case 3. limited link buffers, homogeneous arrivals.

In case 1, we use the following parameters:

average external arrival rates: $\lambda^{(1)} = \lambda^{(2)} = \lambda^{(3)} = \lambda^{(4)} = \lambda^{(5)} = \lambda = 0.05 \sim 1.10$

average service rates: $\mu^{(1)} = \mu^{(2)} = \mu^{(3)} = \mu^{(4)} = \mu^{(5)} = \mu = 1.0$

link buffer sizes: $B^{(1)} = B^{(2)} = B^{(3)} = B^{(4)} = B^{(5)} = B = 0 \sim 3$

input buffer sizes: $N^{(1)} = N^{(2)} = N^{(3)} = N^{(4)} = N^{(5)} = N = 1 \sim 4$

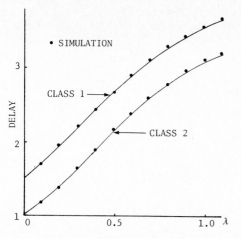

Figure 3
Simulation Results vs. Exact Results

Figure 4
Simulation Results vs. Exact Results

number of permits: $N^{(1)} = N^{(2)} = N^{(3)} = N^{(4)} = N^{(5)} = N = 1 \sim 4$

O-D matrix: $\begin{bmatrix} 0.7 & 0.2 & 0.1 & 0 & 0 \\ 0 & 0.7 & 0.2 & 0.1 & 0 \\ 0 & 0 & 0.7 & 0.2 & 0.1 \\ 0 & 0 & 0 & 0.7 & 0.3 \\ 0 & 0 & 0 & 0 & 1.0 \end{bmatrix}$

Figure 5 shows average network delay against external arrival rate.     Generally
speaking, delay increases with arrival rate, and further increase with N, the number of permits.     From Figure 6 it is also found that total throughput increases
according to arrival rate and N.     In fact, the more permits there are, the more
easily jobs are accepted and subsequently, greater throughput is achieved.     However, it is unavoidable that more throughput causes more network delay.     Throughput and delay are contrary to each other.     Power seems to be a compromising network performance measure for these two, and is shown against arrival rate in
Figure 7.     When B = 0, N = 1 seems to be better setting than the others as a whole.
However, this selection causes unacceptable blocking probability as shown in
Figure 8.     Changing our approach, we can try to find out N which makes power high
or attains an aimed throughput keeping blocking probability low.     For this purpose
Figure 9 is useful.     Next Figure 10 shows the influence of input buffer size on
power under the same parameters as before.     If the number of permits is fixed,
delay gets longer with the size of input buffers because of an increase in admission delay.     On the other hand, throughput hardly increases, and power is dominated mainly by delay.     Moreover, under the same parameters as the above, free
permit routing scheme where permits are sent back to the most congested stage dynamically is tested by simulation in Figure 11, which shows this scheme does not
improve remarkably.

In case 2, parameters are set as follows:

$\lambda^{(2)} = 0.05 \sim 1.10,\ \lambda^{(1)} = \lambda^{(3)} = \lambda^{(4)} = \lambda^{(5)} = 0.3$
$L^{(1)} = L^{(2)} = L^{(3)} = L^{(4)} = L^{(5)} = \infty$
$B^{(1)} = B^{(2)} = B^{(3)} = B^{(4)} = B^{(5)} = 1$
$N^{(2)} = 1 \sim 4,\ N^{(1)} = N^{(3)} = N^{(4)} = N^{(5)} = 2$
$\mu^{(1)} = \mu^{(2)} = \mu^{(3)} = \mu^{(4)} = \mu^{(5)} = 1.0$

$\{P_{ij}\} = \begin{bmatrix} 0.7 & 0.2 & 0.1 & 0 & 0 \\ 0 & 0.7 & 0.2 & 0.1 & 0 \\ 0 & 0 & 0.7 & 0.2 & 0.1 \\ 0 & 0 & 0 & 0.7 & 0.3 \\ 0 & 0 & 0 & 0 & 1.0 \end{bmatrix}$

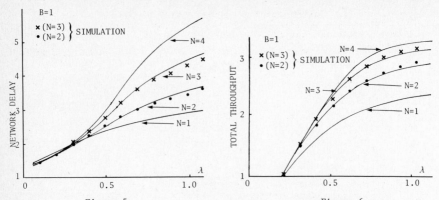

Figure 5.                                    Figure 6.
Network Delay vs. External Arrival Rate  Total Throughput vs. External Arrival Rate

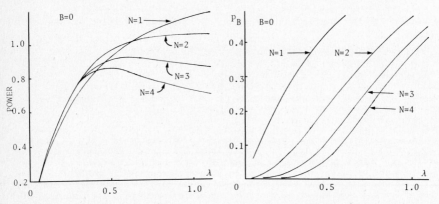

Figure 7.                                    Figure 8.
Power vs. External Arrival Rate   Blocking Probability vs. External Arrival Rate

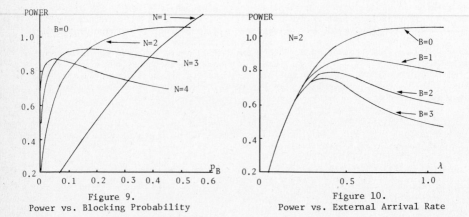

Figure 9.                                    Figure 10.
Power vs. Blocking Probability     Power vs. External Arrival Rate

In this case the effect of our composite control method on an individual stage is considered, and is shown in Figure 12 and 13 where external arrival rate at stage 2 changes while the others are fixed.   An interesting feature can be seen at $N^{(2)} = 4$ that under the considerably high arrival rate, delay abruptly increases, throughput begins to decrease and that power notably decreases.   From these phenomena we may conclude that even if external arrival rate increases unexpectedly at a stage, it is not advantageous to provide more permits for the stage from the macroscopic standpoint.

In case 3, parameters are as follows:

$$\lambda^{(1)} = \lambda^{(2)} = \lambda^{(3)} = \lambda^{(4)} = \lambda^{(5)} = 0.05 \sim 1.10$$
$$\mu^{(1)} = \mu^{(2)} = \mu^{(3)} = \mu^{(4)} = \mu^{(5)} = 1.0$$
$$L^{(1)} = L^{(2)} = L^{(3)} = L^{(4)} = L^{(5)} = 4$$
$$B^{(1)} = B^{(2)} = B^{(3)} = B^{(4)} = B^{(5)} = 1$$
$$N^{(1)} = N^{(2)} = N^{(3)} = N^{(4)} = N^{(5)} = 1 \sim 4$$

$$\{p_{ij}\} = \begin{bmatrix} 1/5 & 1/5 & 1/5 & 1/5 & 1/5 \\ 0 & 1/4 & 1/4 & 1/4 & 1/4 \\ 0 & 0 & 1/3 & 1/3 & 1/3 \\ 0 & 0 & 0 & 1/2 & 1/2 \\ 0 & 0 & 0 & 0 & 1 \end{bmatrix}$$

In this case, our approximation method for the model with finite link buffers is tested in comparison with simulation results.   Figures 14, 15 and 16 show delay, throughput and power with respect to arrival rate, respectively.

CONCLUSION

In this paper, composite congestion control scheme is represented and its performance when applied to a tandem link is analyzed approximately.   Its scheme is mainly composed of isarithmic control method and input buffer limiting.   Our approximation method is validated by simulation results, and it finds that our method can give fairly good approximations with respect to characteristic quantities for engineering purpose.   From numerical results obtained by our method and simulation it finds that composite congestion control scheme is effective.   When some requirements are made, for example, attaining predetermined throughput, preventing delay from excessing maximum acceptable level, suppressing blocking probability less than tolerable level and so on, our composite control scheme and approximation method may  be one of a useful tool from which nearly  optimal control strategy can be derived.

[REFERENCES]

[1] Chou, W. and Gerla, M., A unified flow and congestion control model for packet networks, Proc. of the 3-rd ICCC (1976) 475-482.
[2] Davies, D.W., The control of congestion in packet-switching networks, IEEE Trans. on Communications, COM-20 (1972) 546-550.
[3] Grange, J.L. and Majithia, J.C., Congestion control for a packet-switched network, Computer Communication, 3 (1980) 106-116.
[4] Kleinrock, L., On flow control in computer networks, ICC'78 (1978) 27.2.1-27.2.5..
[5] Pennotti, M.C. and Schwartz, M., Congestion control in store and forward tandem links, IEEE Trans. on Communications, COM-23 (1975) 1434-1443.
[6] Price, W.L., Data network simulation experiments at the National Physical Laboratory 1968-1976, Computer Networks, 1 (1977) 199-200.
[7] Schwartz, M. and Saad, S., Analysis of congestion control techniques in computer communication networks, in: Grange, J-L. and Gien M. (eds.), Flow Control in Computer Networks (North-Holland, Amsterdam, 1978).
[8] Chatterjee, A., Georganas, N.D. and Verma P.K., Analysis of a packet-switched network with end-to-end congestion control and random routing, Proc. of the 3-rd ICCC (1976) 488-494.
[9] Georganas, D.N., Numerical analysis of computer-communication networks with multilevel flow control, Proc. of COMPCON 78 (1978) 4-11.
[10] Wong, J. and Unsoy, M., Analysis of flow control in switched data networks, Proc. of IFIP Congress (1977) 315-320.

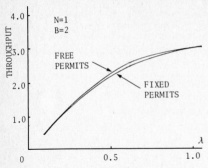

Figure 11.
Total Throughput vs. Arrival Rate

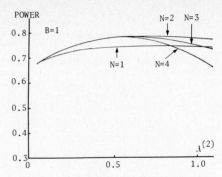

Figure 12.
Power vs. External Arrival Rate

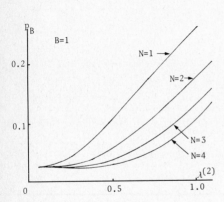

Figure 13.
Blocking Probability vs. External
Arrival Rate

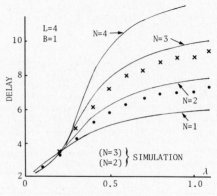

Figure 14.
Network Delay vs. External Arrival Rate

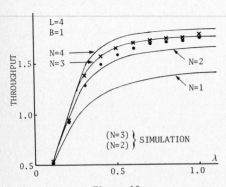

Figure 15.
Total Throughput vs. External Arrival Rate

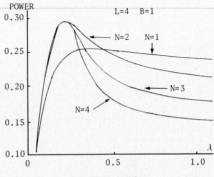

Figure 16.
Power vs. External Arrival Rate

Performance of Data Communication Systems
and their Applications, G. Pujolle (ed.)
© North-Holland Publishing Company, 1981

# LOCAL CONTROL FOR INTEGRATED VOICE/DATA NETWORKS

DR. C. G. OMIDYAR & DR. K. A. SOHRABY

COMPUTER SCIENCES CORPORATION
SYSTEMS DIVISION
6565 ARLINGTON BOULEVARD
FALLS CHURCH, VIRGINIA 22046
U.S.A.

Analytical and simulation models for voice and data packet processing
in an integrated network with poisson arrival and exponential service
are considered. An exact analytical solution for the average delays
of packetized voice and data packets based on two different local
control schemes at each node are presented. Novel results about
packet length and switching probability effects on performance of an
integrated voice and data network are obtained. Simulation models
are used to check the statistics of the proposed models. Finally,
suggestions for further research are described.

## INTRODUCTION

The purpose of this paper is to investigate the problems of sharing the resources
in an integrated voice/data packet-switching network. The integrated voice and
data traffic transmission with the evolution of digital communication networks
has received a great deal of attention, [1], [2]. As voice digitization
technology and the packet switching techniques improve, the inherent cost savings
of integrating voice and data becomes feasible and more attention is focused on
the problem by the agencies operating communications networks which carry the two
traffic types. Many studies so far have put all the effort on the four major
alternatives for integrating voice and data:

1. Circuit -Switching: The traditional switching scheme for telephony which is
   also relatively useful for bulk traffic. Due to long circuit set up time,
   this method is not efficient for interactive data transmission.

2. Packet-Switching: An efficient switching scheme for interactive as well as
   bulk type traffic. With additional efforts for constructing appropriate
   protocol structures, this switching technique happens to be very attractive
   for digital voice transmission in the form of packets as well [9], [10].
   This paper specifically focuses on some analysis regarding this switching
   technology.

3. Hybrid-Switching: Operating cost of a communication network is naturally
   a dominant factor in pursuing different design technologies for the particular application. It has become evident that [1], circuit switching is
   most cost effective when used for traffic requiring high bandwidth but not
   so efficient for traffic characterized in bursts. In this latter case,
   packet switching is most efficient. Hybrid switching techniques then provide
   a desirable alternative for integrating data and voice.

4. Message-Switching: Although this approach may only represent an efficient
   technique in specific applications, recent studies [3], [4], have
   shown its usefulness when implemented through intelligent control and
   decision making processes at communication nodes. Some studies suggest its
   applicability in integrated data and voice environments.

This paper specifically looks at the packet-switching alternative in transmission of packetized voice and data.  Packet-switching provides two basic protocol alternatives in communication networks:

a.    Virtual Circuit Protocol (VCP):  Although shared by both data and voice packets, VCP uses the following concepts:  A source which is the originator of data or voice packets requests a connection through an appropriate control packet.  The control packet establishes the connection by setting up a proper pointer to routing tables while identifying the connection requested through a connection identification.  When the source destination connection is approved, the originator is notified and transmission starts. Its basic characteristic is that the destination receives packets in the same sequence transmitted by the source.  This makes the (VCP) an interesting procedure for packetized voice applications due to critical timing and sequence of packets in recovering the voice information.  Basic differences of this procedure with that of circuit switching are discussed in $\lfloor 1 \rfloor$ . The virtual circuit is disconnected by issuing a connection termination command through either source or destination.  From a link failure point of view, this scheme has some drawbacks.

b.    Datagram Protocol:  Each packet is delivered from source to destination independent of all others.  Packets consult the routing tables at each node and proceed until reaching the destination node.  Although in communication environments with link failure this procedure proves more efficient than (VCP), it has problems of high packet overhead.  This is because each packet should find its way through the network independent of all others (no connection identification is required).

This paper investigates some of the properties in a queuing system handling both data and voice in packet-switching node.

In the experimental work performed on the ARPANET, the problem associated with packetized voice transmission in store-and-forward tandem link was in the area of end-to-end delay $\lfloor 5 \rfloor$ .  In order to examine the probability of sharing the communication links between voice and data packets, we propose the integrated network of Figure (1), where each node is capable of storing packets and forwarding them to the next node.  We will examine several techniques for controlling the flows of voice and data packets in the model of Figure (1), in order to minimize the voice delay.

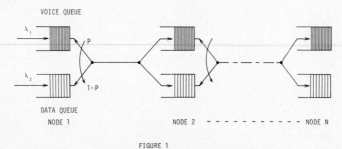

VOICE QUEUE

DATA QUEUE
NODE 1                          NODE 2 - - - - - - - - - - - NODE N

FIGURE 1

NETWORK OF CASCADED NODES

Two different local controls for switching packets at each node have been studied in this paper and their descriptions are as follows:

DYNAMIC FLOW CONTROL

Since voice packets are more sensitive to variable dealy, we choose to give high priority to the voice queue. Theoretically, the set of equations in appendix (A) were written in such a way that voice packets have priority over the data packets, but there is no preemption. Physically it is necessary that the switch changes its position dynamically as the need for serving voice packets arises. The above scheme was examined both by an analytical model (when removing P from the set of equations in appendix (A)) for one node and by a simulation model which is extended to two cascaded nodes.

The static flow control was examined by analytical model and described later. The interpretation of the static control for the steady state solutions is tabulated later for different values of P. It is shown that there exists an optimum point for data packets which minimizes the average delay whereas the voice delay changes inversely with P.

METHODOLOGY AND CONTROL CHARACTERISTICS

The simulation model was constructed of two stage cascaded nodes as shown in Figure (2). The assumption for voice and data packets to arrive at the integrated node (node 1) are according to Poisson process with the rates of $\lambda_1$ and $\lambda_2$. The respective packets are tagged as to their arrival rates so that they may be treated individually and stored in different buffers. If messages are to be composed of fixed-length packets, then voice and data packets contain $\mu_1^{-1}$, $\mu_2^{-1}$ bits respectively. Voice and data messages are transmitted through the channel at a rate of C bits/second thus, packet transmission across the channel (node-to-node) for voice and data are $(\mu_1 C)^{-1}$, $(\mu_2 C)^{-1}$ seconds/packet respectively. The selection of control regime in the simulation and analytical models at each node is based on an isolated adaptive policy which operates independently at each node in order to make use of local data to adapt to dynamic changes.

ANALYTICAL MODEL

In this section a priority queuing model is analyzed. The system considered here represents an infinite queue which receives a mixture of packetized voice and data each following a Poisson process with fixed traffic rates $\lambda_1$ and $\lambda_2$ respectively, Figure (1). It is assumed that the two arrival processes, although identically distributed, represent two independent arrival patterns. The service policy is as follows:

In what is called the static model in this paper, a switch is set for transmission of voice for only (P) fraction of the time and for data during the remaining time which accounts for (1-P) fraction of the time. The static model utilizes full channel capacity C for Transmission of Voice and data packets and it preserves the priority scheme only during (P) fraction of the time whereas, during (1-P) fraction of the time voice packets may arrive and experience delay. The effect of this delay is embedded in the set of equations and it is controlled by (P). When the system is looked at in steady state, on the average at least (P) fraction of the time switch is dedicated to voice transmission and (1-P) to data.

In our dynamic model, voice packets are given higher priority over those of data. Whenever a voice packet arrives at the system, if a data packet is already in process, it is finished being processed and then switched to voice packets (non-preemptive). The switch is turned to those of data packets if and only if there are no voice packets available in the system.

Analytical solutions for processing digital voice and data packets in a store-
and-forward network of tandem links can be obtained by writing a set of
differential difference equations which represent the transition probabilities of
the packets at the first node.

Let $P_{i,j,k}(t)$ be the probability that there are i units of packetized voice in
the voice buffer and j units of data packets in the data buffer and a unit of
voice or data in the transmitting state k = 1,2.  P is, in a sense, the switching
probability such that the voice packets are given priority over the data packets,
but that there is no preemption.

Appendix (A) provides details of the queuing analysis for the control schemes.

DYNAMIC FLOW CONTROL (SIMULATION MODEL*)

In order to study the levels of variable delays for speech packets in an integrated network before the effects become objectionable, we proceed to develop
the integrated simulation model of Figure (2).

Voice packets can be constructed from a high speed digital bit stream at the
first node, where the voice and data packets merge together and compete for
channel access.  Without loss of generality, we may assume that the voice and data
packets are Poisson distributed and their rate of arrivals to the voice and data
buffer are $\lambda_1$ and $\lambda_2$ respectively.  In this model we are focussing mainly on
the packet-switching technique (local control) which utilizes the resources
efficiently and minimizes an end-to-end delay for packet speech.

The interpretation of the dynamic flow control is to give priority to voice
packets if traffic can be found in either queue, but that there is no preemption.

The dynamic local control of the simulation model operates exactly the same as
analytical model except, it was extended to two cascaded nodes (Figure 2).

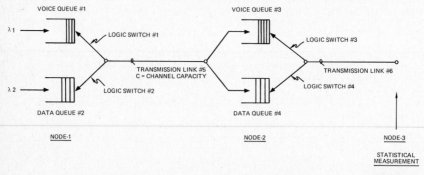

FIGURE (2):  TWO STAGE CASCADED NODES SIMULATION MODEL

STATISTICAL
MEASUREMENT

1 - INTERARRIVAL
   TIME OF VOICE/DATA
   PACKETS.
2 - NO. OF ARRIVALS
   PER T UNIT TIMES.

Moreover, it takes (t) time units to transfer control from voice queue to data
queue (the walk time).  The effect of switching time on performance of the network was evaluated.  The statistical measurements were obtained at nodes 1 and 2
and the results were tabulated in Table 1.

_____

* The model is simulated with General Purpose Simulation System V (GPSSV) on
  INFONET

NUMERICAL RESULTS OF THE ANALYTICAL MODELS

To generalize the results of this study, we adopt the following notations:

$$\rho_1' = P \; \rho_1 = \frac{\lambda_1}{\mu_1 C}$$
Traffic intensity for voice packets with full channel capacity.

$$\rho_2' = (1-P) \; \rho_2 = \frac{\lambda_2}{\mu_2 C}$$
Traffic intensity for data packets with full channel capacity.

$$\alpha = \frac{\mu_1}{\mu_2}$$
Ratio of average data packets length to average voice packet length (both independently exponentially distributed)

Equations (4) and (5) in Appendix (A) characterize different normalized delay components, namely voice and data, respectively. For different static probability values (P) these equations should be numerically solved. Also with ($\alpha$) introduced above as the relative value of data packet size to that of voice behavior should be closely investigated.

Figures (3) and (4) represent the normalized delay per voice and data packet separately versus static switching probability (P). As these figures show for all values of ($\alpha$) as the portion of time dedicated to voice increases voice packet delay decreases, while that of data is concave. Figures (3) and (4) suggest an optimal static control probability (P*) which minimizes data delay while maintaining an acceptable voice delay.

Figures (5) and (6) on the other hand show the results of normalized data packet delays versus ($\alpha$), as introduced above for different traffic intensities. As ratio of data packet length to that of voice increases, service time of each voice packet compared to those of data will be neglegible and the effect of non-preemption will be more evident. In static control the average data delay will decrease. For large voice packet sizes since voice has higher priority, this will increase the average data delay. These figures also show the results of data delay in the dynamic model which generally represent the same characteristics. Data delay under dynamic control is always better than that of static control. Note that in all these results, the switching time between data and voice packets (walk-time) is not included. Figures (7) and (8) show average voice delay decreases and is always lower for higher probability of switching. The dynamic model holds the switch at data queue until the data packet already in the transmitter is served and then switch to voice. Due to longer data packets compared to those of voice, voice delay in dynamic control increases. A very interesting property shown by these results is that the delay trends always increase at $\alpha < 1$ for data packets, and for $\alpha > 1$ data delay is almost unchanged. For voice packets, the reverse of the above is observed for $\alpha < 1$. Dynamic control characteristics also represent similar ($\alpha$) trends. It is immediately noticed that the static control scheme presents a more attractive model than the dynamic since almost always $\alpha \gg 1$. As a practical contribution, a hardware implementation of this multiplexer requires further study.

SIMULATION RESULTS

The start of the simulation run marks the time when the generate blocks start to generate packets at the first node. The simulation run for cases 1 through 5 in Table (1) are 13.65, 14.13, 13.94, 14.18, 14.15 seconds respectively. This time is the relative clock-time which indicates the number of time units elapsed since the start of the simulation run.  In order to reach the steady state solution the indicated results for queue statistics are expected to increase slightly. Delay results are checked with those of the dynamic control of the analytical models and agreed favorably.

TABLE - 1

C = 50 KBPS

SIMULATION RESULTS

| # Cases | P/Sec. $\lambda_1$ | P/Sec. $\lambda_2$ | $(\mu_1 C)^{-1}$ | $(\mu_2 C)^{-1}$ | Transmission Links Average Utilization #5 | #6 | Queue Statistics Average Contents $L_1$ | $L_2$ | $L_3$ | $L_4$ | Average Time/Packet(Sec) $W_1$ | $W_2$ | $W_3$ | $W_4$ |
|---|---|---|---|---|---|---|---|---|---|---|---|---|---|---|
| 1. | 20 | 50 | .005 | .01 | .608 | .628 | .45 | 2.92 | .64 | 3.46 | .022 | .054 | .031 | .065 |
| 2. | 50 | 20 | .005 | .01 | .425 | .452 | 1.7 | .26 | 1.3 | .30 | .036 | .013 | .027 | .015 |
| 3. | 20 | 50 | .01 | .005 | .458 | .431 | .15 | 2.2 | .13 | 1.5 | .007 | .042 | .006 | .020 |
| 4.* | 50 | 20 | .005 | .01 | .428 | .436 | 2.0 | .3 | 1.3 | .3 | .038 | .015 | .026 | .016 |
| 5.* | 20 | 50 | .005 | .01 | .606 | .572 | .5 | 3.1 | .65 | 3.0 | .026 | .058 | .033 | .056 |

*(8 millisecond switching time is included)

## CONCLUSIONS AND SUGGESTIONS FOR FURTHER RESEARCH

Several switching techniques for integration of voice and data packets have been investigated in the literature.  Among those, reference [8] considers the performance of circuit-switching for voice and packet-switching for data traffic, whereas reference [9] considers integration of packetized voice and data over packet-switched networks.  Based on suggested control schemes the sensitivity of the network performance, in particular packetized voice and data packet delays, to the switching parameters along with different packet lengths were investigated.  Results of this study depend on the ratio of data and voice packet sizes.

Numerical values from analytical equations along with simulation experiments resulted in a collection of statistical measurements which provides an intuitive approach to the design of such networks.  These results also provide a quantitative basis for more efficiently using the resources while maintaining an acceptable voice speech.

Other research related subjects are needed to include preemptive schemes and their effects on the switching models described here.  It may be needed to establish special routing and protocol schemes in the event of voice and data traffic recovery due to partial transmission.  It is shown [6] that, for two different arrival rates with no priority imposed on any class of traffic, there exists an optimum switching probability (local control) that minimizes the average system waiting time.  The present paper evaluates the performance of several different local control schemes for packetized voice and data packets at several switching nodes.  The results indicate that in some cases it is possible to achieve a significant improvement over previous suggested schemes.

REFERENCES

[ 1 ]  Gitman, I., Occhingrosso, B., Hsieh, W., and Frank, H., "Sensitivity of Integrated Voice and Data Networks to Traffic and Design Variables", Sixth Data Communications Symposium. November 27, 1979.

[ 2 ]  Gruber, J. G., "Delay Related Issues in Integrated Voice and Data Transmission", Sixth Data Communications Symposium, November 27, 1979, Pacific Grove, California.

[ 3 ]  Sohraby, K. A., "Adaptive Channel Capacity Store-and-Forward Buffers", IEE Computers and Digital Techniques Transactions, December 1979 Volume 2 No. 6, P.P. 233-236

[ 4 ]  Sohraby, K. A., Shaw, L. G., "Communication Networks with Adaptive Capacity Links", IEEE International Symposium on Information Theory, Grignano, Italy June 1979.

[ 5 ]  Casner, S. L., Mader, E. R., and Cole, E. R., "Some Initial Measurements of ARPANET Packet Voice Transmission", National Telecommunications Conference 1978, Alabama, December 1978.

[ 6 ]  Omidyar, C. G., Pickholtz, R., "Local Control for Packet Switching for an N-Station Polling System", Pacific Telecommunications Conference, Honolulu, Hawaii, January 1979.

[ 7 ]  Morse, P. M., "Queues, Inventories and Maintenance," New York: Wiley 1958.

[ 8 ]  Weinstein, C., Malpass, M. and Fischer, M.J., "Data Traffic Performance of an Integrated circuit- and packet-switched Multiplex Structure" IEEE Transaction on communications, Vol. COM-28, No. 6, June 1980.

[ 9 ]  Sencer, M. A. and Baker, D. M., "A Viewpoint on Packet-Switched Voice Networks", Fifth International Conference on Computer Communication, Atlanta, GA, P.P. 287-294, October 1980.

[10 ]  Cohen, D., "On Packet Speech Communication", Fifth International Conference on Computer Communications, Atlanta, GA, P.P. 271-274, October 1980.

[11 ]  Kuemmerle, K., "Multiplexer Performance for Integrated Line and Packet Switched Traffic", Second International Computer and Communications Conference, P.P. 505-515, Stockholm, Sweden, 12-14 August 1974.

APPENDIX A

CALCULATION OF THE AVERAGE NUMBER OF VOICE/DATA PACKETS AND
AVERAGE WAITING TIME FOR THE STORE-AND-FORWARD NETWORK (FIG. 1)

We write a set of differential difference equations for the network of Figure 1 at node 1. The voice packets have priority over data packets since voice transmission is more sensitive to delay variations than data. In the stationary case we have:

$$0 = - (\lambda_1 + \lambda_2) \, P_{0,0,0} + P \, \mu_1 c P_{1,0,1} + (1-P) \, \mu_2 c P_{0,1,2}$$

$$0 = \lambda_1 \, P_{0,0,0} - (\lambda_1 + \lambda_2 + P \, \mu_1 c) \, P_{1,0,1} + P \, \mu_1 c P_{2,0,1} + (1 - P) \, \mu_2 c P_{1,1,2}$$

$$0 = \lambda_2 \, P_{0,0,0} - (\lambda_1 + \lambda_2 + (1 - P) \mu_2 c) \, P_{0,1,2} + (1 - P) \, \mu_2 c P_{0,2,2} \ +$$

$$P \, \mu_1 c P_{1,1,1}$$

$$0 = \lambda_1 \, P_{i-1,0,1} + P \, \mu_1 c P_{i+1,0,1} + (1-P) \, \mu_2 c P_{i,1,2} - (\lambda_1 + \lambda_2 + P \, \mu_1 c) \, P_{i,0,1}$$

$$0 = \lambda_2 \, P_{0,j-1,2} + (1 - P) \, \mu_2 c P_{0,j+1,2} + P \, \mu_1 c P_{1,j,1} - (\lambda_1 + \lambda_2 + (1 - P)$$

$$\mu_2 c) \, P_{0,j,2}$$

$$0 = \lambda_2 \, P_{1,j-1,1} + P \, \mu_1 c P_{2,j,1} + (1-P) \, \mu_2 c P_{1,j+1,2} - (\lambda_1 + \lambda_2 + P \, \mu_1 c) \, P_{1,j,1}$$

$$0 = \lambda_1 \, P_{i-1,1,2} - (\lambda_1 + \lambda_2 + (1 - P) \, \mu_2 c) \, P_{i,1,2}$$

$$0 = - (\lambda_1 + \lambda_2 + P \, \mu_1 c) \, P_{i,j,1} + P \, \mu_1 c P_{i+1,j,1} + (1 - P) \, \mu_2 c P_{i,j+1,2} \ +$$

$$\lambda_1 P_{i-1,j,1} + \lambda_2 \, P_{i,j-1,1}$$

$$0 = - (\lambda_1 + \lambda_2 + (1 - P) \, \mu_2 c) \, P_{i,j,2} + \lambda_1 \, P_{i-1,j,2} + \lambda_2 \, P_{i,j-1,2}$$

where $\lambda_1$ and $\lambda_2$ are the arrival rates of voice and data packets (poisson distributed), $\mu_1^{-1}$, $\mu_2^{-1}$ are the times to transmit a voice and a data packet from
one node to neighboring nodes, C is channel capacity, and P is the probability
of switching the voice packets.

The easiest approach to solve these stationary equations is via the generating
functions we define:

$$F_{i,2} \, (Z) = \sum_{j=1}^{\infty} Z^j \, P_{i,j,2} \quad ; \quad F_{i,1} \, (Z) = \sum_{j=0}^{\infty} Z^j \, P_{i,j,1}$$

then the joint generating function for the voice and data are:

$$G_1(Y,Z) = \sum_{i=1}^{\infty} Y^i P_{i,1} (Z) \quad ; \quad G_2(Y,Z) = \sum_{i=0}^{\infty} Y^i P_{i,2} (Z)$$

and:

$$C(Y,Z) = G_1 (Y,Z) + G_2 (Y,Z) + P_{0,0,0} \qquad (1)$$

where:

$$P_{0,0,0} = 1 - \frac{\lambda_1}{P \mu_1 c} - \frac{\lambda_2}{(1-P) \mu_2 c} \; , \; G_1 (1,1) = \frac{\lambda_1}{P \mu_1 c} = \rho_1 \quad \text{and}$$

$$G_2(1,1) = \frac{\lambda_2}{(1-P) \mu_2 c} = \rho_2$$

The average number of voice and data packets at the first node can be obtained by differentiating equation (1) with respect to Y, Z and set Y = Z = 1 and then use Little's formula to obtain the average delays.

If we multiply the stationary equations with $Y^i$ and $Z^j$ then sum over proper range of i and j we can obtain:

$$G_1(Y,Z) = \left[ - (\lambda_1 + \lambda_2 + (1-P) \mu_2 c - \lambda_2 Z) F_{0,2} (Z) - (\lambda_1 + \lambda_2 - \lambda_2 Z - \lambda_1 Y) P_{0,0,0} \right.$$

$$\left. + \frac{(1-P) \mu_2 c}{Z} G_2 (Y,Z) \right] \Big/ (\lambda_1 + \lambda_2 + P \mu_1 c - \lambda_1 Y - \lambda_2 Z - \frac{P \mu_1 c}{Y} ) \qquad (2)$$

where

$$G_2(Y,Z) = (\lambda_1 + \lambda_2 + (1-P) \mu_2 c - \lambda_2 Z) F_{0,2} (Z) \Big/ (\lambda_1 + \lambda_2 + (1-P) \mu_2 c - \lambda_1 Y - \lambda_2 Z ) \qquad (3)$$

From equation (3) the value of $F_{0,2}(1) = \lambda_2/(\lambda_1 + (1-P)\mu_2 c)$, replacing these values in equation (2) we can check $G_1 (1,1) = \lambda_1 / P\mu_1 c$ as we expected, the average number of digitized voice packets are:

$$L_1 = \rho_1 \left[ 1 + \rho_2 P \mu_1 / (1 - P )\mu_2 \right] \Big/ (1 - \rho_1) \qquad (4), \text{ where } \rho_1 \text{ and } \rho_2 \text{ are}$$

the traffic intensity of the voice and data units. To find $L_2$ the average number of data packets at the first node we can redefine our generating functions such as:

$$F_{j,2} (Y) = \sum_{i=1}^{\infty} Y^i P_{i,j,1} \quad ; \quad F_{j,1} (Y) = \sum_{i=0}^{\infty} Y^i P_{i,j,1}$$

then we can obtain:

$$L_2 = \rho_2 \left[ 1 + \rho_1 (\rho_1 + \rho_2 + \frac{(1-P )\mu_2}{P \mu_1} - 2) \right] \Big/ (1 - \rho_1)( 1 - \rho_1 - \rho_2) \qquad (5)$$

if we check equation (4) and (5) for the cases when $\lambda_1 = 0$ or $\lambda_2 = 0$ we have a M/M/1* queueing model.

---

* M/M/1 Poisson input, exponential service, single server.

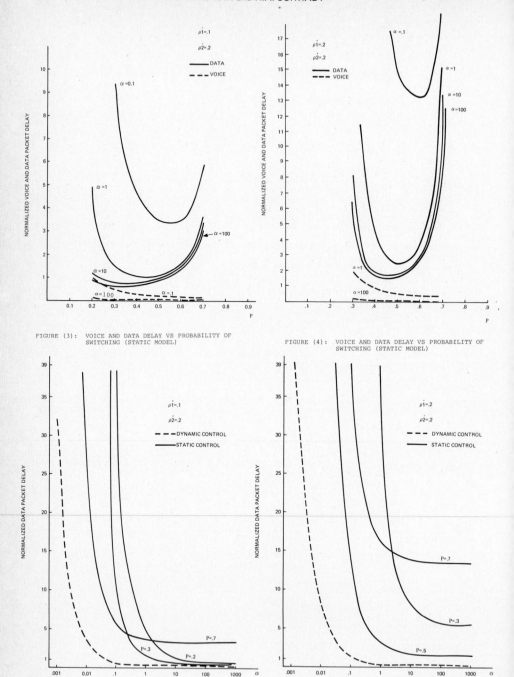

FIGURE (3):   VOICE AND DATA DELAY VS PROBABILITY OF
              SWITCHING (STATIC MODEL)

FIGURE (4):   VOICE AND DATA DELAY VS PROBABILITY OF
              SWITCHING (STATIC MODEL)

FIGURE (5):   DATA PACKET DELAY VS ($\alpha$)

FIGURE (6):   DATA PACKET DELAY VS ($\alpha$)

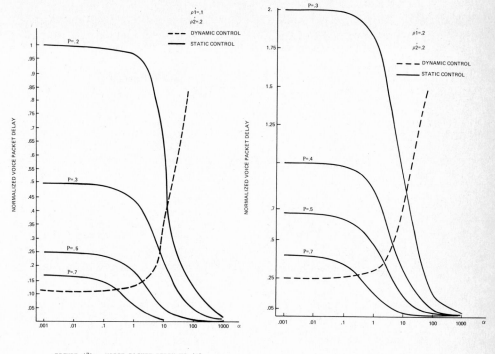

FIGURE (7): VOICE PACKET DELAY VS (α)

FIGURE (8): VOICE PACKET DELAY VS (α)

Performance of Data Communication Systems
and their Applications, G. Pujolle (ed.)
© North-Holland Publishing Company, 1981

A GLOBAL DATA COMMUNICATIONS SYSTEM

Dr. E. I. Muehldorf, TRW Inc., Washington Operations, McLean, VA 22101, USA
Dr. F. J. Prokoski, MIKOS Corp., Falls Church, VA 22042, USA
Prof. Dr. R. Eier, Technical University, A1040 Vienna, Austria

In this paper a world-wide automatic data communication system is
described which is intended for monitoring sensors at many sites world-
wide. The classical steps of system design are described: establishing
communications requirements, approaches to meet the requirements, the
resulting system design, performance evaluation of the system's initial
implementation, possible improvements, and potential expansions.

1. INTRODUCTION

World-wide data transmission has become a technical reality. The global
long-distance telephone system, CCITT data transmission protocols, a wide array of
available modems, microprocessors and associated software, direct distance
dialing (DDD), and satellites provide the technical capability to realize it.
Current regulations, mostly concerned with economic and data privacy issues, may
in some cases impose obstacles on the use of that capability.

A world-wide data transmission system, here designated Worldcom, has been
designed, implemented, and tested. Worldcom is intended for monitoring
functioning and integrity of sensors producing sensitive data placed in various
sites on a world-wide scale. In theory the sensors could be disabled and their
outputs falsified. To eliminate that possibility sensor integrity is continuously
monitored. When an attempt is made to tamper with a sensor, the Worldcom
interface will produce an output deviating from an expected response, which will
be recognized at a central facility. Worldcom will also detect tampering with its
own data transmission and hardware. This is accomplished by encryption and
changes to the encryption keys with each transmission.

This experimental system is for the benefit of mankind, and the non-technical
obstacles have been overcome through special agreements. The intent of this paper
is to consider only available technical capabilities, and not to discuss a particular application or negotiations involved to accomplish it.

The Worldcom's concept is elegant and simple. Sensor Monitors (SM) sense
sensor status and assemble status and integrity data into a common format. The
SMs at a site are periodically interrogated by an On-Site Concentrator (SC), which
stores the data for transmission to a central facility located in Austria. At the
central facility the Central Verification Unit (CU) interrogates the SCs at
different sites in an automatic mode or, on demand, manually.

Microprocessors in the CU and SCs perform many communication functions. They
provide error control, message protection by encryption, and message formatting.
At the CU statistics of abandoned calls are logged to provide statistical
information on the availability and quality of the system's links.

The network of SCs and the CU communicate via the public dial-up telephone
network. The dialing-up of the different sites is randomized. If a connection to
a site cannot be made at the first dialing attempt, automatic follow-up attempts
are scheduled. After a certain number of unsuccessful attempts to contact a site,
an alarm condition is indicated.

2. COMMUNICATIONS REQUIREMENTS

Data Volume. Typically 1536(m+1) bits are exchanged in Worldcom during an
SC-to-CU transaction, where m is the number of SMs connected to an SC. Estimating
that the fully developed system serves 500 sites, that on the average 10 SMs are
connected to each SC, and each SC is polled on the average once every 10 days,
then $3.1 \times 10^8$ information bits/year are transmitted through Worldcom. Allowing for
100% overhead (error control, start and stop bits, acknowledgements) about $1.7 \times 10^5$
bits/day need to be transmitted. Considering time for establishing connections,

unsuccessful contacts, forced waiting periods, about 9.5 hours per day are assumed to be available for data transmission. Thus a minimum data transmission capability of 50 b/s is required. It is estimated the requirement will not exceed 300 b/s in the forseeable future for applications indicated here.

Ground rules. For designing the communications interconnecting the CU and the SCs certain groundrules were adopted:

  a. Data transmission must be very economical
  b. Worldcom must provide truly global coverage
  c. Data must be transmitted in encrypted form
  d. Uncorrected transmission errors must be extremely low.

Economy. Funds for operating the system are limited, and the research and development also had to be accomplished within a tight budget. This requires very cost-effective communications, and rules out a network of dedicated data links. However, by using public communications facilities, economical and safe world-wide data transmission can be accomplished.

Data Protection. Data security is accomplished through encryption and data accuracy through error control. Encryption authenticates messages and prevents insertion of false messages. Encryption must use a derivative of methods available in the public domain, such as the NBS private key system[2]. Error control is required to avoid accidental false messages. An unrecognized error can lead to undesirable and dangerous situations, false alarms can cause interference in sites' operation and loss of confidence in the system. A goal was adopted based on the estimated data volume of $3.1 \times 10^8$ bits/year, and a requirement of less than one uncorrected error in 100 years, or $1:3.1 \times 10^{10}$.

A summary of SC-to-CU communications requirements is given in Table 1.

Table 1.  COMMUNICATIONS REQUIREMENTS

| |
|---|
| High cost effectiveness<br>Usage of public world-wide communications facilities<br>Usage of data encryption<br>Usage of error control<br>Duplex transmission CU/SC for efficient error control<br>Flexible data formats to accommodate encryption and error control<br>Extensive use of automatic direct distance dialing<br>Short messages, typically 16896 bits (2112 bytes)<br>Data rate at least 50 b/s<br>Transmission transaction approximately 6 minutes |

## 3.  COMMUNICATIONS SYSTEM DESIGN

Trade-Off. To choose the public telecommunications facility best suited for Worldcom the following were considered:

  a. The Telex network
  b. Leased lines
  c. Packet switching networks
  d. The public dial-up telephone network.

The Telex network was excluded, because its 5-bit code (CCITT alphabet No. 2) makes it awkward to implement a system with a flexible data format. Furthermore, its maximum transmission rate of 50 b/s leaves no room for growth.
Leased lines were excluded because of cost. Establishing a world-wide leased-line network for connecting about 500 sites would result in a cost somewhere between $1-2M per month - which is impractical.
Packet switching, seemingly ideal for a data transmission system, has some drawbacks which excluded it from use in Worldcom. Each SC would have to be permanently on-line and have the status of a host computer. Furthermore, packet switching is not available in many countries where Worldcom sites would be located.

The logical choice, meeting all technical requirements, is the public dial-up telephone network. It is used to establish short term point-to-point connections between the CU and SC. Interoperable modems meeting CCITT specifications are available for data transmission. The telephone network is commonly available and offers DDD to a large number of countries from Austria (see Table 2). It is constantly being improved through technical innovations, but current equipment will remain usable for a long time to come.

Difficulties with the choice of using the dial-up telephone network which needed to be overcome were not of a technical nature. For example, data transmission on dial-up telephone lines out of Japan was illegal. However, Japan's Ministry of Post and Telecommunications authorized a site for research purposes in Japan. Data transmission on dial-up lines across the borders of the USA has only recently been the subject of revised tariffs.

Generally it was found that for countries where the telephone system is administered by the national postal services, there are no restrictions on data transmission across borders. The message content of the transmission data is not regulated and any encryption scheme can be applied.

Costs. Table 2 shows the costs of telephone calls from Austria. A simple model for communications costs makes the following assumptions:

Table 2. COSTS OF TELEPHONE CALLS FROM AUSTRIA

### (1) DDD Calling Costs from Austria, Status of Early 1980

|  | ZONE 1 | ZONE 2 | ZONE 3 | ZONE 4 | ZONE 5 |
|---|---|---|---|---|---|
| COUNTRIES | Czechoslovakia Federal Republic of Germany (Southern Zone) Hungary Italy (Northern Zone) Liechtenstein Switzerland Yugoslavia (Northern Zone) | Belgium Denmark France Federal Republic of Germany (Northern Zone) GDR Italy (Southern Zone) Luxembourg Netherlands Poland Yugoslavia (Southern Zone) | Finland Greece Ireland Norway Portugal Spain Sweden UK | US Canada Israel | Argentina Australia Japan Union of South Africa Venezuela |
| COST PER MINUTE* OS $ US | 9.58 0.74 | 12.08 0.93 | 14.58 1.12 | 40.42 3.11 | 55.42 4.26 |

*13 Austrian Schillinge (OS) = 1 $ US used for computation of these tables

### (2) Operator Assisted Calls From Austria

| COST COUNTRY** | FIRST THREE MINUTES | | EACH ADDITIONAL MINUTE | |
|---|---|---|---|---|
|  | OS | $ US | OS | $ US |
| Algiers | 120.00 | 9.23 | 40.00 | 3.08 |
| Bulgaria | 75.00 | 5.77 | 25.00 | 1.92 |
| Japan*** | 234.00 | 18.00 | 78.00 | 6.00 |
| Turkey | 105.00 | 8.08 | 35.00 | 2.69 |
| UK*** | 75.00 | 5.77 | 25.00 | 1.92 |
| US*** | 180.00 | 13.85 | 60.00 | 4.32 |
| USSR | 90.00 | 6.92 | 30.00 | 2.31 |

** Representative list - countries requiring operator assistance
*** Listed for comparison - countries which can also be reached via DDD

a. The distribution of sites with SCs in zones 2, 3, 4, and 5 is 5:4:8:8. When using these numbers as multipliers for the costs, the cost for 25 facilities results.
b. 50% of the sites in zone 5 require operator assistance; the cost ratios are thus 0.93 : 1.12 : 3.11 : 5.13.
c. Sites are contacted every 10 days by a 6-minute call.
d. One out of four calls is abandoned because of line trouble.

With these assumptions, the average daily cost per monitored site is:

$$C_D = 1.33 \frac{6}{10} \frac{1}{25} (4.65 + 4.48 + 24.88 + 41.04) = 2.40 \text{ [US\$]} \qquad (1).$$

In this equation 1.33 accounts for the abandoned calls, 6/10 for the minutes per day per facility, and 1/25 adjusts for the fact that the costs are for 25 facilities. Figure 1 shows daily and annual communications costs with the above assumptions as function of the number of sites.

Modem. The CCITT V.21 300 b/s modem was adopted for the design. It is widely available, can be used for full duplex transmission, is certified in many countries, and many years of experience have been accumulated using it. It is robust in operation, and meets all technical requirements for Worldcom.

Dialing Equipment. The automatic dialing equipment selected for the system is the Siemens AWD 8393. This equipment is certified for use in Austria and could also be used for tests in the USA with a protective access arrangement. This choice minimized potential regulatory and certification delays in providing an initial operational capability.

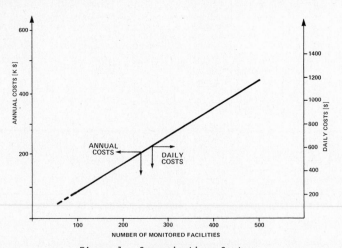

Figure 1.   Communications Costs

System Structure. The system structure is shown in Figure 2. The CU contains a central processing unit which activates the dialing equipment across the CCITT V.24 interface. It also drives a Siemens A 300 modem. For operator assisted dialing the CU issues a prompting schedule. At monitored sites the modems are used in the automatic answer-back mode.

Communications Transaction. The transmission is asynchronous and 8-bit byte oriented. The communications transaction between the CU and an SC is illustrated in Figure 3. It includes dialing, establishing a link, retrieving messages from memory, encrypting, adding error control redundancy, and formatting. At the receiver the messages are temporarily stored and processed by error control routines.

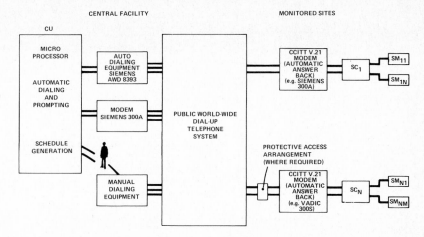

Figure 2.   Communications System Structure

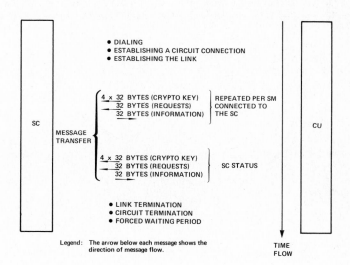

Legend:   The arrow below each message shows the direction of message flow.

Figure 3.   Typical Worldcom Communications Transaction

Error Control.   For Worldcom an extremely low rate of residual errors was adopted; to accomplish this goal retransmission and comparison at the source with automatic repeat request (ARQ) was chosen.   Messages consist of n-bit code words. The use of forward error correction (FEC) in addition to ARQ can greatly reduce the need for message repetition and also reduce the residual error rate.   Worldcom requires duplex transmission for efficient operation.

Effective Rate of Information Transfer.   Use of error control results in transmission overhead in the form of additional bits (redundancy) and/or waiting time between blocks for ARQ.   Thus the information transfer rate is reduced with respect to the bit rate on the communications facility.

The Transfer Rate of Information Bits (TRIB)[2] is:

$$TRIB = \frac{\text{number of information bits accepted at the receiver}}{\text{total time to get those bits accepted}} \quad .$$

The numerator can be expressed as $kpW^p$ and the denominator as $(np/r) + \Delta T$. This leads to:

$$TRIB = \frac{k}{n} \, r \, \frac{W^p}{1 + \dfrac{r\Delta T}{np}} \qquad (2),$$

where k is the average number of information bits per code word, n the number of transmission bits per code word (including redundancy), p the number of n-bit code words per transmission block, r the bit transmission rate over the communications facility, W the probability of correctly receiving an n-bit code word, and $\Delta T$ the delay between p.n-bit transmission blocks required for implementation of ARQ. The factor $k/n^{(1)}$ is the code efficiency, $W^p$ is the success rate for accepting correct words, and $1 + r\Delta T/np$ is the transmission rate reduction resulting from ARQ.

The probability of correctly receiving an n-bit code word is related to the word error rate Q by

$$W = 1 - Q \qquad (3).$$

For t-error correction the n-bit word error rate $Q_t$ can be expressed as[3]

$$Q_t = 1 - \sum_{i=0}^{t} \binom{n}{i} e^i (1-e)^{n-1} \qquad (4),$$

where e is the bit error rate.$^{(2)}$ From this the success rate $W_t$ can be expressed as:

$$W_t = \sum_{i=0}^{t} \binom{n}{i} e^i (1-e)^{n-1} \qquad (5).$$

Without error correction the success rate becomes

$$W_0 = (1-e)^n \doteq 1-ne \qquad (6),$$

and with single-bit FEC

$$W_1 = (1-e)^n + ne(1-e)^{n-1} \doteq 1 - \frac{n(n-1)}{2} e^2 \doteq 1 - \frac{n^2}{2} e^2 \qquad (7).$$

The above approximations yield excellent results for ne $\leq$ 0.1.

The TRIB can now be expressed for transmission without and with single-bit FEC. Without FEC it is:

$$TRIB_{NOFEC} \doteq \frac{k}{n} \, r \, \frac{(1-ne)^{2p}}{1 + \dfrac{r\Delta T}{np}} \qquad (8).$$

---

(1) Redundancy with the use of FEC can be estimated by the Hamming bound. For single-bit FEC $2^{n-k} \leq 1+n$, hence

$$\frac{k}{n} \leq 1 - \frac{ld\ (n + 1)}{n} \quad .$$

(2) The error rate e depends on the modulation scheme used. For FSK the bit error rate e is related to the bit energy to noise density $E_b/N_o$ by [4]

$$e = erfc\sqrt{E_b/N_o}.$$

With FEC one obtains:

$$TRIB_{FEC} \doteq \frac{k}{n} \; r \; \frac{\left(1 - \frac{n(n-1)}{2} \, e^2\right)^{2p}}{1 + \frac{r \Delta T}{np}} \qquad (9).$$

The factor 2 in the exponent of eqns. (8) and (9) is required since the block must be transmitted from the sender to the receiver and then back again.

The TRIB as function of the number of blocks, p, using 32-bit code words, a transmission rate r = 300 b/s, with the delay $\Delta T$ and the bit error rate as parameter is shown in Figure 4. For FEC k=26 is a reasonable assumption, although in reality k < 26 because of block-format overhead. For comparison the figure shows curves with $\Delta T$ = 1s and $\Delta T$ = 5s.

The TRIB function has the following characteristics:

a.  The TRIB has a maximum at a particular transmission block length if stop-and-wait ARQ is used. The block length is a function of the waiting time $\Delta T$, the data rate r, the bit error rate e, and through W also depends on the average number of retransmissions.

b.  Block lengths must be chosen so that transmission is efficient over the expected range of error rates.

c.  Use of FEC greatly improves the TRIB, and it is very useful to combine FEC with stop-and-wait ARQ.

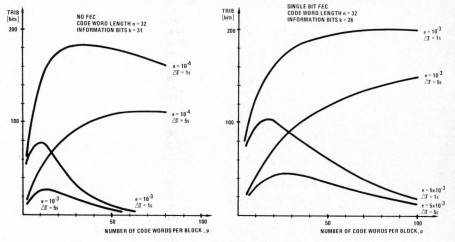

Figure 4.   Transfer Rate of Information Bits in the System

The system design was based on a delay $\Delta T$ of about 1s and an error rate e of about $10^{-3}$. Therefore, the use of FEC is suggested and a protocol which makes use of duplex transmission. The code word length for FEC is n = 32 bits, and with 12 words to a block (p = 12), a block is n.p = 384 bits. From Figure 4 it can be seen, that TRIB values between 100 and 160 b/s can be expected. Without use of FEC the TRIB value would be somewhere between 20 and 80 b/s.

Transmission Block Format and Protocol. The transmission message block has a header consisting of an ACK or NAK character signalling acceptance or retransmission of the block transmitted prior to it, a NUL character, and an STX or EOT character, followed by 32 information bytes, followed by an ETB character. This is a total of 288 information bits, which are expanded to 384 transmission bits to implement error control. To assure communications even under adverse conditions, this transmission block format is under software control and adjustable should the need arise. This flexibility provides the potential to adjust the communications procedure to the conditions existing in different communications paths.

A typical timing diagram of the transmission protocol with error control is shown in Figure 5. For normal conditions ($e \doteq 10^{-3}$) error control with the message block format described above is intended to operate as follows:

   a.  A 288-bit (36-byte) transmission block is segmented into 12 three-byte (24-bit) sections.

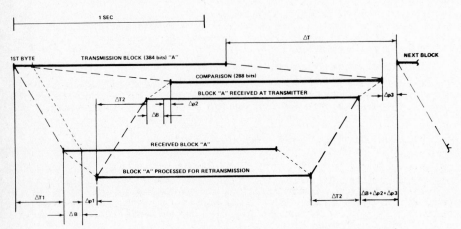

Figure 5.  Typical Systems Timing Diagram for Data Transmission

   b.  Each 24-bit (3-byte) section is padded by two zeros and extended to a 31-bit word of the (31, 26) Hamming code. An additional parity bit produces a 32-bit word with single error correction and double error detection capability. The original 288-bit block thus becomes 384 bits or 48 bytes long (transmission block "A").
   c.  The 48-byte block is transmitted byte-by-byte.
   d.  After receiving the first 32-bits (4 bytes, duration $\Delta$B) at the destination, error processing commences; the three message bytes are extracted and temporarily stored.
   e.  The three message bytes are recoded into four bytes and echoed back to the source. The processing delay for steps d and e is $\Delta$p1.
   f.  At the source the retransmitted block is received (delay $\Delta$B), decoded, processed, and its 24 message bits are compared to the transmitted 24 messages bits (delay $\Delta$p2). The comparison at the source is thus carried out over the original 288 bits as indicated in Figure 5.
   g.  The process described in steps d, e, and f is continued until one 48-byte block has been transmitted, received and completely echoed back.
   h.  At the end of a 36-byte block comparison, the transmitter issues an ACK, NUL, character sequence as header for the next block in case of successful comparison; when an error is detected the old block is retransmitted and preceded by a NAK character (processing delay $\Delta$p3).
   i.  The last block at the end of a transaction contains an EOT character.

With this protocol ARQ virtually eliminates residual errors, while FEC avoids an excessive retransmission rate. The protocol protects against random errors and bursts. To avoid being trapped in a continuous request for retransmission cycle, an upper limit of R consecutive NAKs requesting retransmission of the same block are taken as indication of a bad connection and cause unsuccessful termination of a transaction.

System Performance. The probability of success, S, of a communications transaction, given that a modem-to-modem link-up has been established, is

$$S = [1 - (1 - W^p)^R] \frac{L}{np} \qquad (10),$$

where R is the maximum number of transmissions before the communications trans-action is terminated unsuccessfully, and L is the total message transmitted; W and p were introduced above.[3] For the system implementation suggested by Figures 3 and 5, n = 32, p = 12, R and L are parameters.

When eqn. (7) is used in eqn. (10) and ne < 0.1, then

$$S_{(FEC)} \doteq \left[1 - \left(\frac{pn(n-1)}{2} \ e^2\right)^R\right] \frac{L}{np} \doteq \exp \ - \frac{L}{np} \left(\frac{pn(n-1)}{2} \ e^2\right)^R \qquad (11).$$

The conditions under which the approximation (11) holds reflect parameter values to be chosen for trouble free operation of the system. When FEC is not applied, eqn. (6) is introduced into eqn. (10) and for a n.p-bit transmission block

$$S_{(NOFEC)} \doteq \left(1 - (npe)^R\right) \frac{L}{np} \doteq \exp \ - \frac{L}{np} \ (npe)^R \qquad (12).$$

Comparisons of eqns. (11) and (12) shows that for the design described here the transaction failure rate with FEC is significantly smaller than without FEC.

The limit of the number of allowable retransmission requests, R, can be critical, especially without FEC. Figure 6 shows the success rate as function of the error rate with and without FEC. With FEC two allowable retransmissions (R=3)

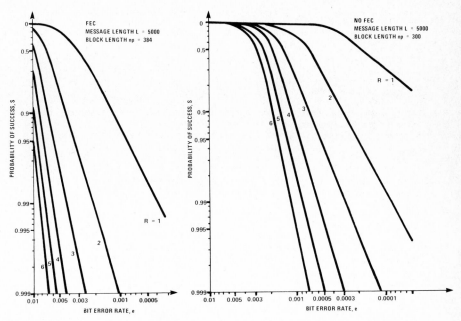

Figure 6. Success of a Communications Transaction

_____
[3] The total number of transmitted blocks is B = L/np.

will guarantee satisfactory operation, and with more retransmissions the system will operate even when the bit error rate is $10^{-2}$. At a block length of 300 bits without FEC, six retransmissions may be needed to produce satisfactory results. For error rates above $10^{-3}$ no satisfactory results can be obtained without FEC; the only option is to reduce the block length when the error rate falls below $10^{-3}$.

An estimate of the order of the magnitude of the residual error rate can be made without too much difficulty. A residual error will remain if an error in the forward path is compensated in the return path. From eqn. (7) the residual word error rate on the forward link with the use of FEC is of the order $(n^2/2)e^2$, and with single FEC plus double bit error detection capability of the order $(n^3/6)e^3$. When the compensating error in the return path is also considered, the residual word error probability with the use of FEC is of the order $(n^2/2)e^4$ and with single FEC plus double bit error detecting of the order $(n^3/6)e^6$ for an undetected error. With $n$ = 32 and $e$ = $5 \times 10^{-3}$ the probability of an uncorrected error is of the order $10^{-7}$ and an undetected error of the order $10^{-10}$. Thus with appropriate processing the ambitious goal of the design can be met even when error rates are above $10^{-3}$.

## 4. RESULTS

The Worldcom has been implemented and was recently tested at 10 sites in eight countries (Australia, Austria, Bulgaria, Canada, Federal Republic of Germany, Japan, United Kingdom, United States of America).

The initial operating capability does not fully utilize all features of the design. The full duplex capability of the V.21 modem is not used, resulting in very slow transmission. The use of FEC has not been implemented, and therefore, data transmission requires many retransmissions and slows down considerably in the presence of error rates above $10^{-3}$, which frequently exist on long distance international traffic. The block length without FEC needs to be kept between 100 and 200 bits in order to keep the success rate of communications transactions during system testing at a reasonable level.

Key problems were identified as:

a. Busy lines in international telephone traffic (depending on locality and time of day)
b. Low signal level (depending on country where the SC is located)
c. Variability of line quality (depending on routing)

Manual dialing. Unattended operation to a station to which manual dialing is required proved not desirable. For trouble-free operation initial voice contact is preferred between operators who initiate data transmission.

Automatic dialing. The following difficulties may be experienced:

a. Waiting between dialing the last digit and its arrival at the far end may vary greatly; this was successfully controlled by inserting separator digits into the dialing sequence. Control in this manner is important since equipment timing-out is subject to regulations.
b. Automatic recognition of the answer tone is strongly dependent on the return signal level, and many connections that human operators would find acceptable are not utilized by the AWD. This can be controlled by modifying time constants determining the dialing process, since the return signal level may increase after the initial hand shaking.
c. Time constants and delays in establishing connections between calling and called modem may cause lock-out or unstable conditions of repeatedly connecting and disconnecting. Such problems usually depend on the specific conditions of telecommunications between the CU and the dialed-up SC and can be overcome by software modification.

Recommendations. Technical insights gained with Worldcom can be employed to improve other world-wide communications systems similar to it:

a. Modifications to fine-tune the time constants and signal level recognition in dialing equipment and modems at each installation.
b. Incorporating test procedures into a system, such as loopback testing, signal level measurement, usage of standard test signals, statistics gathering methods, etc.
c. Improving the data transmission parameters and protocols including: transmission block lengths, maximum repetitions of blocks for error control, use of full duplex transmission, and others.
d. Providing adaptive parameters in the software design which automatically optimize communications between the CU and SC at a site.

## 5. GROWTH POTENTIAL

Worldcom's design was conceived for growth. It can ultimately serve 500 sites world-wide. Using the telephone network and choosing robust 300 b/s data transmission is an important factor for the growth potential.

The system also offers the possibility of monitoring mobile facilities. For this purpose sensors are attached to mobile platforms along with an SC. The facility must also carry a satellite communications terminal. The CU calls the telephone number of the terminal and is connected to the SC. This is currently done via MARISAT for platforms aboard ships, and may be accomplished via other satellite systems for ground-mobile platforms.

A system as described here opens the possibility of constructing data bases of global scope with world-wide access. A communication system as described here has potential applications in a variety of areas:

a. Monitoring UN safeguards and safety sensors [5]
b. International banking
c. World-wide medical information services
d. Argicultural support to developing nations
e. Weather information dissemination.

Through a communication systems approach, as given in this paper, it has become possible at the present time to have reliable, quick access to information on a global scale at very low cost. Mankind can benefit in many ways from application of this technology.

## REFERENCES

[1] M. E. Hellman, An Overview of Public Key Cryptography, IEEE Communications Society Magazine, Vol. 16, No. 6, Nov 1978, p 24-32.

[2] D. R. Doll, Data Communications, Facilities, Networks, and System Design, John Wiley & Sons, NY 1978.

[3] R. W. Lucky, J. Salz, and E. J. Weldon, Jr., Principles of Data Communications, McGraw Hill, NY, 1968.

[4] M. Schwartz, Information Transmission, Modulation, and Noise, 2nd Ed., McGraw Hill, NY, 1970.

[5] F. J. Prokoski, Monitoring of International Nuclear Safeguards, 5th Int. Conf. on Comp. Comm., Oct 27-30 1980, Atlanta, Ga.

Performance of Data Communication Systems
and their Applications, G. Pujolle (ed.)
© North-Holland Publishing Company, 1981

THE PERFORMANCE OF A PACKET SWITCHED NETWORK
- A STUDY OF EURONET

Bryan Alton, Ahmed Patel, Michael Purser, John Sheehan

National Board for Science and Technology
Dublin
Ireland

This work presents some results from a European Commission
contract to monitor the technical performance of EURONET
by a host.  Performance trends are examined, and absolute
figures are analysed and related to network parameters.

## 1.  INTRODUCTION

The Irish National Board for Science and Technology owns a DEC PDP-11/34 computer
connected into Euronet via an X25 interface to the Dublin multiplexor and hence to
the London node (Figure 1).  (There are also other connections to this computer[1]
which are irrelevant to this paper.)  In summer 1980 an agreement was reached with
DG XIII of the European Commission to add software to the basic system to monitor
the performance of Euronet.  This software has been operational since November 1980
and regular four-weekly reports have been produced since December 1980.

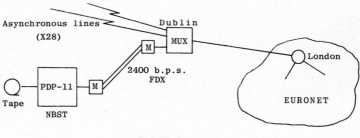

FIGURE 1

The Commission's interest in monitoring Euronet's performance is essentially that
of examining trends:  for example, the effect, if any, on average transit times
over several months as usage of the network increases.  Our interest is perhaps
more in analysing absolute figures, and relating them, where possible, to network
parameters:  for example, the impact of extra inter-nodal 'hops' on call set-up
times;  or the ratio of maximum attained throughput to maximum theoretical throughput of data packets.  Additionally, both are interested in the quality and
reliability of the network:  for example, the proportion of failed or prematurely
terminated calls.

This paper presents the design of our monitoring program;  the measurements of
network performance made by it to meet the requirements outlined above;  and a
discussion of the results obtained.

## 2. MONITORING PROGRAM

The monitoring program is an assembly language task, under our SPEX operating system[2]. It calls system subroutines, provided by our X25 software, to establish, use and clear virtual calls across Euronet. These subroutines converse with the Level 3 task over a buffered interface (Figure 2). The X25 software naturally supports many simultaneous virtual calls. However the monitoring software has been written to generate, and take measurements from, only one call at a time. The data so acquired are written to magnetic tape, which is subsequently analysed off-line by a Pascal programme.

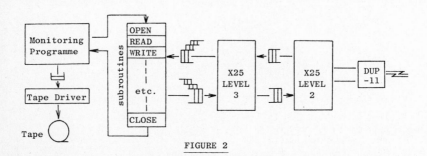

FIGURE 2

The computer is, in principle, on-line to Euronet 24 hours per day. However monitoring takes place only four times per day, once in each of the 3-hour periods 0700 - 1000 - 1300 - 1600 - 1900 hours (CET). On these occasions the monitor runs for approximately one hour and twenty minutes, the starting time within the period being altered from day to day according to a partly random, partly predetermined schedule, so that over a month a proper sample is obtained. When running, the monitor makes 30 calls in each of the first and last periods, and 60 calls in the middle two periods. The interval between packets and the size of the data packets are all randomly and dynamically selected. However, the distributions are such that, on average, 45 data packets of 44 octets are sent per call - or some 2000 octets. This is done to ensure that the budgeted volume and duration costs incurred in using Euronet, are not exceeded.

The calls are made to the Echo facilities at the London, Paris, Frankfurt and Rome nodes, and at the Joint Research Establishment at Ispra. The destination for any particular call is also randomly chosen. This means that, once a call has been set-up, data packets sent by the monitoring programme are returned to it. By placing a sequence number, the time of transmission and a software check sum in each data packet, it is possible to measure round-trip delays, or detect loss, duplication and corruption of data packets. Although normally, one data packet has returned (echoed) before the next is sent, this is not necessarily so; both our software and Level 3 window size allow more than one data packet to be in transit at a time. A consequence of this is that, in the face of line errors and loss of data, retransmissions of Level 2 frames containing data packets can occur either because a timeout has occurred, due to not receiving an acknowledgement to the former, or because a frame error has been detected when receiving a frame subsequent to a lost one. This is not the case for Level 2 frames containing Call Request/Accept packets, because they have no subsequent packets on the same virtual channel which might allow a frame sequence error to be detected - timeouts alone apply. (Of course, traffic on another virtual channel would force Level 2 frames through, and hence allow the detection of frame sequence errors, but this depends on manually established calls, since the monitor itself only has one virtual call extant at a time.

The basic calls made in a monitoring period are "short" calls, of 60 or 120 seconds average duration for periods 2, 3 and 1, 4 respectively.  The following parameters are measured:

- Call set-up delay
- Call duration
- Data packets sent
- Data packets received withot error (echoed)
- Data packets lost at end of call (usually on premature clearing)
- Data packets lost during call
- Duplicated data packets
- Corrupted data packets
- Out of sequence data packets
- Round-trip delay for data packets
- Packet size

Additionally, once a period, one maximum throughput and one long call are made. The maximum throughput call sends data packets as fast as it can, subject to window constraints only.  The long call lasts some 900 seconds on average.

The monitoring programme also records:  failed and aborted calls (and the reasons for them);  a count of the packet types received;  breakdowns of the reasons for clearing calls, for resetting the virtual channel,  and for restarting the interface.  The off-line programme has a complete record for each call on which to work.  Rather than print out everything, it produces three main reports per four -weekly period:

- Four summaries of monitoring results for all destinations, one per period

- Five summaries of monitoring results for all periods, one per destination

- One summary of monitoring results for all periods and all destinations

The above summaries are of short calls and include means, standard deviations, maximum and minimum values and histograms of measured parameters, as appropriate. Additionally, the off-line programme produces:

- One summary of monitoring results for all periods and all destinations for long calls

## 3.  RESULTS: NORMAL OPERATION

Normal operation is when calls are set-up and cleared successfully, and when data packets are sent and their echoes received successfully.  Normal operation includes possible retransmissions at Level 2 and resettings at Level 3.

In analysing call set-up and packet round-trip delays, the following components of delay are considered:

1. Transmission
2. Propagation
3. Modem and multiplexor delays
4. Nodal and host processing
5. Queueing
6. Retransmission
7. Echo process response (At the nodes the echo process has low priority)

Both minimum and average delays are recorded by our monitor.  By considering only minimum delays, it can be assumed that delays due to queueing, retransmission and echo process response are zero.  Furthermore, the modem and multiplexor delays are regarded as part of the nodal processing delays which we hope to calculate.

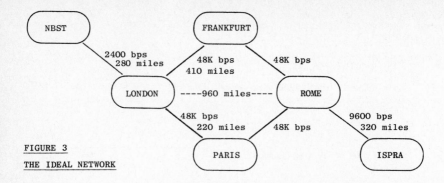

FIGURE 3

THE IDEAL NETWORK

The minimum figures are compared with "ideal" figures. These ideal figures are
obtained by considering the behaviour of packets and frames of equal length to the
real ones, which are subject to the same transmission speed restrictions as the
real ones, but which are supposed to require no processing time in multiplexors
or in nodal or other computers (including our own). The network used for these
ideal calculations is shown in Figure 3. The ideal figures also allow for a
propagation delay of 10 secs per mile, giving the following approximate figures:

|                                      | miles | msecs. |
|--------------------------------------|-------|--------|
| Dublin - London                      | 280   | 3      |
| London - Paris                       | 220   | 2      |
| London - Frankfurt                   | 410   | 4      |
| London - Rome<br>(via Paris or Frankfurt) | 960   | 10     |
| Rome - Ispra                         | 320   | 3      |

### 3.1  CALL SET-UP DELAYS

Figure 4(a) shows a histogram of call set-up delays for all destinations (except
Ispra) for all periods during May 1980. The peaks between 2 and 3 seconds, and
between 8 and 9 seconds are due to timeout-originated retransmissions (see section
2). 7.96% of successful Call Requests take over 2 seconds for this reason. Figure
4(b) shows a histogram of the same calls but over the interval 0 to 2 seconds. It
can be seen that the effect of retransmissions almost doubles the average delay.

Our Call Request packets are 15 octets long on the network access links, and 19
octets within the network; and the Call Connected packets are 3 octets. Allowing
for Level 2 framing (6 octets per packet) and 3 per cent expansion for bit
stuffing:

Call Request transmission delay     =  72 msecs @ 2400 bps
                                    =  18 msecs @ 9600 bps
                                    =   4 msecs @  48 Kbps
Call Connected transmission delay   =  30 msecs @ 2400 bps
                                    =   8 msecs @ 9600 bps
                                    =   2 msecs @  48 Kbps

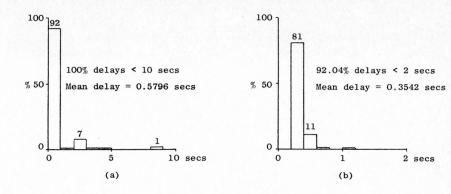

FIGURE 4. CALL SET-UP DELAYS

The following table shows the ideal and minimum call set-up times in msecs for the different destinations. (It should be noted that our real-time clock operates with a 20 msec interval).

|  | London | Paris | Frankfurt | Rome | Ispra |
|---|---|---|---|---|---|
| Ideal | 108 | 118 | 122 | 140 | 172 |
| Minimum | 220 | 280 | 280 | 360 | 480 |
| Difference | 112 | 162 | 158 | 220 | 308 |
| Accounted by: | D+L+N | D+L+2N | D+L+2N | D+L+3N | D+L+3N+I |

These differences between the minimum and the ideal are accounted for by processing delays in Dublin, which we call D; nodal processing delays common to all Call Requests, which we call N; an extra processing delay at London for address validation and billing initialization, which we call L; and a processing delay at the Ispra host, which we call I.

It was found from local loopback testing that D is equal to 13 msec. (Despite the low frequency of our clock, a figure of this magnitude can be accurately obtained through averaging techniques.) Thus:

$$N = ( (162-112) + (158-112) + (220-112)/2 ) / 3 = 50 \text{ msecs}$$
$$L = 112 - 50 - 13 = 49 \text{ msecs}$$
$$I = 308 - 49 - 13 - 3*50 = 96 \text{ msecs}$$

The average values and standard deviations of call set-up delays for all periods for each destination are:

| London | Paris | Frankfurt | Rome | Ispra |
|---|---|---|---|---|
| 416 + 627 | 458 + 686 | 540 + 901 | 645 + 905 | 910 + 1122  msec. |

And for each period for all destinations:

| Period 1 | Period 2 | Period 3 | Period 4 |
|---|---|---|---|
| 562 + 813 | 556 + 748 | 600 + 973 | 597 + 908  msec. |

Finally, we can estimate the bit error rate on the Dublin - London link from
Figure 4(a).  7.96% of call set-up delays are greater than 2 seconds due to Level
2 retransmissions as a result of errors on this link.

Thus bit error rate  =  0.0796 / (No. of bits in Call Request + Accept frames)

$$= 0.0796 / (173 + 74)$$

$$= \sim 3 * 10^{-4}$$

This figure is plausible in view of the bad line quality experienced to London, and
gives us confidence in our calculations !


## 3.2  PACKET ROUND-TRIP DELAYS

Figure 5(a) shows a histogram of round-trip delays for short calls for all periods
and destinations during May 1981.  The peaks due to timeout retransmissions are

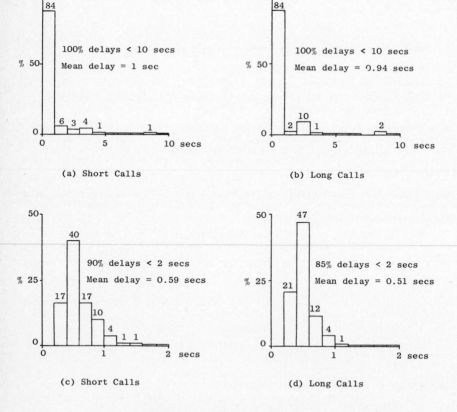

FIGURE 5.  ROUND-TRIP DELAYS

scarcely visible since most error recovery is by retransmissions caused by the detection of sequencing errors at Level 2. This is made clear in Figure 5(b) which applies to <u>long</u> calls, in which the average interval between data packets is longer than the Level 2 timeout value (2 seconds) so that timeout operates before sequencing errors can be detected. The peaks at 2 to 3 seconds and 8 to 9 seconds as in Figure 4(a) are clearly visible. Figure 5(c) is the same as 5(a), except that it focuses on 0 to 2 seconds, and Figure 5(d) is similarily related to 5(b).

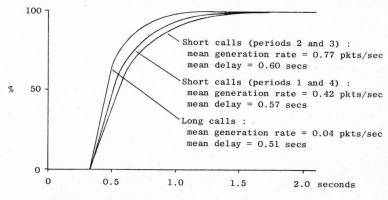

FIGURE 6. CUMULATIVE DISTRIBUTION OF ROUND-TRIP DELAYS

The round-trip delays of less than 2 seconds are shown cumulatively in Figure 6, in which the short calls are categorised according to their packet generation rates. As expected, the graphs are very similar to exponential curves. The reason for the difference in mean delays is twofold: firstly, the greater the packet generation rate the longer the queueing delay; secondly, the greater the packet generation rate the sooner the detection of line errors by out-of-sequence frames, and thus the increased liklihood of retransmitted packets having a delay of less than 2 seconds.

The following table shows ideal and minimum round-trip delays in msecs for packets of 30 data octets:

|  | London | Paris | Frankfurt | Rome | Ispra |
|---|---|---|---|---|---|
| Ideal | 274 | 292 | 296 | 322 | 394 |
| Minimum | 340 | 340 | 340 | 380 | 580 |
| Difference | 66 | 48 | 44 | 58 | 186 |
| Accounted by: | d+n | d+3n | d+3n | d+5n | d+6n+i |

The notation is similar to that used in section 3.1, where:

$d$ = processing delay in Dublin = 15 msec
$n$ = nodal processing delay
$i$ = processing delay at Ispra

From this table we note that the minimum delays to London, Paris and Frankfurt are identical (as determined by our clock). This may be explained by the fact that data packets received at London require acknowledgement at both Levels 2 and 3. Thus a data packet echoed at London is queued behind a level 2 RR frame and a Level 3 RR packet, incurring a threshold delay of 52 msecs for their transmission (d + 52 = 67 = ∿66).  Similarily echoed packets from Paris and Frankfurt are queued behind these acknowledgements at London and experience the same minimum round-trip delay.  Rome, however, because of its farther distance is not affected and we can use the minimum delay obtained to calculate the value of n :

$$n = (58 - 15) / 5 = 9 \text{ msec}$$
$$i = 186 - 6*9 - 15 = 117 \text{ msec}$$

The average values and standard deviations of round-trip delays for all periods for each destination are:

| London | Paris | Frankfurt | Rome | Ispra |
|--------|-------|-----------|------|-------|
| 923 ± 1328 | 955 ± 1287 | 949 ± 1369 | 967 ± 1243 | 2000 ± 2880 |

For the nodal destinations, the difference between the average and ideal delays does not vary from node to node as one might expect.  This indicates that queueing and retransmissions occur largely at the network access points rather than within the network.


3.3  MAXIMUM DATA THROUGHPUT

The limiting factor on throughput is the speed of our Dublin - London link, which is 300 octets/sec.  Our Level 3 window size is three so that, in the absence of errors, we should never be restricted from sending at a maximum rate by flow control considerations.

Maximum attainable throughput  =  Maximum attainable efficiency * 300

where  efficiency = $\dfrac{\text{No. of data octets}}{\text{No. of data octets + No. of control octets}}$

The maximum size packet that the monitor sends is 60 data octets, which requires 9 control octets plus bit stuffing.  As Euronet does not use the piggybacking facility for Level 3 acknowledgements, data packets will be interleaved with RR packets in both directions of the link since traffic is echoed.  This implies an additional overhead of 9 octets for the RR packet.

Maximum attainable throughput  = $\dfrac{60}{(60 + 9 + 9) * 1.03} * 300$ = 224 octets/sec

The best throughput values for each of the destinations during January-May 1981 are:

| London | Paris | Frankfurt | Rome | Ispra | |
|--------|-------|-----------|------|-------|--|
| 207 | 209 | 206 | 211 | 152 | octets/sec |

The maximum throughput attained is 94% of the theoretical maximum.  The 6% difference may be partly accounted for by the fact that we measure throughput by dividing the time difference between sending the first and receiving the last data packet, so our figures should be corrected for one round-trip delay.

It should be noted that the 'maximum' throughput normally attained is 75% on average of the theoretical maximum due to errors on the link.  Our throughput figures could be increased by a substantial 12% were Euronet to avail of Level 3 piggybacking facilities.

## 4.  GENERAL NETWORK QUALITY

Firstly we must note that the quality of the Dublin - London link has been poor. Prior to May, approximately 40% of attempted calls failed to be set-up due to problems at Level 2 (disconnection, reinitialization).  In early May the line was upgraded and we now obtain a link availability in the region of 99%.  In the subsequent analysis we consider only those problems which we know are not related to the local Dublin - London link.

### 4.1  NETWORK FAULTS

Calls may be rejected or cleared prematurely by the network due to internal diffi-culties.  Two causes of clearing have been found to occur:

(a)   "LIB NC"  or  "Network fault"

(b)   "LIB RC"  or  "End of 'Out of order'" , indicating the detection of a network difficulty which has now been corrected.

Both difficulties have resulted in the premature clearing of calls, while only the former has resulted in call rejections - this indicates the short-lived nature of the "LIB RC" difficulty.  Figures are given below for the percentage of calls affected by network difficulties during May.  These clearly show a high rate of failure at the node in Rome.

| Cause of failure | London | Paris | Frankfurt | Rome | Ispra |
|---|---|---|---|---|---|
| "LIB NC" | 0.0% | 0.2% | 0.0% | 1.0% | 2.0% |
| "LIB RC" | 0.0% | 0.0% | 0.0% | 0.0% | 8.8% |

### 4.2  RELIABILITY OF DATA TRANSFER

In almost a million data packets sent by the monitor, only one has ever been duplicated;  none have been corrupted or received out of sequence.  Packet losses have occurred, but always as a result of resetting of the virtual circuit.  The losses of data packets during May was as follows:

| | London | Paris | Frankfurt | Rome | Ispra |
|---|---|---|---|---|---|
| No. of packets lost | 13 | 26 | 0 | 0 | 0 |
| Fraction of total sent | $4.5*10^{-4}$ | $1*10^{-3}$ | 0 | 0 | 0 |
| No. of resets | 2 | 3 | 0 | 0 | 4 |

The cause of all these received Reset Indications was "Reset by Remote DTE". Resetting is found to occur when data packets are being transmitted at a very high rate and when the sending DTE's window size is greater than the receiving DTE's window size - Euronet does not heed the receiver's window size.  We have subscribed for a window size of 3, but by reducing our size to 2 (the preferred Euronet size) we can eliminate occurrences of resetting completely.

## 5.  PERFORMANCE TRENDS

It is interesting to examine the trends in monitored statistics over the five month period between January and May 1981.  Encouragingly, a continual improvement in the networks performance is visible.

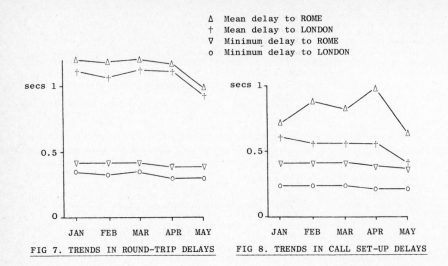

FIG 7. TRENDS IN ROUND-TRIP DELAYS     FIG 8. TRENDS IN CALL SET-UP DELAYS

## 5.1 NETWORK DELAYS

Figure 7 illustrates the trends in minimum and average packet round-trip delays
for the London and Rome nodes (being the closest and farthest nodes). We see that
all the delays decreased over the 5 month period. In particular, minimum delays
were reduced an average 7.5% in April, indicating a substantial decrease in nodal
processing delays. Also noticeable is a 15% reduction in average delays in May,
which may be credited largely to the fact that more Level 2 timeout originated
retransmissions were being initiated at the lower timeout value i.e. at 2 seconds
instead of 8 seconds.

Figure 8 illustrates the trends in minimum and average call set-up delays for the
London and Rome nodes. Excepting the erratic behaviour of average delays to Rome,
the trends are identical to those of the packet round-trip delays.

## 5.2 NETWORK FAULTS

Figure 9 shows the percentage of call failures due to network difficulties. The
peak in clearances due to "LIB NC" for short calls in April corresponds to the
inclusion of Ispra as a monitored destination. The sharp increase in failures due
to "LIB RC" for short calls similarily coincides with the inclusion of Ispra which
is most prone to this type of difficulty.

The intention of "long" calls is to determine the network conditions to which a
file transfer of 15 minutes duration would be typically subjected. Only 80 long
calls are attempted over a four week interval, of which perhaps 40 would not be
rejected or cleared due to Dublin - London Level 2 problems. Although this is not
a very representative sample on which to base a conclusion, the graph of failures
of long calls due to "LIB NC" does indicate a greater susceptibility to clearance
due to network faults (as compared to short calls).

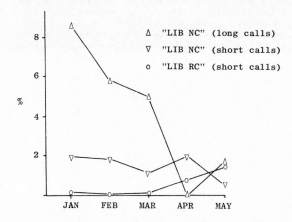

FIGURE 9. TRENDS IN NETWORK FAULTS

## 6. CONCLUSIONS

In our foregoing analysis we have not always included figures for traffic to Ispra as these would obscure the behaviour of the actual network. Based on the use of the echo facilities at the nodes we can make the following three main conclusions:

(i)   The network generally behaves well and consistently, and the trends in its performance are for the better.

(ii)  However, the criteria of 90% of packet transit delays being less than some 800 msecs, and the average delays being some 700 msecs, for an access link of 2400 bps, are not met (See ref. 3, Chapter 5, Page 8). The figures we find, using the Rome node for echoing, are some 1600 msecs and 900 msecs respectively.

(iii) The reason for the failure noted in (ii) above is essentially the problems on the local acess links. If retransmissions due to local line quality were excluded, the design criteria would be met comfortably.

The strength of the network is that of its weakest link.

Our thanks are due to the National Board for Science and Technology (Dublin) and the staff of DG XIII of the European Economic Commission for granting permission to present this paper. The views expressed are, of course, our own.

## References

1.  "Networking Experience at Trinity College Dublin", Alton et al, COMNET '81 IFIP, Budapest.

2.  "The Design of a Real Time Operating System for a Minicomputer. Part I", D. Jennings and W.F.C. Purser, Software Practice and Experience, Vol. 5 147-167 (1975).

3.  Euronet Technical User's Guide.

Performance of Data Communication Systems
and their Applications, G. Pujolle (ed.)
© North-Holland Publishing Company, 1981

# MODÈLE ANALYTIQUE D'OPTIMISATION DE LA STRUCTURE DU SYSTÈME RÉGIONAL DE TRANSMISSION DE DONNÉES

Paraskeva T. Bodourova
Todorka Hr. Kadreva

Institut supérieur de mécanique
appliquée et d'électotechnique
Varna
Bulgarie

Dans cet article les auteurs présentent un modèle
analytique d'optimisation de la structure du réseau
de transmission de données. L'optimisation s'effectue
d'une mahière itérative par minimisation de la valeur de la fonction de but, ayant en vue l'influence
des divers paramètres. L'édification du réseau
d'après l'algorithme décrit est effectuée tant en
réalisant les connections les plus fiables entre les
noeuds de communication à un prix de revient le plus
bas possible du système.

Les systèmes régionaux de transmission de données sont des éléments
spécifiques du Système unifié d'information social /SUIS/ qui est
en voie d'édification dans la République populaire de Bulgarie. Le
SUIS est un système d'information national général automatisé pour
la collecte, traitement et la conservation de l'information de la
gestion, la planification et le compte-rendu du développement social et économique du pays. C'est pourquoi les systèmes régionaux
de transmission des données /SRTD/ ont à accomplir des fonctions
reliées avec la collecte automatique, le traitement et la conservation de différentes sortes d'information. Ils réalisent un traitement à distance de l'information et la liaison des abonnés de SRTD
entre eux et au moyen du réseau des centres d'informatique avec
tous les autres abonnés du SUIS. Le SRTD représente un ensemble de
postes d'abonnés, lignes de communication, des noeuds de commutation et des centres d'informatique - tous pris avec leurs caractéristiques et leurs relations mutuelles. Pour servir le mieux les
abonnés du SRTD il est nécessaire d'assurer:
— un traitement du message dans le centre d'informatique
respectif, tout en observant le temps prévu de réponse et de réac-
tion du système;
— une vitesse définie de transmission de l'information
dans tous les postes de la ligne;
— une vraisemblance nécessaire de l'information obtenue et
une fiabilité du SRTD.

Au moment d'étude et de préparation du SRTD on a en vue l'exigence
assurant le minimum de dépenses pour la construction et l'exploitation du système.

La réalisation des exigences énumerée ci-dessus est obtenue par:
1. Une sélection correcte du genre de la liaison, de la
forme de l'information et la manière de la fourniture des messages.
2. Un choix d'un appareillage convenable de commutation et

de multiplage et d'un système pour leur commande lors de leur utilisation maximale et leur integration.
        3. Création d'une structure optimale du réseau.
        4. Mise au point d'algorithmes optimales de gestion et
d'entretien du réseau.

Par les recherches analytiques accomplies des courants d'information dans les SRTD /1/ et tout les considérant comme système de
service de masse, on donne une idée exacte de leur structure par un
graphe arborescent hiérarchique sans cycle. La structure du SRTD
sous son aspect général est démontré à la figure 1.

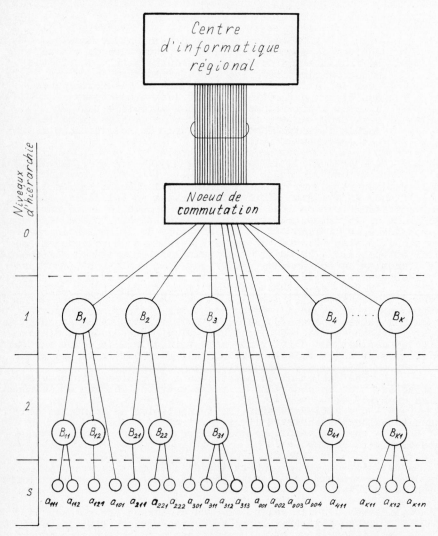

Figure 1
Structure d'un système régional de transmission de données

L'élaboration d'une structure optimale du SRTD, tout en prenant en
considération l'interaction entre les différents éléments du système et ses particularités, est un problème complexe multiextrémal.
A cause de la complexité lors de la résolution de tels problèmes
au moment de l'élaboration de systèmes pareils on prend généralement en considération l'un des paramètres d'évaluation de l'optima-
lité, lequel est compté dans la période de la mise à l'étude et il
est prévu en même temps lors du développement du système une période définie de temps. Le plus souvent ce paramètre est la valeur
du système.

Comme pour les conditions concrètes il n'y a pas encore suffisam-
ment d'expérience dans la mise à l'étude et l'élaboration des
réseaux de transmission de données, nous proposons ci-dessous un
mode opératoire d'optimisation de la structure des SRTD, qui peut
être utilisé avec succes lors de l'élaboration de pareils réseaux.

## DESCRIPTION DE LA MÉTHODOLOGIE D'OPTIMISATION DES SRTD

La méthodologie a été élaborée après avoir accepté quelques conditions restrictives et les définitions suivantes:
    1. Tout abonné n'est lié qu'avec un seul noeud de commuta-
tion /NC/, indépendamment de son niveau d'hiérarchie.
    2. Les liaisons de chaque abonné avec un ordinateur ne se
réalisent que durant le temps de transmission /réception/ de l'information par les lignes de commutation.
    3. Seul le noeud auquel est relié au moins un abonné ou
un noeud de commutation d'un niveau d'hiérarchie inférieur est
accepté comme un noeud de commutation.
    4. Les pannes se produisant dans les différentes parties
du réseau sont indépendantes.
    5. On accepte comme une ligne d'abonnés d'une longueur
jusque 10 km la ligne de cables du réseau urbain téléphonique. Pour
une ligne d'abonnés dont la longueur dépasse 10 km on adopte le
canal téléphonique.
    6. Les faisseaux de canaux entre les noeuds de commutation
et entre les abonnés et les NC sont définis à la base de 1% de
perte d'appel sur eux.
    7. La manière de connection entre les NC dans le réseau
doit être réalisé de façon qu'il puisse assurer le degré donné à
l'avance de fiabilité entre tous les deux noeuds en lui et entre
les NC et le noeud de commutation du niveau zéro de la hiérarchie
– $c1_{ij} < c1_{ij_{donné}}$.

Pour la définition du critère de fiabilité de la structure, reliant
les NC entre eux et avec un ordinateur on prend en considération
les pertes moyennes provoquées par les refus sur les lignes et
l'appareillage de canaux.
    8. Au cause de la plus grande valeur des aménagements de
ligne il est nécessaire de créer le réseau relié le plus court
entre les NC.

L'optimisation de la structure se fait par le contrôle de toutes
les combinaisons possibles de connection des NC et le choix d'une
telle structure, où la valeur du système est minimale avec une garantie de la connection la plus fiable possible entre les NC et le
centre zéro quand les parcours entre eux sont les plus courts.

La fonction de but est exprimée par l'expression:

$$F = min\left[\sum_{k \in M}\sum_{i \in X} w_{ik} c_{ik} b_{ik} + \sum_{k \in M} S_k u_k + S_{NC(0)} + \sum_{f,g \in M} z_{fg} c_{fg}\right] \quad [1]$$

$X = \overline{1,n}$ – ensemble des abonnés du système
$M = \overline{1,m}$ – ensemble des postes qui peuvent être des noeuds
         de commutation $M \subseteq X$

Le système a au moins un NC. Par le numéro 1 est marqué le poste
où se trouve un NC à un niveau égal à zéro, relié au centre d'in-
informatique.

$w_{ik} = \begin{cases} 1 - \text{si l'abonné } i \in X \text{ est branché au } k^{-i\text{ème}} \text{ NC} \\ 0 - \text{si l'abonné } i \in X \text{ n'est pas branché au } k^{-i\text{ème}} \text{ NC} \end{cases}$

$c_{ik}$ – valeur des dépenses pour un seul canal /ligne/ entre
      le $i^{-i\text{ème}}$ abonné et le $k^{-i\text{ème}}$ NC. La valeur comprend
      les dépenses de capital pour la création de la liaison
      et les dépenses annuelles d'exploitation.

$b_{ik}$ – nombre des canaux nécessaires entre le $i^{-i\text{ème}}$ et le
      $k^{-i\text{ème}}$ NC.

$S_k$ – valeur des dépenses pour la création et l'exploitation
      d'une année du $k^{-i\text{ème}}$ NC.

$u_k = \begin{cases} 1 - \text{si le } k^{-i\text{ème}} \text{ poste se forme comme un NC} \\ 0 - \text{dans le cas contraire} \end{cases}$

$S_{NC(0)}$ – valeur d'un NC de niveau nul /zéro/, par lequel
      on établit la liaison avec un ordinateur

$z_{fg}$ – nombre de canaux entre le $f^{-i\text{ème}}$ et le $g^{-i\text{ème}}$ NC

$c_{fg}$ – valeur des dépenses pour un canal unique entre le
      $f^{-i\text{ème}}$ et le $g^{-i\text{ème}}$ NC.

Comme données de sortie on se sert:
     – d'un nombre des abonnés dans le système – n
     – d'un nombre des endroits qui peuvent se former comme un
NC dans le système – m
     – d'une matrice des distances entre les noeuds de commuta-
tion possibles $L = \|l_{fg}\|$
     – d'une matrice des probabilités de fiabilité de la ligne
entre le NC – C1 $= \|c1_{fg}\|$. Chaque élément de C1 est égal à 1 - $K_p$.
$K_p$ est défini par la méthodologie décrite dans /2/, où $K_p$ représente la probabilité du bon état de fonctionnement de la ligne en
ce moment.
     – d'une matrice des valeurs pour la réalisation d'une liai-
son entre les abonnés et le système C $= \|c_{ij}\|$. Dans la valeur $c_{ij}$
entre $i^{-i\text{ème}}$ et $j^{-i\text{ème}}$ abonné du SRTD sont compris les investissements pour la création de la liaison et les dépenses annuelles d'
exploitation. Dans la matrice C prennent part également les éléments de l'ensemble M.
     – d'une valeur du noeud de commutation $C_{NC}$, prise comme $c_{ij}$.

L'algorithme général de la méthodologie pour une optimisation des
SRTD et le programme développé pour les ordinateurs comprennent les
moments fondamentaux suivants:
       1. Introduction des données d'entrée: M,N,NC, $\|c_{ij}\|$, $\|c1_{fg}\|$,
$\|l_{fg}\|$

2. Calcul de la valeur du réseau radial, construit uniquement avec le NC nul.

3. La création successive de toutes les combinaisons de structure des SRTD avec un nombre différent de NC, commençant par les combinaisons $C_m^{(m)}$, $C_m^{(m-1)}$,.....$C_m^{(2)}$. Les numéros compris dans la combinaison consécutive du NC sont exclus du massif $c_{ij}$ jusqu'à la fin de l'itération.

4. On réalise la connection des abonnés avec un NC correspondant d'après la valeur minimale de la liaison tout en observant la condition:

$$\sum_{k=1}^{m} w_{ik} = 1 \qquad i = 1,2,.....,n$$

Dans l'algorithme on a prévu une possibilité d'optimisation de structure où l'on peut interdire des liaisons entre des NC déterminés.

5. Pour la construction d'une structure optimale de fiabilité un processus de n-étape est mis à l'exécution, sans cycles et sur l'algorithme /3/. A chaque pas du fragment on adjoint un des points restés "i" et à ce point on attribue la valeur $c_i$ égale aux pertes moyennes des refus sur la ligne entre le i-ième point et le point O, pourtant $c_0 = 0$. Sous un fragment on entend le sousensemble de postes, y compris le poste O, de manière que tous les postes soient reliés entre eux par des liaisons directes formant une structure sans cycles. Les pertes et les refus sur la ligne entre un poste isolé jusqu'au fragment "k" se déterminent par:

$$\mathcal{G}_{jk} = \mathcal{G}_{jk} + c_k$$

où $\mathcal{G}_{jk}$ – des pertes des refus sur la ligne jusqu'au poste O, du j-ième poste associé au k-ième fragment

$\mathcal{G}_{jk}$ – des pertes des refus sur la ligne entre j-ième poste et le k-ième fragment

$c_k$ – valeur des pertes des refus sur la ligne entre le k-ième fragment et le poste zéro.

A la différence de la méthode de R.K.Prim le fragment comprend à tout prix le pôle O. Au premier pas de l'algorithme avec le poste O est relié ce poste "k", pour lequel $\mathcal{G}_{k0}=$ min. Au chacun des pas suivants vers le fragment déjà crée est associé ce poste "j", pour lequel $\mathcal{G}_{jk} = $ min. Pour $q_{ij}$ on accepte les pertes moyennes, provoquées par les refus sur la ligne entre le i-ième et j-ième poste et les $q_{ii}$ sont les pertes moyennes des refus de l'appareillage au i-ième poste. Cet algorithme est efficace, car il permet de construire, sans calculs répétés, la structure la plus fiable.

6. Pour la chaîne de connection des NC obtenue suivant le point № 5 on détermine le nombre des canaux dans le système à un pourcentage donné de pertes de rappel. La détermination du nombre nécrssaire de canaux, reliant les abonnés au NC respectif et entre les NC s'effectue à la base de l'intensité du traffic. Les analyses réalisées du traffic des abonnés /4/ nous nous font accepter une intensité moyenne du traffic d'un abonné 0,25 Erl. Le flux de l'information entrant sur les canaux est accepté comme le flux de Poisson.

7. On calcule la valeur de la fonction de but pour la

combinaison correspondante de NC d'après l'expression /1/. Un contrôle logique est effectué pour voir si toutes les combinaisons de
connection de NC sont épuisées.

    8. Les résultats définitifs sont imprimés pour la combinai-
son où une valeur minimale de la fonction de but est réalisée par
la connection fiable du NC avec le NC nul.

La méthodologie et le programme des ordinateurs pour l'optimisation
de la structure de SRTD sont expérimentés dans les conditions concrètes du département de Varna. La résolution du problème est obtenue en 40 minutes sur un ordinateur du type 1020 du système
unifié. Les données pour la matrice d'entrée $\| c_{i,j} \|$ sont conformes au
"Pronostic pour un développement scientifique et technique des télécommunications et la nessecité de communications". Pour la détermination des éléments de la matrice C1 on s'est servi des données
de fiabilité des liaisons entre les noeuds de commutation du système /5/. L'exemple comprend 66 abonnés du SRTD.

Grâce à la solution du problème on obtient une structure optimale
du SRTD considéré, le nombre nécessaire de canaux entre les noeuds
de commutation, la répartition des abonnés vers les différents NC
et la valeur du système total. La structure obtenue du SRTD concret
est démontré à la figure 2.

La méthodologie proposée permet, lorsque sont donnés les ensembles
d'abonnées et des NC, les matrices $c_{i,j}$, L, C1 et la valeur du NC,
de déterminer la structure optimale de SRTD à une valeur minimale
de la fonction de but et la connection la plus fiable des noeuds de
commutation avec le NC zéro sans limitation de leur nombre. L'optimisation s'effectue par itération au moyen de la minimisation de la
fonction de but tout en cherchant les voies les plus courtes entre
les NC et le NC zéro. On fait une vérification des combinaisons de
connection possibles des NC.

La méthodologie est développée comme un programme total pour un ordinateur. Elle peut être utilisée par les spécialistes comme un
moyen pratique commode lors de l'élaboration de projets des systèmes
pareils.

BIBLIOGRAPHIE

[1] Bodourova P.T., Petrichka N.T., Etude et analyse de la liaison
    entre les flux d'information et la structure du système régio-
    nal de télétraitement dans le district de Varna, dans Recueil
    de rapports de la III-ième conférence jubilaire scientifique
    "Nouveautés dans la radioelectronique", (Varna, 1975).

[2] Swarzman V.O., Mikhalev D.G., Calcul des caractéristiques de
    fiabilité des chaînes de transmission des données ("Sviaz",
    Moscou, 1975).

[3] Kelmans A.K., Mamikonov A.G., Sur la constructure des struc-
    tures de transmission de l'information, optimales en fiabilité,
    "Avtomatika i télémechanika" tome XXV, № 2 (1964) 207-212.

[4] Rapport technique économique sur le thème 8.2 "Etude des com-
    munications de TBRVIC – Varna avec les terminaux des usines du
    complexe industriel de Devnia" – NCESSI-Varna, 1975.

[5] Kadréva T.H., Bodourova P.T. – Détermination de la fiabilité de
    certaines orientations fondamentales dans le réseau de télé-

communication du district de Varna, destinées de transmission de données, dans Recueil de rapports de la session du Collège naval supérieur VNVMU "N.I.Vaptsarov", (Varna, 1977).

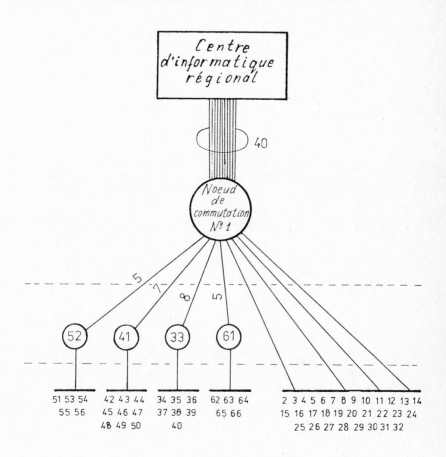

56 – numéro de l'abonné dans l'ensemble d'abonnés du système
5 – le nombre nécessaire de canaux entre les noeuds de commutation

Figure 2
Structure de système régional de télétraitement dans le structure de Varna

Performance of Data Communication Systems
and their Applications, G. Pujolle (ed.)
© North-Holland Publishing Company, 1981

DEADLINE SCHEDULING IN PACKET SWITCHING SYSTEMS WITH DELAY
- ADVANTAGES AND CONSTRAINTS -

Joachim Majus

Deutsche Forschungs- und Versuchsanstalt
für Luft- und Raumfahrt e.V.
Linder Höhe
5000 Köln 90
Federal Republic of Germany

Transmission time is a more and more important requirement
to data communication systems. In data processing systems
deadline oriented scheduling methods are proven to be suitable for achieving desired maximum flow times. Deadline
oriented criteria are discussed with respect to the general
objective of minimizing "bad" cases. Task models with well
known and with recently gained results for deadline-oriented
scheduling methods are described. Specific data communication processes are investigated as to that models, and the
limitations of the known scheduling methods are discussed.

INTRODUCTION:

As much as data communication systems become more and more flexible
the importance of the performance criterion 'transmission time' increases. Time critical behaviour occurs e.g. in satellite systems /5/
and in optical systems /13/. Applied to packet switching systems,
this behaviour can be influenced by priority driven resource allocation. Assigning due-dates or deadlines to the packages and messages
is a tool to achieve a desired transmission time performance.
In the field of data processing and computer performance the advantages of deadline oriented scheduling methods are well known with
respect to the objective of meeting desired maximum flow times
(allowances) for jobs and tasks (/15/, /14/, /10/). On the other
hand, priority driven assignement methods in multiple access communication systems have been implemented. Consequently to various
application situations, models of different complexity are to be
investigated. Though, scheduling methods for the discussed models are
known to be optimum with respect to a specific criterion, they cannot
be applied, in some cases, for the lack of necessary information
esp. on the individual service length (i.e. total transmission
time) of a task.
Constraints ot the applications are discussed.

DEADLINE ORIENTED CRITERIA AND SCHEDULING METHODS:

Assigning desired maximum flow time $D_i$ called 'allowance' /3/ to
task i (transmission task or processing task) gives with its arrival
time $t_{Ai}$ the deadline or due-date $t_{Di} = t_{Ai} + D_i$.
The term 'Deadline' does not necessarily imply the 'hard' deadline,
that must not be overrun in any case. The lateness $L_i$ of a task
measures, how a deadline is met: $L_i = t_{Di} - t_{Ci}$, with the

completion time $t_{Ci}$. Lateness values greater than zero are described by 'Tardiness' $T_i = \max\{0, L_i\}$.
The behaviour of a number of tasks to their deadlines can be
optimized by

1.  minimizing the average lateness $\bar{L}$,
2.  minimizing the maximum lateness $L_{max}$,
3.  minimizing the number or fraction of late tasks $n_L$ ($n_L/n$),
4.  minimizing the average tardiness of the late task $\bar{T}^+$.

Of course, optimizing one of these criteria leads to a worse performance of some of the others. To refer to Kleinrock /9/ you 'have to
borrow from Peter to pay Paul'. It is known from the literature, e.g.
/12/, that minimizing the average lateness is achieved, when the
average flow time is minimized as well, hence, when the throughput
is maximized. This effect corresponds to a smaller number of late
tasks, too, but is payed by a greater maximum lateness (see figure 1).

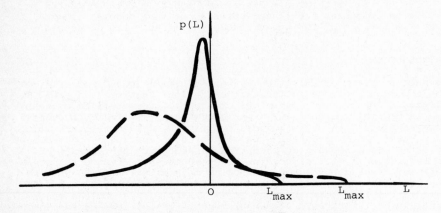

Figure 1:   Lateness Distribution Density with Respect to
            Minimization of Mean and Maximum Lateness.

On the other hand, minimizing the maximum lateness results in a
greater fraction of late tasks and increases the average lateness.
Growing workload, of course, increases the fraction of late tasks
more, when the maximum lateness is minimized, than by minimizing the
mean lateness. Under heavy load a situation could occur, where
almost all tasks are slightly late but no task has a great amount of
lateness, if the maximum is minimized, whereas there are a lot of
tasks in time, but some are intolerable late, if under the same
traffic situation the average lateness is minimized (see figure 2).

The objective of allocating the resource as equitable as possible
gives preference to those methods, which lead to a small decrease in
performance of all tasks rather than to a good average performance
but with a few tasks, suffering from far worse performance. Therefore, minimization of maximum lateness is selected for the primary
criterion of deadline scheduling.

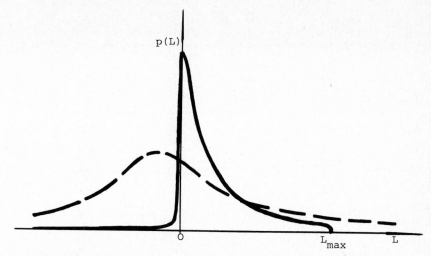

<u>Figure 2</u>:     Lateness Distribution Density by Minimizing <u>Mean</u> or
              <u>Maximum</u> Lateness under Heavy Load Conditions.


As maximum lateness can be investigated in finite independent periods
as in deterministic problems or in stochastic problems with only
finite busy periods, we have the following analogy for the stochastic
cases /3/:
Let P(L) be the probability distribution of L with values
f = P(L), $0 \leq f \leq 1$,
then the 'lateness fractile' is that lateness value, which is not
exceeded with probability f = P(L). Minimizing all lateness fractile
values within an interval $[f^*,1]$, $f^* < 1$, is achieved, when maximum
lateness is minimized in any independent observation period /14/.

Three basic deadline oriented scheduling methods are under discussion:
- Shortest Deadline First (SDF),
- Shortest Remaining Slack Time First (SRSF), and
- Delay Dependent Priority Rule (DDP).

SDF or 'due-date rule' selects the task with the minimum deadline
where deadline is the desired maximum <u>finishing</u> time. SRSF selects
the task with the minimum remaining slack time, where the remaining
slack time is the period from the instant of investigation left to
the <u>start time</u> for service necessary to meet the deadline. That rule
is identical to the so called dynamic priority rule /6/.
DDP applied to deadline scheduling assigns a priority to any task
that depends on the ratio of its total allowance to its momentary
flow time (/9/, /2/, /10/). Thus, any task enters with minimum priority "0" and at its deadline reaches the priority "1", becoming late
its priority is further increasing.

For any of these rules preemption of a lower priority task by a
higher priority task may be allowed or excluded. Preemption is
subsequently considered of the type 'resume repeat' /3/ such as
causing no overhead to the system or to the tasks. But, for SRSF,
preemption includes the danger of 'processor thrashing'. Fore,
whenever one of two or more tasks with equal (minimum) remaining
slack time is selected for service, the remaining slack time of the
waiting task(s) instantaneously becomes the new minimum, requiring
an immediate interrupt of the just selected task, and so on. Thus,
some limitation to the preemption rule must be provided for.


DEADLINE SCHEDULING TO MINIMIZE THE MAXIMUM LATENESS IN STOCHASTIC
AND DETERMINISTIC CASES:


The investigation of stochastic models suffers from problem complexity, whereas some of the results known for deterministic problems
can be transferred to stochastic cases. Immediate results within the
field of stochastic analysis are reported in /14/:
In a one machine model with discrete time steps the due-date rule
with respect to the latest start-time, and thus, identically SRSF
minimizes the lateness fractile L(f), when f tends to 1. Geometrically distributed interarrival times and service times are assumed,
and simulations lead to the same result for Poisson arrivals and
exponentially distributed service times /6/.

The proof for the case of preemptive SRSF with arbitrary interarrival-
time and service time distributions that lead to finite busy periods,
has recently been carried over to the stochastic situation from the
corresponding deterministic results /10/. For deterministic cases
with a finite number of tasks, but arbitrary arrival times, both
preemptive SDF /6/ and preemptive SRSF /10/ have been proven to
minimize the maximum lateness. Thus, we have preemptive SDF being
optimum at stochastic cases with finite busy periods, too. The
calculation for the maximum lateness in a single server model under
SDF is given in the annex.

In the field of deterministic cases we can introduce a second server
into the model, which is cyclically connected to the initial server,
but with a different behaviour:  This server is of the "non-bottle-
neck" type; this is achieved by allowing more equal parallel
machines than tasks are ever simultaneously present at that server
(figure 3). No queue can occur. The service time of a task at this
server can e.g. be interpreted as an independent delay. (For convenience, new tasks arrive only at the first server with limited
capacity and also leave only from that server.)

For deterministic cases of this model, the minimization of maximum
lateness is achieved also by preemptive SRSF, but cannot be guaranteed by preemptive SDF, as is easily demonstrated by counter-
examples /10/. This result holds true for any stochastic case with
finite busy periods by virtue of the above mentioned technique.

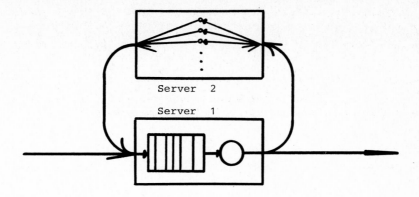

<u>Figure 3:</u>   Open Cyclic 2-Server-System with an Infinite 2nd Server

APPLICATION OF DEADLINE SCHEDULING IN DATA COMMUNICATION SYSTEMS:

The Single Server Problem:   A Packet Switching Link without Acknowledgement:

Satellite links have a transmission delay of about 250 ms caused by a round-trip distance of 2 * 36.000 km. Applied to a packet switching system with an e.g. HDLC-like acknowledgement method, the retransmission delay from the end of the first transmission to the reception of the rejection, which initiates the retransmission, is approx. 0.5 s /5/. In many cases, this problem can almost be prevented by replacing the acknowledgement precedure by a foreward error correction method, which doesn't leave more errors uncorrected than the previous check would leave undetected. For a satellite link with a fairly low initial bit error rate the foreward error correction coding requires only a tolerable part of the channel bandwith /4/. But in many cases, e.g. in the 30/20 GHz region, the initial bit error rate changes drastically. Therefore, we have to investigate both the foreward error correction case described in this section and the acknowledgement case dealt with in the subsequent section. The very small number of still unacceptable packages, e.g. due to errors elsewhere, shall be neglected for this discussion.

To such a packet switching link without acknowledgements SDF and SRSF can both be applied, since it represents the single server case of the model. Due to the far simpler algorithm for SDF, we shall restrict ourselves to that scheduling rule. One of the features of preemptive SDF is exhibited by the fact, that the minimization of the maximum lateness is achieved even, when the maximum desired flow times and the derived deadlines are independent from the individual service times. Thus, we can introduce priority classes, which allocate the shortest allowances to the most time critical packages such as voice packets or network commands. (This is not sufficient for packets to be retransmitted, as shown in the subsequent section.)

The preemption necessary to achieve the desired optimum performance, in general, causes an additional effort, that does not offset the performance decrease due to missing the preemptions, because a preemption requirement occurs only, when a packet arrives with a shorter deadline than that of the packet just being transmitted, which itself has the shortest deadline of all packets in the system. The probability of missing a preemption $P_m$ decreases with the waiting time $W_i$ of the task in service, and decreases as well if that task belongs to a high priority class, but increases with its service time $X_i$:

$$P_m = X_i \sum_{D=D_{min}}^{D_i - W_i} \lambda_D, \text{ with } \lambda_D \text{ the arrival rate of tasks with the allowance D.}$$

The more the workload consists of more and shorter packages, the smaller is the error by missing preemptions. A trade-off between package length and overhead has yet to be done.

The Open Cyclic 2-Server Model with 2nd Infinite Server: Packet Switching With Selective Acknowledgement:

Assuming a satellite link as described in the previous section, an acknowledgement method can be used that rejects a single package, whenever an incorrect package is detected /11/. It is assumed that due to the limited transmission capacity in forward direction, the backward transmission capacity exceeds always the required rejections and no waiting time will occur to the transmission of the rejections. This method causes transmission tasks, which, with random numbers of retransmission $n_r$, consists of $n_r + 1$ transmission bursts interrupted by $n_r$ delay bursts caused by transmitting the rejections. Let $P_n$ be the probability, that any task must be retransmitted n times (e.g. refer to /5/,/8/), then the rate of tasks, which have to be transmitted $n_r$ times, is

$\lambda_n = \lambda * P_n$, where $\lambda$ is the total arrival rate.

But, since one cannot predict the number of necessary retransmissions for a specific task i, the overall transmission time

$X_i = T_i + n_r(T_i + A_i)$, $T_i$ the initial transmission time and $A_i$ the rejection delay

is unknown (figure 4). The deadline assigned to that transmission task is independent of the overall transmission time.

$$\text{Server} \quad 1 \mid 2 \mid 1 \mid 2 \mid 1 \mid ... \mid 2 \mid 1 \mid$$

$$T_{i0} \mid A_{i1} \mid T_{i1} \mid A_{i2} \mid T_{i2} \mid ... \mid A_{in_i} \mid T_{in_i} \mid$$

Figure 4:  An Example Transmission Task with $n_i$ Retransmissions

Applying the cyclic model introduced in section 3, we don't have any other rule but SRSF to minimize the maximum lateness. But, in order to apply SRSF the knowledge of the required service times, in this case the overall transmission times, is necessary. This knowledge, however, is not available using link control procedures with additional retransmission capability such as described above.

It appears to be impossible to treat the probabilistic model of deadline oriented scheduling servers in a cyclic model by the hitherto known analysis methods. Realistic results on the lateness performance of SDF and DDP applied to this model can todate be achieved by simulations or measurements of real world applications only. For a simple workload model with poisson arrival, and exponentially distributed service times, and highly correlated exponential allowances a simulation has shown SDF to be optimum among the three scheduling rules mentioned before with respect to minimization of maximum lateness /10/ (figure 5). (SRSF in this simulation is restricted with respect to preemption).


CONCLUSION

In order to achieve an as equitable delay performance as possible Shortest Deadline First should be applied to package switching channels with foreward error correction to minimize the maximum lateness. This scheduling method can be used too for channels with a large number of retransmissions and yields very good, but not optimum results.

Monitoring the lateness allows for admission control, such that a desired maximum lateness value can be met, e.g. $L_{max} = 0$.
Preemption - though necessary in theory for optimality - cannot be applied here, but a short maximum packet length can partially offset the degradation of performance caused by omitted preemptions.

Performance figures for real world situations are more easily derived from in-situ measurements or simulations than from the very restrictive models that can be treated analytically. But, knowing that a specific scheduling method (SDF) has been proved to be the best possible, when uniform delays are desired, suggests as a logical step the design of experiment configurations applying SDF.


REFERENCES:

/ 1/    Calabrese, D., Fischer, M., Hoiem, B. and Kaiser, E., Modelling a Voice Network with Preemption,IEEE Transactions on Comm. COM-28 (1980) 22-26.

/ 2/    Chamberlin, D. D., Schlaeppi, H. P. and Wladawsky, I., Experimental Study of Deadline Scheduling for Interactive Systems, IBM Journal Res. Dev. (May 1973) 263-269.

/ 3/    Conway, R. W., Maxwell, W. L. and Miller, L. W., Theory of Scheduling (Addison-Wesley, London, 1967).

/ 4/    Eliece, R. J., The Theory of Information and Coding (Addison-Wesley, London, 1977).

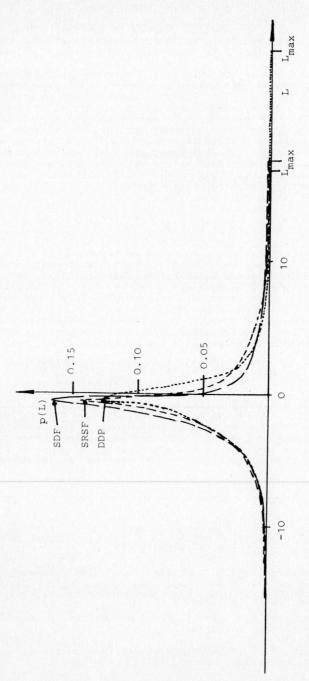

Figure 5:   Lateness Distribution in an Open Cyclic 2-Server System with an Infinite 2nd Server
($\rho$ = 0.9, allowance = 4 * total service time, retransmission rate 1 - $\zeta$ = 0.15)

/ 5/    IBM, COMSAT, PTT France and DFVLR, Computer/Satellite
      Communications Experiment (COMSAT Labs., Clarksburg, Md.,1979).

/ 6/    Jackson, J. R., Waiting-Time Distributions for Queues with
      Dynamic Priorities, Naval Research Logistic Quarterly,
      9 (1962) 31-36.

/ 7/    Jakobs, I. M., Binder, R. and Hoversten, E.V., General Purpose
      Packet Satellite Networks, Proceedings of the IEEE, 66 (1978).

/ 8/    Kaul, A., Performance of High Level Data Link Control in
      Satellite Communications, Comsat Technical Review, 8 (1978),
      41 - 87.

/ 9/    Kleinrock, L., Queueing Systems, Vol. I & II. (John Wiley
      & Sons, London, 1975).

/10/    Majus, J., Deadline Scheduling bei Multiprogramming, (DFVLR,
      Köln, to be published 1981).

/11/    Pujolle, G. and Spaniol, P., The Virtual Subchannel Protocol
      for Satellite Link Communications, in: Schindler,S. and
      Schröder,J. (eds.), Kommunikation in verteilten Systemen,
      Proceedings (Springer-Verlag, Berlin, 1981).

/12/    Rinnooy Kan, A.H.G., Machine Scheduling Problems (Martinus
      Nijhoff, den Haag, 1976).

/13/    Sauer, A., Ein Mehrrechner-Netz mit verteilter Kommunikations-
      steuerung und optischem Bussystem, in: Schindler, S. and
      Schröder,J. (eds.), Kommunikation in verteilten Systemen,
      Proceedings (Springer-Verlag, Berlin, 1981).

/14/    Walke, B., Realzeitrechner-Modelle (R. Oldenbourg Verlag,
      München, 1978).

/15/    Zwass, V., Economically Effective Deadline Scheduling in Multi-
      programming Systems (University Microfilms International, Ann
      Arbor, 1975).

## ANNEX

FORMULA TO DETERMINE THE MAXIMUM LATENESS FOR SINGLE SERVER MODELS
WITH $L_{max} < \infty$ UNDER SDF:

From /10/ we have the result, that SDF minimizes the maximum lateness, whenever a finite maximum lateness occurs. Thus

(i)    $L_{max} = \lim_{f \to 1} (L_j(f))$    for all j.

From the definition of lateness we have

(ii)    $L_j = W_j - S_j$    and

(iii) $L_j(f) = [W_j - S_j](f) = W_j(f) - S_j$     for all j     (see <u>figure A1</u>).

From (i) and (iii) follows that

(iv) $L_{max} = \lim_{f \to 1} (L_x(f)) = \lim_{f \to 1} (W_x(f) - S_x) = \lim_{f \to 1} (W_x(f)) - S_x$,

where $W_x(f)$ represents the fractile of that waiting time distribution, which represents the urgency class x with the initial
urgency number $S_x = E\{S_j\}$ :

Thus, the maximum lateness under SDF discipline is the difference of
the maximum waiting time under FCFS and of the expected value of the
initial urgencies.

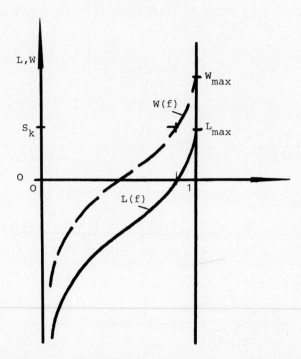

<u>Figure A1</u>:    Fractions of Lateness Distribution for a Waiting Time
                Distribution of Urgency Class k.

Performance of Data Communication Systems
and their Applications, G. Pujolle (ed.)
© North-Holland Publishing Company, 1981

MODELISATION PAR LES FILES D'ATTENTE
D'UN CONCENTRATEUR STATISTIQUE PARAMETRE

Odile MACCHI[*] et Jacqueline ZAMARLIK[**]

[*]LABORATOIRE DES SIGNAUX ET SYSTEMES, CNRS-ESE, Plateau du Moulon,
91190 - GIF SUR YVETTE, France.

[**]LABORATOIRE C.N.R.S., Structure de l'Information GR-22, Université PARIS VI,
4, Place Jussieu, 75005 - PARIS CEDEX.

RESUME :    Le concentrateur statistique reçoit des messages de termi-
            naux asynchrones et il regroupe ces messages en trames pour
            augmenter le nombre de ses entrées.
            Nous présentons et analysons un modèle orginal de concentra-
            teur décrit par deux niveaux de mémoires et dont le fonction-
            nement est lié à deux paramètres notés T et B.
            A chaque ligne d'arrivée nous associons une mémoire et avec
            la période T le concentrateur prélève des paquets de B ca-
            ractères dans chacune des mémoires d'entrée. Ainsi il cons-
            truit périodiquement une trame qu'il range dans la mémoire
            de sortie où elle est prête à être émise.
            L'étude du modèle est celle des files d'attente de l'entrée
            et de la sortie en fonction de la valeur des paramètres T
            et B. Cette analyse définit les conditions de stabilité du
            fonctionnement du concentrateur. Elle met aussi en évidence
            des critères de choix des paramètres T et B pour obtenir un
            temps d'attente minimum ou bien pour relier le plus grand
            nombre possible de terminaux.

0. PRESENTATION DU CONCENTRATEUR.

Un concentrateur est un système de transmission à plusieurs entrées, ce sont les
lignes à faible débit, et à une seule sortie, la ligne à grande vitesse.

Par les ligne basse vitesse il reçoit des terminaux asynchrones des messages séparés par des silences. Le concentrateur statistique regroupe ces paquets de caractères en trames et profite du silence de certains terminaux pour augmenter le nombre de ses entrées.

Nous définissons un modèle original de concentrateur, sa structure plus élaborée que
celle des concentrateurs usuels et ses paramètres de fonctionnement lui donnent une
grande souplesse d'adaptation aux divers objectifs des utilisateurs (attente minimum, nombre élevé de terminaux) et aux évolutions du trafic.

Au cours de ce texte nous décrivons et analysons notre modèle et pour deux exemples
nous précisons le choix des paramètres.

Le concentrateur regroupe les caractères émis par les terminaux, nous commençons
donc cette étude en définissant leur activité.

1. LES TERMINAUX.

Les terminaux émettent les caractères en mode asynchrone sur les lignes à faible
débit d bauds.

Chaque caractère comporte a bits d'information et m bits pour le START, le STOP et la parité, chaque caractère a donc b bits,

$$b = m + a .\tag{1}$$

Les terminaux envisagés émettent les caractères par paquets séparés par des silences; le nombre de caractères par paquet et la durée des silences suivent des lois de probabilité qui dépendent du type d'utilisation du terminal [1]. Nous décrivons un terminal par trois paramètres :

$N_C$, le nombre moyen de caractères par paquet,
$T_C$, la durée moyenne des silences,
$N$ , le nombre moyen de caractères émis par seconde.

Nous avons proposé plusieurs chaînes de Markov [2], [3] pour modéliser un terminal. Tous les modèles donnent une même expression de la probabilité d'activité $P_A$ d'un terminal, qui est la proportion de temps pendant lequel il émet des caractères

$$P_A = 1 - \frac{N}{N_c} T_c \quad \text{ou} \quad P_A = N \frac{b}{d} .\tag{2}$$

Cette probabilité d'activité, ou activité, s'exprime en fonction de N nombre moyen de caractères émis par seconde, de la longueur b d'un caractère et du débit d de la ligne.

## 2. LE MODELE DU CONCENTRATEUR.

Le rôle d'un concentrateur se décompose en trois fonctions :

- il reçoit les caractères
- il regroupe les caractères en trames
- il émet les trames.

Pour donner une très grande souplesse d'adaptation au concentrateur nous séparons nettement ces trois fonctions et de plus nous lions la fonction de regroupement des caractères à deux paramètres ajustables.

### 2.1. La description du modèle

Pour atteindre l'indépendance entre toutes les entrées d'une part et la sortie d'autre part, notre modèle a deux niveaux de mémoires-files d'attente; nous associons donc une mémoire à chaque ligne d'arrivée de caractères, et une mémoire à la ligne de sortie du concentrateur, figure 1.

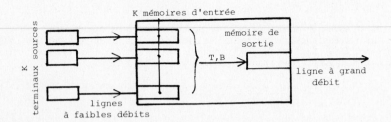

FIGURE 1 : Le modèle du concentrateur

Nous complétons ce modèle en ajoutant deux paramètres de fonctionnement noté T et B. Avec la période T, le concentrateur prélève dans chacune des mémoires d'entrée des paquets de B caractères.

Par ses deux paramètres ajustables et ses deux niveaux de file d'attente notre
concentrateur se différencie des modèles habituels schématisés par un seul niveau
de file d'attente.

Un concentrateur est souvent décrit par une seule file d'attente associée à la ligne à grande vitesse, comme le proposent W. CHU [4] et A. ECKBERG [5]; en arrivant
les messages sont rangés dans cette mémoire. D'autres auteurs comme M. EISENBERG
[6] et P.J. KUEHN [7], associent une mémoire-file d'attente à chaque ligne d'arrivée. Le concentrateur construit des trames, généralement de longueur constante,
en vidant cycliquement les mémoires d'entrée; la trame est émise immédiatement.
C'est un schéma analogue à celui-ci que propose E. GELENBE [8], pour analyser
l'attente dans un multiplexeur.

Pour préciser notre modèle et ses facultés d'adaptation, nous examinons successivement chacune des trois fonctions du concentrateur.

## 2.2. Le concentrateur reçoit les caractères.

La mémoire d'entrée, figure 2, est formée de deux registres à décalages; un premier registre reçoit en série les bits des caractères; quand le bit de STOP est
arrivé le caractère est complet, ses a bits d'information sont transmis en paral-
lèle au deuxième registre, la mémoire d'entrée; là le caractère est prêt à être
prélevé.

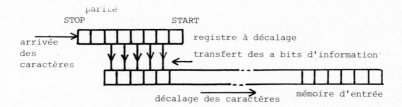

FIGURE 2 : La mémoire d'entrée.

A chaque période T, le concentrateur interroge chacune des mémoires d'entrée pour
prélever un paquet de B caractères. Deux cas sont alors possibles :

   a) la mémoire contient moins de B caractères, aucun n'est prélevé, ils res-
      tent tous en attente.

   b) la mémoire contient au moins B caractères, B sont prélevés, les autres
      restent en attente.

La mémoire d'entrée est une file d'attente.

## 2.3. Le concentrateur regroupe les caractères en trames.

Toutes les trames ont la même structure, deux fanions encadrent la zone d'information.

Pour notre modèle nous choisissons une trame dont la zone d'information a une
longueur aléatoire; cette zone est divisée en autant de tranches qu'il y a de
terminaux et une tranche est allouée à chaque terminal, figure 3. Une tranche a
deux longueurs possibles :

   - a B bits pour le prélèvement de B caractères,
   - e  bits pour le marqueur  de non prélèvement.

tranche du terminal

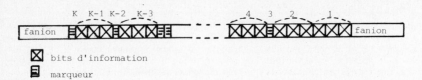

☒ bits d'information

▤ marqueur

FIGURE 3 : Une trame.

Nous notons k le nombre de terminaux reliés au concentrateur.

La longueur $L_k$ d'une trame correspondant à k prélèvements ($0 \leq k \leq K$) a pour expression

$$L_k = F + a B k + e(K-k) ,$$   (3)

où F est la longueur des fanions de la trame.

Périodiquement une trame est rangée dans la mémoire de sortie.

## 2.4. Le concentrateur émet les trames.

La mémoire de sortie du concentrateur comprend deux registres à décalages; le premier registre reçoit les trames à émettre, et le second relié à la ligne à grande vitesse contient la trame en cours d'émission, figure 4.

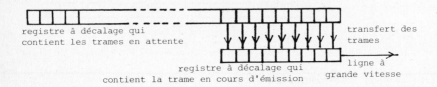

registre à décalage qui
contient les trames en attente

transfert des
trames

registre à décalage qui
contient la trame en cours d'émission

ligne à
grande vitesse

FIGURE 4 : La mémoire de sortie.

Quand une trame arrive dans la mémoire de sortie, deux situations sont possibles:

a) aucune trame n'est en cours d'émission, la mémoire est vide, la trame est émise immédiatement.

b) une trame est en cours d'émission, la mémoire est vide ou non, la trame reste en attente, à la suite de celles qui la précèdent.

La mémoire de sortie est une file d'attente.

Le temps d'émission $\tau_k$ d'une trame de longueur $L_k$ (3) est une grandeur aléatoire, définie par :

$$\tau_k = L_k/D ,$$   (4)

où D est le débit de la ligne de sortie du concentrateur.

Les trames de longueur aléaloire sont émises les unes à la suite des autres. Ainsi nous n'introduisons aucune contrainte dans le fonctionnement du système.

Nous étudions la stabilité du concentrateur; elle dépend de la stabilité des files d'attente de l'entrée et de la stabilité de la file d'attente de la mémoire de sortie.

## 3. LES MEMOIRES D'ENTREE DU CONCENTRATEUR.

Nous faisons plusieurs hypothèses concernant les mémoires d'entrée :

a) les K terminaux sont identiques et statistiquement indépendants,

b) les K mémoires d'entrée sont indépendantes les unes des autres,

c) la mémoire de sortie n'a aucune influence sur les mémoire d'entrée.

Les hypothèses b et c sont justifiées car les files sont de longueur illimitée et les paramètres T et B sont toujours choisis pour que les files d'attente d'entrée et de sortie soient dans un état stationnaire.

### 3.1. L'arrivée des caractères dans la file d'attente pendant une période.

Le fonctionnement du concentrateur est asynchrone de l'émission des terminaux.

Pendant la période T, il arrive au plus $J_c$ caractères dans une mémoire d'entrée,

$$J_c = 1 + \text{Partie entière } (\frac{Td - 1}{b}) . \tag{5}$$

Nous notons ($\Pi_j$, $j \in [0, J_c]$) les probabilités d'arrivée de j caractères au concentrateur. L'étude complète [2], des probabilités $\{\Pi_j\}$ montre que la distribution de Poisson généralement adoptée par les auteurs n'est pas réaliste dans tous les cas.

Au cours de cette étude nous dirons qu'entre deux prélèvement successifs :

- le nombre de clients qui arrivent pendant une période est indépendant du nombre de clients arrivés pendant les périodes antérieures.

- les probabilités $\{\Pi_j\}$ d'arrivée de j caractères sont indépendantes de la période envisagée.

Nous négligeons toute dépendance marginale.

### 3.2. Une file d'attente de l'entrée.

Chaque mémoire d'entrée est une file d'attente définie par :

- une capacité illimitée,
- les clients sont des caractères complets,
- les arrivées des clients pendant une période T suivent la distribution de probabilité $\{\Pi_j\}$,
- B clients sont servis simultanément,
- le temps de service est constant et égal à T,
- la discipline du service est premier arrivé, premier servi.

Pendant la période T, la mémoire reçoit au plus $J_c$ caractères, il paraît donc normal de choisir B inférieur ou égal à cette limite,

$$B \leq J_c . \tag{6}$$

Il est en effet inutile de vouloir prélever plus de caractères qu'il n'en arrive à chaque période.

### 3.3. Etude générale de la file d'attente.

Nous considérons les probabilités de présence $q_r$ de r clients dans la file; $q_r$

s'exprime en fonction des probabilités d'arrivée $\{\Pi_j\}$ des caractères et du nombre B de caractères prélevés. On a la relation

$$q_r = \sum_{j=0}^{J_c} \Pi_j \ q_{B+r-j} \ . \tag{7}$$

La transformée en z de la distribution $q_r$ a pour expression :

$$Q(z) = \frac{(z^B-1) \ \Pi(z)}{z^B - \Pi(z)} \ \sum_{r=0}^{B-1} q_r \ z^r \tag{8}$$

où $\Pi(z)$ est la transformée en z de la distribution $\{\Pi_j\}$.

La relation (8) ne permet pas de définir les B premières probabilités mais seulement les probabilités $q_B$, $q_{B+1}$, ... . En outre la transformée en z d'une distribution de probabilité doit satisfaire deux conditions :

$Q(1) = 1$
$Q(z)$ doit être une fonction holomorphe dans le domaine $|z| < 1$.

## Première condition.

Pour $z = 1$ la fonction $Q(z)$ est indéterminée d'après (8): on applique alors la règle de l'Hospital et la condition devient :

$$\frac{B \sum\limits_{r=0}^{B-1} q_r}{B - \Pi'(1)} = 1 \ . \tag{9}$$

Pour que $Q(z)$ existe il faut donc que

$$B - \Pi'(1) > 0 \ , \tag{10}$$

soit encore

$$B > \overline{n} \quad \text{ou} \quad B > NT. \tag{11}$$

Le nombre B de caractères prélevés doit être supérieur à $\overline{n}$, nombre moyen de caractères qui arrivent pendant une période T. Quand cette condition est réalisée, la relation (9) s'écrit :

$$\sum_{r=0}^{B-1} q_r = 1 - \frac{\overline{n}}{B} \ . \tag{12}$$

Par conséquent la probabilité p de prélèvement d'un paquet de B caractères vaut :

$$p = \frac{\overline{n}}{B} \quad \text{ou} \quad p = N \frac{T}{B} \ . \tag{13}$$

## Deuxième condition.

$Q(z)$ est une fonction holomorphe dans le disque $|z| < 1$ si les racines de module inférieur ou égal à 1 de son dénominateur, (degré $J_c$), sont aussi racines de son numérateur [9], [10]; comme elles ne peuvent être racines de $\Pi(z)$, elles sont racines de $(Z^B-1)$ ou de $\sum\limits_{r=0}^{B-1} q_r z^r$.

Le théorème de ROUCHE [11] donne le nombre de racines de module inférieur, égal ou supérieur à un. On démontre que ce théorème s'applique ici, seulement dans le cas où la première condition (11) est satisfaite. Ainsi le dénominateur a

- une racine égale à 1, racine de $(Z^B-1)$,

- (B-1) racines de module inférieur à 1, racines de $\sum\limits_{r=0}^{B-1} q_r z^r$ , $\tag{14}$

- $(J_c-B)$ racines de module supérieur à 1, notées $z_{B+1}, \ldots, z_{J_c}$.

On pose

$$D(z) = (z - z_{B+1}) \cdots (z - z_{J_c}) .$$ (15)

*Remarque 1* : $Z = -1$ est racine du dénominateur de $Q(z)$ seulement dans deux cas :

$$B \text{ pair avec } \pi(z) = \sum_{s=0}^{S} \pi_{2s} \, z^{2s} ,$$ (16)

$$B \text{ impair avec } \pi(z) = \sum_{s=0}^{S} \pi_{2s+1} \, z^{2s+1} .$$ (17)

*Remarque 2* : $|Z| = 1$ : une racine sur le cercle $|Z| = 1$. Pour traiter ce cas on peut prendre l'exemple de la racine $Z = i$.

Pour que $Z = i$ soit racine du dénominateur de $Q(z)$ il faut par exemple avoir $B=4$ et $\{\pi_j\} = \{\pi_0, 0, 0, 0, \pi_4, 0, 0, 0, \pi_8\}$; cette distribution très particulière ne correspond pas aux divers exemples d'émission de caractères que nous avons envisagés.

Les $(B-1)$ racines de module inférieur à un et la condition (12) déterminent les probabilités $q_0, q_1, \ldots, q_{B-1}$ de présence de $0,1, \ldots, B-1$ caractères dans la file d'attente.

Après simplification de l'expression (8), $Q(z)$ devient

$$Q(z) = -\frac{q_{B-1}}{\pi_{J_c}} \cdot \frac{\pi(z) \cdot \sum\limits_{r=o}^{B-1} z^r}{D(z)} .$$ (18)

Ainsi l'étude de la file d'attente de l'entrée définit la condition de stabilité de la file

$$NT < B$$ (19)

et montre comment les probabilités de présence des caractères dans la file dépendent du nombre B de caractères prélevés et de la période T. En particulier pour toute valeur de la période T,B sera choisi pour satisfaire la double inégalité

$$NT < B \leq 1 + \text{Partie Entière } [\frac{Td - 1}{b}] .$$ (20)

## 3.4. La longueur moyenne de la file d'attente.

Dans cette étude nous nous intéressons essentiellement à la longueur moyenne $\overline{n}_c$ de cette file.

Pour une activité fixée $P_A$ d'un terminal, nous traçons sur le graphique 1, les variations de la longueur moyenne de la file en fonction de la période T et pour plusieurs valeurs du paramètre B. Sur ce graphique nous indiquons $\mathcal{D}_B$ défini comme le domaine des valeurs possibles pour B,données par l'équation (20).

Pour une valeur fixée de B, les courbes $\overline{n}_c(T)$ sont semblables, elles sont la juxtaposition de deux zones :

. zone 1 : $\overline{n}_c$ croît linéairement en fonction de T

. zone 2 : $\overline{n}_c$ a une croissance parabolique douce puis très rapide quand la période T s'approche de la limite de stabilité.

La courbe $\overline{n}_c(T)$ présente un coude à la jonction de ces deux zones pour

$$T = b. \frac{B}{d} .$$ (21)

Tous les coudes des courbes $\overline{n}_c(T)$   sont sur la droite $\overset{\sim}{n}(T)$ d'équation

$$\overset{\sim}{n}(T) = (P_A + \frac{1}{2}) \frac{Td}{b} - \frac{1}{2} . \tag{22}$$

Cette droite traverse le domaine $\mathcal{D}_B$ (20).

Sur le graphique 1 nous remarquons que pour une valeur fixée de la période T, il existe une valeur $\overset{\sim}{B}$ de B, telle que la longueur moyenne de la file est minimum. Si pour chaque valeur de T, on choisit pour B la valeur optimale $\overset{\sim}{B}$, la longueur moyenne de la file d'attente est la juxtaposition des zones 1 rectilignes et des débuts des zones 2 paraboliques; cette courbe est voisine de la droite $\overset{\sim}{n}(T)$.

La possibilité de modifier la valeur de B que nous avons introduite dans notre modèle permet de remplacer la croissance parabolique de la longueur de la file par une croissance linéaire en fonction du temps. Par conséquent en augmentant la valeur de B on élimine les risques de débordement de la mémoire.

Sur le graphique 2, nous traçons $\overline{n}_c(T)$   pour une valeur plus élevée de l'activité du terminal.

L'étude détaillée de la mémoire d'entrée montre, comme les graphiques 1 et 2, que la valeur optimale $\overset{\sim}{B}$ de B doit être choisie en fonction de l'activité du terminal, conformément à la règle

$$\begin{cases} P_A \geq 0,5 \quad , \qquad \overset{\sim}{B} = J_c \quad , \\ P_A < 0,5 \quad , \qquad \overset{\sim}{B} = J_c - 1 \quad . \end{cases} \tag{23}$$

## 4. L'ETUDE DE LA MEMOIRE DE SORTIE.

A chaque période T, le concentrateur construit une trame et il la range dans la mémoire de sortie. Le temps d'émission d'une trame $\tau_k$ (4) est une grandeur aléatoire.

### 4.1. Le temps d'émission des trames.

Aux instants $t_1$, $t_2$, ..., $t_n$ arrivent les trames de 1, 2, ..., n formées de $k_1$, $k_2$, ..., $k_n$ paquets de caractères; leurs temps de transmission respectifs valent $\tau_{k_1}$, $\tau_{k_2}$, ..., $\tau_{k_n}$ .

Nous notons $I_{n,k}$ l'état de prélèvement de la mémoire de rang $k(1 \leq k \leq K)$ au $n$[ième] prélèvement, et

$$I_{n,k} = \begin{cases} 1 & \text{prélèvement (probabilité p)} \\ 0 & \text{pas de prélèvement} \end{cases} \tag{24}$$

Par suite :

$$k_n = I_{n,1} + I_{n,2} + \cdots + I_{n,K} . \tag{25}$$

Les paramètres T et B sont toujours choisis pour que le fonctionnement du concentrateur soit stable; en particulier les K mémoires d'entrée sont indépendantes les unes des autres; c'est à dire que pour $j_1$ et $j_2$ quelconques ($1 \leq j_1 \leq K$ et $1 \leq j_2 \leq K$ ) $I_{n,j_1}$ est indépendant de $I_{n,j_2}$.

Pour l'étude d'une mémoire d'entrée (cf. § 3.1) nous avons supposé que le nombre de caractères qui arrivent pendant une période était indépendant du nombre de caractères arrivés pendant les périodes précédentes, ainsi $I_{n,k}$ est indépendant de $I_{n',k}$ ($n > n'$).

De ces deux hypothèses il résulte que les temps de transmission $\tau_{k_1}$, ..., $\tau_{k_n}$ qui sont proportionnels à $k_1$, ..., $k_n$ sont indépendants les uns des autres.

Ainsi les temps de transmission des trames suivent la loi binomiale $\mathcal{B}$ (K,p).

## 4.2. La file d'attente de la mémoire de sortie.

La mémoire de sortie est une file d'attente dont

- la capacité est illimitée,
- les clients sont les trames,
- les clients arrivent à la période T,
- le temps de service est $\tau_k$,
- la discipline du service est premier arrivé, premier servi.

## 4.3. Etude de la file d'attente.

Sur la figure 5 nous donnons le diagramme de temps de cette file.

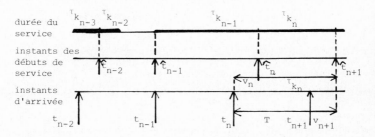

FIGURE 5 : Le diagramme de temps de la file.

Le temps d'attente $v_{n+1}$ de la $(n+1)^{\text{ème}}$ trame s'exprime en fonction du temps d'attente $v_n$ et du temps de transmission $\tau_n$ de la $n^{\text{ième}}$ trame. Lorsque la file est vide, l'attente est nulle.

$$v_{n+1} = \begin{cases} v_n + \tau_n - T & \text{file non vide,} \\ 0 & \text{file vide.} \end{cases} \tag{26}$$

Les probabilités des temps d'attente s'expriment en fonction des probabilités des temps de transmission des trames. La transformée en z de cette distribution de probabilité est, comme $Q(z)$ (8), le rapport de deux polynômes en z.

Cette transformée en z doit satisfaire les mêmes deux conditions

Première condition : pour $z = 1$ la transformée en z vaut un.

Cette condition est satisfaite quand $\overline{\tau}$, le temps moyen d'émission d'une trame est inférieur à la période T de prélèvement :

$$\overline{\tau} < T \tag{27}$$

et $\overline{\tau}$ est défini par l'expression

$$\overline{\tau} = \frac{F + eK + (aB - e)\ Kp}{D} \tag{28}$$

Deuxième condition : la transformée en z est une fonction holomorphe dans le disque $|z| < 1$.

Le théorème de ROUCHE [11] s'applique quand la condition (27) est vérifiée; il nous permet de définir toutes les probabilités de la distribution des temps d'attente, en suivant une méthode analogue à celle exposée au § 3.

### 4.4. Le temps moyen d'attente.

Le temps moyen d'attente $\overline{v}$ d'une trame dans la mémoire de sortie n'a pas une expression analytique simple, mais il est calculable numériquement.

Pour une nombre fixé K de terminaux nous étudions $\overline{v}$ en fonction de p, la probabilité de prélèvement, et en prenant T comme paramètre; sur le graphique 3, $\overline{v}$ est en coordonnées logarithmiques.

A période T constante, toutes les courbes $\overline{v}(p)$ sont semblables et se déduisent les unes des autres par translation. La fonction log $\overline{v}(p)$ croît rapidement pour les faibles valeurs de p; il y a ensuite un domaine de croissance moyenne, pratiquement linéaire; puis à cette plage succède une croissance très rapide quand p s'approche de la limite de stabilité définie par la condition (27).

Dans le domaine de croissance linéaire, le temps moyen d'attente a pour expression:

$$\log \overline{v} = - f(K) (T - \overline{\tau}) , \tag{29}$$

où l'on constate que f(K) est voisin de 1/2 pour K de l'ordre de 20.

Cette relation donne une évaluation du temps moyen d'attente qui est une fonction exponentiellement décroissante de $(T - \overline{\tau})$ temps moyen d'inactivité de la ligne de sortie.

Ainsi la stabilité de la file d'attente de la mémoire de sortie (condition (27)) et le temps moyen d'attente $\overline{v}$ (29), dépendent de $\overline{\tau}$ (28) et par conséquent des valeurs des paramètres T et B.

### 5. LA STABILITE DE FONCTIONNEMENT DU CONCENTRATEUR.

Le concentrateur a un fonctionnement stable si les files d'attente de l'entrée et de la sortie sont dans un état stationnaire. Par conséquent les paramètres T et B doivent satisfaire simultanément les conditions (11) et (27).

En exprimant N en fonction de la probabilité d'activité $P_A$ d'un terminal, grâce à la relation (2), on obtient la double inégalité :

$$\frac{\frac{F+eK}{D} + (K P_A \frac{a}{b} \cdot \frac{d}{D} - 1)}{K P_A \frac{e}{b} \cdot \frac{d}{D}} < \frac{T}{B} < \frac{b}{P_A d} . \tag{30}$$

Nous introduisons et définissons la charge ψ d'un concentrateur par :

$$= K P_A \frac{a}{b} \cdot \frac{d}{D} . \tag{31}$$

Cette charge dépend du nombre K et de l'activité $P_A$ des terminaux, du rapport des débits des lignes d'entrée et de sortie et de la longueur des caractères avec ou sans bits de protocole. La charge est une grandeur intrinsèque au système.

On peut montrer que la double inégalité (30) définit toujours un intervalle non vide pour T/B quand la charge ψ est inférieure à un :

$$\psi < 1 , \tag{32}$$

et seulement dans ce cas.

Nous sommes conduits à définir un nombre limite $K_0$ de terminaux d'activité $P_A$ donnée, qu'il est possible de relier au concentrateur.

$$K_0 = \frac{1}{P_A} \cdot \frac{b}{a} \cdot \frac{D}{d} . \tag{33}$$

## 6. LES CAPACITES D'ADAPTATION DE CE CONCENTRATEUR.

Avec ce modèle dont la structure est plus élaborée que les systèmes habituels nous pouvons atteindre divers objectifs et en particulier minimiser le temps d'attente ou bien relier un très grand nombre de terminaux.

### 6.1. Minimiser le temps d'attente.

Une évaluation des temps moyens d'attente, montre que l'attente dans la mémoire de sortie est nettement inférieure à celle dans la mémoire d'entrée. Par suite le temps moyen d'attente sera le plus faible si dans la mémoire d'entrée l'attente est la plus petite possible, c'est-à-dire si la longueur moyenne de la file est la plus courte possible et par conséquent voisine de la droite $\tilde{n}(T)$ (22).

Pour K terminaux d'activité $P_A$ fixée, nous choisissons la plus petite valeur de la période T qui satisfait la relation (30) et qui correspond à la valeur optimale $\tilde{B}$ de B donnée par les relations (23).

Lorsque la charge évolue, par une variation du nombre K ou de l'activité $P_A$ des terminaux, on doit modifier les paramètres T et B; lorsque la charge $\psi$ croît, il faut augmenter T et B et inversement.

On montre que si la charge $\psi$ reste inférieure à l'unité, il est toujours possible de choisir la période T et le nombre B de caractères prélevés pour que le temps moyen d'attente soit minimum.

### 6.2. Relier le plus grand nombre possible de terminaux.

Le nombre limite $K_O$ (33) de terminaux est indépendant des paramètres de fonctionnement T et B.

Pour tout couple de valeurs T et B, il existe une limite $K_M(T,B)$ du nombre de terminaux, définie par la condition de stabilité (30).

Sur le graphique 4, nous traçons les variations de $K_M(T,B)$ en fonction de T et avec B pour paramètre. Pour une valeur de B, $K_M(T)$ a une croissance rapide suivie d'une plage de saturation voisine de la limite $K_O$. L'ampleur de ces plages croît avec B. L'écart entre les courbes $K_M(T)$ décroît rapidement avec B.

L'étude de $K_M(T,B)$ montre que la limite $K_O$ ne peut être atteinte que si la charge $\psi$ et la probabilité de prélèvement p sont égales à l'unité, mais alors le concentrateur a un fonctionnement instable.

La limite $K_O$ peut seulement être approchée; pour cela comme il paraît très naturel, il suffira de choisir B de quelques unités et une valeur de T correspondante située juste au début de la plage de saturation car c'est un domaine de fonctionnement stable.

Par ces deux exemples d'utilisation d'un concentrateur nous montrons que les deux objectifs contradictoires, peuvent être atteints par un choix judicieux des valeurs des paramètres T et B.

## CONCLUSION.

La période T de prélèvement et le nombre B de caractères prélevés contrôlent la stabilité de notre concentrateur et lui donnent toutes ses facultés d'adaptation.

C'est grâce aux deux niveaux de mémoires que T et B peuvent jouer un rôle fondamental.

Les études des files d'attente définissent les conditions de stabilité du système et donnent les critères de choix des paramètres T et B.

La modélisation de notre concentrateur par deux niveaux de files d'attente donne une très grande souplesse d'adaptation à ce système de transmission.

BIBLIOGRAPHIE.

[1] E. FUCHS, P.E. JACKSON, Estimates of Distributions of Random Variables for Certain Computer Communications Traffic Models. Communication of the A.C.M. Vol. 13, n° 12, dec. 1970. pp. 752-757.

[2] J. ZAMARLIK, Un concentrateur statistique asynchrone et adaptable. Thèse d'état Paris 1980.

[3] J. ZAMARLIK, C. MACCHI, Modélisation et entropie d'un terminal téléinformatique. Théorie de l'Information - développements récents et applications. Colloques internationaux du C.N.R.S. n° 276, Editions du CNRS, Cachan 1977.

[4] W.W. CHU, A study of Asynchronous Time Division Multiplexing for Time Sharing Computer Systems. AFIPS Conf. Proc. Vol. 35, 1969, Montvale, N.J. AFIPS Press, pp. 669-678.

[5] A. ECKBERG, The Single Server Queue with Periodic Arrival Process and Deterministic Service Times. IEEE Trans. on Com. Vol. COM 27, n° 3, March 1979, pp. 556-562.

[6] M. EISENBERG, Queues with Periodic Service and Change over Time. Operations Research Vol. 20, March-April 1972, pp. 440-451.

[7] P.J. KUEHN, Multiqueue Systems with Nonexhaustive Cyclic Service. The Bell System Technical Journal, Vol. 58, n° 3, March. 1979, pp. 671-698.

[8] E. GELENBE, I. MITRANI, Analysis and Synthesis of Computer Systems, Academic Press 1980.

[9] D. WHISHART, A Queuing System with $\chi^2$ Service Time Distribution. Ann. Math. Statist. Vol. 27, 1956, pp. 768-779.

[10] L. KLEINROCK, Queueing Systems, Vol. 1, Theory, John Wiley 1975.

[11] L. TAKACS, Introduction to the Theory of Queues. Oxford University Press, 1962.

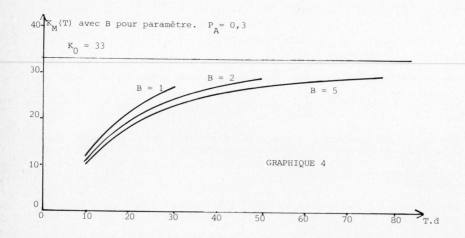

GRAPHIQUE 4

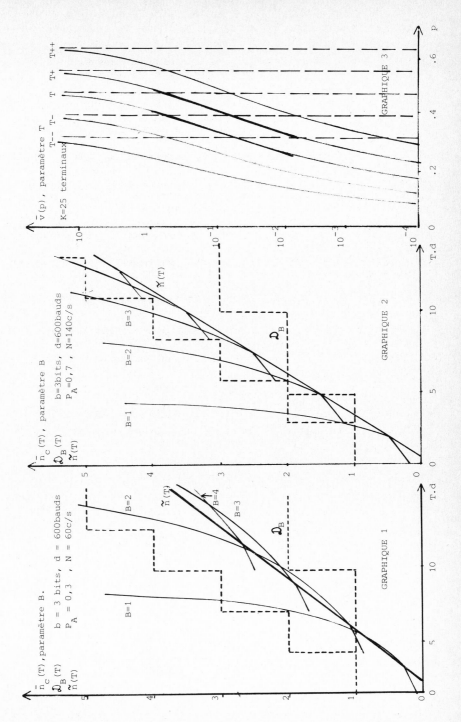

Performance of Data Communication Systems
and their Applications, G. Pujolle (ed.)
© North-Holland Publishing Company, 1981

A SERVICE SYSTEM WITH HETEROGENEOUS USER REQUIREMENTS
- APPLICATION TO MULTI-SERVICES TELECOMMUNICATIONS SYSTEMS

James W. ROBERTS

PAA/ATR/SST
Centre National d'Etudes des Télécommunications
38-40, rue du Général Leclerc
92131 ISSY-LES-MOULINEAUX
FRANCE

The occupancy distribution of a blocked-arrivals-cleared
service system where customers can require more than one
server for the duration of their service is derived in the
case of Poisson arrivals and general service times. This
system is encountered, in particular, in the evaluation
of multi-services telecommunications systems where different
bit rate traffic streams share the same resources although
the results obtained have other applications (dimensioning
of buffers in packet switching nodes, memory requirements in
multiprogramming systems, ...).

INTRODUCTION

The use of digital time division multiplexing techniques for transmission and
switching and the enhanced processing capacity provided by computer control and
highly versatile common channel signalling are considerably extending the communications potential of the existing telephone network. In the future "Integrated
Services Digital Network", new types of communication will compete with telephone
calls for the use of a common pool of transmission channels and switching equipment.
Some new services will have the same bit rate requirement as speech signals, (currently transmitted using Pulse Code Modulation at 64 K bits/s) but others, such as
hi-fi quality sound, high speed data and video communications, will require several "telephone" channels per call.

While the introduction of the ISDN will not become a reality before the network
reaches a certain degree of digital connectivity, the problems posed by the integration of multiple bit rate traffic streams are already being encountered, notably in the introduction of business satellite communications networks like the
French TELECOM 1 system [1]. These problems take the form of evaluating queueing
systems in which customers can occupy more than one server for the duration of
their service time.

Previous studies of such systems [2, 3, 4, 5, 6, 7] are mainly confined to the
simplest hypotheses of Poisson arrivals and exponential service times. In this paper we consider loss systems with general service time distributions. We prove that
the stationary occupancy distribution of a full availability group, already known
for exponential service times [2], is in fact independent of the service time distribution.

It has been pointed out by a referee of this paper that this result is not completely new. The system may be considered as a queueing network with population constraints belonging to the class of networks considered by S.S. LAM in [13]. As such,
the product form for the occupancy distribution may be deduced from the general
theorem proved by Lam, at least for Coxian type service time distributions. The
result presented here goes a little further in including the distribution of the

remaining service time of customers present in the system.

The probability that n servers are occupied is shown to satisfy a simple recurrence relation wich greatly simplifies the calculation of blocking probabilities. Note that this distribution also applies to the example considered in |13|, giving the total memory requirements of all job classes in a multiprogramming system. We have encountered a further example in the dimensioning of buffers in a system transmitting data packets of variable length. As far as we know, this recurrence relation has not previously been reported in the literature.

Lastly, we consider the application of the above results to the evaluation of a more complicated network representing the TDMA system of a satellite such as TELECOM 1 [14]. The method of evaluation based on Monte-Carlo techniques may have application to other problems having a formal analytical solution but for which the number of states is too vaste for direct numerical calculation.

## THE m.M/m.G/R LOSS SYSTEM

We adapt the standard queueing theory notation to indicate the presence of m independent traffic streams, the stream $\nu$, $\nu = 1...m$, being characterised by the following

- a Poisson arrival process with arrival rate $\lambda_\nu$ ;
- a demand per call of $d_\nu$ channels ;
- a service time distribution function $H_\nu(t)$ with mean $\mu_\nu^{-1}$.

These m streams compete for a total of R channels. We assume that there is no restriction on the positioning of available channels : a call requiring d channels will be accepted as long as the total number busy is less than R-d.

Let $x_\nu^t$ be the number of calls of stream $\nu$ present at time t and let $\{\zeta_\nu^t(1),...\zeta_\nu^t(x_\nu^t)\}$ (for $x_\nu^t > 0$) be an arbitrary permutation of the remaining service times of these calls. Define $\zeta_\nu^t(0) \equiv 0$ and write $\underline{\zeta}_\nu^t$ for $\{\zeta_\nu^t(i), i = 0, 1... x_\nu^t\}$.

We prove the following

## Theorem

The process $\{x_1^t, \underline{\zeta}_1^t, x_2^t, \underline{\zeta}_2^t, \ldots x_m^t, \underline{\zeta}_m^t\}$ has the stationary distribution

$$F_R^t (k_1, \underline{t}_1, \ldots, k_m, \underline{t}_m) = \Pr \{x_\nu^t = k_\nu, \underline{\zeta}^t \leqslant \underline{t}_\nu, \nu = 1, \ldots, m\}$$

(1)

$$= \frac{1}{C_R} \prod_{\nu=1}^{m} \left\{ \frac{a_\nu^{k_\nu}}{k_\nu !} \prod_{i=0}^{k_\nu} H_\nu^* (t_\nu(i)) \right\}$$

where $C_R$ is a normalising constant,

$$a_\nu = \lambda_\nu/\mu_\nu, \nu = 1, 2 \ldots m$$

(2)

and

$$H_\nu^*(t) = \mu_\nu \int_0^t (1 - H_\nu(u)) \, du$$

(3)

is the distribution of remaining service time for calls of stream $\nu$, $\nu = 1, 2 \ldots m$.

This is a generalisation of the stationary distribution obtained for a classical

M/G/R loss system and the proof we shall give closely follows a part of the demonstration of this result given by Cohen $|8|$. Indeed we shall use as Lemmas, two classical results for the M/G/∞ system (proved in $|8|$, for example).

Lemma 1

For an M/G/∞ system offered traffic stream $\nu$, the process $\{x_\nu^t, \underline{\zeta}_\nu^t\}$ has the stationary distribution

$$
f_{\nu\infty}^t(k, \underline{t}) = P_r \{x_\nu^t = k, \underline{\zeta}_\nu^t \leqslant \underline{t}\}
$$

$$
= \frac{a_\nu^k}{k!} e^{-a_\nu} \prod_{i=1}^{k} H_\nu^*(t_i)
$$
(4)

Let $x_\nu^a$ and $x_\nu^d$ be the numbers of calls present just before an arrival and just after a departure, respectively. Let $\underline{\zeta}_\nu^a$ and $\underline{\zeta}_\nu^d$ be the vectors corresponding to $\underline{\zeta}_\nu^t$ defined at these arrival and departure instants, respectively. We then have the second lemma :

Lemma 2

For an M/G/∞ system offered traffic stream $\nu$, the processes $\{x_\nu^t, \underline{\zeta}_\nu^t\}$, $\{x_\nu^a, \underline{\zeta}_\nu^a\}$ and $\{x_\nu^d, \underline{\zeta}_\nu^d\}$ all have the same stationary distributions, i.e.

$$
f_{\nu\infty}^a = f_{\nu\infty}^d = f_{\nu\infty}^t
$$
(5)

where $f_{\nu\infty}^t$ is given by Lemma 1.

We first consider the infinite capacity system m.M/m.G/∞. Clearly, the m traffic streams here remain independent and the process $\{x_1^t, \underline{\zeta}_1^t, \ldots, x_m^t, \underline{\zeta}_m^t\}$ has the stationary distribution

$$
F_\infty^t (k_1, \underline{t}_1, \ldots, k_m, \underline{t}_m) = \prod_{\nu=1}^{m} f_{\nu\infty}^t(k_\nu, \underline{t}_\nu)
$$
(6)

with $f_{\nu\infty}^t$ given by (4).

Since the traffic streams are independent, the arrival and departure instants of one stream are arbitrary instants for all the others. We may therefore conclude that the processes $\{x_1^a, \underline{\zeta}_1^a, \ldots, x_n^a, \underline{\zeta}_n^a\}$ and $\{x_1^d, \underline{\zeta}_1^d, \ldots x_n^d, \underline{\zeta}_n^d\}$ also have the stationary distribution (6), i.e.

$$
F_\infty^a = F_\infty^d = F_\infty^t
$$
(7)

The distribution functions $F_\infty^a$ and $F_\infty^d$ correspond to the imbedded processes defined at the arrival and departure instants of any traffic stream. Let $\eta$ be the stream to which the arriving or departing call belongs ($1 \leqslant \eta \leqslant m$) and consider the processes

$$
\{x_1^a, \underline{\zeta}_1^a, \ldots, x_n^a, \underline{\zeta}_n^a, \eta\} \text{ and } \{x_1^d, \underline{\zeta}_1^d, \ldots, x_n^d, \underline{\zeta}_n^d, \eta\}
$$

For the infinite capacity system these processes have the same stationary distribution

$$G_\infty^a = G_\infty^d \ (k_1, \ \underline{t}_1, \ \cdots, \ k_m, \ \underline{t}_m, \ \alpha)$$

$$= \mathrm{Pr} \ \{x_\nu^d = k_\nu, \ \underline{\zeta}_\nu^d \leqslant \underline{t}_\nu, \ \nu = 1 \ \cdots \ m \ \underline{\mathrm{and}} \ \eta = \alpha\} \qquad (8)$$

$$= F_\infty^t \ (k_1, \ \underline{t}_1, \ \cdots, \ k_m, \ \underline{t}_m) \ \cdot \ \frac{\lambda_\alpha}{\displaystyle\sum_{\nu=1}^m \lambda_\nu}$$

since the $(x_1, \ \underline{\zeta}_1, \ \cdots, \ x_m, \ \underline{\zeta}_m)$ are independant of $\eta$ and arrivals form independent Poisson processes.

We are now in a position to consider the finite capacity system, m.M/m.G/R. We adopt the convention that a blocked call generates an instantaneous departure from the point of view of the definition of $\{x_1^d, \ \underline{\zeta}_1^d, \ \cdots, \ x_m^d, \ \underline{\zeta}_m^d, \ \eta\}$.

The latter is a Markov process processing a stationary distribution. The existence of the stationary distribution is obvious by comparison with the corresponding infinite capacity system. Denote this distribution by

$$G_R^d \ (k_1, \ \underline{t}_1, \ \cdots, \ k_m, \ \underline{t}_m, \ \alpha)$$

By the general theory of Markov processes, $G_R^d$ is determined, within a normalising constant, by the equilibrium equations obtained on considering transitions between successive departures. These equations may be written

$$G_R^d \ (k_1, \ \underline{t}_1, \ \cdots, \ k_m, \ \underline{t}_m, \ \alpha) = \qquad (9)$$

$$= \sum p \ (k_1, \underline{t}_1 \ \cdots \ k_m, \ \underline{t}_m, \ \alpha | j_1, \underline{s}_1 \ \cdots \ j_n, \ \underline{s}_m, \ \beta) \ dG_R^d \ (j_1, \underline{s}_1 \ \cdots \ j_n, \ \underline{s}_m, \ \beta)$$

for $\displaystyle\sum_{\nu=1}^m k_\nu \ d_\nu < R.$

where the summation is over all states $(j_1, \ \underline{s}_1, \ \cdots \ j_m, \ \underline{s}_m, \ \beta)$ such that the transition probabilities $p \ (k_1, \underline{t}_1 \ \cdots \ | j_1, \underline{s}_1 \ \cdots)$ are non null. If the departure actually corresponds to the termination of a served call we have

$$\sum_{\nu=1}^m k_\nu \ d_\nu \leqslant R - d_\alpha \qquad (10)$$

and the transition probabilities are non zero only for $j_\alpha \leqslant k_\alpha + 1$ and $j_\nu \leqslant k_\nu$ $\nu \neq \alpha$. The fact of limited capacity in no way intervenes in determining the non null $p \ (k_1 \ \cdots \ \alpha | j_1 \ \cdots \ \beta)$ and we see that for states satisfying (10), equation (9) must also be satisfied by $G_\infty^d$.

Now consider the case where the departure $\alpha$ in fact corresponds to a blocked call. We then have

$$R - d_\alpha < \sum_{\nu=1}^m k_\nu \ d_\nu \leqslant R \qquad (11)$$

In this case the transition probabilities are zero for $j_\nu \leqslant k_\nu$, $\nu = 1, \ldots, m$. The remainder are identical to the transition probabilities of the infinite system linking the state $(j_1, \underline{s}_1 \ldots j_m, \underline{s}_m, \beta)$ just after a departure to the state $(k_1, \underline{t}_1, \ldots k_m, \underline{t}_m, \alpha)$ just before the arrival of the next call of stream $\alpha$. In other words, (9) is satisfied if we replace $dG^d_\infty$ on the right hand side by $dG^d_\infty$ and $G^d_R$ on the left hand side by $G^a_\infty$. But by (8), $G^{d}_\infty = G^a_\infty$ and we conclude that (9) is also satisfied by $G^d_\infty$ for states satisfying (11).

We have shown that (9) is satisfied by $G^d_\infty$ for all states such that $\Sigma k_\nu\, d_\nu \leqslant R$. But $G^d_R$ is the unique solution of (9) within a multiplying constant. We must have, therefore

$$G^d_R = K \times G^d_\infty \tag{12}$$

where the constant K is to be determined by the normalising condition.

Let $F^t_R$ $(k, \underline{t}_1 \ldots k_m, \underline{t}_m)$ be the stationary distribution of $\{x^t_1, \zeta^t_1, \ldots x^t_m, \zeta^t_m\}$. $F^t_R$ may be expressed in terms of the state existing just after the last departure preceding t :

$$F^t_R\ (k_1, \underline{t}_1, \ldots, k_m, \underline{t}_m) \tag{13}$$

$$= \sum q\ (k_1, \underline{t}_1, \ldots, k_m, \underline{t}_m | j_1, \underline{s}_1 \cdots j_m, \underline{s}_m, \beta)\ dG^d_R\ (j_1, \underline{s}_1 \cdots j_m, \underline{s}_m, \beta)$$

for $\Sigma k_\nu\, d_\nu \leqslant R$ where the $q$ $(k_1, \underline{t}_1 \ldots | j_1, \underline{s}_1 \ldots)$ are the appropriate transition probabilities.

As above it may be noted that (13) is also satisfied by $F^t_\infty$ and $G^d_\infty$ (no call is blocked between the epochs d and t). But $dG^d_R = K.dG^d_\infty$ by (12), and we deduce,

$$F^t_R = K \times F^t_\infty \tag{14}$$

The proof of the theorem is completed on substituting for $F^t_\infty$ given by (6) and (4) and writing $C_R = \exp\ \{a_1 + a_2 + \ldots + a_m\}\ /\ K$.

The distribution of the numbers of calls in progress is obtained from (1) on letting $t_\nu(i)$ tend to infinity for $i = 0, 1 \ldots k_\nu$ and $\nu = 1, 2 \ldots m$ :

$$P\ (k_1, k_2 \ldots k_m) = \frac{1}{C_R} \prod_{\nu=1}^{m} \frac{a_\nu^{k_\nu}}{k_\nu!} \tag{15}$$

## OCCUPANCY DISTRIBUTION

The joint distribution (15) is already well known for the case of exponentiel service times, [2], and indeed for the more general case considered in [13]. However, it does not seem to have been noticed that the calculation of the normalising constant $C_R$ defined by

$$\sum_{(\Sigma\ k_\nu\ d_\nu\ \leqslant R)} P\ (k_1, \ldots k_m) = 1 \tag{16}$$

and moreover, the distribution of the total number of busy channels

$$Q(n) = Pr \{\Sigma \; x_\nu^t \; d_\nu = n\} \tag{17}$$

can be obtained by means of a simple recurrence relation.

We have,

$$Q(n) = \sum_{(\Sigma \; k_\nu \; d_\nu = n)} P(k_1, k_2, \ldots, k_m), \quad n = 0, 1, \ldots R$$

So,

$$n \; Q(n) = \sum_{(\Sigma \; k_\nu \; d_\nu = n)} (k_1 d_1 + k_2 d_2 + \ldots + k_m d_m) \cdot P(k_1, k_2, \ldots, k_m)$$

But by (15)

$$k_\nu \; P(k_1 \ldots k_\nu \ldots k_m) = a_\nu \; P(k_1 \ldots k_\nu - 1 \ldots k_m)$$

Therefore,

$$n \; Q(n) = \sum_{(\Sigma \; k_\nu \; d_\nu = n)} a_1 d_1 \; P(k_1 - 1, k_2 \ldots k_m) + \ldots +$$

$$+ \sum_{(\Sigma \; k_\nu \; d_\nu = n)} a_m d_m \; P(k_1, k_2 \ldots k_m - 1)$$

$$= \sum_{(\Sigma \; k_\nu \; d_\nu = n - d_1)} a_1 d_1 \; P(k_1, k_2 \ldots k_m) + \ldots +$$

$$+ \sum_{(\Sigma \; k_\nu \; d_\nu = n - d_m)} a_m d_m \; P(k_1, k_2 \ldots k_m)$$

$$= a_1 d_1 \; Q(n - d_1) + \ldots + a_m d_m \; Q(n - d_m)$$

i.e.

$$\boxed{n \; Q(n) = \Sigma \; a_\nu \; d_\nu \; Q(n - d_\nu)} \tag{18}$$

The normalising condition (16) now becomes $\displaystyle\sum_{n=0}^{R} Q(n) = 1$ \hfill (19)

Note that $\quad B(i) = \displaystyle\sum_{n = R - i + 1}^{R} Q(n)$

gives the blocking probability of a call requiring i channels.

APPLICATION TO THE EVALUATION OF TELECOM 1

The business communications systems of TELECOM 1 has a total transmission capacity of 125 Mb/s, although this is not fully accessible to all users |9|. Earth stations are divided into 5 groups, each group having access to one fifth of the satellite capacity (one 25 Mb/s transponder). Full network interconnectivity is assured by the fact that every station can receive the signals from all five groups. The total incoming bit rate cannot however exceed 25 Mb/s and the stations cannot receive communications from two or more groups at the same time. The system is managed on the basis of a 20 ms time division multiple access (TDMA) time frame.

The traffic capacity of the satellite depends on the probabilities that communications of particular services (telephone, visioconference, ...) cannot be set up because either,

- available capacity is insufficient on the up path,

- available capacity is insufficient on the down path, or

- sufficient bit rate is available on both paths but the idle time slots do not occur simultaneously.

The latter constraint can be particularly important for high bit rate services. In fact, to minimize the effects of such conflicts, communications from say group i to group j may be restricted to a part of the system time frame and/or rearrangement algorithms may be applied to free required time slots by relocating existing communications. One object of the evaluation of the traffic capacity of TELECOM 1 is to compare the efficiency of a number of such time frame management methods.

Considered methods are such that the blocking probability of a communication depends only on the following :

- the required bit rate
- the total demands of communications already in progress between all user groups
- the management method (rearrangement algorithm, path choice restrictions).

System capacity and demands can be expressed as multiples of the lowest common denominator bit rate of the services required. In practice this may be taken as the bit rate of a telephone channel (32 kb/s or 64 kb/s). The time frame may then be viewed as representing a number of channels to be distributed among the various users.

Let $n_{ij}$ be the number of channels required by communications in progress from stations of group i to stations of group j, $1 \leqslant i \leqslant 5$, $1 \leqslant j \leqslant 5$.

An argument on the same lines as that used above (or more simply, an application of the theorem proved in |13|) may be employed to prove the following

Theorem

If communications arrive according to independent Poisson processes, the probability that there are simultaneously in progress calls requiring a total of $n_{ij}$ channels from group i to group j for $1 \leqslant i \leqslant 5$ and $1 \leqslant j \leqslant 5$ is given by

$$P \{n_{11} \ n_{12} \cdots n_{55}\} = \frac{1}{C_A} \prod_{\substack{1 \leqslant i \leqslant 5 \\ 1 \leqslant j \leqslant 5}} Q_{ij} \ (n_{ij}) \qquad (20)$$

where the functions $Q_{ij}$ (n) satisfy recurrence relations (18) (with appropriately defined traffics $a_\nu$ (i, j), etc...) and $C_A$ is a normalising constant.

The various frame management methods satisfying the stated conditions for accepting or rejecting a communication define different spaces of feasible states and are thus differentiated by the value of the constant $C_A$.

An optimal method would be such that only the constraints on available capacity on up and down paths limit the state space, i.e.

$$\sum_i n_{ij} \leqslant R \quad \text{and} \quad \sum_j n_{ij} \leqslant R$$

where R is the available capacity expressed in channels. Algorithms meeting this condition have been studied in another context |10, 11|, but these are not particularly well suited to the present system. Simpler procedures giving a reduced feasible state space are more practicable but need careful evaluation being clearly sub-optimal.


EVALUATION METHOD

Relation (20) giving the state probabilities may theoretically be used to determine the blocking probabilities of the various communications services. However, the number of states is of the order of $R^{25}$ where R is the number of channels per group (R > 300) and direct calculation is clearly impracticable. A Monte-Carlo technique similar to that described in |12| has been used to estimate these probabilities.

For each demande i - j we calculate the function $Q_{ij}(n)$ satisfying

$$n\ Q_{ij}(n) = \sum a_\nu(i,j)\ d_\nu\ Q_{ij}\ (n - d_\nu)$$

$$\sum_{n=0}^{R} Q_{ij}(n) = 1 \tag{21}$$

The $Q_{ij}(n)$ are then probability distributions defined on $\{0, 1, ..., R\}$.

We sample the random variables $n_{ij}$ according to these distributions and constitute a matrix of demands $\{n_{ij}\}$. This sampling procedure generates states wich may or may not be feasible according to a particular time frame management method. However, because of (20) we know that the generation of feasible states is in fact in accordance with the actual occupancy distribution.

Given a feasible state $\{n_{ij}\}$ we then calculate the corresponding available capacities $m_{kl}$ (k = 1 ... 5, l = 1 ... 5). These are defined by the condition $\{n_{ij}\} + m_{kl} \{\Delta_{kl}\}$ is feasible while $\{n_{ij}\} + (m_{kl} + 1) \{\Delta_{kl}\}$ is not, where $\{\Delta_{kl}\}$ is the 5 x 5 matrix with all elements equal to zero except element (k, l) which is equal to 1. To each state $\{n_{ij}\}$ there thus corresponds a matrix of available capacities $\{m_{ij}\}$ (note that the $m_{ij}$ cannot be used simultaneously).

After a sufficient of such samplings, at each of which the available capacities $\{m_{ij}\}$ are recorded, we obtain estimates of the probabilities $B_{ij}(d) = Pr \{m_{ij} < d\}$.

Since arrivals are Poissonian, $B_{ij}(d)$ gives the probability that a call between inlet switch i and outlet switch j requiring d channels will be blocked.

The accuracy of the estimated blocking probabilities clearly depends on the number of feasible states sampled. Following [12], we estimate that, after n samples, the 95 % confidence interval on $B_{ij}(d)$ is approximately $\pm\ 1.961\sqrt{(B_{ij}(d)/n)}$.

REFERENCES

[1]    FLEURY L., GUENIN J.P., RAMAT P.,  Le système TELECOM 1, Echo des recher-
       ches 101 (July 1980).

[2]    GIMPLESON L.A.,  Analysis of mixtures of wide and narrow-band traffic,
       IEEE Trans. Comm. Technol. 13 (Septembre 1965) 258-266.

[3]    YAMAGUCHI T. AKIYAMA M.,  An integrated hybrid traffic switching system mi-
       xing pre-emptive wide-band and waitable narrow-band calls, Electronics and
       Communications in Japan. 53-A  N° 4 (1970).

[4]    AKIYAMA M. YAMAGUCHI T. MORITA T.,  Wide-band and narrow-band traffic inte-
       gration on multistage time division switching networks,  Electronics and
       Communications in Japan. 58-A  N° 12 (1975).

[5]    ENOMOTO O., MIYAMOTO H.,  An analysis of mixtures of multiple bandwidth
       traffic and time division switching networks ; NEC Research and Development
       41 (April 1976)

[6]    KATZSCHNER L., SCHELLER R.,  Probability of loss of data traffics with dif-
       ferent bit rates hunting one common PCM-channel,  Eighth International Tele-
       traffic Congress, Melbourne (1976).

[7]    SAITO T., INOSE T.,  Evaluation of traffic carrying capability in one-stage
       and two-stage time division networks handling data with a variety of speed
       classes, Ninth International Teletraffic Congress, Torremolinos (1979).

[8]    COHEN J.W.,  On regenative processes in queueing theory, Springer-Verlag
       (1976).

[9]    BOUSQUET J.C.,  Time division multiple access with demand assignment for
       intra company network using the satellite TELECOM 1, Fifth International
       Conference on Digital Satellite Communications, Genoa (March 1981).

[10]   ITO Y. URANO Y.,  MURATANI T., YAMAGUCHI M.,  Analysis of a switch matrix
       for an SS/TDMA system, Proc.  IEEE 65  N° 3 (March 1977) 411-419.

[11]   INUKAI T.,  An efficient SS/TDMA time slot assignment algorithm, IEEE
       Trans. Comm. Technol. 27  N° 10 (October 1979).

[12]   HARVEY C. HILLS C.,  Determining grades of service in a network, Ninth In-
       ternational Teletraffic Congress, Torremolinos (1979).

[13]   LAM S.S.,  Queueing networks with population size constraints, IBM J. Res
       Develop. (July 1977).